A POCKET HISTORY OF THE UNITED STATES

A POCKET HISTORY OF THE UNITED STATES

EIGHTH REVISED EDITION

ALLAN NEVINS AND HENRY STEELE COMMAGER
WITH JEFFREY MORRIS

WASHINGTON SQUARE PRESS
PUBLISHED BY POCKET BOOKS NEW YORK

ACKNOWLEDGMENTS

The following acknowledgments are gratefully made: to Everett Dick and D. Appleton-Century Company, Inc., for the quotation from *The Sod-House Frontier*. To the Bobbs-Merrill Company, Inc., for the quotation from Herbert Quick's *The Hawkeye*. To the Macmillan Company for the quotation from "Bryan, Bryan, Bryan" in *Collected Poems* by Vachel Lindsay, copyright 1920 by the Macmillan Company, copyright renewed 1948 by Elizabeth C. Lindsay. To Brandt and Brandt for the quotation from *Western Star* by Stephen Vincent Benét, published by Holt, Rinehart and Winston, Inc., copyright 1943 by Rosemary Carr Benét, copyright renewed 1971 by Thomas C. Benét, Rachel Benét Lewis and Stephanie Benét Mahin.

Cover photographs: Culver Pictures, Inc.

A Washington Square Press Publication of
POCKET BOOKS, a division of Simon & Schuster, Inc.
1230 Avenue of the Americas, New York, N.Y. 10020

ISBN: 0-671-63268-X

First Washington Square Press printing of this Eighth Revised and Enlarged Edition November, 1986

10 9 8 7 6 5 4 3 2 1

WASHINGTON SQUARE PRESS, WSP and colophon are registered trademarks of Simon & Schuster, Inc.

Printed in the U.S.A.

Preface

America emerged out of obscurity into history only some four centuries ago. It is the newest of great nations, yet it is in many respects the most interesting. It is interesting because its history recapitulates the history of the race, telescopes the development of social and economic and political institutions. It is interesting because upon it have played most of those great historical forces and factors that have molded the modern world: imperialism, nationalism, immigration, industrialism, science, religion, democracy, and liberty, and because the impact of these forces upon society is more clearly revealed in its history than in the history of other nations. It is interesting because, notwithstanding its youth, it is today the oldest republic and the oldest democracy and lives under the oldest written constitution in the world. It is interesting because, from its earliest beginnings, its people have been conscious of a peculiar destiny, because upon it have been fastened the hopes and aspirations of the human race, and because it has not failed to fulfill that destiny or to justify those hopes.

The story of America is the story of the interaction of an Old World culture and a New World environment, the early modification of the culture by environment, and the subsequent modification of the environment by the culture. The first European settlers in America were not primitive men, but highly civilized, and they transplanted from their homeland a culture centuries old. Yet the United States was never merely an extension of the Old World: it was, what its first settlers anticipated and its founding fathers consciously planned, something new in history. The unconquered wilderness confronting the pioneer from the Atlantic to the Pacific profound-

ly modified inherited institutions and gave rise to wholly new institutions, and the intermixture of peoples and of races modified inherited cultures and created, in a sense, a completely new culture. The new United States became the most ambitious experiment ever undertaken in the deliberate intermingling of peoples, in religious toleration, economic opportunity, and political democracy—an experiment perhaps still under way.

European historians and commentators, admitting readily enough the substantial virtues of the American people and the value of their political experiments, long asserted that American history was nevertheless colorless and prosaic. It is, on the contrary, dramatic and picturesque, and cast in heroic mold. There are few parallels in modern history to the drama of the swift expansion of small and scattered groups of people across a giant continent, the growth of a few struggling colonies into a continental nation of fifty states, or the spread of a new culture and of new social and economic practices so swiftly to the four quarters of the globe.

ALLAN NEVINS AND
HENRY STEELE COMMAGER, 1942

The first edition of this history was written at the beginning of World War II and was designed to present and interpret the American historical record not only to the English-speaking world, but also to the peoples of all nations who were interested in the evolution of the first constitutional and first democratic society at a time when both constitutionalism and democracy were in mortal peril. In the thirty-five years since its preparation, it has gone through five revisions and enlargements and has been published in most of the languages of the world.

This sixth edition appears as the United States celebrates or recalls two hundred years of independence. The decade since the last edition has been the most challenging, and perhaps the most sobering, in our history since that of the Civil War and Reconstruction. In its preoccupation with war, its susceptibility to large-scale corruption, and its attack upon the integrity of the constitutional system, it discloses interesting analogies to that earlier decade. Thus, this last decade, too, has been a time of trial and disillusionment. It witnessed on *the world stage a meaningless and futile war that did infinite damage to a distant people with whom we had no legitimate quarrel, and did irreparable damage to the social, economic, and moral fabric of our society. It witnessed on the domestic stage the ignominy of Watergate and all its attendant evils. It marked, in a sense, the real end of American innocence—the end of that long era that stretched from the Declaration and the Constitution to the Marshall Plan and the launching of the United Nations, when Americans could consider themselves as in some sense exempt from the truth of History and when they could take for granted that Nature and History permitted them to enjoy higher standards of conduct and of morals than the nations of the Old World could afford to indulge. It marked the end, too, on both the domestic and the international scene, of those concepts of an infinity of land and resources, of geographical and moral isolation, and of a special destiny and a special mission, which had bemused the American mind from Jefferson to Woodrow Wilson and Franklin D. Roosevelt. Whether a United States chastened by experience and matured by failure can adapt herself in the third century of her existence to a new position in the world remains for the future to discover. Clearly she has the capacity to do so: immense natural resources, sound institutions, a proud heritage, and a people as competent to meet challenges and overcome trials as any in the world. There is no reason why she should not emerge from the current crisis more dedicated to the values and potentialities of her Constitution, more ardent in her response to her obligations to be vigilant against usurpations of power, more intelligent in setting the limits on that power, and more magnanimous in its exercise.*

Since the last edition the co-author of this book, the distinguished and beloved Allan Nevins, died, leaving a void that cannot be filled. In preparing the present edition, I have had the assistance of Professor Milton Cantor of the University of Massachusetts.

HENRY STEELE COMMAGER
1976

CONTENTS

MAPS

CHAPTER 1

The Planting of the Colonies

Natural Features of North America

THE HISTORY of English settlement in America began on a beautiful April morning in 1607, when three storm-beaten ships of Captain Christopher Newport anchored near the mouth of Chesapeake Bay, sending ashore men who found "fair meadows, and goodly tall trees, with such fresh waters as almost ravished" them to see. With these ships were George Percy, the active, handsome son of the Earl of Northumberland, and Captain John Smith. Percy records how they found noble forests, the ground carpeted with flowers; fine strawberries, "four times bigger and better than ours in England"; oysters "very large and delicate in taste"; much small game; "stores of turkey nests and many eggs"; and an Indian town, where the savages brought them corn bread and tobacco smoked in clay pipes with copper bowls. For a time these first experiences in Virginia seemed enchanting. Percy's *Observations* describes the delight of the newcomers in the richly colored birds, the fruits and berries, the fine sturgeon, and the pleasant scenery. But his brave narrative, full of a wild poetry, ends in something like a shriek. For he tells how the Indians attacked the settlers, "creeping on all fours from the hills, like bears, with their bows in their mouths"; how the men were seized by "cruel diseases, such as swellings, fluxes, burning fevers"; and how many died of sheer famine, "their bodies trailed out of their cabins like dogs to be buried."

The planting of a new nation in America was no holiday undertaking. It meant grim, dirty, toilsome, dangerous

1

work. Here was a great shaggy continent, its Eastern third
covered with pathless forests; its mountains, rivers, lakes, and
rolling plains all upon a grandiose scale; its Northern stretches
fiercely cold in winter, its Southern areas burning hot in summer; filled with wild beasts, and peopled by a warlike, cruel,
and treacherous people still in the Stone Age of culture. In
many respects it was a forbidding land. It could be reached
only by a voyage so perilous that some ships buried as many
as they landed. But despite all its drawbacks, it was admirably fitted to become the home of an energetic, thriving
people.

North America is a roughly triangular continent, of which
the widest part—a rich, variegated, and, in general, well-
watered area—lies between the twenty-sixth and fifty-fifth
parallels. Here the climate is healthful, with a warm summer which permits of fine crops and a cold winter that stimu-
lates men to activity. Europeans could establish themselves in
most of this area without any painful process of adjustment.
They could bring their chief food crops: wheat, rye, oats,
beans, carrots, and onions. They found in the new land two
novel foods of remarkable value—maize and potatoes. The
"Indian corn," if planted in May, would yield roasting ears
in July and later furnished fodder for cattle, husk beds for
the settlers, and an unequaled yield of grain. Everywhere
game abounded, the deer and bison roaming in millions, the
passenger pigeons darkening the sky with their flocks. The
coastal waters were rich in fish. A search in due time revealed
that North America contained more iron, coal, copper, and
petroleum than any other continent. It had almost boundless
forests. Bays and harbors gave many shelters along the Eastern shore, which in general was low, while broad rivers—the
St. Lawrence, Connecticut, Hudson, Delaware, Susquehanna,
Potomac, James, Pee Dee, Savannah—made it easy to pene-
trate a considerable distance into the interior. A foothold
could be gained and enlarged without excessive hardship.

Certain natural features of the continent were destined to
have a marked effect upon the future course of the American nation. The many bays and inlets on the Atlantic coast
made for numerous small colonies rather than a few large
ones. Fifteen in all were soon established, counting Nova
Scotia and Quebec, and they gave America in its early history a rich variety of institutions. Each clung tenaciously

to its own character. When independence came, the nation built out of thirteen of these units simply had to be a federation. Behind the coastal plain rose a wide, wild mountain barrier, the Appalachian range. It was so hard to cross that the coastal settlements grew fairly thick and sturdy, with well-rooted ways, before the people expended any great strength upon trans-Appalachian expansion. When they did push west, they traversed the mountains to find before them a huge central plain, the Mississippi basin. This, comprising nearly half the area of the United States and more than half of its cultivated land, was so flat that communication was easy; particularly as it was seamed east and west by many navigable streams—the Wisconsin, Iowa, Illinois, Ohio, Cumberland, Tennessee, Arkansas, and Red—and north and south by the great Mississippi-Missouri river system. Settlers covered this fertile basin with comparative rapidity and ease. Men from all parts of the seaboard and all countries of western Europe intermingled in it on equal terms. It became a great pool in which a new democracy and a new American sentiment developed.

Farther west were high plains with so dry a climate that they, with the high Rocky Mountains just beyond, long delayed the onward sweep of settlement. The soil and the gold of the distant Pacific slope attracted a host of adventurous pioneers several decades before these half-arid plains were wrested from the Indians. California was a populous and powerful state at a time when a wide unsettled belt still separated it and Oregon from the older parts of the United States. But this belt did not long remain a solitude. Following the buffalo hunters, the cattle ranchers rapidly covered the plains, while population gradually thickened as the railroads brought the materials needed for the conquest of the treeless country: barbed wire, windmills, lumber, and agricultural implements. Irrigated farms, too, gained in number. By 1890 the frontier had substantially disappeared, and the wild West was no more.

It was inevitable from the beginning that the movement of settlement in America should in general follow east-to-west lines. From the Atlantic seaboard the St. Lawrence and Great Lakes waterway, which offered the readiest access to the interior, ran roughly in an east-and-west direction. The Mohawk Valley break in the northern Appalachians, which in due time furnished a site for the Erie Canal, afforded another east-west route. The Ohio Valley, a third great artery for settlement, roughly follows an east-west line. To a striking degree, emigration all the way from the Atlantic to the Rockies tended to pursue parallels of latitude. It was also inevitable that the French sovereignty over Louisiana, and the Mexican sovereignty over California and the Southwest, should melt away before the advance of English-speaking Americans. Even in colonial days keen-sighted observers pointed out that the people who controlled the Ohio Valley must in time control the Mississippi. It was equally true that the people who controlled the Mississippi basin must eventually control the whole area west of it. With superior numbers and energy, the Americans made the most of their geographical advantages.

It was fortunate for the white settlers that the Indians of North America were too few and too backward to be a grave impediment to colonization. They harassed and at times delayed it; they never stopped it for long. When the first Europeans arrived, the Indians east of the Mississippi probably numbered not more than two hundred thousand. Those of the whole continent north of Mexico certainly did not exceed five hundred thousand. Armed only with the bow and arrow, the tomahawk, and the war club, and ignorant of any military art save the ambush, they were ordinarily no match for well-accoutered and vigilant bodies of whites. For that matter, they had shown little capacity to subdue nature, and, as they lived mainly by hunting and fishing, their resources were precarious. Most of the hundreds of tribes in the fifty-nine recognized "families" north of Mexico were small and could muster no formidable war bands. The most powerful Indian organization was the Five (later Six) Nations of the Iroquois family, whose stronghold was western New York, who had a general council, and who pursued an aggressive policy which made them dreaded by the neighboring Algonquin tribes. In the Southeast the Creeks had set up another strong confederacy of the Muskogean family. Far in the Northwest, on the upper plains, the Sioux had established a somewhat looser organization.

The struggle between the settlers and the Indians in the colonial period passed through several well-marked stages. No sooner were the first colonies planted than most of them came into sharp local conflict with small neighboring tribes. A good illustration is afforded by the fierce, brief Pequot War in New England, which in 1637 ended in the complete destruction of the Pequot tribe inhabiting the Connecticut Valley; another illustration is furnished by the war between the Virginia settlers and Powhatan's tribes, which began in 1622 and also ended in utter Indian defeat. But as the white newcomers advanced, seizing larger tracts of land, the Indians formed extensive tribal alliances for resistance. King Philip, for example, rallied several important New England tribes who fought heroically for two years before they were crushed; while the North Carolina settlers faced a similar combination in the Tuscarora War, and the South Carolina settlers in the Yamassee War. These struggles were stern and extensive and caused the whites many losses in life and property. Finally came the phase of warfare in which the Indians found European allies. Some of the Northern tribes combined with the French; some of the Southern tribes received arms and encouragement from the Spaniards. Fortunately for the English-speaking settlers, the powerful Iroquois Confederacy took a friendly attitude and lent active aid in operations against the French. In the end, the hostile Indians were as decisively defeated in this third phase of warfare as in the preceding two.

The Early Settlers

To THE RAW NEW CONTINENT the first British settlers came in bold groups. The ships that under Christopher Newport sailed into Hampton Roads on the 13th of May, 1607, carried men alone. They laid out Jamestown, with a fort, a church, a storehouse, and a row of little huts. When calamity fell upon them, Captain John Smith showed a nerve, resourcefulness, and energy that in the second year made him president and practical dictator of the colony. Agriculture was slowly developed; in 1612 John Rolfe began to grow tobacco, and as it brought high prices in the London market everyone took it up, till even the market place was planted with it.

Yet growth was slow. By 1619 Virginia had no more than two thousand people. That year was notable for three events.

One was the arrival of a ship from England with ninety "young maidens" who were to be given as wives to those settlers who would pay a hundred and twenty pounds of tobacco for their transportation. This cargo was so joyously welcomed that others like it were soon sent over. Equally important was the initiation of representative government in America. On July 30, in that Jamestown church where John Rolfe several years earlier had cemented a temporary peace with the Indians by marrying Pocahontas, met the first legislative assembly on the continent: a governor, six councilors, and two burgesses each from ten plantations. The third significant event of the year was the arrival in August of a Dutch ship with Negro slaves, twenty of whom were sold to the settlers.

While Virginia was thus painfully managing to survive and grow, a congregation of English Calvinists who had settled in Holland were making plans to remove to the New World. These "Pilgrims," who had been persecuted because they denied the ecclesiastical supremacy of the king and wished to set up a separate Church of their own, had originally come from the village of Scrooby, in Nottinghamshire. In every way they were a remarkable body. They had three leaders of conspicuous ability: the teacher John Robinson, a learned, broad-minded, generous-hearted graduate of Cambridge University; their sage elder, William Brewster, also a Cambridge man; and William Bradford, shrewd, forcible, and idealistic. The rank and file possessed integrity, industry, and sobriety, as well as courage and fortitude. They had endured popular hostility in England; they had withstood loneliness and harsh toil in Holland. Now, securing à patent to settle in America, a ship called the *Mayflower*, and a store of provisions, they prepared to face the rigors of the wilderness. Sailing from Plymouth one hundred and two in number, the Pilgrims on December 11 (Old Style), 1620, landed on the Massachusetts coast. That winter more than half of them died of cold and scurvy. Well might William Bradford write:

But here I cannot but stay and make a pause and stand half amazed at this poor people's present condition. . . . Being thus past the vast ocean and a sea of troubles before in the preparation . . . they had now no friends to welcome them, nor inns to entertain or refresh their weatherbeaten bodies, no houses or much less towns to repair to, to seek for succor. . . . And for the season, it was winter, and those that know the winters of that country know them to be sharp and violent and subject to cruel and fierce storms, dangerous to travel to known places, much more to search an unknown coast. Besides what could they see but a hideous and desolate wilderness full of wild beasts and wild men? . . . What could now sustain them but the spirit of God and His grace?

But the next summer they raised good crops, and in the fall a ship brought new settlers. Their resolution never faltered. When the Narraganset chief, Canonicus, sent them a bundle of arrows in a snakeskin as a challenge to war, Bradford stuffed the skin with bullets and returned it with a defiant message.

Then in rapid succession emerged other English colonies. The parent hive was ready to send forth its swarms. A May day in 1629 saw the London wharves a scene of bustle and cheery excitement; five ships carrying 400 passengers, 140 head of cattle, and 40 goats, the largest body thus far sent across the North Atlantic at one time, were sailing for Massachusetts Bay. Before the end of June they arrived at Salem, where John Endicott and a small group of associates had planted a town the previous autumn. These people were Puritans—that is, members of the Church of England who at first wished to reform or purify its doctrines and who finally withdrew from it—and they opened a great Puritan exodus. In the spring of 1630 John Winthrop reached Salem with eleven ships carrying nine hundred settlers, enough to found eight new towns, including Boston. The Massachusetts Bay colony grew so rapidly that it was soon throwing off branches to the south and west. Roger Williams, a minister of Salem who courageously taught the separation of Church and state, with other radical views, was driven into the Rhode Island wilderness. Here in 1636 he founded Providence as a place of perfect religious toleration. In that year, too, the first migration to Connecticut began under the resolute Reverend Thomas Hooker, who moved a great part of his congregation from Cambridge westward in a body. Another notable colony sprang into existence in 1634, when the first settlement was made in Maryland under the guidance of the liberal-minded Cecilius Calvert, second Baron Baltimore.

Most of the gentlemen who first went thither were, like the
founder, English Catholics, while most of the common folk
were Protestants. Toleration was therefore essential, and
Maryland was a home of religious freedom, attracting people
of varied faiths. Settlers from Virginia drifted into the Albe-
marle Sound region of what is now North Carolina as early
as the 1650's, but it was not until 1663 that Charles II granted
a charter to eight of his favorites for the vast area now embraced by both the Carolinas and Georgia. The proprietors
named both the colony and the first city after their royal
benefactor, and induced John Locke to draw up for them a
Fundamental Constitution which, happily, never went into
effect. Settlers drifted down from Virginia and others, including many French Huguenots, came directly to the coast from
England and the West Indies. Charleston, established in 1670,
speedily became the cultural as well as the political capital
of the colony.

The seat of one rich colony was gained by conquest. The
Dutch had sent Henry Hudson, an English mariner, to explore the river which bears his name—a task executed in
1609. Dutch fur traders had followed him, and in 1624 a
small settlement was effected on Manhattan Island. The province of New Netherland grew but slowly and failed to develop
institutions of self-government, but did leave a permanent
mark in the patroon system of plantations along the Hudson,
in architecture, and in "Knickerbocker" families who were
to play a leading role in the history of New York and of
the nation. Meanwhile, the English never gave up their claim
to the entire coast, and the Connecticut settlements were
anxious for the seizure of their troublesome neighbor. Why
permit this alien element in the very center of British America? Charles II granted the area to his brother, the Duke of
York, who took vigorous action. In the summer of 1664
three warships arrived before New Amsterdam. They carried
a body of soldiers who were reinforced by Connecticut
troops, while forces were promised from Massachusetts and
Long Island. Most of the Dutch settlers, sick of despotic
rule, made no objection to a change of sovereignty. Although
old Peter Stuyvesant declared he would rather be "carried
out dead" than surrender, he had no choice. The British
flag went up over the town renamed New York and, save

for a brief intermission during a subsequent Anglo-Dutch war (1672–1674), it stayed there. Indeed, the British flag now waved from the Kennebec to Florida.

Yet one of the most interesting colonies did not take on firm outlines till late in the century. A number of settlers, British, Dutch, and Swedish, had found their way into the area which later became Pennsylvania and Delaware. When the pious and farsighted William Penn came into control of the region in 1681, he prepared to erect a model commonwealth on the principles of the Quakers—that sect which Voltaire later called the most truly Christian of peoples. In his benevolent fashion, he quieted the Indian title by friendly treaties of purchase. To attract colonists he offered liberal terms, assuring all that they could obtain land, establish thrifty homes, and live in justice and equality with their neighbors. No Christian would suffer from religious discrimination. In civil affairs the laws would rule, and the people would be a party to the laws. He directed the establishment of Philadelphia, his "city of brotherly love," with gardens surrounding each house, so that it would be "a green country town . . . and always be wholesome." In 1682 he came over himself, bringing about a hundred colonists. Pennsylvania throve wonderfully, attracting a great variety of settlers from Britain and the Continent, but keeping its Quaker lineaments.

Roughly speaking, two main instruments were used in this work of transferring Britons and others across the seas and founding new states. It was the chartered trading company, organized primarily for profit, which planted Virginia and Massachusetts. The London Company, so-called because organized by stockholders resident in London, had been granted its charter in 1606 to plant a colony between the thirty-fourth and forty-first degrees of latitude. The Plymouth Company, whose stockholders lived in Plymouth, Bristol, and other towns, was chartered that same year to establish a colony between the thirty-eighth and forty-fifth degrees. These companies could distribute lands, operate mines, coin money, and organize the defense of their colonies. The king, who granted the charters, kept ultimate jurisdiction over the colonial governments. After heavy financial losses, the London Company in 1624 saw its charter revoked, the king mak-

ing Virginia a royal colony. The Plymouth Company promoted various small Northern settlements and fishing stations,
but made no money, and after reorganization asked in 1635
for annulment of its charter, calling itself "only a breathless
carcass."

Yet if neither the London nor the Plymouth Company was
profitable financially, both did an effective work in colonization. The London Company was in a very real sense the parent of Virginia; the Plymouth Company and its successor,
the Council for New England, founded town after town in
Maine, New Hampshire, and Massachusetts. And a third
corporation, the Massachusetts Bay Company, had a peculiar
character and a special destiny. It originated as a body of
stockholders, most of them Puritans, who had commercial and
patriotic motives. Undaunted by the failure of the earlier
companies to pay dividends, they believed that better management would yield profits. Charles I granted a charter early
in 1629. Then a strange development took place. When the
king and High Church party under Archbishop Laud became
masters of the Church of England, many Puritan leaders
wished to emigrate. They had property, social position, and
an independent spirit. They did not wish to go out to Massachusetts Bay as mere vassals of a company in London. Moreover, they hoped to secure liberty to set up the kind of
Church government they liked. Therefore, the principal Puritans of the company simply bought up all its stock, took the
charter, and sailed with it to America. A commercial company was thus converted into a self-governing colony—the
colony of Massachusetts Bay.

The other principal instrument of colonization was the
proprietary grant. The proprietor was a man belonging to
the British gentry or nobility, with money at his command,
to whom the Crown gave a tract in America as it might have
given him an estate at home. The old rule of English law
was that all land not otherwise held belonged to the king,
and America fell under this rule. Lord Baltimore received
Maryland; William Penn, the son of an admiral to whom the
king owed money, received Pennsylvania; and a group of
royal favorites under Charles II received the Carolinas. All
these proprietors were given large powers to devise a government. Lord Baltimore, who had some of the absolutist ideas

of the Stuarts, was averse to giving his colonists any lawmaking power, but finally yielded to a popularly created assembly. Penn was wiser. In 1682 he called together an assembly, all of whom were elected by the settlers, and allowed them to enact a constitution, or "Great Charter." This vested many of the powers of government in representatives of the people—and Penn accepted the scheme.

As soon as it was proved that life in America might be prosperous and hopeful, a great spontaneous migration from Europe began. It came by uneven spurts and drew its strength from a variety of impulses. The first two great waves went to Massachusetts and Virginia. From 1628 to 1640 the Puritans in England were in a state of depression and apprehension, suffering much actual persecution. The royal authorities were committed to a revival of old forms in the Church and determined to make it completely dependent on the Crown and the archbishops. Political as well as ecclesiastical turmoil racked the land. The king dissolved Parliament and for ten years got on without it. He imprisoned his chief opponents. As his party seemed bent on subverting English liberty, many Puritans believed that the best course was to quit the island and build in America a new state. In the great emigration of 1628–1640, some twenty thousand of the sturdiest people of England left home. No fewer than twelve hundred ship voyages were made across the Atlantic with settlers, livestock, and furniture. Boston became one of the important seaports of the world, ministering to an area full of bustle and vitality. Harvard College was founded. Among the settlers were the ancestors of Franklin, the Adamses, Emerson, Hawthorne, and Abraham Lincoln. One striking characteristic of this movement was the migration of many Puritans not as individuals or families but in whole communities. Certain English towns were half depopulated. The new settlements consisted not of traders and farmers alone, but of doctors, lawyers, schoolteachers, businessmen, craftsmen, and ministers. New England became a microcosm of old England, carrying in extraordinary degree the seeds of future growth.

When the Civil War began in England in 1642 the Puritan exodus slackened; but what may be loosely called the Cavalier exodus began soon afterward. It gained volume in 1649, when Charles was beheaded, and continued vigorously until the

Restoration in 1660. As the Puritan migration had lifted the population of New England above thirty thousand, so the Cavalier migration was the main factor in increasing Virginia's population by 1670 to almost forty thousand. And the influx brought a remarkable amount of wealth, for though few of the newcomers were in fact Cavaliers, many were from the prosperous classes. Having capital, they bought and cultivated large estates, and having power or influence, they were often able to enlarge these estates from Royal lands. Virginia, at first predominantly a poor man's colony, became full of the well to do. This immigration brought over some of the greatest names in American history. Lee's ancestors first arrived in Virginia in the 1640's, and Washington's great-grandfather, John Washington, came in 1657. The family traditions of the Marshalls state that their American progenitor had been a captain in the royal forces during the English war and came to Virginia when the royalists were worsted. After the influx we meet in Virginia history such notable families as the Harrisons, the Carys, the Masons, the Carters, the Tylers, the Randolphs, and the Byrds.

But no real social distinction can be drawn between the settlers of Massachusetts and those of Virginia. The people who made both commonwealths great were drawn from the same large middle-class stratum. In England the Washingtons had been simply country squires, who had a tiny manor called Sulgrave in Northamptonshire; one had been mayor of Northampton. John Marshall's great-grandfather seems to have been a carpenter. The first Randolph in Virginia sprang from a family of Warwickshire squires of no great consequence. None of these Cavaliers was of better birth or more gentility than the Puritan John Winthrop, who came of a well-to-do family which owned the manor of Groton in Suffolk. None was of better origin than Sir Richard Saltonstall, who left many notable descendants in New England, or William Brewster, who as an undersecretary of state had been a man of influence at court. The great majority of the emigrants to both Massachusetts and Virginia before 1660 were yeomen, mechanics, shopkeepers, and clerks of modest means; while many in all parts of America were indentured servants, who paid for their passage by a stated term of labor. Their real wealth lay in their sturdy integrity, self-reliance, and energy.

The Rise of Self-Government

WHEREVER THE COLONISTS WENT, they carried with them in theory the rights of freeborn Britons, inheriting the traditions of the English struggle for liberty. This was specifically asserted in Virginia's first charter, which declared that the settlers were to have all the liberties, franchises, and immunities "as if they had been abiding and born within this our Realm of England." They were to have the protection of Magna Carta and the common law. This was a foundation principle of great significance. But to make it effective the colonists had to display constant vigilance and at times to wage a grim struggle. From almost the beginnings of their history, they began to rear their own fabric of constitutional government, contending for a stronger representative system, a control of the purse, and fuller guarantees of personal liberty.

The Virginia legislature, born in 1619, began at once to make a variety of laws. When the Crown revoked the charter of the Virginia Company, the House of Burgesses continued to show undiminished vigor. Indeed, within a few years it laid down certain fundamental rules upon its own rights. It declared that the governor was not to levy any taxes without legislative authority, that the money raised was to be employed as the legislature directed, and that the Burgesses were to be exempt from arrest. A little later the House declared that nothing might contravene a legislative act, while it took steps to safeguard trial by jury. So long as the Commonwealth endured in England, the Virginia legislature was a powerful body. Unfortunately, after the Restoration of the Stuarts it fell into weakness. But against its subserviency to the royal governor there was presently a fierce reaction.

In Massachusetts Bay also a representative system soon evolved. The terms of the charter seemed to give John Winthrop and his twelve assistants power to govern all the settlers. In the fall of 1630 a large body of colonists applied to this governing group to be made freemen of the corporation. It was decided the next year to grant the request; but "to the end that the body of the commons shall be preserved of good and honest men," thereafter nobody should "be admitted to the freedom of this body politic but such as are members of some of the churches within the limits of the same." A theocracy, or church-state, was thus erected. At the same time the twelve assistants resolved that they should keep their seats year after year unless removed by a special vote of the freemen. As they held practically all judicial and legislative powers, this security of tenure created a little oligarchy. The governor, the assistants, and the ministers held the colony in the hollow of their hands.

But a revolt was not long delayed. When a tax for defense was laid on Watertown in 1632, the unrepresented citizens grumbled and refused to pay it for fear of "bringing themselves and posterity into bondage." To pacify such complainants, it was soon decided that the governor and assistants should be guided in laying taxes by a board consisting of two delegates from every town. The foundation of a true legislature was thus laid. This body of town delegates, in fact, meeting with the governor and assistants, made up a one-chambered legislature. When it sat in 1634 it took full legislative authority into its hands, passing laws, admitting new freemen, and administering oaths of allegiance. Thus the second popular body of representatives on the continent had sprung into life. As the unicameral system worked badly, a decade later the legislature divided into two bodies, the assistants making the upper house, the town delegates the lower. For half a century the colony of Massachusetts Bay continued to be a Puritan republic, governed by its own legislators. And when it was made a royal province in 1691 under a new charter, the legislature remained a strong body. The Crown thereafter chose the governor, but the people chose the house, and the house kept a tight grip upon the purse.

Meanwhile, two permanent little republics sprang up on American soil—Rhode Island and Connecticut. The first overflow from Massachusetts Bay had established several towns in the lower Connecticut Valley. In 1639 their freemen met in Hartford and drew up the Fundamental Orders of Connecticut, the first written constitution framed by an American commonwealth for itself, the first, indeed, in the Western world. It provided for a governor, a body of assistants, and a lower house consisting of four deputies from each town, all to be popularly elected. After the Stuart Restoration, Connecticut obtained a charter from the Crown

(1662), but it was drawn in amazingly liberal terms; the freemen were to have power to govern themselves just as they liked, subject only to the vague restriction that no laws should be contrary to those of England. Rhode Island fared equally well. When its towns first drew together, Roger Williams had obtained for them a charter granting the fullest possible powers of self-government. The Restoration made a fresh application necessary. But the new charter of 1663 made Rhode Island, like Connecticut, a little republic within the British Empire, and it remained so until the Revolution. Electing all its own officers, making all its own laws, it was probably the freest community on the face of the earth.

By the year 1700 a general system of colonial government had taken form. Connecticut and Rhode Island held a special status as completely self-governing commonwealths, choosing all their own officers. The other colonies were either proprietary or royal, but no matter which, they had much the same political framework. A governor was appointed by either the king or the proprietor. About him and to some extent supporting him was a council, which outside Massachusetts was also appointed by the Crown or the proprietor. But whereas the governor was nearly always a Briton, the councilors were usually Americans; and though they generally represented the wealthier class, they often had views very different from those of the governor. At first their functions were chiefly administrative and judicial, but they developed more and more into an upper legislative chamber. Every colony had its representative assembly, chosen by those adult males who could meet certain property or other qualifications. This popular house initiated legislation, fixed appropriations, and levied taxes. Its strength lay in its power to represent public opinion and in its control of the purse— the elements which made Parliament so powerful in Britain after 1689.

The colonists had done much for themselves and posterity in winning and holding representative institutions. Three fundamental facts distinguished their political system. The first was the exalted valuation they placed upon written charters as guarantees of their liberties. England had no written constitution. But from the earliest years the colonists had learned to hold sacred the rights written into the charters granted to trading companies, proprietaries, or the people themselves.

This regard for a written system of fundamental law was to have a profound effect on American history. The second important fact was the almost constant conflict between the governors and the assemblies. They represented two antagonistic elements: the governor standing for vested rights and imperial interests, the assembly for popular rights and local interests. Finally, a marked feature of colonial politics was the insistence of the assemblies upon control over appropriations. They contended for a variety of objects—frequent elections, the exclusion of royal officeholders from their ranks, the right to choose their own speakers; above all, they asserted that they alone should grant or withhold appropriations. They met much opposition, but usually they made this demand good.

It was not true that the British colonies suffered from tyranny. By and large, they enjoyed a political freedom that in the seventeenth and eighteenth centuries was unequaled in any other part of the globe. But they did experience much class government. Theocratic New England had its ruling few whose power had to be broken. In the South, patrician landholders and merchants tried to set up a political monopoly.

Now and then, class tyranny raised an especially ugly head—and the colonists struck at it. The first such blow came in Virginia in Bacon's Rebellion of 1676. Indentured servants who had worked out their terms, immigrants tilling frontier farms, the lesser planters, and numerous laborers and slave overseers felt themselves maltreated. After 1670 no landless man had a vote. In various other ways they were deprived of a voice in political affairs. Assemblies sat practically unchanged for long periods—one, 1661–1675, for fourteen years; offices were parceled out to favorites of the royal governor and the richest planters. Education was above the reach of the poor. They were ill-guarded against Indian attacks, for the governor and his associates, with an eye to the fur trade, befriended the savages. Taxes were heavy. Markets were distant from the outer farms, and when the price of tobacco fell, the farmers were left in sore straits.

Finally an Indian attack upon the exposed settlements led to a dramatic revolt. The settlers clamored for protection, and when Governor Berkeley and the coastal planters gave them procrastinating answers, they became outraged. Na-

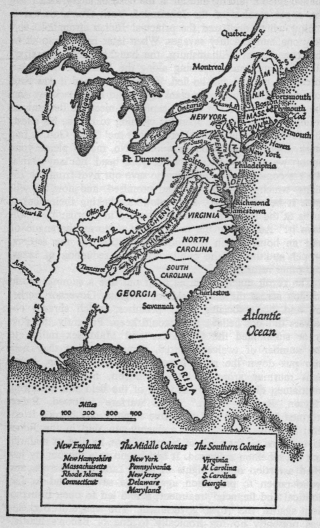

The Thirteen Colonies

New England	The Middle Colonies	The Southern Colonies
New Hampshire	New York	Virginia
Massachusetts	Pennsylvania	N. Carolina
Rhode Island	New Jersey	S. Carolina
Connecticut	Delaware	Georgia
	Maryland	

thaniel Bacon, putting himself at the head of angry men from the upper reaches of the James and York rivers, delivered a blow which destroyed the principal Indian stronghold and slew one hundred fifty savages. When later he went to sit in the assembly at Williamsburg, the haughty governor seized him; but an instant uprising along the heads of the rivers forced his release, and he fled. When he returned it was with four hundred armed men clanking behind him. Berkeley and the council hurried out of the capitol to meet the determined young planter. Tearing open his clothing to expose his chest, the governor exclaimed: "Here! Shoot me! 'Fore God, a fair mark, shoot!" But Bacon answered: "No, may it please your honor, we will not hurt a hair of your head, nor any man's. We are come for a commission to save our lives from the Indians, which you have so often promised, and now we will have it before we go." His followers, shaking their cocked fusils at the assembly windows, shouted in chorus: "We will have it!" Addressing the assembly in a stormy harangue of half an hour, Bacon demanded protection for the settlers, proper auditing of the public accounts, reduction of taxes, and other reforms.

The revolt quickly whirled itself out like a summer storm rushing across the dusty fields of Virginia. Governor Berkeley and his associates made promises, which shrewd observers did not believe they would keep. Presently the governor summoned the Gloucester and Middlesex militia to the number of twelve hundred, demanding that they help him put down the rebel Bacon. Thereupon a deep, indignant murmur arose of "Bacon, Bacon, Bacon," and the militiamen disgustedly walked out of the field still muttering "Bacon, Bacon, Bacon." Open warfare followed. Bacon stormed Jamestown and on a fine summer day burned it entire; he took possession of a twenty-gun ship in the James River. Then, at the crisis of his operations, he died of malaria, and his rebellion collapsed. It had begun as a thoroughly justified assertion of the rights of small farmers, laborers, and frontiersmen to protection against the savages and to fair political and financial treatment; it had led to open insurrection against the royal government. The vengeful Berkeley was presently bowing ironically to one of Bacon's lieutenants as a prisoner: "Mr. Drummond! You are very welcome. I am more glad to see you than any man in Virginia. Mr.

Drummond, you shall be hanged in half an hour." But abortive as the rebellion seemed, it had exemplified the frontier spirit of independence and sturdy self-assertion—the American spirit—in a memorable fashion. It was not forgotten.

Church and State in the Colonies

As THE THIRST for political freedom grew in America, so did the spirit of religious toleration. From early times the British colonies were the homes of many sects which learned to live together harmoniously.

The Church of England was transplanted to Virginia with the first settlers. One of the first buildings erected in Jamestown was that plain church which, now beautifully restored, still looks out over the river. When Lord Delaware came as governor in 1616, he had it repaired and enlarged, so that it became a structure of dignity, with cedar pews, walnut altar, a tall pulpit and lectern, and a baptismal font. Here the planters married the girls who came over by shiploads; here their children were christened. As Virginia grew, new parishes were created and churches erected, to be supported by public taxation as the Established Church was supported in England. For some years every settler was taxed a bushel of corn and ten pounds of tobacco for the clergy. This was not sufficient; and in 1632 the legislature passed an act compelling every settler, in addition to the former contribution, to set aside for the minister his twentieth calf, twentieth goat, and twentieth pig. After the Stuart Restoration the annual stipend in tobacco was made larger and more certain. In addition, the clergy were supposed to have free grants of land, called glebes, and other perquisites. The Anglican establishment was very much a reality in Virginia, as it became in other parts of the South, notably Maryland and South Carolina.

Nevertheless, the Virginia Church was neither a flourishing body materially nor one which impressed itself spiritually or intellectually upon the settlers. Social and economic conditions were unfavorable to its growth. Most parishes were spread out over huge tracts of sparsely settled territory. The boundaries of many, following the riverbanks closely, were from thirty to sixty miles in length. Those who went to church had to travel long distances over execrable roads, or to paddle laboriously for hours up or down the streams. Naturally, attendance was irregular; even George Washington, a devout vestryman, was open to the charge of capricious churchgoing. In bad winter weather the minister would find most of the pews empty. One man complained that he sometimes traveled fifty miles to hold service and found only a handful present. In these sparsely settled parishes, too, the minister's support was often meager. As prices fell, the local taxes, unevenly collected in tobacco and livestock, were inadequate, and when the legislature raised them, the poorer parishes made bitter complaints.

With salaries low, tenure insecure, and many hardships to meet, it was difficult to obtain ministers of ability, piety, and zeal. The best clergymen would not emigrate from England to the colonies; they could find better careers at home. Those who came were often dull of mind, lazy of body, or dubious in morals. We soon find governors and others complaining that the Virginia clergy were "a pack of scandalous fellows," given to "many vices not agreeable to their coats," and addicted to "swearing, drunkenness, and fighting." They were like Fielding's Parson Trulliber. Reform movements were undertaken, one of which led to the founding in 1693 of the second colonial college, William and Mary, primarily as a training school for young ministers. But the establishment remained unsatisfactory down to the Revolution.

In Virginia and other parts of the South the Anglican Church accepted public support, but had no control whatever over the state. In Massachusetts and Connecticut, the Puritan Church was for decades largely identified with the state, exercised a marked control over the government, and, in fact, long maintained a kind of ecclesiastical despotism.

The fundamental reason for the Puritan migration to Massachusetts was to establish a church-state and not to find religious freedom. The Puritans were not religious radicals; they were religious conservatives. In England they had believed in the Church of England, but had wished to modify the absolutism of its hierarchy and to alter it by abolishing Catholic forms, observing the Sabbath strictly, and keeping a close watch upon morals. Failing in their hope to capture the establishment, they sought the American wilderness to set up their "particular Church," supported by public taxation, interwoven with the state, and tolerating no opposition. When Endicott founded the first Puritan church in Salem, two men in his company hauled an Anglican prayerbook out of their luggage and wished to read the services. He promptly put them and their obnoxious prayerbook on board ship and hustled them back to England. The Puritan leaders at once created a close-knit church-state, its authority vested in an aristocracy of iron-willed, able, and despotic Church rulers.

The triumph of this Calvinist church-state, with its harsh discipline, meant that the Pilgrim or Separatist ideal of self-governing congregations was submerged. At Plymouth the Pilgrims had established a little Church democracy, the people managing their religious affairs without deference to bishops or synods. But the Puritans found this anarchical and demoralizing, for they believed in a firmly centralized control.

There were four steps in the erection of this church-state in Massachusetts. The first was a basic provision that unless a man was a member of the Puritan Church in good standing, he could not vote or hold office. The second made attendance at church compulsory for everyone, thus guarding the Church and colony against unbelievers. The third required that the Church and state both approve the incorporation of any new church. No nest of dissenters or unbelievers could set up shop for themselves in any part of Massachusetts; those who wanted a church which did not strictly conform to the Puritan type must emigrate to some other part of America. Finally, a provision for state support made it possible for the state to act with the Church heads in punishing any rebellion or infraction of discipline. The synod of the Puritan churches promulgated, in 1646, what is called the Cambridge Platform, providing that if any church congregation rebelled against the synod, or the Church rules, the civil government stopped the minister's pay, discharged him, and put in his place a man who would conform.

This church-state in Massachusetts, this rule by a combination of priests and magistrates, lasted with gradually declining vigor till 1691, when an improved charter was granted by William and Mary and Massachusetts was made a royal province. The theocracy had just one great achieve-

ment to its credit. The grim Puritan organization resisted
the encroachments of Charles II with a dogged determination which counted powerfully in the development of political freedom in the New World. This resistance did much
to pave the way for the task of achieving political independence late in the next century. But the theocracy had a
number of things to its discredit. It was an oppressive tyranny; it committed some shameful acts of persecution against
Quakers and others; it was hostile to freedom of thought and
speech; and its fanatical temper helped to account for the
Salem witchcraft delusion, during which nineteen men and
women were hanged. As population thickened and new ideas
took root, a strong liberal party had arisen to combat the
conservatives under Increase Mather and his pedantic son,
Cotton, both Boston ministers of renown. It was a happy
moment for America when the theocracy declined.

In Roger Williams and Anne Hutchinson, Massachusetts
sent forth two great apostles of religious liberty. Williams,
a highly educated man who had been graduated from Cambridge University in England, and a most devout Christian,
was a radical opponent of the whole Puritan idea of theocracy. He believed that Church and state should be entirely
separated; that it was folly to try to compel men to attend
church; and that dissenters should be calmly tolerated. The
government, according to his view, should protect all well-
behaved sects alike. Williams, ordered by the Massachusetts
authorities to return to England, instead escaped through the
snows to make Rhode Island a land in which his principles
could be applied. Anne Hutchinson, originally of Salem, and
the first woman to take a prominent part in religious and
political matters, preached doctrines akin to what later, in
Emerson's day, was called transcendentalism. It was the duty
of every individual, she said, to follow the promptings of an
inner supernatural voice; and it was the presence of the
Holy Ghost within, and not any amount of good works or
sanctification, which really saved an individual. Living for
a time in the Rhode Island country, she finally perished in an
Indian massacre in New York.

Throughout the middle colonies, toleration early became
the rule. In New York alone was any serious effort made
to establish the Anglican Church, and even there it almost
completely failed. The great majority of the people belonged

to other sects. As the eighteenth-century historian William Smith wrote, the people were for "an equal, universal toleration of Protestants." The Jews supported a synagogue. In the Quaker colonies of Pennsylvania and Delaware, sects of all kinds were welcomed, and many small and eccentric denominations, chiefly German, found root there. Catholics were not molested, and in Philadelphia the Mass was publicly celebrated. Maryland also was a land where faiths long hostile lived in general concord. In 1649 an assembly which was partly Catholic, partly Protestant, passed a Toleration Act which is one of the great landmarks of religious freedom. It dealt harshly with non-Christians and with Unitarians, but it placed Protestants and Catholics on precisely the same plane. A pregnant phrase was written into Maryland's Toleration Act. Its authors declared that toleration was wisdom because "the inforceing of the conscience in matters of Religion hath frequently fallen out to be of dangerous Consequence." As the decades passed, most colonists became convinced that it was just and prudent to let men worship as they pleased.

CHAPTER 2

The Colonial Heritage

A Developing Americanism

Two MAIN FACTORS may be distinguished in the development of a distinctive American nationality during the colonial period, a character that was already crystallizing when the Revolution began. One factor was a new people—an amalgamation of different national stocks. The other factor was a

new land—a country rich, empty, and demanding as the price
of its bounty only that the newcomers should bring it industry
and courage. By 1775 a distinctly American society, with its
own social, economic, and political traits, was emerging. At
some points it approached closely to the European pattern:
The merchants, professional men, and mechanics of Boston
and New York were not easily distinguishable from similar
groups in London and Bristol. But the great mass of Americans was growing quite distinct from the European type in
the old homeland.

The emigration to America had fortunately taken place in
a way which made the English language and English institutions everywhere dominant, so that the country possessed
a general unity. Neither the Germans nor the French Huguenots set up a separate colony, as they might have done; they
mingled with the first British comers, adopting their language
and outlook. The English migration soon swamped the Dutch
in the Hudson Valley and the Swedes on the Delaware. Yet
this happy unity of tongue and basic institutions coexisted
with a remarkable diversity in national origins.

We should neither exaggerate nor underestimate the amalgamation of peoples in colonial days. At the time of the
Revolution probably over three fourths of the white colonists
were still of British blood; but the infusion of Dutch, German, French, and other Continental stocks was significant.
The first great waves of settlement had been English waves,
and New England and the lowland parts of the South remained almost purely English. But while the original flow
continued, in the eighteenth century two other heavy waves
of emigration came from Europe—the German and the
Scotch-Irish. Each was represented, at the outbreak of the
Revolution, by hundreds of thousands of settlers.

It was the German immigration which first became important. Western German areas, and the Rhineland in especial, were filled with misery and discontent. The ravages
of the French armies under Louis XIV had been of the
most cruel character. They were followed by a systematic
religious persecution of the Lutherans and other sects, reinforced by the political tyranny of the small German princes.
When the government of Queen Anne and her successors offered safety and religious freedom under the English flag, by
tens of thousands the Germans poured into England and her

colonies. An advance guard from Crefeld had come to William Penn's domains as early as 1683, making Germantown a seat of thriving handicrafts. The first paper mill in the colonies was set up there by the Rittenhouse family; beer was brewed and cloth woven. But the real tide began to flow after 1700. Some went to the Mohawk Valley in New York, some to New Brunswick in New Jersey, but most of them to Pennsylvania. As time passed, several thousand Germans and Swiss came in a single year.

So great was this influx that Benjamin Franklin estimated that just before the Revolution one third of the Pennsylvania population was German. Lutheran, Moravian, Mennonite and United Brethren settlements dotted the province. In considerable areas little English was used, and in 1739 a German newspaper was set up at Germantown. Baron Stiegel's iron foundry and glass factory became famous, as did Sauer's printing establishment. But most of the Germans were thrifty farmers whose hard work made the limestone region of Pennsylvania a huge wheat granary. They did not take readily to pioneering, but preferred to buy in a region already settled, protected, and partly improved. They cleared the land thoroughly; they built big, handsome barns before they spent much energy on houses; they kept their stock fat and sleek, their fences high and strong. Living frugally, they sold as much as possible of their produce. The women worked in the fields, but they nevertheless reared large families.

The Scotch-Irish, a more aggressive stock, furnished the chief pioneering element in Pennsylvania, the Shenandoah Valley, and the upland parts of Carolina. They too had fled from oppression at home, for they suffered under the Anglican establishment in Ireland, while the English laws against Irish manufactures were disastrous to their weaving industry. Coming over in shiploads, they brought with them a bitter anti-English feeling. They were more Scotch than Irish, most of them being Presbyterians who had migrated to Ulster within the past century; and the Presbyterian Church organization had given them a natural understanding and love of democratic institutions. Some of them settled in New Hampshire, some in Ulster and Orange counties in New York; but their principal refuge was Pennsylvania and the valleys stretching southward into Virginia and Carolina. Plunging into the wilderness, they lived by hunting, cleared the land, erected log cabins, and hewed the first rough farms out of the forests. These "bold and indigent strangers," as a Pennsylvania official called them, were impatient of legal restraints and of quitrents charged by the Penns and other landowners. They hated the Indians and were quick to quarrel with them. Their acquisitiveness gave point to the old remark: "They kept the Sabbath and everything else they could lay their hands on." They made wonderfully efficient pioneer settlers. Spreading south and west, reaching upland Georgia and penetrating Kentucky before the Revolution, rearing large families, showing marked gifts for politics and Indian fighting, the Scotch-Irish began to lay a strong impress on American life. Among them were names later famous— Calhoun, Jackson, Polk, Houston, McKinley, Wilson.

In the Shenandoah and other interior valleys the Scotch-Irish, English, Germans, Dutch, and others soon mingled their bloods to create a new American people. The last colony to be founded, Georgia, also represented a mixture of peoples. General James Oglethorpe, supported by other philanthropic Englishmen, obtained a royal charter for it in 1732 as a refuge for poor debtors and other unfortunates and as an outpost against Spanish and Indian aggression. To Georgia the paternal trustees brought carefully selected English people, a large body of German Protestants, and a number of Scotch Highlanders. At first slavery was prohibited. All non-Catholic faiths were encouraged, and Anglicans, Moravians, Presbyterians, Anabaptists, Lutherans, and Jews worshiped side by side. The Anglican Church at Savannah was distinguished by two famous ministers, John Wesley and George Whitefield.

Other non-English groups were smaller but not unimportant. The revocation of the Edict of Nantes brought hundreds—possibly thousands—of French Huguenots to the English colonies, and names like Laurens and Legaré in South Carolina, Maury and Latané in Virginia, Delano and Jay in New York, Revere and Faneuil in Massachusetts, suggest how widely they scattered. A sprinkling of Swiss came with the Germans; there were substantial numbers of Swedes and Finns along the Delaware, and, chiefly in the towns, small groups of Italians and Portuguese Jews. The defeat at Culloden, in 1745, sent many Highland Scots in flight to America. Town names like Radnor and Bryn Mawr in Pennsylvania and Welsh Neck in South Carolina remind us that the Welsh too made their contribution. It is clear that even in the colonial era America was something of a melting pot.

The second great factor in shaping a distinct American nationality was the land, and especially the frontier. At the outset the coastal strip itself, impinging on the dark forest, was the frontier. The early settlers were unbelievably inexperienced. The Pilgrims searched the Plymouth thickets for spices and thought the wild beasts they heard might be "lions"; some of the dandies at Jamestown thought they could live there much as in London streets. But the newcomers had to adjust themselves to the primitive wilderness, or die. At the very beginning we meet in Captain John Smith and Miles Standish men whose daring and endurance remind us of such later heroes as Robert Rogers, Daniel Boone, and Kit Carson. From the Indians the settlers learned how to plant and fertilize corn, grow tobacco, cook succotash, make canoes and snowshoes, stalk game, tan deerskins, grow expert in woodcraft. By hard experience the pioneer became hunter, farmer, and fighter all in one. A new agriculture, a new architecture, a new domestic economy, arose. Within a decade there were men in the New World who had little in common with the old neighbors they had left in England—and their children had still less. They possessed a more rugged, practical, homespun outlook upon life. Stephen Vincent Benét caught this in his picture of Dickon Heron:

> I have given no pledge, I have made no vow,
> But they call me Captain Heron now
> And this is a world where a man starts clear
> Once he's paid the price of getting here . . .
> For here is a knight and a Newgate debtor
> And which of the two will prove the better?
> Can you read the riddle? I will not try
> But we live under another sky
> From the men who have crossed the seas.

The frontier was pushed back to the highest navigation point on the rivers by 1700 or thereabouts, back to the Alleghenies by 1765, and on across the mountains just before the Revolution. Successive generations were subjected to its influence and emerged from the experience reshaped as by a gigantic, irresistible mold.

On the frontier a rough equality of social condition was the rule—and, indeed, such equality prevailed generally outside the few large towns. There was no icing on the cake of American society. The English redemptioners working out their passage costs by five years of labor, the poor debtors freed from prison, the Germans fleeing from the ravaged Palatinate, the Scotch-Irish driven out by English mercantile laws—all came with nothing and had to struggle hard for property. As plebeians, they disliked the aristocrats who had obtained large land grants, or who made fortunes from trade and speculation. But no matter how poor, the average settler felt in America a sense of opportunity and independence that he had not known in Europe. This feeling was born of the wide spaces and abundant natural wealth of the country. St. John Crèvecoeur, a French gentleman who came to the American colonies about 1759 and settled down as an "American Farmer," wrote that "the rich stay in Europe, it is only the middling and poor that emigrate." He added: "Everything tends to regenerate them; new laws, a new mode of living, a new social system; here they are become men." And in an eloquent passage he described the emergent Americanism, based on unfettered activity in a land of vast natural resources:

A European, when he first arrives, seems limited in his intentions as well as in his views; but he very suddenly alters his scale. He no sooner breathes our air than he forms new schemes, and embarks on designs he never would have thought of in his own country. There the plenitude of society confines many useful ideas, and often extinguishes the most laudable schemes which here ripen into maturity. . . . He begins to feel the effects of a sort of resurrection; hitherto he had not lived, but simply vegetated; he now feels himself a man, because he is treated as such; the laws of his own country had overlooked him in his insignificancy; the laws of this cover him with their mantle. Judge what an alteration there must arise in the mind and thoughts of this man! He begins to forget his former servitude and dependence, his heart involuntarily dilates and glows, and his first swell inspires him with those new thoughts which mark an American.

But while an American character was developing, down to the eve of the Revolution few of the colonists had any real consciousness of the fact. They thought of themselves primarily as loyal British subjects, secondarily as Virginians, New Yorkers, or Rhode Islanders. As the author of *Virginia Hearts of Oak* wrote in 1766:

> Though we feast and grow fat on America's soil
> Yet we own ourselves subjects to Britain's fair isle;
> And who's so absurd to deny us the name,
> Since true British blood flows in every vein.

By 1750 the thirteen colonies had taken firm root and contained almost 1,500,000 people. They ran the whole length of the coast from the spruce of the Androscoggin Valley to the palmettos of the St. Johns. Each had characteristics of its own, while they fell into four fairly well-defined sections.

One section was New England, a country of small, rocky, well-tilled farms, of lumbering, and of a wide variety of maritime employments: construction of the kind Longfellow described in *The Building of the Ship*, codfishing like that described by Kipling in *Captains Courageous*, whaling as pictured in Melville's *Moby Dick*, and overseas trade similar to that described by R. H. Dana in *Two Years Before the Mast*. Another section was the middle colonies, made up partly of small farms and partly of great estates, with a good deal of small-scale manufacturing, and with lively shipping interests in New York and Philadelphia. A third was composed of the Southern colonies, where large plantations, worked by gangs of black slaves, producing indigo, rice, and tobacco, were the most prominent, though by no means the most common, feature. Finally, there was the most American section of all: the great border strip or back country, stretching from Maine to Georgia, where pioneer hunters, hardy log-cabin settlers, and a sprinkling of more solid farmers pushed toward the interior. This border country was much the same north and south. In western Massachusetts, western Pennsylvania, and western Carolina alike it produced hard-hitting, resourceful men, indifferent to book learning, impatient of restraint, and invincibly optimistic.

The New England Colonies

THE COASTAL SETTLEMENTS of New England displayed
great expansive power. We have already seen that one migration of Massachusetts people founded Rhode Island and another migration founded the twin colonies of Connecticut and
New Haven, later combined into one. A third body of Puritans scattered northward into Maine and New Hampshire,
areas originally claimed by non-Puritan promoters, and there
quickly became dominant. Massachusetts by 1650 asserted
political control over both the New Hampshire and the
Maine settlements, but toward the end of the century the
former were made into a distinct royal province. This marked
expansive quality of New England was to continue generation
after generation and was to send wave after wave of the
descendants of the Puritans westward until they reached the
Pacific.

Throughout the colonial period New England kept a remarkably homogeneous population, its 700,000 people at
the time of the Revolution being almost purely English in
blood. They were generally alike in language, manners, piety,
and ways of thought; little Rhode Island alone standing somewhat apart, for its political radicals and dissenting church
groups gave it a peculiar stamp. The Yankees had sprung
in the main from a remarkably sturdy, independent, and intelligent English stock and took a stern pride in their ancestry—the choice grain sieved out, as one leader put it,
to plant the wilderness. Those who tilled the land or fished
the seas made a comfortable living, while merchants, shipowners, and small manufacturers often accumulated small
fortunes. The foreign commerce of Boston alone employed
six hundred vessels by 1770; the fisheries of Massachusetts,
furnishing large exports to Europe and the West Indies, were
estimated to be worth $1,250,000 annually. With good reason
the codfish was made the emblem of the commonwealth.
Most New England households were self-supporting, weaving
their own cloth, growing their own food, making their own
furniture and shoes. Industry, thrift, hardheaded enterprise,
and a narrow piety were Yankee characteristics; and if the
people were not much liked in other sections, they were
universally respected.

In New England both Church and school held a place of special dignity. All Puritan communities looked to their minister as an intellectual as well as a religious mentor and to the meetinghouse for the greater part of their social intercourse. The clergy were vigorous, aggressive men, strong not only in learning but also in community leadership, and regarded with awe by their followers. They taught damnatory doctrines with gusto, and Jonathan Edwards' word pictures of sinners writhing in the torments of hell were famous. John Cotton declared that he loved to "sweeten his mouth" with a passage of the stern Calvin every night before he slept. But the clergy had to be men of power, rectitude, and erudition. They were deeply versed in theology and the ancient languages. President Chauncy of Harvard, who had the Old Testament read to him in Hebrew in the morning and the New in Greek in the afternoon, commented upon them in Latin; many another minister could have done the same. From the beginning the Puritans provided for public education. For, as the author of *New England's First Fruits* tells us, "one of the things we longed for, and looked after, was to advance Learning, and perpetuate it to Posterity; dreading to leave an illiterate Ministry to the Churches, when our present Ministers shall lie in the Dust." Boston Latin School was opened in 1635, and the next year "it pleased God to stir up the heart of one Mr. Harvard to give the one halfe of his Estate towards the erecting of a Colledge, and all his Library." And in 1647 the Massachusetts General Court enacted "Ye Ould Deluder Satan" law requiring every town of fifty householders to support an elementary school and every town of one hundred householders to set up a grammar school. Connecticut soon enacted similar laws. Though this and subsequent school legislation was widely evaded, it is probably true that education and literacy were more widespread in New England than anywhere else in the seventeenth-century world.

As time passed, the early rigidity of New England life was pleasantly modified. The carrying trade and mercantile interests brought in not only wealth but also new ideas. Lawyers, physicians, and other professional men grew numerous. In Massachusetts and Connecticut the Sabbath, which lasted from six o'clock Saturday till sunset on Sunday, was stringently kept; no travel was allowed, no tavern might

entertain a guest, games were forbidden, and even a knot
of men talking in the streets might be arrested. But new
fashions like periwigs came in, the Anglicans introduced a
merry observance of Christmas, and politics, money-getting,
love-making, and feasting began to play a more frankly
recognized part in life.

A document which gives an unrivaled picture of the great
transition from the old order to the new in Massachusetts is
the diary of Samuel Sewall, who was graduated from Harvard in 1671 and began three years later a record which
he kept up till 1729. This grimly old-fashioned Puritan, who
became Chief Justice, liked a glass of Madeira and a ride
in his chariot, but detested all innovation. As we read his
three volumes, a many-colored vision rises before us. We
see the little city of Boston, solidly built on its neck of land,
with the three hills, the spires, the fortress, and the harbor
crowded with shipping. We hear the watchman call the
hours and the public crier make his rounds. We feel the
shudder that runs through the town when news comes of
pirates on the coast, or of the Comte de Frontenac ready to
descend upon New England with his French and Indian
forces. We see the citizens hunting after stray cows, as
Sewall himself did, "from one end and side of the Town to
t'other"; gathering in groups to discuss the nominations for
council; and streaming to that favorite amusement, a funeral.
When the harbor is solid ice up to the island Castle, we shiver
with the poor churchgoers as we hear the hard-frozen sacra-
mental bread "rattling sadly as broken into the plates." Smallpox runs over the town. Childbirths are numerous, for every
goodwife is a fruitful branch, but child deaths almost keep
them pace. We see training day celebrated on the Common, with the Ancient and Honorable Artillery and other
companies brave in uniforms, great firing and excitement,
and gentlemen and ladies dining in tents on the grass. We
look at the redcoats with disfavor and hear with horror that
the royal governor has given a ball at his palace that lasted
till three in the morning. We join the concourse that goes
out to Broughton's Hill to see malefactors hanged. We see
the constables breaking up ninepin games on Beacon Hill,
or as censorious Puritans called it, Mount Whoredom, and
watch Sewall as a magistrate riding through Charlestown or
Boston on Saturday at sundown ordering the shop shutters

put up. But little by little we see the old Puritan strictness giving way to the modern age.

Crime and pauperism were rarer in thrifty, orderly New England than in other colonies. Indentured servants, at first unknown, became common in the eighteenth century, but they and other laborers found it easy to attain independence, and outside of Rhode Island slavery declined. The town system of government, with all the public business transacted at a town meeting of qualified voters, fostered self-reliance. Boston, New Haven, and other large centers came to have numerous aristocrats with fine houses, coats of arms, and plate, while class lines were real and distinct. But in no part of the world did the common people show a sturdier self-respect.

The Middle Colonies

THE MIDDLE COLONIES had a far more varied, cosmopolitan, and tolerant society, less elevated but also less austere. Pennsylvania, with its sister province Delaware, counted by the Revolution about 350,000 people; New York and New Jersey together possessed not far from that number. As elsewhere in America, the great mass of the people depended upon the soil for subsistence. In the better parts of these provinces the landowners rapidly grew prosperous. Quaker farms in Pennsylvania, for example, boasted of substantial brick houses, rooms wainscoted or papered, heavy furniture, and good china and glassware. The tables, where farmers and their servants ate together, groaned with simple but varied fare. Meat, rare in many parts of Europe, was eaten thrice daily. So rapidly did farm appliances increase that by 1765 Pennsylvania boasted nine thousand wagons. Agriculture was more varied than in other sections; there were a variety of grains and vegetables, fine orchards, all kinds of livestock, and many landowners had their own fish ponds. The Hudson Valley was parceled out into the manorial estates of the Van Rensselaers, Cortlandts, Livingstons, and other aristocrats, who had huge houses with retinues of servants, and whose annual rent days possessed a feudal quality. But Long Island and upper New York were full of small holdings as well.

Besides the tillers of the soil, Pennsylvania and New York had an increasing number of merchants, tradesmen, and mechanics. The carrying trade, devoted chiefly to the export of lumber, furs, grain, and other natural products, and the import of manufactures, sugar, and wines, was extensive and profitable. Just before the Revolution nearly five hundred vessels, with more than seven thousand seamen, plied out of Delaware Bay, while the Hudson and Long Island Sound were full of shipping. Both Philadelphia and New York had become great distributing points for interior trade. One way of making a fortune was to send grain and dried fish to the West Indies, bringing back slaves or molasses; another was to load furs at Albany and exchange them in London for fine textiles, china, or furniture. Small manufactures were gaining a foothold. In Pennsylvania and New Jersey iron furnaces sprang up, and the export of iron products led Parliament to pass an act to suppress rolling mills. New Yorkers made glassware and felt hats; Rhode Islanders specialized in rum. As wealth increased, professional men grew more common. The lawyers of the principal towns achieved political leadership and did as much as any other group to bring on the Revolution.

A more mixed and polished society could be found in New York and even in staid Philadelphia than in New England. The merchants and shippers, keeping in close touch with Europe, dispensed a gay and fashionable hospitality. When John Adams paused in New York on his way to Philadelphia, he was impressed by the splendid houses, fine silver, and elaborate cuisine. That city boasted of its clubs, its balls, its concerts, its open-air pleasure gardens, its coffee-houses, its private theatricals, and its funerals, which sometimes cost several thousand dollars. The Dutch had shown a taste for holidays which the English gradually acquired; wealthy people dressed in the latest London mode, with silks and velvets, powdered wigs and smallswords; and the mixture of sects and races helped ideas to circulate briskly. Philadelphia, with its broad streets and well-swept sidewalks, had a quieter elegance. But it was notable for its public institutions—particularly the College and the American Philosophical Society—and it cultivated those scientific studies in which Franklin, Benjamin Rush, and the botanist William Bartram gained distinction. The largest city in the colonies, it was neat, substantial, and prosperous. It seemed to Thomas Jefferson a more impressive city than London or Paris—and Jefferson was no mean judge. Religious doctrines in New York became so liberal that churchmen complained of the "free-thinking," while politics aroused more passion in that province than anywhere else in British America. In Quaker-dominated Pennsylvania, opinion was more conservative; but just before the Revolution the Quaker ascendancy in politics was violently shaken by the Scotch-Irish and Germans.

Throughout the middle colonies a large population of Negroes added to the color of life. The Quakers were deeply hostile to slavery and in the late colonial period produced one antislavery leader of international renown—that "beautiful soul," as Lamb called him, John Woolman. Nor did slavery flourish among the Scotch-Irish and Germans, who worked hard with their own hands. But it was common in the cities and on the manorial estates along the Hudson. In general, life had an ampler quality in the middle provinces than in New England. The climate, the soil, and the people were more genial. There was nothing else in the North quite like New Year's Day in New York, when salutes were fired at dawn, and gentlemen went about town paying calls, eating delicacies, and consuming so much wine and punch that they often had to be taken home in carriages. There was nothing quite like the reception New York gave to a new royal governor, with pomp and ceremony; or like the celebration on one of the manors when an heir was married.

The Southern Colonies

THE DISTINCTIVE FEATURES of the Southern colonies, and particularly of Virginia and South Carolina, the richest and most influential, were three. They were the almost exclusively rural character of their life, Charleston and Baltimore being the only towns of even slight importance; the prominent place held by large estates, with troops of slaves, imposing mansions, and ostentatious living; and the sharp stratification of society into classes. Among the whites, the upper class was composed of well-to-do and often aristocratic planters, who furnished a singularly able political leadership; the middle class was made up of small planters, farmers, and a few tradesmen, factors, and mechanics; while the lower class was of yeomen and "poor whites." Below all three groups were the slaves, who by 1770 in Virginia numbered somewhat less than half the total population of 450,000, in Maryland fully one third of the population of about 200,000, and in South Carolina outnumbered the whites in the ratio of two to one.

The diffusion of population was partly the result of the plantation system, each estate being to a great degree self-sufficient, and partly of the aversion of Southerners to towns. The great landowners, whose plantations spread along the tidewater rivers, carried on a direct trade with England or with Northern cities, requiring no large mercantile group. Slavery all but crushed the life out of a promising handicraft system. In vain did Virginia pass laws designed to create large towns—one, for example, requiring each county to erect a house in Williamsburg. The largest center in the colony when the Revolution opened was Norfolk, with about seven thousand people, while Williamsburg had only two hundred straggling houses. Colonel Byrd had written of Fredericksburg in 1732 that besides the "top man of the place," it had only "one merchant, a tailor, a smith, an ordinary-keeper, and a lady who acts both as doctress and coffee-house keeper." The situation was much the same elsewhere in the South. Charleston just before the Revolution was a rustic-looking town of fifteen thousand people, half Negroes, with unpaved sandy streets; Baltimore was a rather rude port of about the same size, dependent on its trade in farm products from the "back country." The lack of towns had some unhappy consequences. Boston possessed a newspaper as early as 1690, but it was not until 1736 that the *Virginia Gazette* appeared. No theatrical performance was given by a professional company in Virginia until within twenty-five years of the Revolution; and the dependence of the tidewater section on more enterprising parts of the empire for even brooms, chairs, hoes, and rough crockery aroused complaint among farsighted leaders.

The great plantations of Maryland, Virginia, and South Carolina were scattered through the low country, generally fronting on some river or "run" which afforded water transportation. Each had its family mansion, usually of brick or stone, its storehouses, blacksmith shop, cooperage, and other outbuildings, and its straggling huts of the Negroes' quarters.

Many of the large houses, like General Ringgold's Fountain Rock, William Byrd's Westover, George Mason's Gunston Hall, and John Rutledge's estate near Charleston, were beautifully designed and finished. Inside were paneled halls, fine staircases, and large rooms. The best houses contained handsome mahogany furniture, some made in America but most of it imported from England, heavy silver services with London hallmarks, silk or velvet hangings, good family portraits, engravings (Hogarth being a prime favorite), and considerable libraries. Robert Carter of Nomini Hall had more than fifteen hundred volumes, and the third William Byrd more than four thousand. A good many planters had town houses also in Annapolis, Williamsburg, or Charleston, to which they traveled every autumn in their family coach for a season of balls, dinners, cardplaying, racing, and legislative activities. As a class the planters were often charged with indolence. But the proper care of a great plantation required much labor and anxiety; Washington worked hard in his oversight of Mount Vernon, while Robert Carter of Nomini Hall, whose holdings included sixty thousand acres scattered over Virginia, a textile establishment, a share in an ironworks, various mines, and handicraft shops, was incessantly busy. The planters were also charged with lack of intellectual tastes. But they took a passionate interest in politics, held most of the elective offices, and talked and wrote on governmental questions with extraordinary ability, and a surprising number of them interested themselves in science and achieved election to the Royal Society.

The lesser planters and farmers of the South—typified very well by Thomas Jefferson's father, Peter, who acquired cheap frontier land by surveying and helped clear it himself —were hard-working, intelligent, thrifty men. They hewed away the wilderness, built modest houses, and acquired property; many tilled broad tracts with the aid of slaves; some, like Peter Jefferson, married into the aristocracy. They were a sturdy race, self-reliant and independent in temper, and determined to maintain their British liberties. If they lacked polish and education, they had plenty of hard sense and produced brilliant political leaders of democratic views, like Jefferson, James Madison, and Patrick Henry. Indeed, differences between the upper and middle classes in the South often grew vague, and intermarriage tended to knit the two together. In Maryland particularly, the eighteenth century witnessed a strong tendency to break up cumbersome estates into small, efficient farms. Merchants and attorneys stood on a somewhat lower level than landholders, while shopkeeping was regarded for generations with the same condescension which it then met in England. Business communities like Baltimore and Norfolk stood on a plane distinctly inferior to the colonial capitals. But land speculation flourished among the best circles in the South as well as in the North. The second William Byrd in 1737 founded Richmond by breaking up an estate on the upper James and selling it in town lots.

The lowest white stratum of society in the South was marked off by distinct lines. Some convicts, released debtors, and indentured servants who came over from Europe deteriorated under frontier conditions and made up a body, illiterate, vulgar, and shiftless, which was despised even by the Negroes. Of course, no degradation necessarily attached to an indenture. Many emigrants of high character paid for their passage to America by giving bond service. They included English and Continental craftsmen—cabinetmakers, tailors, silversmiths, jewelers, gunsmiths, and the like—who might have given the South a far greater degree of industrialism but for the rapid spread of slavery. Men of distinction escaped from the Fleet Prison in London by assisted emigration. Convicts were often transported for trivial offenses, and in hard times some Britons would commit small crimes to get sent overseas. When they arrived, their time was sold to the highest bidder. Nevertheless, the South acquired a sizable element of vagabondish, unenterprising, and turbulent folk who made lazy farmers and poor citizens. In due time science was to show that climate, a defective diet, and the hookworm had far more to do with their slovenliness and waywardness than any innate faults. Slavery, too, brought manual labor into contempt. William Byrd, in the record he kept of a surveying expedition (*History of the Dividing Line*), has described with humorous exaggeration these shiftless countrymen, content with rude comforts, hostile to law, taxes, and the Established Church, and fond of "the felicity of having nothing to do."

The Negro slaves were brought chiefly from the west coast of Africa, from Senegambia on the north to Angola on the south. After the close of the seventeenth century, when the monopoly of the Royal African Company was ended, the trade was in the hands of a wide variety of firms and individuals, both American and British. Many fortunes in Boston, Newport, New York, and Southern ports were built upon the traffic. The most active market was probably that maintained at Charleston, with numerous firms competing. Henry Laurens, who was prominent in the business for some years after 1750, wrote that planters would come long distances and eagerly bid fine young Negroes up to £40 sterling. Whereas in the North slaves were commonly sold by the importer directly to the purchaser, for cash, in the South they often went in batches to merchants and other middlemen who bartered them for tobacco, rice, or indigo. Field hands were clothed in coarse garments, housed in rude huts, and worked hard in the fields under severe overseers; household servants had kindlier treatment. Both in the North and South, mulattoes soon became numerous. As slavery increased in the South, few indentured servants or other white laborers could be found working on the great tobacco and rice plantations.

It is clear that New England and the lowland South were very unlike, while the middle colonies had some of the traits of both. New England was adapted to nothing but small farms; lowland Virginia, South Carolina, and Georgia to large plantations. In New England, the people worked in a stimulating climate with their own hands; in Virginia, hard labor under the broiling sun was done by slave gangs driven by overseers. In New England, the small holdings and the great stretches of unoccupied land encouraged parents to divide their estates equally among their children; in the South, the large slave-worked estates could seldom be broken up without economic loss, and men kept them together by laws of primogeniture and entail. In New England, the people associated in compact villages to maintain their church congregations; in most of the South, congregations counted for little and the plantations spread over so wide an area that villages were impossible. While in New England the town was the natural unit of government (though counties were created), in the South the county was all-important. In New England, the general rule was that local officers should be chosen by the people; in the South, some were appointed by the provincial authorities and some selected by an aristocratic clique. Parish vestrymen were not elected by the parishioners, for example, but chose their own successors. The Puritans, though by no means the dour, fanatical, unhappy race they are sometimes painted, were likely to be grimly conscientious and self-disciplined; the Southerners were sunnier, freer, and more pleasure-loving. Between the two, in many respects, stood the middle colonies.

Yet, as the eighteenth century wore on, as population and wealth grew, and as society became more complex, social and economic groupings cut across sectional lines. The merchants of Charleston and Portsmouth, Norfolk and Boston, with their offices full of bustling clerks, their connections with London and Bristol, the West Indies, and the African coast, their handsome houses rich in mahogany, plate, and pier glasses, were much alike. A Laurens and a Hancock would have been at home with each other at once. The mechanics of the seaports—vulgar, boisterous, full of class-conscious radicalism, and ready to sally out of their taverns in a mob on small provocation—were much alike from Carolina to Massachusetts. The small farmers—economical, hardworking, and in countless instances almost wholly self-sustaining—were alike in New Hampshire and Maryland, in Pennsylvania and Virginia. And the pioneers of the border area were everywhere stamped with the same traits.

The Back Country

THE FOURTH GREAT SECTION, the border or back country, came into clear existence during the eighteenth century. It stretched from the haunts of the hardy Green Mountain Boys and the ragged forest clearings of the Mohawk Valley down along the eastern fringes of the Alleghenies, on through the Shenandoah Valley in Virginia, into the Piedmont area of the Carolinas and Georgia. Here lived a rude, simple, and intrepid people who were purely American in outlook.

Buying cheap land at a shilling or two an acre, or taking it by "tomahawk claim," they cleared tracts in the wilderness, burned the brush, and planted corn and wheat among the stumps. They built rude cabins of hickory, walnut, or persimmon logs, notching the timbers into each other at the four corners, chinking the crevices with clay, laying a puncheon floor, and making windowpanes of paper soaked in lard or bear's grease. The men dressed in homespun hunting shirts and deerskin leggings, the women in fabrics made on the spinning wheel and loom set up in every home. They pegged their chairs and tables together from wooden slabs; they ground their meal in homemade block mortars; they ate with pewter spoons from pine trenchers; they went barefoot or wore skin moccasins. Their food was hog-and-hominy, with roast venison, wild turkeys or partridges, and fish from the nearest stream. For defense against Indians the scattered settlers built a fort at some central spring, with bulletproof blockhouses and stockade. They had their own exuberant amusements—merry barbecues at political rallies, where oxen were roasted whole; the "infare" or housewarming of newly married couples, with dancing and drinking; shooting matches, quilting bees, and balls with the Virginia reel. As in the wilder parts of Scotland and Ireland, feuds and sporadic fighting furnished much excitement. On the Pennsylvania border the Scotch-Irish and Germans waged vindictive combats. In Virginia and the Carolinas personal encounters knew no rules, and "gouging" matches made men who had lost an eye no uncommon sight. All border dwellers regarded the Indians with enmity; some tribes were friendly, but in general the settlers waged constant war with the wilderness and the red man and were thus trained to alertness, hardiness, and clannish solidarity.

The border produced picturesque and energetic traders with the Indians, such as George Croghan in the North and the versatile, cultivated James Adair in the Southwest; both friends of the savages, wide-ranging adventurers, and men with a vision of rapid western development. Croghan in late colonial days was active in keeping the Iroquois peaceful in New York, and in opening up the country at the headwaters of the Ohio River; Adair boasted that he was acquainted with two thousand miles of Indian trail. The border produced land speculators like Richard Henderson of North Carolina, who, shortly before the Revolution, resolved to buy much of present-day Kentucky from the Cherokees and convert it into a sort of proprietary colony. It produced daring fighters like Robert Rogers, a Scotch-Irishman of New Hampshire who

made himself the hero of the northeastern frontier in the
French and Indian War, and John Sevier, who in the Tennessee country boasted of "thirty-five battles, thirty-five victories." It produced the archetype of restless pioneers in
Daniel Boone, a North Carolinian of Devon stock, who in
1769 passed through the magic door that pierced the wild
Appalachian wall into Kentucky—the Cumberland Gap. By
a series of lonely explorations in this rich Indian hunting
ground, Boone did much to make the natural attractions of
Kentucky known; and he served Henderson and various
colonizing groups well. But, above all, the border produced
sturdy pioneer farmers who steadily widened the belt of settlement and civilization.

If a land of hardship and peril, the back country was to
many also an area of irresistible novelty and fascination.
The pages of William Byrd exhale an impression of its
natural enchantments. Telling how he ran the boundary
line into the wilderness, he describes the sweet grapes, both
black and white, twining all over the trees; the wild turkeys,
whirring away in flocks on every hand; the multitude of
pigeons, clouding the skies as they passed between the Gulf
and Canada, and sometimes breaking down the larger limbs
of mulberries and oaks. He pictures the fat bears swimming
clumsily across the rivers; the opossums feeding on wild
fruits; the wolves, which "entertain'd" them a great part of
the night; and the slow-grazing buffalo, of which Byrd's party
killed a powerful two-year-old bull. He mentions the sturgeon,
which in summer basked on the surface of the rivers. He tells
of the ledges of purple-and-white marble, the clear streams
pouring over sandy beds where mica gleamed in the sun like
gold, the rich forests of oak, hickory, and locust, the distant
peaks glimmering against the western sunset. He notes the
soft haziness of the sky where the Catawbas or Tuscaroras
had fired the brush to drive out game. He tells of the thrill
of coming upon an Indian encampment, and observing the
grave, dignified demeanor of the braves, often with "something great and venerable in their countenances," and the
comeliness of the copper-colored maidens, neither very clean
nor very chaste, but bashful before the white men. Once the
joys of the wilderness had been tasted, many pioneers preferred it to any other environment.

Culture

BY THE LATTER PART of the colonial period, culture was beginning to thrive bravely in favored communities. New England particularly placed great emphasis upon education. While the colonies were still in their infancy, all except Rhode Island had made some elementary schooling compulsory. Grammar schools and academies flourished. Two colleges, Harvard and Yale, had been established, and two more, Dartmouth and the College of Rhode Island (now Brown), were gaining a foothold. At Harvard, which had commodious brick buildings, a library of five thousand volumes, and good scientific apparatus, the instruction in theology, philosophy, and the classics lagged little behind that of the best European universities.

In the middle colonies, Maryland alone had a system of public education, and it was ill-organized and weak. Both the Quakers and the Germans conducted schools which were to some extent under Church supervision, while Pennsylvania had many private schools, particularly in and near Philadelphia. New York had some good town schools on Long Island and some grammar schools in New York City, but no general system of instruction. In the South, education was largely in private hands. Ministers and others kept a good many private schools; the Virginia rector, Jonathan Boucher, for example, took boys at twenty pounds apiece, among them Washington's stepson. Rich planters there and in the Carolinas hired private tutors from Great Britain and the Northern colonies, who taught reading, writing, practical mathematics, and Latin and Greek. Only two free schools each existed in Virginia and South Carolina. A number of colleges were founded in the middle and lower colonies—William and Mary in Virginia, which trained Jefferson and many another public figure, in 1693; the College of Philadelphia (now University of Pennsylvania), which Franklin did so much to set up, in 1755; the college at Princeton in 1748; and, in 1754, King's College, now Columbia University, in New York, which trained John Jay, Alexander Hamilton, and Gouverneur Morris. Wealthy families in New York and the South often sent their sons to Oxford or Cambridge, lawyers took their dinners at the Inns of Court in London, and doctors and surgeons turned naturally to Edinburgh.

Newspapers, magazines, almanacs, and even books of enduring merit were being published in the colonies. The oldest printing press in America was set up as early as 1639 at Cambridge, and its activity was never interrupted. On the eve of the Revolution Boston had five newspapers, and Philadelphia three. Bookdealers became important colonial figures, and a number of libraries (Boston's was founded in 1656) were established. One Philadelphia publisher in 1771 imported a thousand sets of Blackstone's *Commentaries* and himself issued a thousand more. Two men achieved a lasting European reputation as writers, Jonathan Edwards in theology and philosophy and Benjamin Franklin in science and belles-lettres. Both the wealthy Yankee judge, Samuel Sewall, a conservative, stubborn, industrious administrator, and the cultivated planter, Colonel William Byrd of Virginia, kept diaries which, like John Woolman's *Journal*, will not be forgotten. The simple Quaker farmer John Bartram, a precise scientific observer, was called by Linnaeus the world's greatest "natural botanist"; the indomitably busy Cadwallader Colden of New York gained fame by his *History of the Five Indian Nations;* David Rittenhouse of Pennsylvania became internationally known as an astronomer and mathematician. John Mitchell of Virginia, Fellow of the Royal Society, won eminence in botany, medicine, and agriculture. The learned divine, Cotton Mather, who has been called the "literary behemoth" of New England, published no fewer than 383 books and pamphlets, of which his *Magnalia Christi Americana* (American Wonders of Christ) was almost a library in itself. One historian of the late colonial period, Thomas Hutchinson of Massachusetts, can still be read with pleasure and profit. Good artists were at work in the colonies, and the eminent Benjamin West, going to England shortly before the Revolution, succeeded Sir Joshua Reynolds as president of the Royal Academy.

A vivid idea of the way in which cultural appliances increased may be drawn from Franklin's *Autobiography*. Born in Boston (1706) in a family so large that he recalled thirteen children sitting at table at once, Franklin was largely self-educated. His father, who had come from Northamptonshire in England, had a little library containing, besides books of polemic divinity, Defoe's *Essay on Projects,* Cotton Mather's *Essays to Do Good,* and Plutarch's *Lives.* Apprenticed at twelve to a printer, the bright lad got hold of other books—Bunyan, Locke, Shaftesbury, Collins, and some ancient classics in translation. With a few pence he bought a volume of Addison's *Spectator,* which fired him with an ambition to write essays. When he went to Philadelphia to better himself, he found literature just taking root in that city. Keimer, the printer, was equipped with "an old shatter'd press, and one small, worn-out font of English." After a sojourn in England, the indefatigably enterprising Franklin set himself to improve the Quaker city.

He established a Junto or "club of mutual improvement," which began with nine members and threw out influential branches. He set on foot a circulating subscription library, the first in America (1731), which rapidly expanded. He started a journal designed to avoid contention and to print real news—*The Saturday Evening Post*—and in 1743 the American Philosophical Society. This society, which numbered among its members the most distinguished Americans of that generation and many Europeans of world fame, sponsored far-reaching investigations not only in science but also in education, philosophy, and the arts. He founded an academy which, duly incorporated and enriched by gifts from the Penns and others, grew into the university. Franklin tells us of the remarkable effect of George Whitefield's eloquent preaching, which coaxed money from reluctant Quaker pockets. He tells, too, how in homes like his own, such luxuries as china and silver crept in to replace plain crockery and pewter; and how inoculation for smallpox was introduced—he bitterly blamed himself, when he lost a fine son of four, for neglecting it. Science always interested him; and presently, sending up a kite into the thunderclouds, he was performing the famous experiment which led a French epigrammatist to say that he seized the lightning from the skies. The political activities which justified the second half of the epigram—"and the scepter from the tyrant"—began in earnest when in 1754 he represented Pennsylvania at the first intercolonial gathering, the Albany Congress. From 1753 to 1774 he was deputy postmaster general for the colonies, and his improvement of the mails contributed not a little to American cultural unity. Altogether, Franklin's career showed both how much could be made of the cultural resources of the colonies and how much an able leader could do to strengthen them.

Wealth was accumulating faster and faster; finer houses were being built, luxury in food and dress was increasing, fashionable conventions were growing commoner. By 1750 all along the seaboard a well-to-do society, acquainted with the best European thought, could be found. In Boston and New York, Philadelphia and Charleston, as much elegance was visible as in any British or French towns outside of London and Paris. But at the same time the frontier was steadily being pressed westward, and the first rivulets of immigration were pouring through the passes of the Appalachians into the Ohio and Kentucky country. Hardy pioneers of the border, with their long rifles and keen axes, cared nothing for luxury, fashion, or ideas; their mission in life was to tame the wilderness. Between the fashionable planters and merchants on one side, the Indian-slaying frontiersmen on the other, stood the great mass of plain middle-class people who were the typical Americans of 1775. Yeomen farmers and small planters, brawny mechanics and bustling shopkeepers, they had grown up with no real knowledge of any land but America, and no taste for any but American ways of life. They were loyal subjects of the Crown, admiring England and proud of their British birthrights; but at least subconsciously they felt that America had a destiny of her own.

The Colonial Heritage

PART OF THE HERITAGE that the colonies were to bequeath the young nation is evident at a glance. The fact of a common language, the English tongue, was of immeasurable value. It was one of the great binding elements which made a true nation possible. The long and steadily broadening experience with representative forms of government was another priceless part of the heritage. We may take it rather for granted until we remember that the French and Spanish colonies had nothing to show in representative self-government; the British alone permitted their colonists to erect popular assemblies and to create governments in which both

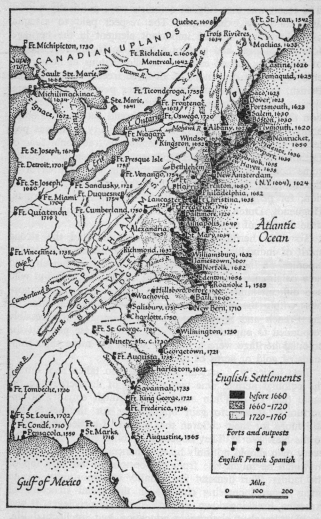

**English Settlements, 1607–1760, and English, French,
and Spanish Outposts, 1760**

electors and representatives had real political responsibility. The result was that English colonists were politically minded and politically experienced. The respect paid to essential civil rights was another important element in the heritage, for the colonists had as firm a belief in freedom of speech, of the press, and of assembly as did Britons at home, and enjoyed a great deal more of all three freedoms than did the British, or, for that matter, any other peoples. The general spirit of religious toleration in the colonies, and the recognition that different sects could and should get on with entire amity, must be included in the roster. Every faith was protected under the British flag; despite the traditional fear of Catholicism in England, Parliament was even charged by some colonials after 1763 with showing excessive favor to that religion. Equally valuable was the spirit of racial toleration, for people of different blood—English, Irish, German, Huguenot, Dutch, Swedish—mingled and intermarried with little thought of any difference.

To these heritages we should certainly add the strong spirit of individual enterprise which manifested itself in the colonies, an individualism noteworthy in Britain herself, and now heightened under the pressure of life in a rich but wild and difficult land. The British never permitted such monopolies within the colonies as had crushed individual effort in the French and Spanish dominions. Enterprise irrepressibly responded to opportunity. Taken together, these parts of the colonial heritage were a treasure worth far more than shiploads of gold or acres of diamonds.

Two basically American ideas had also taken root during the colonial period. One was the idea of democracy, in the sense that all men are entitled to a rough equality of opportunity. It was to gain opportunity for themselves and still more for their children that a host of settlers had come to the New World. They hoped to establish a society in which every man should not only have a chance, but a good chance; in which he might rise from the bottom to the very top of the ladder. This demand for equality of opportunity was to bring about increasing changes in the social structure of America, breaking down all sorts of special privileges. It was to effect marked changes in education and intellectual life, making America the "most common-schooled" nation in the world. It was to produce great political changes, giving the ordinary man a more direct control of government. Altogether, it was to be a mighty engine for the betterment of the masses.

The other basic idea was the sense that a special destiny awaited the American people and that they had before them a career such as no other nation was likely to achieve. This general wealth, the energy of the people, and the atmosphere of freedom which enveloped both imparted to Americans a fresh and buoyant optimism and an aggressive self-confidence. As the "American Farmer," St. John Crèvecoeur, said: "Americans are the western pilgrims, who are carrying along with them that great mass of arts, sciences, vigor and industry which began long since in the East; they will finish the great circle." The idea of a peculiarly fortunate destiny was to be one of the main forces in the swift expansion of the American people across the continent. It was sometimes to have evil effects; that is, it was to lead Americans to rely all too easily upon Providence when they should have been taking painful thought to meet their difficulties— it was to make them complacent when they should have been self-critical. But, along with the idea of democracy, it was on the whole to give American life a freshness, breadth, and cheerfulness that were matched nowhere else. The new land was a land of promise, of hope, of steadily widening horizons.

CHAPTER 3

The Imperial Problem

The French Wars

AS THE BRITISH COLONIES in America grew strong and expanded, they were certain to come into collision with their neighbors north, west, and south, the French and the Spaniards. It was certain, too, that the quarrels of Britain, France, and Spain in the Old World would involve the subjects of these nations in the New, for neither then nor later was America isolated from the rest of the Western world. One of the epic stories of North American history is that of the momentous series of conflicts waged between Latin and Anglo-Saxon, conflicts the more dramatic because they involved not merely peoples but also ideas and cultures. They were wars between absolutism and democracy, between a rigidly disciplined despotism and free institutions, between men of one intolerant faith and men of many mutually tolerant sects. With the vast wilderness for background, with the Indians as participants, with soldiers of high ability—Frontenac, Montcalm, Wolfe, Amherst, Washington—as leaders, they were marked by episodes of savage cruelty, heroic gallantry, and masterful strategy. The prize of this conflict was the control of the continent.

The Spaniards had been the first to gain a strong foothold in North America. Following Columbus' discovery of the New World, they soon effectively occupied the principal West Indian islands. In 1519 the indomitable soldier, Hernán Cortés, with a small army hewed his way to the center of Mexico, defeated the forces of the Aztec emperor Montezuma, and seized the country. Twenty years later another iron-willed Spanish gentleman, Hernando de Soto, landed in Florida (already the scene of several abortive Spanish adventures), defeated the Indians, left a garrison behind him, and with some six hundred men set out on four years of restless wandering across what is now the Southern States, going as far west as Oklahoma and Texas. Other Spanish explorers, notably Coronado, who used Mexico as his base, made expeditions northward in search of legendary wonders, such as the Seven Cities which, situated on great heights, had jewel-studded doorways and whole streets of busy goldsmiths. The Spaniards founded their first settlement in Florida, St. Augustine, in 1565. Before the sixteenth century ended, Spanish soldiers and priests, after bloody fighting, had established themselves in New Mexico, where from Santa Fe thereafter a long line of military governors ruled over the sleepy province. Meanwhile, a hardy Jesuit missionary of Italian parentage, Eusebio Francisco Kino, had explored Lower California and the Arizona country, building chapels and baptizing the wondering Indians. But not until 1769 was California proper occupied by a force of Spanish soldiers, with whom came Franciscan missionaries under Junípero Serra to help found San Diego and Monterey.

The French had not made good their foothold in Canada until just before the English colonists settled in Virginia. To be sure, a *voyageur* of Brittany, Jacques Cartier, had in 1535 carried the French flag up the St. Lawrence to the site of Montreal, and half a dozen years later had made a fruitless attempt to colonize part of the new territory. Indian hostility and the terrible cold of winter sent the settlers home in discouragement. Not until 1603 did the founder of New France appear—Samuel de Champlain, at thirty-six a veteran soldier and sailor, who had narrated his adventures on the Spanish Main so well that the king had made him royal geographer. In 1608 he laid the foundations of Quebec, the first permanent European settlement in New France. For purposes of exploration the next year he accompanied a party of Hurons and Algonquins against the Iroquois, traversed the lake which now carries his name, and near Ticonderoga emptied his musket at hostile savages. The incident has been credited with causing the long enmity of the Iroquois against the French, but that enmity was pro-

duced rather by geography and the fur trade, in which the
Five Nations were natural middlemen between the English
and the Western tribes. The Company of New France,
formed under Richelieu's auspices in 1628, did something to
give energy to the colonizing venture. And when Louis XIV
came into full control of France in 1661, with the sagacious
Colbert his chief minister of state, the royal authorities gave
the Canadian settlements generous support.

The colonial undertakings of the Spanish, French, and
British were alike in being rather haphazard and unplanned,
but they differed sharply in other respects. The Spanish conquests involved the subjugation of a fairly numerous, static,
and industrious body of natives by a small number of enterprising soldiers, traders, and adventurers intent on a rapid
accumulation of wealth. This meant that Spain transferred
many features of the feudal system to America. A few
thousand hardheaded, hardfisted conquistadors, ruthless in
their methods, were soon in control of millions of Indians.
Humane churchmen like Las Casas tried with scant success
to lessen the rigors of their domination. The Spaniards
opened rich mines in which they worked tens of thousands
of Indians to death; they laid out great ranches on which
they raised cattle, with some tropical products—sugar, vanil-
la, cacao, and indigo. The Spaniards were overlords; the Indians, the Negroes (who were soon imported in great numbers, especially into Caribbean lands and Portuguese Brazil),
and the mixed-blood offspring of all three races were serfs
or slaves. The system produced a great deal of wealth; but
this went into a few grasping hands, while the masses remained in poverty. No definite middle class developed. The
Spaniard liked to be a ranch owner, a churchman, or a soldier, but he did not like to be a merchant or industrialist.
Foreigners, and especially Protestants, were rigidly excluded.
As a consequence, toleration never developed. Representative
institutions, at least outside occasional town councils, had
no existence, and all rule came from above.

At the same time, the Spaniards and Portuguese did introduce Christianity to millions of savages; did teach the natives new crafts, a better agriculture, and some rudiments
of European education; did make their lands productive of
millions of cattle; and did establish universities for the
study of the classics and the church fathers. However un-

evenly and roughly, they did spread civilization over vast areas below the Rio Grande.

The French came to America only in small numbers; and their civilization was molded chiefly by geographical and economic conditions, the autocracy of the French government, and the Catholic Church. What they sought was not silver, gold, or ranches, but fish and furs. They penetrated a chilly, inhospitable land, with a roving population of Indians, many of them hostile. The deeper they pushed into the interior, the more furs they could procure. Establishing a number of weak agricultural settlements, they therefore thrust their posts farther and farther into the wilderness, following the main watercourses—the St. Lawrence, the Great Lakes, the Wisconsin, Illinois, Wabash, and Mississippi, and finally even the waters of Manitoba. While the English colonists created self-governing communities and exhibited boundless individual initiative, Paris gave the French colonies a government both despotic and paternal; though daring leaders appeared, the people never learned to stand on their own feet and take care of themselves. While England encouraged men of every faith to emigrate, France allowed none but Catholics to set foot in Canada. When the final struggle came the British colonies had nearly twenty men for every Frenchman; they were well planted, while the French *habitant* peasants, laboring under a feudal *noblesse*, had less sturdy roots in the soil; and they were energetically resourceful, while the French depended upon a centralized authority.

The history of New France passed through five distinct epochs. The first was the thirty-five-year period of beginnings coterminous with the career of the hardy Champlain. After sailing up the St. Lawrence in 1603, the next year he helped found Port Royal (Annapolis) in what is now Nova Scotia. Until his death in 1635 he labored amain to develop Canada as a French colony; to spur on the work of exploration, he himself reaching lakes George, Ontario, and Huron; and to make the fur trade profitable. The second era had for its most prominent feature the missionary activity of a band of devoted men, representing the Franciscans, the Recollects, the Ursulines, and above all the Jesuits. Some, like Isaac Jogues and Jean de Brébeuf, both tortured to death by the Iroquois, showed unconquerable heroism. In their own *Relations* they wrote one of the most inspiring pages of Catholic history. But their most fruitful field of endeavor was destroyed when in 1649–1650 the Iroquois practically wiped out the Huron tribesmen among whom the Jesuits had met their greatest success, while in 1654 the Erie tribe was likewise exterminated. Commercially the colony in this period was a failure. The year 1660 found not more than a few thousand French people precariously settled in all Canada.

The third era was more fruitful. New France became a royal province, with a governor, intendant, and other officials modeled on those of the French provinces. Louis XIV, taking a keen personal interest in its fortunes, furnished generous subsidies as well as orders and advice. Fresh shiploads of colonists were sent out. At Quebec in 1659 arrived the first bishop, François Xavier de Laval-Montmorency, who had resolved that Canada should be ruled by the Church under a regime as strict and austere as that of the Puritan theocracy in New England. His mark is upon Quebec's life still, for, coming into conflict with governor after governor, he usually had his own way.

Finally, however, ambitious ecclesiastics met more than their match when the iron-willed Comte de Frontenac arrived in 1672 as governor and inaugurated the fourth era. A man of tremendous ability and determination, he asserted the dominance of the civil authorities over the Church, temporarily broke the strength of the Iroquois, and fought off the fleet of thirty-four ships which Sir William Phipps led against Quebec in King William's War (1690). During this period the greatest of the French explorers were busy in the Far West—Radisson and Groseilliers, who penetrated beyond Lake Superior; Joliet and Marquette, who mapped much of the upper Mississippi Valley; and La Salle, who descended the Mississippi to its mouth. Before Frontenac died at the close of the century, he had begun to prepare New France for the desperate struggle which all men of vision saw must be fought out with the British. This struggle, running through the Wars of the Spanish Succession and Austrian Succession (Queen Anne's War and King George's War) into the Seven Years' War, fills the fifth and closing epoch in the history of New France.

In the protracted conflict the French had certain advantages. They had been active in taking posts of strategic power. Steadily, by a line of forts and fur-trading posts, they had marked out a huge crescent-shaped empire, stretching from Quebec in the Northeast through Detroit and St. Louis down to New Orleans in the South. They expected to hold and develop this great hinterland, pinning the British to the narrow belt east of the Appalachians. France was a stronger nation militarily than Britain and could send over powerful armies. The highly centralized government of New France was better fitted for conducting war than was the loose association of ill-co-ordinated colonial governments.

But for three principal reasons an ultimate British victory was certain. First, the 1,500,000 people of the British colonies in 1754 were a fast-increasing body, compact, tenacious, and resourceful; while New France had fewer than 100,000 people, brave but scattered and deficient in enterprise. Second, the British held a better strategic position. Operating on inside lines, they could effectively strike westward at what is now Pittsburgh, northwestward toward Niagara, and northward at Quebec and Montreal. They also had the better navy, could more speedily reinforce and supply their troops, and could lay siege to Quebec by water. Finally, they proved able to produce better captains. In Chatham they eventually found a political leader, and in Wolfe, Amherst, and Lord Howe (to whom Massachusetts raised a monument in Westminster Abbey) generals whom the French did not equal; while colonial officers, like the alert Washington, who guided Braddock's army, Phineas Lyman, who repulsed the French at Lake George, and Lieutenant Colonel Bradstreet, who captured Fort Frontenac, won high distinction. Chatham, a true genius, had nearly two years to marshal the Anglo-American effort before France found an able statesman in the Duc de Choiseul.

The seventy years of conflict that reached a climacteric in 1763 were full of stirring events. Arresting figures emerged —on the French side Cadillac, who founded Detroit, Iberville, who challenged the British from Hudson Bay to the West Indies, and Bienville, who founded New Orleans and laid claim to the Ohio Valley; on the British side the alert and aggressive Governor William Shirley of Massachusetts, the dashing fighter Sir William Pepperell, and the shrewd Governor Horatio Sharpe of Maryland. The story included stubborn sieges like that of Louisbourg, twice taken by the imperial forces; sanguinary pitched battles like those fought at Ticonderoga, where first the French and then the British won; sickening Indian raids on border towns like Deerfield, Massachusetts; and grueling wilderness marches. The rout of Braddock by the French and Indians in 1755, as his army was nearing the site of Pittsburgh, was a humiliating disaster. But the defeat was shortly wiped out by Forbes's capture of that strategic position.

In 1759 Wolfe, trying to come to grips with Montcalm at Quebec, took a desperate chance, scaled the high cliffs at night, and brought the enemy to battle on the Plains of Abraham commanding the city. In the ensuing action both he and Montcalm were killed. Not yet thirty-three, the British commander had said the previous night that he would rather have written Gray's *Elegy* than have the glory of beating the French; his real glory was that he forever linked his name with the predominance of the English-speaking peoples in North America, for the capture of Quebec decided the war.

By the treaty of peace in 1763 England took all of Canada from France, and Florida from Spain, which had entered the war against the British Empire. North America from the Atlantic to the Mississippi, with New Orleans excepted, became British. At the same time Louisiana passed from French to Spanish sovereignty. We may note that the final British victories in Canada coincided with equal triumphs under Clive in India; for this was one of the decisive world wars of history, and the French were driven out of India as out of North America.

Imperial Relations

THE TRIUMPHANT Seven Years' War jarred the American colonies into a totally new position with respect to Great Britain. It removed the sharp menace that had been offered by the well-armed French holdings to the north and west, half encircling the colonies as with a jagged scythe. It removed the lesser pressure of the Spaniards to the south. Its campaigns gave many colonial officers and men valuable training in war, and enhanced their self-confidence. It did something to create sentiment for uniting the provinces; a number of proposals for union were broached, the most notable being that drafted by the Albany Congress in 1754, attended by representatives of seven colonies. This plan, which Franklin largely shaped, called for a president general appointed by the king, and a federal council whose members should be chosen by the colonial assemblies. The council was to provide for general defense, control Indian relations, and levy taxes for general purposes, while the president general was to have a veto power. Though the plan failed to gain support, it did much to educate people in the idea of union. So, too, did the spectacle of men from different provinces fighting side by side.

Just as the war lessened the old dependence on Great Britain, so it reduced the respect paid to her. Colonial troops, though badly equipped and ill-disciplined, found on several fields that they could fight as well as the British regulars—and in wilderness fighting could do better. They found many English officers blundering, just as the British found many colonials incompetent; they saw that the brave but inept Braddock would have done well to take young George Washington's advice on Indian fighting. The New Englanders, electing their officers on a democratic basis, thought badly of the aristocratic British system of appointing commanders, and Americans from all colonies resented the system whereby any British officer outranked all colonial officers.

Finally, the victorious close of the war and the huge expansion of the empire raised questions which became a subject of practical dissension between the colonists and the British government. Of deliberate "tyranny" there was none. But the administration of the empire had to be tightened and systematized, and this meant hordes of new officials. Its defense against jealous neighbors had to be provided for, and this meant taxation. Its economic organization under the Navigation Acts or "acts of trade" had to be revised and strengthened.

British administrative control over the colonies had hitherto been extremely lax. Under the Crown, the principal imperial agency of government was the Board of Commissioners for Trade and Plantations, which had taken almost complete form by 1696. The principal ministers were ex officio members, but the bulk of the work was generally done

by a small body of fairly expert and hard-working officials. It
guarded the commercial interests of the mother country and
the colonies, supervised colonial finances and systems of
justice, gave some guidance to colonial enterprise, and proposed new imperial policies. It had certain powers of investigation; it drafted instructions to the royal governors;
it nominated colonial officials when offices fell vacant; and it
could demand reports from these officers. Parliament, of
course, exercised considerable legislative powers over the
colonies. In fact, it was the only body available which could
deal in a large way with the commercial and other relations
of the British Empire, both externally and internally. The
Crown, too, had extensive powers. Not only did it appoint the
governors of the eight royal provinces (for by 1760 only
Rhode Island and Connecticut were self-governing charter
colonies, and only Pennsylvania, Delaware, and Maryland
were proprietary colonies); it could, and often did, disallow
any laws passed by the colonial legislatures. Such vetoes
were normally interposed by the Privy Council, acting on
the careful advice of the Board of Trade and Plantations. The
Privy Council could also sit as a court of appeal in colonial
cases.

The principal parliamentary enactments down to the close
of the Seven Years' War had been the various Navigation
Acts, applying certain economic principles on which the
well-being of the British Empire was supposed to rest. The
mercantilist theory of the times held that the wealth of
a nation was proportioned directly to its stock of property,
gold, or silver; and that individual or corporate enterprise
should be controlled by the state to enhance this power. The
empire was regarded not as a federation, but as a unit, a consolidated state. In this unit it was supposed that the colonies
could contribute to national wealth and power by giving employment to imperial shipping and by producing articles
which Britain would otherwise have to buy from foreign
lands—sugar, tobacco, rice, naval stores and other raw
materials. In return, the mother country could supply manufactures to the colonies, the two main elements in the empire
thus becoming complementary.

As early as 1651 Parliament, alarmed by the growth of
Dutch shipping, passed a Navigation Act which required all

colonial exports to England to be carried in English-owned and English-operated vessels. A series of later enactments enlarged the system. They gave England *and the colonies* a monopoly of the carrying trade of the empire—protecting both against Dutch and other foreign shipowners; required certain colonial exports to the European continent to be transshipped in English ports; and regulated the importation of European goods into the colonies in such a way as to favor English manufactures. London limited colonial enterprise in some directions, but encouraged it in others.

At first these laws were not thoroughly enforced. But when in 1763 Britain undertook a revamping and tightening of the colonial system, the mercantilist statutes were overhauled.

The Problem of Federalism in the Empire

INDEED the whole imperial system was overhauled, and the process, involving as it did a reconsideration of the relations of colonies to mother country, precipitated the Revolution. It is this problem of imperial organization, now first presented in a clear-cut fashion, that gives unity and meaning to much of the complex and confused history of the next generation. How to organize and govern an empire so that the advantages of centralized power and of local autonomy could both be preserved—that was the question, and it was one of the most difficult questions that ever confronted statesmen of any age. Could some system be devised whereby the general government at Westminster would exercise control over all matters of a general imperial nature —war, peace, foreign affairs, Western lands, Indians, trade, and so forth—while the various local governments in Massachusetts, Virginia, South Carolina, and elsewhere were allowed to control all matters of strictly local concern? Could a line between these general and local concerns be drawn with such skill that it would leave the central government with adequate powers and yet not infringe upon the liberties of men in their local affairs?

This was, of course, the problem of federalism. The British Empire of the mid-eighteenth century, in operation and in fact, if not in theory or law, was a federal empire. It was an empire in which powers were distributed between central and local governments. Parliament had, for a century and a half, controlled all matters of general concern; the local assemblies had, from the beginning, exercised practical control over all matters of local concern. Had the empire, somehow, been frozen in 1750 this would have been clear.

But in law the empire was not a federal but a centralized one. In law and theory Parliament had all power. And when, after 1763, British statesmen addressed themselves to the task of reorganizing the empire they fell back upon the legal or theoretical supremacy of Parliament. They insisted, in the words of the Declaratory Act of 1766, that the colonies "have been, are, and of right ought to be, subordinate unto and dependent upon the imperial Crown and Parliament of Great Britain," and that Parliament had "full power and authority to make laws and statutes of sufficient force and validity to bind the colonies and people of America . . . in all cases whatsoever."

Faced with the opportunity to create a real federal system British statesmen muffed the chance. But the problem was not solved in 1776, nor did it end with the separation of colonies and mother country. It was simply transferred to the United States. From 1775 on to 1787 Americans were confronted with the same problem—with the problem of achieving a unified government for general purposes and maintaining intact the autonomy of the state governments over local concerns. The first American effort to solve this problem—the Articles of Confederation—was a failure. Taught by bitter experience Americans tried again, and in the Federal Constitution of 1787 did construct an enduring federal system.

One of the great themes of this Revolutionary period, then, one which we must not lose sight of amidst the smoke of battle and the march toward democracy, is the solution of the problem of imperial organization and the emergence of a federal system. That system, as finally elaborated, was built upon the experience of a century in the British Empire, the debates and discussions in Britain and America after 1763, the trials of war and the tribulations of the Confederation. The final achievement of federalism, in the Constitution of 1787, was one of the great constructive achievements of the age.

General Causes of Discontent

IT IS NOT EASY to say when the Revolution began; but it is certain that it was not in 1775. Years later John Adams tried to distinguish between the Revolution proper and the Revolutionary War, declaring that the former really ended before the latter began. "The revolution was in the minds of the people, and the union of the colonies," he wrote, "both of which were accomplished before hostilities commenced. The revolution and union were gradually forming from the years 1760 to 1776." True enough, but it is equally true that the Revolution—as distinct from the War—was not completed for many years, perhaps not until 1800. Adams' statement that the Revolution was "in the minds of the people" confronts us with the necessity for another distinction. After all, only a minority of the American colonists by July, 1776, had been convinced of the wisdom of seceding from the British Empire. Probably half the Americans at that date still wished to avert a political divorce. Throughout the war, by John Adams' own testimony, fully one third of the colonists remained opposed to the rebellion, and one third were indifferent. It would, therefore, be more accurate to say that the Revolution prior to 1776 was in the minds of part of the people, and the struggle of 1776–1783 was a struggle to impose it on the rest of the people and to make the British government recognize it.

In dealing with the economic causes of the Revolution we have to discriminate sharply among different sections and interests. The Northern merchant had a wholly different set of grievances from the Southern planter, and the Western land speculator from either.

The Mercantile or Navigation Acts injured the Northern colonies far more than the Southern. These Northern colonies had no valuable staples which they could carry direct to England to exchange for manufactured goods. In general, they had to pay for their imports from England with hard money, and to get it they had to trade with the West Indies. They carried wheat, meat, and lumber to the West Indies and in return got cotton, indigo, or sugar. They also got molasses, which they made into rum and traded in Africa for slaves who were in turn sold in the West Indies or the

Southern colonies. In 1733 Parliament passed the Molasses
Act, which by prohibitive levies restricted New England's
trade with the West Indies to the British islands alone. Had
the law been rigidly enforced, the New Englanders would
have suffered heavy losses. But the Molasses Act was evaded
in the most wholesale manner: Rhode Island, for example,
imported about 14,000 hogsheads of molasses annually, of
which 11,500 came from the French and Spanish West Indies. Smuggling was no crime. The English authorities winked
at it, and some of them frankly pointed out that in the end
the money derived from this illicit trade went to English
merchants and manufacturers. The Livingston family in
New York and John Hancock in Massachusetts grew wealthy
from smuggled goods.

The Sugar Act of 1764 was virtually a re-enactment of the
old Molasses Act of 1733 in such terms as to make it enforceable. The old prohibitive and uncollectible rate of six-
pence a gallon was reduced to threepence, and provision
was made for the seizure of all vessels evading the law. Perhaps a rate of twopence would have been justifiable, but
the West Indian lobby in Parliament shoved it up to the
higher figure. This meant a heavy blow to the economic
interests of New England. Rhode Island protested that the
West Indian business was the whole foundation of that
colony's trade with England and that of her 14,000 hogsheads of molasses, the British West Indies could furnish
only 2500 at most. One clause provided that cases under the
Sugar Act could be tried by any vice-admiralty court in
America, which meant that a merchant might find his ship
and crew taken all the way to Halifax for trial. He could
claim no damages if the jury acquitted him. The colonial
leader Jared Ingersoll said that the procedure was like burning a barn to roast an egg—decidedly irritating to the man
who owned the barn.

Another annoyance lay in the fact that the export tax on
continental goods shipped to the colonies from Great Britain
was raised in 1764 from 2.5 per cent to 5 per cent. Customs
officials were ordered to show more strictness, and enforcement was strengthened by various steps—for example, the
stationing of warships in American waters to seize smugglers, and the issuance of "writs of assistance" to enable
Crown officers to search suspected premises.

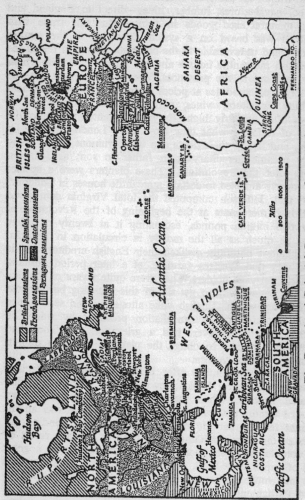

The Domain of Colonial Commerce about 1750

The South was in a wholly different position. It had little or no trade with the West Indies. It sent its staples—tobacco, indigo, naval stores, lumber, hides—direct to England and took manufactured goods in return. But this trade with England was based on a system favorable to the mother country and unfavorable to the colonists. It was in the hands of British mercantile houses and the factors or agents whom they sent out to the provinces. The factors bought tobacco and other commodities at prices often unfairly low; they sold clothing, furniture, wines, carriages, and other goods at prices often unfairly high. Easygoing planters fell into the habit of ordering what they liked from London, paying by notes, and letting their debts run up to ruinous sums. Many debts became hereditary from father to son; as Jefferson wrote after the Revolution: "These planters were a species of property annexed to certain mercantile houses in London."

In fact, Jefferson computed the total Virginia debt owed to British merchants at the beginning of the Revolution at over two million pounds, estimating it at twenty or thirty times as much as all the money in circulation in Virginia. The planters naturally disliked their English creditors in the same way that Western farmers, at a later period, disliked Eastern mortgage holders. They were quite aware of the fact that the easiest way to get rid of this crushing burden was to rebel against the English yoke altogether and seek refuge in the moratorium or cancellation provided by war. The British lenders, however, had a grievance too. They had risked their money to oblige the planters, and two million pounds was a lot to lose.

In the quarter century after 1750, some Southern legislatures passed liberal bankruptcy acts and stay laws which favored debtors. When these reached England the Privy Council almost always vetoed them. The result was an indignant feeling that the rich in England were grinding the faces of the poor. Parliament also tried to stop the resort of the colonies to paper money. Most provinces issued a good deal of paper after 1730, and some made it legal tender; but they met more and more opposition in London. Finally, in 1764 Parliament flatly forbade the colonies to make paper money legal tender for debts, thus creating a new and important grievance of debtor groups all over British America. Another large economic interest was concerned with land speculation and the settlement of the West. In the Western country, wealth was attained in two main ways: by trading with the Indians for furs and by organizing land companies to acquire, parcel out, and sell great tracts of the wilderness. The fur trader and land speculator wished a free hand in those years just as the oil prospector and timber cutter wish a free hand in the West today. Besides these two groups, we find after 1760 another, the colonial veterans of the Seven Years' War who had been granted Western lands as bounties. Virginia in especial had rewarded her soldiers in this fashion, while Governor Dinwiddie had promised 200,000 acres to the troops who would be brave enough to drive off the French from their great holdings in the Ohio Valley.

Many of the plain people of Pennsylvania, Virginia, and the Carolinas were land hungry. By the close of the war it was clear that there would shortly be a great stampede for the West. One land company after another was being organized; the greatest men on the continent—Benjamin Franklin, George Washington, Sir William Johnson—were keenly interested; there was a confusion of claims, purchases, and surveys.

But while this host were clutching at Western lands, the British government was determining upon a new policy of strict control and policing in the West. To keep peace with the Indians, to prevent the colonists from spreading too far west and thus outgrowing English control, and to put an end to the chaos of overlapping claims, it proclaimed in 1763 that all settlement must stop at the crest of the Appalachians. Lands beyond this "Proclamation Line" were temporarily barred off as a Crown domain, and no Indian lands anywhere were to be sold except to the Crown. The theory was that a little delay could do no harm, that the restive Indians should be given time to quiet down, and that lands could then gradually be opened to the colonists. The Board of Trade and Plantations was soon supporting a scheme for a new Western colony called Vandalia. But this proclamation gave offense to the fur traders, the land companies, the bounty holders, and those generally who were hungry for Western holdings, for it seemed to slam shut the door which Americans had just fought the French to force open.

The ecclesiastical grievances of the colonies centered in the relations with the Anglican Church, which was the state-supported Church in all the colonies south of Delaware and in part of New York as well. Three colonies, to be sure, had a Congregational establishment, but although the Congregational establishment was more rigorous, it was the Anglican Church that excited antagonism.

This antagonism rested upon two principal foundations: the fact that many colonists objected violently to paying taxes for the Church and the fact that they feared an Episcopalian hierarchy of political tendencies. Each Anglican clergyman in the South had his parsonage, his glebe, his fixed salary paid by taxes, and his fees. In all the colonies the Episcopalians were decidedly in a minority. In Virginia nearly all the great families of the lowlands—the Washingtons, Lees, Randolphs, Carters, Masons, Carys—were Episcopalians. But west of Richmond, the dissenters—Quakers, Baptists, Lutherans, Presbyterians—were far more numerous. North Carolina had only a handful of Episcopalians, though the authorities tried to make the people support nine Episcopalian ministers. In South Carolina the Church was stronger, but even there the dissenters, with about eighty congregations, were heavily in the majority. No pious dissenter relished paying for the support of an Episcopalian clergyman as well as for one of his own faith.

Another ground for dispute lay in the question of imperial defense. Some Indian fighting was certain, while the French thirsted for revenge, and the Spaniards beyond the Mississippi could not be trusted. The British government did not believe that the colonies could defend themselves. It complained that they had been slow and stingy in raising troops in the recent war and had failed to act in harmony. The only central agency was the imperial government in London. Under George Grenville, therefore, it was shortly decided to keep ten thousand soldiers in North America, paying one third of the cost of maintenance out of colonial taxation. This meant raising about £360,000 a year in the colonies. Grenville, after giving a year's notice and assuring the colonies that he would take a better plan if they offered it, brought in a bill for a stamp tax on newspapers and legal and other documents. Parliament passed it in 1765 "with less opposition than a turnpike bill," and along with it a measure requiring the colonies to furnish the troops with fuel, light, bedding, cooking utensils, and help in obtaining billets. To England this seemed a trifle, but to the colonists the Stamp Act was a clear instance of taxation without representation.

Finally, America was a fertile soil for doctrines of a republican or quasi-republican character. The population for a century and a half had been living in an atmosphere of democracy or "leveling." Economic differences were few; economic opportunity was equally open to all. What aristocracy did exist simply stimulated the growth of democratic principles. There was a little seaboard class or clique which held most of the wealth, and in some provinces, like Virginia and South Carolina, the political power, and against this the rising democracy of the interior conducted a long struggle. The small farmers of the back country, the Scotch-Irish and German immigrants, the laborers and mechanics of the towns, constantly asserted themselves against the older merchants and planters. They did so in the generation before the Revolution with an energy which shocked their superiors, and the same spirit contributed to their revolutionary zeal against the mother country.

When we list the leaders in the revolt against England, we find that they fall into two main groups. One was a set of educated men, writers and thinkers—such men as Samuel Adams, John Adams, John Jay, James Otis, Alexander Hamilton, John Morin Scott, William Livingston, Benjamin Franklin, John Dickinson, Charles Carroll of Carrollton, Thomas Jefferson, George Mason, Willie Jones, and John Rutledge. They were abetted by a set of radicals of poor education or none, sprung from the mechanics and the back-woodsmen—men like Alexander McDougall, Isaac Sears, and John Lamb in New York; like Daniel Roberdeau and George Bryan in Pennsylvania; like Patrick Henry in Virginia; like Thomas Person and Timothy Bloodworth in North Carolina; like Christopher Gadsden and Thomas Sumter in South Carolina. The second group was impetuous, fiery-tempered, and inclined to take radical views of government; they liked a pure democracy, or something near it. They derived their inspiration from intellectuals like Jefferson and Sam Adams, but they gave the Revolutionary movement, once it was fairly started, much of its brute energy. The first group, however, was much more important in starting it. The educated men used voice and pen earnestly, sending out flocks of pamphlets, filling the newspapers with essays, and spreading their political views by public meetings.

These colonial writers and pamphleteers harked back to two powerful groups of British thinkers: the group which had written to justify the doctrines of the Puritan commonwealth and the group which had justified the Whig revolution of 1688. That is, they drew their arguments from Sidney, Harrington, Milton, and, above all, John Locke. The second book of Locke's *Two Treatises of Government* contains the germs of the American Declaration of Independence. Locke maintained that the supreme function of the state is to protect life, liberty, and property, to which every man is entitled. Political authority, he said, is held in trust for the benefit of the people alone. When the natural rights of mankind are violated, the people have the right and duty of abolishing or changing the government. This doctrine is written into the preamble to the Declaration of Independence. "The true remedy of force without authority is to oppose force to it," Locke asserted. He also laid another great foundation stone for the Revolution when he expounded, in his *Letter on Toleration*, the view that Church and state properly occupy separate spheres and should be kept apart. In its healthiest character, he showed, the Church is a voluntary organization, supported freely by its members and not by the taxing power of government.

Locke and the thinkers who stood with him were profoundly admired by all educated Americans interested in politics. The Americans in fact inherited their political philosophy at the very time that the British diverged from it. British constitutional practice after 1688 developed a misshapen and undemocratic system of representation. A ruling oligarchy emerged, resting upon a rotten-borough system, upon the refusal to grant representatives to new manufacturing towns, and upon the systematic disfranchisement of large parts of the population. Disfranchisement and rotten boroughs or their equivalent existed in America, but not to the same extent. In fact, a constant struggle went on in America throughout the eighteenth century to broaden the electorate and to see that new counties and western areas were given their fair representation along with the older settlements. America had a system that was growing more representative; England a system that had grown less representative. Both people believed in natural rights—the Bill of Rights was a great British heritage; but many Britons tended to accept almost absolute Parliamentary authority, while most Americans were quick to reject it or any other absolute authority. When trouble with the mother country began in 1765, Americans found that they had a political philosophy full-fashioned to their needs.

Misunderstanding

SELDOM have two contestants more completely misunderstood each other than the American colonists and British Crown managed to do in the ten years preceding the Revolution. None of the early British steps was inspired by a desire to "tyrannize" over America. The effort to solve the Indian problem, to garrison the colonies for their own protection, and to strengthen the customs service seemed to ministers in London fair and moderate. But to multitudes of Americans these measures looked like a closely geared engine of oppression.

Hard times had followed the Seven Years' War. Men who were out of work and pinched for money wished to find new homes beyond the mountains—and the "Proclamation Line" forbade it. Trade was bad and hard cash very scarce; yet the Crown seized this moment to drain gold and silver out of the country by new tariff levies, strictly enforced. Under the Stamp Act it was meanwhile taxing the colonists without their consent. The moneys thus raised were being used to maintain a standing army, for which most colonists saw no real need; and this grim garrison was in turn to help enforce the burdensome customs regulations and the unfair tax laws. To Crown officers it seemed proper in 1761 to ask the courts for "writs of assistance"—search warrants for dealing with smugglers. But to the colonists these writs, applying to everybody, giving absolute power to officers who held them, and allowing every man's home or shop to be ransacked, were intolerable. The British government had passed certain laws for restricting or forbidding manufactures in the colonies. The Crown thought this fair, for it believed that the empire would prosper best if the colonies concentrated on raw materials and Britain on manufactured goods. But many colonists resented the interference.

And behind these disputes over practical matters lay a theoretical disagreement which gave the whole quarrel depth and created an unbridgeable gulf.

Most British officials held that Parliament was an imperial body which exercised the same authority over the colonies as over the homeland. It could pass laws for Massachusetts as it passed laws for Berkshire. The colonies, to be sure, had governments of their own. But the colonies were nevertheless merely corporations and, as such, subject to all English law; Parliament could limit, extend, or dissolve their governments whenever it pleased. This is not so, said the American leaders, for no "imperial" parliament exists. Their only legal relations, they argued, were with the Crown. It was the Crown which had agreed to establish colonies beyond the sea, and the Crown had provided them with governments. The king was equally a king of England and a king of Massachusetts. But the English Parliament had no more right to pass laws for Massachusetts than the Massachusetts legislature had to pass laws for England. If the king wanted money from a colony, he could get it by asking for a grant; but Parliament had no authority to take it by passing a Stamp Act or other revenue law. In short, a British subject, whether in England or America, was to be taxed only by and through his own representatives.

It must be realized, however, that both in Britain and in America feeling was sharply divided on the main issues; that the developing contest was not so much a struggle between colonies and motherland as a civil conflict within the colonies and also within Great Britain. In Parliament the eminent Whig leaders, Chatham, Burke, Barré, and Fox, leaned strongly toward the side of the American patriots; in the colonies a staunch body of Tories upheld the British government. It must also be realized that some extreme men on both sides were glad to use the quarrel to further their own views. Lord Bute would have been glad to drive roughly over the colonists in order to diminish the spirit of democracy that was expressed by John Wilkes and others in England. Samuel Adams in Massachusetts and Patrick Henry in Virginia were equally willing to use the conflict to advance their radical ideas in colonial politics and remake society on a basis more friendly to the plain man.

Organizing a Revolt

THE REVOLT against the British government was not a vast, spontaneous movement. Instead, it was carefully planned by shrewd men and laboriously and sagaciously executed by some of the most active spirits on the continent. It could never have succeeded if it had been left unorganized. It was in part because the patriots were well organized, and because the Tories or loyalists were not, that the former won the day.

The first step in the movement was the appearance of sporadic and unconnected rioting in resistance to the British measures. The Stamp Act of 1765 produced this response in several colonies. Legislatures protested, and Virginia, especially, passed influential resolutions. But the most effective action was that taken by mobs which in Massachusetts, New York, Virginia, North Carolina, and other provinces destroyed stamps and other property, compelled the stamp collectors to resign or flee, and even menaced the lives of the royal governors. This rioting had much popular support at first, but the orderly and wealthy citizens soon showed their disapproval of it. Organizations called Sons of Liberty also sprang into existence to maintain a popular opposition to Parliamentary oppression.

The second step was the institution of an economic boycott by groups of merchants, sometimes supported by the provincial assemblies. This was called forth by the Townshend Act of 1767, imposing duties on tea, paper, glass, and painters' colors. Merchants and substantial citizens in numerous communities adopted nonimportation or nonconsumption agreements, boycotting the articles on which British taxes had been laid. This measure was adopted in Boston in March, 1768, and spread through the colonies till within two years it had affected all of them. In some colonies English imports fell off by nearly one half; in others the agreements were badly enforced. The movement ended in 1770, when Parliament repealed all the Townshend duties save that on tea.

The third step was the formation of a system of local and

intercolonial committees of correspondence. Sam Adams of
Massachusetts, a born propagandist and organizer, was the
principal leader in this undertaking. He was the most powerful figure in the general assembly of freemen which, meeting in Faneuil Hall, controlled Boston, while he played a
leading role in the Massachusetts legislature. In the summer of 1772 citizens learned that the royal government intended to give both the governor and the superior judges
permanent salaries, thus freeing them from popular control.
A town meeting was summoned and took the step which
"included the whole Revolution." It set up a Committee of
Correspondence to communicate with other towns throughout the province. Soon every locality had a similar committee, and the province was humming like an angry beehive.
The people from Massachusetts Bay to the Berkshires were
brought into a well-marshaled array. A Tory writer later
testified, "This was the source of the rebellion. I saw the
small seed when it was implanted. It was as a grain of mus-
tard. I have watched the plant until it has become as a great
tree." Other colonies set up similar local committees, and
the Virginia Burgesses in 1773 appointed the first of a system of intercolonial committees which rapidly overspread
the whole continent.

The fourth step toward revolt was the creation of revolutionary legislatures, or, as they were generally called, provincial congresses. The old regular legislatures would not
serve the radicals for two reasons. They were in large part
composed of conservative men, property holders attached
to the existing order, and slow to act; and they were partly
under control of the royal governors, who could prorogue
or adjourn them when they liked. The first provincial congresses appeared in 1774, as a result of news of the passage
of the Boston Port Act. The means by which they were created was usually very simple.

In Virginia, for example, news of the Boston Port Act
arrived in May, 1774, and electrified the province. The legislature was sitting at the time. Jefferson, Patrick Henry,
Richard Henry Lee, and four or five others at once held a
meeting in the council chamber. They decided to proclaim
a day of fasting and prayer. This was an unusual solemnity,
for there had been none since the Seven Years' War. They
looked over the precedents of Parliament under Cromwell

and induced the Burgesses to appoint June 1, 1774, as the day. Governor Dunmore promptly dissolved the Burgesses as insubordinate. They marched eighty-nine strong down the long street to the Raleigh Tavern, where in the Apollo Room, the scene of many balls and feasts, they came to order with Speaker Peyton Randolph in the chair. The radical members proposed a new nonimportation agreement. Richard Henry Lee wanted additional steps taken, but some held back—for "a distinction was set up between their then state and when they were a House of Burgesses." But they did not hold back long. On May 29, horsemen from Boston rode in, bearing letters from other colonial capitals. They brought the news that a stoppage of all trade with England was now proposed. Peyton Randolph, with twenty-five Burgesses advising him, decided to call the members of the late House together on August 1; and with this call the first Provincial Convention, or revolutionary legislature, in the colonies was born.

CHAPTER 4

The Revolution and Confederation

The Resort to Arms

LITTLE BY LITTLE the irritation and turbulence in the colonies increased. The presence of British troops in various cities gave the radical leaders an opportunity to excite the populace. In New York in 1770 occurred the bloodless

"Battle of Golden Hill." As Cadwallader Colden put it, "an ill-humor had been artfully worked up between the towns-people and the soldiers"; at length, "some townspeople began to arm, and the soldiers rushed forth from their barracks to support their fellow-soldiers"; and only the interposition of army officers and magistrates prevented a conflict. In Boston a more serious collision took place. The noise of the fife and drum when the two regiments of the garrison changed guard on Sunday angered some puritanical townspeople, while rougher elements liked to jeer and bait the "lobster-backs." As the troops were ordered to show the greatest restraint, this baiting grew more and more impudent.

Finally, on March 5, two soldiers were attacked and beaten by townsfolk. Bells were rung to call people into the streets. A sentinel posted at the customhouse was reviled and pelted with ice and other missiles. When Captain Preston and a small squad came up to protect him, the jeering and pelting increased. "Fire if you dare—fire and be damned!" cried the mob. The troops behaved well until finally somebody clubbed a soldier to the ground, and rising, he discharged his musket. A general melee ensued, and other soldiers, without orders, fired, too. Three men were killed outright and two mortally wounded. As the drums beat for a general turnout of troops, the governor appeared and restored order. One of the mortally wounded men said on his deathbed "that he had seen mobs in Ireland, but never knew troops to bear so much without firing as these had done." Captain Preston and his soldiers were charged with murder; young John Adams had the courage to act as lawyer for the defense and obtain their acquittal. "Judgment of death against those Soldiers," he wrote, "would have been as foul a Stain upon this Country as the Executions of the Quakers or Witches, anciently." The Boston Massacre seemed to many a climactic instance of British tyranny. Its anniversary was solemnly celebrated, and it aroused the populace as nothing had theretofore done.

The British ministry, headed by Lord North, failed to draw the proper lesson from this rising suspicion and hostility. In 1772 another significant incident occurred. The little eight-gun warship *Gaspee*, busy enforcing the laws against smuggling in Rhode Island waters, ran ashore in June near Providence. A body of citizens attacked it, overmastered the crew, and burned the hated craft. All duties imposed by the Townshend Acts had been repealed save that on tea, which was maintained to enforce the principle. Tea drinking practically ceased in the colonies, and the East India Company fell into financial difficulties. To help it, the ministry in 1773 allowed it to send tea to America under conditions which made the product very cheap; but Lord North still insisted on maintaining the threepence-a-pound duty in the colonies, saying that the king regarded it as a test of authority. That test led directly to American revolt. Keen indignation was aroused by what seemed to Americans a subterfuge. The company sent over a number of ships. At every port the people were determined to resist. In Charleston the tea was locked up in vaults; from Philadelphia and New York it was sent back in the ships which had brought it. In Boston excitement ran especially high. On the night of December 16, 1773, a party of about fifty men disguised as Indians, led by Sam Adams himself, boarded the ships, burst open 343 chests of tea, and emptied them into the harbor. No town official attempted to prevent the destruction of property. "This," said John Adams rapturously, "is the most magnificent Movement of all. There is a Dignity, a Majesty, a Sublimity, in this last Effort of the Patriots that I greatly admire. This destruction of the Tea is so bold, so daring, so firm, intrepid and inflexible, and it must have so important Consequences, and so lasting, that I cannot but consider it as an Epoch in History." By this act of violence, which was applauded from Maine to Georgia, Boston threw down its gage at the feet of the Crown—and the British government swiftly took it up.

George III and the majority in Parliament were determined to punish rebellious Boston. Burke and Chatham pleaded for a conciliatory course. But the ministry carried through Parliament a series of five drastic acts. One radically changed the much-cherished charter of Massachusetts by destroying some of its most liberal features. One made the British military commander in America, General Gage, the governor of Massachusetts, with four regiments for his support, and authorized the quartering of troops in the homes of the people. One provided that officers charged with capital crimes while executing their duties might be sent to England, with witnesses, for trial. One shut the port of Bos-

ton to all commerce until compensation was paid for the tea
destroyed and evidence was furnished that the duties would
be loyally paid. Finally, the Quebec Act extended the boundaries of Canada over the entire territory north of the Ohio
and west of the Alleghenies. This last measure was not punitive in character; it had long been in contemplation, was
based on much expert study, the Northwestern fur trade and to put
better regulation of the Northwestern fur trade and to put
the French Catholic inhabitants of the Michigan and Illinois country under a congenial authority. But it was ill-
timed, and the people of the seaboard colonies naturally
thought that it closed the Northwest to them.

These harsh acts of Parliament aroused anger and con-
sternation. The intercolonial Committees of Correspondence
were galvanized into action. Meetings were held, newspaper
articles written, pamphlets scattered broadcast. When the
Virginia legislators, at their Raleigh Tavern meeting, sent out
a summons for an annual congress to discuss "the united
interest of America," the response was instant and enthusiastic. Virginia's Provincial Convention elected delegates,
and other provinces followed. On September 5, 1774, the first
Continental Congress assembled in Philadelphia, with every
colony except Georgia represented. Its fifty-one delegates included Washington, Benjamin Franklin, John Adams, John
Dickinson, and other able men. Studiously ignoring Parliament, they adopted addresses to the king and to the people
of Britain and America. They drew up a stiff declaration
of colonial rights, in which they asserted that the provinces
had "exclusive power" to legislate on their own affairs, subject to a royal veto, but promised that they would agree to
parliamentary acts upon external commerce made for the
bona fide interest of the empire.

But above all, the Continental Congress adopted two measures which pointed straight toward a breach with the British
ministry. One was the preparation of an agreement to be
scattered broadcast, binding its signers to stop within three
months all imports of English goods and within a year all
exports to British ports, including the West Indies. This
meant grim sacrifice. Virginia planters could no longer ship
their tobacco to English consumers; Massachusetts skippers
could no longer engage in the profitable West India trade.
Eleven of the colonies (New York and Georgia holding

aloof) ratified the "association," while in all thirteen energetic local committees undertook to enforce it. They administered oaths, published lists of violators, and sometimes
resorted to the whipping post or tar and feathers. The other
step was the drafting of a resolution—practically an ultimatum—by which Congress not only approved the opposition of Massachusetts to the recent acts of Parliament,
but declared that if force were used against the people of
that colony, "all America ought to support them" in resistance.

A collision had now become inescapable. Either the Acts
of Parliament would be made nullities or force would have
to be used in executing them. Neither side could recede.
Parliament declared that Massachusetts was in rebellion and
offered the Crown the resources of the empire to suppress
the revolt. All over the country arms were being bought and
military companies were drilling. Gage in Boston believed
that the spring of 1775 would bring an attack on his force.
Deciding to seize some illegal military stores at Concord,
on the evening of April 18, he set a column of eight hundred
men in motion. Patriots were on the watch, and a lantern in
the tower of North Church flashed word to Paul Revere
beyond the Charles River, who galloped off to arouse the
countryside. The embattled farmers gathered at dawn with
their muskets on Lexington Common. There was a brief
skirmish, eight Americans fell dead, and the Revolution was
under way. Sam Adams was not far away, and as he heard the
rattle of the guns he exclaimed: "What a glorious morning
is this!"

The Revolutionary War

WITHIN A FEW DAYS an undisciplined and half-armed but
formidable mass of patriot troops besieged Gage and his
army in Boston; within a few weeks the last royal governments were being overturned all over the country. The second Continental Congress, meeting in Philadelphia on May
10 as a frankly rebellious body (though it sent a last conciliatory address to the king), organized the troops about
Boston into the "American continental army" and appointed
George Washington to take command. The fortress of Ti-

conderoga, commanding the main approach to Canada, was brilliantly captured by a force under Ethan Allen, leader of the Green Mountain Boys. As the American lines were pushed closer about Boston, Gage realized that his position could be threatened from Dorchester Heights on the south, and from the hills behind Charlestown on the north. When the patriots took steps on June 16–17 to occupy the latter position, they precipitated the first great battle of the war, Bunker Hill.

Like Bull Run eighty-seven years later, Bunker Hill had an importance out of all proportion to its immediate results. The Americans, about thirty-five hundred strong, had planted themselves during the night on both Breed's Hill, where they built a redoubt, and Bunker Hill. At dawn their activities were observed. Gage called a council of war and, though he might have cut off the American works in the rear, decided to attack them in front. This piece of hardihood was probably inspired by the British impatience for a square stand-up fight. Infantry were landed below the American position, formed in line, and at three o'clock in the afternoon of a broiling day sent to the attack. In full-dress uniform, with knapsack, three days' rations, ammunition, and musket, a total load of perhaps 125 pounds each, they advanced slowly in beautiful order. When they were forty yards from the entrenchments, the Americans, aiming at the waistline, opened fire with terrible effect; the British recoiled, were re-formed, and came on again to meet another murderous fire at twenty yards; they recoiled once more, were again rallied, and this time swept over the entrenchments as the patriots fired their last two rounds. It was magnificent, but it was criminally unnecessary. An equal force, occupying Charlestown Neck under naval protection, could have starved the Americans into early surrender. Altogether, the British losses were 1054 men, the American losses only 441.

The battle proved to the Americans that even without proper organization or equipment, they could repulse the best regular troops of Europe, and they gained enormously in confidence. Howe, in immediate command on the British side, was so sickened by the carnage that he never forgot it. When he replaced Gage, who was recalled to England in disgrace, he showed timidity in pressing American troops to battle that helped cost England the war.

American Disadvantages

THE CONFLICT dragged over six years, with fighting in every colony, and a dozen pitched battles of importance. Repeatedly the patriot forces came close to total disaster. It was difficult for Washington to form a true army out of the mixed and ill-trained forces at his disposal and still harder to hold it together. Loyalist sentiment was widely diffused, and indifference was even more general. In New England, Virginia, and parts of the Carolinas the people showed a vigorous fighting temper. But New York seemed quite as much Tory as patriot; in Pennsylvania the Quakers would not fight, while most Germans were averse to leaving their farmsteads; in North Carolina many upland settlers, hating the lowland people, rallied to battle for the king; and much of Georgia, threatened by the Creeks and grateful for a special royal subsidy, held back from the struggle. At the lowest computation, twenty-five thousand Americans bore arms for the Crown; and had the loyalists been sedulously cultivated, carefully marshaled, and ably led, the outcome of the war would have been different.

The patriot forces were at first wretchedly organized. When Baron von Steuben, a staff officer of Frederick the Great, arrived in 1778 as a volunteer to improve the situation—soon rising to be inspector general—he found the regiments ranging from three to twenty-three companies in strength. The quality of the commissioned officers was poor, for in some colonies any glib-tongued man with a pleasing personality could induce men to enlist under him as captain, or with the use of rum and money might get himself elected to higher rank. Democracy in New England and elsewhere made for insubordination; the farmer or villager who knew his captain as a neighbor was loath to take orders from him, so that Washington wrote that the Yankees regarded their officers "as no more than broomsticks." Nor were many privates moved by any strong sense of responsibility. They felt that they had enlisted for periods terminable at their convenience. When cold winter weather came on, when they heard that crops were ripening without hands to harvest them, or when they grew homesick and discouraged, they slipped out of camp. Washington besought Congress for long-term enlistments, which were authorized in September, 1776; but this by no means fully met the evil. To stiffen the discipline, Washington finally urged Congress to give courts-martial the power to inflict a maximum of five hundred lashes upon offenders.

Repeatedly the army almost faded away. After the patriots took possession of Boston in March, 1776, and Washington transferred his troops to New York, he found that he had only eight thousand men fit for duty; the total British forces were thirty-five thousand, and Howe landed on Long Island with at least twenty thousand effectives. Naturally he had no difficulty in smashing the little force of patriots which he found at Flatbush. There were left in front of him only some fifty-five hundred troops, and he might have overwhelmed and captured them all if he had moved promptly; but he let the opportunity slip until Washington escaped to Manhattan Island under cover of fog. Then came the patriot defeats on Manhattan and at White Plains; and as Washington retreated across New Jersey, his army melted away almost to nothing. The New York and New England militia deserted in droves. He lost much of his food, baggage, and cannon. Before he had reached the Delaware River the New Jersey and Maryland militia had also forsaken him. When he took up winter quarters he had about thirty-three hundred men, half of them men whose steadiness he could hardly trust. Only his daring and skill that winter, in his brilliant blows at Trenton and Princeton, saved the country. He was able to begin the campaign of 1777—"the year of the three gallows," said the Tories—with eleven thousand troops. That was the number he had when he marched through Philadelphia on August 24, 1777, with what one writer of the time called "ragged, lousy, naked regiments." Howe moved on Philadelphia with twenty thousand trained troops, and Washington, defeated at Germantown, was driven back to spend a cruel winter at Valley Forge.

The patriots were also fearfully handicapped by their inability to finance the war effectively. They had no way to float bond issues. Taxation was almost out of the question. No continental agency had power to lay taxes; Congress had to request the thirteen states for tax levies; and since the states were jealous, stingy, and badly governed, they gave but grudging and inadequate help. The whole amount raised for national purposes by state taxation, down to 1784, came to less than six million dollars in specie value, or not two dollars per capita. Loans brought in quite inadequate sums—domestic loans nearly twelve million dollars, loans from abroad (chiefly France, with Holland and Spain contributing) not quite eight millions. The principal reliance of the United States in fighting the Revolution had to be placed upon paper money.

First and last, the country was snowed under with paper bills. They depreciated so rapidly that although their face value ran up to about $240,000,000, the actual return to the treasury in specie was less than $38,000,000. By the spring of 1781 continental notes were so near zero that barber-shops were papered with them and frolicsome sailors returning from their cruises took the bundles of worthless money in which they were paid, had suits of clothes made from them, and paraded through the streets in this tattered finery. Naturally, the depreciating bills were a source of great injustice, discontent, and disorganization. As a contemporary observer, Pelatiah Webster, wrote: "Paper money polluted the equity of our laws, turned them into engines of oppression, corrupted the justice of our public administration, destroyed the fortunes of thousands who had confidence in it, enervated the trade, husbandry, and manufactures of our country, and went far to destroy the morality of our people."

The patriot cause suffered heavily, again, from the keen distrust of Congress by the separate colonies and from their jealousy of one another. It was quite impossible to set up a strong continental government. The colonies were in revolt against a centralized control and believed in local home rule. Moreover, after the first flush of patriotic ardor had passed away they had little sisterly feeling. Virginians disliked the Yankees as a set of vulgar, grasping, and ultra-democratic schemers, and even the reserved Washington wrote caustically of their bad manners. The Yankees thought the Southerners inclined to be proud and aristocratic. Each colony had lived so much to itself that when John Adams rode to the Continental Congress he hardly knew the names of the principal New York and Pennsylvania leaders. Congress had to beg on bended knee for support of the army and the treasury, and its pleas often went unheeded.

Then, too, the Americans had practically no navy—though John Paul Jones soon performed some striking exploits at sea, raiding boldly in British waters. The British held general control of the ocean until 1778, and partial control thereafter. They could attack almost anywhere they liked along a fifteen-hundred-mile coastline. They had plenty of money and supplies; they brought over nearly thirty thousand German mercenary troops; and their officers possessed a superior training in military affairs. It is not strange that at first they confidently expected victory.

American Advantages

BUT THE AMERICANS had great advantages as well as handicaps, and in the end these turned the tide. One lay in the theater of conflict. They fought in their own sparsely populated land, much of it still wilderness, three thousand miles from Britain. An army might be beaten in one place, and another would spring up hundreds of miles away. The British could no more hold down such a vast territory than they could nail currant jelly to a wall. To transport men and supplies over the wide ocean was costly and difficult, while proper strategic management of the whole British force from London was impossible. Another advantage lay in the superb fighting spirit which American troops at certain critical moments did exhibit. These farmer-soldiers, fresh from the hunting path and plow trail, individualistic and erratic, might be exasperating three fourths of the time, but they sometimes fought like men inspired. The Northern troops who rallied to destroy Burgoyne's invading army in 1777, and the Southern soldiers who took defeat after defeat in 1780–1781, always returning to the attack till final victory came, proved that a patriotic yeomanry could be unbeatable. Still another advantage after 1778 was the alliance with France, who was burning to revenge herself upon Britain—an alliance that brought men, money, encouragement, and, at the final crucial moment, command of the coast. And by no means least among the patriot blessings was the stupid mismanagement which Burgoyne, Howe, and Clinton gave the British troops. Wolfe was dead, and no Wellington emerged.

The culminating American advantage was that of leadership—for the Americans had George Washington. Chosen by Congress with little knowledge of his capacities, he proved all in all to the patriot cause its best guide and support. He can be criticized on narrow military grounds. He never handled an army larger than a modern division, he made many missteps, he was defeated again and again. Yet, taking command at forty-three, he became the soul of the war. This Virginia planter and frontier colonel was its informing spirit because of his unflagging patriotism, his calm wisdom, his serene moral courage; because in the gloomiest hours he never lost his dignity, poise, or decision; because he knew how to combine enterprise and caution; because his integrity, elevation, and magnanimity never failed, his fortitude never faltered. He knew how to bide his hour to strike, so that his patient vigilance gave him the title of "Fabius."

He could lose his temper fiercely when provoked beyond endurance, as the traitorous Charles Lee learned at the battle of Monmouth; but in general he had an iron self-control, so complete that when in later years the news of Wayne's terrible defeat at the hands of the Indians was brought him at a presidential dinner party he betrayed no emotion to his guests. Scrupulous in everything, he drove his troops hard and punished army offenses severely, but his justice and devotion to his men won their utter loyalty. When he began his address to the unpaid and discontented troops at Newburgh with the words "Gentlemen, you will permit me to put on my spectacles, for I have not only grown gray, but almost blind in the service of my countrymen," many shed tears. It was characteristic of him that he accepted nothing but his expenses for his Revolutionary services and kept account of these expenses with minute care. When the war was done, like Cincinnatus he thought only of going back to his beloved farm, which he wished to make the best in America; "Agriculture has ever been the most favorite amusement of my life," he wrote. But he remained at the call of duty. Less humanly appealing than some other heroes of the republic, he has remained pre-eminent in the massiveness of his character, the fixed elevation of his aims, and the wisdom and breadth of his mind. Goldwin Smith has justly remarked that the three finest things in the Revolution "are the character of Washington, the behavior of his army at Valley Forge, and the devotion of the better class of loyalists."

Independence

WHAT HAD BEGUN as a war for the "rights of Englishmen" and the mere redress of grievances became in little more than a year a war for independence. This was perfectly natural. At first, Congress warmly protested its loyalty to the Crown. But the bitterness caused by bloodshed and destruction, the resentment aroused by the implacable attitude of George III, and a sense of the natural right of Americans to determine their own destiny soon led to complete separation. Early in 1776 Washington's army raised a distinctive American flag. At the same time a profound effect was being produced by the pamphlet *Common Sense*, written by a brilliant young radical, Thomas Paine, lately come from England. He argued that independence was the only remedy, that it would be harder to win the longer it was delayed, and that it alone would make American union possible. As June arrived, many members of Congress became impatient. A Virginia delegate, Richard Henry Lee, moved a resolution for independence, which John Adams seconded. A committee of five, for whom Thomas Jefferson held the pen, then drew up a formal declaration of independence, which Congress adopted on July 2 and proclaimed on July 4, 1776.

The men who drew up and adopted this epoch-making document were not content with a mere declaration of independence. They confessed to "a decent respect to the opinions of mankind," and they were at pains to set forth in detail the causes that "impelled them to separation" and the philosophy that justified it. Nor were these causes—some twenty-five or thirty of them are listed—cited as in themselves justifying so drastic a step. They were listed, rather, in order to prove, on the part of George III, "a design to reduce them under absolute despotism." It is significant that at the very beginning of their national history Americans took their stand on principles and proclaimed a philosophy.

And what are these principles of government here given

immortal expression? "We hold these truths to be self-evident," wrote Jefferson:

That all men are created equal, that they are endowed by their Creator with certain unalienable Rights, that among these are Life, Liberty and the pursuit of Happiness.—That to secure these rights, Governments are instituted among Men, deriving their just powers from the consent of the governed,—That whenever any Form of Government becomes destructive of these ends, it is the Right of the People to alter or to abolish it, and to institute new Government, laying its foundation on such principles and organizing its powers in such form, as to them shall seem most likely to effect their Safety and Happiness.

What we have here, of course, is the philosophy of democracy, a philosophy which had never before been given so succinct or so eloquent a statement. There are certain things—so the Americans said—that no reasonable man can doubt—self-evident truths. There is the truth that all men are created equal—that all men are equal in the sight of God and equal before the law. There were, to be sure, even as Jefferson wrote, many inequalities in America: the inequality of rich and poor, of men and women, of black and white. But the failure of a society to live up to an ideal does not invalidate the ideal, and the doctrine of equality, once announced, worked as a leaven in American thought.

Another great truth proclaimed in the Declaration is that men are "endowed" with "unalienable" rights—among them life, liberty, and the pursuit of happiness. These are not rights granted to men by some benevolent government and held at the pleasure of that government. They are rights with which all men are born and which they cannot lose. This principle, too, worked as a ferment in the minds of Americans and others, changing their attitude toward authority; for, as the Declaration pointed out, it was precisely to secure these rights that governments were organized in the first place. What we have here is the "compact" theory of government—the theory that men once lived in a "state of nature," that in such a state they were continually in danger, and that in order to protect themselves they came together and set up governments, granting to those governments just enough power to protect their lives, their liberty, and their property. In short, men made government to do good, not evil; made it to protect them, not to injure them. And the moment government failed of the purposes for which it was established, it no longer deserved the support or allegiance of men.

If men could make governments, they could unmake them, for it is their right to alter or abolish a bad government and to institute a new one. And they shortly proved that this was not mere theory. Even as the Revolution was under way, during the stress and turbulence of war, they set about to translate this idea into reality. Meeting together in conventions they did, legally, abolish their old governments and set up new ones; they wrote into their constitutions solid guarantees of life and liberty and happiness. The ideas that had for centuries been the property of philosophers were taken out of the realm of philosophy and made law.

Marches and Battles

THE GREAT DECISIVE BATTLE of the war, its turning point in a military sense, was Saratoga. At the beginning of 1777 the British had large forces in Canada, and a strong army in New York under Howe. Had these troops been concentrated at New York, the Crown could have put thirty-five thousand strongly equipped regulars in the field. If an energetic British commander had then used them to strike relentlessly at Washington's little army of eight thousand continentals in New Jersey, as Grant in 1864 struck relentlessly at Lee in Virginia, the revolt would almost certainly have been crushed. What Washington most dreaded was this concentration of troops to destroy him. But the authorities in London, badly advised by Burgoyne, who had gone home on leave, decided to keep their forces divided. One army, under Burgoyne, was to move from Canada southward upon Albany, at the head of navigation on the Hudson; Howe's army in New York was to move northward up the Hudson to Albany. The king endorsed the plan. Full instructions were then sent from London to the Canadian authorities to launch the northern half of the joint expedition. But no definite instructions were sent to Howe—who moved against Philadelphia instead of Albany.

A radical defect of the Burgoyne scheme was that it pre-

Washington's Campaigns in the Middle States, 1776–1783

vented an irresistible unification of British forces. Another radical defect was that once the northern army had advanced into American territory, it was much too far from its base. When Burgoyne reached Fort Edward in upper New York, he was 185 miles from Montreal, and every forward step put more difficult terrain between him and his supplies. He had to look about for provisions in the surrounding country. At Bennington, in the southern part of what is now Vermont, were large stores of breadstuffs and cattle, guarded only by a few militia. To seize them, and to strike a blow at a district which, he wrote, "abounds in the most active and most rebellious race of the continent, and hangs like a gathering storm on my left," he sent some thirteen hundred Germans and others against Bennington. They ran into a hornets' nest. The yeomen soldiers of New England, mustering two thousand strong under a veteran of the French war named John Stark, overwhelmed them.

Meanwhile, a fast-increasing American army confronted Burgoyne's main force on the upper Hudson. When the two armies clashed at Freeman's Farm on September 19, 1777, the Americans numbered about nine thousand men, the British about six thousand. Other engagements completed the discomfiture of Burgoyne, who was soon mired down in the wilderness, exhausted, and losing heavily while the American army rose to twenty thousand. On October 17, surrounded on all sides, his troops laid down their arms. He had proved the folly of taking an army nearly two hundred miles from its base into a wild country swarming with hostile recruits.

Burgoyne's defeat had far-reaching consequences. At one stroke nearly one fourth of the king's effective troops in America were lost. The Hudson was placed permanently under American control. The patriots took new heart. In Paris, Benjamin Franklin had been laboring manfully to induce Vergennes, the Foreign Secretary, to send aid to the Americans. When news came that Howe was in Philadelphia and that Burgoyne had taken Ticonderoga, French enthusiasm had cooled. But when word arrived of Saratoga, Franklin's friend Beaumarchais is said to have dislocated his arm in hurrying joyously to inform the king. On February 6, 1778, France and the United States signed a treaty of alliance which placed a wholly new aspect upon the war. Already the gallant Lafayette, who came to the United States at his own expense to serve in any capacity, had been made a major general by Congress. Already the kings of France and Spain had made secret loans, with which large quantities of arms and munitions had been purchased. Now the French prepared to send over six thousand excellent troops under Rochambeau to reinforce Washington; they furnished money and supplies in larger quantities; and the operations of the French fleets greatly aggravated the difficulties of the British in supplying their forces.

Having failed to conquer the North, the British turned to the South. Their plan was to seize Georgia, which was notoriously weak, and move irresistibly northward, gaining loyalist aid as they went. In the closing days of 1778 they took Savannah and in 1779 occupied interior areas of Georgia and South Carolina. The Americans sent General Benjamin Lincoln to meet the situation. But he allowed himself to be shut up in Charleston, and in May, 1780, the British captured him, his five thousand men, and the principal Southern seaport together. It was one of the heaviest blows of the Revolution. All South Carolina was soon overrun. A second American commander, the "hero of Saratoga," Horatio Gates, went south to stay the tide. Instead, his little army of three thousand, half of it raw militia, was crushed by Lord Cornwallis at Camden (August 16, 1780). Their total loss in killed, wounded, and captured was two thousand, and Gates did not halt in his flight till he had covered nearly two hundred miles.

But at Kings Mountain a force of a thousand loyalists from western Carolina had meanwhile been defeated by a larger patriot army. A third American commander, Nathanael Greene, far abler than his predecessors, now arrived on the Southern scene. He, too, was defeated—at Guilford Courthouse early in 1781—but he showed astonishing skill in long and rapid marches. Indeed, while in nine months he lost four important battles, he wore the British troops out, and his threats in combination with the hostility of the inhabitants finally forced them back into Charleston and Savannah. Like Washington, Greene lost engagements but won his campaigns.

And while Greene was clearing the lower South, another British army was nearing its doom. Cornwallis left the Cape

Fear country in late spring and moved northward to join the force of the traitor Benedict Arnold in Virginia. After an ineffectual pursuit of American forces under Lafayette, he withdrew to Yorktown at the mouth of the York River, which he fortified. At this time Washington had some six thousand men near New York and Rochambeau had about five thousand at Newport, Rhode Island. Just as Cornwallis retired to the coast, word came from the French admiral in the West Indies, De Grasse, that he could offer his co-operation. Washington saw his opportunity and brilliantly seized it. By marches of magnificent rapidity, he brought a combined American and French army of sixteen thousand men before Yorktown. Cornwallis' eight thousand troops were cut off from escape by sea by De Grasse's fleet. His outer redoubts were taken; his inner defenses were battered down by American artillery. On October 19 he sent his sword to Washington, who ordered it received by General Lincoln, and the British troops stacked their arms while their band played *The World Turned Upside Down*.

The war was now practically ended. For a time King George stubbornly refused to acknowledge defeat. But during 1782 the Southern ports were all abandoned, and the royal forces soon exercised no authority whatever beyond the sound of the garrison bugles in one city, New York.

The Peace Treaty

IN THE TREATY which in 1783 ended the war, Great Britain made generous terms. Had her government chosen, it might have driven a hard bargain as to boundaries. The British fleet under Rodney had just won a decisive victory over the French in the West Indies, and the British forces in New York could not be dislodged. It is true that American riflemen under George Rogers Clark had penetrated the wild country north of the Ohio River, capturing British posts in what is now Indiana, Illinois, and Michigan. Most of this territory, however, was reoccupied by the British before the end of the war. The leading British minister, Shelburne, who dealt with the American plenipotentiaries, Benjamin Franklin, John Adams, and John Jay, might have tried to draw a tight line around the new America. Instead, he conceded to the new republic all the country between the Alleghenies and the Mississippi, with the northern boundary nearly as it now runs; while he handed Florida over to Spain and gave Americans large fishing rights off the Canadian coast.

This generosity bore valuable fruit. Had the British tried to hold a great part of the Northwest, friction with the United States (by no means lacking anyhow) would have been constant and serious. The natural march of the republic was westward, and its expansive energies were exerted in a direction which finally compelled the French to cede Louisiana and the Mexicans to cede the area north of the Rio Grande—but which, especially after 1815, gave little anxiety to the British Empire. Indeed, Canada and the United States expanded to the Pacific side by side and to-day hold the best part of the continent as fast friends and allies.

The Growth of Democracy

IN EXTERNAL RELATIONS, America had accomplished a memorable revolution. Internally an equally important change had taken place. Quite as important as the cutting of the British connection was the profound alteration which these years brought to American society.

Separation from England, of course, meant an immediate gain in political democracy. Governors were now chosen by the people and not by the Crown, the upper chambers of the legislatures were made elective instead of appointive, and laws demanded by the populace were safe from a veto. But equally important were the internal reforms which broadened the suffrage and made representation more equitable. In Pennsylvania a tremendous demand arose in 1775–1776 for two democratic steps; one giving the long-slighted western counties a representation in the Assembly commensurate with their population, the other abolishing the property qualifications and naturalization requirements which had restricted voting to a small favored class. Both reforms were decisively won. In March, 1776, the legislature admitted seventeen additional members, most of them from the western area, while the suffrage was soon broadened to permit any male taxpayer to vote. In some states, like Virginia, the old-settled sections still held an unfair predominance in the legislature, and in others, like Massachusetts, property qualifications were still demanded for the ballot. But in Pennsylvania, Delaware, North Carolina, Georgia, and Vermont the ballot was freed, so that, as one disgusted conservative put it, soon any taxpaying "biped of the forest" might vote.

The dispersion of the loyalists made another great contribution to democracy. Many conservative and propertied Tories had shown dislike for those whom Dorothy Hutchinson called "the dirty mob." Devoted to the old order, they exiled themselves in a passionate mixture of scorn and sorrow. When Howe evacuated Boston, almost a thousand loyalists sailed with him, and another thousand soon followed—their motto, "Hell, Hull, or Halifax." Nearly all the important property owners of the province of New York were Tories. When the British evacuated Charleston, a great crescent-shaped fleet of a hundred ships sailed down the bay with departing loyalists—a magnificent and tragic sight. Upper Canada and the Maritime Provinces received more than sixty thousand refugees, the West Indies thousands more, and England a dejected host. "There will scarcely be a village in England without some American dust in it by the time we are all at rest," wrote one. Following their departure the homely, hard-working farmers, shopkeepers, and artisans were free to create a civilization after their own hearts. Dignity, leisure, and culture thenceforth counted for less, energy and rude self-assertion for more. The pushing trader and speculator were more prominent in American society. Everybody was counted equal, everybody was in a hurry, and nearly everybody thought more of the dollar.

A strong impetus toward democracy was also supplied by the successful attack on three bulwarks of privilege—the destruction of primogeniture and entail, the breakup of great Tory estates, and the overthrow of the Anglican Church establishment wherever it existed. Virginia was the colony in which entail and primogeniture were most firmly rooted. Their effect had been to preserve great family estates intact. As Jefferson said in his *Notes on Virginia*, the province was thus given a set of great aristocratic families, who were "formed into a patrician order, distinguished by the splendor

and luxury of their establishments." The holders of Westover, Shirley, Tuckahoe, and other manorial dwellings looked
out across princely domains. Thomas Jefferson led the attack
on entail in the Virginia legislature and, at almost the first
assault in 1776, swept it away. All estates were thereafter
subject to unrestricted sale. In 1785 Jefferson also succeeded
in abolishing primogeniture. Someone proposed that the
eldest son should get at least a double share. "No, unless he
eats a double allowance of food and does a double amount
of work," Jefferson retorted. When the French traveler, Bris-
sot de Warville, shortly visited Virginia, he was able to
record: "The distinction of classes begins to disappear."
Great estates were rapidly broken up among the sons or
were sold in parcels to newcomers while the children took
the money and went west. Other Southern States—Georgia,
South Carolina, Maryland—rapidly followed Virginia's example.

Similarly, the confiscation of the huge land tracts of the
proprietaries and the rich Tories made for a democratic
system of smallholders. The two principal proprietors were
the Penn family in Pennsylvania and the Lord Baltimore
family in Maryland. In memory of her founder, Pennsylvania granted the Penns £130,000, but Harford received
only £10,000 from Maryland. Virginia confiscated a number of estates, notably that of Washington's genial friend,
the sixth Lord Fairfax. North Carolina seized the Gran-
ville holdings of millions of acres. New York took over all
the Crown lands and in addition fifty-nine specified Tory
estates, including the Philipse holdings of about three hundred square miles. The De Lancey estate in Westchester
and the Roger Morris lands in Putnam County were sold
to more than five hundred holders. The confiscated estate
of Sir John Johnson in upper New York ultimately gave
homes to ten thousand farm people. Massachusetts seized a
number of holdings, including that owned in Maine by Sir
William Pepperell, a baronet who could ride thirty miles
in a straight line on his own land. All the way from New
Hampshire, where Sir John Wentworth lost his domain, to
Georgia, where Sir James Wright suffered the same fate,
small farmers jubilantly moved on to rich lands that would
once have taken them only as tenants.

The religious aristocracy connected with the British re-

gime went down along with the landed and official aristocracy. In New England the special privileges of the Congregational Church, which had nothing to do with the Crown,
persisted. Massachusetts even strengthened them. But in
the South the privileges of the Anglican Church crumbled
away.

The Revolution utterly wrecked the establishment in North
Carolina, where not one of its pulpits was left occupied.
In other states it gave the political radicals, and the dissenting sects like the Baptists and Presbyterians, a golden opportunity. North Carolina adopted a Constitution in 1776
which guaranteed religious freedom and forbade any establishment. South Carolina took the same step in her Constitution of 1778. Georgia did so in her Constitution of 1777.
But the fiercest fight was waged in Virginia. Here the establishment was strongly entrenched, for most of the aristocratic
families were Anglicans. Even such a political firebrand as
Patrick Henry believed that state support of religion was indispensable to piety and good morals. But the dissenting
sects found leaders in two great liberals bred within the
Church of England, Thomas Jefferson and James Madison.

It was easy for these leaders to carry the first trench by
obtaining a guarantee of religious toleration. Madison wrote
into the Declaration of Rights of 1776 the simple principle:
"All men are equally entitled to the free exercise of religion."
But the establishment remained, and a ten years' battle was
required to overthrow it. Jefferson called it "the severest
contest in which I have ever been engaged." Beginning in
1776, he and his friends succeeded year by year in suspend-
ing the ecclesiastical taxes and in 1779 abolished tithes
forever. But their antagonists carried resolutions in 1776
declaring that the question of a general tax levy for all
churches should be reserved, and behind this demand for
a general religious tax rallied a powerful party. In essence
the plan would have established all Christian denominations,
made them equally state religions, and supported them out
of the public purse. Its most redoubtable advocate was the
eloquent Patrick Henry.

The crisis came in 1784–1786. Henry, by his irresistible
forensic power, carried in the House of Burgesses a resolution declaring: "The people of this commonwealth ought
to pay a moderate tax or contribution for the support of

the Christian religion, or of some Christian church or denomination, or community of Christians." But when an effort was made to implement this expression by a specific bill, the opposition rallied all its forces. In a tremendous debate between Henry and Madison, the latter carried off all the honors. The bill was postponed, and this allowed the liberal leaders to wage a campaign of education. In 1786 the measure was finally buried out of sight, and at the same time Jefferson's famous bill for religious freedom was passed—a bill declaring that the government must not interfere in Church affairs or matters of conscience or impose any disabilities for religious opinion. This epochal measure became the cornerstone of religious freedom not only in Virginia, but also in many new states of the West.

Much, too, might be said of the measures soon taken in various states to strengthen the foundations of education. During these years of war and turbulence, Americans managed to found no less than seven new colleges—including Dickinson and Franklin in Pennsylvania, Hampden Sidney and Washington in Virginia, and Transylvania in distant Kentucky—while three states laid the foundations for state universities. Yet at the same time the conflict had a distressing effect upon private schools and colleges. Yale College was for a time closed; so was King's College, now Columbia. As late as 1797 the president of William and Mary was teaching a group of barefoot boys, while in 1800 the Harvard faculty consisted of the president, three professors, and four tutors. During the years 1780–1784 not a single bookseller advertised in the principal newspaper of Boston.

But the Revolution had one happy effect in arousing a general demand for popular training—for free public schools. It was at once seen that democratic self-government required an educated electorate. Governor George Clinton of New York remarked in 1782: "It is the peculiar duty of the government of a free state where the highest employments are open to citizens of every rank to endeavor by the establishment of schools and seminaries to diffuse that degree of literature which is necessary to the establishment of public trusts." Jefferson wrote: "Above all things, I hope the education of the common people may be attended to; convinced that on their good sense we may rely with most security for the preservation of a due degree of liberty." Poverty at first hampered the states, but this new demand in time resulted in far better facilities for elementary instruction than before the war. And of far-reaching importance for education were the provisions of the Land Ordinance of 1785 making available millions of acres of public land as an endowment for public schools.

Lack of a National Government

THE OUTLOOK of the young republic was thus, in many ways, hopeful and progressive. Yet one dark cloud lay on the horizon. The thirteen states had never succeeded in setting up a really *national* government. They had adopted in March, 1781, certain Articles of Confederation, but this system, which was simply a "league of friendship," was feeble and inadequate. No true national executive existed. No national system of courts had been set up. The Continental Congress, which consisted of one house in which each state had a single vote, was too weak to be effective. It could not levy taxes, enlist troops, punish men who broke the laws it passed, or compel the states to observe the treaties it made with other countries. Worst of all, it could not raise enough money to carry on the functions of government or pay interest on the national debt. Yet it is easy to exaggerate the weakness and inadequacy of the Articles. If they did not solve the problem of federalism, they went a long way on the road to a solution, and the division which they made between those powers which were general and those which were local was a sound one. They were an important, even a necessary, step on the road from the independence and sovereignty of the separate states to the federal union of 1789.

The Revolution, in short, had given the American people an independent place in the family of nations. It had given them a changed social order, in which heredity, wealth, and privilege counted for less, and human equality for more; in which the standards of culture and manners were temporarily lowered, but those of equity were raised. It had given them a thousand memories to deepen their patriotism: Washington unsheathing his sword under a Cambridge elm, the bloody slopes of Bunker Hill, the death of Montgomery under the walls of Quebec, Nathan Hale saying "I only regret that I have but one life to lose for my country," the prison ships in the Hudson, Benedict Arnold foiled as he tried to betray his country, the piercing cold of Valley Forge, Marion's guerrilla fighters in South Carolina earning him the nickname of "the swamp fox," Robert Morris, the patriot financier, patiently collecting money for the cause, Alexander Hamilton storming the redoubt at Yorktown, the British fleet sailing out of New York Bay in its grand evacuation.

But the American people still had to show that they possessed a genuine capacity for self-government—for making a success of their republic. They still had to show that they could solve the problem of imperial organization. They had not yet proved it. Their "league of friendship" seemed to be turning into a league of dissension. Their Congress was sinking into utter contempt. The quarrels among the states were growing positively dangerous. No group suffered more from the chaotic state of affairs than the army, which failed to receive the food, clothing, or pay it needed. Its officers had a frequent toast: "Here's to a hoop for the barrel"—and if a hoop were not furnished, the barrel seemed likely to collapse into a pile of staves.

CHAPTER 5

Making the Constitution

An Epochal Achievement

BY COMMON AGREEMENT the United States has one of the most ingenious and effective constitutions ever prepared, a constitution which, unlike Britain's, is written, but which has expanded flexibly with the nation. Gladstone said that "As the British Constitution is the most subtle organism which has ever proceeded from progressive history, so the American Constitution is the most wonderful work ever struck off at a given time by the brain and purpose of man." Actually it, too, was largely an evolutionary product. But it took shape in one of the most remarkable conventions of modern times.

It was probably fortunate that the Articles of Confederation, which the states adopted near the close of the Revolution, were so clearly defective. Had they provided a somewhat better framework of government, Americans might have been content to patch them up, and the country might have labored for many decades under a poor constitution. Because they broke down almost completely, they were thrown aside; because the breakdown sprang from their weakness, the new Constitution was made exceptionally strong. It was fortunate, too, that the breakdown of the Articles coincided with a serious commercial depression in 1785 and 1786. Only a manifest crisis could lead many suspicious Americans to accept a powerful new central government.

Weakness of the Confederate Government

FOR 1786 was the very climax of the critical period. Not only was the country without any really vigorous national machinery of government; the thirteen states had become so disorderly that men spoke of possible war between some of them. They were quarreling over boundary lines—in Pennsylvania and Vermont even breaking heads over them. Their courts were handing down decisions which conflicted with one another. The national government, which should have had the power to lay whatever tariffs were necessary and to regulate commerce, did not. This government should have had authority to levy taxes for national purposes: again it did not. It should have had the sole control of foreign relations, but a number of states had begun their own negotiations with foreign countries. The nation should have had exclusive control over Indian relations, but several states managed the savages to suit themselves, and Georgia began and ended an Indian war.

When internal disorders threatened the security of property in great areas, the sober middle classes grew alarmed. When the depression became heaviest in 1785–1786, it produced intense hardship wherever people lived close to the subsistence level. All along the frontiers money was scarce, markets were prostrated, and crops rotted on the ground for want of takers. People resorted to barter. Debtor groups demanded that the state governments manufacture paper money to move their crops and pay their obligations. They asked for a moratorium on debt collection and for statutes making cattle or grain legal tender. The petition of the town of Greenwich, Massachusetts, in January, 1786, recited that foreclosure sales of land took place daily at one third the true value, that cattle sold at half price, and that taxes during the preceding five years had equaled the whole rental of the farms. Political contest assumed the form of struggles between creditor and debtor classes. In many states the antagonism between poor and well to do became intense. A typical pronouncement was that of a South Carolina group which denounced Governor Rutledge and other aristocrats: "the nabobs of this state, their servile toadeaters the bobs, and the servilely servile tools and lickspittles of both, the bobbetts."

Seven state legislatures were carried by the paper-money forces in 1786. In Rhode Island they passed measures under which every man could satisfy his obligations by practically worthless currency. As a rhymester wrote:

> Bankrupts their creditors with rage pursue;
> No stop, no mercy from the debtor crew.

Since the rag money was a full tender for debts owed to people in other states, Connecticut and Massachusetts indignantly passed retaliatory measures. The paper-money forces failed, however, to carry the two legislatures which dominated all northern New England, those of Massachusetts and New Hampshire; and here armed disturbances broke out. The existing Massachusetts Constitution lodged control of the government in the propertied elements of society. It had erected special defenses for property in suffrage qualifications and officeholding qualifications. The conservative legislature had then levied heavy taxes to pay the Revolutionary debt, which was largely held by specu-

lators. In vain did town meetings and conventions petition
for relief, and the process of foreclosing mortgages and dis-
training on land for the payment of back taxes continued.
It is not surprising that an agrarian uprising occurred. The
adjournment of the General Court in July, 1786, gave the
signal for a "revolt" led by a veteran of Bunker Hill, Daniel
Shays. Shays's Rebellion—as it was called—was in the tradition of earlier agrarian uprisings—Bacon's Rebellion, for
example, or the Regulator outbreaks in western North Carolina on the eve of the Revolution; it was not so much a
revolt against government as a violent protest against conditions that had become intolerable.

The state acted energetically under Governor Bowdoin,
General Lincoln, and some wealthy men who lent their
money in the crisis, and it was easy to stop Shays's march
when he tried to plunder the arsenal at Springfield, and to
scatter his forces. But the brief struggle deeply alarmed
conservative circles all over the nation. It seemed to pres-
age a revolutionary movement toward the left. General
Knox wrote Washington that New England had twelve or
fifteen thousand desperate men who held what would now
be called Communist views. "Their creed is, that the property of the United States has been protected from the confiscation of Britain by the joint exertions of all and therefore
ought to be the common property of all." They had shocked
"every man of principle and property in New England."
Washington, who thought that the Massachusetts authorities
should have been even more rigorous, wrote in evident con-
sternation: "There are combustibles in every state which a
spark might set a fire in." That was the general view. And the
logical inference was that a stronger national government
was needed to help the states deal with disorder. "It is clear
in my mind," wrote Stephen Higginson of Massachusetts to
Nathaniel Dane, "that we cannot long exist under our
present system; and unless we soon acquire more force to
the Union by some means or other, Insurgents will arise and
eventually take the reins from us. We shall inevitably be
thrown into . . . convulsions which will result in one or
more Governments, established with the loss of much blood."

The quarrels of the state governments had already produced severe distress among the groups whose livelihood
depended upon some measure of co-ordination. Merchants

were in desperation over the lack of a uniform currency. They had to deal with a curious hodgepodge of coins minted by a dozen nations, many clipped and short in weight; with counterfeit pieces, and with a maddening variety of state and national paper bills, fast depreciating in value. It was clear that nothing less than a standard national currency would suffice. All exporters bemoaned the lack of protection for their enterprise in trying to market American goods abroad. The feeble Continental Congress had found it impossible to re-establish the old commercial relations with the British Empire and especially with the West Indies. Spain had defiantly closed the mouth of the Mississippi to American commerce, and there was general fear that the government would acquiesce supinely in this move so fatal to the interests of the West. Even at home no means existed by which traders could be sure of collecting money due them. A New Yorker who sued for payment in Pennsylvania was at the mercy of Pennsylvania courts and juries, which naturally stood by their own fellow citizens. The fast-growing body of American manufacturers were at the mercy of price-slashing competition from Europe.

But the worst evils arose from the deliberate impediments raised against commercial intercourse among the states. A number, anxious to prevent the dumping of European goods and to gain revenues, laid tariffs on all imports. Three main stages appeared in the process. During the war, Virginia alone had levied duties upon a broad range of goods, for she maintained a considerable commerce, exporting tobacco and importing various commodities, and could afford to do this. Then in the first three years after the peace all the states, except New Jersey, placed duties on imports, but for revenue only, not protection. Finally, by 1785 New England and most of the Middle States had developed promising home industries and suffered from European competition. They therefore set up protective tariffs.

An element of interstate retaliation quickly crept in. The Southern States and some small Northern States had few manufacturers and needed imported goods. Delaware and New Jersey created free ports for European wares, while Connecticut also passed laws to encourage the direct shipment of European goods. Restrictions were also laid on the movement of vessels, so that New Jersey men, for example, could not cross the Hudson to sell vegetables in New York without paying heavy fees. Naturally, feeling among the states grew savage. North Carolinians, denouncing Virginia and South Carolina, compared their state to a cask broached at both ends. Oliver Ellsworth said that his little Connecticut was like "Issachar of old, a strong ass crouching down between two burdens."

A wide variety of creditor groups besides the merchants and manufacturers deplored the want of any national authority which could place effective restraints upon the "leveling" tendencies of radical legislatures. They included money lenders and mortgage holders who were distressed by state "stay" laws and by the wholesale issues of rag money. They included American holders of British claims, for the radical groups in control of some legislatures and courts had made debts owed to Britons uncollectible. They included many officers and soldiers who had received land warrants in part payment for their Revolutionary services. They included the land speculators who had bought up great areas, either in soldiers' lands or in confiscated lands, at cheap rates, and were anxious to resell them. These landholders wanted a national government strong enough to protect the frontier against Indians, to ensure order in newly settled areas, and to protect titles.

Finally, an important body of holders of Federal and state securities viewed with anguish the chaotic financial conditions of the time and the popular aversion to taxes. In the last fourteen months under the Articles of Confederation, interest on the internal and external debt of the nation was approximately $14,000,000, while the national revenues were only $400,000! Washington summed up the situation when he wrote James Warren in 1785: "The wheels of government are clogged."

The Northwest Ordinance

ONE GREAT SUCCESS was scored by the government of the Confederation. Faced with the question of what to do with the unsettled lands west of the Alleghenies (for the states one by one ceded their claims here to the general government), it devised a wise plan which did much to make the

United States the country it is. It decided to open them to orderly and progressive settlement; to encourage the inhabitants to develop self-government by regular stages; and, finally, to erect new states, similar in powers to the original thirteen. This scheme was embodied in the Northwest Ordinance (1787), which covered the region north of the Ohio and provided for the ultimate creation of from three to five states. Slavery was never to enter. Three regular stages of government were arranged. Congress was first to create a "territory," appointing a governor and judges who were to make laws subject to a Congressional veto. Later, when the population reached five thousand, the people were to have a legislature of two chambers, electing the lower house themselves. Finally, when the territory attained sixty thousand people, it was to be made into a full-fledged state, equal in every respect to the original states. Thus the United States solved its "colonial problem." A pattern was established which the nation followed as it expanded to the Pacific and which finally gave it fifty states.

But in most other ways the Confederation was a disappointment. Washington wrote that the states were united only by a rope of sand, and another observer declared that "our discontents were fermenting into civil war." Congress now had too few members of ability, and its prestige was too low, to enable it to devise a better form of government. Thomas Paine had long before suggested that "a continental conference be held, to frame a continental charter." A few farsighted leaders who gathered to discuss commercial questions brought this about.

Calling the Convention

THE PRELIMINARIES of the Constitutional Convention are a familiar story. While thoughtful men were growing sick of national weakness and the bickerings of the states, a special commercial problem was demanding attention. Maryland held sovereignty over the entire Potomac River, where it divides her from Virginia, to the southern bank. Virginians feared that Maryland would interfere with their free navigation of that noble stream; and in 1785 representatives of Virginia and Maryland met at Mount Vernon with George

Washington to discuss the navigation of the Potomac and Chesapeake Bay. Madison, who was there, had been greatly depressed by the general disorder of commerce and believed that a larger conference should be held with the object of getting the states to vest its regulations in Congress. This body met at Annapolis in 1786; when delegates from only five states appeared, it seemed an utter failure.

Fortunately, one of the delegates was the audacious Alexander Hamilton, who snatched victory out of defeat. He induced the gathering to call upon the states to appoint commissioners who should meet in Philadelphia the following May to consider the situation of the United States and to "devise such further provisions as shall seem to them necessary to render the Constitution of the Federal government adequate to the exigencies of the Union." The Continental Congress was at first indignant over this bold step, but its fatuous protests were cut short by the news that Virginia had elected Washington a delegate. Congress then fell into line, fixing the second Monday in May, 1787, as the date of meeting. During the fall and winter all the states but contumacious little Rhode Island elected delegates.

The delegates were chosen by the state legislatures. Some legislatures were controlled by radical agrarian groups, and in all of them the defenders of state sovereignty were strong. Yet most of them instructed their delegates to create a strong national government, and sent to Philadelphia a body of men who were nationalist in their general outlook. It was after all the "nationalists"—they later called themselves Federalists —who had been so deeply concerned at the breakdown of the Confederation, and who had sent out the original call for the Convention. It was the nationalists, too, who took charge of the Convention. They had the good fortune to have Washington on their side, and Washington was the inevitable choice of all the delegates for President of the Convention; they had the good sense to come prepared with a draft for what was a new constitution, and to make this plan, rather than the old Articles, the one that was considered.

Early May found the delegates straggling into Philadelphia by ones and twos. Washington was characteristically punctual, arriving on the thirteenth; and clad in black velvet, wearing a ceremonial sword, he was immediately a cynosure of attention. Benjamin Franklin on the sixteenth gave a long-remembered dinner for the delegates then in town, broaching a cask of porter that a friend had sent him and doubtless opening plenty of old Madeira. His guests included James Madison of Virginia, diminutive in stature but a giant in his powers of political analysis. A graduate of Princeton, and a lawyer-planter who spent much time in his fine library, he was next to Franklin the most learned member of the Convention, and was to prove the most industrious and constructive-minded of the delegates. Another guest was the sixty-five-year-old George Wythe, who had taught Jefferson, Madison, John Marshall, and other luminaries of the Virginia bar much of their law. Still another was the governor of Virginia, Edmund Randolph, the owner of some seven thousand acres with two hundred slaves.

Among the Pennsylvanians were Robert Morris, the portly banker who had raised the money which kept Washington's armies in the field during the gloomiest days of the Revolution. It was at Morris' handsome house that Washington stayed during the sessions. Gouverneur Morris was there, son of a wealthy New York family, and now a leading lawyer and speculator of Philadelphia. Jared Ingersoll, who had studied in the Middle Temple and risen to be one of the best lawyers in Pennsylvania, was present, and so was James Wilson, a brusque, hardheaded man of Scottish birth and education, the best-read jurist in America. It would have been difficult to assemble at a dinner table anywhere in the world in 1787 more talent and character; certainly no Old World group could have boasted more impressive figures than the grave, dignified Washington and the delightfully wise and benevolent Franklin, who, as a contemporary wrote, seemed "to diffuse an unrestrained freedom and happiness."

It is worth noting that some of those who had been most active in bringing on and fighting the Revolution were not delegates to the Convention. Jefferson was in France; Patrick Henry had refused election; John Adams was minister to England; and those three firebrands, Tom Paine, Sam Adams, and Christopher Gadsden, had not been chosen. The radicals, in short, were not adequately represented. Some historians have laid much emphasis on the fact that the great body of delegates were propertied men and holders of Continental or state securities. But it must be remembered that the great body of Americans belonged to the propertied middle elements. There were, as Benjamin Franklin pointed out, few very rich and very few poor in eighteenth-century America. And it should be added that the Federal Convention was probably the most nearly representative political assemblage to be found anywhere in the Western world at that time.

The Convention at Work

THE CONVENTION was that rare creation, a truly deliberative body. In view of the fact that each state had been allowed to send as many delegates as it liked—for every state voted as a unit—this was remarkable. But for reasons of economy, most states sent small delegations. Only fifty-five men in all attended; some came but for a short time, so that at the close only thirty-nine were present; and a few, including of course Washington, were habitually silent in debate. About half were college graduates, and a heavy majority were lawyers, so that they expressed themselves concisely and well. No verbatim report of debates was kept, and the versions given in the journals of Madison and others doubtless eliminate much verbosity; but no one can read these summaries without being impressed by the logical cogency of most of the utterances. They were aided in their discussions by the rule of secrecy which the Convention strictly kept. Publicity would have magnified the dissensions; it would have tempted members to make speeches for the galleries or press; and it would have laid them open to pressure from their constituents. The sober citizens of Philadelphia deserved praise for their refusal to pry into the Convention's work. Once at his dinner table Franklin mentioned to friends the old fable of the two-headed snake which starved to death because the heads could not agree on which side of a tree to pass; he said he could give an illustration from a recent occurrence in the Convention; but his friends reminded him of the rule of secrecy and stopped him.

At the outset the delegates tacitly agreed that they would not revise the Articles of Confederation, but would write a wholly new constitution. In this they exceeded the authority granted them by the resolution of the Continental Congress, but not the authority which they derived from the state legislatures, for most of these had authorized them to make a constitution "adequate to the exigencies of Union." And as clearly no mere tinkering with the old Articles would achieve this end, the delegates, with—as Madison later wrote —"a manly confidence in their country," went boldly ahead with a new form of government.

In describing the work of the Convention, it is important to lay emphasis upon a few great general considerations. The delegates knew that a complex mechanism had to be set up, that no simple government would suffice. To begin with, they had to reconcile, with scrupulous nicety, two different powers: the power of local control which was already being exercised by the thirteen semi-independent states and the power of the newly created central government. It was a task for which only the history of the British Empire afforded precedent. In the empire as it existed before 1763 there was, to all intents and purposes, a federal system— a division of governing powers between central and local authorities. But the other federations created up to that time had without exception been small in area; they had almost without exception been exceedingly loose; and they had seldom been successful for any long period. James Madison and a few others had made an intensive study of government in general, and of the Greek, Helvetic, and Dutch Confederations in particular, while most of the delegates were well read in political thought. The principle adopted was that the functions and powers of the national government should be carefully defined, while all other functions and powers should be understood as belonging to the states. The powers of the national sovereignty, being new, general, and inclusive powers, simply *had* to be stated.

The Final Handiwork

HAND IN HAND with this process of statement went the construction of the national machinery. Here also a general principle underlay the work. It was understood that three distinct branches of government should be set up, each equal and co-ordinate with the others: the legislative, executive, and judicial powers, so adjusted and interlocked as to permit of their harmonious operation, but at the same time so well balanced that no one interest could ever gain control. This eighteenth-century idea of the balancing of powers was a Newtonian conception of politics. The principle was naturally derived from colonial experience and strengthened by the writings of Locke and Montesquieu, with which most of the delegates were familiar. The American definition of a tyrannical government was one in which a single element assumed a dominant role. It was natural also to assume that the legislative branch, like the colonial legislatures and British Parliament, should consist of two houses. Not everyone believed in a single executive; but the advocates of a plural executive were silenced by an appeal to the general example of the colonies and states.

The decision to set up a legislature of two branches made it much easier to adjust the fundamental, though unrealistic, quarrel in the Convention over the powers of the small states and the large states. The small states asserted that, as under the Confederation, they were entitled to precise equality with their greater sisters; that little Connecticut should never be trampled over by great New York, or little Maryland by great Virginia. The large states asserted that power should be proportioned to size, population, and wealth.

By the compromise finally adopted, the small states were given equal representation with the large in the Senate, but in the House of Representatives the seats were to be based upon population. When it came to the executive, the greatest difficulty lay in fixing upon a mode of election. Should the President be chosen by Congress? That would go far toward making him dependent on the legislative branch, and so upsetting the balance of power. Should he be chosen by popular vote? The people of the United States were scattered over an immense and expanding area, and communications were poor. It would, therefore, be difficult for them to concentrate upon one or a few candidates; a great number of choices would be made, and no one man would have any approach to a majority of votes. It was finally decided, therefore, to set up an electoral college, each state having as many electors as it had Senators and Representatives. This system by no means operated as its authors had intended, for they failed to foresee the development of political parties which immediately took place. As for the third branch, the

Federal judiciary, the judges were to be appointed by the President, by and with the advice and consent of the Senate, for life terms during good behavior.

The ingenuity as well as the wisdom of the authors of the Constitution challenges our admiration. They set up the most complex government yet devised by man, and also the most nicely poised and guarded. Each of the three branches was independent and co-ordinate, and yet each was checked by the others. Congressional enactments did not become law until approved by the President; the President in turn had to submit many of his appointments and all of his treaties to the Senate and might be impeached and removed by Congress. The judiciary was to hear all cases arising under the laws and the Constitution and, therefore, had a right to interpret both the fundamental law and the statute law. But the judiciary were appointed by the President and confirmed by the Senate, while they, too, might be impeached by Congress. Since the Senators were elected by the state legislatures for six-year terms, since the President was chosen by an electoral college, and since the judges were appointed, no part of the government was exposed to direct public pressure except the lower house of Congress. Moreover, officers of government were chosen for such a wide variety of terms, ranging from life to two years, that a complete change of personnel could not be effected except by a revolution.

Some students, treating the Convention as an economic rather than political body, have declared that its chief conclusions favored the property-owning, trading, and creditor "class." But once more we must remember that America in 1787 was a land where nearly all—farmers, planters, shopkeepers, professional men—were well off and class lines few and faint. And security and stability profited everybody, for everybody was interested in stable money, a flourishing trade, the protection of western lands, the firm administration of justice, and the efficient administration of the everyday affairs of government. And as for the Constitution being a "class" document, it is relevant to observe that under its provisions there were no property or religious qualifications for voting or for any Federal office.

The decisions by which the Convention made certain that the Federal government would be strong enough to maintain order and protect property might, under other circumstances, have been dangerously explosive. But most of them were taken after brief and calm debate. The Federal government was freely and fully given the power to lay taxes, thus ensuring it the means to pay the debt so long overdue, to restore its credit, and to raise money for the general welfare. It could borrow money, and lay uniform duties, imposts, and excises, and pass uniform bankruptcy laws. It was given authority to coin money, fix weights and measures, grant patents and copyrights, and establish post offices and post roads. It was empowered to raise and maintain an army and navy. It could regulate interstate commerce. It was given the whole management of Indian relations, of international relations, and of war. If "domestic violence" broke out in any state, and the legislature or governor asked for help, it might intervene to restore order. It could pass laws for naturalizing foreigners. Controlling the public lands, it could admit new states on a basis of equality with the old. It was to have its own capital in a district not more than ten miles square. In short, the national government was strong from the beginning—and was soon to be made still stronger by the interpretations which the Supreme Court gave the Constitution. This strength was a natural reaction from the weakness of the Confederation.

Yet the states also remained strong. They retained all the powers of local government and they regulated most of the daily concerns of the people. Schools, local courts, policing, the chartering of towns and cities, the incorporation of banks and stock companies, the care of bridges, roads, and canals—these and many other matters were in state hands. The states were to decide who should vote, and how. They were mainly responsible for the protection of civil liberties. For a long time many people felt themselves Georgians, or Pennsylvanians, or Virginians before they felt themselves Americans.

Finally, the Convention faced the most important problem of all: how should the powers given to the new national government be enforced? The old Confederation had possessed large, though by no means adequate, powers, on paper. But in practice its powers had come close to zero, for the states paid no attention to them. What was to save the new government from meeting precisely the same obstacles and refusals? At the outset most delegates furnished but one answer—the use of force. Virginia proposed that Congress should be given power to "call forth the force of the Union against any member . . . failing to fulfill its duty under the articles thereof." This was wrong in theory, for force is an instrument of international law. It would have been fatal in practice, for it would have meant civil war. Application of force would quickly have broken up the Union amid bloodshed and destruction.

What, then, was to be done? As the discussion went on, a new and perfect expedient was evolved. The government, it was decided, should not act upon the states at all. Instead, it should act directly upon the people within the states. It was to legislate for and upon all the residents of the country, ignoring the state governments. As Madison wrote Jefferson: "A voluntary observance of the Federal law by all the members could never be hoped for. A compulsive one could evidently never be reduced to practice, and if it could, involved equal calamities to the innocent and the guilty, and in general, a scene resembling much more a civil war than the administration of a regular government. Hence was embraced the alternative of a government which, instead of operating on the States, should operate without their intervention on the individuals composing them. . . ." The Convention adopted as the kingpin of the Constitution the following brief article:

This Constitution, and the Laws of the United States which shall be made in Pursuance thereof; and all Treaties made, or which shall be made, under the Authority of the United States, shall be the supreme Law of the Land; and the Judges in every State shall be bound thereby, any Thing in the Constitution or Laws of any State to the Contrary notwithstanding.

Under this provision, the laws of the United States became enforceable in its own national courts, through its own judges and marshals. They were also enforceable in the state courts, through the state judges and state law officers. This provision breathed a vitality into the Constitution which it might never otherwise have gained, and offers perhaps the best single illustration of that combination of common sense and inspiration, of practical ingenuity and farsighted vision, which marked the instrument as a whole.

On Monday, September 17, after one of the best summer's work yet done by any deliberative assemblage in the world, the Convention held its last meeting.

Only three of the delegates present refused to sign, and most of the members were delighted. The aged Franklin declared that while he did not approve all parts of the Constitution, he was astonished to find it so nearly perfect. He begged any men who did not like some of its features, to doubt their own infallibility a little and accept the document. Dashing young Alexander Hamilton made a somewhat similar plea. He had wished a far more centralized and more aristocratic form of government, but, he asked, how could a true patriot hesitate between anarchy and convulsion on one side, order and progress on the other? Delegates representing twelve states came forward to sign. Many seemed oppressed by the solemnity of the moment, and Washington sat in grave meditation. But Franklin relieved the tension by a characteristic sally. Pointing to the half sun painted in brilliant gold on the back of Washington's chair, he remarked that artists had always found it difficult to distinguish between a rising and a setting sun. "I have often and often, in the course of the session, and the vicissitudes of my hopes and fears as to its issue, looked at that behind the President, without being able to tell whether it was rising or setting; but now, at length, I have the happiness to know that it is a rising, and not a setting, sun."

Ratification

WOULD THE STATES ratify the new Constitution? To many plain folk it seemed full of dangers, for would not the strong central government that it set up tyrannize over them, oppress them with heavy taxes, and drag them into foreign wars? The Convention had decided that it should go into effect as soon as approved by nine of thirteen states. Before 1787 ended, Delaware, Pennsylvania, and New Jersey had ratified, but would six others follow? Great anxiety was felt by the authors of the new system.

The struggle over ratification brought into existence two parties, the Federalists and Antifederalists; those who favored a strong government and those who wanted a mere league of states. The contest raged in the press, the legislatures, and the state conventions. Impassioned arguments were poured forth on both sides. The ablest were the *Federalist Papers*, written in behalf of the new Constitution by Alexander Hamilton, James Madison, and John Jay, a series that has become a classic work on politics. The three states in which the battle proved sternest were Massachusetts, New York, and Virginia. In Massachusetts the strong support of the Boston shipwrights, metalworkers, and other mechanics, reinforcing the lawyers, merchants, and a good part of the farmers, carried the Constitution to victory. In New York the eloquence of Alexander Hamilton finally converted the principal opposing debater, broke down the enemy forces, and obtained ratification by a handsome majority. In Virginia the influence of George Washington (which was powerful everywhere), and the strong arguments of Madison, won the day. By the time that Virginia finally acted, nine other states had given their approval, so that the government was certain to go into effect; but the full support of Washington's state was felt indispensable and was received with tumultuous rejoicings.

Philadelphia mustered a great procession on July 4, 1788, to celebrate the acceptance of the new form of government. One symbolic float showed how the battered scow *Confederacy* (representing the weak government under the Articles of Confederation), with Imbecility for captain, had foundered; another showed the stanch ship *Constitution* ready to take the high seas. And ready she was. Arrangements were made for the choice of President and Congress and for putting the new government into force in the spring of 1789. One name was on every man's lips for the new chief of state, and Washington was unanimously chosen President.

Thus it was that after the gloom of recent years the country witnessed the bright sunrise which Franklin had hailed in Independence Hall. One of the delightful episodes of early American history, at once idyllic and moving, was the journey which Washington made from his beautiful estate on the Potomac to take up the reins of government in New York. He set out in mid-April, as full spring was breaking over the Virginia hills. He moved northward over roads that at some points closely paralleled the route he had taken in 1781 to capture Cornwallis. In every hamlet, town, and city the people poured forth to give him lusty cheers. At Philadelphia cavalry paraded, and he rode under triumphal arches of evergreen and laurel. He reached Trenton on a sunny afternoon, where twelve years earlier he had crossed the ice-filled Delaware in darkness and storm to strike one of his most famous military blows. Here a party of white-clad maidens strewed flowers before him and sang an ode. On the shores of New York Bay he was escorted aboard a handsome barge manned by thirteen men in white uniforms, and as he approached the city thirteen guns boomed; while he landed to find the city filled with joyful crowds, which included many Revolutionary veterans. On April 30, in the presence of an immense multitude, he stood on the balcony of Federal Hall in Wall Street to take the oath of office. The chancellor of New York administered it and then, turning to the crowd, exclaimed: "Long live George Washington, President of the United States!" From the host below rose a thunderous shout.

America in 1789

IT WAS A LUSTY REPUBLIC that was now ready to begin its career. A census taken the year after Washington's inauguration showed that it had nearly four million people, of whom about three and a half million were whites. This population was almost wholly rural. Only five cities worthy of the name existed: Philadelphia with 42,000 people, New York with 33,000, Boston with 18,000, Charleston with 16,000, and Baltimore with 13,000. The great mass of the population lived on farms and plantations or in small villages. Communications were poor and slow, for the roads were wretched, the stagecoaches uncomfortable, the sailing vessels uncertain. But turnpike companies were beginning to be formed (a model road was soon made from Philadelphia to Lancaster), and canals were soon dug. Most people lived comparatively isolated lives, with poor schools, few books, and rare newspapers. The impression which America made upon European travelers was one of rudeness, discomfort, rough manners, and thin culture, along with independence, material well-being, and boundless self-confidence.

Yet culturally as well as materially its condition was improving.

For the country was growing sturdily. Immigration from the Old World came in such volume that Americans sometimes thought that half of western Europe was flowing into the land. Good farms were to be had for small sums; labor was in strong demand and well paid. The government looked with favor on this immigration, and Washington particularly liked the idea of bringing expert farmers over from Britain to teach Americans better agricultural methods. The rich stretches of the Mohawk and Genesee valleys in upper New York, of the Susquehanna in upper Pennsylvania, and the Shenandoah in Virginia soon became great wheat-growing areas. New Englanders and Pennsylvanians were moving into Ohio, Virginians and Carolinians into Kentucky and Tennessee.

Manufactures, too, were growing and were encouraged by state bounties. Massachusetts and Rhode Island were laying the foundation of important textile industries, surreptitiously obtaining their models of jennies and Arkwright machinery from England. Connecticut was beginning to turn out tinware and clocks; the Middle States paper, glass, and iron. But America as yet had no mill towns with a population exclusively devoted to factory work. Indeed, much of the manufacturing was still done in households. Farmers in the long winter evenings could make coarse cloth, leather goods, pottery, simple iron implements, maple sugar, and wooden contrivances. When mills and factories did spring up, the owner often labored alongside his hands.

Shipping was beginning to flourish, and the United States was taking second place on the ocean only to England. Vessels were built in great numbers for the coastal trade, for the codfisheries, for whaling, and for carrying breadstuffs, tobacco, lumber, and other goods to Europe. The Revolution had scarcely ended when the ship *Empress* made a voyage to Canton and brought back news of the possibilities of the China trade, which stirred New Englanders. A new commerce sprang up. It became so brisk that in 1787 five ships carried the Stars and Stripes to China. The Orientals were eager to obtain furs; and some Boston merchants determined to send ships to the Northwest coast, buy pelts from the Indians, carry them to China, and bring home teas and silks.

The new scheme proved successful. What was more, it led the Yankee captain Robert Gray, master of the ship *Columbia*, to enter the great river on the upper Pacific Coast which he named after his vessel, and so lay a basis for the United States' claim to Oregon.

The main impulse of American energy was westward—ever westward. From the oak clearings of Ohio to the pine glades of Georgia the backwoodsman's ax rang out as the drumbeat of advancing hosts. Up the long slopes of the Alleghenies climbed the white-topped Conestoga wagons of the emigrant trains; through the Cumberland Gap into Kentucky wound the buckskin-clad hunters and the pioneers with carts of furniture, seeds, simple farm implements, and domestic animals. In many a rough clearing, where the hickory and walnut trees, tokens of a rich soil, had been killed by girdling, the frontier farmer and his neighbors lifted a log cabin, its timbers chinked with clay, its roof covered with thin oak staves. Year by year the Ohio and Mississippi saw more American rafts and flatboats floating downward to New Orleans with grain, salt meat, and potash. Year by year the western towns, such as Cincinnati on the Ohio, Nashville in the heart of Tennessee, and Lexington in Kentucky, grew more important. Indian warfare, malaria, wild beasts, the roving highwaymen of the remote borders, and other perils had to be faced; hardship, poverty, and disease took a heavy toll. But still ten thousand rivulets of settlement spilled into the wilderness, still the frontier line advanced, still Bishop Berkeley's statement of colonial days held good: "Westward the course of empire takes its way."

CHAPTER 6

The Republic Finds Itself

Organizing the Government under Washington

THE YEAR 1789 found New York blossoming temporarily into a national capital. Its best houses were renovated with all possible elegance; its streets that summer were crowded with Congressmen, expectant officeholders, lobbyists, and spectators. President Washington at first occupied a residence just out of town on Franklin Square and then took the imposing McComb mansion in lower Broadway, with a beautiful reception room. Vice-President John Adams occupied a large house on Richmond Hill. Congress sat in Federal Hall at Wall and Broad Streets—for the nation's first political capital was on the site of its subsequent financial capital. Levees were held and balls arranged. The President gave dinner parties of chilly dignity and went frequently with friends to the theater in John Street. When he visited Congress it was in state, riding in a heavy cream-colored coach, drawn by six spirited white horses of Virginia breed, with postilions and outriders. Citizens were not admitted to the Congressional debates, but knots gathered in the streets outside to discuss the grave issues of the day.

The wise leadership of Washington was indispensable to the new government. Politically, he was not a man of imagination or brilliant initiative; he was a stiff writer and a poor public speaker; he knew little about principles of administration. But he commanded not merely obedience but a sort of awe, and he typified the idea of union as nobody else could. Responsible men of every party and section trusted his fairness, breadth of view, and sagacity. Always dignified, his "republican court" was marked by grave formality. At receptions he would enter dressed in black velvet and satin, with diamond knee buckles, his powdered hair tied in a bag, his military hat under his arm, and a dress sword in a green scabbard at his side. In his relations with Congress and administrative officers he held aloof from party or faction, essaying to represent the national idea alone—though his sympathies were with the Federalists. Vigilant and laborious as ever, he worked by fixed schedules for long hours. He toiled successfully to give the government elevation and principle and to impress upon the country the admonition which he put into his "Farewell Address" in 1796: "Be united—be Americans."

In August, 1790, Congress adjourned to meet again in Philadelphia that December—for Philadelphia, clean, quiet, and sociable as ever, was to be the capital for ten years. Meanwhile, much was done to set national affairs in order.

The organization of the government was no small task. Congress in rapid succession created a Department of State, a Department of War, and a Department of the Treasury. Washington appointed to the first post Thomas Jefferson, just returned from his service as minister to France; to the second post Henry Knox of Massachusetts, a mediocre but popular general; to the third Alexander Hamilton, known for his special knowledge of finance. Congress also established the office of Attorney General, who was at first not a departmental head but merely legal adviser to the government; and Washington filled it with Edmund Randolph, a Virginian. Hamilton and Knox were understood to be of Federalist leanings, Jefferson and Randolph of Antifederalist views. Congress simultaneously moved to create a Federal judiciary and to create the mechanism whereby it would mesh with the state judiciaries. The Constitution itself had provided for a Supreme Court, but left it to the discretion of Congress to create inferior courts. The Judiciary Act of 1789—an act which is almost a supplement to the Constitution itself—set up not only a Supreme Court but also three circuit courts and thirteen district courts; all the judges, like the heads of Federal departments, were to be appointed by the President and confirmed by the Senate. The act provided in detail for appeals from state courts to the Federal courts on all matters concerning the interpretation of the Constitution or the rights of citizens under the Constitution. Thus by the end of 1790 the first three national departments and the national courts were hard at work.

The Bill of Rights

THIS FIRST CONGRESS, which all in all achieved more than any other Congress in American history, had to its credit not only the successful organization of the government, of law, administration, and defense, but also the enactment of the Bill of Rights.

The original Constitution had not contained a specific bill of rights, though a number of rights were guaranteed in the body of the document. This failure to incorporate a bill of rights was not an indication of hostility or indifference to the rights of man by the Framers, but rather of their conviction that particular guarantees of rights were unnecessary. The Constitution, after all, specifically enumerated the powers of Congress, and whatever was not granted was withheld. As no power over the rights of man were granted, it followed therefore that the government had no such powers. This was a sound logical argument, but it did not satisfy the deep emotional demand for solemn assurances that the new government would not be permitted to exercise tyranny. This was Jefferson's view; from Paris he wrote to his friend James Madison that "a bill of rights is what the people are entitled to against every government on earth, general or particular, and what no just government should refuse, or rest on inference."

A number of states had ratified the Constitution with the understanding that it would be promptly amended by the addition of a bill of rights. Many members of Congress were inclined to take this understanding lightly, but Madison—prodded by Jefferson—felt that it constituted a solemn obligation. Shortly after Congress convened he introduced a series of amendments incorporating most of the suggestions that had come up from the states. Twelve of these eventually passed the Congress, and ten were ratified, and came, in time, to be known as the Bill of Rights.

The Federal Bill of Rights was modeled on the more elab-

orate bills of rights of Virginia, Massachusetts, and some of
the other states. Like these, it differed fundamentally from
the historic English bills of rights of 1628 and 1689. For
whereas the English bills of rights addressed themselves almost exclusively to matters of procedural justice, the American not only included procedural guarantees—trial by jury,
no excessive bail, no cruel or unusual punishments, no dep-
rivation of life, liberty, or property without due process of
law, and so forth—but also extended to such things as freedom of religion, speech, the press, and assembly. As limitations on government they were incomparably broader and
more effective than anything to be found elsewhere in the
world at that time.

Though at first the significance of the Federal Bill of
Rights was chiefly symbolic, in time it came to have practical effectiveness as well, and after 1868 its guarantees were
incorporated in the Fourteenth Amendment and thus applied directly to the states.

Alexander Hamilton

As REVOLUTIONARY AMERICA had produced two commanding figures who gained world-wide renown, Washington and
Franklin, so the youthful republic raised into fame two brilliantly able men whose reputations spread beyond the seas
—Alexander Hamilton and Thomas Jefferson. But it was not
the striking personal gifts of these two men, great though
their talents were, which best entitle them to remembrance.
It was the fact that they represented two powerful and indispensable, though to some extent hostile, tendencies in American life: Hamilton the tendency toward closer union and
a stronger national government, Jefferson the tendency toward a broader, freer democracy. The most significant facts
in American history between 1790 and 1830, next to the irresistible westward march, are the triumphs scored by
nationalism and democracy.

Hamilton had been born in Nevis, a little sugar-growing
island of the Lesser Antilles, to a Scottish father and a Huguenot mother. He grew up a man of the Scottish type por-
trayed by Stevenson in Alan Breck of *Kidnapped*—ambitious,
generous, devoted, proud, quick to take offense and to for-

give, of flashing mind and inexhaustible energy. His achievements all arose from his combination of brilliancy, self-confident ambition, and industry. It is noteworthy how precociously he displayed these traits. His father meeting business misfortunes, he had no money to go to college. But a terrible hurricane swept the Antilles, and he wrote a description of it which attracted so much attention that his aunts sent him to the American mainland. He entered King's College in New York, a happy choice, for it threw him into easy contact with the radicals of the town who were leading the revolt against royal authority. By publishing two long pamphlets, one just before he was twenty, the other just afterward, he measured himself effectively against the leading Tory divine of the province. When at twenty-two he became captain of an artillery company, he showed his omnivorous mind by taking his books to camp and studying far into the night.

Besides brilliancy and ambition, Hamilton had other qualities which served him well. He possessed great personal attractiveness. With reddish-brown hair, bright brown eyes, fine forehead, and firm mouth and chin, he was exceptionally handsome, his face animated and pleasant when he talked, severe and thoughtful when he was at work. He liked a lively dinner party and shone in any circle which offered good wine, intellectual companions, and witty talk. As shrewd as he was quick, he had the great quality of *address*—of doing the right thing at the right time. His address made him leader of the New York patriots, it brought him to Washington's notice and made him the general's principal aide, it enabled him to lead a dramatic assault at the siege of Yorktown, it lifted him to the leadership of the New York bar, it rendered him the principal figure in Washington's administration, and it gave him command of a great party. He had remarkable talents as an executive and organizer. He wrote and spoke with dash and vigor. Yet he also showed striking defects. He was excitable, quick-tempered, and when thwarted decidedly petulant. At the battle of Monmouth, when Washington rebuked General Charles Lee for retreating, he leaped from his horse, drew his sword, and shouted, "We are betrayed!" Washington silenced him by the quiet command: "Mr. Hamilton, mount your horse." He quarreled with Washington near the end of the war, wrote his father-in-law a pompous, conceited letter about the incident, and rejected the advances that Washington made to heal the breach. His hot impetuosity, his readiness to embark hastily upon a quarrel, and his petulant arrogance of spirit brought him into unnecessarily harsh conflicts—with Jefferson, disrupting the Washington administration, with John Adams, disrupting the Federalist party, and with Aaron Burr, ending in his own death in a duel.

The keynote of Hamilton's public career was his love of efficiency, order, and organization, a dominant impulse which explains his unforgettable service to the young nation. From 1775 to 1789 he saw spread all about him the evidence of inefficiency and weakness. He thoroughly detested the resulting disorder. As Washington's secretary he was the agent through whom the commander conducted much of his business. We need only glance at Washington's letters for the Revolutionary period to see in what a continual fret the general was kept by the feebleness of the government. He fretted because the states would not supply him with enough troops, because they sent insufficient munitions, clothing and money, because while one part of the country acted energetically, others hung back. He fretted over the lack of discipline in the army, for the troops straggled, looted, and on the slightest excuse often packed up and went home. All this anxiety Hamilton shared. And later, in the dark Confederation years, Hamilton was an active attorney close to the mercantile groups in New York and intimately acquainted with their worries over the obstacles to trade and the insecurity of property. His reading gave him a European rather than an American conception of the proper character of the state, and throughout his life he thought the English the most admirable form of government. It is easy to see why he desired efficiency and vigor in the government—a strong Federal authority.

Thomas Jefferson

WHEN WE TURN to Jefferson, we turn from a man of action to a man of thought. As Hamilton's talents were executive, Jefferson's were meditative and philosophical. Hamilton delighted in setting up strong machinery and watching

its efficient operation; Jefferson delighted in people and in
seeing them contented whether efficient or not. His inefficiency as governor of Virginia has been exaggerated, but he
nevertheless left the office in discredit, and he was not a
particularly efficient Secretary of State. But as a political
thinker and writer, in his own generation he was without a
peer, after the death of Burke, anywhere in the world. When
he suggested the inscription on his gravestone, he proposed
not a record of his offices and acts but of his three major
contributions to thought. The stone reads:

> HERE WAS BURIED THOMAS JEFFERSON
> AUTHOR OF THE DECLARATION OF AMERICAN INDEPENDENCE
> OF THE STATUTE OF VIRGINIA FOR RELIGIOUS FREEDOM
> AND FATHER OF THE UNIVERSITY OF VIRGINIA

Jefferson had been reared in the loose, genial, and carelessly intellectual atmosphere of Virginia. As a youth he
engaged in "dancing, junketing, and high jinks"; he was
fond of riding, observing wild life, and playing the violin;
he read novels—Fielding, Smollett, and Sterne—and was
enthusiastic over Ossian. His later life, full of wide contacts with nature, books, and men, merely stimulated his
intellectual versatility. He acquired a knowledge of half a
dozen languages, of mathematics, surveying, and mechanics,
of music and architecture, and of law and government. He
eagerly gathered a large library and a remarkable collection
of prints. He wrote about plants and animals, about history, politics, and education—and always with originality
and insight. He designed his famous house at Monticello
and the beautiful halls of the University of Virginia. A
lover of talk, deep, discursive, and many-sided, he was one
of the best conversationalists of his time. The sage of Monticello, often putting fifty people up over night, showed as
much courtesy and warmth to a learned Negro as to a European nobleman. Throughout his life he liked freedom,
leisure, and breadth of contacts.

Politically Jefferson's instincts were opposed to Hamilton's, and his training confirmed them. He was identified
for many years with Virginia, first as legislative leader and
then governor. He saw plainly how difficult it was for the
states to meet all the demands upon them. When he went

abroad as minister to France, where he was pressed for repayment of the loans to America, he did realize that a strong national government could be of value in foreign relations, but he did not want it to be too strong in many other respects, frankly declaring: "I am not a friend to a very energetic government." He even said that the weak Articles of Confederation were "a wonderfully perfect instrument." He feared that a strong government would fetter men. He fought for freedom from the British Crown, freedom from Church control, freedom from a landed aristocracy, freedom from great inequalities of wealth. He was an egalitarian democrat. He disliked cities, great manufacturing interests, and large banking and trading organizations—they promoted inequality; and though in his later years he admitted that industrialism was necessary to give the country an independent economy, he believed that America would be happiest if it remained chiefly a rural nation.

Yet it is a mistake to think of Jefferson in terms of "states' rights" or of particularism. He was not only author of the Declaration of Independence and one of the Founding Fathers; he was, all his life, an ardent nationalist. Nowhere was that nationalism more ostentatious than in his attitude toward the West, and it was not wholly fortuitous that while Hamilton stayed in the busy metropolis of New York and yearned to reproduce in America a society and economy modeled on that of England, Jefferson built his beautiful Monticello on a hillside looking westward over the Valley of Virginia. It was Jefferson who had drafted the Ordinances of 1784 and 1785, which provided the basis for the Northwest Ordinance of 1787; it was Jefferson who sent Lewis and Clark out to the Pacific coast; it was Jefferson who bought Louisiana, thereby doubling the size of the new nation. Philosophically and culturally, too, Jefferson was ardently American. He was convinced that the New World was incomparably superior to the Old, and was determined to keep it that way, even at the cost of separation from the Old. For all his own cosmopolitanism, he wanted an America that was culturally as well as politically independent—with its own laws, its own literature, its own schools, its own social institutions. Familiar with the institutions of the Old World—the monarchy, the state, the church, the military, the class system—he wanted none of these for America:

here was to be tried the great experiment in equality and self-government. Convinced that his nation was "advancing rapidly to destinies beyond the reach of mortal eye," he devoted a long life to educating it for that destiny.

Hamilton's great aim was to give the country a more efficient organization. Jefferson's great aim was to give individual men a wider liberty. The United States needed both influences. It required a stronger national government and it required also the unfettering of the common man. The nation would have suffered had it possessed Hamilton alone, or Jefferson alone. It was a piece of great good fortune that it had both men and could in time fuse and to a great extent reconcile their special creeds.

Hamilton's Financial Measures

BECOMING Washington's Secretary of the Treasury, Hamilton carried through a set of measures that made him the greatest finance minister in American history. His program was not only impressive in extent but creative in character. Many men wished to repudiate the national debt of about $56,000,000, or to pay only part of it; against their opposition Hamilton put into effect a plan for reorganizing and paying off all of it. He carried out a plan by which the Federal government took over the unpaid debts of the states, incurred in aid of the Revolution, some $18,000,000 more. He set up a Bank of the United States modeled largely on the Bank of England. He established a national mint. Writing a famous *Report on Manufactures*, he argued in favor of laying moderate tariff duties in order to develop national industries; and Congress did pass a tariff law which, though it imposed only low duties, gave definite aid to American manufacturers. Finally, Hamilton had a law enacted levying an excise tax to be collected upon all distilled liquors.

These measures had an instant effect, which reached in three directions. They placed the credit of the national government on a foundation strong as bedrock and gave it all the revenues it needed. They encouraged industry and commerce. And most important of all, they attached powerful groups of men in every state to the national government. The refunding of the national debt, and the assumption of the state debts, made a host of men who held continental and state paper look to the new government for their money. Manufacturers who depended on the new tariff law for their prosperity looked in the same direction. The national bank secured the support of influential groups of moneyed men, for it made all financial transactions easier and safer. The excise tax not only furnished revenue, but, being collected at every local still, brought home to plain citizens the authority of the Federal government. Altogether Hamilton's policies created a solid phalanx of propertied men who stood fast behind the national government, ready to resist any attempt to weaken it; and it made that government much more impressive than before.

The Northwestern Indians

ONE of the most vexatious problems of Washington's presidency was the pacification of the warlike tribes northwest of the Ohio River. The years following the Revolution witnessed a vigorous renewal of the westward march of pioneers eager for cheap land. Speculators organized a number of companies which obtained large tracts from Congress: General Rufus Putnam's Ohio Company getting one and a half million acres on which Putnam laid out the town of Marietta in what is now southern Ohio, a Scioto Company getting five million acres, and Judge J. C. Symmes of New Jersey taking a million acres on which, in time, the city of Cincinnati rose. The settlers who crowded in to fell trees and erect cabins threatened the best hunting grounds of the Indians. It was clear to the redskins that they must check the influx or lose everything. Word went from village to village: "White man shall not plant corn north of the Ohio."

As white settlers murdered Indians, and Indians slew white men, women, and children, Washington decided to send an expedition of 1500 Pennsylvania and Kentucky militiamen to chastise the tribe of Miamis. Unfortunately, the green leader in charge, Josiah Harmar, led his equally green men into a hornets' nest, was defeated in what is now northern Indiana, and had to retreat with a loss of about 200 lives. Thereupon Washington, in the autumn of 1791, ordered an elderly general of poor health and worse judgment, Arthur St. Clair, to lead a much larger army, including two regiments of regulars, into the Indian country. The result was the worst defeat that any such body had received since Braddock's debacle. In an ambush about a hundred miles north of Cincinnati, in a deep forest, St. Clair's force was cut to pieces, about 700 being killed and many wounded. When Washington heard the news he betrayed the deepest anguish and chagrin. The only possible course was to try again with an abler leader and a more formidable array. This time "Mad Anthony" Wayne, who had gained renown on half a dozen Revolutionary battlefields by his dash and skill, took command; he trained a larger army in the best Indian-fighting methods; and after receiving a reinforcement of 1400 hardy Kentucky militiamen, he led forth much the strongest and grimmest body of fighters ever seen west of the Alleghenies. At Fallen Timbers on the Maumee River, not far from present-day Fort Wayne, he defeated the Indians so decisively that all warfare ceased (August 20, 1794). Wayne became a national hero.

Northwestern settlement at once took on greater volume than ever. Migrants took up farms all along the Ohio, established towns, and flowed into Connecticut's "Western Reserve" on Lake Erie, where they founded Cleveland.

Interpretation of the Constitution: "Implied Powers"

HAMILTON'S MEASURES required an important interpretation of the Constitution. When he brought forward his scheme for a national bank, Jefferson—speaking for all believers in state rights as against national authority, and for those who feared great corporations and a money power —objected. He sent Washington a strong argument. The Constitution, he declared, expressly enumerates all the powers belonging to the Federal government and reserves all other powers to the states; and it nowhere says that the Federal government may set up a bank. This seemed good logic. Washington was on the point of vetoing the bill. But Hamilton submitted a more convincing argument. He pointed out that all the powers of the national government could not be set down in explicit words, for that would mean intolerable detail. A vast body of powers had to be implied by general clauses, and one of these authorized Congress to "make all laws which shall be necessary and proper" for carrying out other powers granted. In reading this clause Hamilton emphasized the word "proper." For example, under the war powers of the Constitution the government clearly had a right to conquer territory. It followed that it properly had a "resulting power" to administer this territory, even though the Constitution said nothing about it. The Constitution said that the government should regulate commerce and navigation; and it followed that it had a "resulting power" to build lighthouses. Now the Constitution declared that the national government should have power to lay and collect taxes, to pay debts, and to borrow money. A national bank would materially assist it in gathering taxes, in sending money to distant points to pay bills, and in borrowing. It was therefore entitled to set up the national bank under its "implied powers." Washington accepted this argument and signed Hamilton's measure.

The Whisky Rebellion; Jay's Treaty

JEFFERSON THOUGHT that Hamilton's excise law of 1791 was "odious" and wrote Washington that it was also unwise, for it committed "the authority of the government in parts where resistance is most probable and coercion least practicable." By this he primarily meant western Pennsylvania. This country was filled with hardy Scotch-Irish. They had no means of getting their grain eastward across the mountains to market; they needed money; and knowing the Scottish art of whisky-making, they set up stills on nearly every farm to produce an easily transported commodity. The excise tax seemed to fall unfairly on this money crop. Moreover, it was inquisitorial. Four counties in the area just south of Pittsburgh were soon being lashed to open resistance by angry leaders. Washington issued a proclamation of warning, but it was disregarded; and in 1794, when the government tried to arrest men who had defied the revenue officers, violence broke out. Mobs forced a Federal inspector to flee for his life and threatened the little garrison in Pittsburgh. The governor should have used the militia, but fearing to make himself unpopular with the western voters, he failed to do so.

Thereupon Washington, closely advised by Hamilton, decided to take stern action. A force of a thousand soldiers could easily have suppressed the "insurrection," which was really nothing more than a disorderly demonstration. But Hamilton was anxious to furnish an illustration of the overwhelming strength of the government. Fifteen thousand troops were therefore called out from Virginia, Maryland, and Pennsylvania—an army almost as large as that which had captured Cornwallis. Marching upon the disaffected area, the soldiery quickly overawed the malcontents. Hamilton went with them and saw that eighteen men were carried to Philadelphia for trial. But only two were convicted, and Washington pardoned them.

This Whisky Rebellion created great excitement, the Federalists extolling the government's stern measures and the Antifederalists denouncing them as arbitrary and militaristic. Unquestionably Hamilton's policy enhanced the prestige of the national authorities. But it is also unquestionable that it aroused much popular antagonism and distrust and was a mistake. As soon as the Jeffersonians came into power the excise was repealed.

Equally unpopular with many was the course of the Washington administration with respect to foreign affairs. In 1793 war began in Europe between France and Britain. Strong feeling was aroused in the United States. The trading classes and many religious people, especially in New England, feared and hated the Republic which had overturned property interests and set up a goddess of reason; the Southern farmers and urban mechanics sympathized with the French. Washington wisely issued a proclamation of neutrality. This was so fiercely denounced that the hotheaded French minister to the United States, Genêt, thought that he could disregard it. He wrote his government that Washington was a weak old man under British influence; he talked of appealing to the populace; and when the government forbade him to use American ports as a base of operation for French privateers, he disobeyed the order. Is he, Washington angrily demanded, "to set the acts of this

government at defiance with impunity"? Genêt was ordered
to return home. But knowing that the guillotine awaited him,
he did better—he stayed in the United States, married the
daughter of the governor of New York, and lived prosper-
ously to old age. His indiscretions had embarrassed the pro-
French party in America. Nevertheless, this party in 1794
began to demand war with England, chiefly on the ground
that the British were illegally seizing American ships bound
for the French West Indies, and that they were holding trading posts in the Northwest Territory in flagrant violation of
the Treaty of 1783.

Nothing could really have been more disastrous to America
at this time than such a war; and to settle a variety of disputes with Great Britain, Washington sent John Jay, an
experienced diplomatist who was now Chief Justice, to
London as envoy extraordinary. He could have made no
better choice. Jay believed that "a little good-natured wisdom often does much more in politics than much slippery
craft." Acting with moderation and enlightenment, he
made a treaty which gained as much as the United States
could rightfully expect. That is, he obtained a promise that
the western posts which the British still held should be
given up within two years. He got the American claim for
damages arising from British ship seizures referred to a commission. Finally, he obtained important commercial privileges in both the British East Indies and West Indies. On the
other hand, the treaty renounced American trade in cotton,
sugar, and molasses to the British West Indies, recognized
the obligation to pay the prewar debts which Americans owed
to British merchants, and failed to provide compensation for
the slaves which the British armies had taken from their
owners during the war. These were not in fact serious defects, but already the notion that America must have the
best of all treaties was fermenting in the American mind,
and the treaty was greeted with a burst of indignation. Jay
was burned in effigy by wild mobs; angry orators and editors
heaped execration upon Washington. But Washington and
Jay were too wise and too philosophic to be moved by a
temporary public clamor. With certain amendments, the
Senate accepted the treaty. Merchants and shipowners again
had reason to look gratefully to the national government.

John Adams

WHEN WASHINGTON RETIRED, in 1797, John Adams, able and high-minded, but stern, obstinate, and full of idiosyncrasies, took the helm. His headstrong, tactless traits made it certain that his presidency would be troubled. Too independent to accept Hamilton's guidance, he had quarreled with that leader even before he entered the presidency. Thus he was handicapped by having a divided party behind him and a divided Cabinet at his side—for the heads of departments took Hamilton's views in party matters. Many Southerners disliked Adams as a New Englander, and party feeling grew intensely bitter. To make matters worse, the international skies became more heavily clouded than ever.

This time it was with France that war threatened. The Directory which governed the French Republic, angered by Jay's treaty, refused to accept the minister whom Adams sent over and actually threatened him with arrest. This humiliating episode aroused strong American feeling. When Adams sent three commissioners to Paris to try to adjust the difficulties, they were met with fresh contumely. Talleyrand, in charge of foreign affairs, curtly declined to deal with them. Confidential agents, later described by the American envoys as X, Y, and Z, suggested that something might be done if they were paid a bribe of $250,000. Finally Talleyrand practically broke off negotiations by a coarsely insulting message in which he accused the United States of double-dealing. The publication of the X Y Z papers, as the correspondence was called, raised indignation in America to an excited pitch. "Millions for defense, but not a cent for tribute," said Robert Goodloe Harper, and the phrase caught the popular fancy. Troops were enlisted, the navy was strengthened, and in 1798 a series of sea battles took place in which American ships uniformly defeated the French. For a time open war seemed unescapable.

In this crisis Adams' stern individualism served the nation well. Thrusting aside Hamilton, who wanted war, he suddenly sent a new minister to France—and Napoleon, who had come to power, received him cordially. The danger of conflict swiftly disappeared. Unfortunately, in home affairs, Adams, meanwhile, behaved with a narrowness and tactless-ness that the American people found unforgivable. He and the Federalist Congress made themselves responsible for four unhappy laws which did much to ruin the administration. The first extended from five years to fourteen the period for which an alien must reside in the United States before becoming a citizen. The second gave the President power for two years to order any dangerous alien out of the country. The third provided that in time of war aliens might be deported, or imprisoned as long as the President decreed, and without trial. The fourth made it a high misdemeanor to conspire against any legal measure of the government, or to obstruct or even to criticize a public officer.

These Alien and Sedition Laws seemed outrageously severe, a gross infringement of personal and civil liberties. Jefferson and Madison, who believed that the Federalists were concentrating a dangerous power in the national government, determined to take a stand against them. They wrote two sets of resolutions, of which Jefferson's were adopted by the Kentucky legislature and Madison's by the Virginia assembly. Setting forth the theory that the national government had been founded by a compact among the states, these Kentucky and Virginia Resolutions declared that a state might take steps to veto an unconstitutional act. Their purpose was not to declare the rights of states but to protect the rights of men.

The year 1800 found the country ripe for a change. Indeed, it proved the year of a great political upheaval. Under Washington and Adams, the Federalists had done a great work in establishing the government and making it strong. Nobody now doubted, as many had in 1789, that the nation and the Constitution would endure. But the Federalists had failed to recognize that the American government was meant to be essentially popular in character. They had followed policies which did much to give its control and benefits to special classes. Jefferson, a born popular leader, had steadily gathered behind him the great mass of small farmers, mechanics, shopkeepers, and other workers. They meant to see that the nation had a people's government, not a government of special interests, and they asserted themselves with tremendous power. In the election of 1800 Adams carried New England. But the opposition swept the Southern States and gained a heavy majority in the Middle States. The clumsy electoral system resulted in a tie between Jefferson and Aaron Burr, a plausible but unprincipled New Yorker of the same party. But the people had manifestly intended that Jefferson should be President, and Hamilton, in one of those fine acts which so frequently marked his career, saw to it that the House of Representatives decided in his favor.

"The tough sides of our Argosie have been thoroughly tried," wrote Jefferson to a friend. "We shall put her on her republican tack, and she will now show by the beauty of her motion the skill of her builders."

CHAPTER 7

The Rise of National Unity

Jefferson's Administration

THE MANNER in which Jefferson assumed the presidency in 1801 emphasized the fact that democracy had come into power. The ceremonies were the first to be held in Washington, which had just been made the capital. It was then a mere forest village on the north bank of the Potomac, its muddy roadways built through bushes and across sloughs, with only a few shabby houses—"most of them small, miserable huts," according to one of the outgoing Cabinet. Gouverneur Morris sarcastically remarked that the capital had a great *future*. "We want nothing here but houses, cellars, kitchens, well-informed men, amiable women, and other trifles of this kind, to make our city perfect." Jefferson, carelessly garbed as usual, walked from his simple boarding-house up the hill to the new Capitol, with a number of friends at his heels. Entering the Senate chamber, he shook hands with Vice-President Burr, his recent unscrupulous rival. Another man whom he distrusted stood at hand, John Marshall of Virginia, a distant kinsman whom Adams had recently appointed Chief Justice. Jefferson took the oath of office and quietly delivered one of the best addresses ever made by an incoming President.

Part of Jefferson's address was a much-needed plea for conciliation. The political canvass just ended had been so bitterly vituperative that many people, especially in New England, believed that Jefferson was an atheist, a leveler, and even an anarchist. He begged the citizens to remember that political intolerance is as bad as religious intolerance and to unite as Americans in preserving the Union, making representative government effective, and developing the national resources. "We are all republicans," he said, "we are all federalists," and added a memorable declaration of faith in freedom: "If there be any among us who would wish to dissolve this Union or to change its republican form, let them stand undisturbed as monuments of the safety with which error of opinion may be tolerated where reason is left free to combat it." The remainder of the address laid down the political principles of the new administration. The country, he said, should have "a wise and frugal government," which should preserve order among the inhabitants, but "shall leave them otherwise free to regulate their own pursuits of industry and improvement, and shall not take from the mouth of labor the bread it has earned." It should preserve the rights of the states. It should seek honest friendship with all nations, but "entangling alliances with none"— a long-remembered phrase. Jefferson promised to sustain the Union "in its whole constitutional vigor," to preserve "the supremacy of the civil over the military authorities," and to support popular elections as the only arbiter short of revolution.

The very fact that Jefferson was in the White House for two terms greatly encouraged democratic procedures throughout the country. He abolished all the aristocratic trappings with which Washington had surrounded the presidency. The weekly levees were given up, court etiquette was rigidly pruned, and titles of honor like "Excellency" were abandoned. To Jefferson the plainest citizen was as worthy of respect as the highest officer. He taught his subordinates to regard themselves simply as trustees for the people. He encouraged agriculture and promoted land settlement by purchasing the Indians' titles and helping them migrate westward. Believing that America should be a haven for the oppressed, he encouraged immigration by a liberal naturalization law. He tried hard to keep peace with other nations, for war would mean more government activity, more taxes, and less freedom. Appointing Albert Gallatin, a far-sighted financier of Swiss birth, his Secretary of the Treasury, Jefferson encouraged him to reduce expenses and pay off the national debt; with the result that by 1806 the national revenues were $14,500,000, the expenses $8,500,000, and the surplus $6,000,000. By the end of 1807 the thrifty Gallatin had reduced the national debt to less than seventy millions. As a wave of Jeffersonian feeling swept over the nation, all commoners rejoiced. State after state was abolishing property qualifications for the ballot and for office and passing more humane laws as for debtors and criminals.

Yet fate turned Jefferson and the country in a direction that he had not intended. By two steps he, the apostle of a strict construction of the Constitution, stretched the powers of the Federal government to the utmost; and, when he left office, the war that he hated lay just ahead.

The Louisiana Purchase: The Burr Conspiracy

ONE OF HIS STEPS doubled the area of the nation. Spain had long held the country west of the Mississippi, with the port of New Orleans near its mouth. But soon after Jefferson came into office Napoleon forced the weak Spanish government to cede the great tract called Louisiana back to France. The moment he did so farsighted Americans trembled with apprehension and indignation. New Orleans was an indispensable port for the shipment of American products grown in the Ohio and Mississippi valleys. Napoleon's plans for a huge colonial empire just west of the United States, balancing the Anglo-Saxon dominion in North America, menaced the trading rights and the safety of all the interior settlements. Even feeble Spain had made a great deal of trouble for the Southwestern country. What might not France, the most powerful nation in the world, do?

Jefferson asserted that if France took possession of Louisiana, "from that moment we must marry ourselves to the British fleet and nation"; and that the first cannon shot fired in a European war would be the signal for the march of an Anglo-American army against New Orleans. Napoleon was impressed by the certainty that the United States and England would strike. He knew that another war with Great Britain was impending after the brief Peace of Amiens and that when it began he would surely lose Louisiana. He was discouraged, too, by his inability to crush the great revolt of the Negro leader Toussaint L'Ouverture in French-ruled Haiti, where in 1802 the insurgents and yellow fever together destroyed a force of twenty-four thousand men. He therefore resolved to fill his treasury, to put Louisiana beyond the reach of the British, and to bid for American friendship by selling the region to the United States. For $15,000,000 this vast area passed into the possession of the republic. Jefferson "stretched the Constitution till it cracked" in buying it, for no clause authorized the purchase of foreign territory, and he acted without prior Congressional consent.

By this happy stroke the United States obtained more than a million square miles and with it the valuable port of New Orleans, picturesque brick and stucco city built on a crescent sweep of the Mississippi, with the dark cypress forest as background. On an autumn day in 1803 a motley gathering on the Place d'Armes—French soldiers in gay uniforms, Spaniards and French Creoles in fashionable dress, pioneers in hunting shirts, tawny Indians, ebony slaves—saw the ensign of France fall and the Stars and Stripes rise. The United States gained a sweep of rich plains that within eighty years was one of the world's granaries. It gained control of the whole central river system of the continent. For the first time Americans could say, as Lincoln said later in Civil War days, that the Father of Waters went unvexed to the sea. Within four years Robert Fulton's introduction of a successful steamboat on the Hudson solved the problem of using these inland waters easily and cheaply. Puffing vessels soon filled all the Western streams, taking emigrants to settle on the land and bringing furs, grain, cured meats, and a hundred other products back to market.

As the end of his first term approached, Jefferson had gained widespread popularity, for Louisiana was manifestly a great prize, business was prosperous, and the President had tried hard to please all sections. His re-election was certain, and in 1804 he actually received all but fourteen of the 176 electoral votes, carrying every state even in New England, except Connecticut. Able to rule his party with a strong hand, he had taken steps to crush the ambitious and constantly intriguing Aaron Burr. The crafty New Yorker, deprived of all share in the distribution of Federal offices and practically read out of the party, turned to a flirtation with the bitterest Federalists of New England. He ran for governor of New York on the Federalist ticket in the spring of 1804, but largely through the opposition of Hamilton—who correctly suspected that Burr and such Yankee schemers as Timothy Pickering were plotting disunion—suffered a humiliating defeat. To obtain revenge, the unprincipled Burr then provoked Hamilton to a duel which, fought at dawn of a July morning on the Jersey shore of the Hudson, ended in Hamilton's death. The loss of so brilliant and beloved a leader threw the community into a paroxysm of angry grief, and Burr had to go into hiding for safety. His career in the East was blasted, but with unchastened insolence he turned to the West for new adventures.

Ordinary prizes and distinctions did not suffice for so overmastering an ambition as Burr's. Rule or ruin was his motto, and he laid plans to found a state of his own. Just where it was to be, and just how he was to create it, are still disputed questions. Many students believe that he intended to collect a little army in the West, descend the Mississippi, seize control of New Orleans, and wrench Louisiana away from the United States. Describing some such intention to British and Spanish officers, he tried to get money from London and Madrid. He told the British that he would place his state under their protection, while he informed the Spaniards that he would make it a buffer state between Mexico and the United States. Neither supported him. But other students believe that Burr's real object was to recruit his army and lead it against the Spanish authorities in Vera Cruz and Mexico City, gaining control of Texas and Mexico. Indeed, he told such leaders as Andrew Jackson of Tennessee, who hated Spain, that this was his intention. Possibly he did

not know himself whether he was aiming at Louisiana or
Mexico; possibly he even aimed at both!

At any rate, Burr came to a fall as complete as Lucifer's.
Loyal men in the Southwest got wind of his conspiracy and
late in 1806 brought charges against him. He was arrested
and sent to Richmond, Virginia, for trial on an indictment
for treason. John Marshall presided over the case, and his
principal rulings were favorable to Burr, while the evidence
was unavoidably vague. Burr was therefore acquitted—but
he was now ruined beyond all redemption.

American Neutrality: The Embargo Act

JEFFERSON made his second extraordinary use of Federal
authority in attempting to maintain American neutrality
during the colossal struggle between Great Britain and Napoleon. He knew that the young and immature republic
needed peace; and as war raged on land and sea, he hoped
to keep the United States outside the circle of flames. Great
Britain was fighting to prevent the conquest of all continental
Europe by a single power. Naturally, commercial warfare
was one of her best weapons. Realizing its value, the British
hastened to blockade Napoleon's empire, and Napoleon retaliated by the Berlin and Milan decrees for blockading Great
Britain. In their combat both powers struck heavy blows at
American commerce. The British acted to cut off the rich
carrying trade of American vessels with products of the
French West Indies and to shut them out of practically the
whole European coast from Spain to the Elbe. The French
ordered the seizure of any American ship which submitted
to British search or touched at a British port. That is, the
war soon reached a point where no American craft could
trade with the broad region controlled by France without
being seized by the British, and none could trade with Britain
without being seized (if it ever got within reach) by France!
Under these conditions commerce was almost impossible.
The British government was fairly rigorous, while the French
confiscated American vessels on the slightest excuse.

What especially aroused American feeling against Great
Britain was the impressment question. To win the war the
British were compelled to build up their navy to a point

where it had more than seven hundred warships in commission, with nearly 150,000 sailors and marines. This oaken wall kept Britain safe, protected her commerce, and preserved her communications with her colonies. It was vital to Britain's existence. Yet the men of the fleet were so ill-paid, ill-fed, and ill-handled that it was impossible to obtain crews by free enlistment. Many sailors deserted and they were particularly glad to find refuge on the pleasanter and safer Yankee vessels. In these circumstances British officers regarded the right of searching American ships and taking off British subjects as essential. They did not claim the right to impress American seamen, but they refused to admit that a Briton could be naturalized into an American citizen. The American view, however, was thoroughly hostile to this claim. It was humiliating for American vessels to lay to under the guns of a British cruiser while a lieutenant and a party of marines lined up the crew and examined them. Moreover, many British officers were arrogant and unfair. They impressed true American seamen by scores and hundreds—ultimately, it was alleged, by thousands.

To bring Great Britain and France to a fairer attitude without war, Jefferson finally had Congress pass the Embargo Act, a law forbidding foreign commerce altogether. It was a grim experiment. First the shipping interests were almost ruined by the measure, and discontent rose high in New England and New York. Then the agricultural interests found that they were suffering heavily, for prices tumbled when the Southern and Western farmers could not ship their surplus grain, meat, and tobacco overseas. Observers compared the measure to a surgeon's amputation of a leg in an effort to save a life. In a single year American exports fell to one fifth their former volume. But the hope that the embargo would starve Great Britain into a change of policy failed—the British government would not budge. As the grumbling at home increased, Jefferson turned to a milder measure. A Nonintercourse Law was substituted for the embargo. This forbade commerce with either Britain or France, including their dependencies, but promised that it would be suspended with reference to either country as soon as that country ceased its attacks upon neutral commerce. Napoleon in 1810 officially announced that he had abandoned his

measures. This was a lie—he was maintaining them. But the
United States believed him and limited its nonintercourse
to Great Britain.

The War of 1812

THIS MADE RELATIONS with Great Britain worse, and the
two countries drifted rapidly toward war. Ill-feeling had
been aroused by various incidents. For example, the British
warship *Leopard* had ordered the American warship *Chesapeake* to give up certain British deserters—though actually
only one was aboard; meeting some hesitation, it fired into
the *Chesapeake* for fifteen minutes and then boarded her, the
decks wet with blood, and took off four men. A little later
the President laid before Congress a detailed report, showing
6057 instances in which the British had impressed American citizens within three years. Indian troubles too entered
into the situation. Northwestern settlers who suffered from
the attacks of a league of Indian tribes formed by the able
chief Tecumseh were convinced that British agents in Canada
were encouraging the savages.

And one motive was thoroughly selfish. Land-hungry
Westerners, ably represented in Congress by the eloquent
Henry Clay of Kentucky, wished to grab all of Canada,
and they were abetted by Southerners under the young
John C. Calhoun who hoped to conquer Florida from Spain,
now Britain's ally, and by other "War-Hawks." The result
was that, with Madison in the White House, war was declared on Britain in 1812.

The War of 1812 was in many ways one of the most
unfortunate events in American history. For one reason,
it was needless; the British Orders in Council that had
caused the worst irritation were being unconditionally repealed just as Congress declared war. For another, the United
States suffered from internal divisions of the gravest kind.
While the South and West favored war, New York and New
England in general opposed it, and toward its end important
New England groups went to the very edge of disloyalty.
For a third reason, the war was far from glorious in a mili-
tary sense.

The American army, which Jeffersonian economy had

kept to fewer than three thousand troops, supported by a rabble of undrilled, undisciplined militia, was in wretched shape to fight. Many regular soldiers were the offscourings of jails and pothouses. Winfield Scott, a young Virginian who had begun his brilliant military career a few years earlier, tells us that the commanders fell into two main groups. "The old officers had very generally slunk into either sloth, ignorance, or habits of intemperate drinking." The newer officers had for the most part been appointed for political reasons; a few were good, but the majority were either "coarse and ignorant men," or if educated were "swaggerers, dependents, decayed gentlemen, and others unfit for anything else." The senior major general when the war began was the incompetent Henry Dearborn, well past sixty, who had never commanded a larger unit in the field than a regiment. The senior brigadier general was James Wilkinson, now known to have been a traitor to the United States, a pensioner of both France and Spain, and an accomplice of Aaron Burr: corrupt, profligate, and insubordinate, he was despised by all who knew him. The only brigadier general who possessed valuable experience was William Hull, who had attained the rank of colonel in the Revolution, but was now infirm and senile. He began the war by surrendering Detroit without firing a shot.

Disaster then followed disaster. The American efforts to invade Canada ended in general failure. During the first year, as a British historian put it, "the militia and volunteers do not seem to have made up their minds whether they wanted to fight or did not." The hardest fought contest on the northern frontier, that of Lundy's Lane near Niagara, was a drawn battle which both sides later claimed as a victory (July, 1814). But as it temporarily shattered American plans for pushing forward into Canada, the British and Canadians had the better title to exultation.

When Napoleon's forces were defeated in Spain, the British were able to reinforce their armies heavily with Wellington's veterans. A seasoned force drove into New York at Plattsburg on Lake Champlain, but the British fleet on those waters was decisively defeated by a youngster of twenty-eight, Commodore Thomas MacDonough, and the British army, its communications thus rendered precarious, was forced to retreat. Another British army of less than five thousand men landed near Washington and met a slightly larger force, chiefly militia, at Bladensburg. The unheroic defenders gave way after losing ten killed and forty wounded and ran for Washington so rapidly that many Britons suffered sunstroke in trying to keep up. In retaliation for the American destruction of public buildings at York (now Toronto), British troops fired the Capitol and the White House. However, when the British fleet subjected Fort McHenry near Baltimore to a long-range night bombardment—shoals making closer fire impossible—it accomplished nothing; and a young Washington attorney, Francis Scott Key, who had been on a British warship trying to arrange an exchange of prisoners, was inspired by the sight of the national flag waving in the morning breeze to write *The Star-Spangled Banner*.

Only at sea did the Americans win any laurels. The navy, systematically built up under Washington and Adams, had acquitted itself magnificently in the short war with France and the operations of 1803–1804 against the Tripolitan corsairs, whose depredations upon American shipping had become intolerable. Unlike the army, it had been blessed with one great early organizer. This was Edward Preble, who gave the Mediterranean squadron a harsh but efficient administration, instilled into his men a spirit of pluck, gallantry, and obedience which became a tradition, and trained young officers like Stephen Decatur to high capacity. Numerically the navy was small, for Jefferson had followed a fatuous policy of building shore-defense gunboats, and in 1810 it numbered only a dozen vessels of any power. But in a series of single-ship actions, like that of the *Constitution* ("Old Ironsides") and the *Guerrière*, the *United States* and the *Macedonian*, the Yankee captains consistently defeated equal or heavier British vessels. On the Great Lakes, too, the Americans proved their mettle. Captain Oliver Hazard Perry, another officer well under thirty, built a fleet on Lake Erie, searched out a small British force, and after a dogged action thrilled the country with his laconic dispatch: "We have met the enemy and they are ours." Yet in the end the stronger British navy established full command of the seas, drove American commerce into shelter, and kept a close blockade of the American coast.

When the war closed, the Treaty of Ghent (1814), negotiated by John Quincy Adams, Henry Clay, and others, said not a word about impressment and neutral rights, ostensibly its chief causes. Only the dramatic and one-sided victory which a bizarre but formidable army of frontiersmen under the veteran Indian fighter, Andrew Jackson, won at New Orleans over a strong British force commanded by Wellington's courageous lieutenant, Edward Pakenham, gave the country any real exultation. This was January 8, 1815, after the peace treaty was signed, but before it was known in America. It made the fiery, imperious Jackson a tremendous national hero.

National Unity

YET NOTWITHSTANDING its inglorious military character, the war did contribute signally to the development of the republic. Begun and continued amid discontent and bickering, it nevertheless strengthened the sentiment of national unity and patriotism. For this several reasons can be assigned. The scattered successes, and especially the naval victories and the defeat of Pakenham's veterans at New Orleans, gave Americans a new basis for pride and self-confidence. They dispelled the feeling of inferiority that Jefferson's "submission policy" had fostered. In the second place, the fact that men of different states again fought side by side, and that a Virginian, Winfield Scott, was the ablest commander the Northern troops found, added to the sense of national unity. The Western troops won some battles that they did not forget, and they had less attachment to their state and more loyalty to the nation than many people of the original thirteen. From this time onward the West counted for much more in American life, and the West was always national in sentiment.

Finally, the people came out of the war disgusted with the unpatriotic temper that some selfish and narrow groups had shown. The malcontents of New England had gone to the very verge of treason, and late in the war had sent delegates to a convention in Hartford to consider setting up a separate union. Though it did not actually go this far, this "Hartford Convention" became a byword of contempt and reproach.

Altogether, this ill-starred war did a great deal to make

the republic more mature and more independent; to knit
it together and strengthen its character. Albert Gallatin asserted that before the conflict, Americans were becoming
too selfish, too materialistic, and too prone to think in local
terms. "The war," he said, "has renewed and reinstated the
national feeling and character which the Revolution had given,
and which were daily lessening. The people have now more
general objects of attachment, with which their pride and
political opinions are connected. They are more Americans;
they feel and act more as a nation; and I hope that the per-
manency of the Union is thereby better secured." Because the
war had been so closely fought, it left little ill-feeling. When
next Britons and Americans met on a battlefield, more than
a hundred years later, it was as comrades in arms and in
sentiment.

Events had proved that no matter which party was in
control, whether Hamilton's Federalists or Jefferson's Democrats, the national unity grew and the power of the central
government increased. This was because the conditions of
national growth demanded it. To acquire Louisiana, to wage
a commercial contest with France and Great Britain, to attack the Barbary pirates, to carry on war with the British—
all this required a vigorous central authority.

During these years, too, the national government was
being greatly strengthened by the decisions of the Supreme
Court. The convinced Federalist, John Marshall of Virginia,
who was made Chief Justice just before Jefferson entered the
presidency, held that office until his death in 1835. The court
had been weak and little regarded; he transformed it into a
powerful and majestic tribunal, occupying a position as important as that of Congress or President. In his tastes and
manners Marshall belonged to the easygoing planter society
of his native state. He dressed plainly, carried his own dinner
home from market, loved cards, punch, and a rollicking game
of horseshoes or quoits. But in ideas he represented rather
the business and professional circles of cities like Boston
and New York. His memorable decisions, the work of a bold
and penetrating mind, showed that he was dominated by two
cardinal principles—one, the sovereignty of the Federal
government; the other, the sanctity of private property.

Marshall was a great judge. His decisions were written
with a masterly logic which in nearly every instance carried

conviction to the reader. Simple in style, they rested upon an impressive learning and an exhaustive analysis. His habit was first to establish his major premise fully; then to go on to the deductions, demolishing every objection to them; and finally state his conclusion, amply supported by citations and illustrations. Master of the Supreme Court, he gave it harmony, so that discordant views and dissenting opinions were rare. But Marshall was more than a great judge—he was a great constitutional statesman. Deciding nearly half a hundred cases which involved clear constitutional issues, he dealt with them on the basis of a well-matured political philosophy. They concerned nearly all the important parts of the Constitution. In consequence, when he finished his long service, the Constitution as the courts applied it throughout the country was in great degree the Constitution as Marshall interpreted it. He may be said to have remolded the instrument according to his own clear vision.

It is impossible to do much more than enumerate his principal decisions. In Marbury vs. Madison (1803), he decisively established the right of the Supreme Court to review any law of Congress or of a state legislature. "It is emphatically the province and duty of the judicial department to say what the law is," he wrote. In Cohens vs. Virginia (1821), he swept aside the arguments of those who declared that the decision of a state court in cases arising under state laws should be final. Pointing out the confusion into which this would lead the country—for the states would take numerous different views as to the validity of laws under the Federal Constitution or Federal treaties—he insisted that the final judgment must be that of the national courts. In McCulloch vs. Maryland (1819), he dealt with the old question of the implied powers of the government under the Constitution. Here he stood boldly forth in defense of the Hamiltonian theory that the Constitution by implication gives to the government powers which it does not expressly state. In Gibbons vs. Ogden (1824), Marshall amplified this doctrine. The Constitution gave to Congress the right to regulate interstate commerce; and in this case arising out of a dispute over steamboat rights on the Hudson, Marshall held that this right of national regulation was to be interpreted broadly, not narrowly. In the Dartmouth College case,

Marshall applied the contract clause of the Constitution to sustain the validity of a corporate charter, denying the state subsequent power to amend it. Altogether, Marshall did as much as any leader to make the central government of the American people a living, growing force.

CHAPTER 8

A National Culture

The Search for a National Character

IT WAS A FACT of immense significance that whereas in the making of most new states—Portugal, for example, or Norway, or Germany, or Italy—the nation came centuries before the state, in the making of the United States the state came before the nation. That is, the United States crystallized politically and administratively before it had acquired most of the traditional ingredients of nationalism. And much of American cultural enterprise has been addressed, consciously or unconsciously, to the task of providing those ingredients —a common history, common songs, stories, legends, heroes, a common literature and art.

From the first, Americans recognized the desirability of an "American" language, literature, and culture. "America must be independent in literature as she is in politics," wrote that ardent nationalist Noah Webster, of dictionary fame, and Governor Sullivan of Massachusetts observed that "it is now full time that we should assume a national character, and opinions of our own." They spoke for a large body of educated opinion. The first generation of American independence witnessed an energetic, almost a convulsive, effort to "create" an American culture. There was to be an American language, and Noah Webster set himself resolutely to champion American speech and prove its superiority to British speech. There was to be an American literature, and Philip Freneau and Hugh Brackenridge and a group of Connecticut poets known somewhat misleadingly as the "Connecticut Wits" tried their best to break away from Old World standards and establish better in the New. There was to be an American education, and the generation of Jefferson and Noah Webster and Benjamin Rush worked tirelessly to make education at once secular and universal. There was to be an American science —Americans were almost inevitably environmentalists and concentrated heavily on geography, botany, and ethnology —and even an American arithmetic, for as Nicholas Pike wrote: "As we are now an independent nation it was deemed proper that we should have an independent arithmatic." The new nation did not quite cut itself off from Euclid, but it did at least take a great leap forward with the decimal system of currency.

Actually little came of this cultural self-consciousness in the first generation after the Revolution. The new independent nation was not yet prepared to provide an independent culture, and literature, art, and architecture remained stubbornly derivative. The "American" language proved to be very much like the English, and in time the English came to be more and more like the American. The many promising journals which were to promote American literature modeled themselves on the great British quarterlies, even the *North American Review*, which dominated the field for many years. American painters like Benjamin West and John Singleton Copley not only studied abroad but lived abroad. It was perhaps in those areas where Americans were least self-conscious—politics and law—that they made the most distinctive contributions. The most impressive literary products of the new nation were not its poems or novels— almost all of them feeble—but such books as *Common Sense* and *The Federalist Papers*, and the public papers of such statesmen as Washington, Jefferson, Madison, and John Marshall. In this first generation, American pre-eminence in the political realm was as indisputable as the Italians' in the artistic or the Germans' in the musical field; statesmanship was the American specialty.

The Birth of an American Literature

NOT UNTIL AFTER the War of 1812 did Americans really begin to achieve a native culture. That war at once completed the American disillusionment with the "Mother Country," encouraged American self-confidence, and turned American interests westward to the vast new areas which came increasingly to seem authentically American. Washington Irving, though he wrote very much in the style of contemporary English essayists, did at least address himself to native themes. His Knickerbocker's *History of New York* has some claim to be considered the beginning of American literary humor; his *Sketch Book* caught and preserved the legends and traditions of the Hudson Valley he knew so well—the legend of Rip Van Winkle and the legend of Sleepy Hollow, for example. After a long period of immersion in England, Germany, and Spain, Irving returned to American themes, gave his countrymen their first substantial biography of Columbus, the first good biography of Washington, and three capital books on the Far West, including the classic account of Astoria.

Irving thought of himself as a cosmopolite, equally happy in the Old World and the New. Not so James Fenimore Cooper, who quite deliberately cultivated American themes and American scenes as a counter to European romantic novels, and engaged with gusto in the literary war with England. It was Cooper who really discovered the literary possibilities of the Indian and the frontiersman and who, in his great Leatherstocking series, provided a record of the clash of red and white civilizations that caught the imagination of the whole Western world. A writer of wide-ranging talent, Cooper wrote a series of sea tales that were to inspire later authors such as Marryat and Conrad, and another series of novels about American society in urban and rural New York that have some claim to be regarded as the first examples of the sociological novel in America. Meantime William Cullen Bryant, whose "Thanatopsis," written at the age of seventeen, heralded the appearance of a genuine poetic talent, was celebrating American nature in poetry and American democracy in editorials for the New York *Evening Post*.

The first great flowering of American literature, however, came in New England, in the years from the mid-1830's to the Civil War. We can date that flowering, with some assurance, from the appearance of Ralph Waldo Emerson's *Nature* in 1836, and its decline, perhaps, from the death of Hawthorne in 1864. Within a few years after the appearance of his first essays, Emerson emerged as the spokesman for the New England, and perhaps the American, mind. Idealistic, optimistic, and original, Emerson spoke with a clarity and a beauty that reached the mind and fired the imagination of the young of every generation. Notwithstanding his debt to German idealism, he was authentically American, and authentically Yankee, in his philosophy; he was, too, the philosopher of all those who had no other philosopher. His *Nature* and *Divinity School Address* constituted the platform of American transcendentalism; his *American Scholar* and *English Traits* (1856) were a literary and philosophical declaration of independence; his poetry showed more originality and perhaps more philosophical depth than any written in America before *Leaves of Grass*.

Emerson was, as one contemporary put it, the cow from which all the others drew their milk. One of those who depended on Emerson and for a time appeared to live in his shadow was Henry David Thoreau, also of Concord. But Thoreau had a mind as independent as Emerson's, and in many ways more original; his *Walden, or Life in the Woods*, read eagerly by each new generation of young men and women, bids fair to outlive anything that Emerson himself wrote, and his essay "Civil Disobedience" inspired such world figures as Leo Tolstoy, Mahatma Gandhi, and Pandit Nehru.

A third inhabitant of the little town of Concord—a town which had some claim to be regarded as the Athens of America—was Nathaniel Hawthorne, a novelist of exquisite sensibility. Hawthorne found in the history of New England material for stories which, in his rich imagination, took on a universal character: *The Scarlet Letter*, *The House of the Seven Gables*, *The Blithedale Romance*, and a host of short stories, such as "The Great Stone Face" and "Ethan Brand," which, like the novels, belong to world literature. And in

The Marble Faun Hawthorne gave us one of the most penetrating of all interpretations of the clash between Old and
New World morality—a theme which fascinated American
writers from Cooper to Henry James.

It was the poets, however, rather than the novelists or
essayists who appealed most to contemporaries and who
are best remembered. For this was the day of Henry Wads-
worth Longfellow, most beloved of all American poets; of
James Russell Lowell, whose *Biglow Papers* showed the literary potentialities of the New England vernacular; of John
Greenleaf Whittier, poet of the New England countryside
and of the abolitionist movement; of the incomparable "Doctor" Holmes, poet, essayist, and novelist, and most learned
of physicians as well. These men, together with theologians
like William Ellery Channing and the "Great American
Preacher," Theodore Parker, and historians like George
Bancroft and William Prescott, created what is still remembered as the golden day of American letters.

Already in the 1850's, however, the center of literary
gravity was shifting to New York. Irving and Cooper and
Bryant lived on into that decade, but their literary talent
was spent; the writers of the 1850's belonged to a new world.
Herman Melville had published no less than five novels
before 1850, but it was with *Moby Dick* (1851) that he
inaugurated what may be considered a distinctively American literature, for *Moby Dick* owed less, perhaps, to the
traditional English novel than any that had been written in
America up to that time. This great allegorical story of the
pursuit of the white whale contained within its tumultuous
pages characters indubitably American but addressed itself
to moral questions that were universal. A few years later
came another authentically American voice. In 1855 Walt
Whitman of Brooklyn published the first of many editions
of *Leaves of Grass.* Unorthodox both in style and in subject
matter, these poems were regarded, in their day, as both undisciplined and shocking. They were in fact most skillfully
contrived, and—at their best—revealed a poetic talent richer
than that of any American poet of the twentieth century;
they were, too, quite orthodox in their romanticism. American poetry—indeed modern poetry—never quite recovered
from the impact of *Leaves of Grass.*

History

IT IS GENERALLY SAID that a common history and tradition, a common sense of the past, is one of the essential ingredients of successful nationalism. If that were true, the new United States would have been in a bad fix, for she had very little history of her own. Her intellectual Founding Fathers set themselves to remedy this situation, to re-create an American past, to discover American traditions, to celebrate American heroes. The story of the struggle for independence and of the writing of the Constitution lent itself wonderfully to this enterprise, and almost before the War of Independence was over Americans were comparing the founders of their nation to Romulus and Remus, to Horsa and Hengist, while in no time at all Washington took his place alongside other legendary heroes like Alfred the Great and Frederick Barbarossa. Indeed at the hands of the egregious Parson Weems, Washington surpassed them all in virtue, in prowess, in dignity, in wisdom. Soon more sober historians were writing the history of the Revolution or collecting the papers and letters of the Founding Fathers.

In 1834 came the first volume of George Bancroft's massive *History of the United States*, every page rejoicing in freedom and democracy, every volume proclaiming the superiority of America to all other nations. Bancroft inaugurated —and for half a century presided over—the golden age of American historical writing. Soon William H. Prescott was re-creating the Inca and Aztec civilizations; soon John Motley was recounting the glorious story of the Dutch struggle for freedom against the Spaniards; soon young Francis Parkman made his historical debut with the *Conspiracy of Pontiac*, the first of a long series of volumes recording the struggle between Spain, France, and England for North America.

Bancroft, Prescott, and Motley were widely read, but it was not from their glowing pages that the average American got his sense of the past. It was rather from the poems of the beloved Longfellow, who threw a romantic aura over the Indians in his "Hiawatha" and over the expulsion of the Acadians in his "Evangeline," and who dramatized the American past in such poems as "Paul Revere's Ride," "The

Courtship of Miles Standish," and many others that entered into the mainstream of American memory. It was from Whittier, with such poems as "Skipper Ireson's Ride," "Snow-Bound," and other poetic re-creations of New England's past; it was from the stories and novels of Nathaniel Hawthorne; it was from the "readings" in Noah Webster's grammar, used for fifty years in every schoolhouse in the country, or the many *Readers* put out by the indefatigable McGuffey brothers; it was from the grandiloquent orations of Daniel Webster, who—legend had it—could outargue the devil himself and whose peroration to the Union, in his Reply to Senator Hayne, was a favorite recitation piece for half a century:

When my eyes shall be turned to behold for the last time the sun in heaven, may I not see him shining on the broken and dishonored fragments of a once glorious Union; on states dissevered, discordant, belligerent; on a land rent with civil feuds, or drenched, it may be, in fraternal blood! Let their last feeble and lingering glance rather behold the gorgeous ensign of the republic, now known and honored throughout the earth, still full high advanced, its arms and trophies streaming in their original lustre, not a stripe erased or polluted, not a single star obscured, bearing for its motto no such miserable interrogatory as, What is all this worth? nor those other words of delusion and folly, Liberty first, and Union afterward; but everywhere, spread all over the sea and over the land, and in every wind under the whole heavens, that other sentiment, dear to every true American heart—Liberty *and* Union, now and forever, one and inseparable!

The Arts

IN ART AND ARCHITECTURE, too, the new nation tried, somewhat self-consciously, to achieve something distinctively national, but without great success. Painting and sculpture remained derivative until well after the Civil War. The first generation of American artists painted by "the light of distant skies"—mostly English and Italian. The youthful Benjamin West had studied in Italy and settled in London even before the Revolution; his studio was the magnet for most of the younger painters of the new republic—Trumbull, Peale, Copley, and Stuart among them. Thereafter budding artists turned to Italy for inspiration and training—Washington Allston, for example, or Thomas Cole, who may be said to have brought romanticism to American painting and who prepared the way for the romanticism of that group of landscape painters known as the Hudson River School. Meantime there was another foreign interlude; for a brief time a school of painters trained at Düsseldorf, in Germany, indulged in orgies of romantic historical and landscape painting at the expense of the new nation: Leutze's "Washington Crossing the Delaware" belongs to this artistic vintage, and so too many of the landscapes of Albert Bierstadt, which helped fix in the American imagination the image of the West as romantic and wild. More nearly native were the paintings of American birds by the neglected genius John James Audubon; the wonderfully authentic Indian portraits by George Catlin and Alfred Jacob Miller; and the genre paintings of George Bingham and William Sidney Mount.

Circumstances were not propitious for the development of sculpture. The New World had neither schools nor teachers, stonecutters nor models. From the first, American sculptors headed for Italy to study under disciples of Canovar or under Thorwaldsen himself, and to learn to imitate these masters. Almost all of the early American sculptors were trained in Italy, and almost all of them persisted in the classical tradition long after it had gone out of fashion in Europe. There was Horatio Greenough, who was best known for his heroic half-draped Washington. There was Thomas Crawford, who did a vast equestrian Washington, and who immortalized many other Founding Fathers in marble, and crowned the Capitol in Washington with a colossal "Armed Liberty." There was Hiram Powers, whose nude "Greek Slave" was something of a scandal in America although it made a sensation when exhibited in the Crystal Palace in London, but whose real contribution was in busts of statesmen and men of letters. And there was William Wetmore Story, son of the great judge, who left a brilliant legal career in Boston to live the life of a sculptor, poet, and social lion in Rome and provided material for a novel by Hawthorne and a biography by Henry James, fame enough for any man.

Architecture, too, was derivative, though a new environment required, and new materials made possible, interesting variations on European styles. The New England town was as nearly perfect a unit as medieval walled cities like Avignon or Murat, at once comely and functional; architects and town planners have not been able to produce anything as satisfactory for the past century and a half. The Georgian style, better called Federal, was a modification of the prevailing English, inevitably smaller and more modest, and relying on wood rather than stone. In Samuel McIntire of Salem and Charles Bulfinch of Boston, New England developed two architects who were able to adapt the contemporary English styles of building and decoration to American needs. McIntire left his imprint on Salem much as Palladio did on Vicenza, while Bulfinch's monument was the Boston State House, whose golden dome Oliver Wendell Holmes regarded as the Hub of the Universe.

Three foreign-born architects—William Thornton, Stephen Hallet, and Benjamin Latrobe—were responsible for the national capitol, based of course on Roman models, and the White House, and with Thomas Jefferson, Latrobe was largely responsible for launching the "Greek Revival" which flourished throughout the country until well into the second quarter of the century and gave a distinctive character to the domestic architecture of the South.

Thomas Jefferson was, in his generation, the most imaginative and resourceful of American architects, the only one who combined landscape gardening with architecture in the great English tradition. He had fallen in love with the Maison Carrée at Nîmes and with the wonderful achievements of Palladio in Vicenza, and he undertook to adapt Greco-Roman and Palladian architecture to the needs of the new republic. Monticello, which he built atop a hill overlooking the Valley of Virginia, was modeled on Palladio's Villa Malcontenta—and then furnished with gadgets characteristically American. The University of Virginia, planned and built and landscaped by Jefferson when he was in his seventies, was—and probably still is—architecturally the most beautiful and harmonious group of buildings in the country.

Education

THE FOUNDING FATHERS knew that their experiment in self-government was without precedent, and they took it for granted that it could not succeed without an enlightened electorate. "Above all things," wrote Jefferson, "I hope the education of the common people will be attended to; convinced that on their good sense we may rely with the most security for the preservation of a due degree of liberty." And John Adams insisted on the necessity of "education for every class and rank of people down to the lowest and the poorest" in order to make sure that the nation would be well governed and united. Benjamin Rush in Pennsylvania, Noah Webster in Connecticut, Governor Clinton in New York, shared these views, and devoted their energies to advancing public and higher education in their communities. Thus Dr. Rush championed schools for girls, contributed greatly to medical education, advocated a national university, and was instrumental in the founding of Dickinson College. Thus Governor Clinton set up the University of the State of New York, and his son De Witt laid the foundations for the public school system of the state. Thus Noah Webster worked ceaselessly for public education, provided the schools with dictionaries, spellers, readers, and histories, and helped found Amherst College. Of all the Founding Fathers it was Jefferson who gave the most time and thought to education, and who made the most important contributions. He devised and tried to carry through a complete system of public education for all the children of Virginia; he was largely responsible for the enlightened provisions of the two western land ordinances for public education; he undertook a sweeping reform of the ancient College of William and Mary; he founded, and in large part stocked, the Library of Congress; he planned and built the University of Virginia, in its day the most progressive institution of its kind in the country.

If provision for public education was somewhat better than any to be found in western Europe at that time, it was still—by modern standards—woefully inadequate. In the New England states the legal requirements for elementary education were widely evaded, and many other states did not even bother with requirements. Yet there was far less illiteracy than in Britain or on the Continent, and most men could read the local newspaper, the almanac, and the Bible. Higher education was not as high as that available in Scotland or Germany or Italy at the time, but it was more easily available, and to proportionately larger numbers, and if colleges like William and Mary, Princeton, and Harvard seemed more like academies than like real universities, we may reflect that they produced such men as Jefferson, Madison, and John Adams.

Notwithstanding the liveliest interest in public education, state and local communities neglected it badly during the first generation of the republic. It was not really until the 1830's that things took a turn for the better, and public education received an impetus from outside—from Swiss and German educators who were revolutionizing education in their countries, and from the reformers who saw ignorance as a stumbling block to their program of moral and social amelioration. Not the first in the field, but easily the most effective, was Horace Mann of Massachusetts. Appointed commissioner of education in 1837, he enforced existing laws, improved the physical facilities and the intellectual standards of the schools, developed the first program of teacher training, and in twelve famous annual reports elaborated a philosophy of the place and function of public education in a democracy whose influence was felt in many parts of the globe. Only a little less important was the work of Henry Barnard of Connecticut, who did for that state and for Rhode Island what Mann had done for Massachusetts, who acquainted American schoolmen with educational developments abroad through the pages of his *American Journal of Education* and in 1867 became the first United States Commissioner of Education. Meantime in Pennsylvania young Thaddeus Stevens—fresh from Vermont—pushed through an act requiring public support for schools, New York State set up the first public high schools and supported the enlightened provisions of the Northwest Ordinance, and public education flourished all through the Old Northwest.

It was in the 1830's that American education first felt the impact of new ideas from abroad. That education was an active, and not a passive, process, that the young would learn better by observing and doing than by repeating lessons from a text, that the teacher was a guide and friend rather than a taskmaster, that the child had a life of his own and would develop at his own pace, that play and exercise were as important to the child as book learning—all of these ideas were first announced by Jean Jacques Rousseau, but put into practice by Pestalozzi in Switzerland and Froebel in Germany. They were ideas that appealed naturally to a democratic people, and to a people which had already acquired the habit of idealizing the young. Soon Bronson Alcott was trying out some of these ideas in his Temple School in Boston; soon Mrs. Carl Schurz and Elizabeth Peabody were setting up kindergartens in America, and Froebel was to say that only in America did his kindergarten fulfill its true purpose.

Progress in higher education was mostly quantitative. The nine colleges that had flourished during the colonial period increased to over twenty by the turn of the century, and thereafter seemed to increase at a geometrical ratio. Most of the colleges were small and poor, with inadequate resources, meager libraries, and teachers more admirable for their devotion than for their competence. But these colleges did what comparable institutions in Europe were not prepared to do: they took in almost all who knocked at their doors, they stressed moral training and civic responsibility, and they taught subjects that were useful as well as subjects that were intellectually respectable.

Three departures distinguished American higher education during the first half of the century. One was the growth of the state university, which was to be seen at its best in the new western states of Ohio and Michigan. Another was the advent of higher education for girls, ardently championed by Mary Lyon, Emma Willard, and Catherine Beecher, who succeeded in setting up the first women's colleges in the Western world. A third was the emancipation of higher education from the traditional requirement of Four Faculties, and the development of miscellaneous institutions to do the varied tasks that desperately wanted doing in this new democracy—an emancipation which reached its climax in the Morrill Act of 1862, which set aside public lands to support agricultural and engineering universities in every state.

CHAPTER 9

Jacksonian Democracy
Sweeps In

The Monroe Doctrine

THE "LITTLE WITHERED APPLEJOHN" James Madison gave
way in 1817 to tall, rawboned, awkward James Monroe, who
presented that not unusual combination, a commonplace man
with a highly distinguished public career. He had held one
position after another—senator, governor, minister to France
and England, Secretary of State—until he became President.
Though the era was rather one of bad feeling than good,
political parties were temporarily in abeyance. Monroe therefore had the distinction in 1821 of being reseated by all the
electoral votes except one, cast by a New Hampshire elector
who wished Washington alone to have the honor of unanim-
ity. Yet Monroe, who lacked magnetism, was never very
popular, and his wife, a stiff, reserved, handsome woman,
was liked far less than the vivacious Dolly Madison. Monroe's two exceptional qualities were his shrewd common
sense and strong will. As John Quincy Adams put it, he had
"a mind sound in its ultimate judgments, and firm in its final
conclusions."

The event of his administration which has given his name
immortality was his enunciation of the so-called Monroe
Doctrine. Two main ideas were bound up in this doctrine
which was actually but part of Monroe's annual message
to Congress for 1823. One was the idea of noncolonization,
an assertion that Europe should be forbidden to establish any

new dependencies in the Western Hemisphere. The other was the idea of nonintervention, a declaration that Europe must no longer interfere in the affairs of New World nations in such a way as to threaten their independence. These ideas arose from two distinct situations.

The first was called forth primarily by the claim of Russia to the territory south of Alaska, reaching down as far as the fifty-first parallel, a pretension which conflicted with American and British claims in the Pacific Northwest. The second was evoked by the threat which the reactionary Quadruple Alliance in Europe offered to the Latin American peoples just liberated by Bolívar and San Martín. The allied powers had taken steps to crush democratic movements in Spain and Italy. Holding a congress at Verona in 1822, they discussed sending forces across the ocean to South America in order to compel at least some of the weak new republics to return to Spanish allegiance. France would take the leading part in such an expedition and might obtain lands of her own.

On hearing the news the brilliant British Foreign Secretary, George Canning, was deeply alarmed. He suggested that the United States and Great Britain take concerted steps to block such intervention; and for a time the American government seemed likely to assent. Jefferson and Madison counseled Monroe in favor of joint action. But John Quincy Adams, as Secretary of State, rightly insisted that the United States ought to move alone, and Monroe finally swung to this view. In his message to Congress he declared, first, that the American continents "are henceforth not to be considered as subjects for future colonization by any European powers"; and, second, that any European interposition "for the purpose of oppressing" the Latin American states, "or controlling in any other manner their destiny," would be treated as evidence of unfriendliness toward the United States. Thus was set up a great landmark in our foreign policy, destined to endure for more than a century.

The Missouri Compromise

ALTHOUGH it had thus far received little public attention, slavery had rapidly been growing into a great power, and in

1819, with startling suddenness—"like a fire bell in the night," wrote Jefferson—it burst upon the public attention. In the early years of the republic, when the Northern states were providing for immediate or gradual emancipation, many leaders had supposed that slavery would presently die out everywhere. Washington wrote Lafayette in 1786 that he devoutly wished that some plan might be adopted "by which slavery may be abolished by slow, sure, and imperceptible degrees," and in his will he emancipated his slaves. Jefferson held that slavery ought to be wiped out by a combination of emancipation and deportation. "I tremble for my country," he declared, "when I reflect that God is just." Patrick Henry, Madison, Monroe, and many others made similar utterances. As late as 1808, when the slave trade was abolished, numerous Southerners thought that slavery would prove but a temporary evil.

But during the next generation the South was converted into a section which for the most part was grimly united behind slavery. How did this come about? Why did the abolitionist spirit in the South almost disappear? For one reason, the spirit of philosophical liberalism which flamed high in Revolutionary days gradually became weaker. For another reason, a general antagonism between puritanical New England and the slaveholding South became evident; they differed on the War of 1812, the tariff, and other great issues; and the South felt less and less liking for the so-called Northern idea of emancipation. But above all, new economic factors made slavery far more profitable than it had been before 1790, and what was originally regarded as a necessary evil became so necessary that it ceased to be an evil.

One element in the economic change is familiar—the rise of a great cotton-growing industry in the South. This was based in part on the introduction of improved types of cotton, with better fibers, but in much larger part on Eli Whitney's epochal invention in 1793 of the "gin" for cleaning cotton. Cotton culture rapidly moved westward from the Carolinas and Georgia, spreading over much of the lower South to the Mississippi River and, eventually, on into Texas. Another factor which placed slavery upon a new basis was sugar growing. The rich, hot delta lands of southeastern Louisiana are ideal for sugar cane; and in 1794–1795 an enterprising New Orleans Creole, Étienne Boré, proved that the crop could be highly profitable. He set up machinery and vats, and the crowds which had come from New Orleans to watch the boiling-off broke into cheers when the first sugar crystals showed in the cooling liquid. The cry "It granulates!" opened a new era in Louisiana. A great boom resulted, so that by 1830 the state was supplying about half of the nation's sugar supply. This required slaves, who were brought, in thousands, from the Eastern seaboard.

Finally, tobacco culture also spread westward and took slavery with it. Constant cropping had worn out the soil of lowland Virginia, once the greatest tobacco region in the world, and the growers were glad to move into Kentucky and Tennessee, taking their Negroes with them. Thereafter the fast-multiplying slaves of the upper South were largely drained off to the lower South and West. This diffusion of slavery relieved many observers, because it lessened the risk of such a slave insurrection as Nat Turner's Rebellion, a revolt of sixty or seventy Virginia slaves in 1831—which, incidentally, did much to increase Southern fear of emancipationist doctrines.

As the free society of the North and the slave society of the South spread westward, it seemed desirable to maintain a rough equality between them. In 1818, when Illinois was admitted to the Union, there were ten slave and eleven free states. In 1819 both Alabama and Missouri applied for admission. Now Alabama by the terms of Georgia's original land cession had to be a slave state, and its admission would restore the balance between slave and free. But many Northerners at once rallied to oppose the entry of Missouri except as a free state. Representative Tallmadge of New York introduced an amendment to the admission bill requiring Missouri to adopt gradual emancipation. A terrific storm swept over the country. For a time Congress, with the free-soil men controlling the House, the slavery men controlling the Senate, was at a complete deadlock. Men even feared bloodshed.

Then, under the pacific leadership of Henry Clay, a compromise was arranged. Missouri was admitted as a slave state, but at the same time Maine was cut loose from Massachusetts and came in as a free state; and Congress decreed that slavery should be forever excluded from the territory acquired by the Louisiana Purchase north of the parallel 36° 30', the southern boundary of Missouri. The skies became sunny again. But every farsighted observer knew that the storm would recur. Jefferson wrote that this fire bell in the night had seemed to him the knell of the Union. "It is hushed, indeed, for the moment. But this is a reprieve only, not a final sentence. A geographical line, coinciding with a marked principle, moral and political, once conceived and held up to the angry passions of men, will never be obliterated; and every new irritation will mark it deeper and deeper."

Two clouds no bigger than a man's hand might have announced to the South the impending tempest. In 1821 a young Quaker named Benjamin Lundy founded in Ohio an antislavery journal called *The Genius of Universal Emancipation*. In 1823 the English reformer, Wilberforce, established an antislavery society which was joined by Zachary Macaulay and other men of note.

The Emergence of Jackson

THE YEAR 1824 found five important candidates for the presidency before the country. Of these five, John Quincy Adams, Clay, and Calhoun were all men of consummate ability, and W. H. Crawford of Georgia was a most astute politician. But beyond question the most popular aspirant was the fifth, Andrew Jackson. Western admirers of the hero of New Orleans regarded him as the greatest living soldier. Some thought that Caesar, Napoleon, and Marlborough were nobodies compared with him. In the East many conservative men distrusted him. They recalled with Jefferson that in the Senate debates he used to choke with rage until he could not speak; they remembered how impetuously as a military commander he had invaded Spanish Florida and how highhandedly he had hanged two Scotsmen there. Adams thought he would make an ideal Vice-President. It would be a dignified office for him; his fame would restore its luster; and there would be no danger that he would hang anybody!

But the election showed Jackson well ahead in the popular vote. No man had a majority of the electoral college, however, and the choice went to the House, which finally selected the learned, experienced, and statesmanlike, but stubbornly untractable, Adams.

Adams entered office with two great national achievements to his credit: for the Monroe Doctrine was primarily his work, while it was he who in 1819 had pushed the Spanish government into a treaty which ceded Florida to the United States. He was a man of extraordinary talents, fine character, and great public spirit, but handicapped by his icy austerity, brusque manners, and violent prejudices. As President he was able to accomplish little, for the virulent hostility of the Jacksonians—who charged that he had reached the White House by a corrupt bargain whereby he received Clay's electoral votes and in return appointed Clay Secretary of State—thwarted him at every turn. Party antagonism has seldom risen higher than in these years. The caustic John Randolph of Roanoke, with a reference to Fielding's *Tom Jones*, spoke of Adams and Clay as "the coalition of Blifil and Black George—the combination, unheard of till then, of the Puritan with the Blackleg." Adams was provoked by such assaults to write in his diary: "The skunks of party slander have been squirting around the House of Representatives, thence to issue and perfume the atmosphere of the Union." He called Randolph "a frequenter of gin lane and beer alley."

During the administration new alignments took shape, the followers of Adams and Clay assuming the name of National Republicans, later to be replaced by that of Whigs, and the Jacksonians giving a new character to the Democratic party. Adams governed honestly and efficiently and strove in vain to institute a national system of internal improvements. His untiring industry is well described in a paragraph of his diary:

The life that I lead is more regular than it has perhaps been at any other period. It is established by custom that the President of the United States goes not abroad into any private companies; and to this usage I conform. I am, therefore, compelled to take my exercise, if at all, in the morning before breakfast. I rise usually between five and six; that is, at this time of year, from an hour and a half to two hours before the sun. I walk by the light of moon or stars, or none, about four miles, usually returning here in time to see the sun rise from the eastern chamber of the [White] House. I then make my fire, and read three chapters of the Bible, with Scott's and Hewlett's Commen-

taries. Read papers till nine. Breakfast, and from nine till five
P.M. receive a succession of visitors, sometimes without intermission—very seldom with an interval of half an hour—never such
as to enable me to undertake any business requiring attention.
From five to half-past six we dine; after which I pass about four
hours in my chamber alone, writing in this diary, or reading papers upon some public business.

The election of 1828 was like an earthquake, the Jacksonians overwhelming Adams and his supporters. So bitter
had feeling become that on arriving in Washington, President-elect Jackson refused to pay the usual visit of respect
to the President, while Adams declined to ride to the Capitol
with his successor.

Jackson's inauguration has long been regarded as opening a new era in American life. It was such an inauguration
as the country had never before witnessed. Washington observers compared it with the invasion of Rome by the bar-
barians. Daniel Webster wrote several days before that the
city was full of speculators, office hunters, triumphant politicians, and plain Westerners and Southerners. People had
come five hundred miles to see their hero made President
and they talked as if the country had been rescued from
some awful danger. As they surged through the streets shouting "Hurrah for Jackson!" many were so boisterous that gentlemen shrank from them. One observer has left a graphic
record:

On the morning of the inauguration, the vicinity of the Capitol
was like a great, agitated sea; every avenue to the fateful spot
was blocked up with people, insomuch that the legitimate procession which accompanied the President-elect could scarce make
its way to the eastern portico, where the ceremony was to be
performed. To repress the crowd in front, a ship's cable was
stretched across about two-thirds of the way up the long flight of
steps by which the Capitol is approached on that side, but it
seemed at times as if even this would scarce prove sufficient to
restrain the eagerness of the multitude, every man of whom
seemed bent on the glory of shaking the President's hand. Never
can I forget the spectacle which presented itself on every side, nor
the electrifying moment when the eager, expectant eyes of that vast
and motley multitude caught sight of the tall and imposing form
of their adored leader, as he came forth between the columns of

the portico; the color of the whole mass changed as if by a miracle; all hats were off at once, and the dark tint which usually pervades a mixed map of men was turned, as by a magic wand, into the bright hue of ten thousand upturned and exultant faces, radiant with sudden joy. The peal of shouting that arose rent the air and seemed to shake the very ground.

But the most characteristic scene of the day was that which followed the ceremony. The motley concourse of enthusiastic Democrats made a rush for the White House. Everyone knew that refreshments were to be distributed there; everybody wanted to see the new President at home. Barrels of orange punch stood ready, but the crowd upset the waiters with pails and glasses. They forced Jackson against the wall, so that his friends had to link arms to protect him. They stood in muddy boots on the satin-covered furniture. "I never saw such a mixture," wrote Justice Story. "The reign of King Mob seemed triumphant."

Jackson's Ideas

JACKSON was one of the few Presidents whose heart and soul were completely with the plain people. He sympathized with and believed in them partly because he had always been one of them. He had been born in utter poverty. His father, a poor Ulster-Scots linen draper, who had come to the woods of North Carolina and cleared a farm, died while Andrew was still unborn; the family was unable to buy him even a headstone. His mother became a poor-relation housekeeper to a brother-in-law. The boy, reared in hardship and insecurity, dressed in the cheapest linsey-woolsey, and subject to a nervous disease, was probably humiliated again and again. A childhood sense of inferiority may help to explain his explosive temper, his keen sensitiveness, and his lifelong sympathy with the oppressed. As a mere lad, he fought in the Revolution, which cost the lives of two brothers, and which instilled in him a lasting distrust of the British.

Jackson also imbibed, partly from his Western frontier environment and partly from unfortunate personal experiences, an intense distrust of Eastern capitalistic organizations. After studying law, he went to Tennessee, where he tried to push forward in the world. He bought and sold land, traded in horses and slaves, and for a time owned a general store. A lawyer almost had to be a trader in that area, for he received many fees in bearskins, beeswax, leather, cotton, and land. In 1798 Jackson bought nearly $7000 worth of goods in Philadelphia, selling land to pay for them to a merchant whose notes (endorsed by Jackson) presently went to protest. This saddled him with a heavy debt, and he paid it with a feeling that somehow the financial system of the East had victimized him. He had not gambled; he had simply taken some of the paper circulating among Philadelphia merchants, and when the fog blew away the merchants had his land and his cash.

Moreover, as a frontier lawyer, planter, and merchant Jackson learned that the East exercised absolute sway over much Western commerce. He had to sell his cotton, corn, and hogs down the river in New Orleans; he had to buy general merchandise for his Nashville store in Philadelphia. In both cities the markets kept fluctuating. He might send his orders to Philadelphia and find that prices of goods there had risen to a ruinous level. He might send his produce down the Mississippi and find the bottom had fallen out of the market. At both ends of the line the men who controlled credit grew fat, while Jackson and his neighbors had difficulty in making both ends meet. From this fact grew a distrust and hatred of banks—the same distrust that has always marked the West. The money power, Jackson believed, was paid too much for its services. It was monstrous that easy-living bankers in Philadelphia and New York should have power to ruin the hard-working people of Tennessee.

In the third place, Jackson had the Western faith that the common man is capable of uncommon achievement. Westerners believed that an upstanding man who could command a militia company, run a plantation, and make a good stump speech was fitted for almost any office. They did not believe for a minute that the great prizes of public life were reserved for the rich, the well born, and the educated. The coon hunter had as good a right to them as the Harvard graduate. They had some reason for this view. In Tennessee the Indian fighter Jackson, whose wife smoked a corncob pipe and who spelled Europe "Urope," got a training that made him a great national leader. In Illinois was growing up a lanky rail splitter who was totally ignorant of drawing-room manners and Latin conjugations, but who was destined to save the Union. Jackson had seen the backwoodsmen whip Wellington's veterans. He had seen self-made men like Benton and Clay dominate the national Congress. He knew the tremendous energy of the West and its strength of character.

Altogether, Jackson's main creed can be summed up in a few phrases: faith in the common man; belief in political equality; belief in equal economic opportunity; hatred of monopoly, special privilege, and the intricacies of capitalistic finance.

Two principal elements could be distinguished in the heterogeneous Democratic party supporting Jackson. Much the largest was composed of the agrarian voters of the nation, the pioneers, farmers, small planters, and country shopkeepers. The trans-Allegheny West, which by 1830 had roughly one third of the population, was marked by special characteristics. It was highly nationalistic in feeling; the new areas had less state feeling, more attachment to the Union, than the thirteen original states. In the West, moreover, political equality was taken for granted. Almost every adult white male there was eligible to vote and to hold office. Restrictions on suffrage long survived in the East, and the movement to abolish them was denounced with horror by such conservatives as Webster in Massachusetts, Chancellor James Kent in New York, and John Marshall in Virginia. But Alabama and Missouri, Indiana and Illinois, gave every white man the vote.

The West, again, liked a direct form of democracy. Jackson's followers attacked the old method of nominating presidential candidates by Congressional caucus and supported the new method of direct nominating conventions, which became firmly established in 1836. They preferred elected judges to appointed judges. Finally, the agrarian voters of the West were interested in a new set of political demands. They disliked banking institutions under Eastern control; they favored the debtor as against the creditor; and they hated anything like monopoly, from steamboat and bank charters to patent rights. They wanted the right to buy public lands cheap and on easy terms.

The other prominent element in the Jacksonian democracy was the mass of toilers in Eastern towns and cities. Stimulated by the Embargo, the War of 1812, and the protective tariff, factories were beginning to grow important in New England and the Middle States. The Merrimack Valley and the region around Providence became thriving textile centers. Lowell in Massachusetts had about five thousand factory hands in 1830. By that year a great part of New York's two hundred thousand people were workers in the factories and shipyards. Most immigrants—English, Irish, German—found the Democratic party more congenial than the Whig. The new working classes converted New York from a Federalist to a Democratic city with a rush and made Philadelphia and Pittsburgh centers of Jacksonian sentiment. They formed many unions (at first usually called trade associations) in this Jacksonian period, and under such leaders as the fiery William Leggett fiercely assailed the reactionary courts which punished strikes under the old conspiracy laws. They warmly applauded Jackson when in 1836 he established the ten-hour day (for the Massachusetts factories then worked men twelve or fourteen hours daily for five dollars a week) in the national shipyards.

Jackson's Measures

ONCE IN POWER, Jackson vigorously carried his main ideas into practice. Objecting to the way in which Congress was voting money for local roads and canals, he sharply checked these raids on the treasury by his "Maysville veto" —disapproving a road from Maysville to Lexington in Kentucky. He dealt sternly with South Carolina when it attempted to nullify the protective tariff of 1828. At a Jefferson Day banquet in 1830 he looked the South Carolina leader, Calhoun, squarely in the eye as he gave an immortal toast: "Our Union—it must be preserved." When South Carolina continued on her willful course, he showed in 1832 that he meant business by sending General Scott and a naval force to Charleston and by issuing a proclamation in which he declared that "disunion by armed force is treason." He was ready to hang Calhoun if necessary, and in later years regretted that he had not. Daniel Webster, in a masterly speech, overwhelmed South Carolina's principal champion in the Senate, Robert Y. Hayne; and his peroration, "Liberty and Union, now and forever, one and inseparable!" became a national rallying cry. Fortunately, South Carolina, unable to unite the South, gave up nullification as Clay, always a friend of peace, arranged a compromise in the reduction in the tariff.

Jackson fought a desperate and successful battle with the second Bank of the United States, overthrowing that citadel of Eastern finance and monopolistic power. Its head, the dexterous Nicholas Biddle, was supported by Henry Clay and the Whigs. On the whole, the bank had been well conducted and had rendered valuable services to the nation. But Jackson, disliking a centralized money power, in 1832 sternly vetoed a bill for its recharter. The next year, removing the government deposits from the bank, he placed them with leading state banks, so that these would be able to take over the functions of the central institution. Beyond question the bank had meddled with politics; beyond question it was also a private monopoly which had unduly enriched a small group of insiders. Public sentiment was behind Jackson, and though he had to fight hard to bring his whole party behind him, he killed Nick Biddle's great bank.

In other matters also the President acted with stern decision. When France suspended payment on certain obligations to the United States, he recommended the seizure of French property and brought her to terms. He roughly removed the Indians from Georgia, and brushed aside an attempt by the Supreme Court to intervene on behalf of the helpless natives. But when Texas revolted against Mexico and appealed to the United States for annexation, he wisely took a waiting attitude. To the end of his second term he retained his vast popularity.

Other Democratic Tendencies

THE GREAT NEW DEMOCRATIC WAVE which surged forward in Jackson's day involved masses of the population which Jeffersonian democracy had not touched. The thirties were the decade in which manhood suffrage spread through most of those states which had hitherto imposed some property restriction. And manhood suffrage meant an increased interest in national affairs. In 1824 the aggregate vote cast in the presidential election was only 356,000; in 1836 it rose to 1,500,000; and in 1840 the vote was 2,400,000—seven times as much as only sixteen years earlier. While part of this increase resulted from the growth of population, most of it could be traced to the unshackling of the ballot and the mounting interest in politics. Presidential electors ceased (except in South Carolina) to be chosen by the legislatures, and were elected by popular vote. In national affairs a more rapid rotation in office became the rule. Jackson, frankly announcing his belief in this, displaced many political opponents. Though he made fewer removals than later Presidents, he accepted the rule defined by William L. Marcy of New York: "To the victors belong the spoils."

Manners were becoming more democratic, less formal and punctilious. Foreign observers were shocked by the general tobacco spitting, the rapid feeding at table, the impertinent curiosity, the widespread bumptiousness and bragging, and the nervous hurry of the Northern cities. American culture was stamped also by recklessness and violence. As was natural in a fast-developing country, the job in hand seemed more important than human life. Steamboats and railroads paid little attention to safety. Dueling had become common, and in the South and West, family feuds, marked by free use of the bowie knife and pistol, were frequent. In areas where courts and law officers were undependable, lynching naturally took root. When William Henry Harrison was elected President by the Whigs in 1840, the party had to pretend that this educated and moderately wealthy man, living as a country gentleman on his two thousand acres near Cincinnati, was really a rough pioneer who had dwelt in a log cabin, drinking hard cider. Yet actually the average level of manners was not lower than in the early days of the republic. They were worse than the manners of the aristocracy had then been; but they were better than the manners of the ignorant and brutish workingmen. The old cleavage so sharply visible between the good deportment of the gentry and the wretched deportment of the "mob" had been largely obliterated.

Life was growing more democratic in many ways. A cheap press was arising. Imitating the penny papers of London,

Benjamin Day in 1833 launched the New York *Sun* at popular prices, while two years later James Gordon Bennett achieved a more spectacular success by founding the sensational New York *Herald*. The first popular magazine also appeared in the Jacksonian era, for *Godey's Lady's Book* was established in Philadelphia in 1830; while the first widely read literary monthly, the *Knickerbocker*, emerged three years later. In education a tremendous battle was being fought for free public schools, nonsectarian, publicly controlled, and tax supported. In this struggle Horace Mann of Massachusetts took the lead. It was a much fiercer battle, in fact, than later generations would suppose. On the one side were ranged democratic and humanitarian men, intelligent workers, Calvinists, and Unitarians; on the other side stood men of aristocratic views, penurious conservatives, the Lutheran, Catholic, and Quaker supporters of parochial schools, many planters and farmers, and teachers in private schools. After bitter fighting, one by one the states were forced into line. A New Englander declaimed, "Reading rots the mind"; an Indianian asked to have inscribed on his tombstone, "Here lies an enemy to free schools." But laws permitting any county or town to levy a tax for free public schools were followed in the Middle States and the West by laws compelling local units to do so.

Even religion, as it followed the frontier westward, became democratized. The sects which flourished most in the West were the Baptists, the Methodists, the Campbellites, and the Presbyterians, all of which were democratic in their form of government and grew more so. The first three sects in particular emphasized two religious elements which the frontier liked: an appeal to the emotions, with much shouting, singing, and fervent prayer; and the idea of personal conversion, which led to enthusiastic revivals and uproarious camp meetings of the kind described in Mark Twain's *Huckleberry Finn*. Literature, too, revealed democratic tendencies. Bryant, Fenimore Cooper, and Washington Irving were all ardent supporters of Jackson. Cooper's books on Eastern society, and Irving's volumes on the Far West, alike stressed democratic ideas. Popular works like David Crockett's *Autobiography* (1834) and Augustus B. Longstreet's *Georgia Scenes* (1835) revealed the influence of the frontier.

The first volume of George Bancroft's *History of the United States* unmistakably "voted for Jackson."

The Age of Reform

"IN THE HISTORY OF THE WORLD, the doctrine of Reform had never such scope as at the present hour," wrote Emerson in 1841. All previous reformers had respected some institutions—the church or the state, or history or tradition. "But now all these and all things else hear the trumpet and must rush to judgment—Christianity, the laws, commerce, schools, the farm, the laboratory; and not a kingdom, town, statute, rite, calling, man, or woman, but is threatened by this new spirit." It was indeed the day of infinite discontent and of infinite hope. "A restless, prying, conscientious criticism broke out in the most unexpected quarter"—it is Emerson again. "Am I not too protected a person? Is there not a wide disparity between the lot of me and the lot of thee, my poor brother, my poor sister?" Every man you met on the streets of Boston—for the reform movement had its capital there—might pull out from his waistcoat pocket some petition, some protest, some call for a convention, some plan for a utopia, for "we are to revise the whole of our social structure, the state, the school, religion, marriage, trade, science, and explore the foundations of our own nature." And that is just what the reformers did.

The reform movement of this middle period was, to an astonishing degree, the product of a philosophy—the philosophy of Transcendentalism. That philosophy, to which almost all the reformers subscribed with varying degrees of commitment, had come originally from Germany, via Coleridge in England, but in America it suffered a sea change. It held that men must acknowledge a body of moral truths, that these truths were intuitive, subjective, and a priori, and thus that they *transcended* more sensational proof. Thus it instinctively—and logically—rejected all secular authority —the authority of the church or the Scriptures, of the state, or law, or convention—unless that authority could be squared with those truths which God had planted in the mind and heart of man. The most important of these great intuitive truths were—as the "Great American Preacher," Theodore

Parker, put it—the infinite benevolence of God, the infinite beneficence of Nature, and the divinity of man.

Now if these concepts were true—and who could challenge them as long as they were intuitive?—it followed that any departure from them was contrary to God and to Nature. If man was divine, it was wicked that he should be held in slavery, his soul corrupted by superstition, or his mind clouded by ignorance. Let us then restore men to that divinity with which God endowed them. Let us give freedom to the slave, well-being to the poor and the miserable, learning to the ignorant, health to the sick; let us give peace and justice to society. As Emerson put it: "The power which is at once spring and regulator in all efforts of reform is the conviction that there is an infinite worthiness in man, which appears at the call of worth, and that all practical reforms are the removing of some impediment."

And that is what the reformers set themselves to do, with an energy, a dedication, a passion—almost a fanaticism—that has no parallel in our history: to remove impediments. Superstition was an impediment, and led by clergymen like Emerson, Theodore Parker, William Ellery Channing, and George Ripley, they tried to rid the church of dogma and ritual and return to the great principles of morality that were to be found in the hearts of men. Ignorance was an impediment, and Horace Mann and Henry Barnard set themselves to create a true system of public schools, while Mary Lyon and Catherine Beecher addressed themselves to the problem of the education of girls. Poverty was an impediment, and the intellectuals joined forces with labor to improve the condition of the "dangerous and perishing classes of society," and of the working men and women in factories and mills, and to protect helpless women and children from the rush of the industrial revolution. Property was an impediment, and two-score utopias did away with private property altogether, while other reformers concentrated on the more sensible solution of a wider distribution of land. The subjection of women was an impediment, and a dozen reformers—Theodore Parker, Wendell Phillips, Thomas Wentworth Higginson among them—joined forces with intrepid women to campaign for women's rights before the law, in politics, and in the professions and the schools. The thoughtless inhumanity of man to man was an impediment, and Dorothea

Dix led a crusade on behalf of the insane, the "Chevalier" Howe started up the Perkins Institution for the blind, Thomas Gallaudet established a school for the deaf, Edward Livingston called for a reform of the penal code, Charles Loring Brace dramatized the tragic lot of urchins in the streets of the great cities, and Neal Dow fought "Demon Rum." War was an impediment, and men like Elihu Burritt and William Ladd worked out schemes of universal peace, while William Lloyd Garrison championed non-resistance and Charles Sumner announced that there was no war that was honorable, no peace that was dishonorable. The state was an impediment, and while some attempted to withdraw altogether into private utopias, others set about to limit the authority of the state by higher law or to counsel—with Thoreau—the doctrine of civil disobedience. Slavery was the greatest of all impediments, and in the end almost all the forces of reform movements were absorbed in the crusade against slavery.

"What is Man born for, but to be a Reformer, a Remaker of what man has made, a renouncer of lies, a restorer of truth and good?" So asked Emerson at the beginning of the era of reform. And when, with the Civil War, that era drew to a close and materialism took over, the great editor-reformer Horace Greeley looked back upon it and concluded that "though the life of the Reformer may seem rugged and arduous, it were hard to say that any other was worth living at all. . . . Not to have been a Reformer is not to have truly lived."

CHAPTER 10

The West and Democracy

The Moving Frontier

ONE OF THE FORCES which did most to shape American life from the beginning was the frontier, which may be defined as the border area whose sparse population (not more than six to the square mile) was engaged chiefly in clearing and breaking land and building homes. Moving across the continent as population advanced from the Atlantic to the edge of the Great Plains, it profoundly affected the American character. It was more than a line—it was a social process. It encouraged individual initiative; it made for political and economic democracy; it roughened manners; it broke down conservatism; it bred a spirit of local self-determination coupled with respect for national authority.

When we think of the frontier we think of the West. But the Atlantic coastal strip was the first frontier and long contained frontier areas; Maine, which drew forty thousand settlers from older New England in 1790–1800, was frontier country for a generation after the Revolution. The second frontier was the region about the headwaters of the coastal rivers and just over the Appalachians. The close of the Revolution found the border in western New York, where two capitalists in 1787 obtained title to six million acres of wild lands; in the Wyoming Valley of Pennsylvania, where Connecticut settlers established homes; about Pittsburgh, which in 1792 had 130 families and "36 Mechanics"; in the eastern Tennessee area, where in 1784 independent-minded pioneers organized the short-lived "State of Frank-

175

lin"; and in upland Georgia. Then by 1800 the Mississippi and Ohio valleys were becoming a third great frontier region. "Hi-o, away we go, Floating down the river on the O-hi-o," became the song of thousands of emigrants. In the spring after the writing of the Constitution, Rufus Putnam had taken the first emigrants westward to found Marietta on the northern bank of the Ohio, thus opening an area of about two million acres transferred by Congress to the Ohio Company. That same year another group of land speculators founded Cincinnati. Population was meanwhile pouring into Kentucky and Tennessee with startling rapidity. The first year after peace, ten thousand settlers entered Kentucky; and the first national census in 1790 gave it and Tennessee together a population of over a hundred thousand.

Without pause the westward stream flowed over the whole Northwest and Southwest. By 1796 Kentucky and Tennessee were full-fledged states, and Ohio, with a belt of settled lands along the Pennsylvania border and Ohio River, was about to become one; by 1820 Indiana and Illinois, in the Northwest, Louisiana, Alabama, and Mississippi in the Southwest, were all states. The first frontier had been tied closely to Europe; the second was tied to the coast settlements; but the Mississippi Valley was independent, and its people looked West rather than East.

The Frontier Settlers

NATURALLY the frontier settlers were a varied body of men, but early observers distinguish three main groups. In the van of emigration marched the hunter or trapper. An English traveler named Fordham pithily described the wilder sort of pioneer, usually unmarried:

A daring, hardy race of men, who live in miserable cabins, which they fortify in time of war with the Indians, whom they hate but much resemble in dress and manners. They are unpolished but hospitable, kind to strangers, honest and trustworthy. They raise a little Indian corn, pumpkins, hogs, and sometimes have a cow or two, and two or three horses belonging to each family. But the rifle is their principal means of support.

When they heard the sound of a neighbor's gun, it was time to move on. Fenimore Cooper has given a good picture of the pioneer hunter in Natty Bumppo, and of the backwoods life in *The Prairie*. These men were dexterous with the ax, rifle, snare, and fishing line; they blazed the trails, built the first log cabins, held back the Indians, and so made way for a second group.

This second body Fordham describes as the first true settlers, "a mixed set of hunters and farmers." Instead of a cabin, they built a "log house," which had glass windows, a good chimney, and partitioned rooms, and was as comfortable as any English farm cottage; instead of using a spring they sank a well. An industrious man would rapidly clear land of timber, burning the wood for potash and letting the stumps decay. Growing his own grain, vegetables and fruit, ranging the woods for venison, wild turkeys, and honey, fishing the nearest streams, looking after some cattle and hogs, he would worry little over the loneliness and roughness of his life. The more enterprising bought large tracts of the cheap land on the theory that it was wise, as a character in Edward Eggleston's *Hoosier Schoolmaster* put it, to "git a plenty while you're agittin' "; then, as land values rose, they sold their acres and moved westward. Thus they gave way to the third group, the most important of all.

The third body included not only farmers, but also doctors, lawyers, storekeepers, editors, preachers, mechanics, politicians, and land speculators—all the materials to furnish the fabric of a vigorous society. The farmers were the most important. They intended to stay all their lives where they settled and hoped their children would stay after them. They built larger barns than their predecessors and then sounder brick or frame houses. They constructed better fences, brought in improved livestock, plowed the land more skillfully, and sowed more productive seed. Some of them erected flour mills, sawmills, or distilleries. They laid out good highways, built churches and schools. As towns grew up, many of this third group, as bankers, merchants, or land dealers, became men of wealth. In short, they represented the more enduring forces in American civilization. So rapidly did the West grow that almost incredible transformations were accomplished within a few years by this third wave. Chicago in 1830 was merely an unpromising trading village with a fort; before some of its first settlers died it was one of the largest and richest cities in the world.

Many different peoples mingled their blood in the new West. Farmers of the upland South were prominent, and from this stock sprang Abraham Lincoln and Jefferson Davis, born in Kentucky log cabins in the same year. Hardheaded Scotch-Irish, thrifty Pennsylvania Germans, enterprising Yankees, and men of other origins played their part. All these people had two traits in common—individualism and democracy. By 1830 more than half the Americans had been brought up in an environment in which Old World traditions and conventions were absent or very weak. Men in the West had to stand on their own feet. They were valued not for family, inherited money, or years of schooling, but, like the castaways in Barrie's *The Admirable Crichton,* for what they could do. People could get farms for a price not beyond reach of any thrifty person; government land after 1820, as we have seen, could be obtained for $1.25 an acre, and after 1862 for merely settling on it. They could easily get the tools to work it. Then, as Horace Greeley said, they could "grow up with the country." This equality of economic opportunity bred a sense of social and political equality and gave natural leaders a chance to come quickly to the front. It should be added that the sea was practically another frontier in its effect upon American character. Vessels were small and had small crews, while many fishing ships and whalers were worked on a partnership basis. Initiative, courage, individual vigor, and hard sense were the requirements of a good pioneer hunter, frontier farmer, or Eastern sailor alike.

Frontier Virtues and Vices

BY CONTAGION and example this democracy and individualism became marked traits in the cities of the young republic. The upright independence that the Englishman William Cobbett lauded immediately struck European visitors to New York and Philadelphia. These observers noted that workmen did not tip their hats and say "sir" to earn a shilling. The very porters accepted a job with the attitude of men conferring a favor. Cobbett mentioned approvingly that

American servants wore no livery and usually ate with the family and were called "help." He saw only two beggars in America, and both were foreigners. One of Ralph Waldo Emerson's most truly American essays is that on "Self-Reliance." He speaks of the typical Yankee of the day who, going West, was by turns farmer, storekeeper, land dealer, lawyer, Congressman, and judge, a jack-of-all-trades, always landing on his feet. It was not an overdrawn portrait. One of the ablest Civil War generals, W. T. Sherman, was in turn cadet, soldier in the Mexican War, banker in San Francisco, lawyer in Leavenworth, farm manager on the Kansas frontier, head of a military college in Louisiana, and then soldier again.

But if the frontier fostered virtues, it also bred vices. The frontier folk were in general unruly, impatient of discipline, and too aggressively self-confident—too "brash." Many of the military defeats of the War of 1812 were attributable to a frontier dislike of training and discipline. Frontier-trained Americans were inclined to do everything with hurried crudity. So many tasks needed performing that careful finish seemed a waste of time. Americans hurried up rough frame houses instead of durable stone and brick structures, they built rough roads, they made makeshift bridges, they gutted rather than cultivated the soil. New York had fire bells clanging all night because its houses burned like tinder, while in 1836 two of the city's largest business buildings actually collapsed. Railroad collisions and steamboat explosions were frequent. Naturally, little attention was paid to manners or culture; the frontier had no leisure for them. And worst of all, frontier life was marked by a deplorable amount of outright criminality. Some of the scum of society swirled out to the border. Men developed ungovernable tempers and had a taste for settling their quarrels with fists or pistols. Officers of justice had to possess iron nerve and a quick trigger finger.

The Indian Wars

THE UNDISCIPLINED CHARACTER of the frontiersmen had especially tragic consequences in their dealings with the Indians. They constantly encroached on Indian lands in defiance of treaty; they destroyed the game on which the Indians depended for food and clothing; and many were ready to slay any redskin on sight. When the Indians tried to defend themselves, war ensued. Of course, the savages were often aggressors, but the inexorable westward thrust of the whites was the principal cause of the many conflicts. The most bloodcurdling wars were with the Creeks in the South, where Andrew Jackson won a bloody victory; with the Seminoles in the Florida swamps and thickets; and with Tecumseh's followers in Indiana.

Young Abraham Lincoln was a captain in the Black Hawk War, an especially brutal affair. Some spokesmen for Black Hawk's tribe, the Sauk and Fox Indians, had ceded to the government their title to about fifty million acres. The chief and a great part of the tribe denied the validity of this cession. Before a threat of force Black Hawk withdrew from his corn lands in Illinois to the west bank of the Mississippi. But his tribe suffered from hunger, and next spring they recrossed the river in order to join the friendly Winnebagos in Wisconsin and raise corn there. They had a childlike faith that their amicable intentions would be understood. But the whites immediately attacked them; Black Hawk retreated, making offers of peace, which the two thousand militia ignored. His despairing followers were driven through southern Wisconsin to the Mississippi again, where men, women, and children were mercilessly cut to pieces as they tried to cross. "It was a horrid sight," wrote one rifleman, "to witness little children, wounded and suffering the most excruciating pain, although they were of the savage enemy." This was the frontiersman at his worst.

The idea of a general removal of the Eastern Indians to the Great Plains beyond the Mississippi, long thought to be uninhabitable by white men, was officially adopted under Monroe and energetically pursued under Jackson. Congress authorized the President to exchange lands in the West for the older Indian holdings. An "Indian Country" was created, running at first from Canada to Texas. To this area the Northern Indians were removed without much difficulty. But in the South, where the tribes were larger and stronger, the Indians offered a stubborn resistance, and the result was tragic. The so-called Five Civilized Tribes—Creeks, Choctaws, Chickasaws, Cherokees, and Seminoles—loved their homes. Many of them, especially the Creeks and Cherokees, had learned to be thrifty farmers, had built good houses, acquired herds of cattle, erected gristmills, and educated their children in missionary schools. They clung to their lands to the last, some being driven away only by force. Traveling in great part by wagon and on foot, they suffered from hunger, disease, and exposure, and many died. By 1840, however, nearly all the Indians east of the Mississippi had been taken to their new homes in what is now Oklahoma.

This removal facilitated the complete peopling of the Mississippi Valley, the richest and most distinctive part of the country. Wisconsin, the last state east of the Mississippi, was admitted in 1848. Already a tier of states had been erected west of the river, for after Missouri's entry in 1821, Arkansas became a state in 1836 and Iowa ten years later, while Minnesota Territory was organized in 1849. The panic of 1837, in large part a product of overdevelopment in the West, checked the onward movement only briefly. Cyrus H. McCormick, inventor of the reaper, set up a factory in Chicago in 1847 and began turning out machines that made it easy to cover the Western prairies with grain. Railroad building began and soon threw a mesh of tracks over the level region. In 1854 seventy-four trains a day ran into Chicago, which already boasted itself the largest primary grain market in the world. That year saw the Galena and Chicago Railroad carrying three thousand emigrants a month to Iowa, while other thousands traveled by road. Germans, Scandinavians, and Britons helped fill the upper valley and took homes in Texas or Arkansas as well. An English observer was startled in 1854 to find St. Paul in far-off Minnesota a city of seven or eight thousand, with four or five hotels, half a dozen good churches, wharves at which three hundred steamers arrived annually, and "good streets with sidewalks, and lofty brick warehouses, and stores, and shops, as well supplied as any in the Union." New Western leaders came into prominence before 1850; such men as Stephen A. Douglas and Abraham Lincoln in Illinois, Thomas Hart Benton and David R. Atchison in Missouri, Jefferson Davis in Mississippi, and Sam Houston, the hero of the Texan War for Independence, in the Lone-Star State.

The Settlement of the Nearer West

A MAJOR PART was played in the development of the Mississippi Valley by several great avenues of transportation. The first main artery to the West was the Cumberland Road, begun in 1811 and built for the most part with Federal money. Running from Cumberland, Maryland, over the mountains to Zanesville and Columbus in Ohio, and Terre Haute in Indiana, it was finally pushed on to Vandalia in Illinois. When completed its length was about six hundred miles; sixty feet wide, it had in the center a paved strip of twenty feet constructed on McAdam's principles.

Over this "National Pike" ran the Western mails, with special postage. Inns sprang up at convenient distances. The stream of colonists swelled until in summer passengers were never out of sight. "Hundreds of families are seen migrating to the West with ease and comfort," wrote one observer in 1824. "Drovers from the West with their cattle of almost every description are seen passing eastward seeking a market. Indeed, this great thoroughfare may be compared to a street through some populous city—travelers on foot, on horseback, and in carriages are seen mingling on its paved surface." The road connected at Wheeling with the Ohio River, and this also became a crowded artery of travel. At first it was navigated by flatboats, barges, and arks, which "managed to keep up with the current," and took grain, venison, peltry, pork, and flour down to New Orleans. Nicholas Roosevelt, of a family later famous, built a steamboat which in 1811 ran from Pittsburgh clear through to New Orleans and back, and he soon had many imitators.

The most famous highway to the West was the Erie Canal, which linked the Hudson River and Atlantic Ocean with the Great Lakes, thus providing a water road into the very heart of the continent. Men had dreamed of such a highway even in the eighteenth century. It would enable emigrants and trade to flank the wild Appalachian chain. But the task of digging nearly four hundred miles of canal was so formidable that leaders shied away from it. Finally, the indomitable New Yorker De Witt Clinton carried on a campaign to convert the vision into reality. He gained the governorship, began the work in 1817, and after arduous years saw "Clinton's Ditch" completed. A joyous celebration in 1825 welcomed the first procession of boats, and before an acclaiming multitude Clinton poured a kegful of Lake Erie water into the Atlantic. The canal, which made Buffalo a thriving port, and along which new towns and cities sprang up, confirmed New York in her position as leader of American trade and finance.

More important than that, however, was its contribution to Western growth. New Englanders and New Yorkers traveled westward on it in a steady stream. This flood of migrants built up Cleveland, Detroit, and Chicago into bustling cities, and gave great parts of the Northwest a decidedly Yankee flavor. It was responsible in itself for a striking shift in the American population, and it did much to help save the Union, for before the Civil War broke out it had tied the upper Mississippi Valley securely to the North Atlantic states. In this it was aided by Pennsylvania's system of canals. Stung to emulation by the success of Clinton's Ditch, the Pennsylvanians spent about forty million dollars upon a transportation system which linked Philadelphia with Pittsburgh, two hundred miles away. In part they used rivers and canals, while they surmounted the high Allegheny ridges by a series of inclined planes, up which boats, cargo, and passengers were hauled by steam. It was a heroic enterprise, and though it almost bankrupted the state, it did a useful work and helped make Pennsylvania one of the leading industrial states.

Population movements tended roughly to follow the parallels of latitude. Alabama and Mississippi were settled mainly by Southerners; Michigan and Wisconsin mainly by Northerners. In Ohio, Indiana, and Illinois, the two currents met, the Southern stream, crossing the Ohio, and the Northern stream, pouring along the Erie Canal and Great Lakes, peaceably mingled. Cities like Columbus, Indianapolis, and Springfield were built up by the two stocks, who intermarried with each other and with European immigrants. Thus of the five men who dominated Illinois politics in the middle period, Abraham Lincoln and Orville Browning came from Kentucky, David Davis from Maryland, Lyman Trumbull from Connecticut, and Stephen A. Douglas from Vermont; whatever their political differences, all were clearly products of this "valley of democracy."

The Trans-Mississippi West

WHEN WE TURN to the vast country west of the Mississippi, we find that its settlement offers an even more colorful story. It was first made known to the nation by the exploring expedition which in 1803 Jefferson sent clear to the Pacific under Meriwether Lewis and William Clark, two young Virginians with a great deal of frontier experience. This famous undertaking, which wrote an immortal chapter in geographical discovery, was financed by a Federal appropriation of only $2500! Jefferson had always been keenly interested in the wonders of the West. He had written at length about the Indians, whom he admired, and of the discovery of remains of the mammoth in the Ohio Valley. When he sent Lewis and Clark into the wilderness his object was twofold. In addition to scientific inquiry he expected these men to open up the Missouri River country to American fur traders. At that time the Indians of the area carried their furs into Canada to sell to British dealers. They would find it far easier, Jefferson thought, to send the pelts down the river to American buyers.

Both objects were accomplished. Lewis and Clark, ascending the Missouri, crossing the Rockies, and descending the Columbia to the Pacific, accomplished an epic bit of exploration, which has been called "incomparably the most perfect achievement of its kind in the history of the world." They encountered little real danger, for they evaded the warlike Sioux. Covering about two thousand miles on the outward trip in eighteen months, they carefully mapped and described the country. They also laid a basis for American competition with the rich British fur-trading companies and proved the feasibility of an overland route to the Pacific. Immediately after their return Clark helped found the Missouri Fur Company, with a chain of forts on the river. It prospered and grew. And soon afterward John Jacob Astor's energetic American Fur Company entered the Northwestern field. It had hitherto traded chiefly about the Great Lakes, but Astor now resolved to plant a trading post at the mouth of the Columbia. In 1811 a ship of his, called the *Tonquin*, rounded Cape Horn, sailed north, and founded Astoria (about which Washington Irving later wrote a de-

lightful book), while an expedition across the continent by
land reached the same point the next year.

This was a good beginning. And the development of the
West and its trade was hastened by three picturesque occurrences early in the 1820's. One was the opening of a
brisk trade along the Santa Fe Trail to the far Southwest,
then in Mexican hands. An enterprising Missourian, William Becknell, got together a trading party of about seventy
men, placed goods on horses and mules, and, traveling eight
hundred miles over a rough, dangerous country, sold his
wares in the Mexican outpost of Santa Fe at a handsome
profit. The next year he took wagons on the long journey.
Other traders imitated him, and the celebrated Santa Fe Trail
was fairly open. The traders who used it encountered
many perils, for much of the country was semi-desert, parched
by heat and drought; they had to ford difficult rivers; and
they were likely to be attacked by hostile Comanche, Arapa-
ho, and Cheyenne Indians. While large groups of eighty or
a hundred men were fairly safe, small groups of ten or twenty were likely to be overwhelmed. In time the pioneers beat
out an American road which did much to win the Southwest
for the republic.

The second remarkable occurrence was the founding of
the Rocky Mountain Fur Company in 1822 by William
Ashley, a St. Louis general of militia, who advertised for a
hundred young men to ascend the Missouri and remain
about its headwaters for one to three years. This was the
first company which depended primarily upon trapping by
its employees rather than upon trading with the Indians.
Among its men were some of the greatest figures in Western
exploration, including Kit Carson, who as trapper, hunter,
Indian fighter, scout, and guide was to meet a series of
adventures which make his life read like a romance, and
Jedediah Smith, who was unsurpassed as an explorer. The
third occurrence was a military expedition up the Missouri
in 1823 to frighten the Arikaras and other fierce Indians
into submission. This "Missouri Legion," fitted out by the
national government and the St. Louis fur traders combined,
made it clear that the United States would protect the fur
seekers.

Missionary activity also helped greatly in the penetration
of the Far West. The churches had long been active in

frontier work, but a curious incident in 1831 gave new stimulus to their zeal. The Indian tribes on the upper Columbia had learned from British traders some rudiments of religion and wished to obtain further information. The Nez Percé sent four leading men to William Clark in St. Louis to ask for the Book of Heaven. When church journals published the story, keen interest was aroused. The Protestants sent several clergymen, with supporting parties, into the far Northwest, and they established a mission in the Willamette Valley and another near the junction of the Snake and Columbia. The leading figure in this effort was the devoted Dr. Marcus Whitman. These missions did a good deal to Christianize the Indians. They set up model farms, showing the savage converts how to build houses, clear the fields, and grow crops. The enthusiastic letters they wrote about the scenery and climate, meanwhile, fired the interest of relatives and friends; and soon annual caravans of settlers were crossing the plains and mountains to the Oregon country.

The Oregon Trail

THE FIRST EXPLORERS and fur traders who journeyed from the Missouri River to the Columbia vaguely traced a route which in time became definite as the Oregon Trail and which by the middle forties was a great highway. Some two thousand miles in length, it abounded in dangers and difficulties. Starting at Independence on the Missouri, it traversed the rolling plains to the Rockies, crossed them by the relatively low South Pass, and went on through barren and mountainous stretches to Fort Hall on the Snake River, whence the trail ran through the almost impassable Blue Mountains to the Umatilla River and down to the Columbia. An alternative route beyond Great Salt Lake led to California. The first emigrant train to set out for the Pacific was promoted by John Bidwell and, numbering about eighty men, women, and children, successfully wound its way through the wild country to Oregon in 1841. This was the advance guard of an astonishing movement. In 1843 occurred the "Great Emigration," when not fewer than two hundred families, comprising a thousand people, crossed the plains and mountains, driving hundreds of cattle with them, and reached their goal.

At two miles an hour the ox-team caravans could make twenty-five miles on good days; on bad days but five or ten. In 1845 the human rivulet following the Oregon Trail rose to a broad stream. More than three thousand people came into the Willamette Valley that year.

It was an epic migration, this Oregon movement. "Catch up, catch up!" would ring out the cry at dawn; and the long lines of covered wagons, marshaled by chosen leaders, would be got into motion. At nightfall they camped in a circle, the wagons, baggage, and men on the outside, the women, children, and animals within. Sentries were carefully posted. Food was cooked, clothes were washed, on the way. Courtships were carried on, children were born, the feeble died and were buried in unmarked graves. When worn oxen and mules could no longer drag the heavy wagons, dearly prized possessions had to be left by the trail. To some who met Indians, grizzlies, the dreaded cholera, or bitter weather, the trip might be a prolonged agony. Others found it exhilarating. "It was a long picnic, the changing scenes of the journey, the animals of the prairie, the Indians, the traders and trappers of the mountain country," wrote one. This mass movement made Oregon an American community, doing as much as diplomacy to secure it to the United States in 1846. It peopled that far-off country so effectively that it was organized as a territory in 1849 and became a full-fledged state only ten years later.

The Mormons

BY FAR THE MOST STRIKING and important of the religious settlements in the West was that of the Mormons in Utah. The traditions of individualism, dissent, and evangelism in America had led to the formation of numerous curious sects. Most of them were offshoots of existing bodies. But the Mormons were a wholly new organization. The creator of this Church of Latter-Day Saints was Joseph Smith, a youth of upper New York, who asserted that one day in 1820 he retired to the woods to pray for salvation; that two glorious personages appeared to him and asked him to wait for a full restoration of the Gospel; that in time an angel named Moroni came and told him of a record, engraved on buried plates of gold, containing the sacred history of the ancient inhabitants of North America; and that with the aid of instruments presented by this angel, he translated the history. It was published in 1830 as the *Book of Mormon*. A church was organized in that year and grew rapidly. Its headquarters, after various vicissitudes, were transferred to Illinois. Here the Mormons built on the banks of the Mississippi the prosperous city of Nauvoo, founded a university, and commenced erecting a great temple. They also adopted polygamy. Antipathy to this practice and to their religion, together with economic and political jealousies, caused an outbreak of rioting. A mob took Smith and his brother from the county jail and shot them; and soon afterward the Mormons, now led by the able Brigham Young, were expelled from the state. They crossed the Mississippi, resolved to find peace and safety in the Far West.

The upshot was a remarkable exploit in the settlement of what many thought a desert region. Brigham Young led his people across the plains and into the valley of the Great Salt Lake, where, surrounded by high mountain ranges, he found fertile land, a healthful climate, and enough water for irrigation. He directed the laying out of fields, selected the site for a city, and saw to communications with the East. The first year witnessed some scarcity, but after that Utah offered a rude plenty for everyone. Farms and irrigation ditches soon extended up and down the whole valley. Brigham Young exercised a despotic power, but his wisdom and benevolence made it endurable. He and his church officers organized the marketing of Utah products; they controlled settlement, choosing sites for new towns and sending each just the craftsmen it needed; and they made Salt Lake City, with its fine broad streets, its rills of sparkling water, and its temple and tabernacle, one of the most interesting places in America. It was the first American experiment with a planned economy, and it was successful. Polygamy for a time continued, serving a sound colonizing purpose—for women were in the majority among the converts, and the frontier had little place for unmarried and childless women. By 1850 Utah was organized as a territory. But polygamy likewise delayed its organization as a state; not until almost fifty years later—and after the Mormons had given up the practice—was it admitted to statehood.

The Annexation of Texas

THE ANNEXATION OF TEXAS, and the conquest of California and the Southwest from feeble Mexico, finally rounded out the American domain in the West. Within a few years in the 1840's the United States extended its boundaries over some of the richest and most scenic regions of the continent. Various writers have treated this wresting of territory from Mexico as immoral aggression. James Russell Lowell said that the South wanted Texas just to have "bigger pens to cram slaves in." This is unjust. A natural process brought about the addition of this territory to the United States— a process well hit off by the phrase "manifest destiny."

Texas, at first a part of the Mexican Republic, was a land as large as Germany with but a few ranchers and hunters. It early attracted many Americans and some Britons, Stephen F. Austin planting the first Anglo-American settlement in 1821. Free lands, easily accessible to the Southern States, were the principal bait. The Mexican government was inefficient, corrupt, and tyrannical. In 1835 the American settlers rose in revolt and after a number of battles won their independence. One episode was the capture by the Mexicans of the Alamo, a fort in San Antonio, where every American defender was killed: "Thermopylae had its messenger of defeat; the Alamo had none." Once established, the Texan Republic flourished and attracted many fresh American settlers. For a time the United States refused to consider any proposal for annexing the country. But for a number of reasons many Americans gradually changed their minds. For one, they thought it a duty to expand over the unpeopled and undeveloped West. For another, they felt that the Texans were a kindred people whose natural place was under the American flag. For a third reason, they feared that Great Britain might intervene in Texas and try to establish a protectorate. And finally, pocket motives were at work. Northerners wished to sell farm products and manufactured goods in Texas; shipowners saw that their vessels could make profitable voyages to Galveston; Yankee mill owners wished to have cheap Texas cotton to spin. Many Southerners wanted to migrate and yet were unwilling to leave the American flag.

In the national election of 1844 a majority of the voters showed, by their support of the expansionist candidate James K. Polk, that they were ready to take the little republic into the Union, and early the next year it was annexed.

The Mexican War and the Acquisition of California and New Mexico

MEANWHILE many Americans were equally intent upon gaining control of California by the same peaceful means. They thought this possible because of its peculiar position. In 1845 California had a meager population of but eleven or twelve thousand people, clinging tightly to the coast. They had no money, no army, no political experience. They had more Spanish blood than the Mexican masses and regarded themselves as physically and intellectually superior and they were only nominally dependent upon Mexico. Indeed, they would have thrown off the Mexican authority altogether had it not been for their family jealousies and an old feud between northern and southern California. As it was, Mexico provided no courts, no police, no regular postal facilities, and no schools. Communication between California and Mexico City was rare and uncertain. So frankly did Mexico recognize that its sovereignty was a mere shadow that by the middle forties it showed a disposition to sell the region to Great Britain. Year by year the American element in California was growing in numbers and aggressiveness. American ships had long traded on the coast, while emigrants who wished to settle in the golden climate and make money from cattle and wheat had begun crossing the mountains in the 1830's. By 1846 California had twelve hundred foreign residents, most of them Americans. No wonder that some men believed California would drop like a ripe pear into the outstretched hand of the United States—that no force would be needed.

Perhaps it would have done so had not the Mexican War broken out in the summer of 1846. The remote cause of this conflict was the increasing distrust between the two nations, while its immediate cause was a dispute over the boundary of Texas. The United States found it a short and brilliant conflict. One American army under Zachary Taylor was sent

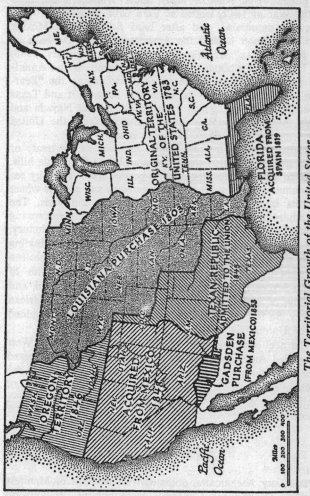

The Territorial Growth of the United States

into northern Mexico, captured the fortified city of Monterey, and defeated a large Mexican force in the stubborn battle of Buena Vista. Another army under Winfield Scott, hero of the War of 1812, landed at Vera Cruz, pushed westward over the mountains, and after hard fighting took Mexico City. Here Scott hoisted the American flag in "the halls of the Montezumas." When peace was made, in February, 1848, the United States obtained not only California, whose American residents had meantime revolted and set up the "Bear-Flag Republic," but also the huge area between it and Texas called New Mexico, which included the present Nevada and Utah. Altogether, in this country and in Texas the United States gained about 918,000 square miles.

It also gained a treasure house, for even as the treaty of peace was ratified gold was discovered in the California hills. At once a host of fortune hunters poured forth, some by sea and some by overland trail, to the canyons and gulches where nuggets could be washed out in troughs and pans. The mountains filled with roaring camps; San Francisco sprang overnight into a lusty little metropolis, full of vice, luxury, and energy; and California was converted in a twinkling from a sleepy, romantic community of Spanish-American ranchers into a hustling and populous commonwealth of Anglo-Saxons. These "days of old, and the days of gold, and the days of '49" were among the most colorful in all American history. So fast did California grow that in 1850 it was added to the Union as a state.

The acquisition of these broad new stretches in the West compelled Americans to take an interest in various neglected problems—the problem of the Caribbean; the problem of the Pacific; the problem of an isthmian canal; and above all the problem of slavery, which threatened to expand into the whole area.

The Pacific Frontier

To MANY AMERICANS, obsessed with the idea of Manifest Destiny, Oregon and California were but way stations on the road to the Pacific and Asia. President Pierce announced that he did not intend to be restrained by "any timid forebodings of evil from expansion," and Senator Thomas Hart Benton asserted that it was the duty of the United States "to reanimate the torpid body of Asia." A natural steppingstone to Asia was Hawaii. When Captain Cook discovered the Hawaiian (then named Sandwich) Islands, back in 1778, he had been accompanied by a Connecticut Yankee, John Ledyard, and it was the same Ledyard who had first seen the possibilities of trade between the Northwest coast and the mainland of China. Within a few years New England ships carrying furs from the Oregon country to China were stopping at the port of Honolulu, and soon those whalers whose epic Herman Melville was to write were putting in at Hawaii for repairs and supplies. By the 1840's, what with merchantmen from Salem and Boston with rum and Yankee notions, whalemen from Nantucket, missionaries living in white frame houses behind white picket fences, Honolulu was almost an outpost of New England. In 1842 Secretary of State Webster announced that the United States would not permit the annexation of the islands by any other power, and a few years later Secretary Marcy negotiated a treaty of annexation to the United States which fell through only because of the untimely death of the reigning King Hamehameha III. Meantime American naval, economic, and missionary interest grew apace, and it became clear that annexation was only a matter of time.

It was during these years, too, that America made its first gestures of official interest in the Far East. Sailing ships from Salem and Boston had been familiar in Chinese ports and in Java and Sumatra ever since the earliest days of the republic, but not until 1844, when Caleb Cushing negotiated a treaty giving American ships access to and privileges in certain Chinese seaports, were commercial relations with China regularized. A few years later American interest in China was dramatized when a Salem adventurer, Frederick Townsend Ward, was made commander of the "Ever Victorious Army" which put down the great Taiping Rebellion. The island kingdom of Japan had been for centuries sealed against European intercourse, but in 1853 Commodore Perry —brother to the hero of Lake Erie—sailed an expedition into Tokyo Bay; the following year he returned to negotiate a treaty opening up Japan to trade with the West: this was the famous "opening of Japan" which was to have such mixed consequences a century later.

If the United States was to be a Pacific power—and after the acquisition of Oregon and California that was inevitable —something would have to be done to provide speedier and safer communications than sailing around Cape Horn. The obvious alternative was a railroad or a canal across the Isthmus of Panama. In 1846 President Polk negotiated a treaty with Colombia guaranteeing the neutrality of the province of Panama in return for the assurance of free transit across the isthmus. To deal with the substantial British interests in Central America, Secretary Clayton negotiated, in 1850, the Clayton-Bulwer Treaty, whereby the United States agreed to joint control of any canal that was constructed across the isthmus, and Britain gave up her territorial rights in Central America. It was to be another half-century before American engineers built the canal—and then only after the abrogation of the Clayton-Bulwer Treaty. Meantime American businessmen hurriedly constructed a railroad across the narrow but dangerous isthmus to meet the needs of the thousands of fortune hunters hurrying to the gold fields of California. In 1855 the soldier of fortune William Walker led a filibustering expedition into Nicaragua, and from the presidential chair of that tentative republic tried to revolutionize the whole of Central America. He was frustrated by Commodore Vanderbilt, who headed up a rival gang of operators; in 1860 he was captured and executed by a Honduran army.

CHAPTER 11

The Sectional Struggle

Slavery: The "Peculiar Institution"

HALF A DOZEN YEARS before the Civil War the shrewd New York observer, Frederick Law Olmsted, visited one of the first-rate cotton plantations in Mississippi. He found a large and handsome mansion; nearly fourteen hundred acres planted to cotton, corn, and other crops; and two hundred hogs. Of the one hundred thirty-five slaves, nearly seventy worked in the fields, three were mechanics, and nine were house or stable servants. They labored from dawn to dark, with Sundays and sometimes Saturdays free. In summer the hoe gang thus spent sixteen hours in plodding labor, with one short interval at noon for rest. The food allowance was a peck of corn and four pounds of pork apiece each week, supplemented by vegetables, eggs, and poultry grown by the slaves themselves. Every Christmas molasses, coffee, tobacco, and calico were generously distributed. The Negroes got their own fuel for their little cabins from a wooded swamp, where on Sundays they could also cut puncheons for sale, using the money to buy small comforts. A black driver walked about among the field hands, urging them on, cracking his whip, and sometimes letting the lash fall lightly on their shoulders. The white overseer told Olmsted that discipline was good, though he had just sold a slave who tried to stab him. "His niggers did not very often run away, he said, because they were almost sure to be caught. As soon as he saw that one was gone he put the dogs on."

This was a typical plantation of the better sort. Olmsted,

like other observers, found plantations where slavery was
harsher and more brutish; he could have found some where
it was kindlier. Critics indicted slavery because of the over-
work, the occasional floggings, the cruel disruption of families by sales, the denial of education and advancement to
the blacks. Defenders extolled it because it protected the
worker in unemployment, sickness, and old age, because it
freed the South from strikes and labor clashes, because it
Christianized a heathen people and gradually elevated them,
because (they said) it made masters chivalrous and servants
loyal. As an economic institution, slavery had both attackers
and supporters. Olmsted, like the North Carolina writer,
Hinton Rowan Helper, author of *The Impending Crisis,*
thought that it impoverished the South, but many Southern
leaders explained the backwardness of their section in terms
of Northern aggrandizement. Socially, Northerners declared
that slavery injured blacks and whites alike, but most Southerners deemed it the only feasible method of controlling the
great mass of Negroes and maintaining white supremacy.

Actually few Americans, North or South, really understood the nature of the peculiar institution which one side
was so bitterly attacking, the other so passionately defending.
For the most important fact about American slavery was
that it was Negro slavery: most of the features that characterized it were connected with race rather than with legal
status. The whole institution was designed largely to regulate the relationships of black and white rather than of
master and slave, and though the status of the Negro was
completely changed by the Civil War and the Thirteenth
Amendment, the economic and social relationships of Negroes and whites were not greatly changed for another three
quarters of a century. Most of the arguments advanced to
justify slavery would have applied with equal force and
relevance to the doctrine of white supremacy formulated
after the Civil War; most of the abolitionist criticism of the
peculiar institution could have been polished up for postwar
use. When the Yankees argued that slavery retarded Southern progress, when they placed upon it responsibility for the
backwardness of agriculture, of industry, of education, in the
South, they were really talking about the presence of cheap
and ignorant black labor—a situation that persisted long after
emancipation. Some Southerners understood this, but in-

stinctively rather than intellectually, and they were unable to explain that slavery was a transitional stage in the evolution of race relationships. And because Northerners did not appreciate this they too did not understand what was involved in emancipation and doomed themselves to grave disappointment in its results.

By 1850, when the total population of the country exceeded twenty-three millions (it passed that of Great Britain during the next decade), the total number of slaves was 3,200,000. In South Carolina and Mississippi they exceeded the whites in number; in Louisiana they nearly equaled the whites, and in Alabama were roughly three sevenths of the population. The South had large areas where slaves were not one tenth of the people, the Appalachian Mountains all the way from Maryland to Alabama being largely free from them. It had other areas where they were heavily predominant. Just north of Charleston they constituted eighty-eight per cent of the population, on the Georgia seacoast eighty per cent, in central Alabama nearly seventy, and in one belt along the lower Mississippi River more than ninety. The slave population was greatest where the climate was hot, the soil flat and rich; it was least where the land was mountainous or barren. Only a minority of Southerners held slaves. Out of a total white population of about six millions in 1850, the census revealed but 347,725 owners. Although most of the blacks were held in small groups, in the cotton, sugar, and rice country of the lower South three or four thousand families owned a majority of the slaves, lived on the best lands, and enjoyed three fourths of the income. Howell Cobb of Georgia, for example, with a thousand Negroes, raised cotton on ten thousand acres. Political power and intellectual leadership were similarly concentrated in a small and generally aristocratic group.

Beginning about 1830, sectional lines had steadily hardened on the slavery question. Abolitionist and above all free-soil feeling grew more powerful in the Northern states. The fiery William Lloyd Garrison founded his *Liberator* in Boston in 1831. But Garrison's importance has been much exaggerated; an equally effective part was played in the movement by a stalwart Ohio group led by the evangelist C. G. Finney and the agitator Theodore D. Weld. and a New York group led by Arthur Tappan. They were able organizers of

the demand for "root-and branch" emancipation. Persecution
simply threw oil on the flames. When Elijah P. Lovejoy,
trying in 1837 to defend his abolitionist press against a mob
in Alton, Illinois, was murdered, the crusade gained intensity. Interferences with civil rights convinced many able
men that the cause of human freedom was broadly involved.
The eloquent Wendell Phillips of Boston was inspired to join
the movement by a mob attack on Garrison; the wealthy
Gerrit Smith of upper New York by an assault on an antislavery meeting in Utica; the able Salmon P. Chase of
Ohio by attacks on the press in his own state. At no time did
the root-and-branch abolitionists command much popular
strength. But the free-soil men, who insisted that slavery
must not expand one inch farther, grew into a host. Meanwhile, in the South various leaders declared slavery a positive
good. Thomas Dew, of William and Mary, published a book
defending it; Governor Hammond of South Carolina in 1835
pronounced it "the cornerstone of our republican edifice";
Calhoun, pointing to ancient Athens, asserted that slavery
offered the firmest basis for a splendid culture.

From an early date keen-sighted men saw that this sectional dispute endangered the Union. John Quincy Adams
in the House repeatedly warned the South that secession
would mean war and that "from the instant your slaveholding states become the theater of war, civil, servile, or foreign,
from that moment the war powers of the Constitution extend
to interference with the institution of slavery." Lincoln was
to verify that prophecy.

The Rising Storm

THE MOMENT the Texan question and Mexican War made
huge annexations of Southwestern territory certain, the slavery quarrel entered upon an acute phase. The fire bell in the
night, to use Jefferson's phrase, again clanged ominously. Up
to 1844 slavery had merely asserted its right to continue
unmolested where it existed. It had been given limits by the
Missouri Compromise and had not overstepped them. Now
when it declared its right to expand, a host of Northerners
rose in opposition. They believed that if kept within close
bounds it would ultimately decay; they asserted that Wash-

ington, Jefferson, and other founders of the republic had held this view; and they pointed to the Ordinance of 1787, forbidding its expansion into the Northwest, as a binding precedent. As Texas already had slavery, she naturally entered the Union as a slave state. But California, New Mexico, and Utah did not have it. When the United States prepared to take over these areas, a Pennsylvania Democrat named David Wilmot attached to an appropriation bill a proviso declaring that slavery should forever be prohibited in any territory which might be acquired from Mexico. The House passed the Wilmot Proviso; the Senate defeated it.

To Southerners it seemed bitterly unfair that an area which they had helped gain by their blood should not be open to them and Northerners alike, one group free to take in slave property as the other was to take in machine property. To free-soilers it seemed outrageous that virgin territories should be opened to an institution that blighted free enterprise and offended their moral sense.

A constitutional question was bound up with this political issue. Did or did not the Constitution permit Congress to exclude or regulate slavery in the national territories? Congress had repeatedly done so; but the instrument was vague, and Calhoun and other Southern radicals asserted that slavery followed the flag into the common domain and could not be shut out. For the first time, in the campaign of 1848 a powerful Free-Soil party appeared. It nominated Martin Van Buren for President and closed its platform with the ringing words: "We inscribe on our banner 'Free Soil, Free Speech, Free Labor, and Free Men,' and under it will fight on, and fight ever, until a triumphant victory shall reward our exertions." The party polled an impressive vote. Largely because of its activities, the Democrats were defeated, and the Whig party elected its last President, the war hero Zachary Taylor.

During and after the campaign it became clear that the lower South would secede before it submitted to the Wilmot Proviso. It was equally clear that Northern antislavery men would never yield to Calhoun's demand that slavery enter all parts of the new acquisitions. Some compromise was imperatively required. One group of moderates suggested that the Missouri Compromise line of 36° 30' be extended to the Pacific, with free states north of it and slave states to the south. Another moderate group, led by Lewis Cass of Michi-

gan and Stephen A. Douglas of Illinois, proposed to refer
the question to "popular sovereignty." That is, the national
government should take its hands off; it should allow settlers
to flock into the new country with or without slaves; and
when the time came to organize the region into states, the
people should determine the question for themselves. When
Congress met at the end of 1849, Southern men openly threatened withdrawal. Robert Toombs of Georgia shouted, apro-
pos of one Northern bill: "If it should pass, I am for disunion!"

Compromise of 1850

IN THIS CRISIS Henry Clay, for the third time, halted a
dangerous sectional quarrel with a well-wrought compromise.
His plan proposed that California be admitted as a free
state, that New Mexico and Utah be organized as territories
without legislation either for or against slavery, that a more
efficient machinery be set up for returning fugitive slaves to
their masters, that the slave trade be abolished in the District
of Columbia, and that Texas be compensated for some territory ceded to New Mexico. Both sides would have to give
up something. Most of these proposals came originally from
Douglas, but Clay welded them together, and his backing
was indispensable. His prestige in all sections, his eloquence,
his deep earnestness, and the influence of his courtly, charm-
ing personality were needed to carry them to victory.

The debates by which the Compromise of 1850 was hammered into final shape were among the most impressive in
American history. The Senate then possessed three parliamentary giants, all approaching the grave—Clay, Webster,
and Calhoun. It possessed a galaxy of young men of high
talent—Stephen A. Douglas, Jefferson Davis, William H.
Seward, and Salmon P. Chase. Of these men Calhoun and
Davis opposed the compromise as unfair to the South. The
former wrote an impressive argument, declaring that to
prevent tragic conflict the grievances of the South must be
remedied. One by one, he said, the cords which bound the
North and South together were breaking. Already the Methodist and Baptist churches had broken into two parts. "If
the agitation goes on, the same force, acting with increased

intensity, will finally snap every cord, when nothing will be left to hold the states together except force." Too weak to read his speech, he tottered into the Senate to hear it delivered by a Virginia colleague. Seward and Chase opposed the compromise as unfair to the North. But Clay was magnificently supported by Daniel Webster. In a powerful speech on March 7, the last great oration of his life, Webster pleaded "not as a Massachusetts man, nor as a Northern man, but as an American," for unity. Peaceable secession he declared impossible. His support of the fugitive slave provisions of the compromise outraged radical antislavery men in New England and required high courage; but it was a statesmanlike act—his last great service to the nation. In the end the moderate spirit of Clay, Douglas, and Webster triumphed. The compromise measures were passed, and the country breathed a sigh of heartfelt relief. Zachary Taylor would probably have vetoed the bills, but he had died in early summer, and his successor, the dim and forgotten Millard Fillmore, gladly signed them.

For three short years the compromise seemed to settle nearly all differences. A majority in both Whig and Democratic parties cordially supported it. Yet under the surface the tension remained and grew. The new Fugitive Slave Law deeply offended many Northerners. They refused to take any part in catching slaves; instead, they helped fugitives to escape. The "underground railroad" from slavery to freedom became more efficient and unabashed. Some slaves escaped from coastal areas by ship. Some, traveling by night and guided by the North Star, walked from their plantations to the Ohio River and were thence helped into Canada. Some followed the Appalachian chain into Pennsylvania. The Northern states became honeycombed with shelters for runaways, and men like Levi Coffin, the so-called president of the "underground railroad," helped scores to reach safety. In 1850 about twenty thousand escaped slaves who had settled in Northern communities were subject to recapture, but efforts to seize men often provoked riots.

Harriet Beecher Stowe was inspired by the Fugitive Slave Law to write *Uncle Tom's Cabin*, which, appearing in book form in 1852, painted a dark picture of slavery so vividly that it aroused deep feeling in both North and South. Mrs. Stowe had lived in the border city of Cincinnati and visited

in the homes of Kentucky planters. She did full justice to
the many humane and generous slaveholders; her one brutal
slave driver, Simon Legree, was of Yankee origin. But she
showed how inseparable cruelty was from slavery and how
fundamentally irreconcilable were free and slave societies.
Her book was translated into more than a score of languages, sold more than a million copies in the British Empire, and when converted into a play thrilled huge audiences.
The rising generation of voters in the North was deeply
stirred by it.

Then in 1854 the old issue of slavery in the territories
was torn open again, and as the quarrel became more bitter,
new leaders stepped forward to take command of both sections. The radical Southerners were determined to get rid
of the Missouri Compromise, closing the whole upper Missouri Valley to slavery. When steps were taken to achieve
this, the North roused itself like an angry giant.

The country beyond the Missouri River which now com-
prises the fertile states of Kansas and Nebraska was already
attracting settlers. If the Indians were removed and a stable
government instituted, it promised a rapid development. The
old idea of a "great American desert" in this area had been
exploded by the explorer John C. Frémont and others; and
many Northerners believed that if the region were organized
as a territory, settlers would flock in and a railroad could be
built through it from Chicago to the Pacific. This would
forestall a Southern project for a railway striking westward
from New Orleans. Early action was required, for the Southern route ran through well-settled Texas and New Mexico
Territory, it was little exposed to Indian attack, and public
lands were available for grants to railroad builders. Nobody
was more eager to clear the Northern line than Stephen A.
Douglas, who lived in Chicago, was an active real-estate
speculator, and had become chairman of the Senate Committee on Territories. But he met stern opposition. Under
the Missouri Compromise all this country was closed to
slavery, and Missouri objected to letting Kansas, which ad-
joined her on the west, become a free territory. It would be
all too easy for Missouri slaves to run away to this free area.
Moreover, Missouri would then have three free neighbors
and, yielding to an already strong movement, would probably
soon become a free state herself. For a time Missourians in

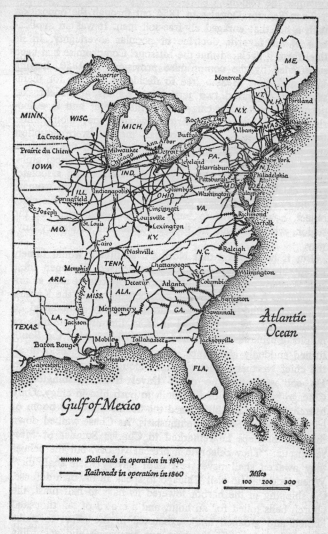

| Railroads in operation in 1840 |
| Railroads in operation in 1860 |

Miles
0   100   200   300

Growth of Railroads to 1860

Washington, backed by Southerners, blocked all efforts to organize the region.

Then Senator Douglas in 1854 cut through the opposition with a bill that enraged all free-soil men. It was an application of his favorite doctrine of popular sovereignty. In its final form it declared that the Missouri Compromise had been superseded by the compromise provisions in 1850, leaving Utah and New Mexico free to decide on slavery for themselves; it organized two territories, Kansas and Nebraska, permitting settlers to carry slaves into them; and it authorized the inhabitants to determine whether they should enter the Union free or slave. Douglas' motives were doubtless mixed. He was accused of currying favor with the South in order to gain the presidency in 1856, and his political ambitions were unquestionably strong. His Democratic associates were chiefly Southerners; he had married a Southern woman; he did not dislike slavery or object to its extension. His chief object, however, was to hurry on the development of the region, whose climate he thought unsuitable to slavery anyway.

But if he believed that Northern sentiment would tamely accept his plan, he was quickly undeceived. To open these rich Western prairies to slavery struck millions of men as unforgivable. Angry debates marked the progress of the Kansas-Nebraska Bill. The free-soil press violently denounced it. Northern clergymen assailed it from literally thousands of pulpits. Businessmen who had hitherto befriended the South turned suddenly about-face. Mass meetings were held in all the chief Northern cities to attack Douglas and his measure. He confessed that he could travel from Washington to Chicago by the light of fires built to burn him in effigy. On a March morning the bill passed the Senate amid the boom of cannon fired by Southern enthusiasts. As Chase walked down the Capitol steps he remarked to Charles Sumner of Massachusetts: "They celebrate a present victory, but the echoes they awaken shall never rest until slavery itself shall die." When Douglas did visit Chicago to speak in his own defense, the shipping in the harbor lowered its flags to half mast, the church bells tolled for an hour, and a crowd of ten thousand hooted and groaned until, exhausted in the effort to make himself heard, he finally drew out his watch and according to some auditors exclaimed: "It is now Sunday morning; I am going to church and you can go to hell!"

The immediate results of Douglas' ill-starred measure were momentous. The Whig party, which had straddled the question of slavery's expansion into the territories, sank to its death, and a powerful new organization, the Republican party, rose instead. Idealistic, full of enthusiasm, attracting young men of brains and vigor, appealing alike to Eastern business and Western farmers, it was formidable from the beginning. Its primary demand was that slavery be excluded from all the territories. In 1856 it nominated the dashing John C. Frémont, whose five exploring expeditions into the Far West had won him deserved renown, and with the rallying cry of "Free Men, Free Soil, Frémont," swept a great part of the North; had it carried Pennsylvania in the October elections, it might even have won over the Democratic nominee, James Buchanan. Such free-soil leaders as Seward and Chase rose to greater influence than ever, and along with them appeared a tall, gaunt attorney of Illinois who showed a marvelous power of logic in discussing the new issues—Abraham Lincoln.

A speech which Lincoln made in Peoria on October 16, 1854, was the best statement of free-soil principles thus far presented. He said that he had no desire to interfere with slavery where it stood. "If all earthly power were given me, I should not know what to do as to the existing institution." He declared that Congress had no more moral right to repeal the Missouri Compromise, a great sectional compact, than to repeal the law against importing slaves from Africa. He asserted that all national legislation should be framed on the principle adopted by the fathers of the republic, that slavery was an institution to be restricted and ultimately abolished. And he contended that the popular-sovereignty principle was false, for slavery in the West was the concern not merely of the inhabitants there, but of the whole United States. "What better moral right have thirty-one citizens of Nebraska to say that the thirty-second shall not hold slaves than the people of thirty-one states have to say that slavery shall not go into the thirty-second state at all?"

The flow of Southern slaveholders and Northern anti-slavery men into Kansas produced a sharp conflict, with savage episodes of guerrilla warfare. Steps were taken in both sections to send forward settlers to hold the country, the Emigrant Aid Society in the North being especially diligent. They went well armed. The popular Brooklyn clergyman Henry Ward Beecher, attending a meeting at which a deacon called for weapons for one company, declared that a Sharpe's rifle was a greater moral agency than the Bible; and from this remark sprang the familiar phrase, "Beecher's Bibles." It was soon clear that the North held the advantage. The proximity of the large free-soil population of the upper Mississippi Valley, and the risks of taking slaves into a region that might soon be free, assisted it. However, many "border ruffians" crossed the river from Missouri to cast illegal votes or to intimidate Northern settlers, while the slaveholding forces had the support of the Buchanan administration in Washington. The conflict, therefore, dragged on, arousing ever-keener feeling throughout the country. When the blundering Buchanan tried to induce Congress, Democratic in both branches, to admit Kansas under the Lecompton Constitution authorizing slavery, a new storm swept the North, and Douglas himself indignantly broke with the President.

Meanwhile, many Northerners who felt that the bargain made in the Compromise of 1850 had been broken by the South refused to carry out the Fugitive Slave Act, which was part of that bargain. "No slave-hunt in our borders, no pirate on our strand! No fetters in the Bay State, no slave upon our land!" wrote the poet John Greenleaf Whittier. Mob interference in behalf of fleeing Negroes became more common. Many Northern states passed "personal liberty laws" which openly nullified the Federal statute. When in 1855 the slave Anthony Burns was caught in Boston, some of the city's most distinguished leaders hastened to his defense. Angry men poured in from all eastern Massachusetts, threatening crowds filled the streets, and it required the united force of the city police, the state militia, and the national army and navy to drag one poor black man back into slavery.

Drifting into War

YEAR BY YEAR the nation moved closer to war. A great drum seemed to beat out the march to conflict, stroke after stroke. In 1856 a hot-headed South Carolina member of Congress, Preston Brooks, attacked Sumner of Massachusetts at his Senate desk and hammered him so heavily with his cane that Sumner was an invalid for several years. The provocation, a grossly abusive speech by Sumner, had been great, but the act was indefensible. Early in 1857 Chief Justice Taney and a majority of the Supreme Court declared in the Dred Scott case that Congress had no power to exclude slavery from the territories. It was a bad interpretation, badly argued. At once the free-soil press and politicians attacked the court with unprecedented bitterness, declaring they would see to it that in good time it changed this mistaken construction. "Hereafter," wrote the poet-editor William Cullen Bryant, "if this decision shall stand for law, slavery, instead of being what the people of the slave states have hitherto called it, their peculiar institution, is a Federal institution, the common patrimony and shame of all the states, those which flaunt the title of free, as well as those which accept the stigma of being the Land of Bondage; hereafter, wherever our jurisdiction extends, it carries with it the chain and the scourge—wherever our flag floats, it is the flag of slavery. If so, that flag should have the light of the stars and the streaks of morning red erased from it; it should be dyed black, and its device should be the whip and the fetter. Are we to accept, without question, these new readings of the Constitution . . . ? Never! Never!"

In 1858 occurred the memorable series of debates in Illinois between Lincoln and Douglas, both seeking a seat in the Senate. Outwardly, these debates had little dignity. Douglas, a squat, powerful man with a huge head, and Lincoln, an awkward, lanky giant whose homely countenance was surmounted by a shock of rough black hair, presented an extraordinary contrast. But no arguments in the English language have more shrewdness, luminosity, or Saxon force than those which they presented. They did much to awaken the country to the significance of the issues. Moreover, Lincoln succeeded in forcing Douglas to reiterate, with emphasis, his belief that the Dred Scott decision did not necessarily overthrow the principle of popular sovereignty in the territories. True, the Supreme Court had held that neither Congress nor territorial legislation could interfere there with slavery. But Douglas explained that in hostile communities slavery could not survive unless protected by positive police regulations, and that by simply refusing to pass such laws, a community could blight and destroy it. When Southerners heard this bold avowal, many took sides with Buchanan in reading Douglas out of the Democratic party. He won the senatorship, but after this year Lincoln was a national figure.

Then in 1859 came the raid of John Brown at Harpers Ferry, a fanatical invasion of Virginia by a little group who hoped to liberate and arm the slaves. This quixotic and criminal enterprise completely failed. The South was justly outraged by the attack. But when Brown and six followers were hanged, many Northerners exalted the old abolitionist into the seat of a martyr to liberty. And within two years soldiers were to march to battle to the tune of *John Brown's Body*.

One underlying fact which made these events desperately serious was that North and South had now grown into sections that were widely unlike, economically, socially, and politically. The South was almost wholly rural, with but one considerable city, New Orleans. Great parts of the North had become urbanized, and New York was fast approaching a population of a million. The South had very little manufacturing, though a few such enterprises as the Tredegar Iron Works in Richmond flourished; its textile mills actually handled less cotton than the single town of Lowell in Massachusetts. The North, on the other hand, was now full of thriving industrial establishments, turning out iron, textiles, shoes, watches, farm implements, and a thousand other products on a large scale, building ships, packing meats, and milling flour, and growing steadily in technical skill. Nearly all the heavy stream of European immigration (2,452,000 in the decade 1850–1860) stayed in the North and West, the Irish settling in the cities, many Germans and Scandinavians going to the farms, the British scattering everywhere. Already this section had a painful problem of labor management and another of slums. The South would have welcomed immigration, but got little, for immigrants did not care to compete with Negro slaves. Railroad construction was far more advanced in the North than the South. Three trunk lines from the East were built over or around the Appalachians—the Erie, completed from New York to the Buffalo area in 1851; the Pennsylvania, completed from Philadelphia to Pittsburgh in 1852; and the Baltimore and Ohio, completed from Baltimore to Wheeling in 1853. The greatest of the Western lines was the Illinois Central, endowed by a rich land grant of 2,600,000 acres and linking Chicago with the Gulf. Of the twenty thousand miles of railroad built in 1850–1860, most was in the North.

An increasing body of Northerners believed in protective tariffs, while the rural South, wanting its manufactured goods cheaply, detested them. The North was interested in a quicker distribution of the public lands to small holders. A mighty demand for free homesteads to all settlers was arising: "Vote yourself a farm!" became a popular cry. The South wished to see the national domain held and sold only for good prices. The North wanted an efficient national banking system; the South, which accumulated little capital, was hostile to centralized banking. Socially the North, despite growing extremes of wealth and poverty in the large cities, was more democratic than the South, where the slaveholding oligarchy held most of the wealth and power.

Yet these differences, important as they were, would not have divided the sections had not fear and prejudice exaggerated them and demagogy exploited them. The South was keenly aware of the fact that an almost insoluble race problem underlay the slavery problem. It "had the wolf by the ears," as Jefferson said, and could neither hold him nor let him go. The abolitionist agitation engendered a fear that the North would attack slavery where it already existed, disrupt the historic labor system of the South, and array race against race to the destruction of both. Much Northern criticism was indeed of a selfish, canting type, unconstructive and incendiary. On the other hand, even reasonable Northerners like Lincoln feared that radical Southerners would try to spread slavery over the whole nation. They feared, too, that the lower South would attempt to reopen the slave trade, as some of its leaders advocated; and that in an effort to expand its system, it would lead the nation into wars to conquer Cuba, or Mexico, or Central America. The Ostend Manifesto of 1854, an irresponsible statement in favor of Cuban annexation signed by the three Democratic ministers whom President Franklin Pierce had sent to Great Britain, France, and Spain, had aroused a distrust of Southern imperialism. So had the filibustering expeditions of the reckless William Walker in Central America.

Many Northern editors, clergymen, and politicians exaggerated the evils of slavery and the intentions of slaveowners. Many Southern fire-eaters exaggerated the evils of industrial society and the aims of the free-soilers. A wise New York leader said that if the worst agitators on both sides could be packed into a stagecoach and plunged beneath the Potomac for fifteen minutes, sectional peace might be secure; but that was too optimistic a view. Others would quickly have taken their places.

Lincoln's Election: Secession

REPUBLICAN VICTORY IN 1860, which precipitated Southern secession, was made possible by a schism in the Democratic party. Behind this schism lies one of the most dramatic stories of American political history.

For years a growing body of Southern extremists had been demanding that Congress pass laws protecting slavery in the territories. When Douglas declared that the Dred Scott decision giving slavery free entry into all territories could be rendered meaningless by hostile local laws, the demand for this protection was redoubled. It was voiced by Jefferson Davis of Mississippi, William L. Yancey of Alabama, and Robert Toombs of Georgia, three spokesmen of the cotton kingdom. In the Senate early in 1859 Albert G. Brown of Mississippi reiterated the demand and, turning to Douglas, asked where he stood. "If the territorial legislature refuses to act," he asked, "will you act? If it passes laws hostile to slavery, will you annul them, and substitute laws favoring slavery in their stead?" The South, he said, called for action —"positive, unqualified action." Other Southerners rose to support him.

But Douglas was not to be intimidated. Brown's demand, he declared, was an infringement upon popular rights in the territories. Never in American history had Congress passed either a criminal code for any territory or a law protecting property in a territory. From 1789 onward Congress had left these matters to the territorial legislature. Why should it break its sound rule now? The Democratic party had for years declared that it stood for Congressional nonintervention in the territories. Why should it forsake that sound doctrine now? "If," asserted Douglas, "you repudiate the doctrine of nonintervention and form a slave code by act of Congress when the people of a territory refuse it, you must step off the Democratic platform. . . . I tell you, gentlemen of the South, in all candor, I do not believe a Democratic candidate can ever carry any one Democratic state of the North on the platform that it is the duty of the Federal government to force the people of a territory to have slavery when they do not want it." Jefferson Davis rejoined that Congress must assert the rights of American citizens and that when a territorial legislature did not perform its proper functions in protecting property, Congress must do it. "Not at all," exclaimed Douglas. "If Oregon will not enact statutes to encourage mules, I won't pass a law in Washington to force mules on them; if Oregon will not encourage longhorn cattle, I will not force cattle on them; and if Oregon will not accept slaves, I will not force slaves on her people."

This was the rock on which the Democratic Convention in 1860 split, this and the feud between Douglas and supporters of the Buchanan administration. The delegates met in Charleston, the very center of aggressive slavery sentiment—the city of Calhoun, of Hayne, of R. B. Rhett and his radical *Mercury*. They met to continue the battle between Douglas and Davis which had now raged in the Senate for two years. If Douglas won, the Democratic party could continue as a truly national organization, strong in the North and West as well as South. If Davis won on his platform of forcing unwilling communities to foster slavery, the Democrats would become a sectional party, strong only in the South. For a time it seemed that a compromise candidate might be placed on a noncommittal platform. But such Southern extremists as Davis, Yancey, Rhett, Toombs, and Judah P. Benjamin of Louisiana were following a policy of party rule or party ruin.

"Gentlemen of the South," exclaimed Douglas' spokesman, Pugh of Ohio, when the extremists tried to force their demand into the platform. "You mistake us—you mistake us—we will not do it." A majority of delegates stood firm against the Davis-Yancey doctrine. Thereupon the Alabama delegation rose in protest and walked out of the hall. The South

212 THE SECTIONAL STRUGGLE

Carolina delegation followed; others from the lower South fell into line. With the party split complete, the Charleston Convention adjourned without making any nominations. Its two fragments shortly organized as separate conventions, the Southern radicals nominating John C. Breckinridge of Kentucky, their opponents nominating Douglas. The significance of the split was greater than many realized at the time. Not merely had the Democrats made their defeat certain. One more of the great bonds holding North and South together had parted.

The Republican party went into the campaign with perfect unity. In an enthusiastic convention in Chicago it nominated its most popular Middle Western figure, Lincoln; and his disappointed rivals, Seward and Chase in the van, loyally rallied behind the rail splitter. Party spirit had been wrought up to a high pitch. A stern determination, an evangelistic ardor, animated the millions of voters who had proclaimed that they would allow slavery to spread no further. The party was successful, too, in enlisting such strong support from capitalist groups that it was far better provided with money than four years earlier. The brief, disastrous panic of 1857 had stimulated the demand in industrial communities for a protective tariff; it had increased the demand in commercial and financial circles for a better banking system. The Republican party promised to satisfy these yearnings. Simultaneously it appealed to land-hungry Northerners with a pledge that it would enact a law granting free homesteads to settlers. Economically, in short, it offered powerful attractions to important American groups. In Pennsylvania, which the Republicans had lost in 1856, the tariff plank helped mightily toward victory. In the old Northwest the internal-improvement program won thousands of votes. In the central West the homestead plan was equally potent.

On Election Day Lincoln polled 1,866,452 votes, Douglas polled 1,376,957, Breckinridge received 849,781, and John Bell of Tennessee, who had run on a platform of sectional conciliation, 588,879. Lincoln had a minority of the popular vote but in the electoral college a decisive majority. The popular vote was unquestionably for the restriction of slavery, but also for union and peace. Breckinridge, the only

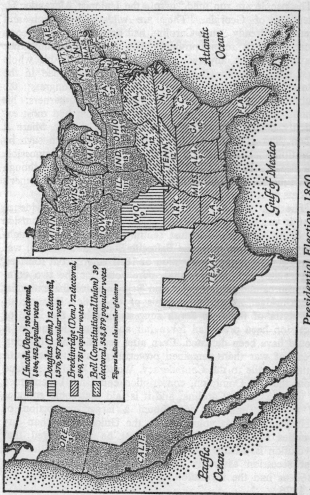

Lincoln (Rep.) 180 electoral,
1,866,452 popular votes

Douglas (Dem.) 12 electoral,
1,376,957 popular votes

Breckinridge (Dem.) 72 electoral,
849,781 popular votes

Bell (Constitutional Union) 39
electoral, 588,879 popular votes

Figures indicate the number of electors

Presidential Election, 1860

secession candidate, received less than one fifth the total vote.

In the South, however, the extremists were in control. "The people are run mad," wrote the Unionist Alexander H. Stephens of Georgia. "They are wild with passion and frenzy." Already South Carolina had determined upon secession. Why? It seems probable that neither the South nor slavery stood in any real danger. During nearly his whole first term, Lincoln (if the Southern states remained in the Union) would face a hostile majority in Congress; the Supreme Court, too, was dominated by Southerners; his hands would be tied. For that matter, Lincoln had most explicitly denied any intention of molesting slavery where it stood. Slavery could not be abolished in the South save by constitutional amendment, and that would be impossible for decades to come. Yet the step was taken—taken though its sequel was certain. "Men will be cutting one another's throats in a little while," Stephens prophesied.

The step was taken, but there is no conclusive evidence that it was supported by the majority of the people outside of South Carolina. Unionist sentiment was strong throughout the South—even in the Palmetto State—and so, too, was peace sentiment. In the election of 1860 voters from fourteen slave states had cast 124,000 more votes for the two compromise candidates, Douglas and Bell, than for the extremist Breckinridge. A careful analysis of the voting in some of the states of the deep South suggests that had the issue of secession been presented for a fair and open referendum, it would have been defeated. Even after secession and the outbreak of war there remained powerful groups in the South bitterly hostile to the Confederacy. Western Virginia seceded from the Old Dominion, conscription could not be enforced in western North Carolina, and it is said that some counties of eastern Tennessee contributed a larger proportion of their population as volunteers in the Union army than any counties in the North. Yet it must be remembered that revolution is usually the work of determined minorities and that secession assuredly had as wide popular support in 1860 as had the revolution against the rule of George III in 1776.

The lower South was actuated by a variety of motives: hatred of the North, pique over its defeat in the election, unwillingness to accept the verdict on the territories, a dream of brighter and better days under its own flag. Above all, it was moved by fear—fear that its institutions and its peculiar civilization would be rudely overthrown by an abolitionist-minded government. South Carolina, leading the way on December 20, 1860, declared that the North had elected as President a man "whose opinions and purposes are hostile to slavery." Mississippi, following her, asserted that the Northern people "have assumed a revolutionary position toward the Southern states." And the Southern extremists, who did not think the North would actually fight, saw that it was now or never. Nullification had been stamped out by President Jackson. Secession by a single state was impossible. The North was growing steadily more powerful in relation to the South. If this crisis were permitted to pass without an attempt at establishing Southern independence, no such opportunity would recur. A Southern Confederacy might gain a strong place among the nations of the world and could soon expand southward around the Caribbean. Early in February, 1861, delegates of seven seceding states met in congress at Montgomery, Alabama, formed the Confederate States of America, and elected Jefferson Davis its provisional President.

Three other states of the reluctant upper South and Arkansas, loyal to their section, were soon to follow. Last-minute attempts were made at compromise. But the most promising of these, John J. Crittenden's plan for returning to the Missouri Compromise line of 36° 30', foundered on the refusal of Lincoln (standing firm on principle) to let slavery enter any territory. At dawn on April 12, 1861, the Southern guns opened on Fort Sumter in Charleston Harbor.

CHAPTER 12

The Brothers' War

Men and Resources

"IT IS ENOUGH to make the whole world start to see the awful amount of death and destruction that now stalks abroad. Daily for the past two months has the work progressed and I see no signs of a remission till one or both the armies are destroyed. . . . I begin to regard the death and mangling of a couple thousand men as a small affair, a kind of morning dash—and it may be well that we become so hardened." So wrote General William T. Sherman to his brother on June 30, 1864. He added: "The worst of the war is not yet begun." That sentence was true for Georgia, whose farms and towns he was about to lay waste in a broad swath of destruction all the way from the mountains to the sea. It was true for Virginia. It was almost true for Grant's and Lee's armies, their bloodiest fighting just under way. Yet the country had entered upon this conflict in a lighthearted spirit, Northerners shouting "On to Richmond!" and Southerners vaunting their chivalric superiority over the Yankee "scum," both sides dreaming that the conflict would be short and glorious.

The shock of conflict at Fort Sumter had at once united the North and also the South. A wave of fury tore Virginia from the Union and placed her in the Confederacy; the Old Dominion gave the South its capital, for Jefferson Davis and his government arrived in Richmond late in June, 1861, and its ablest leader, for Robert E. Lee, hero of Cerro Gordo and Chapultepec in the Mexican War, former superintendent at West Point, and commander of the department of Texas, found the call of his state stronger than that of the nation. Tennessee swung into the Confederate roster. In the North the upper Mississippi Valley, declaring that it would never have "a line of customhouses" between it and the Gulf, took a vigorous stand with the Union. Far-off California did the same. The border states of Maryland, Kentucky, and Missouri hesitated, for they were bitterly divided in sentiment. For a few days the secessionists controlled Baltimore and at one time seemed about to seize control of St. Louis. But in the end the three states of Francis Scott Key, Henry Clay, and Thomas Hart Benton stood by their old allegiance. North and South, party lines temporarily melted away. Douglas symbolically held Lincoln's hat when the new President stepped forward to deliver his first inaugural; Alexander H. Stephens, a lifelong Unionist, became Vice-President of the Confederacy.

Each side had certain advantages. The North was far stronger in population, industrial resources, and wealth. The census of 1860 showed that the twenty-three states under the Stars and Stripes (not counting West Virginia, soon organized out of the loyal counties of Virginia, or Kansas, soon admitted to the Union) had about twenty-two million people, as against eleven states and a little over nine million people under the Stars and Bars. And the Southern population included more than three and a half millions of Negroes. The Northern railway system comprised about twenty-two thousand miles, the Southern only nine thousand. The North held a tremendous advantage in its industrial development, for New York alone produced in 1860 a value of manufactured goods more than twice, and Pennsylvania nearly twice, that of the whole Confederacy. In the last three years of the conflict the North made nearly all of its own war supplies, while the South had to depend on foreign guns, foreign drugs and surgical equipment, and to a great extent on foreign ammunition. The North kept control of the navy and, with it, the ocean. It had a more adaptable and variegated economy. It had the strength lent by immigration, which declined until Gettysburg and then rapidly swelled again.

The South had in its favor the martial spirit of its people, the easy seizure of numerous forts and arsenals, the superior

efficiency and organization of its agriculture, the fact that it
was fighting on the defensive, and the ability of its armies
to operate on inside lines. It had in its favor, above all, the
fact that in order to achieve success it did not have to win
the war in a military sense—did not have to invade and conquer the North. All that it needed to do was to fight long
and hard enough to persuade the North that it could not
itself be conquered. It could afford to lose battles and even
campaigns; it could afford to suffer defeat after defeat. The
Confederacy would win if it could convince Northern
opinion that a Union victory would cost too much and that
it was better, after all, to allow the erring sisters to depart.
Many believed that the South also possessed a great advantage in controlling the world's main cotton supply—
that Britain, needing this cotton to keep her mills busy,
would intervene on the Southern side. Time showed that
this was a miscalculation and that Britain needed Northern
wheat no less than Southern cotton.

A sublime defiance animated the South even in disaster,
but it was matched by Northern determination. The Southern generals were on the whole abler and more experienced
than those of the North; but President Lincoln proved a far
greater statesman than Jefferson Davis, who possessed intellectual distinction, dignity, and austere earnestness, but
lacked breadth, and sometimes allowed temper, impatience,
and personal prejudices to warp his judgment. All in all, the
North was easily the stronger; and the South's great hope
lay in the difficulty of subjugating a territory so huge, a
population so large and irreconcilable as its own.

Those Northerners who believed the war would be short
were taught their lesson by Bull Run. An army of about
thirty thousand, hastily whipped into shape at Washington,
was set in motion against a Confederate force of about the
same size lying behind the deep-gullied Bull Run in northern
Virginia. The Union forces on July 21 drove through the
Confederate center, only to meet a smashing attack from
the fresh Confederate right wing commanded by General
"Stonewall" Jackson. All but the regulars stampeded in a
wild flight back to Washington, choking the roads with men,
guns, abandoned baggage, and Congressmen who had come
in the hope of seeing a sort of picnic victory. Other Northern
reverses followed in Missouri, and at Ball's Bluff on the

Potomac, where Oliver Wendell Holmes, later of the Supreme Court, was wounded. Both sides girded themselves for a desperate struggle.

In the end the war dragged over four years, closing only when the South lay in utter exhaustion. Its cost in money, property loss, and lives was frightful. The North is estimated to have enlisted about two million men altogether, and when the last shot was fired had about a million in the field. The South is estimated to have enlisted something less than a million men; no one will ever know the exact number. On the Union side about 360,000 men died in action, from wounds or disease; on the Confederate side the dead have been computed at 258,000. Great parts of the South were laid waste. The Shenandoah Valley was ravaged from end to end; Sherman destroyed fifty millions' worth of public buildings and hundreds of millions' worth of private property in Georgia; cities like Columbia, Richmond, and Atlanta were gutted by fire; railroads were torn up and factories smashed. With its old labor system destroyed and its physical property shattered, the South was economically prostrate. Though the North was enjoying a great industrial boom when the war closed, it too had suffered more than it at first realized.

The Campaigns

FOUR MAIN FRONTS or theaters of action may be distinguished: the sea, the Mississippi Valley, Virginia and the Eastern-seaboard states, and the diplomatic front. The first may be briefly dismissed. At the beginning of the conflict practically the whole forty-ship navy was in Union hands, but was scattered and demoralized. An able head in Washington, Gideon Welles (best remembered now for his invaluable diary of the war), quickly reorganized and strengthened it. Lincoln proclaimed a blockade of the Southern coast, and although this was at first extremely weak, by 1863 it became highly effective. It prevented shipments of cotton to Europe and the importation of munitions, clothing, and medical supplies that the South sorely needed. Meanwhile, a brilliant naval commander, David G. Farragut, had emerged and conducted two remarkable operations. In one

he took a Union fleet of wooden sloops into the mouth of
the Mississippi, ran past two strong forts, and forced the
surrender of New Orleans, the Confederacy's largest and
wealthiest city. In another he forced his way past the
fortified entrance of Mobile Bay, captured a Confederate
ironclad, and sealed up the port. Ironclads were now beginning to supplant wooden ships. One of the anxious moments
of the war occurred in March, 1862, when the new Confederate ironclad, *Merrimac,* issued from Norfolk, Virginia,
destroyed two Union frigates in Hampton Roads at the
mouth of the James River and seemed ready to attack Washington or New York. Fortunately, an armored Union vessel
of curious design, "a cheesebox on a raft," the *Monitor,*
which had been built in New York and hurried South, appeared in the nick of time, attacked the champion, and put
a stop to its career. The Union navy gained another smart
victory when a roving Confederate cruiser built in England,
the *Alabama,* was sunk by the *Kearsarge* off Cherbourg.
The navy served the Union well in blockading the South, in
helping capture important coastal points, in amphibious
warfare on the Mississippi, the Tennessee, the Red, and
other inland streams, and in sinking or capturing Confederate commerce destroyers.

In the Mississippi Valley the Union forces won an almost
uninterrupted series of victories. Ulysses S. Grant, an Illi-
noisan of dogged tenacity, unimaginative but with a clear
grasp of the main principles of strategy, had been put in
command of strong Western forces. He began with the
breaking of a long Confederate line in Tennessee by capturing Forts Henry and Donelson on the Tennessee and
Cumberland rivers, thus making it possible to occupy most
of the western part of the state. The important city of Nashville had to be abandoned by the Confederates, and Union
troops were able to advance to the southern boundary of
Tennessee—that is, some two hundred miles into the heart
of the Confederacy. Here the Southern troops concentrated
under Albert Sidney Johnston and the dashing P. G. T.
Beauregard, who had commanded at Charleston and ordered
the attack on Fort Sumter. In April, 1862, they delivered
a blow which came near routing Grant. By a swift attack
they caught his army unprepared at Pittsburgh Landing on

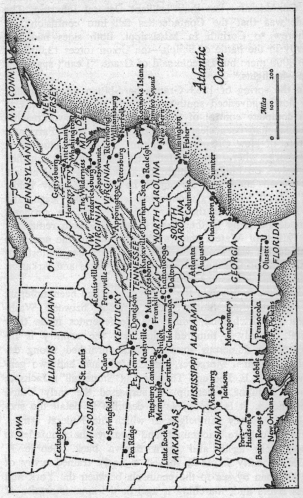

Points of Importance in the Southern Campaigns, 1861–1865

the Tennessee River, its back to the swollen stream, its
front unfortified. The sudden onslaught almost overwhelmed
the Union forces. Just in time Grant was reinforced, while
the Confederates lost their brilliant General Johnston. The
result was that the Confederates fell into confusion and
withdrew to Corinth in Mississippi. Both sides had lost
heavily in the battle of Shiloh—the Union forces 13,000 out
of 63,000 men; but Lincoln said of Grant, "I can't spare this
man—he fights."

In the spring of 1863 Grant's hard-bitten troops steadily
but slowly advanced southward. Their great object was to
gain complete control of the Mississippi, the lower reaches
of which had been cleared of Confederates after Farragut's
capture of New Orleans. For a time Grant was blocked at
Vicksburg, where the Confederates had strongly fortified
themselves on bluffs too high for a successful naval attack.
But by an audacious movement he took his army below
and around Vicksburg, conducted a six weeks' siege, and
on July 4 captured the town together with the strongest
Confederate army in the West. Now, as Lincoln remarked,
the Father of Waters went again unvexed to the sea. The
Confederacy was broken in two, and it became almost impossible to bring supplies from the rich Texas and Arkansas
country east across the stream.

Meantime in Virginia the Union troops had been suffering
one defeat after another. The distance between Washington and Richmond, which the Confederates made their
capital, is only a hundred miles, but the country is in-
tersected by numerous streams which furnished strong defensive positions. Moreover, the Confederates had two generals, Robert E. Lee and Thomas J. ("Stonewall") Jackson,
who in brilliant leadership far surpassed the early Union
commanders. It is impossible to describe in detail the succession of bloody campaigns in which the Federal armies,
trying to capture Richmond and destroy the Confederate
forces, were again and again thrown back. George B.
McClellan early in 1862 moved a finely trained army of
100,000 men by sea to the peninsula between the York and
James rivers and, marching it against the smaller armies of
Lee, fought the desperate Seven Days' Battles before Richmond. At one time his troops could hear the clocks striking

in the steeples of the Confederate capital, but they finally
retreated with heavy losses. The blundering John Pope failed
in the second battle of Bull Run (August 29-September 1,
1862) and was driven back toward Washington, while the
North feared for its own safety. Another Union commander,
the hapless Burnside, failed when, attempting to storm the
heights behind the town of Fredericksburg, he was repulsed
with terrible slaughter. Still another was beaten as ignominiously at the bloody battle of Chancellorsville; but there the
Confederates lost Lee's right arm, the indomitable Jackson,
whose bold raid in the Shenandoah Valley in 1862, defeating
a whole series of Union forces and throwing panic into
Washington, was perhaps the most thrilling exploit of the
war. Up to the summer of 1863 the Confederates had all
the best of it in the East.

Yet not one of these Confederate victories was decisive;
the Union government simply mustered new armies and
tried again. If the Union armies were unable to capture
Richmond, the Confederates had no better success when
they took the offensive. In August, 1862, Lee thought the
time was ripe to strike into the North, but McClellan met
him on the field of Antietam, in western Maryland, and
fought him to a standstill. It was a drawn battle—but Lee
withdrew, and Lincoln, desperately anxious for a victory,
thought it enough of a success to justify the announcement
of the Emancipation Proclamation. Again the following
summer, after the crushing defeat of the Union troops at
Chancellorsville, Lee struck northward and invaded Pennsylvania. His army almost reached the capital of the state,
and Baltimore and Philadelphia were thrown into great
alarm; but a stronger Union force intercepted his march at
Gettysburg. Here, in a three-day battle on July 1–3, Lee's
75,000 veterans made a valiant attempt to hurl back the
88,000 men under George S. Meade. Had they struck with
smashing celerity, while the Union forces were concentrating, they might have won the contest. In the end they had
to fight against a stronger army occupying better positions.
Pickett's desperate charge on the final day, facing a terrific
fire, was one of the most gallant efforts in the history of
war. But it failed, and next day, as Lee's veterans, after
losses which permanently crippled them, sullenly fell back

to the Potomac, it was clear that the "high tide at Gettysburg" had been the high tide of all Confederate hopes.

Grant's army was then taking possession of Vicksburg. The blockade of the Southern coasts had become an iron cordon which few vessels pierced. The Confederacy, its factories running short of machinery and materials, its railroads falling into decay, was nearing the end of its resources. The Northern states, on the other hand, seemed more prosperous than ever, their mills and factories running full blast, their farms exporting bumper crops to Europe, their man power being restored by immigration.

In southeastern Tennessee the final phase of the Mississippi Valley campaigns also went decisively against the Confederates. Chattanooga, a busy railroad junction in this area, was only less vital to the Confederacy than Richmond and Vicksburg. Commanding railways that ran southwest, southeast, and east, and so placed that it blocked the path of Union armies southeastward around the Great Smoky Mountains, it was one of the portals to the lower South. A Union force under W. S. Rosecrans reached Chattanooga early in September, 1863, and found itself faced by a strong Confederate force under the incompetent Braxton Bragg. In a terrific battle at Chickamauga, Bragg almost won the day, but was finally held to a costly deadlock by General George H. Thomas, a Virginian who had stood by the Union. Rosecrans then allowed himself to be shut up in Chattanooga, and Grant had to be sent to the rescue. In November, ably supported by Sherman and Thomas, Grant fought and won the battle of Chattanooga, part of his force driving the Confederates from Missionary Ridge in an impetuous charge that could not be halted. The Union troops were thus placed in a position to begin that advance into Georgia which Sherman carried to so triumphant a conclusion the next year. It was in May, 1864, that Sherman cut loose from his bases and, at the head of an army of one hundred thousand veterans, moved into Georgia. When General Joseph E. Johnston failed to stop him by a series of skillful defensive maneuvers, President Davis unwisely put his favorite, John Hood, in command. In vain Hood flung himself against the invader; on the first of September he was forced to evacuate Atlanta, and now the whole of Georgia lay open to Sherman. Then came the march to the sea, famous in song and story, and on December 22 Sherman captured the seaport of Savannah and presented it to President Lincoln as a "Christmas present." Johnston, hastily restored to command by Davis, retreated skillfully to the Carolinas; with forty thousand men Hood swung back into Tennessee, where, in the sanguinary battles of Franklin and Nashville, he was all but annihilated by Thomas, who once again proved himself one of the greatest of Union commanders.

It would have been far better for the South had it recognized its impending defeat and tried to make terms with the magnanimous Lincoln. But feeling had become too bitter to permit that. The Confederacy fought on until further resistance became almost impossible. It lost its last hope of French and British intervention in 1863. The Union government had great advantages on the diplomatic front, it used them skillfully, and after Gettysburg no European minister would bet on a losing cause. Moreover, in 1862 Lincoln had issued his Emancipation Proclamation, making the extirpation of slavery one of the main objects of the war; and this rallied the moral sense of the British masses to his side. The impoverished working people of Lancashire, deprived of cotton by the Union blockade, gave a memorable proof of their devotion to principle when they stood unshakably for the Union.

Early in 1864 Grant was brought east and made commander of all the Union armies. In battle after battle, collectively called The Wilderness, he relentlessly hammered at Lee, gradually wearing down the main Confederate force. General Sherman had already begun his campaign to subjugate Georgia. After occupying Atlanta early in September, then moving onward to the sea, systematically destroying stores, railways, and other property on a sixty-mile front, and finally emerging at Savannah, he turned northward, captured Columbia, and compelled the surrender of Charleston. And that same autumn of 1864 the dashing cavalry commander Phil Sheridan destroyed the agricultural resources of the Shenandoah Valley so completely that "a crow flying over it would have to carry his own rations." Finally, Lee had to abandon Richmond and on April 9, 1865, surrendered his army at Appomattox.

Internal Conflicts

MUCH MIGHT BE SAID about the internal conflicts in both
the North and South during these years of fearful exertion.
On neither side did the government show high efficiency.
The armies were filled by crude, blundering, inequitable
methods. Conscription laws were passed, but were not fairly
and democratically drawn; and in the North, where men
were allowed to buy substitutes, they resulted in angry draft
riots. Both sides were plagued by internal political squabbles.
The Republican "radicals," led by Thaddeus Stevens of Pennsylvania, Ben Wade of Ohio, and Charles Sumner of Massachusetts, assailed Lincoln as too feeble in his conduct of the
war, too slow to adopt emancipation as one of its objects,
and too mild in his measures for reconstructing Louisiana
and other conquered states. In the South such governors as
Joseph E. Brown of Georgia and Zebulon Vance of North
Carolina gravely impeded the Richmond authorities by their
mulish insistence on state rights. On both sides, but particularly in the North, politics played an unhappy part in army
appointments. They pushed forward incompetents like Benjamin Butler and Ambrose Burnside, while brave and efficient leaders like Thomas were neglected. On both sides
desertions became widespread and in the end gravely crippled the Confederate armies.

The North accused the South of terrible abuses at Libby
Prison in Richmond, Andersonville in Georgia, and other
prisons; but the Northern camps were bad enough. Favor-
itism, fraud, and corruption flourished in both sections.
Washington became full of dishonest contractors, speculators, lobbyists, and other birds of prey, while some schem-
ing Southerners made fortunes at the expense of their
dying cause. The depreciation of paper money in the South
carried prices to insane heights and ruined great numbers
of hard-working people. In the North a pronounced inflation encouraged wild gambling and risky enterprises and
helped to grow a crop of blatant millionaires. Altogether,
the war had its very seamy side. But it also had its innumerable tales of heroism and devotion, of philanthropic
effort and patriotic sacrifice.

Robert E. Lee: Abraham Lincoln

To THE SOUTH war gave an immortal hero in Robert E. Lee, the knightliest of commanders. The brilliance of his leadership, the devotion of his service, the humanity he displayed throughout the conflict, and his magnanimity in accepting defeat and urging the Southern people to become loyal partners of their late enemies must always arouse admiration. His very faults were the defects of his virtues, for he was too courteous and considerate to make stubborn subordinates bend to his will. A better strategist than a tactician, he showed acuteness in divining the plans of his opponents, analytical keenness in using military intelligence, and sound judgment in estimating the power of military units and positions. By virtue of his power of organization, his conscientious attention to details, his tender care for his men, his daring, and his fine presence, he inspired confidence and won the devotion of his troops. Like Washington, he had a self-control that he seldom lost, and then but briefly. This Christian gentleman was great in victory and defeat, in war and in peace. Surviving the conflict but five years, he devoted himself to the restoration of the South and the reconciliation of the sections.

To the North the war gave a still greater hero in Abraham Lincoln. In its early months few perceived the true stature of this rough-looking Western lawyer, homely, awkward, and ill-schooled. His second Secretary of War, Edwin M. Stanton, for a time called him a gorilla—though he later declared that he was the greatest leader of men who ever lived; the hostile press spoke of him as an imbecile. Little by little the nation came to comprehend his deep sagacity, founded upon careful study and hard thinking; his intense love of truth, his inexhaustible patience, and his boundless generosity of spirit. If he seemed at moments to hesitate and vacillate, time always proved that he had known how to wait for the national advantage, how to combine strength with tact. Understanding the American people, he knew when to move forward boldly. He was the most honest of leaders and, though a skillful politician, never resorted to unfair measures. He constantly appealed to the intelligence, never the ignorance, of the electorate.

He was charitable in thought and deed and during all
the agony of the conflict he never uttered a vindictive word
against the Southern people. He was anxious above all to
weld the country together as a union not of force, but of
hearts; and even as the Union armies were winning their
last victories, he proposed to pay the South handsomely for
its slaves. His foreign policy showed dignity, integrity, and
firmness. Though he had to use unprecedented powers, he
believed fervently in democratic self-government and knew
how to inspire the loyalty of his people. Though he exercised the authority of a czar he commanded the complete
faith of the masses. His eloquence grew with the need for
it, and his Gettysburg Address, the Second Inaugural Address, and some of his letters are among the finest treasures
of English prose. His murder on April 14, 1865, less than
a week after Appomattox, was a tragic misfortune to victor
and vanquished alike. As James Russell Lowell wrote:

Never before that startled April morning did such multitudes
of men shed tears for the death of one they had never seen, as
if with him a friendly presence had been taken from their lives,
leaving them colder and darker. Never was funeral panegyric
so eloquent as the silent look of sympathy which strangers exchanged when they met that day. Their common manhood had
lost a kinsman.

The Heritage of the War

UNDER A NEW, untried, and unevenly equipped leader,
Andrew Johnson, the nation had to face the trying problems of readjustment and reconstruction. They were not
made easier by the widespread demand for vengeance
which burst forth immediately after Lincoln's assassination.
They were quickly complicated by selfish political and economic considerations—by the desire of the Republican party
to exploit the situation in order to perpetuate its power, and
by the wish of selfish business groups to use the situation to
their own advantage. Manufacturers who wanted high
tariffs, bondholders who wanted to be certain of interest
payments in gold, railroad builders who wanted land grants,
all rallied behind the Republican regime.

The war left the country a mixed heritage of good and evil results. It had saved the Union and given it an "indestructible" character, but the Union that emerged from the fiery cauldron was not the Union of the Fathers. It had abolished slavery forever, but by violence, and with little thought for the welfare of the freedmen or of the society in which they had to live and the economy which they had to share. It had struck down an aristocratic oligarchy in the South, but there was no other class ready to assume the responsibilities of government which that class had so largely monopolized, and the South was, for a generation, bereft of its natural leaders. Lincoln had pleaded for government of, by, and for the people, but no fair-minded observer could conclude that the war had advanced democracy in any immediate sense.

The war left a hatred between North and South that lasted for decades—the hatred that Lincoln had hoped to sweep away. It made many people more intolerant, especially in political affairs. Republican demagogues in the North long waved the "bloody shirt" to catch votes; that is, they appealed to the prejudice against Southern Democrats. The opposing section, on the other hand, became a "solid South" under the Democratic banner, raising its grievances for generations, and romanticizing its past—slavery, the plantation system, and the war. This intense partisanship was most unfortunate. Not until twenty years after the war ended did a Democrat enter the White House; not until nearly fifty years had elapsed did a man of Southern birth, Woodrow Wilson, become President. The war gave the North a body of veteran soldiers who held great voting power. They presently began to demand pensions from the government, and obsequious politicians ladled out the public money to them with eager carelessness. The conflict had an unhappy effect, too, on the social and moral fiber of the country. It brought into prominence a class of men who were eager for money and power, coarse in their tastes, and unscrupulous in their acts. The great mass of Americans, of course, remained hardworking, conscientious, and patriotic. But a vulgar, brassy, greedy element was more conspicuous than ever before.

Reconstruction in the South

NOW THAT THE SOUTH had been defeated, it had to be
"reconstructed," that is, restored to its proper relationship
with the Union. This painful process, already under way in
Tennessee and Louisiana as early as 1862, dominated the
political scene from Appomattox to 1877. Had Lincoln lived,
he would have insisted on his policy of "malice towards
none, charity for all," and on his view that the whole question of the constitutional position of the seceded states—
whether they were in the Union or out of it, whether they
had committed legal suicide, or forfeited their constitutional
rights—was "bad as the basis of controversy and good for
nothing at all, a merely pernicious abstraction." In all likelihood he would have won both public opinion and Congress
to this sensible and benign view.

But Andrew Johnson did not enjoy either the influence
or the authority of Lincoln. He was President by accident;
he was an ex-Democrat at the head of the Republican party;
he had few friends in Congress; for all his loyalty and stubborn integrity he had no appeal to the public. He had grown
up in the rough and tumble of Tennessee politics, and never
quite adapted himself to the very different circumstances
of the presidency; his conduct in public was undignified, and
his relations with Congress rash and tactless. He quarreled
with Congress over bills to aid the Negroes through a Freedmen's Bureau, and to protect them by a Civil Rights Act, bills
which, he thought, unduly invaded the authority of the
states. Letting himself be outmaneuvered and discredited by
the Radical leaders of Congress, he lost control of the political situation, and his leadership was repudiated in the
Congressional elections of 1866.

Congress, enraged by his intransigence on Reconstruction
and other issues, passed over his veto a bill forbidding him
to dismiss certain officeholders without its consent. The law
was probably unconstitutional, and the President tried to
test it by dismissing his disloyal Secretary of War, Edwin
Stanton. Thereupon the Radicals, in February, 1868, impeached him for "high crimes and misdemeanors," tried him
before the Senate, and came within one vote of ejecting him
from the White House. Only the courage of a few inde-

pendents like Trumbull of Illinois and Fessenden of Maine saved the Congress, and the country, from the fateful consequences of this disgraceful attack upon the constitutional integrity of the presidency.

In a broad way the purpose of Reconstruction was threefold. It was first, and quite simply, to wind up the affairs of the Confederacy, get the Southern states back in the Union, repair and reanimate the shattered mechanisms of national politics and administration. It was, second, to assure the newly emancipated Negro not only his freedom but his political and civil rights. A third purpose was to preserve and prolong Civil War legislation dealing with tariffs, western lands, banking, currency, and finance, and similar interests, by strengthening the Republican party in the South and throughout the nation.

There were two obvious ways of achieving these objectives, one constitutional, the other political. The first was to write into the Constitution itself guarantees for the perpetuation of the verdict of Appomattox and for civil and political rights for Negroes. These were to be achieved by amending the Constitution. The Fourteenth Amendment, which passed the Congress in 1866, made clear that the Negro was a citizen, provided that no state should abridge the privileges or immunities of citizens of the United States or deprive any person of life, liberty, or property without due process of law, or deny to any person the equal protection of the laws. And in 1869 Congress passed the Fifteenth Amendment, granting the franchise to freedmen, and authorized future Congresses to enforce the grant by "appropriate legislation."

The second method to secure the ends of Reconstruction was to implement these constitutional guarantees through civil rights legislation, and to strengthen the Republican party in the South by building up a Negro following and by winning over the business, railroad, and other interests that, in the old days, had attached themselves to the Southern Whigs.

Was Reconstruction punitive? There was a good deal of loose talk about punishing the South and her leaders for secession and war, but in fact there was less of this than might have been expected. For almost a century now Southerners have interpreted the Reconstruction era as one of unmitigated ruthlessness, and have insisted that the victorious North imposed upon the stricken South a Carthaginian peace. Yet no other great rebellion of modern times was put down with so little formal punishment of the vanquished, or so few acts of retribution, and no other rebellious groups were permitted to resume their positions and their power so speedily after defeat. Looking back now over a century of history, and keeping in mind the savage repressions of rebellions in China, Spain, Russia, and even Cuba, we are forced to conclude that the conduct of the victorious North toward the defeated South was on the whole magnanimous.

It is unnecessary to trace in detail the vicissitudes of Reconstruction. The moderates, somewhat blunderingly led by President Johnson, had inherited the policy of Lincoln. They wanted to bind up the wounds of war, persuade the Southern states to try the experiment of Negro suffrage, and get Southern states back into the Union. The Radicals, led by implacable opponents of the Southern "slaveocracy" such as Thaddeus Stevens of Pennsylvania or Ben Wade of Ohio, and by idealists such as Charles Sumner of Massachusetts, were less concerned with the rights, and the votes, of the Negro. They proposed to delay full restoration of the South until such time as Southerners had made clear that they fully accepted the consequences of defeat, and that they would interpose no obstacles to the realization of Negro rights or to other features of the Radical program.

President Johnson launched the moderate program by issuing a generous amnesty proclamation, and setting up provisional governments in the Southern states. These were required to write new constitutions and to get the states back to normal. While Southerners were ready enough to accept the conciliatory parts of this program, they balked at giving the Negro either the vote or any substantial civil rights; on the contrary, the "reconstructed" legislatures proceeded to enact a series of Black Codes designed to "keep the Negro in his place," which was, of course, a subordinate one. Congress responded with the Fourteenth Amendment. One by one the Southern legislatures rejected the amendment, and the issue was joined. Was the South or the North to dictate the terms of Reconstruction?

Victory at the polls in 1866 strengthened Radical determination and aggressiveness. When Congress met the following spring, it wiped the Reconstruction slate clean and started over again. First it re-established military rule in the South, organizing the ex-Confederate states into five military districts under major generals. These military commanders were in turn to register "loyal" voters, Negro and white, who would then set up new governments prepared to do the bidding of Congress. Readmission of the states—that is, the seating of their representatives in Congress—was made dependent on ratification of the Fourteenth Amendment, and then on the Fifteenth Amendment, which prohibited the states from disfranchising the Negro merely because he was a Negro.

The military governments quickly bowed out in favor of reconstructed governments controlled by a coalition of newly enfranchised Negroes, Southern whites prepared to come to terms with reality, and Northern "carpetbaggers" who flooded into the South for political or business purposes that did not always bear close examination. These "Radical" governments in turn controlled the Southern states for varying periods of from one to six or seven years. They were, in many cases, extravagant, incompetent, and corrupt—as were some of the Northern state governments during the Reconstruction years as well. But they carried through important reforms, and they do not deserve the obloquy that had been heaped upon them.

Little by little Southern whites won back "home rule." In part they did this by violence and intimidation. They created secret societies like the Ku Klux Klan, which compelled many carpetbaggers to return to the North, and frightened Negroes away from polling places; it was a resort to secrecy and violence which provided pernicious precedents for the coming years. In part they "redeemed" their governments by winning back control of the old political machinery—for after all it was the native whites who had the political experience and the political skills. And in part they found friends and allies in the North—Democrats who wanted a reunited party, businessmen who wanted to build railroads and get industry going, and ordinary citizens who were simply tired of the prolonged disorder in the South and said, with General Grant, "Let us have peace." State after state was reconquered by the Southern Democrats until, by 1876, only three—Louisiana, Florida, and South Carolina—remained in the hands of the Radicals.

The election of 1876 was one of the closest and most disorderly in American history. The Democratic candidate, Samuel Tilden of New York, emerged with a clear plurality of the popular vote, and, on the face of the returns, a clear majority of the electoral college vote as well. But returns from four states were in dispute; if all of these votes went to the Republican candidate, Rutherford B. Hayes, he would be elected. An electoral commission appointed to settle the dispute awarded all of the votes to Hayes by a strict party vote. Would the Democrats—now probably the majority party—accept what seemed to them like a "steal"?

In this crisis leaders of the two parties came to a tacit understanding. If the Democrats acquiesced in the findings of the electoral commission and allowed Hayes to become President, he would, in turn, undertake to withdraw all the Federal troops from the South, appoint a Southerner to his cabinet, and support substantial appropriations for a program of internal improvements in the South. Hayes took the oath of office, and Federal troops were duly withdrawn from the South. It was the end of Reconstruction; it was, too, for all practical purposes, the end of any serious effort to protect the Negro in his constitutional rights. The "bargain" brought peace—or calm—to American politics, but it crippled the Negro for three quarters of a century and committed the South to the Democratic party.

As we look back on the period of civil strife and turmoil between 1850 and 1877, it seems an almost unmixed tragedy. The country would have fared far more happily if, as Lincoln long hoped, the abolition of slavery could have taken place gradually and with due compensation to the slaveholders. That would have given time to educate the Negroes and the whites to their new relative step in society. It would have spared the nation the six hundred thousand vigorous young men who (out of a population of thirty-one millions) lost their lives in the conflict, and the millions of children they would have brought into the world. It would have saved the South stupendous ruin; it would have saved both sections the coarsening effects so clearly revealed in the "gilded age" of money-getting and vulgarity after the war. Yet there is no reason to suppose that the program could have been carried out. At no time was the South prepared to give up slavery peacefully, and it is relevant to remember that as late as February of 1865 Delaware voted against compensated emancipation.

Yet, even beyond the items already mentioned, the page shows credit entries. The storm unified the nation and knit it into one great whole as no slower process could have done. Socially and economically the South now became more closely akin to the North. The war did much to deepen and mature the national character; literature and education became in various ways more adult. And the conflict gave the country a set of memories, poignant and dramatic, to quicken its heart and lift its imagination. For centuries to come it would recall them with a thrill—the firing on Fort Sumter; the duel of the *Merrimac* and *Monitor;* the irresistible sweep of Stonewall Jackson through the Shenandoah, a trail of defeated Union armies behind him; the gunboats running the Mississippi below Vicksburg in a storm of shot and shell; the death grapple of Pickett's gray host with Hancock's blue line on Cemetery Ridge; the storming of the heights above Chattanooga by troops whom even Grant's order could not stop, a feat that surpassed Balaklava; the desperate valor of Hood's tattered veterans as they assaulted the Union ranks at Franklin, six thousand of them dead or wounded within two hours; the *Kearsarge* circling about the *Alabama* till she sank beneath the waves; Lee with his jeweled sword, Grant in his common private's dress, shaking hands at Appomattox; Lincoln walking through the fire-blackened streets of Richmond; the thousand-mile funeral given the remains of the martyred President; the grand review as the endless ranks of the Eastern and Western armies rolled up Pennsylvania Avenue in the closing scene of the war. It was an epic story, and it will be remembered as long as men cherish the past.

CHAPTER 13

The Emergence of Modern America

The Impact of War

THE CIVIL WAR worked a revolution in American society and economy, North as well as South. Although the roots of modern America go deep into the prewar years, we can date its actual emergence from the war itself. That conflict gave an immense stimulus to industry, speeded up the exploitation of natural resources, the development of large-scale manufacturing, the rise of investment banking, the extension of foreign commerce, and brought to the fore a new generation of "captains of industry" and "masters of capital." It enormously accelerated the construction of the railway and telegraph network and ushered in the railroad age. It put a premium upon inventions and labor-saving devices and witnessed the large-scale application of these to agriculture as well as to industry. It threw open vast new areas for farming and grazing, developed fresh markets for farm produce, and inaugurated both the agricultural revolution and the farm problem. It created conditions favorable to the growth of cities and offered work to the hundreds of thousands of immigrants who soon crowded into the New World. In the South, defeat largely destroyed the planter class, freed the Negro, revolutionized farm economy, brought a new middle class to the fore, and laid the foundations for that New South which was to emerge during the next generation. In

the North it opened up new fields to investment and to speculation, created a host of war millionaires, and hastened the
process of the concentration of control of resources, industry,
and finance in the great urban centers, the subordination of
the South and the West to the Northeast, and the creation
of new class distinctions to take the place of the old.

In the generation after Appomattox the pattern of our
present society and economy took shape. Growth—in area,
numbers, wealth, power, social complexity, and economic
maturity—was the one most arresting fact. The political
divisions of the republic were drawn in their final form, a
dozen new states were admitted to the Union, and an American empire was established. In a space of forty years population increased from thirty-one to seventy-six million; fifteen million immigrants—an ever-increasing proportion of
them from southern and eastern Europe—poured into the
Promised Land, and great cities like New York, Chicago,
Pittsburgh, Cleveland, and Detroit doubled and redoubled
their size. In swift succession the Indians were harried out of
their ancient haunts on the high plains and in the mountains
and valleys beyond and herded into reservations, the mining
and cattle kingdoms rose and fell, the West was peopled and
farmed, and by the end of the century the frontier was no
more. Vast new finds of iron ore, copper, and oil created
scores of great industries, small business grew into big business, the corporation became the effective instrument of the
new economy, the trust and the holding company its characteristic form of organization. Great banking houses, like that
of the Morgans, moved quietly into a commanding position
in the national economy. The railroad network was all but
completed, mileage increasing from thirty to some two hundred thousand and giving the nation the greatest railroad
system of any country in the world. Labor organizations,
few and feeble before the war, increased in membership and
established firmly their place in the economic order, and industrial conflicts, heretofore small and sporadic, became organized and threatening. The small republic became a world
power, expanding into the Caribbean and the Pacific, while
its industry, eager for markets, and its bankers, zealous for
investments, developed new techniques of economic imperialism. No other generation in American history witnessed
changes as swift or as revolutionary as those which trans-

formed the rural republic of Lincoln and Lee into the urban industrial empire of McKinley and Roosevelt.

A new series of problems, complex and baffling, confronted an American people too inexperienced to understand their character, too busy to give them careful thought. The most urgent of these were the problems of the distribution of wealth, the control of vast and powerful aggregations of capital, the maintenance of political democracy under the impact of an undemocratic economy, large-scale unemployment and labor troubles, urban crowding and the assimilation of the foreign-born, the decline of farm income and the increase in farm tenancy, the conservation of natural resources rapidly being exhausted by reckless exploitation, the responsibilities of overseas rule and world politics, and the accommodation of political institutions, organized for the needs of a small rural republic, to the challenging demands of a great industrial nation.

The Transformation of the South

THE IMPACT OF WAR and of defeat on the South was immediate and cataclysmic. Devastation without parallel in American history greeted the eyes of the veterans in gray as they trudged wearily home after Nashville and Appomattox. Large parts of Virginia and Tennessee had been ravaged by contending armies; Sherman had cut a sixty-mile swath through the heart of Georgia and South Carolina; Hunter and Sheridan had swept the rich valley of Virginia; vast areas of northern Alabama, Mississippi, and Arkansas lay in ruins. Proud cities like Richmond, Charleston, Columbia, and Atlanta had been gutted by fire or battered by bombardment. Bridges were down, roads neglected, hundreds of miles of railroad track torn up, rolling stock was destroyed, quays and docks were rotted. Normal economic life was almost paralyzed. Confederate money was worthless, and the only specie was that which had been hoarded or which the Union army brought into the conquered country. Banks had closed their doors, insurance companies were insolvent, industries and business ruined, and a large part of the cotton which had been stored in warehouses was put to the torch or confiscated by the military authorities.

Civil government had all but disappeared, and there was no effective authority to collect taxes, run the schools, maintain the roads, or enforce the laws against the marauders and guerrilla bands who harried the countryside. Churches had been burned and congregations dispersed; the endowments of colleges lost, their libraries and laboratories destroyed: the librarian of the University of Alabama managed to save just one book—the Koran—from the torch. Most public schools were closed, and education was at a standstill.

Even agriculture was in a desperate state—thousands of farms abandoned, fences down, ditches growing up in weeds, dams and levees broken, horses and cattle dead or stolen, plows rusting in the fields, the labor system disorganized. The Carolina rice industry was permanently ruined, salt water inundating the fields; the sugar industry of Louisiana was destroyed. In 1870 Virginia had two million acres less in tobacco than in 1860; not again until 1879 did the South raise a cotton crop as large as that of the year of secession. During the winter of 1865 starvation was imminent throughout large sections of the South, and whites as well as blacks were supported by the Federal army or by the newly organized Freedmen's Bureau. As the Southern poet, Sidney Lanier, wrote, "Pretty much the whole of life has been merely not dying."

Reconstruction brought new woes and new burdens almost as heavy as those of war. The Confederate debt had been swept away and with it, of course, the investment which patriotic Southerners had made in their cause, but the South was expected to bear its share of the national debt as well as of the current expenses of the national government: in addition it was assessed a heavy excise tax on cotton. This was perhaps neither unjust nor exorbitant, but as much cannot be said for the debts and taxes of state and local governments. During the carpetbag regime, millions of dollars were wasted in extravagances, millions were stolen outright, and additional millions insouciantly poured into dubious railroad and business ventures which rarely repaid ten cents on the dollar. Wealth had declined, in some sections, by more than one half, but taxes and debts mounted inexorably. Carpetbag and radical regimes increased the public debt of South Carolina from five to twenty-nine million, that of Arkansas from three to fifteen, that of Louisiana from eleven to almost fifty.

Yet all this should not persuade us to condemn too hastily the Reconstruction governments. The task of repairing the devastations of the war was inevitably costly, and much of the property that had formerly borne the burden of taxes—railroads, banks, and industries—had been swept away, so almost the entire burden of taxation fell upon the land. Public services, long neglected in the South, now made new and increased demands on government; these were, for example, the first governments that attempted to provide public education for all the children of the state. Corruption and incompetence doubtless accounted for a substantial part of the high taxes and indebtedness, but so too did the practice of white "Redeemer" governments of underwriting railroads and other business ventures. And as for corruption, it was to be found in both races, both parties, and all classes.

Nor should we fail to appreciate the constructive side of Radical reconstruction: the establishment of public schools, of charitable and humane institutions, the encouragement of immigration, the distribution of lands to Negroes, and the gestures—condemned to frustration—toward political democracy. It remained for later governments to pick up where the Radical governments had left off, and to try to assure a greater degree of equality and justice to all elements of Southern society.

Vigorously the defeated South turned to the task of physical reconstruction and to the rehabilitation of its agricultural economy and the restoration of the institutions of civilized society. "As ruin was never before so overwhelming," the Georgia editor, Henry Grady, later recalled, "never was restoration swifter." Richmond, Charleston, and Columbia rose from their ruins, and six months after the end of the war a visitor to Atlanta reported that a new city was springing up with marvelous rapidity. Railroad tracks were relaid and new roads pushed into the Southwest, bridges rebuilt, dams and levees restored; ships once more put into the harbors of Norfolk and Charleston and Mobile; country merchants, small-scale traders, and, in time, banks and insurance companies began operations.

Old factories were reopened, and capital was attracted to new industries—often at usurious rates. Vast stands of white and yellow pine furnished the basis for a flourishing lumber industry. Union soldiers who had passed through Durham, North Carolina, and helped themselves to some of the tobacco made by Washington Duke wrote back for more, and the basis of the great North Carolina tobacco industry was established; by 1888 Durham had the largest tobacco factory in the world and was shipping ten million pounds of tobacco every year. Flour and grist mills sprang up to provide for local needs; the fertilizer industry, so essential to cotton growing, was re-established. Rich coal and iron deposits were uncovered in Tennessee and northern Alabama. Birmingham, which was a cotton field in 1870, became within two decades a city of fifty thousand, the center of a booming iron industry, served by six trunk-line railroads. By 1890 the South was producing one fifth of the pig iron of the entire nation. Other towns like Chattanooga, Durham, Winston-Salem, and Danville grew into thriving manufacturing cities.

A textile industry had flourished in the seaboard South ever since William Gregg had opened his cotton mills at Graniteville, South Carolina, in 1846. Like most other industries, however, it had been completely disorganized by the war. In the decade of the seventies it began once more to forge ahead, taking full advantage of the combination of cheap labor, proximity to water power, and easy access to raw materials. Scores of little factories, financed almost entirely by local capital, sprang up along the upcountry of the Carolinas and Georgia. By 1890 South Carolina had half a million spindles, and the whole South could boast almost four times that number; New England industrialists were already worried about competition from that section. And by 1890, too, the South had the beginning of a labor problem which was to grow in seriousness with the passing years.

The Southern textile industry remained local and took on—largely from necessity—a curiously feudal character. Attracted by what seemed to be high wages and steady work, whole families moved in from the rundown farms to the near-by mill villages, bringing with them their labor habits and attitudes developed in farming. They took long hours for granted and they took for granted, too, that the whole family—women and children as well as men—would

share the work. These mill villages, straggling on the edge
of some town, were owned and controlled by the operators
who had built the mills. Workers lived in company houses,
went to company churches and schools, bought their food
and clothing from company stores, were brought into the
world by company doctors and buried by company preachers
in a company cemetery. It was a new feudalism, and though
it worked well enough in its early years, it was fraught with
trouble for the future.

Yet notwithstanding the rise of the iron, lumber, tobacco,
and textile industries, the South remained predominantly
rural and agricultural; before 1900 it could not boast a single
city, except New Orleans, with a population of one hundred
thousand. Even its industries were closely connected with
agriculture: tobacco and textile production was large, but
the value actually added by manufacture was comparatively
small. The vast majority of Southerners stayed on their
farms, growing staple crops. But agriculture, too, had suffered disorganization during the war, and, too, had to go
through a period of readjustment.

The great planters had been most impoverished by the
war and reconstruction. With their capital in slaves swept
away, their labor force disintegrated, taxes and overhead
costs mounting, the majority of them were forced to break
up their plantations or to let them go under the hammer
to pay taxes and debts. The result was a sweeping revolution in landholding: with good land selling for three or four
dollars an acre, thousands of small farmers enlarged their
holdings, tens of thousands of poor whites, freedmen, landless mechanics, and shopkeepers were able to satisfy their
earth hunger and become landowners. In 1860 there were
some 33,000 farms in South Carolina; twenty years later
the number had soared to 94,000. In 1860 there were fewer
than 600 farms in Mississippi under ten acres in size; within
a decade the number had increased to more than 11,000.
Throughout the South, plantations of one thousand acres
or more declined by over one half, and the average size of
farms dropped from 335 to 153 acres in the space of twenty
years. At the same time, new rich lands were being taken
up in Arkansas and Texas, and soon Oklahoma was thrown
open to settlement. King Cotton, who had, for a time, been

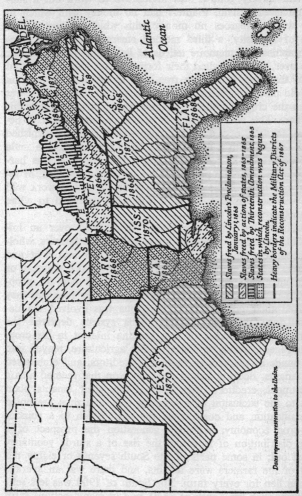

Emancipation and Reorganization of the Southern States

Legend:
- Slaves freed by Lincoln's Proclamation, January 1, 1863
- Slaves freed by action of states, 1863–1865
- Slaves freed by Thirteenth Amendment, 1865
- States in which reconstruction was begun by Lincoln.
- Heavy borders indicate the Military Districts of the Reconstruction Act of 1867

Dates represent restoration to the Union.

toppled from his throne, re-established and expanded his empire.

With slavery gone it was imperative to work out a substitute labor system. Planters had no money with which to pay wages; Negroes no money with which to rent farms. Out of necessity, a third method emerged: countless autobiographies and memoirs tell us of its origin. When the war was over, planters called their former slaves about them, told them that they were now free, and asked them to stay on the old place and work. Wages were out of the question, but when the crop was in, the planter would divide up with his workers. This was the origin of the share-crop system. It became, in time, organized and regularized. Farmers furnished their tenants with a cabin, land, tools, fertilizer, and a mule and undertook to keep them going until the crop was harvested. The share-cropper gave his labor and received, in return, one third of the crop. The system seemed to work well and was so convenient that it was soon extended to white tenants as well as to black.

Actually this share-crop plan, which tided over an impossible situation, developed great evils. Small farmers, wholly dependent upon staple crops, usually fell into debt and became a species of chattel, mortgaged to the planters or merchants who carried them. Because they had no property to pledge as security for the supplies they received, they pledged their growing crop, and thus was evolved the demoralizing "crop-lien" system. This system deprived the average tenant farmer of any genuine interest in his crop, encouraged slovenly and unscientific agriculture, played into the hands of planters or merchant creditors, and embittered the tenants. Because cotton was one crop that seemed a safe investment, creditors often insisted that their tenants plant that to the exclusion of everything else, and thus prevented diversification and condemned the deep South to a ruinous one-crop economy. Within a generation the prospect of a wide distribution of land and the rise of a sturdy yeomanry faded out; in some parts of the South seventy or eighty per cent of the farmers were tenants, and there was an average of one lien for every farm. The South of 1900 was less self-sufficient than the South of 1860, and in many sections farm wealth had actually declined over the years. Only when agricultural education and improved sanitation came with the

Rockefeller Foundation and Smith-Lever Act did the rural South take a secure turn for the better.

The Negroes, too, found that while they were legally free, they were not actually free. Congress, which decreed their freedom, quickly abandoned them to their former masters. After 1877 it did nothing to provide them with political rights, social equality, or economic security, but wasted its efforts rather on the futile task of guaranteeing them political equality. For a year or two after the war, the blacks were like refugees in a war-stricken land. Thousands of them took to the roads, wandering aimlessly from county to county: it is safe to say that more families were broken up by the first year of freedom than by any year of slavery. Thousands of them died of disease and starvation or were the victims of violence. Eventually, through the efforts of more responsible Southerners and with the co-operation of the Federal authorities, order was restored; when the Negroes found that they were not to get the "forty acres and a mule" which they fondly thought had been promised them, they returned to the one thing they knew—farming.

Some of the more enterprising made their way to the North or to the rising industrial towns of the South, but the vast majority of them became share-croppers, and as such they found that life went on for them much as it had before the war. They plowed the soil and cut cotton on white men's farms; they lived in the same ramshackle cabins, ate the same corn meal and collards and salt pork, wore the same tattered shirts and faded blue jeans, that they had always known. They did not try to vote or to send their children to the white folks' school or to get "beyond themselves" socially, or if they did, they were quickly taught a lesson.

The most encouraging development in the South of this postwar generation was the emergence of a middle class of independent small farmers, shopkeepers, businessmen, merchants, bankers, industrialists, and professional men. These were freed, now, from the incubus of slavery, and they freed themselves, in part at least, from the psychological incubus of "the lost cause." They were willing to forget the South of moonlight and gardenias and to recall Gettysburg and The Wilderness with pride rather than with bitterness. They set about to integrate the Southern with the national economy and to rebuild their shattered social institutions. Colleges were reopened, Robert E. Lee setting an example to the whole South by taking the presidency of struggling little Washington College in Virginia. States democratized their educational system, providing, on paper at least, for universal free public education in the elementary grades, though secondary education was pretty much reserved for whites. Churches were re-established, and with the growth of Negro congregations soon boasted a larger membership than before the war. There were notable advances in social legislation, in provision for the poor and the infirm, and feeble gestures toward labor legislation. Economically and politically the South knit itself once more into the national fabric.

The Revolution in the North

WHILE THE SOUTH was painfully rebuilding its economy and adjusting itself to new industrial and agricultural institutions, the North forged energetically ahead. Northern industry and finance, more fully than any other groups, harvested the fruits of victory. From its beginning the Republican party had been committed to high tariffs, internal improvements, railroad land grants, and free farms. Before the attack on Fort Sumter it was unable to translate any substantial part of this program into law. But after the secession of the Southern states there was no longer any effective opposition in the halls of Congress, and war furnished the occasion for a speedy enactment of the whole program. The Morrill tariff of 1861 sharply reversed the long downward trend of duties and established rates frankly protective; subsequent acts raised tariff walls still higher, and by the end of the war the average duties had been increased from eighteen to forty-seven per cent. Northern manufacturers were established in a position well-nigh impregnable; not until 1913 was an administration able to effect any substantial reduction in tariff rates. Further to encourage the business interests, Congress shortly repealed the income tax—never very high—and removed wartime taxes on coal, iron, and corporations. Under a series of railroad laws Congress subsidized the construction of transcontinental roads with loans of over sixty million dollars and outright gifts of over one hundred million acres of public lands—grants lavishly supplemented by state and local committees.

Favored by these auspices and stimulated by the insatiable needs of war and the equally insatiable needs of an expanding population, business and industry flourished as never before. "The truth is," wrote John Sherman to his brother, the General, "that the close of the war with our resources unimpaired gives an elevation, a scope, to the ideas of leading capitalists far higher than anything ever undertaken in this country before. They talk of millions as confidently as formerly of thousands." Certainly there was scope if not elevation to their ideas. Industry responded enthusiastically to the myriad needs of the armed forces and to the even greater demands of a war economy. Twenty thousand miles of track were laid in a decade, most of it in the West, and transcontinentals were pushed across the plains and the mountains with dizzy speed. Telegraph lines were strung from city to city and soon crossed the continent; cables were laid across the Atlantic; and within fifteen years the telephone added a new means of lightning-quick communication. The McCormick harvester works at Chicago could not keep up with the greedy demand for harvesting machines coming from the prairie lands of the Middle West; factories at Akron and Canton, Ohio, turned out tens of thousands of mowers; by the mid-seventies factories along the Middle Border were sending out barbed-wire fencing to the farms of the high plains. The McKay boot and shoe industry, the great packing plants at Chicago and Cincinnati, the flour mills of the Twin Cities, the breweries of Milwaukee and St. Louis, the iron and steel mills of the Pittsburgh region, the oil refineries of Ohio and Pennsylvania, and a hundred others worked day and night to meet the orders that poured in on them.

The end of the war saw no let-up in industrial activity. In the five years after Appomattox almost every industrial record was shattered. More coal and iron ore, silver and copper, were mined, more steel forged, more rails were laid, more lumber was sawed and more houses were built, more cotton cloth was woven, more flour milled, more oil refined, than in any previous five years in our history. In the decade from 1860 to 1870, the total number of manufacturing establishments increased by eighty per cent and the value of manufactured products by one hundred per cent. The industrial revolution was an accomplished fact.

Bankers and investors profited along with the industrialists. By the National Banking Acts of 1863 and 1864 Congress swept away the independent banking system dear to Jacksonian democrats and substituted one more favorable to private bankers. To give a clear field to the notes of the national banks, state-bank notes were taxed out of existence. During the war the government had issued several hundred million dollars in paper money, and, secured only by the credit of the government, this rapidly depreciated in value. By its decision to halt further issues of these "greenbacks," call in a good part of them, and bring the value of the rest up to par, Congress endorsed a policy which gave much-needed stability to the national currency, but which had a deflationary tendency fraught with hardship to debtor groups and particularly the Western farmers.

Speculation in greenbacks and in government bonds created many respectable fortunes. During the darkest period of the war, in mid-summer of 1864, greenbacks had sold for as little as thirty-nine cents on the dollar, but they were still legal tender for the purchase of government bonds. When Congress pledged itself to the payment of both principal and interest on these bonds in gold, it was clear that those canny enough—and, we must in all fairness add, patriotic enough—to have risked their money in the investments would realize a handsome profit. Repayment in gold was only the honest redemption of a clear pledge. But the fiscal policy of the government did more than anything else to accentuate class lines, for it meant that while soldiers were paid in greenbacks worth fifty or sixty cents in gold, bondholders would be paid in dollars worth one hundred cents in gold; while farmers borrowed dollars worth fifty or sixty cents, they would be called upon to pay back dollars worth one hundred cents. It meant that the whole nation could be called upon to pay a national debt which had appreciated to almost double its original cost.

Fortunes could be made then in banking and in financial speculations. But it was in railroads, mining, lumber, meat packing, iron and steel, oil, and similar investments closely tied up with the war or the opening up of the West that the greatest fortunes were made. Soon the names of railroad builders like Vanderbilt, Stanford, and Harriman, of packers like Armour and Swift, of lumber kings like Weyerhaeuser, of iron masters like Andrew Carnegie and Abram S. Hewitt, of oil princes like John D. Rockefeller, were household words, supplanting the names of statesmen or of men of letters in popular esteem. The war redistributed national wealth with a lavish and careless hand, creating thousands of respectable and hundreds of disreputable fortunes. Money gained an enhanced influence over the governments, state and Federal; money greased the ways into social favor, and soon the Vanderbilts and Goulds were as acceptable as the old Knickerbocker families; money built the fine mansions that lined Fifth Avenue, New York, and Michigan Avenue, Chicago. Money financed colleges and universities, like the new Johns Hopkins, Stanford, and Chicago; supported churches and missions; patronized orchestras and art museums. The concentration of wealth was naturally greatest in the industrial areas; the three states of New York, Pennsylvania, and Massachusetts paid sixty per cent of the income tax of 1864. But everywhere, East, West, and even in much of the South, the standard of living rose.

The farmers, too, got something from the war and the postwar boom, though less than they thought. The Republican party had rallied support with the cry "vote yourself a farm" and promptly after it took over the government, it re-enacted the Homestead Law that a Democratic President had earlier vetoed. By the terms of this act anyone might have 160 acres of public land by agreeing to cultivate it for five years. This enlightened legislation did enable several hundred thousand farmers to locate on the virgin soil of the West, and it thereby advanced economic democracy. Yet at the same time, larger areas were given to the railroads and other corporations or sold to land companies and speculators. Most of this, in turn, went eventually to farmers—but at a price. Congress passed the Morrill Act at the same time, granting several million acres of the public domain for the endowment and maintenance of agricultural and industrial colleges in all the states. Great state universities, like Iowa, Michigan, Minnesota, are monuments to the wisdom of the act.

But agricultural expansion during and after the war was not dependent upon governmental subsidies or encourage-

ment. The needs of the army, of the growing population of
the cities, and of hungry millions abroad, all provided a
stimulus to the growers of wheat and corn and to the dairy-
men and cattlemen. Railways, pushing rapidly across the
plains, gave access to unspoiled land, and the harvesters and
plows and mowers and twine binders just then brought onto
the market made it possible for one man—or boy—to do the
work formerly performed by two. In the two decades after
the election of Lincoln the production of corn, wheat, oats,
and barley more than doubled, and so, too, did the number
of cattle, sheep, and swine. As agriculture actually declined
in New England and the South, most of this advance was
in the Old Northwest and the trans-Mississippi West. During
the war decade Missouri increased her population by over
fifty per cent and emerged with almost two million people—
the fifth state in the Union. Nebraska, admitted to statehood
in 1867, counted almost half a million inhabitants by 1880.
The Dakotas, where the Sioux ranged undisputed during the
war, had a farming population of more than half a million
fifteen years later. Wool production had moved from Vermont to Ohio, and soon the Mountain States of the West
would take the lead; Iowa, Kansas, Nebraska, Minnesota, began to figure in the census as leading wheat and corn producers. The agricultural domain was moving irresistibly westward.

Yet, as if in anticipation of the future course of the economy, the farmers profited less by the boom years than did
any other class except the workers, and they were the first
to feel the impact of hard times. Overexpansion led to overproduction; the purchase of larger farms and of expensive
agricultural implements with which to farm them meant a
load of debt which could be carried only while high prices
obtained. The farmers of the older-settled East felt keenly
the competition from the new soil of the West; the farmers
of the West, favored by rich soil, were far from markets and
at the mercy of the railroads. As in ages past, the farmers
toiled long hours under the hot sun, lived without the comforts of community life, and in the end had little to show
for their labors.

Workingmen, alone of the major groups, failed to reap
any material rewards from the war. Toiling ten or twelve
hours a day in the coal pits and at the steel furnaces, work-

ing the looms and the shoe machines, building ships and laying tracks, they had contributed greatly to Union victory, and from their ranks, too, had come a large proportion of the men who did the actual fighting. Under the impact of war and of soaring prices some of the labor organizations shattered by the panic of 1857 were pieced together again. Labor had need of organization. Wages had gone up, to be sure, but prices had gone higher, and conservative estimates suggested that the majority of workingmen were worse off in 1865 than they had been in 1860. With the return to civilian life of over a million soldiers and the sharp upswing in immigration, competition for jobs became keen, and skilled craftsmen hastened to organize to protect their skills. The short-lived Knights of St. Crispin, a shoemakers' guild, was one such organization, and its early demise proved the futility of fighting against machinery and the factory system. More interesting were two larger and more amorphous combinations—the National Labor Union and the Knights of Labor, both dating from the sixties, both representing efforts to unite the most varied labor, farmer, and reform groups.

Yet the vast majority of workingmen remained outside these organizations and suffered all the vicissitudes of a rapidly changing economic structure and, shortly, of panic and depression. The government, so zealous to legislate for business groups, did little for laboring men. In 1868, to be sure, it established an eight-hour day on public works, but this admirable example was not widely followed. And against this gesture may be set the failure to regulate immigration or to provide any protection for immigrants.

Politics

THE MOST SIGNIFICANT THING about the politics of the postwar years was their insignificance. Other administrations —those of Pierce and Buchanan, for example—had been dull and incompetent; it was reserved for the Grant administration to be incompetent and corrupt. Statesmanship, never more sorely needed than in the crisis of national reconstruction, gave way to politics, and politics were shot through and through with partisanship, privilege, and corruption.

The basic principle of reconstruction politics was the establishment in power of the Republican party. That party, it is well to remember, was relatively new and almost wholly sectional. During the war it had things all its own way and entrenched itself firmly in power. But with the end of the war and the return of some—and by the year 1871 all—Southern states to the Union, the prospect of continued Republican control of all branches of the government was dimmed. For throughout this period the Democratic party remained numerous and strong, even in the North, while the war and especially reconstruction made the South solid for the Democrats. If Northern and Southern Democrats could be brought to agree on candidates and policies, there was every likelihood that they would sweep the Republicans out of office and recapture control of the government.

What was at stake was not only party supremacy, but also the maintenance of those policies to which the party was committed and which it had already so boldly advanced. What was at stake was the new tariff wall, the national banking system, the program of railroad subsidies, and, perhaps most important of all, the policy of currency stabilization and of gold payment on government obligations. These economic questions were, of course, hopelessly tangled up with emotional ones—like rewarding those who had been loyal and punishing those who had been disloyal—and social ones—like the position of the Negro. In the end it was the Negro who was most readily sacrificed, and who gained least and lost most in the political shuffle.

The grand strategy and the tactics which the Republicans had to adopt, then, were clear enough. To preserve and advance the economic policies already so auspiciously inaugurated required that the party be kept in office until those policies were so thoroughly established that they could not be reversed. Tentative steps had already been taken in the temporary denial of suffrage and officeholding to large numbers of Confederate leaders and the exclusion from the halls of Congress of representatives from the more recalcitrant Southern states. But obviously this could not go on indefinitely. A promising policy seemed to be to build up a Republican party in the South. The basis of such an organization would have to be those elements among the whites who had long opposed the ruling classes in the South—the poor and underprivileged who might welcome an opportunity to make their voices heard. Numerical strength could be assured only by conferring the suffrage upon the Negro—and seeing to it that he voted right. This was attempted, first by the reconstruction acts and then by constitutional amendments.

The program was neat enough, but it failed to work. Military reconstruction stiffened Southern opposition; even more important was the attempt to exploit the Negro politically. For Republicanism thereby became identified with the notion of racial equality—a notion intolerable to most Southerners at this time. So these ill-advised politics, instead of strengthening the Republican party in the South, weakened it. As soon as Federal military authority was withdrawn, the Republican organizations collapsed and Southern Democrats quickly found ways to withhold the vote from the Negro. Thereafter the Southern Democrats had things all their own way. From 1880 to 1928 no state of the Confederacy cast its electoral vote for a Republican presidential candidate.

If the economic program of the Republican party could not be permanently insured by military reconstruction or by the constitutional requirement of Negro suffrage, it could be protected by another provision newly written into the Constitution. During the early stages of reconstruction, while the radicals were still quarreling with President Johnson, a joint committee of Congress had formulated an omnibus amendment designed to define citizenship, protect the civil rights of freedom, disfranchise Confederate leaders, and guarantee the Federal and invalidate the Confederate debt. This was the famous Fourteenth Amendment, the first article of which provided that:

No State shall make or enforce any law which shall abridge the privileges or immunities of citizens of the United States; nor shall any State deprive any person of life, liberty, or property, without due process of law; nor deny to any person within its jurisdiction the equal protection of the laws.

These memorable phrases did in time what Republican policies had failed to do: they threw constitutional sanction around the property and the practices of great business corporations. For the courts, in due time, interpreted them to mean that no state might so legislate as to deprive corporations of property or of fair returns on that property. This interpretation, to be sure, was not fully developed until the decade of the nineties—just in time to meet and stem the rising tide of Populism.

The Grant administration concerned itself chiefly with the maintenance of reconstruction policies that would keep the South subordinate to the North and Democrats subordinate to Republicans. In this it was largely successful. It had behind it the immense prestige of victory and of Grant himself, and its tenure of power was prolonged by the persistent distrust of any party that was connected with slavery and secession, and strengthened by the support of the business interests which it had served. Yet these advantages were, in time, forfeited. Grant was a great soldier, but a sorry chief executive, and except in the realm of foreign affairs his administration presents a record of egregious failure. Young Henry Adams, viewing the course of American history from Washington to Grant, said that Grant made evolution ridiculous.

Shortly after his accession to power, stories of corruption in high places became rife, and proved not without foundation. The Union Pacific, the nation's pride, had been financed by a group of crooked promoters who hired Congressmen to do their bidding; the Navy Department openly sold business to contractors; the Department of the Interior was a happy hunting ground for land thieves; the Indian Bureau sold post traderships to the highest bidders and neglected the welfare of its wards; the Treasury Department farmed out uncollected taxes to tax gatherers who made a good thing of it; the customhouses of New York and New Orleans were permeated with graft; a "whisky ring" in St. Louis defrauded the government of millions in excise taxes, and a gang of boodlers in the national capital vied with the carpet-bag regimes of the South in extravagance and waste. "It looks," wrote one Republican Senator with understandable exaggeration, "as if the Republican party were going to the dogs. . . . I believe it is today the most corrupt and debauched political party that ever existed."

This corruption, riddling the administration, had a clear connection with wartime confusion and with the era of inflation and speculation which followed Appomattox. For Grant it forfeited in time the confidence—though not the affection—of the people of the North. Grant had come to office with greater repute than any President since Jackson, and the Republican party with the greatest opportunity for constructive work of any party since 1789. Within four years the party was split, and a Liberal Republican organization, dedicated to reform and reconciliation, in the field. Even though the Democrats joined the Liberal Republicans, they were not strong enough to unseat Grant, but two years later the Democrats captured control of the lower house, and in 1876 its candidate polled a quarter million more votes than the Republican candidate for the presidency. The politics of acquisition was by no means ended, but not again for half a century was the nation to be shamed by corruption in the executive office and in the Congress.

CHAPTER 14

The Rise of Big Business

The Foundations of the Industrial Empire

JEFFERSON had dreamed of a great rural republic, filled with an independent yeomanry, of a nation as free from the degradation of great cities and the slavery of the factories or coal pits that he had seen in England as from the serfdom that had horrified him in France and Italy. "While we have land to labor," he wrote, "let us never wish to see our citizens occupied at the work bench, or twirling a distaff." He had founded, so he believed, an agrarian democracy and provided, through the Louisiana Purchase, for its expansion. Here was land enough, he said, "for the thousandth and thousandth generation." He had defeated Hamilton at the polls and confounded, so he thought, the Hamiltonian plan to create a United States in the image of contemporaneous England. The nation was to turn westward, across the mountains and the prairies and the plains, not eastward across the ocean; it was to be a farmers' paradise, not a merchants', bankers', or industrialists' preserve. And as Jefferson's successors moved into the White House and his followers took over the Congress, his dream seemed well on the way to fulfillment. As the nation's boundaries were pushed westward to the Pacific and southward to the Rio Grande, the agricultural domain expanded far more rapidly than the industrial machine. Even in 1860 the nation was still overwhelmingly rural, and many observers viewed the Civil War not as a contest between a rising industrialism and an expanding agriculture but as a struggle between King Cotton and King Wheat.

Yet in the end it was Hamilton who won, at least on the economic front. It was his opinion on the bank that was accepted, his brand of mercantilism that was adopted, his *Report on Manufactures* that became the American gospel. A century after Hamilton fell on the dueling field of Weehawken, the United States was the greatest industrial nation in the world. It had uncovered more coal and iron ore, forged more steel, drilled and refined more oil, laid more tracks, built more factories, than any other nation on earth. A century after the Sage of Monticello went to his well-earned rest, the value of manufactured products was five times that of farm products, financial titans and industrial barons dictated policies in Washington, and the farmer seemed in danger of becoming a peasant.

This swift transformation of American economy was entirely natural, though it was assisted by governmental policies. The bases of American industrial development were six: raw materials vaster and more varied than vouchsafed to any other people except possibly the Russians; inventions and techniques for converting the raw materials into manufactured products; a transportation system of water and rail fully adequate to the demands of an expanding economy; a domestic market rapidly expanding with the increase in population and the growth of foreign markets; a labor supply con-

stantly renewed through immigration; the absence of vexatious tariff barriers between states or sections, protection
against foreign competition, and the maintenance of direct
and indirect governmental subsidies. To these fundamental
factors should perhaps be added the spirit of enterprise and
the atmosphere of optimism which from its beginnings distinguished the people.

The industrial revolution was based on coal, oil, iron,
and eventually electricity. In the mountains of Pennsylvania and West Virginia, under the prairie grasses of Illinois, along the slopes of the Great Smokies, under millions
of acres of Kansas, Colorado, and Texas, were inexhaustible
quantities of anthracite and bituminous coal: New Mexico
alone boasted enough to keep American factories going for
a century. By 1910 the nation was mining five hundred
million tons a year, but less than one per cent of its available reserves had been tapped. In the second great basic
source of energy, oil, the United States was almost equally
rich. The opening of fields in Texas, Oklahoma, Kansas,
Illinois, and California dispelled any fear of the early exhaustion of this essential resource. Iron ore, too, was abundant—all around the rim of Lake Superior, in the South
where rose the Tennessee Coal and Iron Company, in the
West where the Colorado Fuel and Iron Company grew
powerful. Careful estimates after exploitation had been under
way for half a century indicated that reserves would last at
least two centuries more. And nature had given the United
States greater potential water power than any other nation,
a power fully adequate to the industrial needs of a population
of three hundred millions.

A striking fact in the history of natural resources in the
United States is that many of them were made available,
on a large scale, only after 1850. Iron ore had been mined
since the early colonial period, but it was the opening up
of the northern Michigan and Lake Superior fields that gave
the United States supremacy in iron and steel. Colonel
Drake struck oil in western Pennsylvania in 1859. Within
five years annual production had increased to more than
two million barrels, thousands of drills and hundreds of millions of dollars had been sunk, and the rush to the "oil
regions" rivaled the gold rush to California a decade earlier.
Copper had been mined in Michigan since the opening of

that country, but it was not until the eighties that the rich veins of Montana and Arizona were exploited; soon after the Anaconda Mine was opened in 1882, the whole of Montana was a battlefield in the "war of the copper kings," contending not only for industrial monopoly, but for political control as well. The opening up of rich silver deposits in Colorado in 1859, in Nevada and Montana in the sixties, profoundly affected the economic structure and financial policy of the country. The lead mines of Missouri and the Galena region of Illinois had been famous before the Civil War; but it was not until the seventies that the great increase in lead production made possible its widespread use for piping and printing. Portland cement came on the market in the 1870's; the electrolytic process made aluminum commercially available in 1887, and by 1900 production exceeded seven million pounds. When Henry Adams visited the World's Columbian Exposition in 1893, he saw the dynamo and concluded that its discovery was the most important event in modern history; by the turn of the century American engineers were harnessing it to great dams and preparing to substitute electricity for steam.

Americans probably patented more numerous and more ingenious inventions than any other people. Between 1860 and 1900 no fewer than 676,000 patents were granted by the United States Patent Office: since that time the number has reached almost astronomical figures. Important inventions dated back to the end of the eighteenth or the early years of the nineteenth century—Eli Whitney's cotton gin, Robert Fulton's steamboat, Elias Howe's sewing machine, Charles Goodyear's vulcanized rubber, the harvester invented almost simultaneously by Cyrus McCormick and Obed Hussey. But the large-scale production of new appliances awaited the development of the steel industry and the application of electricity to industry.

A brief enumeration of the most spectacular of the new inventions suggests their role in the making of modern America. Before the Mexican War, Samuel F. B. Morse, an American Leonardo who had turned from painting to science, had worked out the principles of electrical telegraphy and persuaded Congress to subsidize the stringing of wires from Washington to Baltimore; in 1856 the Western Union Company was organized to exploit the invention, and soon it and other companies were netting the continent with their poles and wires. Efforts to lay an Atlantic cable began in the middle fifties, but not until 1866 did the *Great Eastern* uncoil a permanently successful cable from Newfoundland to Ireland: the Associated Press promptly transmitted the entire speech of William of Prussia to his Parliament at a cost of almost six thousand dollars, so that Americans could appreciate the advantages of applied science! In 1876 a Scottish immigrant, Alexander Graham Bell, exhibited a telephone instrument, and within a few years a phone box was in every business office, and the streets of the great cities were all but darkened with overhead wires. A quarter of a century later, the American Telephone and Telegraph Company was incorporated with a capitalization of a quarter of a billion dollars.

Improvements in transportation kept pace with the expansion of the nation. The use of automatic block signals, the air brake, the car coupler, and, after 1900, of steel cars made railroad travel less perilous; the introduction of the Pullman sleeping car made it more comfortable. Throughout the early eighties Americans were experimenting with electrical railways, and before the end of the decade perhaps a score of cities—among them Baltimore, Boston, and Richmond—had streetcars operated from overhead trolleys. The invention of the gasoline motorcar came in the nineties. Henry Ford, whose engineering skill and business acumen did so much to make it a universal necessity, recalled that at first

It was considered to be something of a nuisance, for it made a racket and scared horses. Also it blocked traffic. For if I stopped my machine anywhere in town a crowd was around it before I could start up again. If I left it alone, even for a minute, some inquisitive person was always trying to run it. Finally I had to carry a chain, and chain it to a lamp post whenever I left it anywhere.

This same decade witnessed S. P. Langley's bold experiments with the "flying machine" which, within the lifetime of those who derided it, was to alter the destinies of nations.

Invention quickened the tempo of business, introduced large numbers of women and "white-collar workers" into offices, and enlarged the importance of communication. The telephone speedily became an essential adjunct to every office and store. The typewriter, joint product of two Milwaukee inventors, Sholes and Glidden, was placed on the market in 1873, and the next year Mark Twain was hammering out a letter: "One may lean back in his chair and work it. It piles up an awful stack of words on one page. It don't muss things or scatter ink blots around." In time the machine became ubiquitous, and every business office had its quota of young lady typists. Adding machines and cash registers insured accuracy in accounting; addressographs made it possible to bombard the public with unsolicited advertising and propaganda; the card catalogue helped make American libraries the best and most convenient in the world. The linotype composing machine, the Hoe rotary press, and the electrotype process worked a revolution in the printing of newspapers and books.

Electricity, so important to industry, transportation, and communication, intimately affected the social life of the nation. In 1878 a young Ohio engineer, Charles Brush, patented an arc lamp which was promptly adopted by a few enterprising cities for street lighting. More practical was the incandescent lamp which Thomas A. Edison had ready in time to illuminate his home when Garfield was elected President. The commercial possibilities of electric lighting were enormous. In 1882 Edison constructed a generating and distributing station in New York, and within a few years astute businessmen were obtaining exclusive franchises to furnish electricity to cities—and the power fight was in the making. In the nineties Edison experimented with a motion-picture machine; a decade later the commercial history of the movies began, and this powerful agency was launched upon a career of conquest which was to carry American speech, manners, and mores to the uttermost corners of the globe. Radio broadcasting, equally important in its social implications, came into effective use just after the First World War; two decades later every home had its radio set. The telephone, the electric lamp, the movies, the radio added immeasurably to the pleasure and scope of life and for better or worse did much to break down isolation and standardize social habits. Because their practical utilization required large investments of capital and large-scale organizations, they did much to accelerate the growth of big business.

Forty years after the completion of the first transcontinental line, the railroad network was substantially complete and was carrying a billion tons of freight every year; the merchant marine had recovered from the long depression sufficiently to make the American flag familiar once more on the seven seas; fifty million tons of ore and grain were passing through the Sault Sainte Marie Canal; and the Panama Canal was about to marry the Atlantic and Pacific. The looms of Europe clamored for American cotton and their operatives for American wheat and pork; in the half century after Appomattox the United States ran up a cumulative favorable balance of trade of more than two and a quarter billion dollars, and by 1910 her annual exports had passed the two-billion mark.

The supply of labor continued to fill the demand, and most of it was cheap. From the farms and the country villages, from the ranks of women and of children, from the teeming cities of Italy, Austria, and Poland, millions of workers poured into the industrial centers. In the thirty years after 1870 the total number of wage earners increased from twelve to twenty-nine million, but those engaged in manufacturing from less than three to seven million. More illuminating was the fact that the proportion of women in industry increased from one eighth to one fifth and that in the same period the number of child workers between the ages of ten and fifteen rose to one and three-quarter millions. An ever-greater number of immigrants were recruited from the poorer and less skilled peoples of southern and eastern Europe; the first decade of the new century brought in two million of the unhappy peoples of the Dual Monarchy, another two million from Italy, and a million and a half from Russia. Most of them were willing to work for whatever they could get; the average annual wage in manufacturing in 1909 was slightly over five hundred dollars. Even if a dollar then bought six pounds of beefsteak, this was too little.

One element in the pattern of rising industrialism remains to be considered: the role of government. Throughout the generation after the Civil War the business interests were in charge not only of the national, but also of state legislatures. The system of protective tariffs, established during the war as an emergency measure, was continued, and the iron, steel, copper, marble, woolgrowing, textile, and chinaware industries were particularly favored beneficiaries. The Congressional grant of subsidies to railroads was imitated by states and local communities, until altogether the railroads reaped a harvest of some three quarters of a billion dollars in land, stock, tax exemptions, and other gratuities. Government authorities took a complacent attitude toward land grabbing, and toward timber cutting, and cattle grazing on the public domain; numerous fortunes were founded on exploitation of the property of the nation. Congress showed little inclination to regulate private enterprise, and the courts gave substantial immunity to restrictive legislation coming from the states. Not until after the turn of the century was the philosophy of "rugged individualism" effectively challenged.

Iron and Steel

WE MAY TRACE the interrelation of these factors in what proved to be the most important chapter in American industrial development, the story of iron and steel. Iron had been mined in America from the earliest colonial days. In 1619 John Berkeley built an iron forge on Falling Creek, Virginia; a century later William Byrd wrote a lively account of his *Progress to the Mines* of the West. In the Bay Colony an enterprising company obtained free land, tax exemption, and a monopoly for constructing a forge. Ethan Allen, leader of the Green Mountain Boys, built a blast furnace in the Litchfield Hills of Connecticut; forges in eastern Pennsylvania turned out cannon balls for Washington's hard-pushed continentals; and the Sterling Forge, near West Point, cast the greatest of the chains which were strung across the Hudson to bar the British fleet. The most important of the early ironworks were in the Ramapos of northern Jersey, the state where, in later years, Peter Cooper was to establish a great industry and Abram Hewitt was to introduce the open-hearth process of making steel. After 1800 flourishing ironworks sprang up west of the Alleghenies, at Pittsburgh, where there was a fortunate combination of ore, coal, limestone, and wood for charcoal; here forges were built in time to cast cannon balls for Commodore Perry and General Jackson.

Yet these early smelters and forges were small affairs. As late as 1850 the pig-iron production of the entire country was only one-half million tons a year and the manufacture of steel was negligible. Prospects for increased production were not encouraging, for the supply of iron ore was inadequate, and the cost of making steel prohibitive. Then came one of the most dramatic revolutions in the history of industry. In 1844 surveyors, running the boundary between Wisconsin and upper Michigan, noticed that their compasses swung crazily from side to side. They reported great outcroppings of black ore. For generations the Indians had told stories of a fabled mountain of iron; in 1845 a Chippewa chief with the name of Madjigijig guided a copper prospector to the Marquette range, overlooking Superior, and soon hundreds of frantic fortune hunters were pouring into the wilderness, staking out claims to copper and iron. Transporting the heavy ore by rail was difficult and expensive; a water route was essential. Michigan proposed a canal around the rapids of the St. Marys River, connecting Huron and Superior, but even Henry Clay, father of the American system, ridiculed the idea. "It is a work beyond the remotest settlement of the United States, if not the moon," he said. Private enterprise and the driving energy of young Charles Harvey built the canal. It was open to ships in 1855 and before long floated more traffic than any other canal in the world. Docks were built at Marquette, Ashland, and Escanaba, and, after the opening of the Menominee range, crowding the western shore of Lake Michigan, and the wonderfully rich Gogebic range straddling the Michigan-Wisconsin boundary, fleets of mighty "red-bellies" carried millions of tons of ore to distant mills.

Before long, the deposits on the northern peninsula were to be dwarfed by those west of Lake Superior; the whole of that vast lake, indeed, was rimmed with iron. A surveyor stumbled on the Vermilion range in the 1870's; in 1884 Eastern capital had built a railroad connecting it with the Lakes, and in twenty-five years the Vermilion shipped out thirty million tons of ore. Meanwhile the five Merritt brothers of Duluth had been cruising the wilderness west of the lake. Seventy-five miles northwest of Duluth, on the watershed of the continent, they found the Mesabi, "grandmother of them all," the most fabulously rich iron range in the world. This was in 1890, and two years later a rickety railroad pushed through timber and brush and swamp and carried out a million tons of ore. Within a decade the Mesabi had poured forty million tons into the giant converters of Pittsburgh and Chicago.

These iron-ore deposits of northern Minnesota had advantages possessed by no other deposits elsewhere in the world and were largely responsible for American supremacy in iron and steel production. They were practically inexhaustible. The iron ore lay not in rocky veins, deeply imbedded in the earth, but in loose deposits just below the surface; as one of the Merritt boys said, "If we had gotten mad and kicked the ground right where we stood we could have thrown up sixty-four per cent ore, if we had kicked hard enough to kick off the pine needles." The ore was unusually pure; it could be lifted out by great steam shovels; and it was sufficiently close to the Great Lakes for shipment to the industrial and coal areas at low cost.

But how transform the red ore into white steel? In the little town of Eddyville, Kentucky, some years before the Civil War, an ironmaker, William Kelly, hit on the fantastic notion that he could turn iron into steel by blowing cold air through it, and proved that it wasn't fantastic at all. A little later the English engineer, Henry Bessemer, had the same idea. He not only proved it, but successfully applied it. The Bessemer process as finally perfected was simplicity itself. The molten iron ore was poured into a pearlike container, through which cold air was forced. The oxygen of the air and the carbon and silicon of the iron waged a titanic battle with shrieks and roars, while the mouth of the converter belched fire like some fabulous dragon, its flames leaping forty or fifty feet into the air, and changing color from red to violet, from orange to white. In ten minutes the battle of the elements was over, the impurities of the iron ore had burnt out, and the converter was tipped over to pour the flaming steel into molds. In time a new process for steelmaking, the open-hearth, supplanted the Bessemer, but for the last quarter of the century the Bessemer was supreme.

Iron ore, coal, and science made possible the steel industry; all that was needed to insure its success was enterprise, skill, and capital. Andrew Carnegie had come as a boy of twelve from Dunfermline, Scotland, his father, a master weaver, ruined by the advent of the factory system. There were relatives in Pittsburgh, and to that booming city at the juncture of the Allegheny and the Monongahela the family turned. Andrew got work as a bobbin boy, graduated to a steam boiler, to the telegraph office, and finally to the Pennsylvania Railroad. He was honest, clever, industrious, and wide-awake, and the charm of manner which never deserted him won the confidence and friendship of older men. Before he was thirty he had an income of forty or fifty thousand dollars a year from shrewd investments in oil and iron, express and sleeping-car companies. It is indicative of his vision and boldness that in 1865 he decided to abandon his other interests and concentrate on iron. Within a few years he had organized or bought into companies for making iron bridges, rails, and locomotives. When he was thirty he moved to New York and began to act as salesman for his many companies and as broker for numerous railroad and iron interests.

Although Carnegie was slow to adopt the Bessemer process, when he did see it his conversion was complete; and the plant which he built in 1875 on Braddock's battlefield on the banks of the Monongahela was the greatest in the country. Within a year it was turning out more Bessemer steel than all the other American mills combined. Alert for every new improvement, quick to take advantage of hard times to buy up or to ruin his rivals, closely allied with the Pennsylvania and other railroads, aided by astute lieutenants like H. C. Frick and Charles Schwab, Carnegie was in a strategic position to assert his leadership in the steel industry. Year by year his empire grew—new mills, coke and coal properties, iron ore from Superior, a fleet of Great Lakes steamers, a port town on Lake Erie, and a connecting railroad. It was in effect a vertical trust. His iron and steel industry was intimately allied with a dozen others; it could command favorable terms from railroads and shipping lines; it had capital enough for expansion, the best workingmen, and the shrewdest managers. Nothing like it had ever been seen before in America, though the empire Rockefeller was building was to be just as mighty. Capitalized in 1878 at one and a quarter million dollars, its profits rapidly mounted to five million a year. When in 1900 the business was recapitalized at 320 million, it was turning out three million tons of steel a year with annual profits of forty million dollars.

One important element remained—labor. Again the experience of the iron industry, and of the Carnegie Company, is typical. The iron miners of the early years were recruited chiefly from Cornwall and Wales; then came Swedes and Finns, and after them a flood of Slavs and Magyars. The same progression could be traced among those who fired the furnaces and lifted the fiery balls of molten steel into the molds. A survey of 1907 showed more than two thirds of the laborers in the Carnegie mills foreign-born and the vast majority of these from southern and eastern Europe. They were tough—and they needed to be, working twelve hours a day, seven days a week, in an inferno of heat and noise. Because there was a plentiful supply of unskilled workers, unions seldom made progress in the industry, and when they did they were put down savagely.

In the rise of this industry, then, were all but one of the essential ingredients for world leadership: raw materials, transportation, science and invention, managerial skill and enterprise, cheap labor, and finally, with the growth of railroads and the use of structural steel for building, assured markets. The one additional element temporarily needed was protection against foreign competition. A tariff whose terms were dictated by the ironmasters took care of this; twenty-eight dollars a ton on steel rails was prohibitive, and even Carnegie came in time to admit that it might well be lowered.

These auspices presiding, American iron and steel forged ahead. By 1890 production surpassed that of Britain; by 1900 the United States was making more steel than Britain and Germany combined. By 1920 American blast furnaces were forging twenty-seven million tons of pig iron and forty-two million tons of steel, and the demands of the Second World War revealed that productive capacity could be stepped up, when necessary, to eighty-five million tons.

In one final respect, too, the history of the Carnegie Company illuminates the rise of big business in the United States. The enterprising Scotsman had long dominated the industry, but it was quite impossible for him to exercise a monopoly over the natural resources, transportation, and industrial plants involved in the making of steel. Rockefeller owned the most valuable of the Mesabi mines and a fleet of Great Lakes steamers; the Tennessee Coal and Iron Company ruled vast holdings in the South; new steel companies, like the Federal, the Pennsylvania, the American Steel and Wire, rose to challenge the pre-eminence of the Carnegie. Stung by competition, Carnegie threatened to acquire new mines, build a larger fleet of freighters, and embark upon the manufacture of tubes, barbed wire, tin plate, and a hundred other wares. A ruinous war loomed in the industry, and steel men turned, in dismay, to thoughts of combination. Carnegie preferred to sell out at his own price rather than fight; he was an old man, and he had long wanted to retire and give away his money. He listened willingly to the suggestion that he merge his holdings with a new organization which should embrace most of the important iron and steel properties in the nation. In 1901 the United States Steel Corporation was born, with a capitalization of $1,400,000,000—a sum larger than the total national wealth a century earlier. It was appropriate that the banking house of J. P. Morgan engineered the combine and that John D. Rockefeller realized large profits from his efficient development of the Mesabi.

Trusts and Monopolies

THE ORGANIZATION of the United States Steel Corporation illustrated a process that had been under way for thirty years and that was to continue unabated until the present time. This was the combination of independent industrial enterprises into federated or centralized empires. The Carnegie Company, at the height of its power, had been merely one of some six hundred iron and steel establishments; the United States Steel Corporation was designed to absorb or eliminate most of these and to make two thirds of the steel products of the country. Within another generation two hundred giant corporations did half the corporate business of the nation, while three hundred thousand smaller ones did the other half.

The United States of Lincoln's day was a nation of small enterprises. A monopoly was practically unknown; the old

Astor Fur Company and the newly organized Western Union
were the nearest things to it since the weak royal monopolies
of colonial days. Many communities, especially in the North,
were substantially self-sufficient. Furniture came from the
local cabinetmaker, shoes from the neighborhood shoemaker,
meat from small butchers, carriages from community carriage
makers. Manufacturing and mining were spread thin; more
than two thousand factories made plows and cultivators and
reapers; Pennsylvania alone had over two hundred oil re-
finers, and one hundred proprietors divided the wealth of the
Comstock lode. Forty years later all this had changed. The
International Harvester Company made almost all the farm
implements; the Standard Oil had a practical monopoly of
refining; and two or three Eastern corporations owned and
mined the Comstock.

The change had begun during the Civil War and went
on with mounting speed after the seventies. Astute businessmen realized that if they could bring competing firms into
a single organization they could reduce costs and—what was
more important—control prices. The primary instrument
to achieve these ends was the corporation, then came the
pool, and then the trust. The corporation was a device to
create a fictitious person who could enjoy the legal advantages but avoid most of the moral responsibilities of a human being. It enjoyed a permanent life, the power to float
issues of stocks and bonds, limited liability for debts, and,
subject to charter restrictions, the right to do business everywhere in the nation. The trust was, in effect, a combination
of corporations whereby the stockholders of each would
place their stocks in the hands of trustees who would manage
the business of all. In time the term "trust" came to mean
any large business combination. The advantages of trusts,
too, were obvious. They made possible large-scale combination, centralized control and administration, the elimination
of less efficient units, the pooling of patents, and, by virtue
of their capital resources, power to expand, to compete with
foreign business companies, to bargain with labor, to exact
favorable terms from railroads, and to exercise immense influence in politics, state and national.

Combination was a world-wide phenomenon, but it was
more pronounced in the United States than anywhere else
except perhaps Germany. That was in part because of the

vast resources awaiting exploitation. But there were other
reasons. The completion of the railroad system assured a
national market for manufactured products. Patent laws gave
a monopoly on crucially important processes. Generous land
grants and a liberal interpretation of land laws played into
the hands of companies big enough to undertake large-scale
exploitation of timber, copper, or coal. The Federal system
enabled a company to incorporate in a state where laws were
liberal and do business in other states, and the protective
system prevented foreign competition.

It was the Standard Oil Company that led the way. While
oil producers of western Pennsylvania were engaged in cutthroat competition, a silent, austere young businessman of
Cleveland, Ohio, went quietly about buying up the local refineries and welding them into a single company. "The American Beauty rose," his son later said, "can be produced in its
splendor and fragrance only by sacrificing the early buds
which grow up around it." In 1872 Rockefeller took advantage of the organization of the short-lived South Improvement Company, and of favorable rebates from the New York
Central and the Erie railroads, to obtain complete mastery
of oil refining in Cleveland. That done, he moved on to take
control of refining in New York, Philadelphia, and Pittsburgh. A superbly efficient marketing system was built up.
Control of the pipe lines followed, and within a decade
Rockefeller had a practical monopoly of the transportation
and refining of petroleum. In 1882 the Standard Oil Company emerged as the first great trust; dissolved by the Ohio
courts, it promptly reincorporated as a holding company
under the more generous laws of New Jersey and proceeded
unperturbed on its way. Before 1900 Rockefeller had brought
order out of the chaos of the oil industry, eliminated most
of his competitors, amassed a fabulous fortune while reducing prices, and created the greatest monopoly in the country.

Other trusts and monopolies followed rapidly; the cotton-
seed oil in 1884, the linseed oil in 1885, the lead trust and
the whisky trust, and the sugar trust in 1887, the match
trust in 1889, the tobacco trust in 1890, the rubber trust in
1892. Aggressive businessmen, following in the footsteps of
Rockefeller and Carnegie, began to mark out princely domains for themselves. Four great packers, chief among them
Philip D. Armour and Gustavus F. Swift, established a "beef

trust." The Guggenheim interests got control of the copper deposits of Arizona and of Butte, Montana, where "the richest hill in the world" produced about two billion dollars' worth of copper in thirty years. The McCormicks established pre-eminence in the reaper business, and when their position was threatened formed a combine, the International Harvester Company, that all but monopolized the field. The Duke family built up a great tobacco trust. In silver, nickel, and zinc, in rubber, leather, and glass, in sugar, salt, and crackers, in cigars, whisky, and candy, in oil, gas, and electricity, the story was the same. A survey of 1904 showed that 319 industrial trusts, capitalized at over seven billion dollars, had swallowed up about 5300 previously independent concerns, and that 127 utilities (including railroads), capitalized at over thirteen billion dollars, had absorbed some 2400 smaller enterprises.

The life of the average man, especially if he was a city dweller, was profoundly changed by this development. Almost everything he ate and wore, the furnishings of his house, the tools he used, the transportation he employed, were made or controlled by trusts. When he sat down to breakfast he ate bacon packed by the beef trust, seasoned his eggs with salt made by the Michigan salt trust, sweetened his coffee with sugar refined by the American Sugar trust, lit his American Tobacco Company cigar with a Diamond Match Company match. Then he rode to work on a bicycle built by the bicycle trust or on a trolley car operating under a monopolistic franchise and running on steel rails made by United States Steel. Yet it is probable that his food was better, his transportation more efficient, than a generation earlier. What the average man noticed most was the effect of trusts on the business life of his community. Local industry dried up, factories went out of business or were absorbed, mortgages were placed with Eastern banks or insurance companies, and neighbors who worked not for themselves but for distant corporations were exposed to the vicissitudes of policy over which they had no control.

It was not only in manufacturing and mining that this process of combination and consolidation was under way. It was even more spectacular in the realms of transportation and communication. The Western Union, the earliest of the large combinations, was followed by the Bell Telephone System and eventually by the giant American Telephone and Telegraph. Gruff old Commodore Vanderbilt had early seen that efficient railroading required the unification of lines and in the sixties had knit some thirteen or fourteen separate railroads into a single line connecting New York City and Buffalo; during the next decade he acquired lines to Chicago and Detroit, and the New York Central system came into being. Other consolidations were already under way, and soon most of the railroads of the nation were organized into trunk lines and "systems," controlled by Vanderbilt, Gould, Harriman, Hill, and the bankers Morgan and Belmont. E. H. Harriman brought together the Illinois Central, the Union Pacific, the Southern Pacific, and half a dozen other lines and dreamed of creating a nationwide consolidation. It was a banker, J. P. Morgan, who came closest to making that dream real.

The rise of the house of Morgan illustrates the final and perhaps most important development in the process of combination—the creation of the so-called "money trust." In 1864 Junius Spencer Morgan, who had long been engaged in selling American securities to English investors, placed his son J. Pierpont Morgan in charge of an American branch of the house. A few years later young Morgan went into partnership with the old banking house of Drexel, in Philadelphia, and in 1873 the firm of Drexel, Morgan and Company was strong enough to divide with Jay Cooke the refinancing of three quarters of a billion of the national debt. The spectacular failure of Jay Cooke that same year left the Morgan house in a strong position, and when, a few years later, it disposed of a vast quantity of New York Central stock abroad, its reputation was made. This tie-up with the New York Central pointed the way to the major financial activity of the house for the next twenty years.

All through the eighties Morgan reorganized and refinanced railroads, extending his influence more widely into this key field. The panic of 1893 threw half the mileage of the country into the hands of receivers, and railroad men everywhere turned to "Jupiter" Morgan to rescue them from their difficulties. In part because the business was highly lucrative, in part because it was essential to maintain the soundness of the securities which he had sold abroad, he responded. When the clouds of the panic finally blew away,

the Morgan interests dominated a dozen major railroad lines
—the New York Central, the Southern, the Chesapeake and
Ohio, the Santa Fe, the Rock Island, and many others.

Meantime the Morgan interests had expanded into other
fields, until by the first decade of the century there was
scarcely a major business in which the house did not exercise a decisive influence. Morgan had financed the Federal
Steel Company and put through the gigantic deal which resulted in United States Steel. He had brought together the
warring manufacturers of agricultural implements and
emerged with the International Harvester Company. He
had organized American shipping in the ill-fated International Mercantile Marine Company and helped finance General Electric, American Telephone and Telegraph, the New
York Rapid Transit Company, and a dozen other giant utilities. In 1912 a Congressional committee found that the banking houses dominated by the Morgan and the William Rockefeller interests held 341 directorships in railroads, shipping,
and insurance, with aggregate resources of twenty-two billion
dollars. "The great monopoly in this country," said Woodrow
Wilson somewhat rhetorically, "is the money monopoly."

What was the significance of the growth of combinations
and the rise of trusts? It created a system of absentee ownership more far-reaching than anything known heretofore to
American history—vast properties of coal, copper, iron, timber, railroads, owned and directed by New York corporations. It centered in the hands of a few men power over the
fortunes of millions of people greater than that wielded by
many monarchs. It concentrated economic dominance of the
nation in a small section of the Northeast, creating a new
sectionalism to take the place of the old. It separated ownership from management, lodging it in tens of thousands of
stockholders who had little sense of responsibility and knew
nothing about the financial or the labor policies of their
companies. It created new aggregations of capital powerful
enough to influence policies of state and even the national
legislatures, foreign as well as domestic. It undoubtedly eliminated a great deal of cutthroat competition, achieved greater
efficiency, released money for necessary improvements and
for research, and made possible mass production and lower

prices—but all at a heavy cost, until society had learned the necessity and the techniques of regulation.

The Government Steps In

ANDREW CARNEGIE called all this "triumphant democracy"; others were quite ready to admit that it was triumphant, but not at all sure that it was democracy. Indeed, as they looked about them and saw a large part of the natural resources, the industries, the railroads, and other utilities controlled for the profit of a handful of men, they began to doubt that democracy could survive. Exorbitant charges, discrimination, and wholesale land grabs by the railroads, the malpractices of Rockefeller, Carnegie, and others in crushing competitors, the savage power with which many giant corporations beat down labor, the pocketing by the trusts of the savings that came from science and invention, the spectacle of corporation agents lobbying favorable laws through state legislatures and corporation lawyers finding loopholes in state tax or regulation laws, all aroused widespread alarm and bitterness.

Monopolies had long been illegal at common law, and many state constitutions contained clauses forbidding their existence. But these constitutional prohibitions were almost entirely ineffective. During the eighties many states wrote more stringent laws on their statute books, and some went as far as to dissolve trusts with a particularly malodorous record. But a trust dissolved in one state might incorporate in another, where laws were more lenient and enforcement was lax, and continue to do business at the same stand. Clearly this was a matter for Federal rather than state regulation.

As early as 1876 the millionaire philosopher, Peter Cooper, running for the presidency on the Greenback ticket, warned that "the danger to our free institutions now is only less than in the inception of the rebellion. . . . There is fast forming in this country an aristocracy of wealth, the worst form of aristocracy that can curse the prosperity of any country." With the return of prosperity in the late seventies agitation died down, but by the eighties the country was once more trust conscious. By 1884 there was an Anti-

Monopoly party in the field, but in the excitement over the prospect of the return of the Democrats to power, it attracted few votes. Another four years, and the organization of half a dozen major trusts made the country alert to the danger. President Cleveland told Congress that "corporations, which should be carefully restrained creatures of the law and servants of the people, are fast becoming the people's masters," and both major parties went on record as opposed to monopolies in any form.

The first practical result of all this agitation was in the regulation of railroads. As early as the 1870's outraged farmers had clamored against the railroad monopoly, charging that it gouged them with excessive freight charges, gave poor service, and held millions of acres off the market for speculative purposes. At the behest of farm organizations like the Grange, Midwestern states placed on their statute books laws limiting the rates that the roads might charge, and outlawing such practices as rebates, special rates to favored shippers, charging more for a short than for a long haul over the same road, and free passes. This legislation was promptly challenged by the railroads on the ground that it deprived them of their property "without due process of law" and that it infringed upon Congressional control over interstate commerce.

In a series of remarkable decisions in 1877, notably Munn vs. Illinois, the courts sustained the state legislation on the ground that any property "affected with a public interest" or devoted to a public use is subject to regulation by government. But with respect to the problem of the encroachment of the state on the domain of Federal regulation the position of the court was ambiguous. Later decisions, however, made it clear that while states could regulate commerce entirely local in character, they could not touch it if it had in any way an interstate character. That was under the exclusive control of the national government. And as most commerce was interstate this put the issue squarely up to the Congress.

Congress responded with the Interstate Commerce Act of 1887. This act, designed as much to save the railroads from the evil results of rate wars and rebates as to protect the public, prohibited pooling, rebates, discrimination in rates or services, and required that all charges should be "just"

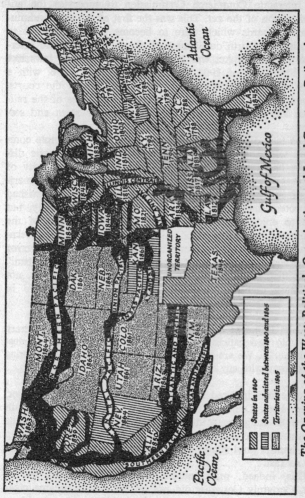

The Opening of the West: Political Organization and Land Grants to Railroads

and "reasonable." More important than these somewhat vague prohibitions and requirements was the provision for an Interstate Commerce Commission to supervise the administration of the act. This was the first of the many administrative boards which were to become so important as to constitute a fourth department of the government. The Interstate Commerce Act was long ineffective, but new laws like the Elkins Act of 1903 and Hepburn Act of 1906, with a more rigid enforcement by the Commission and the courts, served in time to weed out the worst malpractices of the railroads and to establish effective control over rates and services.

The task of regulating railroads was relatively simple compared with that of regulating trusts. Perhaps the basic difficulty had its origin not in the vastness and complexity of business but in the confusion of the American mind. Americans feared big business, but they admired it, too. They wished to protect themselves against the dangers of monopoly, but also to enjoy the benefits of mass production and of the elimination of costly duplication. They believed in government regulation of business, but believed with equal fervor in the virtues of private enterprise and "rugged individualism." What they really wanted to do was to purify the trusts, not to smash them. As President Theodore Roosevelt said in one of his later trust messages:

Our aim is not to do away with corporations; on the contrary these big aggregations are a necessary part of modern industrialism. . . . We are not attacking corporations, but endeavoring to do away with any evil in them.

His dilemma inspired a shrewd parody by the nation's jester, Finley Peter Dunne: "Th' thrusts are heejous monsthers built up by th' inlightened intherprise ov th' men that have done so much to advance progress in our beloved counthry. On wan hand I wud stamp them undher fut; on th' other hand, not so fast."

This, indeed, represented the national attitude: not so fast. Certainly Congress did not go fast. As it became clear that the states could not singly cope with the trust problem, Congress was forced to take action. The Sherman Antitrust Act of 1890 outlawed all contracts, combinations, or conspiracies in restraint of trade, and all monopolies. It was widely supposed that this legislation would give the government a club over such giant corporations as the Standard Oil and combinations like the whisky and sugar trusts. But when the government tried, rather feebly, to break up certain monopolies, such as the sugar trust, the courts sustained them, and they went merrily on their way. "What looks like a stone wall to a layman is a triumphal arch to a lawyer," said the irrepressible Dunne. So impressive was this judicial defeat that the decade after the Sherman Act witnessed the formation of some of the largest and most notorious trusts.

With the organization of United States Steel the storm of public disapproval broke. From the press and forum came torrents of criticism. Books like Ida Tarbell's *History of the Standard Oil Company* and Russell's *The Greatest Trust in the World* (the beef trust) sold by the tens of thousands, while exposures of the iniquities of big business filled the new popular magazines like *McClure's*, *Everybody's* and *Collier's* and pushed their way into the pages of the old respectable ones. So widespread and violent was this criticism that the first decade of the century has been called "the era of the muckrakers."

The demand for the more effective enforcement of the antitrust laws was irresistible, and Theodore Roosevelt responded with enthusiasm. "As far as the antitrust laws go," he said, "they will be enforced, and when suit is undertaken it will not be compromised except on the basis that the government wins." To the astonishment of Wall Street the President directed his Attorney General to break up a trans-Mississippi railroad combination engineered by the three greatest railroad overlords, Morgan, Harriman, and Hill— and was successful in the Northern Securities Company case. Action followed swiftly against the meat-packer trust, the tobacco trust, and the Standard Oil Company, and in each the government emerged victorious.

Yet these victories were more sensational than substantial. Dissolved, the constituent elements in the great monopolies found other ways to maintain a community of interest. Nor, aside from the creation of the Bureau of Corporations, effectively applying "pitiless publicity" to corporate malpractices, did Roosevelt do anything to strengthen the antitrust laws. Notwithstanding his success in the courts and his public denunciation of "malefactors of great wealth," the trusts were stronger when he went out of office than when he came in. Apparently John D. Rockefeller was right when he said: "The combination is here to stay. Individualism has gone, never to return."

CHAPTER 15

Labor and Immigration

The Laborer and His Hire

THE EXPLOITATION of the rich resources of the country, the mechanization of industry, the rise of monopolies, poured a steady stream of wealth into the hands of a small body of farsighted businessmen and a larger number of shrewd investors. But it profited little the workingmen upon whom the drudgery all fell. Labor was one of the basic factors in the growth of big business, but in the division of profits it was conspicuously left out. It was left out, too, when the social rewards were distributed: workingmen rarely lived on "the right side of the tracks," they were not asked to join the country clubs, and their leaders were ignored by the colleges and universities that every year bestowed honorary degrees on masters of capital. New sources of wealth should have meant its wider distribution, but that was long in coming; the application of labor-saving machinery should have meant shorter hours, but that, too, was long an unattained ideal; science should have insured the workingmen safer and pleasanter working conditions, but most of them continued to work in hot, noisy, ill-ventilated factories, or surrounded by dangers in mines and quarries, and the toll from industrial accidents and diseases mounted frightfully year by year. Crowded into the slums of the big cities, exposed to depression and unemployment, competing with hordes of unskilled hands from abroad or from the South, the lot of the workers was far from enviable. Nor did they find it easy to improve their condition. Organization and strikes were regarded with suspicion, and in legislatures and Congress the toilers had few representatives.

Indeed, some of the developments which contributed most to the growth of industrial America were a positive disadvantage to labor. Two of these we can note briefly: the mechanization of industry and the rise of the corporation. Mechanization tended, on the whole, to lower the standards of labor. The skills which workingmen had painfully acquired ceased to have their old-time value, for the machine could do better, cheaper, and quicker most of the things the trained artisan had done. The creative instinct of craftsmanship was largely destroyed, and workingmen were reduced to a mere part of a mechanical process, automata performing every minute of the day some monotonous and deadening operation. As Upton Sinclair described it in *The Jungle:*

Each one of the hundreds of parts of a mowing machine was made separately, and sometimes handled by hundreds of men. Where Jurgis worked there was a machine which cut and stamped a certain piece of steel about two square inches in size; the pieces came tumbling out upon a tray, and all that human hands had to do was to pile them in regular rows, and change the trays at intervals. This was done by a single boy, who stood with eyes and thoughts centred upon it, and fingers flying so fast that the sounds of the bits of steel striking upon each other was like the music of an express train as one hears it in a sleeping car at night. . . . Thirty thousand of these pieces he handled every day, nine or ten millions every year—how many in a lifetime it rested with the gods to say. Near by him sat men bending over whirling grindstones, putting the finishing touches to the steel knives of the reaper; picking them out of a basket with the right hand, pressing first one side and then the other against the stone, and finally dropping them with the left hand into another basket. One of these men told Jurgis that he had sharpened three thousand pieces of steel a day for thirteen years.

Machinery had a tendency, too, to usurp the place of the worker in the economy of industry. It represented an enormous capital investment, it could work twenty-four hours a day seven days a week, and it came to determine working conditions; the fact that furnaces had to be kept going continuously was decisive in maintaining the twelve-hour day in the iron and steel industry for half a century. Machinery was in part responsible, finally, for a great deal of unemployment. It is probably true that in the end machines made more jobs than they eliminated, but it was not always the same people who got the new jobs, and there were usually agonizing periods of want before older men found new work. Large-scale unemployment is a product of the machine age.

The growth of the giant corporation as employer, too, often worked to the disadvantage of labor. Small-scale industry had close relations with its workingmen and with its community. Workers could bargain more successfully with local employers than with some distant and impersonal organization. Theodore Roosevelt put this well:

. . . The old familiar relations between employer and employee were passing. A few generations before, the boss had known every man in his shop; he called his men Bill, Tom, Dick, John; he inquired after their wives and babies; he swapped jokes and stories and perhaps a bit of tobacco with them. In the small establishment there had been a friendly human relationship between employer and employee.

There was no such relation between the great railway magnates, who controlled the anthracite industry, and the one hundred and fifty thousand men who worked in their mines, or the half million women and children who were dependent upon these miners for their daily bread.

And a New England mill owner, testifying before a Senate committee, succinctly remarked: "I never do my talking to the hands. I do all my talking with the overseers."

Several other factors, unique to the United States, conditioned the welfare of labor. The first of these was the passing of good cheap land a generation or so after the Civil War. It would be an exaggeration to say that the West had served as a "safety valve" for labor discontent or as a refuge for very many workingmen. But it is clear that for two or three generations the open land did drain off the surplus population of the countryside, the villages, and even the cities, and the immigrants from abroad. Had the five million immigrants who came over between 1850 and 1870 all stayed in the industrial cities of the East instead of scattering over the country, the position of labor would have been vastly worse than it actually was. With the rise in the cost of farming and the disappearance of good cheap land, surplus population did stay in the industrial areas. Farming was no longer a practical alternative to the factory. Labor could no longer escape the problems of an industrialized society, but was forced to stand and face them.

A second factor, peculiar to the United States among industrial nations, was continuous and unrestricted immigration. In the forty years from 1870 to 1910 more than twenty million people poured into the country. Even subtracting the women and children—many of whom toiled—this meant that every year several hundred thousand recruits joined the ranks of labor, eager for work in the mills and the mines, at almost any wages and under almost any conditions. Nor was this the only competition that confronted Northern labor. From the South, after the turn of the century, came tens of thousands of sturdy Negroes ready to take their places beside the Poles, Italians, and Hungarians. Not every newcomer from abroad or from the South displaced a worker; in boom times there was work enough for all, and the newcomers as often pushed native labor to the top as out. Yet for many years the general tendency of this mass movement was to drive down wages, depress standards, and disintegrate labor unions.

A third factor—again one unique to the United States—was the existence side by side of a national economy and a Federal political system. The problems of labor—in the coal industry, in textiles, in iron and steel mills—were much the same the nation over, but the power to deal with them was lodged, until very recent years, in the states alone. Competition was nationwide, but the right to regulate wages and hours was only state-wide. Thus labor might win important concessions in the textile industry of New England or the garment shops of New York only to have them nullified by a shift of these industries to states where laws were less exacting. After the advent of the New Deal, to be sure, all this was changed. The Federal government found ways to establish national control over the whole field of industrial relations.

One final consideration merits attention: the deep suspicion which many Americans entertained toward labor unions, and their unwillingness to approach the problems of labor with the same sympathy with which they regarded the problems of industry. Lillian Wald, head of a famous New York settlement house, recalled that in her early years on the East Side labor unions were feared "as Socialists were later, and as Communists are now."

The Sherman Antitrust Act was applied first and most effectively to labor: that was typical of the whole situation. Many Americans, until recent years, assumed that combination in business was good sense, but looked on combination of labor with disapproval; took for granted that business would participate in politics, but thought it un-American for labor to do so; approved government aid to industry, but insisted that government aid to labor was socialistic or a surrender to pressure groups; held that investors had a natural right to a fair return on their investments, but assumed that a workingman had no right to any return on his labor but what he could wrest from a reluctant employer, and that unemployment was an act of God. These attitudes changed as the nation became educated to the problems of modern industrialism, but they lingered long enough to place serious obstacles in the path of organized labor.

Yet we must not draw too somber a picture of the condition of labor during the industrial era. For the most part there was work enough for willing hands, and wages, though far from adequate, were high enough to keep a family in food, clothing, and shelter of a sort. There was no "laboring class" in the United States in the sense that there was in many European countries, while there was always the opportunity to shift from job to job, and even from one income group to another. An Englishman visiting the United States just after the Civil War commented perspicaciously on this:

A workingman in this country is situated very differently from one of his own class at home; if he has the means he goes where he pleases without carrying a certificate of character in his pocket. Indeed it would be just as admissible in the social code for a man seeking work to demand a character of the "Boss" he may apply to, as that he should be asked for one. In these matters Jack is as good as his master. . . . This country has had the rare advantage of growing into national greatness without having had to pass through the ordeal of feudalism, or being trammeled in her progress by the tyrannical influence arising from pride of Caste.

Latter-day sociologists were to discover that there were indeed classes in the United States, and to distinguish neatly between middle-middle, upper-middle, and lower-middle, but at no time was American society ever stratified like the European. There were no legal divisions or distinctions; class did not betray itself by accent nor did it follow religious lines; and an open society made it relatively easy for the more enterprising to move from class to class. Free public education enabled the children of laborers to rise in business or the professions, and the ballot was a potential weapon whereby workingmen could, if properly aroused, compel legislators to pass friendly laws.

In Union There Is Strength

THE MORAL of the organization of business was not lost on labor. There had been labor unions, of a sort, ever since the early days of the republic, but these had been for the most part local and weak. During the fifties a number of strong craft unions were established—the Typographical is the oldest and most important—but these embraced only a minute percentage of the working class, and many of them petered out during reconstruction and the black depression that followed the panic of 1873.

During the postwar years three types of labor organizations emerged. The first was the industrial union, best represented by the Knights of Labor. The second was the craft union and the subsequent federation of craft unions into the American Federation of Labor. The third type was the radical socialists or revolutionary labor groups, numerically unimportant but persistent. At no time before the late 1930's did any or all of these organizations embrace a majority of

American workingmen. Large segments of the working population—farm labor, migratory labor, domestic workers, white-collar workers—remained outside the circles of organization.

The most important and the most interesting of early labor organizations was the Noble Order of the Knights of Labor, founded in 1869 but dating its real history from 1879, when Terence Powderly became Grand Master. The most striking characteristics of the Knights were its democracy and its broad social and economic outlook. It was open to all workingmen—skilled and unskilled, farmers, mill hands, miners, and artisans; only gamblers, saloonkeepers, bankers, lawyers, and stockbrokers were excluded! Its purpose was "to secure to the toilers a proper share in the wealth that they create; more of the leisure that rightfully belongs to them; more societary advantages . . . all those rights and privileges necessary to make them capable of enjoying, appreciating, defending, and perpetuating . . . good government." These gleaming ends were to be realized not through strikes or violence, but by political agitation, education, and workers' co-operatives. The program of the Knights was radical but diffuse: an eight-hour day, the abolition of child labor, public ownership of utilities, income and inheritance taxes, and land reform. The combination of starry-eyed idealism with gentlemanly persuasion to effect radical economic changes was not effective, but when after 1885 the Knights resorted to strikes, they really got somewhere. Membership increased by leaps and bounds. Within a year they boasted seven hundred thousand members, and flushed with success they backed an ill-planned general strike for the eight-hour day. In Chicago the strike helped inspire a grand meeting at Haymarket Square, where some unknown anarchist threw a bomb which killed numerous policemen. Though the Knights were not responsible for the outrage, public opinion connected them with it. This, the failure of various strikes, and inherent weakness of organization sent the Order into a decline; when the Knights tied up with the Populist party, in 1892, the decline became a demise.

Meanwhile a new organization was rising to power: the American Federation of Labor. In 1863 a Dutch Jew, Solomon Gompers, decided to give up his London cigar-making shop and try his luck in America. He brought with him a thirteen-year-old son, Samuel, who promptly went to work rolling cigars. The next year the boy joined the Cigar-makers' Union; and from that time the life of Samuel Gompers was identified with union labor, and the history of union labor in the United States with Samuel Gompers. He had no formal education, but the cigar-making shop gave him a thorough training in labor history and economics. "The nature of our work," he later recalled,

developed a camaraderie of the shop such as few workers enjoy. It was a world in itself—a cosmopolitan world. Shopmates came from everywhere—some had been nearly everywhere. . . . In the shop there was also reading. It was the custom of the cigar makers to chip in to create a fund for purchasing papers, magazines, and books. Then while the rest worked, one of our members would read to us for perhaps an hour at a time, sometimes longer. In order that the reader might not be the loser financially, each one of the other men in the shop gave him a definite number of cigars.

Thus Gompers familiarized himself with the writings of the British reformers, and the German and Russian Socialists. There was practical education, too: by bitter experience with strikes, hard times, and the inadequacy of existing unions, Gompers learned the necessity of a practical, hardheaded labor policy. He saw the necessity of discipline, of building up large reserve funds with which to finance strikes and weather depressions, and of avoiding any commerce with politicians, radicals, or doctrinaires. In 1881 he brought together the representatives of various trade-unions in a Federation of Organized Trade and Labor Unions of the United States and Canada. Five years later this organization became the American Federation of Labor.

The A. F. of L. was closer to contemporaneous British labor organizations than to the American Knights of Labor. Unlike the Knights it was a craft union, limited in membership to the aristocracy of labor, and made up of a series of self-governing trade-unions, federated much as are the American states. Unlike the Knights, too, it was eminently practical and opportunistic in its policies. "We have no ultimate ends," said one of its spokesmen. "We are going on from day to day. We are fighting only for immediate objects." Those objects were for the most part higher wages and shorter hours, though such related matters as child labor, sanitation and health laws, the prohibition of contract and convict labor, and the exclusion of Chinese immigrants were not ignored. Throughout its long and successful history, however, the A. F. of L. was to be conservative, opportunistic, and somewhat exclusive. Eschewing politics, co-operating with capital whenever possible, supporting strikes with the reserve funds built up by high dues, maintaining strict discipline, and gaining public confidence by its sober policies, the A. F. of L. weathered hostility, hard times, and rivals; and when Gompers accepted its presidency for the last time in 1924, he could take satisfaction in a membership of almost three million.

The third type of labor organization remained significantly weak. Socialism and Communism have long backgrounds in American history, but their earlier manifestations had been for the most part in such Utopian experiments as Brook Farm; perhaps the nearest thing to a socialistic order that America had known had been the Mormon commonwealth of Utah and labor played little part in that. In the seventies a shadowy secret organization known as the Molly Maguires terrorized the anthracite fields of Pennsylvania, where working conditions were atrocious, until it was stamped out by force. In the seventies, too, German intellectuals, more familiar with the teachings of Karl Marx and Ferdinand Lassalle than with American labor, tried to establish an American Socialism, but with little success. The arrival of Johann Most in 1882 gave to the left-wing branch of labor a revolutionary slant. Most, who had been hunted out of Germany and of England, attempted in vain to win American workers over to a policy of violence.

In time the radical labor groups emancipated themselves from their foreign entanglements; the Industrial Workers of the World, formally organized in 1905, was thoroughly indigenous, though it borrowed something from the syndicalist teachings of Forel. Notwithstanding some successes in the lumber and mining camps of the West and in the textile centers of the East, the I.W.W. never had any real numerical strength, and its hostility to the First World War in 1917–1918 put it out of business, except in the lumber camps of the Northwest and among the migratory farm workers.

Labor Conflicts

THE STORY of American labor is checkered with strikes and violence. From the beginning labor has had to fight for most of its gains: for the right to organize, to strike, to picket, for shorter hours and higher wages, for safe working conditions and accident compensation, for abolition of child labor, injunctions, yellow-dog contracts, the stretch-out system and the company-store racket, for immigration restriction and the closed shop. Mostly the fight has been waged in the industrial arena, sometimes in the domain of politics. And in this prolonged and bitter warfare labor has for the most part stood alone, while business has found powerful allies in public opinion, the police, and the courts. Confronted with such formidable opposition labor has lost or compromised more strikes than it has won, but its victories have been sufficiently numerous to encourage the continued use of the strike as a weapon. Yet the resort to force in industrial relations is as much a monument to the failure of reason as is the resort to force in international relations.

From 1881 to 1905 there occurred no less than thirty-seven thousand strikes, most of them brief and local, some of them prolonged and nationwide. The most spectacular strikes of this period were the railroad strike of 1877, which first introduced large-scale industrial violence to Americans; the strike at the McCormick Harvester works in 1886, which culminated in the tragedy of the Haymarket riot; the Homestead strike of 1892, which was marked by a pitched battle on the banks of the Monongahela; the great Pullman strike of 1894, which tied up half the railroads of the nation; the terrible Cripple Creek war in the Colorado coal fields; and the anthracite-coal strike of 1902, which threatened to paralyze industry throughout the country and which was finally settled only by the intervention of President Theodore Roosevelt. It is neither possible nor profitable to trace their history in detail, but we may select one of them, the Pullman strike of 1894, as in many respects representative of them all.

It started in the "model" town of Pullman, Illinois, where workingmen lived in comfortable company houses (at rents one fourth higher than corresponding houses elsewhere), bought company gas and water, and traded at company stores—at a handsome profit to George Pullman and his stockholders. With the depression of the early nineties, wages were slashed in order to keep up generous dividend payments, and when representatives of the workers appealed to Pullman to arbitrate the wage question, they were summarily dismissed. The workers promptly laid down their tools. The newly organized American Railway Union, under the leadership of young Eugene V. Debs, made the cause of the Pullman workers its own, directing its members not to handle any Pullman cars. With this action, war between the railroads and the workers was on—and it covered half the nation. Within a few weeks transportation throughout much of the North and West was paralyzed, and a metropolitan daily, anticipating the method used to break the strike, announced that this was "a war against the government and against society." Alarmed at the apparent success of the strike, and determined to smash the nascent railway union before it could cause further trouble, an employers' organization, the General Managers' Association, demanded that the Federal government intervene to maintain uninterrupted railway service.

In this appeal the Association was successful. President Cleveland's Attorney General was Richard Olney, a former railroad attorney who was completely sympathetic to the operators' point of view. He responded to their demand with a sweeping injunction against all strike activities. Disorder promptly broke out, but whether by the strikers, *agents provocateurs*, or hoodlums, has never been determined. Governor Altgeld of Illinois was ready to maintain order with state militia, but without giving him an opportunity to act President Cleveland ordered Federal troops to Chicago. The injunction broke the strike, and the soldiers almost broke the labor movement. Debs refused to obey the injunction and was jailed for contempt of court. Altgeld protested that the Constitution had been violated when Federal soldiers were thus sent into the state, but was rebuked by Cleveland and repudiated by the courts. Thus all along the line the railroads appeared victorious.

But subsequent investigations of Congressional committees and of students have sustained the strikers—and Altgeld —on almost every point. The industrial feudalism of the town of Pullman was condemned, the strikers were largely acquitted of responsibility for disorder, the General Managers' Association was branded as arrogant and lawless, the policy of Olney improper, the use of the injunction of dubious legality, and the employment of Federal troops unnecessary and improper. This unhappy episode brought into sharp focus many of the forces that conditioned the position of labor all through these years: the insolence of a great corporation, the role of the sympathetic strike, the use of the Antitrust Act and of the injunction to curb labor, the hostility of the courts, and the tendency of government authorities to side with capital rather than with labor.

By 1900 labor had won most of its basic rights—the right to organize, to strike, to bargain collectively—and made some progress in its campaign for better working and living conditions. Yet it was clear that these gains were limited to a small segment of the working population and that they hardly touched the larger questions of security for the workers and the welfare of society as a whole. It was gradually becoming clear that the labor problem was not isolated from other social and economic problems and that society had a legitimate stake in the welfare and security of its workers. Where industry failed to pay a living wage, society had somehow to make up the difference. Where it failed to provide employment, society had to take care of the unemployed. Where it maimed workingmen or wore them out, prematurely, society had to support them. The labor of women and children was not merely an issue between them and their employers, for it involved the future of the race. It was a question, too, how long society could afford the luxury of industrial warfare, for whoever emerged victorious, society was always the loser.

In the struggle for social reforms labor had powerful allies among the social workers, the Protestant clergy, the scholars and intellectuals. In any history of the war against industrial abuses and the slum the names of Jacob Riis, newspaper reporter extraordinary, Jane Addams of Chicago's Hull House, Washington Gladden, Unitarian clergyman, John R. Commons, professor at the University of Wisconsin, must loom large. They worked unceasingly to enlighten the public upon the social cost of child labor or the danger of the tenements and to stir sluggish legislatures into action. In some states the reformers were notably successful—Massachusetts, New York, Wisconsin, Oregon—but the problem was difficult. For where more advanced states set high standards they invited industry to move to backward states where no such limitations existed.

Yet there was real progress. By the First World War most states had—at least theoretically—prohibited the labor of small children; many had set an eight-hour limit to the labor. of women, established systems of accident compensation, provided for careful inspection of factories and mines, prohibited the yellow-dog contract or the use of private detectives and private police in industrial disputes, and in other ways displayed social alertness. We cannot trace this legislation in detail, but it is well illustrated by the history of child-labor laws.

By 1900 child labor had become a public scandal. One and three-quarters million children between the ages of ten and fifteen were then gainfully employed. Many were working in factories and mines, others in canning establishments, beet fields, or cranberry bogs. One investigator found 556 children under twelve working in eight cotton mills; another found children six and seven years old canning vegetables at two o'clock in the morning. John Spargo, whose *Bitter Cry of the Children* shocked the nation, thus describes what he saw in the Pennsylvania and West Virginia coal mines early in the century:

Crouched over the chutes, the boys sit hour after hour, picking out the pieces of slate and other refuse from the coal as it rushes past the washers. From the cramped position they have to assume most of them become more or less deformed and bent-backed like old men. . . . The coal is hard and accidents to the hands, such as cut, broken, or crushed fingers, are common among the boys. Sometimes there is a worse accident; a terrified shriek is heard, and a boy is mangled and torn in the machinery or disappears in the chute to be picked out later, smothered and dead. Clouds of dust fill the breakers and are inhaled by the boys, laying the foundations for asthma and miners' consumption. I once stood in a breaker for half an hour and tried to do the work a twelve-year-old boy was doing day after day. . . . I could not do that work and live, but there were boys of ten and twelve years of age doing it for fifty and sixty cents a day.

Some of them had never been inside of a school; few of them could read a child's primer.

There were state laws against these evils, to be sure, but they were inadequate and easily evaded. Thus South Carolina finally worked up to a twelve-year limit for factory labor but permitted exceptions where this limit imposed a hardship upon families! And when Maryland required all persons under sixteen wanting to work to apply for a permit, applications were more numerous than the total number of persons under sixteen enumerated in the previous census! Legislation rarely affected anything but factory labor, leaving quite unprotected the hundreds of thousands of children working as messenger boys, bootblacks, and hands in berry fields or canning establishments—which were not held to be factories. Not until 1909 did an American state—Delaware—provide that "no child under the age of fourteen shall be employed or suffered to work in any gainful occupation."

The inadequacy of state laws led to a demand for Congressional action. In 1916 Congress responded with a law forbidding the shipment in interstate commerce of the products of child labor. The problem seemed solved—but the courts blandly announced that this law was beyond the powers of Congress and therefore void. Three years later Congress tried again, this time by trying to tax out of existence the products of child labor. Once more the courts interposed their veto: Congress could not do indirectly what it might not do directly. To be sure, twenty years later the Supreme Court confessed that this was all a mistake, but the harm was done. All through the prosperous twenties child labor continued, and the census of 1930 showed more than two million boys and girls under eighteen gainfully employed. Then the New Deal cut across constitutional dialectic and practically ended the scandal.

Through these two methods—collective bargaining and legislation—labor vastly improved its position. Business, too, began to take a more enlightened view of the labor problem and to set its own house in order. No longer would any businessman say with the railroad manipulator, Jay Gould: "Labor is a commodity that will in the long run be governed absolutely by the law of supply and demand." The "law of supply and demand" had been amended on behalf of manufacturers, bankers, and farmers; now it was to be amended on behalf of labor.

The Melting Pot

MOST AMERICANS have never properly appreciated the role of immigration in their history. They think of immigration as a "problem," and usually as one that has come to the fore only in the last half century or so. And when they think of immigrants, they conjure up a picture of olive-skinned Italians or bearded Jews or Polish peasant women with bright shawls coming down the gangplank onto Ellis Island. They do not think of the Pilgrim Fathers or of French Huguenots or of Scotch-Irish; certainly they do not think of poor black folk enduring the hell of the Middle Passage.

Yet all Americans, except Indians, are immigrants or the descendants of immigrants: the Colonial Dames and members of the Order of Cincinnati as well as the Polish steel workers of Gary or the Negroes of Harlem. Immigrants came, to be sure, at different times, in different circumstances, from different parts of the globe. But all of them went through the same experience of being uprooted from their old homes and transplanted to a new one. All, even the ignorant and lowly, brought their strength, culture, and faith. All of them are ingredients in the giant melting pot of America.

We have already seen something of the various streams that went to make up the population of colonial America. All through the early years of the republic emigration from the Old World to the New continued, most of it voluntary. From 1820, when records were first kept, to the beginning of the Civil War, about five million newcomers from Ireland, England, and Germany threw in their lot with the Americans. Even the war did not seriously retard the stream of immigration, and after Appomattox it swelled to a torrent. The American population of 1870 was, consequently, a very heterogeneous one. Out of one thousand Americans, in that year, 435 were native-born whites of native parentage, 292 native-born whites of foreign or mixed parentage, 144 foreign-born whites, 127 Negroes; one Indian and one Chinaman rounded out the number. Between 1870 and 1920 almost twenty million more immigrants came to the United States. Yet the proportions of the foreign-born and native-born population remained substantially the same. Perhaps the most striking changes were the decline in the relative number of Negroes and the increase in the number of Mexicans.

But one very important fact about the changing character of the American population struck every observer. That was the sharp increase in the number of those whose homes or whose fathers' homes were in the nations of southern and eastern Europe. During the seventies and the eighties the majority of immigrants continued to come from those nations which had in the past furnished so many—Great Britain, Germany, and the Scandinavian countries. But even during these years there was a small stream of the "new" immigration. Enterprising steamship companies established direct connections with Naples, Danzig, Memel, Fiume, and Athens, and retained thousands of agents in Italy, Poland, and the Dual Monarchy to drum up steerage passengers. Enterprising corporations arranged to meet the immigrants at Ellis Island and take them to mining regions or factory towns. As the pressure of population became less acute in Great Britain, Germany, and Scandinavia, the trek to the New World slowed down. But the "new" immigration increased by leaps and bounds. The first decade of the new century, for example, brought only 340,000 immigrants from Ireland, and another 340,000 from Germany, but it brought over two million from Italy and another two million from the states of Austria-Hungary. Before the bars were finally put up, Italy had sent us more than four and a half million of her sons and daughters, Austria-Hungary four million, Russia and Poland three and a quarter million.

To all of these newcomers—to those who fled religious persecution and sought freedom to worship as they would, to those who ran away from military service and from wars, to those who longed for a more democratic society, to those who hoped to escape grinding poverty and share in the fabulous riches of the New World—America was the Promised Land. All, whatever their reasons for taking the step, were caught up in the great adventure; all dreamed of a better life, and most of them helped build such a life for themselves and for their children.

The "old" immigration had spread out pretty evenly throughout the North and West, and had gone, in about equal numbers, into farming and industry. But because it took money to start a farm, because the best land was gone, because there were jobs in the cities, and colonies of their own people and Catholic churches, the "new" immigrants congregated in the industrial centers of the East and Middle West. By 1900 two thirds of the foreign-born were living in towns and cities, and by 1920 this proportion had increased to three fourths. In New York City were hundreds of thousands of Italians, Poles, Russians, and Jews; Italians and French Canadians lived in large numbers in sedate Boston; Russians in Quaker Philadelphia; Russians and Poles in Cleveland; Scandinavians in St. Paul and Minneapolis; while Chicago presented as variegated a racial pattern as any other city on earth. In small industrial towns like Fall River, Scranton, or Hamtramck, the percentage of foreign-born was even higher than in the larger cities. What this meant was that newcomers from southern and eastern Europe were finding work in the mines, mills, and factories. As early as 1910, for example, three fourths of the coal miners of Pennsylvania were foreign-born; of these the overwhelming majority were Italians, Poles, and Slovaks. In 1920 the foreign-born constituted one eighth of the total population, but one third of those employed in factories and more than one half of those working in mines.

What did the immigrants contribute? Most of all, themselves—their strength, their work, their faith. They owed much to their adopted country, and that country owed much to them. They did the hard, grueling work that had to be done if the resources of the nation were to be developed rapidly and cheaply. They broke the prairie sod; they laid the tracks for the transcontinentals; they dug the iron ore, coal, copper; they felled the lumber of the Northwest forests. But their contribution was not only that of unskilled labor. They gave richness and color to American life and in some fields added greatly to her cultural heritage. In music and arts they supplied a large part of the creative impulse. In 1930 there was not a major orchestra in the country whose leader bore an Anglo-Saxon name.

Yet immigration has created its problems, too. Labor felt

it in the form of competition for jobs: as one labor leader said, "Our living is gauged by immigration; our wages are based on immigration; the condition of our family is gauged by immigration." City governments felt it in new problems of housing, sanitation, and police. The school system felt it in the problem of illiteracy and of social adjustment. Yet the assimilation of the foreign-born was not difficult, despite the fears of many representatives of "native stock" who trembled at "accents of menace alien to our air." The average immigrant was pathetically anxious to become an American. The experience which Mary Antin describes in her *Promised Land* was shared by hundreds of thousands of them:

The apex of my civic pride and personal contentment was reached on the bright September morning when I entered the public school. That day I must always remember, even if I live to be so old that I cannot tell my name. To most people their first day at school is a memorable occasion. In my case the importance of the day was a hundred times magnified on account of the years I had waited, the road I had come, and the conscious ambitions I entertained. . . . Father himself conducted us to school. He would not have delegated that mission to the President of the United States. He had waited the day with impatience equal to mine, and the visions he saw as he hurried us over the sun-flecked pavements transcended all my dreams. . . . At last the four of us stood around the teacher's desk; and my father, in his impossible English, gave us over in her charge, with some broken word of his hopes for us that his swelling heart could no longer contain.

It was the children of the immigrants, rather than the immigrants themselves, who raised problems of assimilation and adjustment. Many were truly uprooted and demoralized. At home they lived in one world, outside the home in another and alien world. They were still tied to the Old World, through their parents—and often through their Church—but this connection was derivative and unreal. Often they revolted against their old inheritance before they had learned to embrace the new. The public school was the great solvent, but sometimes the school accentuated differences instead of rubbing them out. The "second-generation" Americans presented more problems of social maladjustment, of violence and crime, than the first.

Around 1900 there developed a widespread feeling that it was time to call a halt on unrestricted immigration. Labor resented the competition of unskilled and easily exploitable laborers; "old-stock" Americans feared that the racial strain was being debased by so many Slavic and Mediterranean newcomers; the average man thought that the United States had people and problems enough without inviting more. As early as 1882 Congress had stopped immigration from China, and that same year it had excluded those designated as "undesirable"—the sick, the mentally defective, the immoral, anarchists, and others. This may have had some qualitative but it had no quantitative effect; what was needed was a screen which would have both. The formula proposed was the literacy test. As illiteracy was almost nonexistent in the British Isles, Germany, and Scandinavia, while it was very high in Italy, Poland, Russia, and other states of southern and eastern Europe, this seemed to have the advantage of cutting down the total number of "new" immigrants without seriously affecting the "old" immigration.

Three Presidents—Cleveland, Taft, and Wilson—vetoed bills favoring a literacy requirement for admission to the United States, on the ground that this was a test not of ability but of opportunity. In 1917, however, Congress finally had its way and wrote a literacy test into the immigration laws. With the end of the World War and the prospect of large-scale emigration from the devastated nations of Europe, the problem appeared one of exclusion rather than mere restriction. In a series of laws, 1921, 1924, and 1929, Congress set a quantitative limit—eventually 150,000—upon those who might come from abroad. The restriction did not apply to immigration from Canada or Mexico or the states of South America, but a strict interpretation of the provisions forbidding the entry of any who might become public charges effectively cut down on immigration from these countries as well.

Thus, by 1930, an era in American history came to an end. The United States was still a melting pot; but, itself becoming crowded in many areas, it could no longer be a Promised Land on the old free terms to the poor and oppressed of other nations.

CHAPTER 16

The West Comes of Age

Opening Up the Last West

WHILE THE SOUTH was recovering from the agony of war and the chaos of reconstruction, while the North was gearing its economy to the factory and the machine, changes even more spectacular were taking place in the trans-Missouri West. In 1860 this region, comprising roughly half the total area of the United States, was for the most part a wilderness. The new state of California, to be sure, boasted a population of almost four hundred thousand; in the Willamette Valley were some fifty thousand Oregon pioneers; the Mormon commonwealth, clustered around the Great Salt Lake, numbered another forty thousand, while along the banks of the upper Rio Grande lived a straggling agglomeration of some ninety thousand Pueblo Indians, Mexicans and white adventurers. The rest of this imperial expanse was the land of the Indians—the warlike Sioux and Blackfoot and Crow of the northern plains, the Ute and Cheyenne and Kiowa of the middle region, the cruel Comanche and Apache of the arid south—the numerous tribes whose names have sung themselves into American folklore. Mounted on fleet ponies, living off the vast herds of buffalo which provided everything from food to fuel, these roamed the plains, mountains, and deserts, undisturbed except by each other or by the mountain lions and coyotes.

Thirty years later all this was changed. The Indians had been defeated and subjected to the dubious process of civilization. The bellowing herds of buffalo had been wiped out. Miners had ranged over the whole of the mountain country, panning the clear streams whose very names are poetry—the San Joaquin, the Beaverhead, the Belle Fourche, the Bitter Root, the Sweetwater—tunneling into the earth, establishing feverish little communities in Nevada, Montana, Colorado, and even the Black Hills of Dakota. Railroads had pushed boldly across the unbroken prairie sod, found passes through the towering Rockies, and linked the Atlantic with the Pacific. Cattlemen, taking advantage of free grass, railroads, and new markets, had laid claim to a vast grassland kingdom stretching from the Panhandle of Texas to the upper Missouri, and sheepmen competed with them in the valleys and on the mountain slopes. Then farmers swarmed into the plains and the mountain valleys and closed the gap between the East and the West. By 1890 the frontier was gone, a solid band of states stretched across the continent, and five or six million men and women farmed where the antelope and prairie dog had played.

Why had the conquest of this immense region been so long delayed; why, when it came, did it proceed with such breathless speed? For two centuries Americans had pushed steadily westward from the Atlantic Coast—into the "Old West" of colonial days, across the Appalachians, down the Ohio, and into the Mississippi Valley. By 1850 the frontier of population had reached approximately the ninety-fifth meridian—and there, for the first time in American history, it stopped its progressive march. Instead of moving regularly forward, it leaped the plains and Rockies and established itself along the waters of the Pacific. The explanation lies in geography and climate. European peoples had come from countries of woods and rivers, and they found in the New World woods and rivers and abundant rain for their crops. But the Great Plains confronted them, for the first time in two centuries of experience, with something new. This was the land of little water. Rainfall was scanty, and there were long periods of drought; the streams were shallow and uncertain, and there was little timber for houses or fences. It was no wonder that the early pioneers passed all this by and pushed out to the well-watered, well-timbered Pacific Coast.

Not until the farmer fashioned tools to adapt himself to a new environment could he hope to conquer the Great Plains.

The adaptation came, and in time. Railroads provided transportation; barbed wire was made available for fencing; deep-drilled wells and windmills supplied water; dry farming and irrigation solved, in part, the problem of farming where the rainfall was inadequate for the kind of cultivation to which the farmers had been accustomed. With these new tools the pioneer could live, raise crops, and plant permanent communities on the plains. Out of the experience came not only new ways of farming, but also new ways of living—new social and economic and cultural institutions.

The great trans-Missouri West, though largely unsettled, was not unknown. Intrepid pathfinders like Lewis and Clark and John C. Frémont had explored it; trappers and fur traders, working for the Northwest or the Astor fur companies, or on their own, had familiarized themselves with it; merchants and traders along the Santa Fe Trail had opened up the way to the Spanish Southwest; missionaries, Protestant and Catholic alike, had labored with the Indians. Pioneers along the Oregon Trail, Saints on the Mormon Trail, fortune hunters on the California Trail, had blazed highways across it; the army had built forts to protect immigrants and traders; surveyors had mapped the country for railway routes; and even as the new era opened President Lincoln was signing a bill providing for the construction of the first transcontinental.

Ever since the 1840's, visionaries had dreamed of a railroad to span the continent, but not until the rush of population to California did the problem become urgent. After that there was acrimonious debate over its route. Southerners wanted a road that would link lower California and Texas with New Orleans or Memphis; Northerners plumped for a road that would tie the Northwest in with St. Louis or Chicago. Surveys were made, but the controversy was not settled until the withdrawal of the Confederate States gave the Northern advocates a free hand. The Pacific Railway Bill of 1862 incorporated two railroads—the Union Pacific and the Central Pacific. The Union Pacific was to build westward from Council Bluffs, Iowa, the Central Pacific eastward from California, until they met. To make possible so gigantic an undertaking the Federal government gave the two roads some twenty-four million acres of the public domain, and loans which came eventually to about sixty-five million dollars.

Spurred on by these endowments, and by additional gifts from state legislatures, the directors pushed energetically ahead with their plans. A Herculean task confronted them. Some 1700 miles of track had to be laid through a wilderness of prairie, mountain, and desert, inhabited only by hostile Indians. The engineering problem of the Central Pacific was particularly arduous. There was no labor available, and eventually some ten thousand coolies were imported from distant China. Every pound of iron rail, every car, every locomotive, every piece of machinery, had to be shipped around Cape Horn or over the Isthmus of Panama: at one time the company had fifty ships chartered just for this purpose. There were no roads over the Sierras, and thousands of tons of equipment, including massive locomotives, were hauled in giant sleds over the snowdrifts. Food, powder, supplies of all kinds, followed the same toilsome route. Roadways had to be blasted out of cliffs, bridges thrown over gorges, and in the space of sixty miles fifteen tunnels bored through the Sierras. When deep snow threatened to halt all construction, ingenious engineers constructed thirty-seven miles of snowsheds, and under these the work went on.

The engineering task of the Union Pacific was less difficult —in part, perhaps, because in General Grenville Dodge it had one of the greatest living engineers. His labor force was made up of Irish workers and veterans from the Union and Confederate armies who were quick to exchange picks for rifles when Indians appeared. Under his driving leadership the road pushed out at the rate of two, three, even four miles a day, one construction gang laying ties, another swinging the rails into place and spiking them down.

On May 10, 1869, the two roads joined at Promontory Point, Utah, and the whole nation joined in the celebration as the marriage was solemnized by the driving of golden and silver spikes. It was a great engineering feat, an epic story of tenacity, ingenuity, and courage. "When I think," wrote Robert Louis Stevenson,

how the railroad has been pushed through this unwatered wilderness and haunt of savage tribes . . . how at each stage of the construction, roaring, impromptu cities, full of gold and lust and death, sprang up and then died away again; how in these uncouth places pigtailed Chinese pirates worked side by side with border ruffians and broken men from Europe, talking together in mixed dialect, mostly oaths, gambling, drinking, quarreling, and murdering like wolves . . . and then when I go on to remember that all this epical turmoil was conducted by gentlemen in frock coats and with a view to nothing more extraordinary than a fortune and a subsequent visit to Paris, it seems to me as if this railway were the one typical achievement of the age in which we live. . . . If it be romance, if it be contrast, if it be heroism that we require, what was Troy town to this?

There were romance and heroism, to be sure, but there were "a fortune and a visit to Paris," too. Indeed the achievement which brought such pride brought at the same time a sense of shame. The directors of the Union Pacific, not content with government largess, organized a dummy construction company and voted that company fraudulent contracts that netted them profits running into millions of dollars. The "Big Four" of the Central Pacific—Huntington, Stanford, Crocker, and Hopkins—organized their own construction company and milked their road to the tune of more than sixty million dollars; each of them left over forty millions at his death. Both groups of directors engaged in wholesale bribery; both groups saddled their roads with such debts that the government had to whistle for its loans and the communities which they served had to pay exorbitant charges for a generation to come.

Meantime many other transcontinentals were projected and four completed. Aided by a Congressional grant of forty million acres of public land, Jay Cooke inaugurated and Frederick Billings and Henry Villard completed the Northern Pacific, which, in 1883, linked Lake Superior with Puget Sound. Two other transcontinentals were scarcely less fortunate in land grants—the Santa Fe, which followed the old trail from Kansas into New Mexico and then struck across the desert to lower California; and the Southern Pacific, which ran from New Orleans to Los Angeles and San Francisco. These roads, as well as others which pushed their way into the West, received grants not only from the Federal government, but from states and counties as well. Only one of the transcontinentals was built without any government aid—the Great Northern. This road, the creation of the Canadian-born J. J. Hill, paralleled the Northern Pacific from St. Paul to Seattle. Financially it proved the soundest of them all, and in its economic and social policies the most beneficent. Hill was indeed an empire builder and the Great Northern functioned pretty much as the Massachusetts Bay Company functioned in the seventeenth and the Ohio Company in the eighteenth century. It transported the colonists to the land, carried them through the first year, built churches and schools, and grew up with the country.

The Mining and Cattle Kingdoms

IT WAS THE MINERS who established the first outposts of the Far West. The discovery of gold in California had transformed that commonwealth from a pastoral outpost of New Spain to a thriving American state and had opened up new and varied economic activities—farming, shipping, railroading, and manufacturing. That experience was to be repeated again and again in the history of the mining kingdom; in the rush to the Pike's Peak country in 1859, to Alder Gulch and Last Chance in Montana and the banks of the Sweetwater in Wyoming in the middle sixties, to the Black Hills of the Dakota country in the seventies. Everywhere the miners opened up the country, established political communities, and laid the foundations for more permanent settlements. As the gold and silver played out or fell into the hands of eastern corporations and the mining fever abated, the settlers would perceive the farming and stock-raising possibilities around them or find work on the railroads that were pushing in from the East and West. Some communities remained almost exclusively mining, but the real wealth of Montana and Colorado, Wyoming and Idaho, as of California, was in their grass and their soil. Even in mineral wealth the value of the precious metals which had first lured adventurers was shortly exceeded by that of the copper and coal and oil which were so abundant.

The decline of the mining kingdom was as swift as its rise, but it left an indelible impression on the American mind. The mining camps were wonderfully picturesque. A new strike would bring thousands of fortune hunters swarming to some wilderness outpost. Within a few days hundreds of tents and ramshackle huts would rise along the banks of some stream or straggle up the slope of the mountain where the wealth was hidden. Every other house might be a saloon or a dance hall, where bad liquor was dispensed at fifty cents a drink and hurdy-gurdy girls entertained the bewhiskered miners. Lawlessness was not as prevalent as the romantic writers have imagined, but there were few of the amenities of civilization, and the life of the camp was barbarizing. Yet in time the mining communities became orderly enough.

The mining kingdom did more than advertise the agricultural riches of the West, attract settlers, and furnish material to later novelists and moving-picture producers. It precipitated the Indian problem, brought in the railroads, poured a stream of riches into the coffers of eastern investors, added some two billion dollars of precious metals to the nation's wealth, thus enabling it to redeem its greenbacks in specie, and introduced the "money question" into American politics.

Even while the miners were grubbing in the hills of Nevada and Montana, a new and more important chapter was being written in the history of the West. This was the rise of the cattle kingdom. The physical basis of the kingdom was the grasslands of the West, stretching unbroken from the Rio Grande to the northern frontier, from Kansas and Nebraska into the Rocky Mountain valleys. Here millions of buffaloes had roamed at will, but within two decades the buffalo was to become almost extinct and its place taken by even more millions of Texas longhorns and Wyoming and Montana steers.

For a century Spanish dons and missionaries had raised cattle in northern Mexico, along the Rio Grande, and in the valleys of southern California, but these were valuable only for local consumption and for their tallow and hides. With the coming of the railroads, the establishment of packing houses in St. Louis, Kansas City, Omaha, and Chicago, and the advent of the refrigerator car, it became profitable to improve the breed and drive the cattle north to markets. Beginning immediately after the Civil War, the long drive became an annual institution. Tens of thousands of cattle pounded out the Chisholm, the Pecos, the Goodnight, the Bozeman trails, and roaring cattle towns like Abilene and Cheyenne sprang up at terminal points of the new railroads. Meanwhile cattlemen had found that they could winter the cattle on the rich grasses of the North, and the empire expanded into Colorado, Wyoming, and Montana. Texas had the most cattle, but Wyoming was the most typical cowmen's commonwealth. Here, for years, there was no interest to compete with the cattle interest, and the Wyoming Stock Growers' Association ruled unchallenged.

In the beginning almost anyone could start a herd, by picking up a few cows and calves and letting them graze on public lands. But within a short time the big cattlemen and cattle companies—many of them organized in the East or in Britain—got control of the industry by helping themselves to the public grasslands or leasing lands from the Indian tribes and fencing in water holes and streams. One cattle company had fenced in one million acres of public land in Colorado; another had entirely surrounded Jones County in Texas; the Cheyenne Indians had leased four million acres of their lands to one group of cattle companies, and the civilized tribes of the Indian Territory had surrendered six million acres to a single company. Cattle barons ruthlessly barred small competitors and waged relentless war on the sheepmen whose sheep cropped the grasses so close that they ruined the pasture.

The cattle kingdom, like the mining, had its romantic side, and the remembrance of this has persisted in the American consciousness after the cattle kingdom itself has vanished. The lonely life on the plain, the roundup, the hieroglyphic brands, the long drive, the stampede, the war with cattle rustlers, the splendid horsemanship, the picturesque costume designed for usefulness, not effect—the wild life of the cow towns like Abilene and Cheyenne, all have found their way into American folklore and song. Children array themselves now in imitation cowboy suits, moving-picture ranchmen shoot down rustlers with unerring aim, and the whole country sings what was reputed to be President Franklin Roosevelt's favorite song:

> Home, home on the range,
> Where the deer and the antelope play
> Where seldom is heard, a discouraging word,
> And the skies are not cloudy all day.

The Coming of the Farmers

CATTLE AND SHEEP RAISING were natural to the High
Plains, and many cattlemen were convinced that it would be
a mistake for the farmers to attempt to establish themselves
in this country. Early in the century Zebulon Pike had reported that "on the rivers Kansas, Platte, Arkansas, and their
various branches, it appears to me to be only possible to introduce a limited population . . . the inhabitants would find
it most to their advantage to pay attention to the multiplica-
tion of cattle, horses, sheep, and goats," and half a century
later a United States Senator, opposing the admission of
Kansas to the Union, declared that "after we pass the Missouri River, except on a few streams, there is no territory fit
for settlement or habitation." These generalizations have
proved erroneous, yet subsequent events have revealed that in
large sections of the arid West, farming is unprofitable. The
cattlemen, in any event, were sure that they held a title deed
from Nature herself to all the grasslands of the West. By fair
means or foul they flouted the land laws, fenced in vast areas,
monopolized watercourses, and tried to stem the advance of
the farmer.

But it was a losing fight. Cattlemen might scare off individual "nesters" but they could not permanently defy the
Federal government, and when Presidents Arthur and Cleveland ordered the barbed-wire fences cut and the grasslands
thrown open to homesteaders, the game was up. During the
seventies and eighties the railroads had opened up access to
the whole of the plains country and engaged in large-scale
colonizing activities. The Northern Pacific, with forty million
acres to dispose of, flooded Europe with advertisements describing the almost tropical richness of the Western soil
(hence Jay Cooke's "Banana Belt"), and Cooke's successor,
Villard, had at one time over eight hundred agents abroad
drumming up land sales. The Santa Fe brought in thousands
of Russian Mennonites; the Southern Pacific attracted Germans and Scandinavians; Hill built up his empire by lending
money to impecunious farmers, subsidizing scientific farming,
building churches and schools. Indian resistance was broken,
and the remnants of defeated tribes were harried out of the
land or herded into reservations. Factories dotting the edge

of the plains region turned out the millions of miles of barbed wire and the thousands of windmills and drills which made farming in the arid land possible. Eight million immigrants poured into the country, population increased by twenty-two million; the pressure on the older-settled regions was heightened while the domestic market for farm produce expanded.

These auspices presiding, the decades of the seventies and the eighties witnessed a veritable stampede into the plains country. Hamlin Garland remembered that when he went to stake out a claim in Dakota:

Trains swarming with immigrants from every country of the world were haltingly creeping out upon the level lands. Norwegians, Swedes, Danes, Scotchmen, Englishmen, and Russians all mingled in this flood of land-seekers rolling toward the sundown plain, where a fat-soiled valley had been set aside by good Uncle Sam for the enrichment of every man. . . . The street swarmed with boomers. All talk was of lots, of land. Hour by hour as the sun sank, prospectors returned to the hotel from their trips into the unclaimed territory, hungry and tired but jubilant.

Similar scenes were enacted all along the plains. In two decades Minnesota increased her population threefold, Kansas fourfold, Nebraska eightfold, while Dakota jumped from fourteen thousand to half a million, and imperial Texas, with two and a quarter million inhabitants, was toppling ancient Massachusetts out of sixth place in the population lists. Altogether during this twenty-year period the population of the predominantly farming states of Minnesota, Kansas, Nebraska, the Dakotas, Colorado, and Montana increased from one million to about five millions—a rate of increase eight times that of the country as a whole. As the great Tocqueville had said half a century earlier, "This gradual and continuous progress of the European race onward toward the Rocky Mountains had the solemnity of a providential event. It is like a deluge of men, rising unabatedly, and driven daily onward by the hand of God."

By the close of the eighties the tidal wave of migration onto the plains had spent its force and in some places begun to ebb. Hard times and drought drove many ambitious farmers out of the arid lands of western Kansas and Nebraska and the Dakotas and back to the East. The rate of population increase slowed up perceptibly: Nebraska, for example, gained only four thousand inhabitants during the nineties, Kansas only forty thousand—whereas elsewhere the additions were scarcely greater than could be accounted for by the natural increase of a fertile population.

Yet the most spectacular chapter in the history of the opening of the West was still to be written. For half a century pioneers had gazed hungrily at the rich land between Texas and Kansas, given over as a permanent reservation to the Five Civilized Indian Tribes. By the mid-eighties pressure for the rich bottom lands of the Arkansas, the Canadian, the Red, and the Washita and for the rolling prairie land between them was so strong that the government could no longer resist it. Indian rights were purchased, and in April, 1889, the territory was thrown open to settlement. The rush into the new country was frantic. A few years later there was a similar rush when the Cherokee Strip of northern Oklahoma was thrown open to settlement. As Marquis James, in *Cherokee Strip*, recalls it:

Well, sir, in this race there were thousands of horses and thousands of riders and drivers, and they stretched in a line across the prairie as far as you could see. Papa asked me to look to the east and look to the west and imagine all those horses strung out ready to break. Most of the horses were under saddle. The others were hitched to every kind of rig. Light rigs—buckboards, spring wagons and sulkies—were the best. But there were covered wagons, lots of them, and even people on foot.

They broke with a yell and at first you couldn't see a thing for the dust that was raised where the grass had been trampled away along the starting line. In this blinding cloud the wheels of rigs locked and there were spills at the very start. When the racers got out on the grass, the dust went down, except along the Chisholm Trail. The riders took the lead, mostly, with the fastest driving horses and lightest wagons next. And on they went. There were no roads, mind you, except the Trail, and no bridges. You got down and up draws and across creeks and ravines and gullies as best you could. Or you headed them. Wagons stuck in the streams and stalled in the draws. Rigs broke down from the rough going. By and by the horses that had been ridden or driven too hard began to play out. Horses that had started slower began to edge ahead. . . . With five miles

to go to Enid, of the thousands who started about a hundred
held the lead. Most of the others were far behind, some dropping
out all the time to stake claims along the Trail or to veer east
or west. The rest pressed on to get nearer Enid. The hundred
leaders dwindled to fifty, nearly all on horseback, though a few
buckboards were still keeping up.

By 1900 this new territory had a population of almost eight
hundred thousand.

The mining kingdom and the cattle kingdom had disappeared; now the frontier, too, was gone. There were still
mines in the West, to be sure, but they were well-regulated
businesses, owned and operated by Eastern corporations.
Millions of cattle still ranged over the grasslands from Texas
and New Mexico to Montana and the Dakotas, but the open
range was gone and cattle raising was just one of a number
of economic interests. There was still land in the West, too,
but it was for the most part in the mountains or in country
so arid that only irrigation could make farming profitable.
More and more, in its economic structure, the West was
assimilated to the rest of the country.

Politically, too, that assimilation proceeded apace. Nevada
had been admitted to statehood as early as 1864—chiefly because Lincoln thought that he might need her electoral votes.
Nebraska achieved statehood in 1867, and Colorado came in
as the Centennial State in 1876. Then there was a long delay,
while the last West filled up and political parties jockeyed
for control of the new territories. At last, in 1889–1890, the
bars were let down and an Omnibus Bill admitted six Western
states—the two Dakotas, Wyoming, Montana, Idaho, and
Washington. Utah, long populous enough for statehood but
regarded with suspicion because of Mormon control, came
in a few years later; Oklahoma in 1907, and the two Southwestern states of Arizona and New Mexico in 1912. Thus the
political boundaries of the nation were drawn in their permanent pattern, and the process so auspiciously inaugurated with
the Northwest Ordinance of 1787 was brought to completion.

In their political organization the Western commonwealths
resembled the Eastern. The familiar form of government—a
tripartite division of powers, a bicameral legislature, the
town and county system of local administration—was everywhere adopted. In some respects, however, the new state con-

stitutions did differ from the older ones. They were far more detailed, more carefully drawn, and on the whole more liberal. Most of them provided for some form of woman suffrage, prohibited trusts and monopolies, regulated railways, and established progressive labor standards. Yet neither the philosophy that inspired them nor the energy that animated them was fundamentally different from that common to the whole of the United States.

Life on the Last Frontier

THE FRONTIER had always spelled hardship and danger, and the last frontier was no exception. For the men and women who left the towns or the wooded farms of the East to try their luck on the High Plains, life was always hard and often bitterly disappointing. The work was harder, the rewards more meager, than on the farms of the Ohio or Mississippi valleys. For some the limitless prairie, stretching out to the farthest horizon, the great billowing clouds, the gorgeous sunsets, had their own beauty, but for most the plains seemed drab and monotonous. In the summer the burning sun beat down remorselessly on the plowmen or the harvesters, and the dry, hot winds sweeping up from the south made even the nights all but unbearable. The winter descended swiftly and with cruel cold, temperatures dropping to twenty and thirty below zero; blinding blizzards sometimes raged for days on end, leaving the carcasses of thousands of cattle strewn over the prairie, killing or maiming men and women unfortunate enough to be caught in them; sometimes men got lost fumbling their way from their house to their barn.

The men had their work and their ambitions; the drudgery and loneliness bore hardest on the women. Many of them, reared in comfort back East, made their first homes in dugouts or sod cabins, dark and badly ventilated, the windows and doors covered with blankets or hides, every rain making puddles on the bare floor. The rude frame houses that succeeded these primitive structures were more comfortable but scarcely less ugly. Set out on a treeless prairie, small, hastily built, painted a dull leaden gray, they were hot in summer, cold in winter, cheerless all the time. The trees and bushes and flowers that had been part of the East were missing, though in time some were planted and—when water was available—tended. There was little water to spare for gardening, however, little to spare even for housecleaning and washing. In times of drought, when the corn dried up and the vines withered and the wells gave out and the south wind blew a flinty dust into every corner and crevice of the house and the temperature stayed up in the nineties day and night, even the most courageous lost heart.

Almost worse than the heat and dirt and drudgery were the loneliness and isolation. Cut off from the pleasures of social intercourse, the consolations of the church, the help of doctors, many a frontier wife—like Beret in Ole Rolvaag's great *Giants in the Earth*—became unbalanced. Children were born with the aid of kindly neighbors—or often without any aid; infant mortality, as the pathetic little cemeteries bore witness, was cruelly high. Sickness was always dreaded, for medical aid was hard to come by and costly. Polluted water caused typhoid; cholera, pneumonia, and measles were common, while accidents took a heavy toll. Harassed country doctors performed heroic operations, often without anesthetics and with the crudest of surgical instruments. Everett Dick tells of one young doctor who performed his first appendectomy without anesthetic, and by the light of a kerosene lamp; when the lamp broke the operation was continued in the flickering light of a smoking flame.

Life in the towns offered more variety and sociability, but it too was drab and isolated. The typical plains town of this period was a small and tentative affair, its inhabitants dreaming of a magnificent future but ready to pack up and move to a more promising location at a moment's notice. Picture a narrow muddy street, with wooden sidewalks ending abruptly at the edge of the prairie, lined on either side with a row of ramshackle frame houses, their gray paint blistered by the sun. The most prominent structures are the saloons, the general store, the livery stable, the hotel, and the station where every day the townsfolk gather to await the train that brings in the newspapers and magazines, the mail-order catalogues, the letters from friends and family back East, the occasional drummer or loan agent or grain buyer. At one end of the street is a church—usually Methodist or Baptist or Presbyterian—where once a month a hard-pressed and poorly paid clergyman dispenses hell-fire and brimstone. Across from it, set back in a square ill-kempt yard, is the grammar school, a rude two-roomed affair, with wooden benches for the scholars, a chair and a desk for the teacher—some young lad back from a year at the normal school or some spinster or widow lady in need of a job. A few of the more progressive townsfolk have planted trees, and here and there a row of sunflowers or hollyhocks or a morning-glory vine shows where some housewife has made a brave attempt to create beauty. Children, clad in calico or denim, play in the back yards or gaze in fascination at the work of the blacksmith; bewhiskered men, in the ubiquitous overalls, lounge in the general store or at the livery stable, talking over the prospect for crops or the price of corn or chewing the cud of politics.

There is little crime or vice, but a good deal of drunkenness and—on Saturday night, when the farm boys come in after a week of labor—numerous brawls. Occasionally there is a big gathering, on the Fourth of July or at a Grange picnic, when all the townsfolk and the farmers from far around hitch up their horses and buggies and ride out to the banks of the nearest river for a prolonged celebration. Everett Dick, in *Sod-House Frontier, 1854–1890,* describes such a Fourth of July celebration at Blue Springs, Nebraska:

A committee of three was appointed to catch catfish . . . by the Fourth these men had over a thousand pounds of large catfish penned up in the mouth of a nearby creek. . . . Another committee of three built a brush canopy and secured boards at a sawmill for a forty foot table and a dance platform. A large pile of logs was gathered from the timber for fuel. The promoters sent to Brownsville, forty miles away, for a two hundred and fifty pound hog which furnished an abundance of lard to fry the fish. A corn crusher was improvised of sheet iron. There was much good cornbread even though the meal was not grated fine nor bolted. There was a sumptuous repast of catfish and corn dodger with a little white bread which a few had brought for dessert. On the afternoon of the third people began to come. By the next day there were one hundred and fifty people. They came walking, riding in ox wagons, and any way they could get there. The ladies were dressed in sunbonnets and plain dresses. There was but one silk dress in the whole crowd; some of the men were barefoot. The flag was run to the top of a pole seventy feet high; the Declaration of Independence was read; and after a sumptuous meal had been served, the fiddles, brought from over an area of eighty miles, were tuned up and the dance began.

Some of these little towns flourished and prospered. Streets and sidewalks were paved, brick and stone replaced the wooden structures, a new hotel, an opera house, banks and stores, a high school, all testified to prosperity and civic pride. Others languished and died; in Kansas alone two thousand geographical names have disappeared from the map. The success or failure of a frontier town was determined pretty much by the railroad—and by politics; and the county-seat wars of the plains country were notorious.

This last frontier, like earlier frontiers, was thoroughly democratic. Most of the new communities adopted some form of woman suffrage—Wyoming had led the way as early as 1869. Some of the new constitutions provided for the initiative, and the referendum on public questions, and most officials—even judges—were chosen by popular election. Democracy was most apparent, however, in social rather than in political relationships. Anyone who dressed better than his neighbors, who put on airs, who flaunted domestic help, was looked upon with suspicion. The banker, the storekeeper, the lawyer, the farmer, and the liveryman sat together in their shirt sleeves in the town square and occupied the same benches in church, and all children went to public schools and the more ambitious of the young men and women to near-by denominational colleges or to the normal schools and state universities that were early provided by every Western commonwealth. Many races mingled in these frontier communities—British, Germans, Norwegians, Bohemians, a sprinkling of Jews, along with native Americans from bordering states; and there was universal toleration for differences of race, language, and creed. In many respects this last frontier was the most democratic and the most American of all frontiers.

CHAPTER 17

The Farmer and His Problems

The Agricultural Revolution

THE INDUSTRIAL REVOLUTION has long been considered the basic fact of modern history. The revolution in agriculture, however, was just as important. The triumphs of the iron-makers, the railroad builders, the engineers, the captains of industry, and the masters of finance have excited the imagination of two generations of Americans, but the triumphs of the farmers and the "hunger fighters," if less spectacular, have been no less remarkable. Of course the two revolutions —the industrial and the agricultural—were interdependent. Without machinery and railroads, the agricultural revolution could not have taken place; without the flood of grain flowing into the warehouses of the great cities, the industrial revolution would not have been possible. For centuries men had struggled to raise enough food for their sustenance, and the growth of population itself had been controlled by the amount of food available. For centuries the specter of famine had been a familiar one, and famine itself had exacted its toll of millions of lives: it was one of the Four Horsemen of the Apocalypse and perhaps the most dreaded. The nineteenth century freed most of mankind from the haunting fear of inadequate food, and for that emancipation American farms were largely responsible.

In the forty years from 1860 to 1900, three times as much land was brought under cultivation as in the previous two hundred years of American history. Production kept pace with this increase in acreage. The two million farms of 1860 produced something under 200 million bushels of wheat, a little less than one billion bushels of corn, and about four million bales of cotton; the six million farms of 1900 raised over 655 million bushels of wheat, well over two and one-half billion bushels of corn, and almost ten million bales of cotton. In this same period the population of the nation more than doubled—and most of the increase went to the cities—but the American farmer grew enough grain and cotton and raised enough beef and pork and clipped enough wool not only to supply American workers but to send ever-increasing surpluses to feed and clothe Europeans.

Two basic factors largely explain this extraordinary achievement. The first was the expanse of the agricultural domain into the West; the second the application of machinery and science to the processes of farming. With the first we are already somewhat familiar. The new West of the plains and the mountain valleys was predominantly a farming region, and within a miraculously short time it took the lead in the agricultural production of the whole country. The wheat belt moved westward from the states along the Ohio River to the Missouri Valley. Illinois, Indiana, Wisconsin, Ohio, Virginia, and Pennsylvania were the leading wheat-producing states in 1860; by 1900 only Ohio still lingered uncertainly among the six leaders, and a decade later it too had disappeared from the list. The shift in corn production was not quite so striking, but here, too, the movement was from the Ohio to the Mississippi Valley. The story of cotton is much the same: by the turn of the century Texas was far in the lead among the states, and not far from half the total cotton crop was raised west of the Mississippi. And during these same years the armies of cattle and sheep moved irresistibly onto the grazing lands of the plains and the mountains.

This westward movement of farming spelled hardship, of course, for the farmers of the East and the seaboard South. Unable to compete with the rich virgin soil of the West, burdened with higher taxes and investment charges, farming in these regions entered upon a decline from which it has never entirely recovered. Much of tidewater Virginia was given over to broom sedge and became that Barren Ground which Ellen Glasgow has described in her novel; large areas in Pennsylvania and New York reverted to wilderness or to a playground for vacationers. Hundreds of thousands of acres of New England were abandoned to brush and forest: in the half century after the Civil War, farm land under cultivation in this section declined by almost fifty per cent. A traveler through New England in 1889 wrote:

Midway between Williamstown [Massachusetts] and Brattleboro [Vermont] I saw on the summit of a hill against the evening sky what seemed a large cathedral. Driving thither, I found a huge old-time two story church, a large academy, a village with a broad street, perhaps 150 feet in width. I drove on and found that the church was abandoned, the academy dismantled, the village deserted. The farmer who owned the farm on the north of the village lived on one side of the broad street, and he who owned the farm on the south lived on the other, and they were the only two inhabitants. All of the others had gone—to the manufacturing villages, to the great cities, to the West. Here had been industry, education, religion, comfort and contentment, but there remained only a dreary solitude of forsaken homes.

Territorial expansion alone could not account for the sharp upswing in farm production, which was out of proportion to the increase in land under cultivation or of men engaged in farming. The explanation lies rather in the increased efficiency of farming. It was a curious fact that the mechanization of agriculture lagged considerably behind the mechanization of industry. The factory hand and the miner of 1800 were using tools unknown to their fathers and grandfathers, but the farmer of 1800 tilled the soil much as had his ancestors a thousand years earlier. His plow was a crude wooden or iron contrivance pulled by a single horse or ox; he sowed wheat and planted corn and potatoes by hand; he weeded with a hoe, harvested his grain with sickle or scythe, flailed it on the floor of his barn, shucked and shelled his corn by hand. It was as much as a family could manage to farm eight or ten acres, even when the womenfolk and the children turned in to help.

The first important American invention—Eli Whitney's cotton gin—profoundly affected agriculture and worked a revolution in the whole economy of the South. Yet the cotton gin had to do with the processing rather than the growing of cotton. Actually, except for such operations as plowing, cultivating, and spraying, cotton long remained relatively immune to machinery. Other crops were more fortunate, but for

most of them, the application of machinery was long delayed. Yet there was incessant experimentation. The story
of the plow is typical. The first patent for a plow was taken
out in 1797, and since that time some twelve thousand more
have been issued. The initial problem was to find a plow that
could cut and turn the soil cleanly, without becoming clogged
with earth or breaking against roots and stones. Jefferson experimented, and his moldboard, designed to cut resistance to a
minimum, won the gold medal of the Royal Agricultural Society of Paris. In 1837, John Deere, on the prairie of Illinois,
faced his wooden plows with steel sufficiently tough to break
the virgin sod, and soon his products were in wide demand.
The Oliver chilled plow, which came on the market in the
late sixties, combined a smooth steel surface with a tough iron
base and seemed to answer all the needs of the prairie farmers. Thereafter improvements were legion.

The story of the reaper is even more illuminating. The
farmer of 1800, using a handle sickle, could hope to cut half
an acre of wheat a day if he worked hard enough; with the
cradle, thirty years later, he might cut two acres a day. But
with such primitive tools he could not grow grain on a large
scale, and he could not have invaded the plains country of
the West. Early in the 1830's two farmers were experimenting
with a mechanical reaper, Obed Hussey and Cyrus McCormick; and by 1840 both were performing the miracle of cutting five or six acres of wheat a day with their curious machines. Hussey moved to Baltimore to make and market his
reaper; McCormick, more farsighted, headed west to the
young prairie town of Chicago. Here, in 1847, he established
his reaper factory and began turning out machines. By the
Civil War the McCormick works had sold a quarter of a
million reapers, and by supplying a machine that would release men for the army, this transplanted Virginian did as
much to insure Union victory as any general.

Every year witnessed some improvement in the reaper.
The backbreaking task of gathering up the grain and binding it into sheaves was eliminated by a moving platform
upon which the grain was deposited into the hands of men
who stood on a footboard and bound it up. Then in 1872
came an automatic wire binder and a few years later the
Appleby twine binder. Meanwhile threshing machines had
been perfected, and in the sixties and seventies these giant

monsters, each with its thrashing gang, moved from farm to farm along the Middle Border. Herbert Quick describes the scene on an Iowa farm:

All rules were suspended during thrashing time. The morning when the McConkeys began thrashing, the house was aroused and alive at three o'clock, electrified by the arrival of the machine, which had run late the evening before at a neighbor's and was pulled in before dawn. . . . The great red machine stood between the high, hive-shaped stacks. The ten horses were standing hitched to the five long wooden sweeps of the horse-power. The driver stood on the board platform in the center with his long whip in his hand. The pitchers had climbed the stacks with their forks, the handles polished by long contact with hard hands, their three tines inserted into the top sheaves of the stack. . . . A deep growl, like that of a bulldog magnified fifty diameters, filled the air, and as the cylinder gathered speed it rose from a bass to a baritone, and then to a tenor of a volume which sang over four square miles of haze-obscured prairie. The feeder looked up at the pitchers, saw the man who pitched to the machine, with his next bundle ready to fall on the table, saw Frank with his band-cutter's knife ready to slice softly through the band of it, and then, he moved the first two sheaves gently over between the open lips, deftly twitched their butts upward, and the great operation was on.

In the eighties came the revolutionary reaper-thresher, or combine, which reaped, threshed, cleaned, and bagged the grain all in a single continuous operation. Drawn by twenty or forty horses—later by a steam or gasoline tractor—it could harvest seventy or eighty acres in a single day.

In every department of agriculture, with the notable exception of cotton picking, machinery came to the aid of the farmer. Mechanical corn planters, corn cutters, huskers, and shellers, the De Laval cream separator, the manure spreader, the potato planter, the hay drier, the poultry incubator, the fertilizer, and a hundred other inventions immensely lightened the labor of the "man with the hoe" and increased his efficiency. With the combines four men could do the work formerly done by three hundred—and do it better. The cornhusker replaced eight men with one, the corn sheller fifty; the time required to harvest a ton of hay was reduced by four fifths. And the twentieth-century application of steam, gasoline, and electricity to farming released millions of acres formerly devoted to pasturage and still further cut down human labor and increased agricultural efficiency.

It was the Middle West and the Far West that absorbed most of the new harvesters and threshers and tractors as fast as they could be manufactured. In the East, farms were too small, agriculture too diversified, to justify investment in expensive machinery; in the South, cotton and tobacco did not yield to mechanized cultivation and labor was cheap. The value of farm machinery increased from a quarter of a billion dollars in 1860 to three and a half billions in 1920, but most of this increase came in the region west of the Mississippi. The farmers of Iowa alone, in 1920, had a larger investment in machinery than did the farmers of all New England and the Middle Atlantic states combined; the average value of machinery on a South Dakota farm was $1500; on each of the farms of the cotton belt, $215.

The mechanization of farming made it possible for the farmer to feed a growing number of city dwellers and to send abroad a surplus which in turn helped finance industrial and railroad expansion. For the farmers themselves it was not an unmixed blessing. It involved many of them in expenditures heavier than they could afford, forced them to expand their operations to justify those investments, and to concentrate on staple crops. It gave the large farmers a distinct advantage over their small competitors and hastened, at once, the development of "bonanza" farming and of tenancy. The small self-sufficient farm of the fifties, with its fields of wheat, corn, and oats, its vegetable patch, its henhouse and pigpen, its eight or ten cows pasturing in the meadow, gave way to the large wheat or cotton holdings of the twentieth century, dependent even for food supplies on the grocery store.

Scarcely less important than machinery was science. From the beginning American agriculture was extensive rather than intensive, for it seemed easier to take up new land than to preserve the old. Yet the rapid exhaustion of the soil of the tidewater South frightened the planters, and Washington and Jefferson were merely the most prominent of the many Southerners who attempted to meet this crisis by introducing new plants, rotating crops, and improving their livestock.

"The greatest service which can be rendered to any country is to add a useful plant to its culture," wrote Jefferson. But these early reforms were largely in vain, for the opening up of the vast trans-Appalachian lands and the invention of the cotton gin made it more profitable for farmers to move on to fertile lands than to attempt to restore the fertility of old soil by more careful husbandry. The "mining" of new land, perhaps an inevitable part of the frontier economy, was to be repeated again and again on successive frontiers.

The Federal government made its first appropriation specifically for agriculture in 1839; but the real beginning of government interest dates from the passage of the Morrill Land-Grant College Act of 1862. This provided an endowment for agricultural and industrial colleges out of the public domain: for each Congressman that it sent to Washington a state was entitled to thirty thousand acres of land. Under this act, state after state established agricultural colleges independently or in connection with a state university, and these eventually pushed research in scientific farming. Equally important was the Hatch Act of 1887, appropriating generous funds for the creation of agricultural experiment stations throughout the Union. At the same time direct appropriations for the research activities of the Department of Agriculture mounted into the millions of dollars. By 1930 some seven or eight thousand scientists were working for these various governmental agencies on a bewildering variety of research projects, and contributions of the most far-reaching importance were coming from their experimental farms and laboratories.

Typical of these "hunger fighters" was Mark Alfred Carleton, who brought the great Kubanka and Kharkov wheats to western America. Farming and teaching in Kansas, Carleton saw, year after year, how the drought and the black rust killed off all but the hardiest wheat that the plains farmers could grow. But he saw, too, that the Russian Mennonites, whom the Santa Fe Railroad had brought in to settle on its lands, had better luck with their wheat, and he discovered that they grew it from seed which they had brought all the way from their homelands. All wheat was, after all, an importation; and Carleton was convinced that the secret of hardy, drought- and rust-resisting grain was to be found somewhere in the Ukraine or the steppes of Eurasia.

In 1898, with the blessing of the Department of Agriculture, he headed for this Promised Land. Finally, in the Turgai steppes, just west of the Ural River—where climate and topography were strikingly like that of western Kansas— he found what he was looking for: the Kubanka wheat. On the plains it grew more bushels to the acre than the Fife and Blue Stem and proved miraculously immune to the black rust. But it was in the region from Minnesota north to the Saskatchewan that the Kubanka scored its greatest triumphs; curiously enough, it did not take to the southern plains. So once more Carleton betook himself to Russia, and in the Ukraine, near the Kharkov where forty years later Germans and Russians were to slaughter each other by the thousands, he found the Kharkov wheat. By 1914 half the winter wheat of the country was of the Kubanka or Kharkov varieties.

Other hunger fighters made scarcely less important contributions. Marion Dorset conquered the dread hog cholera and George Mohler the mysterious hoof-and-mouth disease which had worked such havoc with cattle. From North Africa J. H. Watkins brought back the Káffir corn, and from Turkestan Niels Hansen imported the yellow-flowered alfalfa. Luther Burbank, in his California laboratories, produced scores of new fruits and vegetables, and David R. Coker, on his South Carolina experimental farm, proved that long-staple cotton could grow in the piedmont and upland country. At the University of Wisconsin Stephen Babcock invented a milk test for determining the butterfat content of milk. The Negro scientist, George Washington Carver, working at the Tuskegee Institute, found hundreds of new uses for familiar products like the peanut, the sweet potato, and the soybean. And Seaman Knapp rescued the rice industry from its postwar decline by introducing new varieties from the Orient and inaugurated a far-flung system of demonstration farms which pointed the way to improved agricultural methods throughout the South.

Hard Times on the Farm

WITH EVERY YEAR the American farmer tilled the soil more efficiently and raised larger crops. Industrious, intelligent, blessed with rich land, ingenious machinery, and ready markets, he should have been prosperous and happy. But his lot was hard and grew steadily harder. At the close of the most wonderful century of agricultural expansion in all history the farmers, instead of being the "chosen people of God"—as Jefferson phrased it—had become a major economic problem. What is the explanation of this paradox?

The farm problem is complex, presenting itself to the Southern planter, the grain grower, the corn and hog farmer, the cattleman, the dairyman, and the orchardist in very different guises. It appeared at one time as a railroad problem, at another as a money question, and at still another as a question of land policy; it involved sectional interests, party programs, and international relations. Yet basic to almost every aspect of the farm problem were certain unchanging factors. Chief among them were the exhaustion of the soil, the vagaries of nature, overproduction of staple crops, decline in self-sufficiency, and lack of adequate legislative protection and aid.

The soil of the South had long been exhausted by tobacco and cotton culture and by the use of ignorant farm labor. In the older parts of that section millions of acres reverted to scrub, while water running down undammed gullies washed away millions of tons of rich topsoil every year. Something of the cumulative impoverishment of the Southern soil is suggested by the fact that the South uses seventy per cent of all the fertilizer sold in this country and that the expenditures of South Carolina farmers for fertilizer come to one fourth the value of their cotton crop. In the West, too, erosion and wind storms ravaged the land. Much of the High Plains was unsuitable for farming or even for the kind of grazing that was practiced there, and where the land was overfarmed or overgrazed the "dust bowl" spread.

Recurring droughts spelled disaster to the plains farmers. Over a period of sixteen months in 1859–1860 not one good rain brought relief to the farmers of Kansas and Nebraska, and the ruined pioneers who had come out with such high hopes had to be rescued by Eastern charity. Again from 1886 to 1890 there was a prolonged drought which drove the Kansas-Nebraska frontier back a hundred miles. Mari Sandoz has described it in her graphic account of her father, Old Jules:

The drought exceeded all probability. Corn did not sprout. On
the hardland fringe the buffalo grass was started and browned
before the first of May. Even lighter soil south of the river produced nothing. The sandhills greened only in stripes where the
water-logged sand cropped out. The lake beds whitened and
cracked in rhythmical patterns. Grouse were scarce and dark-
fleshed. Rabbits grew thin and wild, and coyotes emboldened.
Covered wagons like gaunt-ribbed gray animals moved eastward,
the occupants often becoming public charges along the way.

And while prolonged droughts burned up the farms, heavy
blizzards wiped out the cattle on the High Plains and in
the mountain valleys.

Scarcely less menacing were the insect pests and plant
diseases. Of the insects the boll weevil was undoubtedly the
worst. This scourge, crossing the Rio Grande from Mexico
in 1892, thereafter progressed at about fifty miles a year
until it had infested the whole cotton kingdom. The farmers of Enterprise, Alabama, erected a monument to it for
its success in forcing diversification of crops, but during the
years of its worst ravages it cut cotton production over wide
areas by more than fifty per cent. All efforts to eradicate the
weevil have been in vain, and only by early planting and the
lavish use of poison can the cotton farmers hold it in check.

The insect pests of the plains were legion, but the most
terrifying was doubtless the grasshopper. It was in 1874
that the plains farmers had their first experience with the
grasshopper plague—an experience that was to be repeated
again and again. Stuart Henry described how the 'hoppers

ate up every bit of green vegetation from the Rocky Mountains
to and beyond the Missouri River. I recall that when coming
home late one afternoon for supper I stepped back surprised to
see what became known as the Rocky Mountain locusts covering
the side of the house. Already inside, they feasted on the cur-
tains. Clouds of them promptly settled down on the whole country—everywhere, unavoidable. People set about killing them to
save gardens, but this soon proved ridiculous. Specially contrived machines, pushed by horses, scooped up the hoppers in
grainfields by the barrelful to burn them. This, too, was non-
sensical. Vast hordes, myriads. In a week grain fields, gardens,
shrubs, vines, had been eaten down to the ground or to the bark.
Nothing could be done. You sat by and saw everything go.

The chinch bug, corn borer, and alfalfa weevil were almost equally destructive.

The farmer was selling his produce in a world market—in competition with the farmers of Russia, the Argentine, Canada, Australia—and buying in a protected market. The price he got for wheat, or cotton, or beef was determined in Liverpool; the price he paid for his harvester, his fertilizer, his barbed wire, his shoes and clothes, his lumber and furniture, was fixed by trusts operating behind a protective tariff. His costs were going inexorably up—the cost of what he used on the farm, the cost of freight, the cost of the money he borrowed, the cost of government. Fresh land and machinery enabled him to produce more every year, but his income was not going up appreciably. In the years of greatest agricultural expansion, 1870–1890, the value of American farm products increased only half a billion dollars; in this same period the value of manufactures increased by six billion dollars. Prices of most farm products moved irregularly downward. Wheat that brought a dollar a bushel throughout the seventies fell to fifty cents in the mid-nineties. Cotton declined from seventeen cents a pound in 1873 to nine cents twenty years later, and then tumbled to six. Substantially the same story could be told for corn, oats, barley, tobacco, and other farm produce; the average value per acre of ten leading crops was fourteen dollars in the early seventies, nine dollars in the early nineties.

Perhaps the most serious of all the economic handicaps under which the farmer labored was the rising cost of money. When he went to the local banker or mortgage agent to borrow money he found that he was expected to pay from eight to twenty per cent on his loan. The situation came home to him in an even more injurious fashion in declining prices. If we think in terms of the cost of the dollar rather than the cost of farm commodities we can more readily understand this. In 1870 the farmer could buy a dollar with a bushel of wheat, two bushels of corn, or ten pounds of cotton. By 1890 it took two bushels of wheat, four bushels of corn, or fifteen pounds of cotton to buy a dollar. The farmer who borrowed a thousand dollars in 1870 could repay his loan with a thousand bushels of wheat; if he let the mortgage run to 1890 it cost him two thousand bushels of wheat to get rid of it.

In the face of these adverse conditions it is not surprising that the mortgage indebtedness of the American farmer increased by leaps and bounds. By 1890 over ninety thousand farms in Illinois were mortgaged, one hundred thousand in Nebraska, and still more in Kansas. Most of these mortgages were held in the East; inhabitants of New Hampshire alone had some twenty-five million dollars in Western mortgages. Tenancy, too, was on the upgrade. The average for the whole country was twenty-eight per cent, but in the South and the West the proportion was appreciably higher.

These were the chief ingredients of the farm problem. The failure of the farmer to use the government as an instrument to protect his interests was as much a consequence as a cause of his malaise. Although farmers constituted half the population of the nation, they rarely sent one of their number to Congress or even to the state legislatures, and when in the early nineties farmers like Senator Peffer and Congressman Simpson did get to Washington they were looked upon as curiosities. Men who wrote the national laws were much more zealous to serve the interests of manufacturers, bankers, and railroad men than to take care of the farmers, and legislation reflected this zeal. The protective tariff may have helped business, but it made the farmer pay more for almost everything that he bought. The banking and currency legislation written into the statute books was a boon to bankers and investors, but a terrible burden to farmers. Laws designed to regulate trusts and railroads were so written or interpreted that they caused little inconvenience to those interests, and when agrarian states tried their hand at stricter laws, courts threw them out. Even legislation designed ostensibly to assist the farmer, such as the Homestead Act, proved disappointing; up to 1900 more land had been sold directly or through railroads and speculators than had gone to homesteaders. Thus by the end of the century homesteaders had patented about 80 million acres, but the railroads had received—from the Federal and state governments —180 million acres, the states had been given 140 million acres, and another 200 million acres—much of it Indian lands—had been put up for sale to the highest bidders.

Thirty years after Appomattox, then, the American farmer had expanded his domain over the whole continent and, with the latest machinery and the help of science, increased his production to the point where he was ready to feed the Western world. And he was on the road to peasantry.

The Farmers Organize

BUSINESS, banking, even labor, were organizing; it was high time for the farmer to follow their example. Yet nothing was more difficult. The farming interest consisted of millions of units, each operating separately, each in a sense competing; the farmer was naturally an individualist who did not take kindly to outside control; and neither the soil nor the weather could be effectively regulated. In the end, control of farm production did not come until the Federal government moved in. Meanwhile, if the farmer expected to save himself from exploitation by railroads, trusts, mortgage companies, and middlemen, he had to take action himself.

The first nationwide farmer organization was the Grange, or Patrons of Husbandry. In 1866 a government clerk, Oliver Kelley, made a long trip through the war-ravaged South, and what he saw persuaded him that the poverty, backwardness, and isolation of the farmer could be ameliorated only by common action. With a few friends he organized the Patrons of Husbandry, a social and educational order designed "to develop a higher and better manhood and womanhood among ourselves. To enhance the comforts and attractions of our homes and strengthen our attachments to our pursuits. . . . To make our farms self-sustaining." A few Granges, as the local branches were called, were set up in New York and Pennsylvania, but as long as the order remained in the East it made little progress. In 1869 its headquarters were moved out to the Middle West, and during the hard times of the early seventies it spread like wildfire. By 1873 there were Granges in almost every state, and membership had reached three quarters of a million. Its greatest strength was in the Middle West, but it flourished in the South, too, and along the Pacific Coast.

Kelley's idea was that the Grange should be chiefly a social organization. Women were admitted as well as men; an elaborate ritual was copied in part from the Masonic; there were to be monthly meetings devoted to education, patriotic celebrations, and festivities. The great object was to break down the isolation of the farmer, introduce color and interest into his life, bring about an interchange of views, and build up a solidarity of interests. In all this the Grange was highly successful. Grange papers found a wide circulation, Grange libraries distributed farm publications, Grange lecturers addressed meetings in country schoolhouses, and Grange picnics became an established institution. Hamlin Garland, recalling one of these picnics, wrote:

It was grand, it was inspiring—to us, to see those long lines of carriages winding down the lanes, joining one to another at the cross-roads, till at last all the granges from the northern end of the county were united in one mighty column advancing on the picnic ground, where orators awaited our approach with calm dignity and high resolution. Nothing more picturesque, more delightful, more helpful, has ever risen out of American rural life.

But it was inevitable that when farmers came together, even for fun, they should talk business and politics. Talk led to action, and soon many of the state Granges set up co-operative marketing organizations, stores, loan agencies, and even factories. These were not always well run and they encountered from the beginning fierce opposition from established business. Yet they saved their members a good deal of money: the Iowa Grange, for example, shipped five million bushels of grain to Chicago at savings of from ten to forty per cent and by co-operative buying saved its members one hundred dollars on each reaper that they bought. To meet this kind of competition, and to serve directly the needs of the Grangers, the mail-order house of Montgomery Ward was established.

Of course the Grangers went into politics, too, notwithstanding the prohibition against political action in their Constitution. In a number of Midwestern states they elected their members to the legislature and pushed through so-called "Granger laws" regulating railroad and warehouse charges and outlawing some of the grosser abuses of the railroads such as the practice of charging more for a short haul, or the indirect bribery of giving passes to legislators and judges. These laws, challenged in the courts, were upheld in a series of decisions known collectively as the Granger Cases, in 1877, decisions which laid down the great constitutional principle that

when private property is affected with a public interest it ceases to be juris privati only. . . . Property does become clothed with a public interest when used in a manner to make it of public consequence and affect the community at large. When therefore one devotes his property to a use in which the public has an interest he, in effect, grants to the public an interest in that use. . . .

Yet nowhere did the Grangers organize as a political party, nor did they succeed in building up anything like a "farm bloc" in Congress.

With the failure of many of their business enterprises and the frustration of their legislation, and with the return of relative prosperity in the late seventies, the Grange petered out. It was later revived, but as a purely social and educational organization. Meantime some of the discontented farmers drifted into the Greenback party—an ill-assorted conglomeration of farmers, laborers, and doctrinaire reformers —which in 1880 chose as its presidential candidate an old Granger leader, James B. Weaver of Iowa.

The real successors to the Grange, however, were the Farmers' Alliances, the most belligerent farm organizations in American history. The Alliances had their origin in the depression of the late eighties and the early nineties. Times were harder than ever before. Drought descended on the stricken plains, and went on, year after year; the share-crop and crop-lien systems plunged the South into misery; wheat fell to fifty cents a bushel, cotton to six cents a pound; it was cheaper to burn corn for fuel than to ship it to market. And in Washington purblind Congressmen, sensitive only to the demands of business, fastened upon the country in 1890 the McKinley tariff, the highest it had ever known, maintained an inflexible banking and credit system, and voted away hundreds of millions in pensions and "pork-barrel" legislation. Stimulated by governmental injustice, the Alliance movement spread like an epidemic, and by 1890 the various Alliances had not far from two million members.

The Northwestern and the Southern Alliance were in

many respects like the earlier Grange. They undertook elaborate educational programs, circulated books like Henry George's *Progress and Poverty* and Edward Bellamy's *Looking Backward*, published Alliance newspapers—Kansas alone had over a hundred—sent out lecturers to advise farmers on the latest developments in scientific agriculture and to agitate for remedial legislation, and established farmers' institutes and study clubs. They embarked, too, upon far-reaching economic programs. The Texas Alliance sponsored co-operative buying, marketing, and warehousing; in the Dakotas the Alliance underwrote crop insurance; in Illinois it organized a series of farmers' exchanges. Some of these undertakings were successful and saved farmers millions of dollars in profits and middlemen's charges; others, confronted with the implacable hostility of the banks and the railroads, failed.

And before long the Alliances gave birth to a crusading political party. From the beginning they had called for a program of political reform: government ownership of railroads, cheap money, the abolition of national banks, prohibition of alien landownership, reduction of the tariff, and the creation of a "subtreasury" scheme to provide easy credit to farmers. This last was particularly interesting. It called for the construction by the Federal government of warehouses in every agricultural county, where farmers might store their produce, receiving in exchange certificates worth eighty per cent of the market value of the produce. This scheme would give the farmer credit at a very low rate of interest, enable him to hold his crops off the market until the price was advantageous, and inflate the currency—thus enhancing the value of the crop. When first advanced, it was denounced as a harebrained and socialistic device; within a generation it was adopted, in all essentials, by the Federal government.

Between 1890 and 1892 the Alliance was metamorphosed into the Populist party—the most colorful of American political parties. The rank and file of the party was recruited from the farmers of the South and the West, but it embraced many other minority groups—the remnants of the Knights of Labor, of the Greenback and Union Labor parties, advocates of woman suffrage, Socialists, single-taxers, silverites, and professional reformers. Its strength was concentrated on the Middle Border, and from that region, too, came its leaders. Chief among these was the Minnesota Irishman, Ignatius Donnelly, farmer, orator, agitator, discoverer of the lost continent of Atlantis, champion of the Baconian theory, author of the popular novel *Caesar's Column,* who for twenty years had troubled the waters of American politics. From Kansas, the hotbed of Populism, came Senator William Peffer, whose long flowing beard reminded observers of a Hebrew prophet and whom young Theodore Roosevelt denounced as "a well-meaning, pinheaded, anarchistic crank." And from Kansas, too, came the greatest of the women revivalists— Mary Ellen Lease, who eloquently implored the plains farmers to "raise less corn and more hell." Down in Georgia the cadaverous, redheaded Tom Watson, "sage of Hickory Hill" and self-appointed successor to Thomas Jefferson, rallied the tenant farmers and the mill hands to the Populist standard and sent shivers running up and down the spines of all the Southern Bourbons. And in Nebraska a young Democrat named William Jennings Bryan was urging his party to fuse with the new Populist organization.

Never before in American politics had there been anything like the Populist revolt which swept the prairies and the cotton lands in the early nineties. "It was a religious revival, a crusade, a Pentecost of politics, in which a tongue of flame sat upon every man, and each spake as the spirit gave him utterance," wrote one witness; it was "a fanaticism like the Crusades," another recalled. After a hard day in the fields, farmers hitched up their buggies and with their wives and children jogged off to the Grange or the schoolhouse and applauded the impassioned oratory of their grass-roots leaders. "Wall Street owns the country," declaimed Mary Lease. "It is no longer a government of the people, by the people, for the people, but a government of Wall Street, by Wall Street, and for Wall Street. Our laws are the output of a system that clothes rascals in robes and honesty in rags." And outraged farmers voted new declarations of independence. "The history of the United States," read one of them, "for the past twenty-eight years is a history of repeated injuries, tyranny, and usurpation, unparalleled in the history of the world, and all laws enacted having a direct object; viz., to establish a moneyed aristocracy on the ruins of a once free America."

The elections of 1890 swept the new party into power in

a dozen Southern and Western states and sent a score of
homespun Senators and Representatives to startle the staid
halls of Congress. Flushed with this success, the party
planned even greater triumphs. On Independence Day of
1892 a thousand enthusiastic and sweating delegates met
at Omaha to select a presidential candidate and endorse Ignatius Donnelly's perfervid preamble to a boldly progressive
platform:

We meet in the midst of a nation brought to the verge of moral,
political, and material ruin. . . . The fruits of the toil of millions are boldly stolen to build up colossal fortunes for a few . . .
and the possessors of these, in turn, despise the republic and endanger liberty. From the same prolific womb of governmental
injustice we breed the two great classes—tramps and millionaires.

The Populists polled over a million votes. But it was
Grover Cleveland who went to the White House, not James
B. Weaver, who had led so many lost causes. The winds of
revolt blew in from the sun-baked cotton fields of the South
and the hot, dusty prairies of the West, but the old parties
went their accustomed way. Nothing less than an earthquake could shake them out of their smug apathy. That earthquake was not long in coming.

1896

TIMES WERE BAD, in 1892, and they grew steadily worse.
No sooner had portly Grover Cleveland taken the oath of
office for the second time than a major panic burst upon
the country. Business houses crashed, banks closed their
doors, railroads went into the hands of receivers, factories
shut down, trade languished, creditors foreclosed their mortgages. In the cities long lines of unemployed waited outside
soup kitchens, and in the country the army of tramps added
thousands of recruits. This was worse even than the panic of
1873, more widespread and more devastating in its effects.
In the face of this disaster the government followed the
traditional policy of noninterference in economic disturbances. Cleveland was an able leader, honest, courageous,
and well intentioned, a fine exponent of Manchester liberal-

ism in fighting corruption and special privilege. In his first term (1885–1889) he had made an admirable record. But he was wedded to the prevalent philosophy of *laissez faire*. His program was still one of tariff reduction and administrative reform, and he rejected most suggestions of remedial economic legislation. He believed that the storm had to blow itself out; that the depression could best be cured by automatic forces. For two years matters grew steadily worse. The year 1894 witnessed the great Pullman strike, the march of Coxey's army of the unemployed on Washington, and a further collapse of farm prices. From the cotton, corn, and wheat fields came a ground swell of revolt. The Southern and Western wing of the Democracy threatened to bolt the old party, and when in 1894 Cleveland barred the road to an inflationary measure, the old war horse from Missouri, Richard Bland, announced that "we have come to the parting of the ways." That fall a host of discontented Democrats joined hands with the Populists, who rolled up a vote of almost a million and a half.

Many anticipated a repetition of the 1854–1856 crisis, when the decrepit Whig organization had disintegrated and the vigorous young Republican party had taken over. But the astute leaders of the Western Democrats were not yet ready to give up, while in the South the Democrats had become so completely identified with white supremacy that no third party stood a chance. Instead of going over to the Populists, the radical leaders of the Southern and Western Democrats therefore moved to capture the party organization. "Then," as Bryan later described it, "began the struggle. With a zeal approaching the zeal which inspired the Crusaders, who followed Peter the Hermit, our silver Democrats went forth from victory unto victory."

The agrarian Democrats elected to make their fight on the money question. This has often been considered a mistake, yet it is doubtful whether any other issue could have appealed to so many voters or have lent itself so readily to dramatization. The money question of that time was complex, yet it will not be too misleading to suggest that it boiled down to the question of inflation versus deflation. For years, while the population and the business of the nation grew, the government had been following a policy of contracting the currency. In the year 1873, just before the production of the

silver mines of the West began to threaten to depreciate the
value of money, Congress, by a purely routine measure, de-
monetized silver—that is, refused to purchase or to coin
any more of it. Then in 1878 and again in 1890 the government was forced into such extensive purchases of silver that
the maintenance of a gold basis for the currency of the
United States became seriously endangered. A succession of
Presidents, backed by all the conservative forces of the
nation, were resolved to uphold this standard. Cleveland in
especial waged a titanic—and successful—battle for it. It
was this money policy, so many farmers were convinced,
that was chiefly responsible for low prices. Restore silver,
coin all that was mined, open the mints to all the precious
metal in the world, and the value of money would fall back
to normal, prices would soar, prosperity would return. So
argued the silverites.

The conservative hard-money men remained convinced
that such a policy would be financially disastrous. Inflation,
once begun, could not be stopped, and the government itself
would be forced into bankruptcy. Only the gold standard
offered stability. More than this, they talked themselves into
believing that the gold standard was not only sound finance
but sound morals, and they most unjustly denounced the
silver dollar as a "dishonest" dollar. It was an old quarrel—
this controversy over cheap money—and an ever-new one.

On strategic grounds much was to be said for making the
fight on the issue of free silver. Silver-mine owners, facing
bankruptcy, could be counted on to help finance a campaign.
The silver interest was all-powerful in half a dozen sparsely
populated Western states which were normally Republican
and which commanded a disproportionate vote in the electoral college; if these could be swung into the Democratic
column they might turn the election. Easy money would appeal to the vast debtor class throughout the country and to
some workingmen as well as to farmers. Silver, finally, had
an emotional quality that would be easily exploited. Gold
was the rich man's money; silver the poor man's friend.
Gold was the money of Wall Street and of Lombard Street;
silver of the prairies and the little towns.

But it was not enough to have an issue; the silverites
had to have a candidate. "All the silverites need," wrote the
New York *World*, "is a Moses. They have the principle, they

have the grit, they have the brass bands and the buttons and the flags, they have the howl and the hustle, they have the votes, and they have the leaders so-called. But they are wandering in the wilderness like a lot of lost sheep because no one with the courage, the audacity, the magnetism, and the wisdom to be a real leader has yet appeared among them."

In William Jennings Bryan of Nebraska they found their Moses. A delegate to the tumultuous Chicago convention of 1896, he was slated to speak on the money question. And as he climbed to the platform, that sweltering night of June 8, he was stepping forth to national fame:

We do not come as aggressors. Our war is not a war of conquest; we are fighting in the defense of our homes, our families, and posterity. We have petitioned, and our petitions have been scorned; we have entreated, and our entreaties have been disregarded; we have begged, and they have mocked when our calamity came. We beg no longer; we entreat no more; we petition no more. We defy them! . . .

So spoke "the boy orator of the Platte," and every sentence evoked a frenzy of applause. And when he delivered his famous peroration, the hall shook with such a Niagara of noise as had never before been heard at any American gathering:

If they dare to come out in the open field and defend the gold standard as a good thing, we will fight them to the uttermost. Having behind us the producing masses of the nation and the world, supported by the commercial interests, the laboring interests, and the toilers everywhere, we will answer their demand for a gold standard by saying to them: You shall not press down upon the brow of labor this crown of thorns, you shall not crucify mankind upon a cross of gold.

Bryan might have been nominated even without this speech, for he had made a careful preconvention campaign and was in many respects a logical candidate. After the speech his nomination was a foregone conclusion. The victory of the silver wing of the Democrats was complete. They wrote the platform, they named the candidate, and they forced the Populists to come over to them.

With this campaign the engaging figure of Bryan steps into the national arena, and off and on for two decades he held the spotlight. He was in some respects the most remarkable political leader since Henry Clay. Magnificent in appearance, with coal-black hair, black flashing eyes, and a voice of mellifluous beauty, quick-witted, intelligent, fearless, he captured the imagination, the worshipful devotion, of millions of plain people. He had grown up on a farm, attended a country college, moved to the plains country, and there practiced law and politics; he was a devout Presbyterian, and his political speeches were studded with apt quotations from the Scriptures; he was a plain democrat, unspoiled by success, sincerely devoted to the public interest as he saw it, and convinced that the voice of the people was the voice of God. Though his limitations were many, for he was not widely nor deeply read, and was far from being an original or profound thinker, he was a highly representative American.

The campaign of 1896 was more bitterly fought than any since Jackson's day. Bryan's task seemed at first insurmountable. His party was split wide open, its titular chieftain, Cleveland, in opposition and most of its Eastern leaders flocking into the Republican camp. The Democrats, too, were unjustly blamed for the three-year depression. Ranged against Bryan were almost all the forces of respectability: business, the universities, the press, the money power. Mark Hanna, boss of the Republican party, drummed up a campaign fund which has been estimated at from three to seven million dollars; against this the Democrats could match less than half a million. In only one respect did the Democrats have a clear advantage—in Bryan himself. Crisscrossing the country from New England to the West, riding hot, dusty day coaches, speaking eight and ten times a day, appealing to laborers and farmers, to liberals and progressives, he made the most spectacular campaign in American history.

It was magnificent, but it was not enough, for, as Mrs. Henry Cabot Lodge wrote:

The great fight is won, a fight conducted by trained and experienced and organized forces, with both hands full of money, with the full power of the press—and of prestige—on one side; on the other, a disorganized mob, at first, out of which burst into sight, into hearing, and force—one man but such a man! Alone, penniless, without backing, without money, with scarce a paper, without speakers, that man fought such a fight that even those in the East can call him a Crusader, an inspired heretic—a prophet! It has been marvellous. Hampered by such a following, such a platform . . . he almost won.

In the end William McKinley won by more than half a million votes. The West and the South, the combination which had swept Jefferson into power and supported Jackson and Douglas, had failed. For that matter, McKinley and the Republicans carried such Middle Western states as Illinois, Iowa, and Wisconsin, and such Far Western states as California and Oregon. But Bryan and Bryan's campaign were to become legendary. In Vachel Lindsay's words:

> Prairie avenger, mountain lion,
> Bryan, Bryan, Bryan, Bryan
> Gigantic troubadour, speaking like a siege gun,
> Smashing Plymouth Rock with his shoulders from the West.

And the ideas of the Populists and agrarian Democrats were ultimately, without a single important exception, to be written into legislation. They were to change the course of American history.

CHAPTER 18

The Age of Reform

The Challenge to Democracy

WHEN Bryan came to write the history of the campaign of
1896 he called it *The First Battle*. The title was an inspiration. For that battle, though it ended in defeat for the forces
of agrarian democracy, was the beginning of the progressive
campaign. Before the war was over, the armies of farmers
and workingmen swept over state after state in one victorious campaign after another, carried the bastions of reaction by storm, planted their banner triumphantly atop the
White House, and restored the national government to its
traditional democratic course.

For this was the Progressive Era—these two decades between Bryan's first battle and Woodrow Wilson's second. It
was marked by revolt and reform in almost every department
of American life. Old political leaders were ousted and new
ones enlisted; political machinery was overhauled and mod-
ernized; political practices were subjected to critical scrutiny,
and those which failed to square with the ideals of democracy
were rejected. Economic institutions and practices—private
property, the corporation, the trust, great fortunes—were
called before the bar of reason and asked to justify themselves or to change their ways. Social relationships were re-
considered—the impact of the city, immigration, inequalities
in wealth, the growth of classes, all came in for critical attention. Almost every notable figure in this period, whether
in politics, philosophy, scholarship, or literature, derives his
fame in part from his connection with the reform movement:

336

Weaver, Bryan, La Follette, Debs, Roosevelt, and Wilson in the political arena; William James, Josiah Royce, and John Dewey in philosophy; Thorstein Veblen, Richard Ely, and Lester Ward in scholarship; William Dean Howells, Frank Norris, Hamlin Garland, and Theodore Dreiser in literature. The heroes of the day were all reformers. Courageously, defiantly, they manned the battlements of democracy and even sallied out to make new conquests. Not since the forties had there been such a ferment in the intellectual world; not since then had reform been so firmly in the saddle.

And what was it all about, this fine frenzy of reform? What was it that so troubled the waters of American life? We have already seen something of the problems of the farmer and of the workingman. But these, distressing though they were, were symptoms rather than causes. The problem was not economic merely, nor was it confined to these two great interests of agriculture and labor. It affected every aspect of American society.

The fact is that the promise of American life was not being fulfilled. Here in this New World was to have been created a society where freedom and equality were assured to all, a state where liberty was everywhere protected. This was, to be sure, a dream, but it was not a pipe dream, nor were the creators of the American republic visionaries who took refuge in the opium of false hopes. Never before in history had nature vouchsafed to men so rich an opportunity, never before had there been sounder reason to suppose that men might create for themselves an earthly Eden. In the beginning the American people were indeed, in the words of Turgot, "the hope of the human race."

This hope had not been fulfilled. Americans were better off than their contemporaries overseas, but they were worse off than they should be. The material achievements of the nation were impressive, but the social and cultural achievements disappointing. As President Wilson said in his First Inaugural address:

The evil has come with the good, and much fine gold has been corroded. With riches has come inexcusable waste. We have squandered a great part of what we might have used, and have not stopped to conserve the exceeding bounty of nature . . . scorning to be careful, shamefully prodigal as well as admirably efficient. We have been proud of our industrial achievements, but we have not hitherto stopped thoughtfully enough to count the human cost, the cost of lives snuffed out, of energies overtaxed and broken, the fearful physical and spiritual cost to the men and women and children upon whom the dead weight and burden of it all has fallen pitilessly the years through. . . . With the great Government went many deep secret things which we too long delayed to look into and scrutinize with candid, fearless eyes. The great Government we loved has too often been made use of for private and selfish purposes, and those who used it had forgotten the people.

This was not because wicked men had done evil things; it was not because powerful men had rejected democracy and set out to destroy it; it was not because tyranny or despotism had been established in the place of liberty. No, the causes were more subtle than that. The basic difficulty was one common to the whole Western world. Science and machinery had outrun social science and political machinery. The practices and principles inherited from an eighteenth-century rural republic were no longer adequate to the exigencies of a twentieth-century urban state. This was true in the political realm, where the fear of government persisted into the period when only government could adequately control the forces that machinery had let loose on society. It was true in the moral realm, where old notions of personal responsibility were threatened by the rise of the impersonal corporation. It was true in the social realm, where the habits of rural life in a homogeneous society were no longer applicable to the exigencies of urban life in a highly heterogeneous society.

Growth itself had created a host of problems. The farm domain grew beyond the bounds which nature had fixed; immigrants poured in faster than they could be absorbed; cities grew so fast that they could not house or adequately govern their teeming populations; factory production increased beyond practicable consumption; business became so big that nobody could fully understand it or manage it; a few men became so rich that they did not know what to do with their money—and society had not yet learned how to relieve them of their burden.

These were the fundamental difficulties, but few men were

perspicacious enough to appreciate them. What the reformers saw, rather, was poverty, injustice, and corruption; what they saw was the land question, the labor question, the woman question, the money question. So they girded themselves to battle with the slums; they cleaned up politics; they busted trusts and fought "malefactors of great wealth"; they waged war on the "demon rum," on child labor, on sweatshop labor; they led crusades for the Indian, for the Negro, for the "little brown brothers" of our new island possessions; they devised new machinery for government—the initiative, the referendum, woman suffrage, primary elections, corrupt-practices acts, and the merit system; they saved the forests and the water resources, and beautified the cities. Hundreds of societies to do good sprang up and flourished. The presses groaned with books exposing the iniquities of the present order and presenting blueprints for a better one. Magazine editors struck pay dirt with articles exposing everything everywhere—the Standard Oil Company, or the Beef Trust, or *Frenzied Finance*, or *The History of Great American Fortunes*, or *The Shame of the Cities*. Novelists like Theodore Dreiser, Frank Norris, and Brand Whitlock turned from romance and local color to problem novels and moral sermons. Poets abjured their "triolets, villanelles, rondels, rondeaus" and, with Edwin Markham, discovered "the man with the hoe." Scholars emerged from their ivory towers to grapple with social problems—to discuss, with Veblen, the theory of business enterprise, or, with Lester Ward, to take up the cudgels against *laissez faire*. Preachers rediscovered the social gospel and troubled respectable parishioners with a literal reading of the New Testament or with speculation about what would happen "If Christ came to Chicago."

All this was thoroughly in the American grain. It was in protest and revolt against conditions in old England that the Pilgrims and the Puritans had come to New England; colonial leaders in turn—Roger Williams, Nathaniel Bacon, Jacob Leisler—had revolted against tyranny or intolerance when established here; the nation had been born from a revolution, and its national heroes—Jefferson, Franklin, Sam Adams, Thomas Paine—were rebels, not only against the mother country, but also against the ruling classes at home; the great writers and preachers and philosophers of New England in the forties and fifties—Emerson and Whittier, Garrison and Parker—enlisted in the fight for equality and liberty. To inquire, to challenge, to protest, to prove all things and hold fast that which was good, was native to the American character.

Both in philosophy and in methods the new reform movement differed markedly from the great crusade of the second quarter of the century. That earlier crusade was rooted in religious philosophy, embraced universal reform, and was indifferent to politics. The reform movement of the 1890–1912 period was highly secular, lacking in any consistent philosophy, fortuitous and almost haphazard in its objects and interests, journalistic, and intensely political. There was, to be sure, a common faith in democracy and in human nature, but even that was less pervasive in the later than in the earlier period. It is suggestive that while almost all of the crusaders of the "Golden Age" remained faithful to their radical principles, many of the journalists and politicians connected with the progressivism of the nineties later found refuge in the camps of the enemy.

Two main currents of reform merged during these years. One had its origin in the agrarian West, concerned itself largely with economic issues, and revealed occasional flashes of real radicalism. The philosophers of this Western protest were Henry George, author of *Progress and Poverty*, and Edward Bellamy, whose *Looking Backward* envisioned a Utopian economy; its political spokesmen were Altgeld and Donnelly, Bryan and La Follette. The other current was Eastern, and even English, in origin and addressed itself to problems such as tariff reform, the merit system, and anti-imperialism. Its intellectual spokesmen were E. L. Godkin, editor of the powerful New York *Nation*, George William Curtis, and President Charles W. Eliot of Harvard University; its political representatives were Carl Schurz, Abram S. Hewitt, Grover Cleveland, and Woodrow Wilson.

The Crusade for Social Justice

IN 1890 a Danish immigrant, Jacob Riis, working as a reporter for the New York *Sun*, brought out his book *How the Other Half Lives*. It was an unvarnished account of conditions in the teeming slums of New York, and it pictured the overcrowding, the dirt, disease, crime, vice, and misery of the "other half" who had fallen behind in the march of democracy. Soon newspapermen in other cities were making similar reports, and the nation awoke to a realization that the challenge of the city was no less urgent than the challenge of the farm.

The city, as Lord Bryce observed in his *American Commonwealth*, was the one conspicuous failure of American democracy. Here the extremes of wealth and poverty were most flagrant, slums crowding the marble palaces of the rich, beggars haunting the doorways of luxurious restaurants. Here corruption was most unashamed, "rings" and "halls" fattening on the public treasury, selling public franchises, exploiting crime and vice. Here the saloon and the house of ill-fame were protected and encouraged by the politicians and the interests who profited by them, while criminal gangs like the Whyos of Mulberry Bend, New York, or the Lake Shore Push of Cleveland went their predatory ways undisturbed by police interference. Here sweatshops testified to the exploitation of women, newsboys and bootblacks to the failure to take care of the children. Here the problems of public health, housing, education, and government were most acute.

It was the housing problem that first commanded the attention of reformers, for this was one that concerned not only the wretched slum dwellers, but all of the inhabitants of the cities. In the decades after the Civil War the population of cities had grown far more rapidly than housing facilities, and the result had been the development of tenements—rickety wooden structures, five or six stories high, dark, ill-ventilated, and filthy, breeders of disease and nurseries of vice. In New York City alone, in 1890, probably half a million persons lived in these "slums"—where the death rate was four times that of the more fortunate parts of the city. One typical block on the lower East Side contained 2781 persons—but not a single bathtub. Of the 1588 rooms, one third were without light or ventilation and another third gave upon "twilight air shafts." Let Riis describe one of these slums of lower Manhattan:

Suppose we look into one, No. — Cherry Street. Be a little careful please! The hall is dark, and you might stumble over

the children pitching pennies back there. Not that it would
hurt them; kicks and cuffs are their daily diet. They have little
else. Here where the hall turns and dives into utter darkness is
a step, and another, another. A flight of stairs. You can feel your
way if you cannot see it. Close? Yes. What would you have? All
the fresh air that even enters these stairs comes from the hall
door that is forever slamming and from the windows of dark
bedrooms that in turn receive from the stairs their sole supply
of the elements. . . . That was a woman filling her pail by the
hydrant you just bumped against. The sinks are in the hallway,
that all the tenants may have access—and all be poisoned alike
by their summer stenches. Hear the pump squeak? It is the lullaby
of tenement house babes.

The "battle with the slum" was really a long campaign,
waged on many fronts. Pleading the hazards from fire and
epidemics, reformers like Richard Watson Gilder persuaded
reluctant legislators to outlaw the worst of the tenements
and require proper ventilation and sanitation in the others.
To take children off the streets and away from gangs and
give them a better chance at health and decency, playgrounds were built in the most crowded sections of cities,
fresh-air funds provided vacations to the country, milk de-
pots distributed free milk to those unable to buy it, day
nurseries relieved working mothers of anxiety for their children, Visiting Nurses' Associations gave free medical and
nursing care, and organizations like the Young Men's Christian Association and the Boy Scouts provided healthy and
normal outlets for youthful energies.

Indomitable social workers like Jane Addams and Lillian
Wald, inspired by the example of Toynbee Hall in London,
established settlement houses in the slums of the great cities.
The Settlement House undertook to deal, in human and
compassionate terms, with those whom Theodore Parker
had called the perishing and dangerous classes of society—
the newly arrived immigrants, lost in an alien world, the
out-of-work and the penniless, the victims of industry which
took no responsibility for their welfare, or even for their
bodies crippled by their machines, the broken old men and
women abandoned by their children, the waifs playing in
the streets and the alleys and the young in trouble with their
parents, or their church, or the law, the flotsam and jetsam
of the new cities that were growing too fast to give any

thought to justice or mercy or beauty. The Settlement House was, said Jane Addams, "an experimental effort to aid in the solution of the social and industrial problems engendered by the modern conditions of life. It is an attempt to relieve, at the same time, the overaccumulation at one end of society and the destitution at the other."

That Hull House, on Chicago's West Side, was the most successful and the most famous of all the Settlement Houses can be attributed to the genius of Jane Addams, most understanding, most persuasive, and most effective of all social workers. She had founded Hull House in 1889, had made it not only a refuge for the poor and the lost, but a training school for the young, and a laboratory for sociologists and philosophers. Under her guidance Hull House became a community center for the whole of Chicago, an art school, a music school, a drama school, a theater, a rehabilitation center, and—at another level—a center for training social workers in the techniques of social service and of realizing social ends through legislation. Out of Hull House radiated all kinds of reform activities: it served as a kind of clearing house for civil liberties, it sponsored legislation protecting women and children in industry, it helped set up the first juvenile courts in the country. Hull House became a world institution and Jane Addams—St. Jane as she was known to thousands—a world figure, first in the war against poverty and crime, first certainly in peace (she was the first woman to win the Nobel Peace Prize), and first in the hearts of her countrywomen and countrymen.

One of the most urgent problems that engaged the attention of reformers was that of crime, and particularly of mounting juvenile delinquency: the decade of the eighties had witnessed a fifty per cent increase in the number of prison inmates, and child offenders constituted one fifth of these. The United States had a long and honorable record of interest in penal and prison reform, but notwithstanding the efforts of enlightened critics like Edward Livingston, Dorothea Dix, and Frederick Wines, the penal code of many states remained harsh, and prison conditions in some states reminded visitors forcibly of the "Black Hole of Calcutta." The old notion of punishing offenders rather than reforming them died hard, and so, too, did police brutality, the third degree, and the practice of applying one law to the rich and the powerful, another to the poor and the friendless. Governor Altgeld of Illinois, who had pardoned the Haymarket "anarchists," had argued that society rather than individuals was guilty when crimes were committed, and had worked heroically for the reform of the penal code of the state. One of his disciples, Mayor "Golden Rule" Jones of Toledo, took the same attitude—and found opportunity to dramatize it.

He was always going down to the city prisons or to the workhouses [wrote Brand Whitlock] and talking to the poor devils there quite as if he were one of them. . . . And he was working all the time to get them out of prison, and finally he and I entered into a little compact by which he paid the expenses incident to their trials . . . if I would look after their cases. . . . For instance, if some poor girl were arrested and a jury trial were demanded for her and her case were given all the care and attention it would have received had she been some wealthy person, the police, when they found they could not convict, were apt to be a little more careful of the liberties of individuals; they began to have a little regard for human rights and for human life.

But such measures, of course, were palliatives rather than reforms. More important was the adoption, by the turn of the century, of the indeterminate sentence and the probationary system. Inspired by the example of Thomas Mott Osborne, some of the worst prisons were cleaned up and a determined attack was launched upon the chain gang and the system of leasing convict labor, widely prevalent through the South. Special courts were set up, too, for child offenders. Judge Ben Lindsey, who for a quarter of a century presided over the Juvenile Court of Denver, Colorado, attracted nationwide attention by the success with which he cut down juvenile delinquency. The campaign against capital punishment was, however, a failure.

One obvious cause of crime and poverty—so it was thought —was the saloon, and these years witnessed a concerted attack upon the "demon rum" that ended, finally, in national prohibition. The origins of the temperance movement go back to the early years of the republic, and before the Civil War thousands of men had "signed the pledge" of total abstinence and several New England states had experimented with legal prohibition. The postwar years, however, brought an increase in the consumption of beer and of hard liquor, and, in the cities, of saloons; by 1900, places like New York, Buffalo, and San Francisco confessed one saloon to every two hundred inhabitants. Some of these were merely "the poor man's club," but many of them were run with a total disregard of temperance or even decency in drinking. Sunday closing laws were ignored, high license fees evaded, and the liquor interest entered everywhere into a corrupt alliance with the worst elements in politics and society.

To meet these conditions a Prohibition party entered the field as early as 1869, but was ineffectual. Far more effective were such organizations as the Women's Christian Temperance Union, the Anti-Saloon League, and the evangelical churches, notably the Methodist. These were not satisfied with political agitation, but carried on a ceaseless propaganda, in the press, the church, the lecture hall, and the school. The militant leader of the prohibition forces was, for many years, Frances Willard, who carried the war into the enemy's country by leading temperance ladies into saloons, where they would sing psalms and fall to their knees in prayer.

By the end of the century these methods had dried up seven states, all of them rural, and had introduced "local option" to a great many more. During the early years of the new century the prohibition movement made great headway, and by the time of the First World War two thirds of the population lived under dry laws. Only the cities were recalcitrant. Whether the drys could ever have carried these battlements in normal times is uncertain, but the World War played into their hands. At the beginning of the war Congress, for reasons of economy, efficiency, and morality, prohibited the manufacture or sale of intoxicating liquors, and before this law expired prohibition was written into the Federal Constitution. There it remained for more than a decade, a "noble experiment" that failed. In 1933 it was repealed, and the problem returned to the states.

The States Point the Way

THE HISTORY of all these reform movements pointed to one unmistakable moral: private individuals and organizations could accomplish little except through legislative channels.

Discouraged by her experiences with private charity, Josephine Shaw Lowell, founder of New York's Charity Organization Society, and active in many good works, decided to withdraw from them all. "I think," she explained, "there is far more important work to be done for working people. Five hundred thousand wage earners in this city, 200,000 of them women and 75,000 of these working under dreadful conditions or for starvation wages. That is more vital than the 25,000 dependents. . . . If the working people had all they ought to have, we should not have the paupers and the criminals. It is better to save them before they go under than to spend your life fishing them out when they're half drowned, and taking care of them afterwards."

Charity was obviously a mere palliative, and even the humanitarians who distrusted political action usually ended up in the legislative chambers, hat in hand, asking for aid. Slum clearance, prison reform, workmen's compensation, conservation, the salvation of children, prohibition—all required legislative action. And if more fundamental reforms were to be obtained, they too must come through the agency of the state.

The first great battles of the reform movement were fought out in the states, and these continued to be the battlegrounds of reform even after many issues had been transferred to the national arena. Under the American constitutional system, it cannot be too often repeated, the states were presumed to have jurisdiction over almost all matters of a social character. The hours and wages of labor, the conditions of factory work, the welfare of women and children, prisons, reform schools and charitable institutions, education, the suffrage, municipal government—all of these things were matters of state, not Federal, concern. The New Deal, to be sure, changed all this, but it took a national catastrophe to justify and a bold administration to attempt that change, and it was effected only over the determined resistance of the Supreme Court.

The states, then, were the laboratories of reform. It was here that most of the subsequent national reforms were first tested; it was here that they justified themselves on principle and proved their inadequacy in practice. The states, too, were the training schools for the reformers who later performed on the national stage. Theodore Roosevelt went

to school in New York City and at Albany before he moved
on to Washington; La Follette learned the economics of railway and trust regulation in Wisconsin before he tried to
apply them to the nation; Wilson made his reputation as a
liberal as governor of New Jersey before he justified it as
President of the United States; Charles Evans Hughes, George
Norris, and Franklin D. Roosevelt—all served an apprenticeship in their states.

What was the nature of the reforms carried out by the
states? Many of them had to do with the democratization of
political machinery: the initiative and referendum, the secret
ballot, the direct primary, and direct election of Senators,
corrupt-practices acts, provision for municipal home rule, and
woman suffrage. Others were directed toward economic objectives: railway and trust regulation, public-utility commissions, tax reforms, regulation of hours and conditions of
labor, workmen's compensation, and prohibition of the labor
of children. Still others had broad social connotations: educational reforms, public-health programs, the conservation of
natural resources.

The immediate problem was to get control of the governments. It is a nice question whether the state or municipal
governments were more corrupt. Everywhere the field for
corruption was vast and inviting, and the rewards were almost limitless. State legislatures and city councils had in their
control the granting of valuable public-utility franchises, the
fixing of railroad and utility rates, the control of insurance
practices, the assessment and collection of taxes, the award
of juicy highway-construction contracts, the power to protect
or destroy the saloon. Hundreds of millions of dollars were
involved, and business was prepared to pay well for favors,
exemptions, or protection. Payment was not always in the
form of outright bribery; it might take the form of political
advancement, or contributions to political campaigns, juicy
contracts to relatives of complaisant legislators, or lucrative
legal business to attorneys who saw the light. Whatever form
it took, it was usually effective, as reformers learned to their
dismay.

A grand jury investigating conditions in Missouri at the
turn of the century concluded that "for twelve years . . .
corruption has been the usual and accepted thing in state
legislation, and that, too, without interference or hindrance."

The verdict might have been applied with equal truth, at one time or another, to almost every state in the Union. From New Hampshire to California, from New Mexico to Montana, legislators were up for auction. Everywhere the great corporations had their lobbyists who engaged in shameless bribery or, where that failed, in blackmail. In the Yankee state of New Hampshire, as Winston Churchill tells in his *Coniston* and *Mr. Crewe's Career,* the railroads ruled supreme; the *Octopus* of Frank Norris' powerful novel of California was the Southern Pacific. The "copper kings" corrupted Montana; railroads and insurance companies bought up the New York assembly. Even in a small frontier commonwealth like New Mexico, an unholy alliance of two or three railroads, coal-and copper-mining companies, timber and land speculators, and the great ranchmen, completely dominated the state. Coal companies seized thousands of acres of the most valuable mineral lands, lumber companies looted the national forests, ranchmen grazed thousands of cattle and sheep on the public domain, railroads and mines defeated labor laws, and all escaped taxation.

It would be repetitious and confusing to attempt to rehearse the war on corruption or trace the coming of political reforms in the various states. The history of one commonwealth will illustrate—though somewhat optimistically—what was happening widely throughout the Union. Wisconsin, in the 1880's, was a flourishing and enlightened state, but her government was run by a triumvirate of bosses—Boss Keyes, the millionaire lumberman, Philetus Sawyer, and the railroad attorney, John Sponner—who dominated state politics through the caucus and convention system. The whole state, according to Frederic C. Howe,

was a feudatory of the railway, lumber, and franchise interests, which, with the machine of federal officeholders, nominated and elected governors, United States senators and congressmen who, in turn, made use of their power to enrich their creators. Federal and state patronage was used for the same ends. The biennial session of the legislature was a carnival for the benefit of the few. Politics was a privileged trade, into which ambitious men entered only when approved by the state machine. Few believed any other methods were possible, and no one challenged the rule of the oligarchy which distributed elective as well as appointive offices for the maintenance of its political and industrial power. There was no organized protest. The press was indifferent or controlled.

Stirred by the currents of reform sweeping across the prairie states in the eighties, young Robert M. La Follette, fresh from the state university, decided to take a hand. Without machine support, he fought his way into Congress and in four successive terms justified the confidence which the common people had come to cherish for him. Defeated in the Democratic landslide of 1890, La Follette turned to state politics. The people were with him, but the machine would have none of him, and on three successive occasions boss-ridden conventions turned him down for more complaisant candidates. From this experience La Follette learned the necessity of abolishing the caucus and convention system and putting in the direct primary.

Finally in 1900 "Fighting Bob" forced his nomination upon a reluctant convention and was swept triumphantly into the governorship. For the next quarter of a century—with a brief war interlude—he and his followers dominated the state, making it the most democratic, the most progressive, and the best governed in the Union. The "Wisconsin Idea" as formulated and applied by La Follette in the first ten or twelve years of the century was not mere windy doctrine, but a practical and coherent program. It enlarged democracy through the direct primary, the initiative and referendum, the recall of all but judicial officials, the prohibition of corrupt election practices, publicity for and limitation on campaign expenditures, municipal home rule, civil-service reform, and the creation of bureaus of experts to advise on administration. To protect the citizens of the state against exploitation by corporations, La Follette set up commissions to regulate railway and other public-utility charges, forced the railroads and the great timber companies to pay their just share of taxes and to cough up back taxes which they had evaded, and provided for a state income tax and state insurance on savings-bank deposits. To safeguard labor there were workmen's compensation laws, the prohibition of child labor, and the limitation on the hours of labor for women. Agriculture was encouraged by the reduction in railroad rates, by a far-reaching conservation and water-power program, and by vigorous support to the experiment stations and demonstration farms connected with the state university.

Nothing was more interesting than the manner in which La Follette made the university the nerve center of the state. President Van Hise, himself a scientist of note, brought to the school on the shores of Lake Mendota one of the most distinguished faculties to be found in any institution of higher learning in the world. Even more important, he brought the notion that it was the function of the university to serve the people of the state. Its economists served on railway and tax commissions; its political scientists drafted legislative bills; its historians cultivated local history; its engineers planned road-building programs, its school of agriculture taught animal husbandry to practical farmers, carried on investigations which saved the farmers of the state—and of the nation—hundreds of millions of dollars, and was chiefly instrumental in making Wisconsin the Denmark of the New World.

Here was an experiment in practical progressivism which excited the interest of the whole nation. La Follette proved that reform did not need to be doctrinaire and that scholars and scientists could make contributions to practical politics. He showed how a state could regulate public utilities without incurring the charge of socialism and how such regulation could be profitable for the utilities as well as for the public. He revealed the possibilities of a state as a laboratory for political experiments and pointed the way not only for other states but for the nation.

Theodore Roosevelt and the Square Deal

ADMIRABLE as was the achievement of states like Wisconsin, it was clear that most of the problems to which reformers addressed themselves could not be solved in the insulated compartments of the Federal system. Only if reforms were projected on a national scale could they be effective, and only the national government was powerful enough to insure their success. Congress had indeed already enacted some legislation of a mildly progressive nature—the Pendleton Civil Service Act of 1883, the Interstate Commerce Act of 1887, the Antitrust Act of 1890, the Erdman Act for the arbitration of labor disputes on railways in 1898. But these and similar laws were largely ineffective for two reasons: they did not go far enough and they were not rigorously enforced. They were, in short, gestures, sops thrown out by a reluctant Congress to appease public opinion.

For a generation the Federal government had been chiefly in the hands of Republican leaders who, acquiescent in the *laissez faire* philosophy of the period, were indifferent to most of the newer social and economic demands. Without exception they were friendly to big business, while they catered to Civil War veterans with generous pension legislation. Pressure groups and special interests held a sway that was seldom broken. The Republican Presidents—Grant, Hayes, Garfield, Arthur, Harrison, McKinley—were estimable men; Hayes and Garfield had strong liberal tendencies; but as a group they lacked vision and creative thrust. The one Democratic President, Cleveland, had strength of character, unyielding courage, and a program of reform in the public interest. He reformed the Federal departments, reclaimed vast areas of public land from corporation control, fought pension grabs and other special legislation, invigorated the civil service, and even forced through Congress a reduction of the tariff with an income-tax law attached—a law which was promptly annulled by the Supreme Court. But Cleveland's tenure was broken and troubled. In the great industrial states and to some extent in Washington, the real control was exercised by men like Platt of New York, Quay of Pennsylvania, and Hanna of Ohio, whose concept of statesmanship was satisfied in serving their corporation masters and rewarding their party henchmen. Most Congressmen of this generation were party hacks; they filled the *Congressional Record* with their oratory and, arrayed in frock coats and high hats, decorated many a platform, but the average American would find it difficult to recall a single law which they passed that made any marked difference in the course of the nation's history.

The agrarian forces under Weaver and then Bryan genuinely frightened the Old Guard of both parties, and the ground swell of revolt in many states indicated that reforms could not be too long delayed. Then came the Spanish War, and reform was, for the time, forgotten. The campaign of 1900 was waged on the somewhat unrealistic issue of imperialism, and McKinley, who, not so much through clever-

ness as through confusion, had managed to be on both sides
of the question, was triumphantly re-elected, while Bryan was
for the second time repudiated. With prosperity at full tide,
it looked as if the country were in for another long experience with the philosophy of acquiescence in the current order.

Then, on September 6, 1901, McKinley was shot by an
anarchist, and with his death, a week later, the whole outlook of American politics was changed. For in young Theodore Roosevelt, so dramatically elevated to the presidency,
the country found a leader of remarkable stimulation and
power, and the progressive movement a national leader.
Roosevelt had been born to wealth, reared among moneyed
Easterners, and educated at Harvard. Yet he was thoroughly
democratic and passionately interested in reform. He was,
at the same time, a political realist, an ardent nationalist,
and a faithful Republican. After Jefferson he was the most
versatile of American Presidents, though without quite Jefferson's intellectual depth or subtlety and equally without
his philosophical idealism and his vision. He had ranched,
hunted big game, written numerous books, served in the
New York State legislature, administered the New York City
police, helped manage the Federal civil service, directed the
navy, commanded the Rough Riders in Cuba, and made a
first-rate governor. He read omnivorously, was interested in
everybody, and had opinions on everything. He had a knack
of coining memorable phrases, and his earnestness, strenu-
osity, and picturesqueness made him an incomparably effective preacher of civil righteousness. Like Andrew Jackson,
he had a genius for winning the confidence of the plain man
and making all his battles seem dramatic. Like Jackson, too,
he believed that the President was closer to the people than
the Congress and that executive leadership was essential for
getting things done. But unlike Jackson he had no suspicion
of the expert in civil service.

Within a year Roosevelt had shown that he understood the
great changes sweeping over America and meant to deal with
them in a statesmanlike way. He was not a radical, but an
enlightened conservative; he did not want to revolutionize
the existing economic system, but to save it by weeding out
the abuses that had crept into it. He was determined to prove

that the government was supreme over business and to give the plain man more of a "square deal."

In these undertakings Roosevelt made use of the public sentiment generated by the Populist movement, by the progressive impulse flooding in from states and cities, and by a valiant band of "muckrakers" whose books and magazine articles exposed graft and corruption, the malpractices of business, the "social evil," the suppression of racial minorities, and a host of other evils that afflicted American life. The muckrakers were not only themselves an instrument of reform, but their astonishing popularity was a symptom that the public was ripe for their message.

"The great development of industrialism," said Roosevelt, "means that there must be an increase in the supervision exercised by the Government over business enterprise." In his enforcement of the antitrust laws Roosevelt early furnished an example of such "increase in supervision." His before-noted attacks on the Northern Securities combination and the oil and tobacco trusts, and creation of the Bureau of Corporations as a vigilant policing agency, taught big business a healthy respect for the government.

But the trusts were by no means the only interests that felt his "big stick." The extension of government supervision over the railroads constituted one of the positive achievements of the Roosevelt administration. Roosevelt himself called railroad regulation the "paramount issue" and by incessant pressure succeeded in forcing through two major regulatory bills. The Elkins Act of 1903 made published rates the standard of lawfulness and shippers equally liable with railroads for rebates, and under its provisions the government successfully prosecuted the great Chicago packing houses and the Standard Oil Company. More important was the Hepburn Act of 1906, which gave the Interstate Commerce Commission real authority in rate regulation, extended the jurisdiction of the Commission to storage and terminal facilities, sleeping cars, express companies, and pipe lines, and forced the roads to surrender their interlocking interests in steamship lines and coal companies. By the end of the Roosevelt administration rebates had practically disappeared and railroad rates had ceased to be a pressing problem.

The use of the "big stick" in the affairs of labor was dramatic and in its moral effect significant. Under presidential prodding Congress pushed through a Workmen's Compensation Act for government employees, child-labor laws for the District of Columbia, and safety-appliance legislation for railroads, while the President himself saw to it that the eight-hour day on government work, which had been something of a mockery, was enforced. More spectacular was Roosevelt's intervention in the great anthracite coal strike of 1902. After a long struggle the United Mine Workers, under the leadership of the youthful John Mitchell, had succeeded in winning important concessions; when the mine operators abrogated these, the miners struck. The operators were led by a representative of the paleolithic age of American industry, George Baer, who announced that "the rights and interests of the laboring man will be protected and cared for, not by the labor agitators, but by the Christian men whom God in His infinite wisdom has given control of the property interests of the country." When they refused to arbitrate it looked as if the country would face winter without fuel. At this juncture Roosevelt stepped in with a threat that he would take over the mines and run them with soldiers unless the operators came to terms. The threat was effective, and the miners won increased wages and shorter hours.

Of more permanent interest to the average American was the pure-food and drug legislation placed on the statute books in 1906. For years meat packers and food and drug manufacturers had been selling adulterated foods and dangerous drugs and patent medicines to the public. Popular indignation was aroused by a series of exposures by Dr. Harvey Wiley, chief chemist of the Department of Agriculture, and by Upton Sinclair's shocking revelation of conditions in the Chicago stockyards, *The Jungle*. Congress responded with a Meat Inspection Act and a Pure Food and Drugs Act which went far to eliminate the worst abuses.

Easily the most important of Roosevelt's achievements on the domestic front was in the conservation of natural resources. The country had long been deluded by the concept of infinity with respect to its forests and its soil; at the end of the century it awoke to a realization that three quarters of the forests were gone, much of the mineral wealth had been wasted, water power was being exploited for private profit, and the soil was being washed away by floods or blown away by dust storms. Roosevelt's love of nature and his familiarity with the West gave him a personal interest in conservation. In his first message to Congress he announced that "the forest and water problems are perhaps the most vital internal problems of the United States" and he recommended a far-reaching program of conservation and reclamation. Taking advantage of the Forest Reserve Act of 1891, Roosevelt set aside some 150 million acres of land as a forest reserve and withdrew from public entry another 85 million acres in Alaska and the Northwest, pending study of their forest and mineral wealth. At the same time he placed forest conservation under the control of the vigorous and enlightened Gifford Pinchot. A Reclamation Act of 1902 provided for large-scale irrigation projects at the expense of and under the supervision of the Federal government, and under the terms of this act work was soon under way on the great Roosevelt Dam in Arizona, the Arrowrock Dam in Idaho, and the Elephant Butte Dam on the Rio Grande. All this was, to be sure, only a beginning, but the precedents established and the public interest aroused made possible the far more elaborate programs of succeeding administrations.

By 1908 Roosevelt had served one term as successor to McKinley, one in his own right. He was at the height of his popularity and could doubtless have had another term for the asking. But he hesitated to challenge the third-term tradition and chose, instead, to pick a successor to carry out "my policies." His choice fell on the learned and able William Howard Taft, and that choice was ratified first by the Republican nominating convention and then, after a dull contest with Bryan, by popular election.

Taft had been judge of the Circuit Court, Governor General of the Philippines, and Secretary of War. In all these administrative posts he had acquitted himself well, but in none had he revealed any political talent or any really creative liberalism. He was genuinely anxious to continue the Rooseveltian program, and his accomplishments were not negligible. He stepped up the prosecution of trusts; strengthened the Interstate Commerce Commission; established a postal-savings bank and a parcel-post system; expanded the merit system in the civil service; and sponsored the enactment of two amendments to the Federal Constitution—one providing direct election of Senators, another authorizing an income tax. Yet against these progressive achievements must be set policies and gestures of a reactionary stamp. The most striking of these were the acceptance of a tariff whose protective schedules outraged liberal opinion, the dismissal of Gifford Pinchot as head of the Forestry Service, the opposition to the entry of Arizona into the Union because her constitution provided for the popular recall of judges, and the growing reliance on the ultraconservative wing of the party.

By 1910 Taft had succeeded in splitting his party wide open, and a landslide swept the Democrats back into control of the Congress. Roosevelt, anxious to give his successor a free hand, had gone off to Africa to hunt lions; now a popular ditty voiced the hope of his followers:

> Teddy, come home and blow your horn,
> The sheep's in the meadow, the cow's in the corn
> The boy you left to tend the sheep
> Is under the haystack fast asleep.

Roosevelt did come back, after a triumphal tour of Europe, and liberal Republicans like La Follette and Pinchot hurried to pour their indignation into his attentive ear. Roosevelt was not yet ready to act, but La Follette was, and in 1911 he began his campaign to win the Republican nomination. That campaign evoked such widespread support that Roosevelt decided to cash in on it; early in 1912 he announced that "my hat is in the ring." There followed a spirited campaign between Roosevelt and Taft, in which the former won all the popular support and the latter most of the delegates. At the Chicago convention the party steam roller flattened out T. R.'s vociferous supporters and gave the nomination to Taft. Roosevelt denounced the action as "naked theft" and promised to make a fight on an independent ticket. A few weeks later twenty thousand of his hysterical followers met in Chicago, organized the Progressive party, and named their beloved leader its candidate.

The Democrats watched all this with unrestrained enthusiasm. For many years they had wandered with Bryan in the political wilderness; now they caught a glimpse of the Promised Land. Competition for the presidential nomination was keen. The conservatives rallied behind an old war horse, Champ Clark of Missouri, Speaker of the House;

the liberals shouted and voted for a newcomer, Woodrow Wilson, Governor of New Jersey. In the end it was Bryan who dictated the choice, poor Bryan who had never been able to win the presidency himself but who now, at the most dramatic moment of his career, threw his powerful support to Woodrow Wilson, and thus assured him of that nomination which, in 1912, was equivalent to election to the presidency.

CHAPTER 19

The Rise to World Power

New Forces and Horizons

WHEN WE CONSIDER American political history in the generation after the Civil War we meet a spate of dramatic occurrences: reconstruction, the Granger movement, the felling of the spoils system, tariff battles, the Populist upsurge, the rise of progressivism. When we consider industrial history we encounter an equally crowded era: the building of imperial railroad systems, the growth of trusts, the birth of huge new industries, the feats of captains like Rockefeller, Carnegie, Morgan, and Hill. By contrast foreign relations offer a thin chronicle. Only two or three striking episodes give color to the years between the French evacuation of Mexico under American pressure in 1867 and the sinking of the *Maine* off Havana in 1898. "What have we got to do with abroad?" a parochial-minded Congressman of this period is supposed to have ejaculated.

Yet the field was more important than it seemed, for in-

exorably certain facts of direct concern to every American
were emerging. The United States was becoming a true
world power, with a heavy interest in the peace, order, and
prosperity of the more and more interdependent family of
nations. It was also becoming aware of a special relationship with Great Britain. Because the Monroe Doctrine, commercial expansion, and, after 1899, the Open Door in the
Orient demanded an ocean dominated by freedom-loving
powers, because of natural business ties with its best cus-
tomer, and because of a common interest in the promotion
of democracy, the United States moved toward closer association with the British Empire. At the same time, the United
States assumed a more sternly protective attitude toward
Latin America. With manufactured goods as well as raw materials demanding outlets, it gave more attention to the development of overseas markets. Partly for commercial and
strategic reasons, partly from idealistic motives, partly from
pride of power, it swung to an exuberant expansion overseas.

Long before the Spanish-American War the United States
had begun to show consciousness of its position as a true
world power. Under Presidents Arthur and Cleveland it
began building a strong modern navy. By 1890 the "white
squadron" was an object of keen national pride. The total
exports of the United States by 1880 exceeded $835,000,000
and twenty years later were roughly $1,400,000,000. No
nation could ship so much outside its borders without taking
a lively interest in foreign affairs. For a time after the Civil
War the old fever for expansion had seemed almost completely gone. After the purchase of Alaska in 1867 most
citizens felt that the American flag waved over enough territory, and Grant's effort to annex Santo Domingo was overwhelmingly defeated in the Senate. But gradually expansionist
sentiment again rose. When Germany tried to lay greedy
hands on Samoa, the United States stood firm with Great
Britain in asserting its rights there. A three-power protectorate was set up, and in a division at the end of the century
the United States took all the islands but the two largest, receiving the long-coveted harbor of Pago Pago. In Hawaii,
where Americans had obtained control of the sugar-growing
industry, the United States obtained in 1887 the exclusive
right to use the priceless Pearl Harbor as a naval station. Six
years later an effort to effect the annexation of Hawaii was

on the verge of success when Cleveland's reaccession to power halted it—for he rightly thought that the methods used were improper. But thereafter the Hawaiian Islands were controlled by resident Americans until in 1898 they definitely passed under the American banner. Meanwhile, in 1889 the United States brought delegates from nearly a score of southern republics to the first Pan-American Conference in Washington. American influence was reaching farther and farther from home.

In the thirty years after the Civil War most of the international controversies of the United States were naturally with the only other major power in the Western Hemisphere, Great Britain. Some of them were grave. But the significant fact is that they were all settled by arbitration or adjudication, and in such a way as to improve Anglo-American feeling.

The whole list of friendly settlements is impressive. Strong antagonism to Britain had been aroused in the North during the Civil War. Much of it was unfounded; the British recognition of Confederate belligerency was quite correct, the British navy pursued a policy which on the whole favored the North, and the British masses even in the hard-hit cotton-spinning districts of Lancashire stood with Lincoln. But Tory unfriendliness and the ravages of British-built or -equipped cruisers under the Confederate flag were angrily remembered. For a time after the war, as leaders like the fanatical Charles Sumner pressed exaggerated claims for damages, a clash seemed possible. Fortunately, the United States had one of the wisest of all its Secretaries of State in Hamilton Fish. Under his leadership, a plan was worked out for submitting the American claim for damages wrought by the *Alabama* and other cruisers to arbitration. The first great international tribunal of modern times met at Geneva; in 1869 it closed the whole controversy by awarding the United States $15,500,000; and the British promptly paid this moderate sum. At the same time a minor boundary dispute between the United States and Canada, involving a few islands on the Northwest coast, was arbitrated; a few years later a dispute over fishery rights in the North Atlantic was adjusted by a joint commission. In the late 1880's a new controversy arose over the question of whether Canadians had a right to share in the capture of Alaskan fur seals in the Bering Sea. The State

Department bumptiously insisted that these waters were a *mare clausum* under exclusive American jurisdiction. Once more the quarrel was submitted to an international board of arbiters, which decided in favor of the British.

Most telling of all was the amicable settlement of the Venezuelan boundary dispute which flared up so dramatically and dangerously in the closing days of 1895. This dispute came to a head with startling suddenness. On December 16, 1895, few men in America or Britain dreamed of any serious friction between the two nations. On December 17, the public of both countries was thunderstruck by the news that President Cleveland had sent Congress a message which contained an implied threat of war against Britain. How came such a message to be possible?

There had long been an unsettled boundary between British Guiana and Venezuela. Repeatedly the United States had proffered its good offices to bring about a decision. But the Venezuelan pretensions were absurdly exaggerated; and the British refused to arbitrate the claims except west of the so-called Schomburgk line, surveyed half a century earlier. Many Americans suspected the British of land-grabbing designs at the expense of a weak nation. Finally, in the summer of 1895 the State Department sent London what Cleveland called a "twenty-inch gun note," which in effect accused Great Britain of violating the Monroe Doctrine and asked for a categorical answer on arbitration. "Today the United States is practically sovereign on this continent," asserted the note. When the long-delayed British answer came, it denied that the disputed frontier had anything to do with the Monroe Doctrine, pointed out certain historical errors in the American note, and once more refused arbitration. Cleveland was "mad clear through." He at once sent Congress a message declaring that an investigating commission should be hurried to Venezuela to determine the true boundary line, and when it had finished, the United States "must resist by every means in its power" any encroachments on land assigned to Venezuela.

For a time many feared the worst; jingo elements in America had a field day. But the ultimate results of the episode proved happy. The British people and government showed remarkable restraint, while the Kaiser's telegram to the Boer leader Kruger came early in 1896 to divert their ttention to other topics. Powerful American newspapers, led by the New York *World*, condemned Cleveland's rash act. Commercial and religious bodies rose in opposition. Professional circles were grieved and resentful. Multitudes on both sides of the Atlantic declared that war was unthinkable. Messages of friendship and confidence were exchanged. Some 1300 British authors appealed for American amity; more than 350 members of Parliament asked for the arbitration of all disputes. In the end, Britain and Venezuela, using the good offices of the United States, agreed to an arbitration which excepted those areas held by either nation for fifty years or more. The whole affair cleared the air between England and America, increased their mutual respect, and showed how powerful were the attachments which operated beneath the surface of politics.

It was well that this was so. The foreign policy of the United States was more and more clearly in the grip of powerful new forces. The republic was about to play a role on a larger stage, and Anglo-American antagonism had to be discarded for Anglo-American harmony.

The Spanish-American War

THE LAST DECADE of the nineteenth century found imperialist sentiment running high in most great nations. The partitioning of Africa was being concluded; China seemed about to be torn in pieces for the benefit of the powers. Some of the roots of imperialism were economic, for growing populations and expanding industrial systems demanded new markets. Some were political, for rival nations sought strength in overseas dependencies. Some were naval; Alfred T. Mahan's books had emphasized the value of chains of naval bases. Some were religious and ethical, for evangelical churchmen felt it a Christian duty to spread light in dark places, while reformers talked of the white man's mission of uplifting backward peoples. Still other roots were purely emotional; sensational newspapers whipped up a taste for adventure in foreign spheres. In the United States the panic of 1893 and the re-election of the anti-imperialist Cleveland had done something to check the spirit of jingoism and expansionism. By 1897, with the depression wearing away and Cleveland discredited, this spirit was resurgent. It found its opportunity when a bloody rebellion in Cuba gained impressive headway.

The Spanish government in Cuba had long been corrupt, tyrannical, and cruel. Year after year it had drained the island of at least two fifths of its annual income, diminishing its productive capacity and impoverishing the people. The Spaniards practically monopolized the government, paying themselves outrageous salaries and indulging in a system of continuous thefts. Almost intolerable levies were placed upon industry and commerce. Abusive excise taxes burdened agriculture and mining, while the tariff gave Spanish manufacturers and traders a monopoly which they exploited by charging ruinous prices for goods. Life and property were unsafe. Any Cuban might be summarily arrested and "shot while trying to escape." The courts were tools of the Spanish rulers, and a lawsuit was usually another name for robbery. The press was muzzled. The Church, which was in the hands of Spanish prelates, was corrupt, inefficient, and out of sympathy with the plain people. Its reactionary hierarchy kept such a strangulating grip upon education that illiteracy was general. A heavy standing army had to be supported by the people. Revolt lay always just underneath the surface; a ruinous guerrilla war dragged itself out through most of the decade of the seventies, and when in 1895 a heavy depression, accentuated by an American tariff upon sugar, fell upon the island, the suffering masses could no longer be restrained. The patriot José Martí raised his flag and soon the whole country was aflame.

Although both the Cleveland and McKinley administrations made an earnest effort to keep neutral, it became clear that if the war were prolonged America would have to intervene. The economic effects on the United States were serious; about fifty million dollars of American capital was invested in Cuba, while trade with the island before the revolt had amounted to $100,000,000 a year. When Cuban revolutionists used the United States as a base for military expeditions, Madrid complained. But the situation was hard to meet, and the ineffectiveness of the Spanish blockade was an important factor. American citizens in Cuba suffered losses of property, liberty, and even life, and Washington offered vigorous remonstrances over their treatment. Above

all, American feeling was deeply stirred by the savagery
with which the war was being waged on both sides and by
the brutality of Spanish policy. After the able but ruthless
Valeriano Weyler was sent out to crush the revolt, the struggle became increasingly barbarous. Both sides laid waste
the country and massacred their prisoners. Wanton outrages
were committed upon helpless noncombatants. In the fall
of 1896 Weyler turned certain towns and cities into concentration areas, driving women, children, and old men
within stockaded quarters where they perished like flies. By
the end of 1897 more than half of the 101,000 people of
Havana Province who had been placed in concentration
areas were dead; and the American consul general reported
that, in the island as a whole, 400,000 inoffensive women
and children had been beggared and reduced to the condition of wild animals—buried by the hundreds daily from
starvation and fever.

The Spanish government poured troops into Cuba until
by the beginning of 1898 it had 200,000 men there. Its
Foreign Office attempted to organize a league of European
powers to prevent the United States from interfering; cold-
shouldered by Russia and actively opposed by Great Britain,
it received some encouragement from Germany, Austria-
Hungary, and France. But by 1898 the sands were running
out. Congress was growing clamorous for decisive action.
Public sentiment, responsive in part to the naked facts of
the situation, in part to the clamor of a sensational press
led by William Randolph Hearst's New York *Journal,* was
ready for war. President McKinley and the group of big-
business Senators who were his closest advisers wished to
avoid a conflict. But political considerations and a belief
in the right of the popular will to rule placed limits upon
McKinley's resistance to pressure. The stupid Spanish minister in Washington, Dupuy de Lome, did not help matters
when in February he let the Hearst press get hold of a
letter in which he called McKinley "a would-be politician,"
"a bidder for the admiration of the crowd" and a man guilty
of bad faith with Spain. A week later the battleship *Maine*
was blown up in Havana harbor with a loss of 260 lives.
Whether this was the work of irresponsible Spaniards, or
of Cubans acting as *provocateurs,* it rendered war almost
unavoidable. The Spanish government made hasty last-

minute concessions. Properly seized upon, they might have resulted in the peaceful liberation of Cuba. But McKinley believed it too late for further delay, and on April 11 sent Congress a war message. It was unquestionably a popular war; it was clearly a needless war.

No other American conflict ever brought such quick returns in a certain kind of glory as the Spanish-American War. Fighting began on May 1, 1898, and was all over in ten weeks. Not a single reverse of any importance occurred. On May Day Dewey steamed into the unmined waters of Manila Bay at dawn, approached the Spanish fleet—which he outranged—until the distance was perfect, remarked, "You may fire when you are ready, Gridley," and put the enemy out of action without losing a man. The event was fitly celebrated by the Kansas versifier who wrote:

> Oh, dewy was the morning,
> Upon the first of May,
> And Dewey was the admiral,
> Down in Manila Bay.
> And dewy were the Spaniard's eyes,
> Them orbs of black and blue,
> And dew we feel discouraged?
> I dew not think we dew!

Troops equivalent to a single army corps were landed near Santiago, Cuba, won a rapid series of engagements, and brought the port under fire. Admiral Cervera's fleet of four armored cruisers plunged out of Santiago Bay and a few hours later was a row of smashed hulks along the coast —with but one American seaman killed. General Miles's army landed on Puerto Rico and marched through it as if on a holiday parade. Mr. Dooley wrote of the conquest of the island as "Gineral Miles's Gran' Picnic and Moonlight Excursion in Puerto Rico."

The American people accepted the war with a lighthearted patriotism. Every band played Sousa's new air, *The Stars and Stripes Forever*, and every piano strummed the ragtime march, *There'll Be a Hot Time in the Old Town Tonight*. Party lines were forgotten as Bryan served as colonel of a Nebraska regiment. The last vestiges of wartime antagonism between North and South melted away in the fire of national feeling; and Joe Wheeler, the famous Confederate cavalry leader, fighting before Santiago, exclaimed that a single battle for the Union flag was worth fifteen years of life. From Boston to San Francisco whistles blew and flags waved on the hot July day when word came that Santiago had fallen. Newspapers rushed their correspondents to Cuba and the Philippines to see the fun, and these writers trumpeted the renown of a dozen new national heroes. There were "Fighting Bob" Evans of the *Iowa,* who took Cervera on board after his defeat; Captain Philip of the *Texas,* who as a Spanish vessel sank said, "Don't cheer, boys; the poor fellows are dying"; Lieutenant Victor Blue, who plunged into the Cuban jungle to gain information on Spanish forces, and Captain R. P. Hobson, who sank the collier *Merrimac* in a vain effort to plug the mouth of Santiago Bay. Above all other heroes loomed George Dewey, to whom the grateful nation gave a home in Washington, and Theodore Roosevelt, leader of the Rough Riders, whose war record helped him to a more famous Washington house. It seemed an ideal war. Its casualty lists were short, it cost no great debt, it raised American prestige abroad, and the nation emerged with its pockets full of booty.

Yet when scrutinized closely it had less creditable sides. Its glory was won at the expense of a helpless foe, for enemy resistance was pitiable. The Spanish navy was so ill-equipped and demoralized that it hardly inflicted a scratch on American ships. The 200,000 troops in Cuba were so handicapped by bad leadership and wretched transport that only 12,000 could be placed in Santiago when American forces approached that city. Our victories were attributable in part to dash and courage, but in still larger part to Spanish weakness. And the background of these victories was a record of bureaucratic corruption, inefficiency, and bungling which seemed to reflective citizens highly discreditable. The War Department was so badly mismanaged that its head was shortly forced out of the McKinley administration, giving place to a leader who put it and the army on a high plane of efficiency—Elihu Root. The army death rate from disease was a grave reflection not only upon its medical branch, but upon American sanitation and health services in general. Notwithstanding a series of one-sided victories over the Spaniards, naval marksmanship had proved atrocious, and naval gunnery had to be taken sharply in hand. The paralyzing grip of politics upon the war services in Washington was once more demonstrated. Altogether, Theodore Roosevelt was right in calling the conflict the War of America the Unready. The army was soon raised to a strength of 100,000, a permanent General Staff was created, the navy was rapidly enlarged, and professional services in both branches were strengthened. By taking the lessons of the war to heart, the United States was helped to prepare adequately for the ordeal of 1917–1918.

Peace with Spain was rapidly arranged by a meeting of commissioners in Paris. Only two points of controversy arose. The Spanish representative tried to insist that Cuba should assume responsibility for debts which Spain had contracted upon a pledge of the island revenues; and they argued that Spain should keep all or a part of the Philippines. But on both points the American delegation stood firm. Cuba was reborn a debt-free republic. The entire Philippine archipelago was ceded to the United States, and with it Puerto Rico. By this acquisition of overseas territories, peopled by stocks alien in language, culture, and political tradition, America seemed to enter upon a new path. Vehement objections were raised by the anti-imperialists, led by Bryan, Carl Schurz, E. L. Godkin, Mark Twain, and Senator George Frisbie Hoar; the poet William Vaughn Moody cried out in anguish:

> Lies! Lies! It cannot be! . . .
> Tempt not our weakness, our cupidity!
> For save we let the island men go free,
> Those baffled and dislaureled ghosts
> Will curse us from the lamentable coasts
> Where walk the frustrate dead . . .

But that the treaty met general approval was shown by the election of 1900, which returned McKinley to power by increased majorities. Time was to prove that the overseas responsibilities which the United States assumed were in part merely temporary and that at heart the nation remained nonimperialistic. As the years passed, it chose to reduce its overseas holdings, not to enlarge them.

Nevertheless, the Spanish-American War did mark a turning point in American history. At last the nation recognized itself as a world power; less and less it felt isolated and self-centered, more and more it played a leading role in broad international arrangements. It consciously became one of the tutors of backward peoples. Under such proconsuls as General Leonard Wood, it undertook huge tasks of reorganization, reform, and development in the Philippines, Cuba, Puerto Rico, and a little later in Panama. With races like the Igorot and Moros, Americans took up the training of what Kipling called "new-caught, sullen peoples, half-devil and half-child." The conquest of yellow fever as a result of experiments in Cuba by Dr. Walter Reed and others of the army medical staff was a triumph alone worth the whole cost of the war. For centuries "yellow jack" had destroyed life throughout all tropical areas, and it had been a standing menace to our Southern ports. Until the Spanish conflict the United States had tacitly depended on the British navy for maintenance of the Monroe Doctrine; thereafter it insisted on a navy able to maintain the Doctrine unaided. The war, and particularly the sixty-eight-day voyage of the battleship *Oregon* from the Pacific Coast round the Horn to Cuban waters, brought home to everybody the necessity for an isthmian canal. Finally, the struggle did something to increase Anglo-American friendship and to chill German-American relations, for the British celebrated the American victories almost as their own, while a German squadron which kept a jealous watch at Manila had given Dewey anxiety and irritation.

The Open Door: Rooseveltian Diplomacy

THE FIRST POSTWAR TOKEN of a new attitude in world affairs was the enunciation of the Open Door principle. China, defeated by the Japanese in 1894–1895, had become the prey of European powers, which descended upon her to seize economic privileges and territorial concessions. Russia took practical possession of northern Manchuria; Germany leased the port of Kiaochow, gaining economic control of Shantung Province; France obtained various favors. Both the United States and Great Britain watched this looting with alarm. They valued Chinese trade and feared the

erection of high commercial barriers. Just before the
Spanish-American War began, the British suggested joint
Anglo-American action to preserve free commercial opportunities in China, but the State Department was chilly. Then
in 1899 Washington swung to a different position. Manufacturing and trading interests exerted pressure for a firmer
policy in the Orient and recalled that the Bureau of Foreign
Commerce had termed China "one of the most promising"
spots for "an American invasion of the markets of the
world." Missionary interests lent their voice. A timely book
by Lord Charles Beresford on *The Breakup of China* aroused
much feeling. Various men were at work behind the scenes;
and finally in September, John Hay, Secretary of State,
asked nations with spheres of interest in China to promise
that they would not levy special tariffs, harbor dues, or railway charges within these spheres. Though most of the
answers contained some qualifications, Hay early in 1900
announced the "final and definitive" assent of the powers
to a policy of the "open door" in China.

After Theodore Roosevelt in 1901 succeeded to the presidency, with first Hay and then Root as Secretary of State,
American foreign policy fell into two main sections. One
part of it centered about the new insular possessions and
the Panama gateway and was primarily a consequence of
the Spanish-American War and the resultant emergence
of the United States to a position where it felt more vulnerable in both the Atlantic and Pacific. The other part of
it represented certain personal adventures of Roosevelt in
world diplomacy and signalized the arrival of the United
States at the position of a world power. These adventures,
of which Roosevelt's use of his good offices in 1905 to end
the Russo-Japanese War and his participation in the Alge-
ciras Conference of 1906 were the chief, need be given
little attention. Both were spectacular, and from Roosevelt's
point of view both were successful. Neither was really necessary; Russia and Japan might have settled their quarrel at
some different place than Portsmouth, New Hampshire,
and Henry White need not have been sent to support France
in her historic duel with Germany over North African ports
and privileges. It was Roosevelt's foreign policies affecting
the Philippines, the Caribbean islands, and Panama which
were genuinely important to Americans.

And, we may add, his policies respecting Anglo-American relations; for though men did not suspect it, in two titanic wars the hopes of democracy, nay of civilization itself, were soon to rest upon the collaboration of two great English-speaking powers. The United States, a somewhat shivering newcomer in the bleak arena of world affairs, saw clearly enough that the support of the British navy was highly desirable. Great Britain, for her part, was faced on every hand by the menace of German might. In international trade, German competition; in Africa, German demands for a share; in Asia, German hostility to the Open Door; in Europe, Germany's Triple Alliance and German naval ambitions. It is by no means certain that Germany was without territorial ambitions in the West Indies or Latin America —some of her leaders would have liked a naval base there. For evident reasons the United States and Britain found themselves more and more clearly in accord in the Far East, the Caribbean, and on the maritime highways, where they maintained what was later called "the Atlantic system."

As it became plain that the United States was determined to construct an isthmian canal, the British government made generous concessions to help clear the way. The old Clayton-Bulwer Treaty (1850) had provided that the two nations should possess equal privileges in any canal and that neither should fortify it. Negotiations between Secretary Hay and the British ambassador in Washington resulted in the Hay-Pauncefote Treaty, duly ratified in 1901. Providing that the United States might "construct, maintain, and control" the canal (though no discrimination in rates was to be permitted), it represented a surrender by the British of all their old treaty rights. No *quid pro quo* was asked, and the gesture was duly appreciated by Americans. A little later Great Britain took a course upon the Venezuelan debt question which again pleased Washington. Three powers, Britain, Italy, and Germany, had claims against the disreputable government of President Castro. In the fall of 1902, failing to get payment in any other way, they agreed upon a line of "co-operative coercion." Germany, Britain, and Italy blockaded the Venezuelan coast, seized some gunboats, and bombarded two forts. The United States was willing to see Venezuela frightened, but nothing more. When Great Britain perceived that her course was irritating

American opinion, she receded. A debate was arranged in the House of Commons to denounce joint action with Germany, and the ministry declared it wished to avoid any use of force. The American people contrasted the British attitude favorably with the tactics of the Germans; and later Roosevelt told a dramatic story (inaccurate, but perhaps not wholly unfounded) of how he had got Dewey and the fleet ready for action to persuade the Kaiser to back down.

Early in the century the British government, again, helped settle the Canadian-Alaskan boundary in a fashion which gratified Americans as much as it irritated Canadians. Under the old Anglo-Russian treaty of 1825, the boundary of the Alaskan panhandle was to follow "the summits of the mountains situated parallel to the coast" in such a fashion as to leave Russia a coastal strip thirty miles wide. The United States inherited this strip. The question was whether it ran in a jagged line around the heads of the deep inlets on the coast or cut in a straight line across their heads. The Canadians hoped to be given harbors at some of these heads. After much discussion the matter was referred to a panel of jurists representing Britain, Canada, and the United States. Roosevelt, intent upon winning, waved the big stick. But this was not really necessary; right was with the Americans, and the British jurist Lord Alverstone consistently voted with them. Finally, when in 1906 the British navy was redistributed in three main fleets, Mediterranean, Channel, and Eastern Atlantic, the squadron long based on Bermuda to cover the West Indies was recalled. German threats had forced this move, but the United States, with its now powerful navy, appreciated having a free hand in the Caribbean.

It did so in part because the Panama Canal was then under way. "I took Panama," Roosevelt told a Western audience in 1912. "It was the only way the canal could be constructed." The first half of the statement is almost literally true. By a law enacted in 1902, Congress authorized the President to buy up the rights of the old French canal-digging company in Panama, to obtain from Colombia perpetual control of a strip of land in that state from the Atlantic to the Pacific, and to begin digging the great ditch. Negotiations were opened with Colombia. But that republic, knowing that Panama was one of its greatest assets, was unwilling to part with it for a mess of pottage. A treaty drawn up in Washington for American control of a six-mile strip was defeated by the Senate in Bogotá. Such defeats had been common enough in the United States, where the American Senate had made mincemeat of more than one important compact. But Roosevelt denounced it as an outrage, characterizing the Colombian politicians as greedy and corrupt. He was determined to have the canal site before the Congress met again in December, for he feared that if he did not, some of his plans might be upset. Two other powerful elements wanted immediate action. One was the French company, which had a stake of forty millions in an early sale. The other was the people of Panama, who feared that if the United States did not soon begin the canal there it would be constructed in Nicaragua instead. The result was that the idea of a revolution in Panama occurred to a great many persons at once. The *Review of Reviews,* edited by a close friend of Roosevelt, blossomed out with an article, "What If Panama Should Revolt?" Talk of an outbreak filled the air in Washington, and cruisers were dispatched to the Panama coast. French agents were busy on the isthmus. On November 3, 1903, immediately after the arrival of the warship *Nashville* at Colón, the State Department sent a cable to American consuls on the scene:

"Uprising on Isthmus reported. Keep Department promptly and fully informed. Loomis, acting."

The consul at Panama, who was no fool, wired back: "No uprising yet. Reported will be in night. Situation critical." An hour or two later he reported:

"Uprising occurred tonight, 6, no bloodshed. Army and navy officers taken prisoners. Government will be organized tonight."

American marines were landed and stopped Colombian troops from dealing with the revolt. A minister from Panama was promptly received in Washington, and with extraordinary speed the little new republic signed a treaty giving the United States the coveted strip for ten millions down and a reasonable annual rental. Roosevelt later remarked: "If I had followed traditional conservative methods I should have submitted a dignified state paper of probably two hundred pages to Congress and the debate would be going on yet. But I took the Canal Zone and let Congress

debate, and while the debate goes on the canal does also."
So it did. Within a decade, thanks to the engineering genius
of Colonel George W. Goethals and the sanitary genius of
William C. Gorgas, the canal was ready for operation. But
Roosevelt's crude methods had shocked and alarmed public
sentiment throughout Latin America.

Theodore Roosevelt was actuated by a genuine desire for
better relations with the Latin republics, but both his policies and their results were very mixed. When the third Pan-
American Conference was held at Rio de Janeiro, he sent
Secretary Root for a good-will tour of South America to
make clear our friendship with Latin America. He treated
the Monroe Doctrine as a vital protection to the southern
republics. But he added to this Doctrine a famous corollary
which deeply disturbed many of them. Pointing out that
since the United States would not permit European powers
to take rough action with unruly little nations which de-
faulted their debts, seized alien property, or maltreated alien
residents, he declared that this placed an unescapable responsibility on American shoulders. Uncle Sam himself
would have to see that such republics behaved. He illustrated this principle in his treatment of Santo Domingo.
When that nation was threatened in 1904 with intervention,
he induced it to let him establish an American financial
receivership. This set a precedent for the erection of a
number of virtual protectorates in the Caribbean area. The
policy made for peace and order, but it inspired fears in
Latin America that the United States was embarking on a
predatory course.

In the Pacific, also, Roosevelt followed a course which
had mixed results. Japanese-American relations were beginning to become a source of anxiety. The President intervened in a controversy between Japan and the city of San
Francisco, which was giving discriminatory treatment to
Japanese in the schools. By his best endeavors he smoothed
the ruffled feelings of the Japanese, obtained a "gentlemen's
agreement" to prevent immigration of Japanese laborers,
and induced the San Francisco authorities to follow a more
politic course. But because he thought that a warning was
proper, he sent the fleet on a tour of the world in which it
stopped at Japanese ports, receiving there a courteous wel-

come. This was in the spirit of one of his most-quoted utterances: "Speak softly, and carry a big stick."

As the years passed it became more and more clear that the United States was not only a world power, but one of the three or four greatest world powers. It took a prominent part in both of the Hague Conferences for the promotion of world peace. It gave moral support all over the globe to democratic principles and freedom of commercial intercourse. Despite Roosevelt's occasional untactfulness and Taft's "dollar diplomacy"—that is, the promotion of American trade and investments by diplomatic means—it made progress in winning the confidence of Latin America. Despite occasional pinpricks, it steadily grew closer to Britain and the great British Commonwealth overseas. When the First World War began, it was in a measure still isolated. Notwithstanding its isolation, it was quickly drawn into that terrible maelstrom.

CHAPTER 20

America Comes of Age

The Watershed of the Nineties

THE YEARS from roughly 1890 to the First World War constitute a watershed in American history. On the one side lies an America predominantly rural and agricultural, traditionally isolationist, still rooted in eighteenth-century optimism and eighteenth-century equalitarianism. On the other lies an America in world affairs, deeply troubled with problems that had long seemed to be the lot of the Old

World, and passing through convulsive changes in economy, society, and culture.

With the decade of the nineties a new America came on as in flood tide. That decade witnessed the passing of the frontier, the end of the Civil War generation and of the issues of Reconstruction that had long bedeviled American politics, and the rise of the New South. It saw the coming of the "new" immigration, the completion of the transcontinental railroads, the political organization of the last of the western territory, a crisis in agriculture, the large-scale organization of industry and a parallel organization of labor, the first serious recognition by government of its responsibility for the national economy, the beginnings of expansion into the Caribbean and the Pacific areas, and the advent of America as a world power.

It witnessed, too, a comparable revolution in the world of ideas, though this cannot be dated so precisely. During most of the nineteenth century Americans still lived in the afterglow of the Enlightenment. They continued to believe, most of them, in the Jeffersonian notion of an "overruling Providence which by all its dispensations proves that it delights in the happiness of man here and his greater happiness hereafter." They accepted unquestioningly the notion of progress, and of the special exemption of the American people from most of the burdens of history, and their special and manifest destiny in history.

Toward the end of the century this bright vision was clouded by new teachings of science and philosophy. The orderly universe of the Enlightenment was shattered by the impact of Darwinian biology and the new physics, and by literary and philosophical ideas coming out of Continental Europe. All of this led to an intellectual ferment, a questioning of familiar ways and a search for new formulas such as had not been known since the 1840's.

The problems which emerged in the nineties, and the new ideas and theories formulated to meet them, were to dominate the American scene for another half-century—problems of isolation and internationalism, of agricultural decline and urban growth, of the conservation of natural resources, of trusts and monopolies and the danger of class warfare, of the contrasts of progress and poverty, and of accommodating social thought to the teachings of evolution.

Religion and Philosophy

It was in 1859 that Charles Darwin published his *Origin of Species;* from that date the doctrine of evolution made its way, with varying speeds, throughout the Western world. The new dispensation found favor at once with American scientists—Asa Gray had even anticipated Darwinian findings—and among philosophers too, but it took a long time, and a protracted and bitter quarrel, before theologians would admit Darwin to their universe. It is not, however, the hostility but the ultimate acquiescence that is most astonishing. For the implications of evolution were, after all, revolutionary. It substituted natural processes and the survival of the fittest for Special Creation and Providential Direction. Even the "High Criticism" had not quite prepared the American mind for this, nor had the benevolent teachings of the Transcendentalists.

For a generation Protestant churches were wracked by the contest between "fundamentalists," who clung to the Biblical version of creation, and the "modernists," who were willing to interpret the Scriptures by the light of science. Even the secular authority entered into the struggle; a number of Southern states prohibited the teaching of evolution in the schools. Meantime enlightened theologians like Henry Ward Beecher of Brooklyn and James Freeman Clark of Boston, together with philosopher-scientists like Thomas Huxley in England and John Fiske in America, managed to reconcile religion and evolution. Evolution, they taught, was "God's way of doing things," no more beyond His power than Special Creation, and easier for mere humans to understand. Gradually the more liberal Protestant churches were won over, but until well into the twentieth century the Presbyterian and Lutheran churches were adamant in their opposition to the new teachings, while the Roman Catholic Church, growing every year in numbers and power, repudiated the whole of "modernism."

The philosophical response to the new scientific findings was "instrumentalism," or, as it came to be known in America, "pragmatism." Formulated by a group of New England thinkers, the most distinguished of whom were William James and John Dewey, it speedily conquered most of the citadels of academic philosophy and achieved a popularity denied to most philosophies. Pragmatism was less a philosophy than a way of thinking about philosophy. It regarded truth not as absolute but as relative, and William James summed it up aptly in his phrase "Damn the Absolute." Truth, as the pragmatists saw it, was not fixed and final, but still in the making. "The truth of an idea," wrote James, "is not a stagnant property inherent in it. Truth *happens* to an idea. It becomes true, it is made true by events." The best test of truth was to be found in its consequences, for—it is James again—"the ultimate test of what a truth means is the conduct it dictates or inspires."

This meant that the emphasis of pragmatism was everywhere on evolution, growth, and change. The pragmatists accepted the fullest implications of organic evolution, and assumed that the social organism was as much subject to the evolutionary processes as the physical. "Damn the Absolute" therefore applied not only to the world of formal philosophy, but also to the world of law, politics, economics, social thought, art and aesthetics, and even morals. This new way of looking at philosophy, and at the whole social order, quickly worked a revolution in American thought. It carried with it an irreversible shift from the deductive to the inductive, from the intuitive to the experimental, from principle to practice, and from form to function.

Social Thought

THIS REVOLUTION can be observed in every department of social thought. Educators, under the leadership of John Dewey, embraced what came to be called "progressive education," which meant a shift from the notion of the child as object to the child as subject, and from learning by "heart" to learning by hand—that is, by doing. Lawyers and jurisprudents like Louis Brandeis and Justice Holmes ceased to regard the law as "a brooding omniscience in the sky," rejected legal absolutes, looked with scepticism on the tyranny of precedents, and concluded that law was a creation of society and that its purpose was to serve the needs of society. Political scientists like Woodrow Wilson and Walter Lippmann abandoned such abstractions as Sovereignty, the State, or Natural Law, and turned their attention instead to parties and administration and public opinion. They concluded, with Wilson, that

Government is not a machine, but a living thing. It falls not under the theory of the universe, but under the theory of organic life. It is accountable to Darwin, not to Newton. . . . Government is not a body of blind forces, it is a body of men. Living political constitutions must be Darwinian in structure and in practice.

Economists similarly rejected the traditional laws to which generations past had subscribed—the law of supply and demand, for example—and under the leadership of scholars like Thorstein Veblen and John R. Commons, studied instead the actual operation of economic institutions, practices, and malpractices. Sociologists, the most distinguished of whom was doubtless the scientist-civil servant Lester Ward, broke with the widely popular doctrines of "Social Darwinism"—doctrines which seemed to teach that man was the helpless creature of his environment—and taught instead that man was in command of the environment and could use political and legal instruments to change it.

We are told [said Ward] to let things alone, and allow nature to takes its course. But is not civilization itself, with all it has accomplished, the result of man *not* letting things alone, and of his *not* letting nature take its course? . . . Every implement or utensil, every mechanical device . . . is a triumph of mind over the physical forces of nature in ceaseless and aimless competition. All human institutions—religion, government, law, marriage, custom—together with innumerable other modes of regulating industrial and commercial life, are only so many ways of meeting and checkmating the principle of competition.

Literature

EMERSON had pronounced a declaration of intellectual independence as early as the 1830's, but a distinctive American literature was long in coming. We can date an American literature, with some confidence, from Whitman's *Leaves of*

Grass of 1855, and with ever greater confidence from Mark Twain's *Innocents Abroad* of 1869. The first to exploit the possibilities of the American vernacular, to understand the character of the common man—and boy—north and south and west, to give expression to an authentic American humor, Mark Twain was authentically and indisputably American. "Emerson, Longfellow, Lowell, Holmes, I knew them all, and all the rest of the sages, poets, seers, critics, humorists," wrote William Dean Howells, "but Mark Twain was sole, incomparable, the Lincoln of our literature." Much of his writing was autobiographical. *Roughing It* described his experiences as secretary to the Territorial Government of Nevada during the war years; *Life on the Mississippi* was an account of his experiences as a pilot learning the great river and the country that it traversed, and the society that lived on its boats or along its banks. In 1884 came the greatest of his achievements, *Huckleberry Finn;* all modern literature comes from *Huckleberry Finn,* said Ernest Hemingway, and the aphorism is more nearly true than most. It was, with the possible exception of *Moby Dick,* the first major novel so unmistakably American that it could not have been written elsewhere.

The same "valley of democracy" that produced Mark Twain produced his friend and associate William Dean Howells, the most versatile and representative of all American men of letters. In some forty novels, thirty plays, a dozen books of criticism and biography, and hundreds of essays and reviews in leading journals, Howells provided the most comprehensive picture of middle-class American society to be found in the whole of our literature. Probably no other modern novelist except Balzac ever made so elaborate and so faithful a report on his society as did this gentle Ohioan transplanted first to Boston and then to New York. He drew genre pictures of the New England countryside, the best of all portraits of the "self-made" businessman, the extravagant life of the Ohio frontier, the rough and tumble life and work in New York City, the proprieties of the suburbs, and the clash of cultures in European resorts. "Stroke by stroke and book by book," Henry James wrote to him, "your work was to become for our whole democratic light and shade and give and take, in the highest degree documentary." Howells was not only one of the most representative American novelists; he was, too, at the same time, the leading American literary critic. He edited the great *Atlantic Monthly*, introduced Ibsen, Zola, and Turgenev to American audiences, discovered and sponsored younger writers like Stephen Crane and Frank Norris.

The third of the major novelists who emerged during the seventies and reached maturity in these transition years was Henry James, brother of the philosopher William James. Where Mark Twain wrote of the life of the great river, of the mining camps and rundown plantations, and Howells of middle-class America, Henry James took for his theme the sophisticated interrelationships of American and European society. The best of his novels—*The Portrait of a Lady, The American, The Ambassadors, The Wings of the Dove*—explore the themes of clashing standards of manners and morals; very often they are cast into a pattern of New World innocence and Old World corruption. Of all American novelists between Hawthorne and Faulkner, James was most completely preoccupied with moral problems. Because James wrote of characters and subjects alien to the average American, and in a style intricate and sophisticated, he achieved little popularity in his own lifetime; since his death, in 1916, he has been elaborately rediscovered and is now acknowledged to be one of the greatest American men of letters.

Mark Twain, Howells, and James came to maturity before the full impact of the Darwinian philosophy made itself felt. It was the next generation that responded almost convulsively to that philosophy, or, perhaps, to those European literary currents of naturalism and Freudianism which in turn owed so much to that philosophy. That response could be read in the naturalistic novels of Jack London, Frank Norris, and Stephen Crane, in the stories of agrarian revolt by Hamlin Garland, in such Freudian poems and stories as Edgar Lee Masters' *Spoon River Anthology* or Sherwood Anderson's once-famous *Winesburg, Ohio*. It was perhaps Theodore Dreiser who responded most sensitively to these new currents of thought, and to others, like Marxism, as well. In a long series of great sprawling novels—*Sister Carrie, The Titan, the Financier, An American Tragedy*—Dreiser interwove the themes of the survival of the fittest, Freudian psychology, the turbulent life of the great city, and the fierce struggles of the robber barons of business and finance.

For a long time the story of American poetry could be

told pretty much in terms of Walt Whitman, who went from strength to strength during the war and postwar years. But Whitman, even in later poems like "By Blue Ontario's Shore," "Thou Mother with Thy Equal Brood," and "Passage to India," remained rooted in Emersonian idealism. The new poets who came to maturity in the nineties and the early years of the new century reflected, as faithfully as the novelists, the impact of Darwinism and Freudianism. Most distinguished of them was E. A. Robinson; like Hardy and Francis Thompson in England, he was conscious of man's tragic fate and of the obligation to meet it with fortitude, and to wrest some sense of spiritual victory from physical defeat. He presented this view of life in a series of shorter poems laid in an imaginary (but very real) Tilbury Town, and later in the great Arthurian trilogy—*Merlin, Lancelot,* and *Tristram*—which can bear comparison with any other poetic celebration of that theme. The dramatist and poet William Vaughn Moody —best remembered for his lyrical "Gloucester Moors" and for his poems of protest against the Philippine War—shared Robinson's philosophy, as did so many of the younger poets who came to maturity in the second decade of the new century.

That was the real poetic renaissance—a flowering such as had not been known since New England's golden day. "The fiddles are tuning up all over America," wrote John Butler Yeats, and so they were—but particularly in the Middle West. There was Carl Sandburg, a young Swedish-American giant, who had discovered the poetry of the city, the stockyards, the factory, and the mine and who responded to it all with a Whitmanesque "The People, Yes." There was Edgar Lee Masters, whose *Spoon River* was a kind of Freudian Greek anthology. There was Vachel Lindsay, a minstrel who wrote poems to be sung, and whose "Chinese Nightingale," "General William Booth Enters into Heaven," and "The Congo," added a new dimension to our poetry. The Missouri-born T. S. Eliot and the Idaho-born Ezra Pound both achieved world fame as expatriates. There were the lyric poets like Edna St. Vincent Millay and the exquisite Elinor Wylie, who wrote perhaps the most moving love sonnets in American literature. And with the appearance in 1913 of *A Boy's Will,* the foremost poet of the new generation made his bow: Robert Frost. Classicist and modernist, traditionalist and innovator, Frost defies easy definition or classification. He belonged to no school, participated in no movement, but went his way quietly, perfecting a style deceptively simple, growing each year in moral strength and philosophical depth. No American poet since Longfellow was so widely read, or so deeply loved.

The Arts

"By the sixties," writes critic Lewis Mumford, "architectural anarchy had reached a point at which disorder had resulted almost in physical brutality and ugliness conducted a constant assault and battery wherever one turned one's eyes." Architecture continued rootless and derivative until the eve of the twentieth century, one Old World style succeeding—or merging with—another in bewildering confusion. Jefferson and Latrobe had popularized the Greek Revival, which, in the forties and fifties, gave way to the "Italian villa" style and then to various forms of Gothic. Henry H. Richardson introduced the Romanesque, which was almost ludicrously unsuited to the American scene, but in Trinity Church in Boston and the Marshall Field warehouse in Chicago he provided examples that had both distinction and integrity. Richard Hunt returned from Paris with a passion for the French Renaissance; the favorite architect of the new rich, he built palatial palaces modeled on French châteaux or city houses that resembled the *hôtels de ville* of Paris and Bordeaux. In 1892 Hunt and his associates chose the classical style of architecture for the Columbian Exposition at Chicago, and enlisted the ablest artists in the country to join in the classical revival: Louis Sullivan, Stanford White, Daniel Burnham, and, as landscape artist, Frederick Law Olmsted, who had laid out Central Park in New York City. It was the most beautiful exposition of modern times, but its beauty was almost wholly derivative. As one of the architects said to young Frank Lloyd Wright: "The American people have seen the Classics on a grand scale for the first time; I can see all America constructed along the lines of the Fair, in noble, dignified, classic style." Soon it was. Washington adopted the classical as the official style for public buildings, and classicism spread over the country, to colleges, libraries, railroad stations, and banks.

A distinctively American architecture began with Frank Lloyd Wright, who had early taken to heart the admonition that form should follow function, and who thought of buildings not as separate architectural entities but as parts of an organic whole which included the land, the community, and the society. In a very real way the houses of colonial New England and some of the Southern plantations had been functional, but Wright was the first architect to make functionalism the authoritative principle for public as well as for domestic building. As early as 1906 he built the Unity Temple in Oak Park, Illinois, the first of those churches which did so much to revolutionize ecclesiastical architecture in America. Thereafter he turned his genius to such miscellaneous structures as prairie houses, schools, office buildings, and factories, among them the famous Larkin Building in Buffalo and the Johnson Wax Works in Racine, Wisconsin. The most original of all American architects, Wright was, too, the most philosophical, the one most deeply and continually concerned with the social implications of his craft.

American painting, too, long remained dependent on French and Italian inspiration, but gradually in the postwar years a group of painters emerged whose style was authentically American. The Civil War produced the first and long the most distinguished of these: Winslow Homer. Homer had been sent to the front by *Harper's Weekly* to do sketches of camp life and battles, and he did these with a skill which still stirs our imagination. After the war he turned to genre painting, and in such pictures as "Morning Bell," "Snap the Whip," and "The Carnival," he lifted that art to its highest levels. As with Whitman, his middle and late years were his most creative. In the eighties he took up residence on the Maine coast, and there painted the sea and the wilderness; "The Undertow," "Eight Bells," "Gulf Stream," had a vigor and an originality heretofore unknown in American painting.

Homer's great contemporary Thomas Eakins was as fascinated by character as Homer was by nature, and his interest in character was as catholic and as democratic as that of Whitman, whose portrait he painted. Like the Dutch painters of the seventeenth century, he found nothing foreign to his brush: young men swimming or rowing, surgeons operating, professors lecturing, singers on the concert stage, scientists in their laboratory, prizefighters in the ring. "I never knew but one artist, and that's Tom Eakins, who could resist the temptation to see what they thought ought to be rather than what is," said Walt Whitman.

At the turn of the century came a school of realists who were the artistic equivalents of Stephen Crane and Theodore Dreiser—men like Robert Henri, John Sloan, George Luks, and George Bellows. They were, for the most part, disciples of Eakins; they painted life where they found it—children playing under the "El," girls drying their hair on the roof of a tenement, the habitués of McSorley's bar, the Staten Island ferry. Known derisively—and then affectionately—as the Ash-Can School, they were the American equivalents of Toulouse-Lautrec and Edvard Munch.

The most distinguished of American painters preferred to live and work abroad. James McNeill Whistler had led the way even before the Civil War; in the seventies he settled in London and there painted those wonderful "Nocturnes" and "Symphonies" that brought him first contumely and then world fame. Another expatriate was John Singer Sargent, the most dazzling technician and the most fashionable portrait painter of his generation; to be painted by Sargent became the equivalent of wearing a decoration! A third expatriate, the wealthy Mary Cassatt of Philadelphia, was the only American to be accepted by the Impressionists as one of them. A disciple of Degas, friend and patron of Manet and others, she is remembered for her exquisite paintings of children, her early experiments with Japanese techniques, and for her imaginative patronage of the Impressionists at a time when they were generally looked upon with indifference.

Education

THE FOUNDING FATHERS, it will be remembered, assumed that the democratic experiment could not possibly succeed without an enlightened electorate. From the first, therefore, education became something of an American religion and—with such holidays as occur even in religion—remained that to our own day. The Civil War retarded education in the South, but greatly stimulated it in other parts of the country.

The stimulus came particularly in the realm of higher education. First, the Morrill Land-Grant Act of 1862 set aside 30,000 acres of land for each Congressman for the support of the "agricultural and mechanical" arts, and under its enlightened provisions land-grant colleges were set up in every state of the Union. Such affluent institutions as Cornell, Massachusetts Institute of Technology, Purdue, and Michigan State owe their early support to this law. Second, the Reconstruction years saw the creation of the first real universities in America: Harvard, made over from a college to a university by Charles W. Eliot, in 1869; Cornell University, founded by Ezra Cornell and guided by the distinguished scholar-statesman Andrew D. White in 1868; and the Johns Hopkins University, an entirely new foundation dedicated to graduate and professional work, opened in Baltimore in 1876. Thereafter came other new foundations: Clark University in Massachusetts, the Leland Stanford University in distant California, the University of Chicago, founded and munificently endowed by John D. Rockefeller in 1892.

Three developments in higher education during the half-century after Appomattox are of lasting interest. First was the rapid growth of technological and professional education to meet the urgent demands of a complex industrial and urban society—new schools of technology, engineering, architecture, law, and medicine. Second was the provision for graduate study such as had long existed in France and Germany: the reformed Harvard and the new Johns Hopkins quickly took the lead in this field, but the state universities did not lag far behind. Third was more adequate provision for the education of women, the establishment of new women's colleges such as Vassar, Wellesley, and Smith, and the adoption of co-education in all the new state universities outside the South and in many of the private institutions as well. At the same time newly established schools like Howard University in the nation's capital, Fiske University in Nashville, and Hampton Institute in Virginia undertook to provide college and professional training for Negroes.

These developments were made possible in part by the emergence in this generation of the most remarkable group of educational statesmen in our history: Andrew Dickson White of Cornell, who conceived the idea of a university where any student could study any subject; Charles W. Eliot, who transformed Harvard from a college to a university, introduced the elective system, and raised standards in all the professional schools; Daniel Coit Gilman, who planned and guided the destinies of the new Johns Hopkins; James B. Angell of Michigan, who made that school the model of state universities; Charles Van Hise, who was responsible for the "Wisconsin idea" of integrating the university with the commonwealth; William Rainey Harper, who overnight made the new University of Chicago one of the leading centers of learning in the world; and Booker T. Washington, the great Negro leader, who in 1882 founded the Tuskegee Institute.

Notwithstanding the pioneer work of Horace Mann and Henry Barnard in the generation before the Civil War, public education stagnated. As late as 1870, while 7 million pupils were formally enrolled in public schools, average attendance was only 4 million and the average number of days of schooling 78; a mere 80,000 students were to be found in the high schools. Not until the beginning of the twentieth century did the situation materially improve. By 1920 some 21 million boys and girls were attending elementary schools and over 2 million were in the high schools.

The most important development was the general acceptance of those reforms which came to be called—somewhat misleadingly—progressive education. This new philosophy of education owed something to the teachings of eighteenth- and nineteenth-century German educators, and more to the new philosophy and psychology associated with William James. It was the pragmatist philosopher John Dewey who formulated the new body of thought in one of the most famous of all educational tracts, *School and Society* (1899), and who, from his professional chair at the University of Chicago and then at Columbia University, sent out hundreds of ardent disciples who spread the new educational gospel. Progressive education shifted the emphasis from teaching to learning, from subject matter to the training of the child, and from education as a "preparation for life" to education as an essential part of life itself. Within a generation or so progressive education had conquered the country; after the Second World War it fell into some disrepute, but that was chiefly because—as with so many successful philosophies—its teachings had come to be accepted as the common sense of the matter.

CHAPTER 21

Woodrow Wilson and the World War

Woodrow Wilson

WOODROW WILSON was in many respects the most remarkable figure in American politics since Jefferson. A scholar and an intellectual, unaccustomed to the hurly-burly of public life, he was nevertheless astute, hardheaded, and resourceful. A visionary and an idealist, he was at the same time the most thoroughly realistic and adroit political leader since Lincoln. He was a moralist in politics and in international affairs, and in him the spirit of his Covenanter ancestors was reborn. With an old-fashioned courtliness went a hot-tempered belligerence, with passionate devotion to principle a stubborn fierceness in maintaining it. His speeches had none of the homely quality of Bryan's or the forthright vigor of Roosevelt's, but they had a soaring eloquence and a poetic beauty unmatched since Lincoln. He was a student of politics, had written several capital books on government, and had his own well-matured notions of the nature of the presidential office, of the party system, and of the place of the United States in the world of nations, and he was prepared to put these notions into effect. "Clean, strong, high-minded and cold-blooded," as Secretary Lane observed, he was also intellectually arrogant, uncompromising, and, when crossed, resentful. Impersonal in his relations, he attracted men to him as to an abstract principle, and he never permitted personal affection to interfere with his policies or forgave a friend who failed to measure up to his high standards.

Most of Wilson's life had been spent in academic cloisters, as professor of politics and president of Princeton University. In 1910 the Democratic bosses of New Jersey put him forward as gubernatorial window dressing, and he took over the whole political shop. Within two years he had driven the bosses from the political temples and transformed New Jersey from one of the rotten boroughs of American politics into a model commonwealth, and in the process he had perfected many of the techniques he was later to use with such skill—the audacious boldness, the disarming candor, the ostentatious idealism, the insistence upon his own position as party leader, the appeal over the heads of politicians to the people themselves, and the strategy of swift and relentless attack. It was Wilson's spectacular achievement in New Jersey that made him a national figure, brought him the support of men like Bryan, and gave him the presidential nomination; it was his own transparent sincerity and his matchless campaign eloquence that carried him to victory over Roosevelt.

Wilson's inaugural address was at once a challenge and a promise. "No one can mistake," he said, "the purpose for which the nation now seeks to use the Democratic party. It seeks to use it to interpret a change in its own plans and point of view." Then followed a program of constructive reform to achieve the New Freedom, a program at once bold and comprehensive. "We have itemized," said Wilson, "the things that ought to be altered," and he mentioned "a tariff which makes the government a facile instrument in the hands of private interests," a banking and currency system perfectly adapted to "concentrating cash and restricting credits," an industrial system which "restricts the liberties and limits the opportunities of labor," an agricultural economy inefficient and neglected, and the exploitation of natural resources for private gain. On its positive side the government was to be "put at the service of humanity"—in safeguarding the health and the welfare of women and children and of the underprivileged.

These reforms were to be achieved deliberately and efficiently. Yet the process of reform was "no cool process of mere science."

The nation has been deeply stirred, stirred by a solemn passion, stirred by the knowledge of wrong, of ideals lost, of government too often debauched and made an instrument of evil. The feelings with which we face this new age of right and opportunity sweep across our heartstrings like some air out of God's own presence where justice and mercy are reconciled and the judge and the brother are one. We know our task to be no mere task of politics, but a task which shall search us through and through. . . .

The New Freedom in Action

THESE WERE LOFTY IDEALS, eloquently phrased; could this scholar, so miraculously elevated to the presidency, translate them into law? He quickly showed that he meant business. Congress was called into special session, and when it convened, Wilson, reviving an almost forgotten custom, addressed it in person. "The tariff duties must be altered," he said. "We must abolish everything that bears even the semblance of privilege." This was a dangerous issue. There had been no real break in the protective system since the Civil War; Cleveland had obtained only minor concessions from the protectionists, and the astute Roosevelt had avoided the issue altogether. Underwood of Alabama and Hull of Tennessee had their bill all ready, however, and under executive prodding the House passed it promptly enough. But when the Senate took it up, the lobbyists swarmed over the capital like harpies, and observers predicted a repetition of the 1890 fiasco, when a proposed tariff reform emerged from Congress so mutilated that Cleveland denounced it as smacking of "party perfidy and party dishonor" and refused to put his name to it. Then in a public letter Wilson lashed out at the lobby. "It is of serious interest to the country," he said, "that the people at large should have no lobby . . . while great bodies of astute men seek to create an artificial opinion and to overcome the interests of the public for their private profit." The reprimand was effective, and six months after he took office Wilson had the satisfaction of signing a tariff bill which faithfully reflected platform promises and campaign pledges by effecting the first genuine downward revision in over fifty years.

The country sat up and took notice: here was an executive who meant what he said and did what he proposed. Wilson did not give his party pause; even while Congress was wrestling with the tariff schedules, he reminded it of his inaugural promise to reform "a banking and currency system based upon the necessity of the government to sell its bonds fifty years ago and perfectly adapted to concentrating cash and restricting credits." This issue, like the tariff, was packed with political dynamite. The nation had long suffered from an inflexible credit and currency system; almost everyone agreed on the diagnosis, but few on the cure. During the Roosevelt administration there had been stopgap legislation permitting the national banks to issue emergency currency, and a Monetary Commission had submitted an elaborate series of reports on the banking practices of other nations. But a thorough overhauling of the banking system was long overdue. The bankers rallied to write a law which would continue them in control; Bryan, who had long argued that the money question was the paramount issue, was determined that the government should control credit. Wilson, who knew little about the technical aspects of banking but who had not studied in vain the history of the first and second Banks of the United States and the later experiment of the independent-treasury system, sided with Bryan. "Control," he said, "must be public, not private, must be vested in the government itself, so that the banks may be the instruments, not the masters of business and of individual enterprise and initiative." The Federal Reserve Act which emerged from prolonged debate fulfilled these requirements. It decentralized the banking system, affording better banking facilities to the neglected South and West, and provided in Federal reserve notes an elastic currency under government control. The Federal Reserve System came just in the nick of time; without it, the government could scarcely have weathered the crisis of the World War.

A third major legislative achievement of the new administration was in the regulation of trusts. The Sherman Act had been more effective against labor than against great industrial combinations, and recent investigations had revealed that the movement toward concentration of control in industry, transportation, and banking was going on apace. As soon as tariff and banking legislation was out of the way, Wilson moved to implement his campaign pledges. The Clayton Antitrust Act of 1914 carefully defined a number of malpractices, prohibited discriminations in price which might tend to create monopolies, forbade the tying together of large corporations by "interlocking directorates," and made corporation directors personally liable for infractions of the antitrust laws. A gesture—perhaps an intention—to exempt labor from the operation of the act was largely frustrated by the courts. At the same time a Federal Trade Commission was set up to investigate business operations, hear complaints of unfair methods, and stop harmful practices by issuing "cease and desist" orders.

The farmers and labor were not forgotten. A Federal Farm Loan Act made credit available to farmers at low rates of interest, and a Warehouse Act, authorizing loans on the security of staple crops, gave substantial effect to the old subtreasury scheme of the Populists. The La Follette Seamen's Act of 1915 emancipated the hard-driven common seamen from the tyranny under which they had long suffered, and the Adamson Act of the following year established an eight-hour day for railroad labor. Two acts designed to end the scandal of child labor in industry got through the Congress only to be nullified by the Supreme Court on the ground that Congress lacked power to regulate labor either under the taxing or under the commerce power. Twenty-two years later the Court, in a rare act of public penance, acknowledged that it had gone astray in the earlier decision, and permitted Congress to put an end to child labor.

Thus in three years Wilson had pushed through more important legislation than any President since Lincoln. He had revealed unsuspected possibilities in the executive leadership of Congress and presidential leadership of party. He had proved that democracy could function, swiftly and effectively, in a crisis.

A Democratic Foreign Policy

WILSON'S FOREIGN POLICY departed as sharply from that of his predecessor as did his domestic. Roosevelt had cheerfully wielded the "big stick" in foreign affairs, Taft had encouraged what came to be known as "dollar diplomacy."

These policies had unquestionably brought the United States a greater measure of influence in world affairs, but at the cost of antagonizing the nations of Latin America and of imperiling our own welfare by involving us in fortuitous diplomatic and business adventures in which we had no genuine interest. One of Wilson's first official acts was to withdraw official approval from a proposed bankers' loan to China because he "did not approve the conditions of the loan or the implications of responsibility." That same week he announced his purpose "to cultivate the friendship and deserve the confidence" of the Latin American republics, and a short time later, in his Mobile address, gave a specific repudiation of dollar diplomacy and a promise that the United States would never again seek territory by conquest. Circumstances were to involve the United States in the affairs of several of the Caribbean and Central American republics, but throughout his administration Wilson steadfastly refused to make intervention an excuse for exploitation.

The difficulties of the Wilsonian policy were amply illustrated by relations with Mexico. For thirty-five years that unhappy land had groaned under the tyrannical rule of Porfirio Diaz, who reduced his own people to peonage while he sold out his country to foreign mining and business interests. In 1911 the middle classes and peons rose in revolt, drove Diaz out, and placed a liberal, Francisco Madero, in the presidency. It looked like the dawn of a new day for Mexico, but within two years a counterrevolutionary movement under the leadership of Victoriano Huerta overthrew and assassinated Madero. The foreign oil, railroad, mining, and land-owning interests, which saw a return of the fat days of Diaz, were jubilant, and most of the great powers hastened to recognize the new President. But not Wilson. He felt that to recognize Huerta would be to condone murder, and he was unmoved by the importunities of American businessmen who were interested primarily in their own profits. "We hold," he said, anticipating the position he was to take later in a greater crisis, "that just government rests always upon the consent of the governed, and that there can be no freedom without order based upon law and upon public conscience and approval." This policy of basing recognition upon moral considerations was criticized then and later as a departure from correct practice and the dictates of expediency. As the

German Emperor remarked, "Morality is all right, but what about dividends?" But Wilson realized, as did Franklin D. Roosevelt a generation later, how fatal were the consequences that might follow an acquiescence in lawlessness or a recognition of the fruits of violence. He did not perhaps fully appreciate the difficulties of making recognition dependent upon judgment of moral differences between opposing parties, always delicate and complex, and usually illusive.

Wilson not only refused recognition to the bloody-handed Huerta; he brought Britain around to support his policy— a support won through timely concessions `on the Panama Canal tolls question. Relations with Mexico, however, rapidly worsened, and when Huerta arrested some American sailors at Tampico, Wilson hastily landed marines at Vera Cruz. War appeared inevitable, but Wilson had no intention of permitting the situation to get out of hand, and by drawing a distinction between the Mexican people—whom he wished to befriend—and the Mexican government—which he was determined to destroy—succeeded in restraining the war clamor at home while maneuvering Huerta into an untenable position. Then he seized the opportunity of the Mexican crisis to dramatize his policy of treating the Latin American republics as equals by invoking the aid of Argentina, Brazil, and Chile in settling the dispute. When these sided with the United States, Huerta was forced to flee the country, and Carranza, leader of the constitutionalists, came into power. Even after that, difficulties continued, and when the Mexican bandit chief Pancho Villa raided Columbus, New Mexico, Wilson sent an expeditionary force under General Pershing to punish him. Carranza resented the invasion, and American chauvinists clamored for war, but peace was maintained and Mexico allowed to work out her own salvation. The policy of "watchful waiting," denounced as pusillanimous, had succeeded in its dual object of aiding Mexico and gaining the confidence of Latin American republics.

Elsewhere in the Caribbean, however, Wilsonian policies failed to square with principles. On the whole there was very little to choose between Wilson's conduct toward Nicaragua, Santo Domingo, and Haiti and that of the previous administrations. The treaty which Bryan negotiated with Nicaragua so severely curtailed the sovereignty of that Latin country that it was formally denounced by the Central American Court of Justice. Bryan's minister to Santo Domingo acted as if he were governor-general over that country; and the marines who landed in Haiti and exacted a heavy toll of Haitian lives were not ultimately to depart until 1930.

In two other fields the Wilson administration revealed its interest in the maintenance of peace and the sanctity of treaty agreements. Bryan, who now presided over the State Department, had long been convinced that all international disputes were susceptible to arbitration, and with Wilson's blessings he drew up and negotiated "cooling-off" treaties with foreign nations. These provided for arbitration and conciliation of all issues—not excepting those involving national honor—and for the suspension of all war preparation for a "cooling-off" period of one year. Thirty such treaties were negotiated, twenty-two went into effect; Germany conspicuously refused to accept one. And in 1915, when Japan, already headlong on that policy of ruthlessness which was eventually to lead to war with the United States, presented her infamous "twenty-one demands" to China, the State Department protested that these constituted a flagrant violation of the Open Door and of international law.

The World War and Neutrality

IT WAS EUROPE that presented the most serious threat to American peace. On June 28, a Serbian patriot fired a shot whose echoes reverberated around the world; within five weeks all Europe was locked in the greatest war of modern times. The American reaction was one of incredulity and bewilderment. When President Wilson formally proclaimed American neutrality, he spoke for a unanimous nation; even when he counseled neutrality in thought as well as in action he expressed the attitude of the majority of Americans.

Yet Americans could no more be indifferent to the struggle of 1914 than they could to the struggle of 1939, and neutrality, whether of mind or of governmental policy, proved in the end impossible. American feeling was from the beginning violently enlisted. The great majority of the people hoped that Britain and France and Belgium would win. A hundred ties of culture, tradition, common institutions, and common outlook existed with the British people; memory of

French aid in the Revolution and admiration for the gallant resistance of the French and Belgian peoples were only less potent. Comparatively small elements, chiefly German-Americans who responded to the call of blood, and Irish-Americans who had an inherited hatred of Britain, sympathized with the Central Powers. German policy in the Pacific, in China, in the Caribbean, the ruthless acts of German militarists and the arrogance of German intellectuals and statesmen, had alienated Americans long before the war, and the unprovoked invasion of Belgium confirmed their worst suspicions of Germany. It was clear, too, that the Germans stood for absolutist ideas in government and society, and that if they dominated Europe they would be certain to come into conflict, sooner or later, with democratic America.

These two considerations—sympathy for the Allies, fear of the consequences of German victory—were in the end decisive in controlling American policy. Economic considerations re-enforced sentimental and political ones. The American people loaned huge sums of money to Britain and France. American industry rapidly geared itself to Anglo-French war needs, supplying enormous quantities of guns, shells, high explosives, and other materials, and reaping heavy profits. American banks acted as purchasing agents for the Allies, floated Allied loans, and established Allied credits in the United States. American agriculture, recovering from a sharp prewar depression, found ready and profitable markets for cotton, wheat, and pork in England and France. Trade with the Central Powers, meantime, was negligible, and the British blockade effectively controlled trade with neutrals as well.

Yet it was not these economic considerations that persuaded Wilson and the American people of the necessity of war, but rather the German policy of "frightfulness." Submarines were used to sink merchant ships, and they could not save the lives of crew or passengers. When the British vessel Lusitania was sent to the bottom in 1915 with the loss of more than eleven hundred lives, 128 of them American, a wave of horror and anger swept the country. Germany promised to mend her ways, and Wilson kept the nation at peace, but those who believed that America should prepare for war increased in numbers and determination. Meantime, Wilson himself had come to see that the only way to keep the United States out of the war was to bring the war itself to an end. All through 1916 he worked ceaselessly to persuade the belligerents to state their war aims and to pave the way for the organization of the postwar world.

In the presidential election of 1916 Wilson was successful, largely because he had "kept us out of war." Yet he had given no commitments for the future, no promise to buy "peace at any price." Indeed, as early as January, 1916, he had warned the American people in words that the war lords of Germany would have done well to heed:

I know that you are depending upon me to keep this nation out of the war. So far I have done so and I pledge you my word that, God helping me, I will—if it is possible. But you have laid another duty upon me. You have bidden me see to it that nothing stains or impairs the honor of the United States, and that is a matter not within my control; that depends upon what others do, not upon what the government of the United States does.

Early in 1917 the Germans, sure that they could starve England out in six months and that American help could not become effective in that time, announced the reopening of unrestricted submarine warfare. Within a few weeks eight American vessels were sent to the bottom, and the nation was aroused by the revelation of a plot to involve the United States in a war with Mexico and Japan. The preservation of both honor and peace had become, it appeared, "an impossible and contradictory thing," and on April 2, Wilson appeared before the Congress and asked for a declaration of a state of war:

It is a fearful thing to lead this great peaceful people into war, into the most terrible and disastrous of all wars, civilization itself seeming to be in the balance. But the right is more precious than peace, and we shall fight for the things which we have always carried nearest our hearts,—for democracy, for the right of those who submit to authority to have a voice in their own Governments, for the rights and liberties of small nations, for a universal dominion of right by such a concert of free peoples as shall bring peace and safety to all nations, and make the world itself at last free. To such a task we can dedicate our lives and our fortunes, everything that we are and everything that we have, with the

pride of those who know that the day has come when America
is privileged to spend her blood and her might for the principles
that gave her birth and happiness and the peace which she has
treasured. God helping her, she can do no other.

On Good Friday, April 6, 1917, the United States went to
war.

War

"FORCE, force to the uttermost, force without stint or limit,"
President Wilson had promised, and the nation hastened to
fulfill this promise. In no previous war had the government
revealed greater intelligence or efficiency nor the American
people more energy, resourcefulness, and inventive genius.
Wilson proved one of the greatest of war Presidents, controlling every aspect of the war effort, maintaining morale at
home and abroad, never losing sight of the ultimate objectives
for which the nation was fighting. He was ably assisted by
his War Secretary, Newton D. Baker, his Secretary of the
Treasury, William McAdoo, and by Bernard Baruch, chairman of the War Industries Board. The government had to take
steps far more drastic than any contemplated in any previous
war, and it did so with dispatch and energy. It became dictator over industry, labor, and agriculture. It took over the
railroads and the telegraph lines. Food was needed, and farm
production was increased by one fourth; fuel was needed,
and coal production was raised by two fifths. By loans and
taxes the government raised some thirty-six billion dollars,
lending ten to its Allies and spending the rest at home. Above
all, the government concentrated on winning the battle of
the Atlantic—which, in the spring and summer of 1917, appeared all but lost. By seizing interned German ships, com-
mandeering neutral and taking over private shipping, launching a colossal shipbuilding program—more than three million
tons in a single year—and by heroic anti-submarine measures,
the battle was won.

Conscription had been voted early, and before the war
was over, the registration of some twenty-five million men
suggested something of the immense man-power resources
of this Western democracy. But could the United States

train and equip an army and ship it to France in time to
stem the tide of German advance? That was the great question of 1917 and 1918.

The first American contingent landed in France in June,
1917—hurried over for its effect on morale rather than for
military purposes. On July 4, the little army paraded down
the Champs Élysées, the red, white, and blue fluttering in the
breeze. Brand Whitlock described the scene:

I heard the band; it was playing *Marching Through Georgia*. I
could not withstand that! And so downstairs, and out into the
Rue de Rivoli bareheaded. There was the crowd sweeping along
the street below the great iron fence of the Tuileries, from curb
to curb, with no order, men, women, children, trotting along,
hot, excited, trying to keep up with the slender column of our
khaki-clad regulars, who marched briskly along. French soldiers
in their light blue trotted beside them, as closely as they could
get, looking at them with almost childish interest and wonder,
as boys trot hurrying beside a circus parade. Our soldiers were
covered with flowers—and always the steady roar of the crowd
and now and then cries of *Vive l'Amérique.*

But this was merely a token force; the real American army
was still in the training camps back in the United States.
It was desperately needed, for in 1917 the war had taken
a turn for the worse. In October the Italian army was
smashed at Caporetto, and the Allies had to hurry reinforcements to stem the Austrian advance. A month later the
Russians, already torn by revolution, caved in and sued for
peace. Forty new German divisions, drawn from the Russian and Balkan fronts, were hurried to France. By the
spring of 1918 the Germans had clear numerical superiority
in the West and girded themselves for the knockout blow
against the decimated and weary armies of Britain and
France. In March, 1918, came the first major offensive;
within a week the Germans had smashed through the British
Fifth Army, capturing ninety thousand prisoners and immense stores. In April came another great drive, and General Haig issued his memorable appeal: "With our backs to
the wall, and believing in the justice of our cause, each one
of us must fight on to the end." A third offensive was launched
in June, and, with the Germans on the right bank of the

Marne, the Allies placed Marshal Foch in supreme command and advised President Wilson that "there is great danger of the war being lost unless the numerical inferiority of the Allies can be remedied as rapidly as possible by the advent of American troops."

Already the race with time had begun. The United States government girded itself for a Herculean effort. Shipping was given priority over everything, and one massive convoy after another sailed from American ports, laden with khaki-clad doughboys. In March, 80,000 were shipped overseas; in April, 118,000; in May, almost 250,000. By October the American Army in France numbered over one and three-quarter million soldiers.

They came just in the nick of time. First at Mondidier and Cantigny and then at Belleau Wood, they proved their mettle, and the German Command, which had discounted American help, reluctantly admitted that "the American soldier proves himself brave, strong, and skillful. Casualties do not daunt him." But the great crisis was still ahead. At midnight of July 14, the Germans launched their long-awaited offensive on the Marne, designed to crack the last Allied line and open the path to Paris, only fifty miles away. They thundered across the Marne, everywhere successful except where they ran into fresh American divisions. "Right here on the Marne," wrote the German Chief of Staff, Walther Reinhardt, "we well-nigh reached the objectives prescribed for our shock divisions. . . . Especially all divisions of the Seventh Army achieved brilliant initial successes, with the exception of the one division on our right wing. This encountered American units. Here only did the Seventh Army . . . confront serious difficulties. It met with the unexpectedly stubborn and active resistance of fresh American troops. While the rest of the divisions . . . succeeded in gaining ground and tremendous booty it proved impossible for us to move the right apex of our line, to the south of the Marne, into a position advantageous for the development of the ensuing fight. The check we thus received was one result of the stupendous fighting between our 10th Division of infantry and the American troops." And he added ruefully, "The Americans appear inexhaustible." By the eighteenth the German attack was played out, and Foch called upon the Americans to counterattack. This they did, and with spectacular success. "The tide of war," wrote General Pershing, "was definitely turned in favor of the Allies."

In September came the attack on the Saint-Mihiel salient. "The rapidity with which our divisions advanced over-whelmed the enemy," wrote General Pershing. Casualties reached seven thousand, but the Americans wiped out the salient and captured sixteen thousand prisoners to boot. And the next month an American army of over a million took a leading part in the vast Meuse-Argonne offensive, which, in the end, cracked the vaunted Hindenburg line and shattered German morale.

Meantime Wilson, by an eloquent definition of the war aims of the democracies, was doing scarcely less than the armed forces to insure victory. From the beginning he had tried to sow dissension in Germany by insisting that our fight was not with the German people but with their tyr-annous and autocratic government. He had insisted, too, that the peace terms ought not to include annexation of unwilling peoples or money payments of a punitive nature. And in a message to Congress of January, 1918, he had sub-mitted the famous Fourteen Points as the basis for a just peace. These embraced: open covenants openly arrived at; freedom of the seas in peace and in war; the removal of economic barriers between nations; the reduction of arma-ments; an impartial adjustment of colonial claims; co-opera-tion with Russia in the establishment of her own national policy with institutions of her own choosing; a readjustment of the boundaries of Europe with due attention to the prin-ciple of the self-determination of peoples; and the establish-ment of a "general association of nations" to afford "mutual guarantees of political independence and territorial integrity."

With their armies beaten back and their allies on the verge of collapse, and with fresh American troops pouring up to the front in seemingly limitless numbers, the German government saw that only an immediate peace could pre-vent the invasion of German soil. It turned therefore to Wilson and appealed to him to negotiate on the basis of the Fourteen Points. While diplomatic fencing was still under way, mutiny and revolution at home made further German resistance impossible. The Kaiser abdicated and fled, and on November 11 the war came to an end.

The League and Isolationism

THUS FAR Wilson had proved a leader of consummate skill. But as the war ended he made a succession of missteps. He appealed to the people to elect a Democratic Congress, and in resentment at this partisan act they chose Republican majorities in both chambers. He decided to go to the Peace Conference in person, thus offending many Americans who believed that the President should never leave national soil, and in doing so he ultimately lowered his prestige in Europe. He failed to place any prominent Republican—or indeed any man of first-rate ability—on his Peace Commission. And while he committed these errors of judgment, war weariness, a renewed suspicion of Europe, a sense of disillusionment, and party animosity were engulfing the country. As he sailed for France, ex-President Roosevelt, bitter and defiant, warned "our Allies and our enemies" that "Mr. Wilson has no authority whatever to speak for the American people at this time."

The treaty makers—Wilson, Lloyd George of Britain, Clemenceau of France, Orlando of Italy, and a host of lesser statesmen—met at Paris in an atmosphere of hatred, greed, and fear—hatred of the enemy, greed for colonies and reparations, fear of Bolshevism. The peace that was concluded was a dictated, not a negotiated, peace. The Treaty of Versailles fastened war guilt upon Germany, wrested from her all of her colonial possessions, provided for territorial readjustments on all of her borders, and imposed upon her heavy indemnities. Other treaties created or recognized new states which had come into existence in accordance with the Wilsonian principle of self-determination—Czechoslovakia, Yugoslavia, Poland, Finland, among others. In accepting these terms Wilson was forced to compromise on some of his Fourteen Points; he was willing to do this only because he was firmly convinced that all errors would be rectified through the machinery of the League of Nations.

For Wilson had succeeded, against the most formidable opposition, in sewing the League of Nations into the treaty arrangements. The idea of an association of nations was not a new one, and many persons from many lands had contributed to the clarification of that idea. But the League of

Nations that was ultimately established was Wilson's creation. Its function was "to promote international cooperation and to achieve international peace and security." Membership was open to all nations; control was to be lodged in a Council dominated by the Great Powers and in an Assembly in which all members were represented. The members of the League pledged themselves to "respect and preserve as against external aggression the territorial integrity and existing political independence" of all members—the famous Article Ten—to submit all disputes to arbitration, and to employ military and economic sanctions against nations resorting to war in disregard of the League. In addition, provision was made for disarmament, the government of mandated colonies, and the creation of a Permanent Court of International Justice and an International Labor Bureau.

When Wilson returned to the United States with the Versailles Treaty and the League, he found opposition widespread and fierce. Many Republican leaders—like the embittered and intensely partisan Senator Lodge—saw in the issue an opportunity to defeat the Democrats and humiliate Wilson. Personal dislike of the President swayed a number. German-Americans, Italian-Americans, and Irish-Americans all found their own reasons for denouncing the terms of peace. To some vengeful people the treaty seemed too easy upon Germany; to many liberals it seemed too harsh. A substantial number of conservative Americans feared entanglement in European quarrels and recalled that for more than a century the nation had in general kept aloof from Old World affairs.

Yet there is evidence that a majority of the people—and certainly a majority of the more enlightened groups—approved the League, and at no time did the treaty lack a majority in the Senate. Even the two thirds necessary for ratification might have been obtained had Wilson been willing to compromise on Article Ten, which extremists interpreted as a limitation on national sovereignty. But this he was unwilling to do. "Article Ten," he told a Senate committee, "seems to me to constitute the very backbone of the whole covenant. Without it the League would hardly be more than an influential debating society." But the Republican opposition was unconvinced, and Wilson took the issue to the people. As he crusaded through the West his health

gave way, and on September 25 he suffered a paralytic stroke
from which he never recovered. The great cause that he espoused was lost. In March, 1920, the Senate, by its final
vote rejecting the treaty and the League Covenant, condemned the United States for years to come to a sterile and
unheroic isolationism.

The election of 1920 swept the Republicans back into
power by an unprecedented majority, and they hastened to
make isolation a party principle. Broken in health but not
in spirit, Wilson retired to watch, with profound disillusionment, that breakdown of collective security he had predicted. He had lived, like that James Petigru whose epitaph
he so admired,

> Unawed by opinion
> Unseduced by flattery
> Undismayed by disaster

and like him

> He confronted life with antique courage,
> And Death with Christian hope.

Not until a second world war, even greater than the first,
had shaken the very foundations of the firmament were men
to recognize the validity of the principles for which he had
fought so gallantly.

CHAPTER 22

From "Normalcy" to Depression

Normalcy and Isolation

THE DEFEAT OF WILSON, the repudiation of the New Freedom and of internationalism, set the stage for the appearance of isolation and *laissez faire*, and these two forces dominated it for the next decade. The Republican party, to be sure, had not taken a clear stand on the League, but sought refuge, rather, in a masterly obfuscation of that issue. But the decisive majority which the party commanded in the 1920 elections convinced most leaders—and certainly the weak-willed President Harding—that the isolationists spoke for the people, and placed men like Senators Johnson, Borah, and Lodge in positions of strategic strength while it tended to discredit such international-minded Republicans as Hughes, Root, and Taft. Once in power the Republicans hastened to give official status to isolationism.

This was something new, both in the history of the Republican party and of the nation. Never before had the United States so cavalierly betrayed the hopes of mankind: the traditional American policy had been rather one of fulfillment of the promise of world leadership. Nor had the Republican party ever before committed itself to isolation. Grant and Seward had urged expansion into the Caribbean and the Pacific; Blaine had espoused Pan-Americanism; McKinley had led the nation to war on behalf of the Cubans and acquired new colonies in the Pacific; Theodore Roosevelt had claimed for the nation a dominant position in world power politics. The Republican tradition was one of imperialism and internationalism.

But now the party stood committed to a narrow nationalism and an evasion of responsibility comparable to that which afflicted Britain in the middle of the nineteenth century. Yet real isolation was impossible, and the United States could not remain aloof from affairs elsewhere in the world. Actually, during these years of Republican rule, the government took an active part in bringing about the solution of some of the more vexatious problems that disturbed international relations. President Harding sponsored a conference on naval disarmament—with some success. His successor, Coolidge, obtained the support of sixty-two nations to the Pact of Paris, outlawing war as an instrument of international relations. The Young Plan and the Dawes Plan for the settlement of reparations had their origins in the United States, and President Hoover took the lead in proposing a moratorium on war-debt payments. All of the Republican Presidents urged American membership in the World Court—though in vain—and all of them made tentative gestures toward co-operation with some of the work of the League of Nations.

But these gestures toward disarmament and peace were more than counterbalanced by American aloofness from the real work of the League and by the steady growth of economic nationalism. It was, indeed, in the economic realm that isolationism had most serious consequences. Fearful of foreign competition, eager for foreign markets, and infected with the notion of economic autarchy, the nation embarked upon a neomercantilistic policy fraught with danger not only to itself but also to the whole world.

As early as 1920, a Republican Congress rushed through an emergency tariff bill designed to raise a wall of protection against foreign products. In his veto message President Wilson urged common sense on this matter. "If there ever was a time when America had anything to fear from foreign competition," he said, "that time has passed. If we wish to have Europe settle her debts—governmental or commercial —we must be prepared to buy from her. Clearly this is no time for the erection of high trade barriers." But this sage advice the Republicans chose to ignore, and no sooner were they in complete control of the government than they enacted the Fordney-McCumber tariff, raising duties to unprecedented heights and effectively preventing European nations from selling America their goods. Eight years later the still recalcitrant Republican majority pushed through the Smoot-Hawley tariff, highest in American history, and, over the protest of almost every respectable economist in the country, Hoover signed it. These tariffs not only closed the American market to the products of European farms and factories but led to retaliatory tariffs which closed European markets to American goods.

This was only one aspect of the economic question: another and equally important was the financial. The war and postwar years witnessed the transformation of the United States from a debtor to a creditor nation. During the period of war and reconstruction, the government had lent some ten billion dollars to Allied and associated nations; in the twenties, private investors poured an additional ten or twelve billions into the investment markets of Europe, Asia, and Latin America. How were these debts to be serviced and, ultimately, repaid if the United States would not permit debtors to sell to them? To this pertinent question the Republican statesmen had no ready answer.

Throughout the twenties, Republican policy was conditioned by these two contradictory considerations. Toward foreign indebtedness the administration adopted an attitude of adamantine stubbornness. There were, to be sure, generous concessions on interest, but on the repayment of principal the government was firm; as President Coolidge remarked, "They hired the money, didn't they?" But as long as American tariff walls were unbreached, repayment was all but impossible. Indeed, the only way Germany was able to continue reparation payments and other countries to buy American goods was by further borrowing.

In the domestic arena, the Harding administration inaugurated the reign of "normalcy"—and Harding's idea of normalcy was a return to the good old days of Mark Hanna and McKinley. This was not, as is sometimes supposed, pure *laissez faire*, but rather a felicitous combination of two policies—one, freedom of private enterprise from governmental restraint, and the other, generous subsidies to private enterprise. Government withdrew from business, but business moved in and shaped most government policies.

On the positive side the record is impressive. The tariffs of 1922 and 1930 constituted a practical guarantee against foreign competition. The Department of Commerce, under the indefatigable Herbert Hoover, engaged actively in opening up new markets abroad and justified the boast that it was "the world's most formidable engine of foreign-trade conquest." In the domestic field the Department co-operated actively in the organization of some two hundred trade associations and cartels much like those later organized under the National Recovery Administration. "We are passing," said Hoover sententiously, "from a period of extreme individualistic action into a period of associated activities." Generous subsidies were voted to the merchant marine and to aviation companies carrying United States mail. The Treasury Department under Andrew Mellon brought about a repeal of the excess-profits tax, heavy reductions in surtaxes and normal income taxes, and a lowering of the estate taxes. The theory was that this would stimulate business, but unhappily it also stimulated the speculative craze of the late twenties.

At the same time traditional *laissez faire* was honored no less faithfully. The railroads, which the government had operated with striking success during the war, were returned to private owners, and on generous terms. A large part of the war-built merchant marine was turned over, at ridiculously low prices, to private companies. The Sherman and Clayton Antitrust Acts were practically suspended, both executive and judiciary taking the position that they were not called upon "to repeal economic laws." The most characteristic expression of *laissez faire* came in connection with proposals for government construction and operation of hydroelectric plants. In 1916 President Wilson had authorized, as a wartime measure, the construction of dams at Muscle Shoals, on the Tennessee River, to furnish power for nitrate plants. After the war the disposition of these plants and dams became a matter of prolonged and bitter controversy. Conservatives contended that they should be turned back to private owners; progressives, under the leadership of the courageous Senator George Norris of Nebraska, insisted that they be continued under government ownership and operation. In 1928 a bill calling for government operation passed the Congress, only to be vetoed by President Coolidge. A similar measure passed in 1931 was defeated by President Hoover, whose veto message perfectly expressed that philosophy of "rugged individualism" to which he and his party subscribed:

I am firmly opposed to the government entering into any business the major purpose of which is deliberate competition with our citizens. . . . It is destructive of equality of opportunity of our people; it is the negation of the ideals upon which our civilization has been based. . . . I hesitate to contemplate the future of our institutions, of our country, if the preoccupation of its officials is to be no longer the promotion of justice and equal opportunity but is devoted to barter in the markets. That is not liberalism, it is degeneration.

This concern for equality of opportunity would have come with better grace had the Harding and Coolidge administrations shown a sincere and sustained interest in the welfare of labor and farmer groups. But these administrations were interested only in the "businessman," and their conception of business was a narrow one. Neither the farmers nor the workingmen shared the piping prosperity of the twenties. There was a brief but sharp break in farm prices in 1921; by the mid-twenties a gradual decline set in and continued without interruption until the operation of the New Deal reforms became effective. Between 1920 and 1932 farm income declined from fifteen and one-half to five and one-half billion dollars. Some eight hundred million bushels of wheat, in 1920, brought about one and one-half billion dollars; a slightly smaller crop in 1932 brought less than three hundred million dollars. Thirteen million bales of cotton, in 1920, were sold for just over one billion dollars; the same cotton crop, twelve years later, sold for less than half a billion dollars. The same story could be told for most other crops. Meantime the price the farmer paid for his machinery, his fertilizer, or his mortgages remained the same. The result was to be seen in the mounting figures of farm tenancy and mortgage foreclosures. By 1930 forty-two per cent of the farms of the country were operated by tenants, and the total mortgage indebtedness had risen to over nine billion dollars, while in the five years between 1927 and 1932 not less than one tenth of the farm property of the nation was foreclosed at auction.

Yet in the face of this situation the Harding and Coolidge administrations, so eager to place the government at the disposal of business, evinced an attitude of indifference to the farming interests. The first Republican solution to the farm problem was a tariff on agricultural products; since the United States exported rather than imported farm produce, the solution was irrelevant, to say the least. Concrete proposals looking to governmental subsidies and crop control that had the support of farmer organizations were rejected by presidential vetoes. In time, President Hoover set up a Farm Board with power and funds to aid the orderly marketing of crops; but though this accomplished some good, it fell short of the mark.

Politically this era of "normalcy" was one of dullness and mediocrity, unrelieved except by the spectacular scandals of the Harding and the internecine party battles of the Hoover administrations. Never before had the government of the United States been more unashamedly the instrument of privileged groups; rarely had statesmanship given way so unreservedly to politics. Warren G. Harding, an amiable but weak Senator from Ohio, was nominated to the presidency because no one knew anything against him, and elected because the country was weary of Wilsonian idealism. In the two and a half years of his tenure of office his easygoing acquiescence in the exploitation of government by big business and his tolerance of gross corruption amply justified the expectations of those who looked for an end to idealism. Calvin Coolidge who succeeded him was a thoroughly limited politician, dour and unimaginative, thrifty of words and ideas, devoted to the maintenance of the *status quo*, and morbidly suspicious of liberalism in any form. Herbert Hoover, who came to the presidency in 1929, was a man of far greater ability, with a reputation as an efficient executive, an international-minded statesman, and a great humanitarian; in four years he lost all this and managed to make more serious errors of judgment than any President since Grant.

PRESIDENTIAL ELECTION, 1928

Hoover (Rep) 444 electoral, 21,392,190 popular votes
Smith (Dem.) 87 electoral, 15,016,443 popular votes

Figures indicate the number of electors

PRESIDENTIAL ELECTION, 1932

Hoover (Rep) 59 electoral, 15,761,841 popular votes
Roosevelt (Dem.) 472 electoral, 22,821,857 popular votes

Figures indicate the number of electors

Presidential Elections, 1928 and 1932

Society and Culture in the Postwar Years

THESE THREE PRESIDENTS, each so different in personality
and character, represented well enough the dominant forces
in American society during the postwar years. The idealism
of the Wilson era was in the past; the Rooseveltian passion
for humanitarian reform was in the future. The decade of the
twenties was dull, bourgeois, and ruthless. "The business of
America is business," said President Coolidge succinctly, and
the observation was apt if not profound. Wearied by idealism
and disillusioned about the war and its aftermath, Americans
dedicated themselves with unashamed enthusiasm to making
and spending money. Never before, not even in the McKinley
era, had American society been so materialistic, never before
so completely dominated by the ideals of the market place or
the techniques of machinery. It was an age of bigness and of
efficiency, and popular admiration went out to these things:
the stockbroker, the salesman, the advertiser, and the moving-picture star were the popular heroes. The nation grew
in population by seventeen million and grew in wealth even
more spectacularly; if the wealth was unevenly distributed,
there seemed enough to go around and men talked glibly
about the "new era" with a chicken in every pot and two
cars in every garage. Cities were bigger, buildings taller,
roads longer, fortunes greater, automobiles faster, colleges
larger, night clubs gayer, crimes more numerous, corporations more powerful, speculation more frenzied than ever
before in history, and the soaring statistics gave to most
Americans a sense of satisfaction if not of security.

It was an era of conformity and of intolerance with nonconformity, and the literary figure accepted by most Americans as most representative was Sinclair Lewis' George
Babbitt, who believed everything that he heard and read. It
is a striking fact that the public did not react violently to the
scandals of the Harding administration or penalize the party
responsible for them; it visited its displeasure rather upon
those who exposed these scandals or who criticized the
"American" way of life. The seeds of intolerance had been
planted during the war; after the war they sprouted in strange
and terrifying form. Nationalism was chauvinistic; isolationism took on moral and intellectual as well as political charac-

ter. There was widespread hostility to foreigners and to foreign ideas. Aliens suspected of radical notions were rounded up and deported by the scores; legislatures were "purged" of socialists; and states tried to enforce loyalty to political and economic institutions by law. The Ku Klux Klan, which boasted a membership of millions, dedicated itself to that notion of Aryan supremacy which European dictators were to take up a decade later, and its hooded Klansmen intimidated Catholics, Negroes, and Jews. Hostility was directed against the critics of American business practices, embracing, indiscriminately, labor leaders, liberal economists, socialists, pacifists, or "agitators" of any stripe who dared to question the ethics of business. In two notorious cases—that of Mooney and Billings in California and of Sacco and Vanzetti in Massachusetts—there seemed a tragic miscarriage of justice; in the second case, particularly, the prosecution seemed disposed to punish the defendants, who were philosophical anarchists and draft dodgers, for their radical activities rather than any proved crimes of violence. Sacco and Vanzetti were executed in 1927. A thorough sifting of evidence at a later date convinced many that Sacco was guilty of the murder charged, Vanzetti—an eloquent idealist—innocent.

Yet it is easy to exaggerate both the extent and the depth of this intolerance. It is proper to remember that it was inspired by a misguided zeal for democracy rather than by hostility to democracy. And throughout the entire period the current of dissent and protest ran strong and deep. No intolerance went unrebuked; no victim of injustice was too humble to raise up men to champion his cause. Perhaps the most interesting thing about the Mooney-Billings and Sacco-Vanzetti cases is the fact that they inspired eloquent and courageous protests—successful in the one case, unsuccessful in the other. Liberal magazines like *The Nation* and *The New Republic* commanded a substantial circulation and influence; poets and novelists who preached the gospel of revolt enjoyed wide popularity; the colleges and universities remained centers of freedom of thought and inquiry. And throughout all these years the courts stood stanchly for the protection of personal liberties and the guarantees of the bills of rights. This was the era of Brandeis, Cardozo, and Holmes.

The most important factors conditioning social development during this generation were the growth of cities and the acceleration of technological changes. By 1930 over half the population of the country lived in towns and cities, and a substantial part of it in the great metropolitan areas. The cities were the centers of industry and business, of government, of entertainment, of education, of literature and the arts. Urban ideas and ways of life spread out over the countryside. Under the impact of the movies, the radio, the automobile, syndicated newspaper features, national advertising, and a host of other influences, provincialism gave way to standardization. Even in humor, perhaps the most characteristic form of national expression, the tall story of the frontier gave way to the sophisticated anecdote or cartoon purveyed by *The New Yorker* magazine.

Of the many forces making for standardization, the automobile, the moving picture, and the radio were easily the most important. They were, indeed, the most important factors in the social life of this decade. Of the three, the automobile was the oldest and, in some respects, the most significant. Henry Ford had built a "gasoline buggy" back in the mid-nineties, but it was not until the second decade of the new century that Ford's famous Model T and other cheap cars came on the roads by the hundreds of thousands. In 1920 there were some nine million automobiles in use; ten years later the number had increased threefold. The automobile broke down isolation, sped up life, discovered new ways to spend leisure, gave a new freedom to youth, created vast new industries, gave work to millions of men, stimulated a nationwide road-building program, provided serious competition to the railroads, and exacted an annual toll of life and limb as high as that of the Civil War. Within a few years the automobile ceased to be a luxury and became a necessity, perhaps *the* necessity.

The movies and the radio, both relatively new, were scarcely less important than the automobile. Moving pictures date from the early years of the century, but they did not become a big-time business until the First World War or attain their immense influence until the advent of "talkies" in 1927. By the end of the decade, between eighty and one hundred million persons went to the movies every week—and a very large proportion of these were children. It was from the movies that the rising generation got many of its ideas about life, usually romantic and highly misleading; the day of violence was still ahead. To many the moving pictures offered an escape from drab reality into the never-never world of romance, where wickedness was always punished and virtue always rewarded, where all women were beautiful and all men handsome and acrobatic, where riches brought happiness and poverty contentment, and where all stories had a happy ending. Directly and indirectly the movies exercised an incalculable influence. They set the styles in dress and coiffures, in furniture and interior decoration, they originated popular songs, they taught manners, inculcated morals, and created popular heroes and heroines. Their influence spread throughout the world, and they proved perhaps the most powerful instrument of American cultural and social imperialism. To rapt moviegoers of the British Isles, of Russia, of Malaya, of the Argentine, they carried a picture—sometimes a caricature—of American life.

The radio was equally influential as an instrument for entertainment, education, and standardization. Radio developed rapidly during the First World War, and the first commercial broadcasting station began business in 1920. Within a decade almost every family in the nation was able to tune in on comic shows like Amos 'n' Andy, on news broadcasts, or on music. The radio, like the movies, was a big business, and like the movies, too, it was geared to mass consumption and had to fit its programs to popular interest: a study of radio programs would reveal as much about the popular mind as would any other study. In two fields the radio aimed at something more than popular entertainment. It undertook educational programs—rather feebly, to be sure—and it broadcast news and political campaigns. It is interesting to note that the radio remained, with very few exceptions, a private enterprise, supported not by taxes, as in all European countries, but by advertisers. Whether Americans paid too high a price for freedom from government control of the radio is a matter about which opinions differed.

The Great Depression

HERBERT HOOVER assumed office under auspices more favorable than those which had attended any other President since Taft. To all appearances the country had never been more prosperous or society more healthy. Stocks soared to dizzy heights, and every month hundreds of millions of dollars in new securities were snapped up by avid investors who hoped to share in the wonderful new game of making something out of nothing. Factories could not turn out automobiles, refrigerators, radios, vacuum cleaners, and oil burners fast enough to keep up with the insatiable 'demand for new gadgets; railroads groaned with their burdens; hundreds of thousands of new houses, in fantastic colonial, Tudor, Gothic, Spanish, pueblo, and modernistic styles, sprang up in the suburbs of great cities or in the new industrial towns of the South and the West. Colleges and moving-picture theaters were jammed; furnishing men with sporting goods and women with cosmetics became a big business; while advertising rose from the level of a business to the higher levels of a science and an art. Every day some new and marvelous technological improvement or scientific advance gave assurance of still better times ahead. It was the New Era, and if the farmers and the unskilled workers did not share in its benefits, all that would come later. And it was appropriate that the New Era was to be ushered in by a man who had made his reputation as an engineer, had proved himself a humanitarian, and had revealed his understanding of the business civilization by his yeoman work as Secretary of Commerce. "We in America," Hoover boasted, "are nearer to the final triumph over poverty than ever before in the history of any land," and almost everyone expected that Hoover himself would celebrate that "final triumph." But fate was unkind.

For, with dramatic and outrageous abruptness, came the crash of October, 1929. On the twenty-fourth over twelve million shares changed hands in a delirium of selling; on the twenty-ninth came catastrophe. Sound stocks like the American Telephone and Telegraph, General Electric, and General Motors lost from one hundred to two hundred points in a single week. By the end of the month stockholders had suffered a paper loss of over fifteen billion dollars; by the end of the year the shrinkage in securities of all kinds had reached the fantastic sum of forty billion dollars. Millions of investors lost their life savings. But the spiral of depression did not stop here. Business houses closed their doors, factories shut down, banks crashed, and millions of unemployed walked the streets in a vain search for work. Hundreds of thousands of families lost their homes; tax collections dropped to the point where cities and counties were unable to pay schoolteachers; construction work all but ceased; foreign trade, already badly hit, declined to an unprecedented low.

What were the causes of this panic and the long depression that followed? It is neither very satisfying nor very illuminating to say that depression is a normal part of the business cycle, though where government does not step in to control the excesses of individualistic enterprise that is correct enough. In the case of the 1929 panic there were factors that led, clearly enough, to the collapse. In the first place, the productive capacity of the nation was greater than its capacity to consume. This was largely because too large a part of national income was going to a small percentage of the population who promptly turned it back into savings or investment, and not enough of the income to the labor, farmer, and white-collar classes upon whose continued ability to buy the whole business system rested. In the second place, the tariff and war-debt policies of the government had pretty effectually cut down the foreign market for American goods, and with the world-wide depression of the early thirties that market collapsed. In the third place, easy credit policies had led to an inordinate expansion of credit, a vast extension of installment buying, and unrestrained speculation. Government and private debts totaled between one hundred and one hundred and fifty billion dollars, and speculation had pushed stock and property beyond their true value. Finally, the persistent agricultural depression, the continuous industrial unemployment, and the uninterrupted tendency toward concentration of wealth and power in many great corporations produced a national economy fundamentally unhealthy.

Whatever the explanations, it was soon clear that the nation was in the grip of the most ruinous depression in its history. The panic of 1837 had lasted three or four years; that of 1873 had dragged on for five years; the dreadful depression of 1893 came to an end in the spring of 1897; while the panics of 1904, 1907, and 1921 were short-lived affairs. But the great depression of 1929 lasted almost a full decade. It was unprecedented in length and in the wholesale poverty and tragedy which it inflicted upon society. And in another respect, too, it differed from earlier depressions: it was clearly the product of abundance, not of want. More completely than any other depression it was a monument to the breakdown of the system of distribution of wealth and of goods and to the failure of business leadership.

Since the depression arose not out of natural causes but out of artificial ones, it called insistently for aggressive governmental action. But this was not forthcoming. President Hoover, who at first believed (like millions of others) in automatic forces of recovery, did not entirely repudiate the obligation of the government to act, but he did hold that relief was exclusively the concern of private charity and of local governments. "As a nation," he said, "we must prevent hunger and cold to those of our people who are in honest difficulties," but he doggedly rejected specific proposals of direct national relief to the unemployed or the starving. He adopted from the first the policy of minimizing the extent of the depression and, when that was no longer possible, embraced the theory that prosperity was "just around the corner." On the positive side, the Hoover administration contented itself with a series of partial specifics: a program for the construction of roads, public buildings, and airways, a $300,000,000 appropriation for farm loans, the Glass-Steagall Act enlarging the credit facilities of the Federal Reserve system, and above all, the creation of the Reconstruction Finance Corporation, with two billions to lend to banks, railroads, insurance companies, and industrial concerns.

Unhappily, these measures proved inadequate, and the situation went steadily from bad to worse. By 1932 the number of unemployed had mounted to over twelve million; over five thousand banks had closed their doors; commercial failures totaled thirty-two thousand; farm prices had fallen to the lowest point in history; the middle class was in danger of being wiped out; national income had declined from over eighty billion in 1929 to forty billion. The whole economy of the nation seemed to be disintegrating, and the people were in an ugly mood.

Americans are not prone to revolution, and in this crisis they turned hopefully to a different leadership. A group of Republican Progressives, led by Senators Norris, La Follette,

Costigan, and Cutting, had challenged Hoover's policies, but they were not strong enough to wrest control of the party from the Old Guard. Of necessity the country looked to the Democrats for salvation. In 1930 the Democrats swept the Congressional elections, and in 1932 they prepared to take over the presidency. The Republican Old Guard, which had learned nothing from the depression, defiantly renominated President Hoover, who appealed once again to "rugged individualism" for a solution to the national crisis. The Democrats presented the ebullient and magnetic Franklin D. Roosevelt, who as governor of the Empire State had revealed himself a resourceful, courageous, and humane leader and astute politician, and who promised the nation a "new deal." In the November elections Roosevelt rode triumphantly into the White House on the crest of a popular majority of seven million votes.

CHAPTER 23

Franklin D. Roosevelt and the New Deal

The Man and the Problem

AMERICAN DEMOCRACY has always managed to find great leaders in time of great crisis. Sometimes, as in the case of Washington, the choice has been reasoned and deliberate; at other times, as in the cases of Lincoln and Theodore Roosevelt and Wilson, it has been largely fortuitous. It cannot be said that Franklin Roosevelt was an unknown quantity when first elected to the presidency; it can be asserted that few of those who so hopefully voted for him realized that in Roosevelt they had a leader who as spokesman for democracy and nationalism was the peer of Lincoln, as a leader towards a better world order the peer of Wilson.

Roosevelt had made his reputation as an efficient and socially minded Governor of New York, but behind that lay a long apprenticeship in politics. A man of wealth and of distinguished family, a graduate of Groton School and of Harvard, he had early decided to follow the example of his kinsman in the White House, by taking an active interest in politics. His early ventures were distinguished by two qualities which characterized him later: devotion to progressive principles and a talent for commanding the confidence of people from all walks of life. He had served in the New York State Assembly, been Assistant Secretary of the Navy under Wilson, and run for the vice-presidency in 1920. Then he was stricken with infantile paralysis. Slowly he fought his way back to health, and during the years of retirement from active politics he studied American political history and built up through correspondence and personal contacts a wide and devoted following. In 1928 he ran ahead of his ticket in capturing the governorship of New York State and two years later was triumphantly re-elected by an even larger majority. With this background and experience, Roosevelt was probably the best-informed Democratic leader in the country in 1932.

But the new President had other qualities besides experience and knowledge. He had an instinctive faith in the common people as profound as Bryan's, a rationalized faith in democracy as profound as Wilson's. He was politically astute, understood the art of leadership, and had an instinct for the jugular vein of great issues. Like Jefferson, he was opportunistic as to means, tenaciously consistent as to ends; compromised on nonessentials but rarely on essentials; and knew that politics was an art as well as a science. He was not deluded by the notion that society could be remade by blueprints or that statecraft could be watered down to a kind of scientific management or engineering project. He knew the American past, understood the world in which he lived, and had given thought to the organization of the world of tomorrow. He trusted politicians but did not distrust experts; was sensitive to public opinion but did not hesitate to mold it or fear to challenge it. Sometimes he seemed distressingly casual about major decisions; but he had broad interests, indefatigable energy, and an infectious buoyancy which he communicated to those about him and, eventually, to the whole people. These great assets far more than offset his faults: a certain superficiality, a casual way of dealing with grimly serious issues, an aristocratic contempt for money and monied men, and a cavalier attitude toward problems of public finance.

Roosevelt's inaugural address was a promise of what was to come, as significant, though not as eloquent, as Wilson's First Inaugural. The nation, he asserted, was fundamentally sound; "plenty is at our doorstep, but a generous use of it languishes in the very sight of plenty." The fault was in the "money-changers" and "self-seekers"; these had been driven from the temples, and the task ahead was one of restoration. To that task the President dedicated himself: to the relief of poverty and want, the restoration of the balance between agriculture and industry, the supervision of banking and security practices, the readjustment of international economic relationships, and the inauguration of the policy of the good neighbor. "I am prepared," he said boldly, "to recommend the measures that a stricken nation in the midst of a stricken world may require. These measures . . . I shall seek within my constitutional authority, to bring to speedy adoption." And if Congress should fail to respond, "I shall ask the Congress for the one remaining instrument to meet the crisis—broad executive power to wage a war against the emergency as great as the power that would be given me if we were in fact invaded by a foreign foe." And he concluded:

We face the arduous days that lie before us in the warm courage of national unity, with the clear consciousness of seeking old and precious moral values; with the clean satisfaction that comes from the stern performance of duty by old and young alike. We aim at the assurance of a rounded and permanent national life. We do not distrust the future of essential democracy.

This inaugural address served formal notice on the nation that there was to be a New Deal. That New Deal was long overdue. For over a decade, now, politicians had played with marked cards, and business had gathered in almost all the chips. Roosevelt proposed to restore the rules of the democratic game. To many contemporaries the New Deal seemed like revolution. Actually it was deeply conservative—conservative in the same sense that Jeffersonian and Wilsonian democracy had been conservative. It aimed to protect, against violence from the left or from the right, the essentials of American democracy—to conserve natural and human resources, to preserve the balance of interests under the Constitution, security, and liberty.

In philosophy the New Deal was democratic, in method evolutionary. Because for fifteen years legislative reforms had been dammed up, they now burst upon the country with what seemed like violence, but when the waters subsided it was clear that they ran in familiar channels. The conservation policy of the New Deal had been inaugurated by Theodore Roosevelt; railroad and trust regulation went back to the eighties; banking and currency reforms had been partially achieved by Wilson; the farm-relief program borrowed much from the Populists, labor legislation from the practices of such states as Wisconsin and Oregon. Even judicial reform, which caused such a mighty stir, had been anticipated by Lincoln and Theodore Roosevelt. And in the realm of international relations the policies of the New Deal were clearly continuations of the traditional policies of strengthening national security, maintaining freedom of the seas, supporting law and peace, and championing democracy in the Western world.

The New Deal in Action

WHEN FRANKLIN ROOSEVELT assumed office on March 4, 1933, the depression was at its lowest ebb and the economic system of the country on the verge of complete collapse. Roosevelt met the crisis with boldness and vigor, and before his first term had ended he had forced through a more varied and more important body of legislation than had any of his predecessors since Washington. The New Deal that the Roosevelt administration gave the country was made up in part of measures for recovery and relief, in part of measures for reform: many, to be sure, partook of both purposes, and it is not always possible to determine where recovery left off and reform began. In the realm of relief the government assisted hard-pressed business by Federal loans that soon aggregated billions of dollars. It set on foot a broad program of spending on public works and loans for housing, roads, bridges, and local improvements, in order to stimulate business and provide employment. It set up elaborate systems of unemployment relief and, by 1940, had spent some sixteen billion dollars on direct relief and an additional seven billion on various public works. It inaugurated a far-reaching program for the conservation of natural resources, one of the chief instruments of which was the Civilian Conservation Corps, which gave work to some three million young men. It came to the aid of the railroads, brought about consolidation of facilities, and financed long overdue improvements. Through Federal sponsorship of writers' projects, theaters, concerts, and the decoration of public buildings, it gave aid to distressed writers, artists, and musicians, thus greatly enriching the cultural life of the nation. Many of the long-range reforms in agriculture and industry were designed likewise for relief.

Mistakes were naturally made, some of them serious. The National Recovery Administration, or NRA, proved a failure even before the Supreme Court destroyed it in 1935. The devaluation of the dollar did little to raise prices, its main object. A great deal of money was spent wastefully, and the national debt grew at a rapid rate. Much internecine quarreling marked the Administration. But the broad record was good.

Looking in the direction of permanent reform was much of the banking, water-power, farm, labor, social-security, and political legislation. The New Deal closed the banks and reopened them under stricter supervision and with government guarantees of bank deposits. It abandoned the gold standard and devalued the dollar in order to achieve a mild controlled inflation and thus raise commodity prices. It set up careful control of the selling of stocks and bonds and other securities. It broke up the great holding companies which had obtained control of a large part of the business of supplying the country with electric light and which had often been manipulated for the benefit of a few insiders. It formulated codes of fair practices for business, designed to end wasteful competition. It raised taxes on the income of the rich and of corporations, plugged up loopholes in the tax laws, and cleared up much of the confusion that had long obtained with respect to the taxation policies of state and Federal governments.

Roosevelt Re-elected:
Fresh Emphasis on Reform

LATE in the presidential campaign of 1936, Roosevelt's staunch supporter James A. Farley predicted that he would carry every state but Maine and Vermont. His optimism was justified. Running against an estimable but colorless governor of Kansas, Alfred M. Landon, Roosevelt won the largest popular plurality in history, 27,480,000 votes to Landon's 16,675,000, and obtained 528 votes in the electoral college against his rival's 8. The President's strength in the cities was especially remarkable, and the ten states which contained the dozen largest cities of the nation now came near controlling a national election. Roosevelt had defeated not only the Republicans but a Lincoln League which included such conservative Democrats as John W. Davis and Alfred E. Smith.

Powerful reactionary forces, Roosevelt declared in his last important campaign speech, were trying to restore a hear-nothing, see-nothing, do-nothing government. "They are unanimous in their hate for me—and I welcome their hatred." It was true that groups which specialized in hatred and prejudice, and leaders who appealed to passion instead of reason, had become alarmingly prominent in the country. They had been created by the sufferings of the depression, the natural temptation to experiment with panaceas, the emotionalism of fervent supporters and still more fervent opponents of Roosevelt's sweeping measures, and fears of coming change. The spectacle of Old World turmoil made its contribution, for 1936 witnessed Japanese aggression against China and the outbreak of the Spanish Civil War.

One extremist group, Huey Long's Share-the-Wealth Society, represented a dying spasm. Long, first governor of Louisiana and then Senator, had been assassinated in the fall of 1935, ending the threat of a semi-fascist regime in the state. His demagogic views were maintained by a small following which combined with the groups led by Dr. Francis Townsend and Father Charles Coughlin to put a ticket headed by Representative William Lemke of North Dakota in the field in 1936. Townsend had invented a scheme for paying revolving pensions to every person of sixty or older; Coughlin had used the radio to preach isolationism and hatred or distrust of foreign nations. When Lemke's total vote failed to reach 900,000, his motley organization fell apart. He, like Dr. Townsend, was an essentially well-meaning, harmless person; not so much could be said for Coughlin or for the tub-thumping Gerald L. K. Smith, a Louisiana minister who avowed some of Huey Long's worst views. As for the Liberty League, Herbert Hoover's use of it in violent denunciations of Roosevelt's policies helped bring it into discredit, and the election killed it.

The tidal wave of 1936 naturally gave the Roosevelt administration increased self-confidence. The course of events both at home and abroad was shaping a change in policy. The first harsh exigencies of the depression having passed, it could give more attention to reform as distinguished from recovery; and the world turmoil forced it to adopt a more dynamic foreign policy.

Four large fields of New Deal reform merit particular attention: agriculture, labor, social security, and administration. In agriculture the objects were to raise commodity prices to the pre-World War level, to reduce farm production to a point where it would eliminate ruinous surpluses, to encourage the maintenance of soil fertility, to make credit more easily available to farmers, to rescue tenant farmers and those on marginal lands, and to open up new markets abroad and at home for farm products. All of these objectives were in considerable part achieved. An Agricultural Adjustment Act, looking to the voluntary reduction of production of certain staples in return for governmental subsidies, was passed in 1933. It was voided three years later by the Supreme Court, whereupon the Congress passed a second and better farm-relief act. This provided that the government would make money payments to farmers who would devote part of their land to "soil-conserving" crops. By 1940 nearly six million farmers had joined in this program and were receiving subsidies that averaged more than a hundred dollars for each farmer. The new act likewise provided commodity loans on surplus crops, storage facilities to ensure an "ever-normal granary," and insurance for wheat. The resultant decrease in the production of staple crops and the opening up of new markets succeeded in raising the prices of agricultural commodities: by 1939 farm income was more than double what it had been in 1932. A Farm Credit Administration made credit available at almost nominal rates of interest; a Farm Security Administration undertook to finance farm ownership for tenant farmers and the rehabilitation of marginal farmers.

In the field of labor the New Deal enacted a whole series of epoch-making laws. The National Recovery Act of 1933 attempted to spread work, shorten hours, raise wages, and end child labor, guaranteed the right of collective bargaining, and outlawed yellow-dog contracts. It was voided by the Supreme Court in 1935, but its labor provisions were improved upon in two great basic laws: the Wagner Act of 1935 and the Fair Labor Standards Act of 1938. The Wagner Act guaranteed to workers the right to set up and bargain through unions of their own choice, forbade employers to discriminate against any member of a union, and set up a Labor Relations Board to adjudicate all labor disputes. The law aroused violent controversy, but gave labor a better deal than it had ever before enjoyed. Under its auspices the old A. F. of L. was revitalized, and a new and vigorous labor organization came into being—the Congress for Industrial Organization. This C.I.O. revived the industrial unionism of the old Knights of Labor and succeeded in organizing the steel, textile, automobile, and other industries heretofore all but invulnerable to unionization. By 1940 membership in trade unions had increased to nine million and by the close of the war to almost fifteen million. A Fair Labor Standards Act was designed to put "a ceiling over hours and a floor under wages." It fixed forty hours as the normal minimum week and forty cents an hour as the normal minimum wage; the limitation on hours was to remain the same for the next generation, but the minimum wage rose steadily. This act likewise outlawed child labor in industries engaged in interstate commerce—a prohibition happily sustained by the Supreme Court.

Of fundamental importance, too, was legislation to give

security to the unemployed, the aged, and the disabled. Up to this time these matters had been left to the states. Some states had enacted effective unemployment insurance and old-age-pension schemes, but it was clear that the states singly were unable to handle the problem, which was, after all, national in dimensions. At the insistence of the President, Congress, in 1935, enacted a series of Social Security Acts providing pensions for the aged, unemployment insurance, benefit payments to the blind, to dependent mothers, and to crippled children, and appropriations to public-health work. These programs were to be financed partly by employers, partly by workers; to be operated by the states and supervised by the Federal government. Notwithstanding widespread initial opposition, the social-security program soon commanded all but universal support, and in subsequent years its provisions were made more generous and its scope was enlarged.

Among its most significant achievements were the creation of the Tennessee Valley Authority to develop the resources of one of the great interior basins of the country through the use of government-owned hydroelectric dams and through a broad program of economic and agricultural rehabilitation. This highly successful venture was followed by similar, though less ambitious, ones in the Far West and widely copied abroad.

Finally, the Roosevelt administration inaugurated important and far-reaching reforms in administration. The executive department, which had grown in a helter-skelter fashion and which was inefficient and extravagant, was partially reorganized—though much remained to be done. The Hatch Act of 1939, perhaps the most important civil-service reform measure since the original reform act of 1883, prohibited "pernicious political activities" on the part of governmental employees and struck at the corruption and extravagance of political parties. And in 1937 the President, deeply concerned by an unprecedented series of Supreme Court decisions nullifying most of the New Deal measures, proposed a plan to "reform" the Court. The method was to bring about the retirement of aged justices and infuse new blood into the Court; the purpose to persuade the Court to return to the great tradition of Marshall and Story and Holmes—the tradition that interpreted the Constitution as a flexible instrument of government rather than as a barrier to government. Roosevelt's specific proposal was sharply criticized and eventually defeated. Meanwhile, however, the personnel of the Court began to change, and before long, taking a more enlightened view of the legislation enacted by the other equal and independent branches of the government, it reversed most of its earlier paralyzing decisions. The great debate which Roosevelt initiated on the Court, though productive of much confusion and rancor, in the end did something toward educating the nation to the real character of the American constitutional system and persuading the Court to respect more realistically the constitutional provisions for the separation and equality of the three branches of government and to accommodate itself to American democracy.

The Shadow of War

ROOSEVELT'S DOMESTIC PROGRAM, like Wilson's, was harshly interrupted by the clamor of foreign affairs, and before his second term was well under way it was clear that international problems would have to take precedence over domestic. Beginning in the twenties and continuing unbated into the thirties, the system of collective security which President Wilson had so hopefully projected disintegrated. For this breakdown the United States must bear some responsibility. The policy of isolation which she had so confidently embraced deprived the League of the moral and practical support of the greatest and most independent of world powers; tariff policies contributed to world economic collapse; withdrawal from the Far East appeared to invite a continuation of Japanese aggression; and agitation for disarmament discouraged a realistic attitude toward the problems of naval and military preparedness among the democracies.

The roots of the Second World War go deep down into the decade of the twenties. Japan felt that the League of Nations had slammed shut the door to further expansion and resented the power of Britain and the United States in the Orient. Italy was discontented with the fruits of her belated participation on the side of the Allies, and her new swashbuckling leader, Benito Mussolini, hungered and thirsted after glory. Germany was resentful of defeat and restless under the restrictions of the Versailles Treaty. Economic depression, the pressure of growing populations, social confusion and demoralization, all prepared the way for new leaders impatient with the slow processes of peaceful readjustment and for new philosophies which challenged the assumptions and conclusions of the old. Japan, to be sure, had little need for a new philosophy; she needed only weapons with which to implement the old. Italy turned to Fascism. Germany, after a decade of confusion, permitted a fanatical Austrian veteran of the first war, Adolf Hitler, to organize a revolutionary National Socialist party and seize the reins of government. By the early thirties all three nations had organized totalitarian governments and all three were prepared to repudiate not only the Versailles and subsequent treaties, but the whole structure of international law and order.

Thereafter events moved with alarming speed. Each of the totalitarian powers took the path of aggression. Each built up its military machine, threatened its weaker neighbors, embarked upon imperialistic ventures. Most of these ventures were rationalized on plausible grounds and carried through in a manner that greatly enhanced the prestige of the aggressors but did not challenge too sharply the opposition of the democratic powers. Japan, in 1931, invaded Manchuria and set up the puppet state of Manchukuo, from which vantage point she flanked Siberian Russia to the north, China to the south. Italy, which had already consolidated her position in the Dodecanese, seized Fiume, and enlarged her boundaries in Libya, inaugurated the revival of the Roman Empire by warring on Ethiopia and in 1935–1936 reduced that ancient but weak and backward country to subjection. Germany repudiated the Versailles Treaty, reoccupied the Rhineland, and boldly undertook large-scale rearmament. The League protested, diplomats deplored, and democratic leaders declaimed, the victims suffered, but no nation or group of nations interposed an effective barrier to totalitarian ambitions.

Most Americans watched these developments with indifference—an indifference tinged, to be sure, with disapproval. This was, they felt sure, just another chapter in the age-old story of rival imperialisms. No more than most Englishmen did they understand the revolutionary nature of the forces now unleashed in the world. They did not realize that they were confronted here with a menace more dangerous, more explosive, than any before in modern history. They congratulated themselves, rather, that they were safely out of it all, protected by two great oceans, self-sufficient, rich, and powerful.

It was difficult for most Americans to understand the real nature of the threat that hung over them and over the whole world. It was no mere military threat. The United States had met military threats before and emerged triumphant. It was a new thing, new and incomprehensible. The Americans were an easygoing people who had never known defeat or demoralization; the notion of evil, as Santayana observed, is foreign to the American mind. They could not believe that a new philosophy had emerged which repudiated and warred on their way of life and their inherited values.

The core of the American, and of the English, philosophy of government is the individual. The individual is the source of government. He has rights and liberties in society: the right to worship as he will, to speak and to write, to go about his own business, choose his own work, marry whom he will, rear his family as he will, undisturbed by the state. No matter how socialized his thinking, administration, or business became, the ultimate objective of his government, his society, and his economy remained the creation and protection of the free man.

To this philosophy totalitarianism, as practiced by Italy, Germany, and Japan, opposed one diametrically different. Totalitarian philosophy subordinated the individual to the state or to the race. In the Fascist and Nazi systems the individual was relatively unimportant, his liberties, his rights, his property, his ambitions and hopes, his social and family relationships, insignificant.

As the real nature of totalitarianism became clear, Americans grew increasingly apprehensive, and as Germany, Italy, and Japan renewed their aggressions, striking down one smaller nation after another, apprehension turned to indignation. In 1936–1938 came the martyrdom of Spain, where the armies and planes of Mussolini and Hitler aided the Nationalists in overthrowing the Republican regime, while the democracies stood by, paralyzed with indecision. Even as the victorious foreign legions were battering at the gates of Madrid, Japan precipitated the "China incident" which was to drag out for many years until it merged into a general world war. In 1938 came Hitler's violent incorporation of Austria into the Reich, and the Greater Germany was under way. Czechoslovakia was next, and before the democracies had recovered from the shock of the Austrian annexation, Hitler was demanding the cession of the Sudeten region of the little democracy which Britain and the United States had helped create. Frightened, the leaders of Britain and France appealed for an arbitration of the issue. When arbitration was rejected, Mr. Chamberlain flew to Munich and there surrendered Czechoslovakia to the German war lords. "It is peace in our time," said Chamberlain on his return, but Winston Churchill said, "Britain and France had to choose between war and dishonor. They chose dishonor. They will have war."

The American reaction to all this was not one which future generations will recall with pride. Disillusioned with the results of the last war, fearful of involvement in a new one, confident that any decision as to war or peace lay entirely in their own hands, they at first adopted a policy of peace at any price. Hastily they abandoned many of those rights which their fathers and forefathers had twice fought to preserve, and announced to the world that in no circumstances could any belligerent, victim or aggressor, look to them for aid. All this was embodied in the neutrality legislation of 1935–1937 which prohibited trade with or credit to any belligerent.

President Roosevelt, who, like Secretary of State Cordell Hull, disapproved this legislation, made the mistake of signing it. Then as the international situation worsened, he set himself to instill in the American people a realization of the nature of the thing that was abroad in the world, and to arm America, morally and materially, to meet and overcome it. Speaking at Chicago in 1937, he called for a moral quarantine against aggressor nations, only to be met with the charge that he was playing politics and exposing the nation to involvement in "foreign" wars. He denounced Japanese aggression in China, built up friendly relations with Latin American countries and with Canada, and urged upon Congress the imperative necessity of larger appropriations for arms. "Peace by fear," he warned the dictators, "has no higher or more enduring quality than peace by the sword," and he refused to confess fear or to be intimidated by force. As the totalitarian policy became more aggressive, the American spirit hardened against it.

The Coming of the War

BRITAIN TOO, humiliated by Munich and outraged by the subsequent destruction of Czechoslovakia, was feverishly rearming, for it was clear, at last, that the policy of appeasement was bankrupt. But Hitler did not choose to wait until Britain and the United States had achieved military equality with Germany. All through the spring and summer of 1939 he thundered against Poland, demanding the cession of Danzig and the Polish Corridor; his position was immeasurably strengthened when, in midsummer, he concluded an alliance with the most powerful of Continental nations, Russia. Then, even while negotiations with Poland were still under way, Hitler struck. On September 1, his armies rolled across the frontier while his planes rained death and destruction upon Polish cities. Two days later Britain and France, faithful to their commitments, declared war upon Germany.

In two weeks Germany had overrun Poland, Russia advancing from the east to complete the conquest of the hapless nation. Then ensued a long stalemate, which many Americans fatuously characterized as a "phony" war. By spring Hitler was ready for the second round. Without warning, his armies moved into Denmark and on to Norway. The British attempt to rush aid to the sturdy Norse ended in failure, and within little more than a month the resources of most of Scandinavia were in German control. On May 10 Germany turned westward and struck at neutral Holland and Belgium and at France. The *Blitzkrieg* lasted a little over a month, and when it was over Holland had been conquered, the Belgian army had surrendered, and France itself had fallen, while a British Expeditionary Force, hastily rushed across the Channel, was rescued only by a miracle of energy and heroism.

Britain stood alone. But it was no longer the Britain of

Munich or Britain of the futile Norwegian campaign. It was a Britain that remembered that for a thousand years no invader had ruled her soil. "Come three corners of the world in arms, and we shall shock them," Shakespeare had boasted, and the proud boast was echoed now by Winston Churchill, the great leader into whose hands had been entrusted the destiny of the nation and of the cause of freedom:

We shall prove ourselves once again able to defend our island home, to ride out the storm of war, and to outlive the menace of tyranny, if necessary for years, if necessary alone. . . . Even though large tracts of Europe and many old and famous states have fallen or may fall into the grip of the Gestapo and all the odious apparatus of Nazi rule, we shall not flag or fail, we shall go on to the end, we shall fight in France, we shall fight on the seas and oceans, we shall fight with growing confidence and growing strength in the air, we shall defend our island, whatever the cost may be, we shall fight on the beaches, we shall fight on the landing grounds, we shall fight in the fields and in the streets, we shall fight in the hills; we shall never surrender, and even if, which I do not for a moment believe, this island or a large part of it were subjugated and starving, then our Empire beyond the seas, armed and guarded by the British fleet, would carry on the struggle, until, in God's good time, the New World, with all its power and might, steps forth to the rescue and liberation of the Old.

America Abandons Neutrality

"IN GOD'S GOOD TIME"—but when would it be? The attack on Poland precipitated the greatest debate since slavery days, carried on not only in the halls of Congress, but in every newspaper, in every public hall, in every home in the land. Roosevelt moved energetically for the repeal of the neutrality legislation and, after prolonged discussion, he was able to wrest from a reluctant Congress the "cash-and-carry" legislation which did, at least, make American resources available to the fighting democracies as long as they could pay for them. The fall of France convinced most Americans at last of the might of the German military machine, and the air attack upon Britain that summer and fall brought home to them the realization that if Britain fell America would stand alone against the most formidable military coalition in history.

Confronted with this possibility, Congress voted astronomical sums for rearmament, an agreement was reached with the Latin American republics extending collective protection to the possessions of the democratic nations in the New World, the United States and Canada set up a joint Board of Defense, and peacetime conscription with military training for almost a million men was inaugurated. More important even than these moves was the dramatic agreement between Roosevelt and Churchill whereby, in return for fifty overage destroyers, Britain leased to the United States a series of naval bases extending from Newfoundland to British Guiana. It was, said Roosevelt, the most important step in our national defense since the Louisiana Purchase, and Churchill added that "these two great organizations of the English-speaking democracies, the British Empire and the United States, will have to be somewhat mixed up together in some of their affairs for mutual and general advantage." It was a prophetic observation.

Roosevelt had mapped out the course which the nation would follow: would he be able to hold it to that course? In the summer of 1940 the American people were called upon to choose a President who would guide them through the dangerous years ahead. The Democrats, boldly abandoning the anti-third-term tradition, once more named Franklin Roosevelt their candidate. The Republicans, meeting in an atmosphere of confusion, selected a newcomer to politics, Wendell Willkie of Indiana and New York. The Democratic party and its leader had committed themselves irrevocably to the policy of aid to Britain—a policy which might well lead to war. Would the Republican party and the new, inexperienced candidate espouse the opposite policy? Willkie attacked the New Deal on its domestic side, but resolutely refused to play politics with the issue of aid to Britain. On this crucial issue he ranged himself on the side of the President, supported conscription, applauded the destroyer deal, and promised that if he were elected there would be no turning back on the road which the President had marked out and the Congress followed. It was a great and statesmanlike decision and it revealed that in Wendell Willkie the Republican party had found a leader of courage, wisdom, and vision.

In the November elections Roosevelt was re-elected and, confident now of popular support, pushed vigorously ahead with his policies. When the Congress met in January he presented it with a proposal designed to circumvent the remaining limitations of the neutrality legislation—the lend-lease bill. This measure provided that the United States might lend or lease any defense articles or facilities to any nation whose defense was vital to that of the United States. After protracted debate the measure was passed, and under its wise provisions a stream of planes, tanks, raw materials, foodstuffs and other articles began to flow across to Britain and her allies. This measure was clearly unneutral, but the United States, committed now to the defeat of Germany, was not to be stayed by the niceties of international law. Other equally unneutral acts followed—the seizure of Axis shipping, the freezing of Axis funds, the transfer of tankers to Britain, the occupation of Greenland and, later, of Iceland, the extension of lend-lease to the new ally, Russia, and—eventually, after a series of U-boat attacks on American shipping—the presidential order to "shoot on sight" any enemy submarines.

Another sign of the ever closer association between America and Britain was in the joint formulation of democratic war aims. On August 14 Roosevelt and Churchill met in mid-Atlantic and there drew up the Atlantic Charter, containing certain principles upon which they based "their hopes for a better future for the world." These principles were: no territorial aggrandizement; no territorial changes that do not accord with the wishes of the people involved; the right of all people to choose their own form of government; the enjoyment by all states of access to trade and raw materials; economic collaboration between nations; freedom of the seas; and the abandonment of the use of force as an instrument of international relations. Here were Wilson's Fourteen Points in new, and simpler, dress.

It seemed as if the United States was drifting into war with Germany, but it seemed, too, as if that drift might be a prolonged one. The United States had made its decision, but was not yet bold enough to submit it to the fortunes of war. Meantime tension mounted in the Far East. Japan had already formally joined the Axis and now, taking advantage of British and American involvement in the European war, was pushing boldly ahead with her "New Order"—an order in which the Nipponese were to rule the entire Orient and the Pacific as well. A policy of appeasement having proved futile, both Britain and the United States adopted toward Japan a more resolute attitude. This was equally futile. The Japanese war lords were in control now, they had tasted victory, they were confident of greater victories ahead. In November, 1941, while the Russians were battling heroically before Moscow and Leningrad and the British fighting to keep open the sea routes of the Atlantic, Japan poured troops into French Indo-China and prepared air bases along the border of Thailand. On December 6 the situation was so critical that President Roosevelt addressed a personal appeal to the Emperor of Japan to join in arriving at a solution which would maintain the peace.

It is improbable that the Emperor ever received this message. For Japan was ready now for the most desperate throw of the dice in modern history. On Sunday, December 7, she struck with devastating ferocity at American outposts in Hawaii, Guam, Midway, Wake, and the Philippines. War had come.

CHAPTER 24

The Second World War

The Grim Outlook

THE MOST TITANIC CONFLICT in history, with the fate of democratic institutions in the balance, reached what Winston Churchill called one of its grand climacterics with

Pearl Harbor. That the Japanese won a spectacular victory at Pearl Harbor, and in the Philippines, is clear; it is equally clear that by their attacks on American territory they violated one of the basic principles of warfare: if you strike a king, strike to kill. The assault on Pearl Harbor knocked out the United States Pacific fleet, but it did not knock out the United States. On the contrary, it united that nation as nothing else could have done, dedicated all its resources and energies to war, put its giant productive capacity into high gear, and inspired in its people an implacable determination to fight on to victory. Within six months of Pearl Harbor the combined naval and air forces of the United States inflicted on the Japanese at Midway the first major naval defeat they had ever suffered; within one year the nation that was to have been knocked out launched successful offensives on opposite sides of the globe—the Solomon Islands and the shores of North Africa.

Yet the situation in December, 1941, was dangerous, and the prospect bleak. Everywhere the battered Allies stood on the defensive; everywhere the Axis powers were triumphant. Hitler controlled the whole of Western Europe except the Iberian peninsula, and his mighty armies had thrust hundreds of miles into Russia, which seemed at the point of collapse. Italy dominated the Mediterranean, and her legions were swarming across North Africa and threatening Egypt and the Suez Canal. The Japanese had subdued a large part of China; now they prepared to sweep down Malaya and across the Dutch East Indies, conquer the Philippines, threaten India to the east, Australia to the south, the Aleutians and Alaska to the north.

In the Old World only Britain and Russia still held out against the Axis: Britain, torn and bleeding from her wounds, battered ceaselessly from the skies and threatened with starvation; Russia beaten to her knees, her territory ravaged, her cities and factories destroyed, her armies decimated. In December, 1941, it seemed not only possible but probable that Germany would drive through the Caucasus or North Africa to the east, Japan smash through China and Burma to the west, and the two great Axis powers link up in India, with three quarters of the globe at their feet.

Yet if somehow immediate disaster could be averted the long-range view was not quite so desperate. Some forty

countries were associated in the United Nations, and among
these the greatest, most populous and most powerful nations
on the earth—the United States, Britain, Russia, China, India
and the British Dominions among them. The Allies had
superiority not only in man power but in productive capacity
and, as it proved, in scientific and inventive genius as well.
The one thing they needed to ensure ultimate victory was
time. The Axis had prepared for this war for a decade and
in China, Spain, and Africa had waged it for half that period;
everywhere they had seized the initiative and held it. Given
time, the Allies could mobilize their immense resources and
bring them to bear on the enemy. But would they be given
time?

In two respects the Allies enjoyed a marked advantage
over the Axis powers. In the first place they were united in
fact as well as in name. They not only shared their resources and their military and scientific techniques, but—
with the exception of Russia and China—they actually
merged them. The Axis, by contrast, had no real unity.
Germany, Italy and Japan fought separate and independent
wars; there was no grand strategy, no Combined Chief of
Staff, no effective interchange of weapons or even of information. The second Allied advantage was in leadership. In
this great crisis of history both Britain and the United States
found leaders fit for their responsibilities and worthy of the
causes they represented. Winston Churchill proved himself
the greatest war leader the British people had known since
the younger Pitt; Franklin D. Roosevelt emerged as the most
effective of all war-time Presidents. Both commanded support and inspired admiration not only in their own country
but throughout the civilized portions of the globe.

There was, too, a third advantage, one whose significance
becomes clearer with the passing years. The Axis powers
fought the war with the weapons of tyranny, suppression and slavery: nonconformity was punished with
obloquy, criticism was silenced, independence and originality smothered, dissent punished with death or the concentration camp. But in all the English-speaking nations,
liberty flourished in war as in peace: the democratic
processes were uninterrupted, criticism was encouraged,
originality and independence commanded a premium. Thus
the Axis powers earned the hatred of all the peoples they

conquered, and were unable to protect themselves against their own inevitable mistakes. The Allies could count on the support of the peoples they sought to liberate, and enjoyed the inestimable advantage of open debate over policies and strategy, of the voluntary and whole-hearted support of all segments of their populations, and of contributions from original and independent minds.

At the very outset of the war—indeed even before Pearl Harbor—the Allies made two basic decisions. The first was to give priority to the defeat of Germany. The argument was simple enough: Japan could wait, Germany could not. If the United States concentrated on beating Japan—as many shortsighted Americans thought it should—Germany might knock out both Russia and Britain, leaving this country to fight on alone against three quarters of the globe. But if Russia and Britain could be saved and Germany defeated, then Japan must inevitably fall before the united power of the victorious Allies. This was the plan that was adopted, and this was the plan that succeeded.

The second decision was to make the war in fact a combined operation: to plan jointly all major military, political, diplomatic and economic policies; to pool resources; to merge armies and navies in a single command as far as was possible. The pattern for all this had already been set by the destroyer-bases deal and by lend-lease; it was developed during the war, though without the co-operation of Russia, through the Combined Chiefs of Staff; it achieved its most dramatic success in the co-operative production of the atom bomb.

Thus conscious not only of their own immeasurable strength, but of the fact that, in the words of Roosevelt, "the vast majority of the members of the human race are on our side," and that they were fighting in a cause that was just, the Allied powers faced the future with no sense of discouragement or despair, but with undismayed courage and confidence.

Military and Industrial Preparation

IN THE LAST ANALYSIS the outcome of the war would depend on two things: weapons and tools, and the men who wielded them. For as Francis Bacon said, centuries ago, "Walled towns, stored Arcenalls, and Armories, Goodly Races of Horse, Chariots of Warre, Ordnance, Artillery and the like; all this is but a sheep in a Lions Skin except the Breed and disposition of the People be stout." Fortunately for the cause of freedom, the breed and disposition of the British and American people were stout. And fortunately, too, if they were not already adequately equipped with "Arcenalls and Armories, Ordnance, Artillery and the like," they were prepared to produce them, and everything else needed for modern war, in lavish abundance.

The United States, certainly, was better equipped for this than for any previous war in which she had fought. Preparation had begun in the thirties, with the authorization of a two-ocean navy, and after the outbreak of the war in Europe a ceaseless stream of orders from abroad as well as from Washington had geared a large part of American industry to war production. The destroyer-bases deal and the subsequent occupation of Greenland and Iceland had given the nation air and naval bases halfway across the Atlantic; lend-lease had not only supplied the Allies with desperately needed food and war material, but converted American factories to war production; peacetime conscription, enacted in 1940 and re-enacted by a slim margin the following year, had provided a trained army of one and a half million officers and men. And already the United States and Britain had exchanged scientific secrets and techniques and were co-operating on such things as radar and atomic research.

The impact of actual war, therefore, did not catch the United States by surprise or require any radical change in the American economy, as in 1861 and 1917, for example, but merely an acceleration of what was already under way. The first task was to build up the armed services to wartime needs, and to equip them with vast quantities of the most modern weapons of war. This was done speedily and efficiently. The draft was extended to embrace all men between the ages of 18 and 45, and altogether during the war some 31 million men registered, over 17 million were examined, and almost 10 million were inducted into service. Counting voluntary enlistments, 15,145,115 men and women served in the armed forces between Pearl Harbor and V-J day; about 10.4 million in the army, about 3.9 million in the navy, about six hundred thousand in the marines and almost a quarter of a million in the coast guard. This vast army had to be housed, fed, trained, equipped, transported and maintained at a high degree of strength, health, efficiency and morale thousands of miles from home, and all this on a scale that dwarfed anything the United States had ever before undertaken.

In the First World War the United States had been able to ferry about two million soldiers to France, but these were dependent on Britain and France for a large part of their weapons and equipment. In the Second World War the United States was called on to transport well over twice that number of men to battlefields scattered over the globe —many of them in enemy hands—and not only to equip and maintain these armies but to contribute to the maintenance of the armies and air forces and to the civilian economy of Britain, Russia, China, the Free French, and others as well. All this required not only man power and weapons but a merchant marine large enough to maintain the flow of supplies to distant countries; engineering facilities to build camps, roads, harbors, air fields, and pipe lines; a medical corps to protect soldiers and sailors from a host of new diseases and to control epidemics; and above all a navy strong enough to dominate the seven seas and an air force able to carry the air war to the enemy.

Fortunately America's productive capacity was larger than that of all the enemy nations combined, and proved equal to the responsibilities placed upon it. President Roosevelt had called upon the United States to become "the arsenal of democracy," and the nation responded. The enormous energies of the whole people were speedily channeled into war production, and all of its activities—manufacturing, farming, mining, transportation, communication, finances and even science and education—were in some measure brought under new or enlarged governmental controls. Great new industries were created overnight, notably in the manufacture of magnesium and synthetic rubber, while others, such as aircraft and shipbuilding, were enormously expanded. The Far West, with its proximity to the Pacific war, made unparalleled strides in industrialism, and in population as well. Huge sums of Federal money were poured into the construction and enlargement of plants

for war purposes and the national government became the
owner of emergency shipyards and of facilities for the
manufacture of rubber and of aluminum, together with a
multitude of lesser establishments. Universities and industrial research laboratories were commandeered for the development of hundreds of new techniques, gadgets, and
inventions and for research in such things as radar, sonar,
the proximity fuse and the atom bomb.

With employment at an all-time high, three million
women added to the payrolls, labor working overtime and
foregoing strikes, and labor, management, capital, and government all co-operating, American industry shattered all
production records, exceeding the expectations of friend and
foe alike.

In the five years from July, 1940, to the defeat of Japan
in August, 1945, American factories and shipyards turned
out almost 300,000 military planes, 86,000 tanks, three
million machine guns, 71,000 naval ships of all kinds and
55 million tons of merchant shipping, and more barrels
of oil, more feet of lumber, more tons of steel and of
aluminum, than ever before in history. They produced
enough airplanes, tanks, jeeps, trucks, field telephones, rubber tires, radar sets, aluminum landing strips, and a thousand other things to supply not only the needs of their own
war machine, but the needs of Britain and to some degree
of Russia as well. Thus to Britain went thousands of planes,
over 100,000 trucks and jeeps, six million tons of steel and
a billion dollars' worth of ordnance, while Russia got over
400,000 trucks, 50,000 jeeps, 7000 tanks, and 420,000 tons
of aluminum. By the end of the war the lend-lease account
showed that the United States had supplied foodstuffs and
war material to the value of fifty billion dollars; the reverse
lend-lease account, largely in services and facilities, came
to about eight billion.

The most spectacular achievements were doubtless in the
aircraft and shipbuilding industries. "The Americans can't
build planes, only electric ice boxes and razor blades,"
Hermann Goering had said, but as with so many of his
prophecies this one was confounded. Although aircraft production got off to a slow start, once it was under way it
surpassed all expectations. Only some 23,000 military planes
had come off the assembly lines in the eighteen months

before Pearl Harbor, but in 1942 production reached 48,000 planes, in 1943 86,000, and in 1944 over 96,000. Every year, too, the planes produced at Willow Run or the Glen Martin plant outside Baltimore or the Douglas plant in southern California, were larger, faster, and more elaborate. American production, supplemented by British, assured the Allies of mastery of the air over Europe and in the Pacific as well by 1944. By the end of that year the aircraft industry, employing over two and one half million workers and turning out craft valued at some twenty billion dollars, had become the largest single industry in the country. So far had the United States come since the days of the Wright brothers at Kitty Hawk!

Equally remarkable was the success of the shipbuilding program upon which depended in so large a measure the outcome of the war. All through 1941 and 1942, U-boats took a heavy toll of shipping on the Atlantic, American and British alike, and for a time it seemed as if Hitler's plan to isolate Britain and deny America access to any part of the Old World might succeed. Not until the end of 1942 did Allied shipbuilding replace current losses. By building ships in great segments, by the use of electric welding, and by other innovations, the time for constructing a 14,000-ton freighter was reduced from months to weeks. The first so-called Liberty ship, the *Patrick Henry*, was launched in September, 1941; two years after Pearl Harbor American shipyards had delivered 2700 merchant ships of all types— the Liberty, the Victory, tankers, and others—with a total of 27 million deadweight tons. These, together with the substantial contributions from British shipyards and the Allied triumph in the Battle of the Atlantic, assured Allied supremacy on the high seas and made possible the survival of Britain and the ultimate invasion of the continent.

Labor as well as capital contributed its full share to the winning of the war. Immediately after Pearl Harbor the President called a conference representing workers and management, which adopted a perfectionist pledge of no strikes and no lockouts until the end of the war; the two great labor organizations, the A. F. of L. and the C.I.O., accepted this on the understanding that the cost of living, too, would be held down. Sharply rising prices, however, soon forced the newly established War Labor Board to apply the so-called

Little Steel formula—a wage increase of approximately fifteen per cent designed to meet rising prices. Labor complained, with some justice, that this was not enough and that business and the farmers were both profiting greatly by the war. Yet though wages did not rise as fast as labor thought right, full employment and generous overtime pay brought labor's earnings to an all-time high and left labor organizations in a stronger position than ever before. The great unions faithfully observed the no-strike pledge. The only serious labor difficulties came in the coal mines, where John L. Lewis four times led his United Mine Workers out on strike; but even with these interruptions coal production remained adequate.

Farmers, too, performed prodigies of production during the war years, and were loyally assisted by their cattle, hogs, and chickens. Working under severe handicaps of labor shortages and inadequate supplies of farm machinery, the farmer broke all agricultural records. Between 1939 and 1944 the productivity of American farms increased by one fourth, and in 1944 farmers raised 477 million more bushels of corn, 324 million more bushels of wheat, 500 million more pounds of rice, than in 1939, while the increase in cattle, hogs, and dairy products was even more astonishing.

Concentration on war production inevitably dislocated the civilian economy, yet Americans experienced fewer dislocations and suffered fewer hardships than did the peoples of any other major belligerent. There was no such total mobilization of man and woman power as in Britain or Russia, no such sweeping controls of the national economy, and no serious scarcities of essentials. The government rationed important categories of foodstuffs and consumer goods, but Americans generally ate better than ever before, and—except for the discomforts of housing shortages—lived as well. Income and corporation taxes were stepped up to unprecedented heights, but there was no limit on profits; national income left after taxes doubled between 1940 and 1945, and the depression, because a thing of the past, was almost forgotten. Almost every segment of American society except the clerical and professional classes—labor, farmer, businessman, and investor—enjoyed unprecedented prosperity. The national debt soared to over 250 billion but, in accordance with current economic theories for once popular with all classes alike, the debt was handed on to later generations to pay, and the national credit stood as high as at any time in American history.

Defense in the Pacific

PEARL HARBOR, together with the destruction of most of the American air force in the Philippines, and the sinking of the British battleships *Repulse* and *Prince of Wales,* constituted a major disaster. Yet worse was ahead. Within two months Japan had swept through Indo-China and Thailand and down the Malay peninsula, taken the great bastion of Singapore, breached the Malay barrier—Sumatra, Java, Borneo, the Celebes, and Timor—seized Rabaul east of New Guinea, pushed on to the Solomon Islands, and threatened Australia. Other Japanese forces had cut through Burma, isolated China, and stood along the borders of India. Three days after Pearl Harbor the Japanese had swarmed onto Luzon in the Philippines; by January they had seized Manila; and in the next four months they overcame heroic American and Filipino resistance on Bataan, stormed the island fort of Corregidor, and conquered the whole of the Philippines. Thus by the spring of 1942 they were masters of a large part of Asia, dominated the western Pacific, and controlled the teeming millions and the fabulous resources of oil, rubber, and tin of Indonesia. In all history no other conqueror had achieved victories so great at a cost so small.

Yet the Pacific witnessed a swift rally of American, British, and Australian forces. Although the Pacific Battle Fleet had been knocked out, all but two of its lost battleships were ultimately salvaged and fought another day, while most of its destroyers and its three great carriers were intact. With these as a nucleus, naval power was swiftly accumulated, and air reinforcements ferried to Hawaii, Australia, and the outlying islands still in Allied possession. By repulsing Japanese air attacks on Ceylon and building up strength along the Burma border, the British saved the central bastion of India, while General MacArthur, escaping from Corregidor, set up headquarters in Australia and began to build up ground and air forces there for an eventual counteroffensive.

American strategy called for holding operations until sufficient strength had been gathered for an amphibious attack along the north coast of New Guinea to Halmahera and the southern Philippines, and a series of naval attacks "up the ladder" of the Solomons, the Gilberts and Marshalls, the Marianas, and the Bonin Islands to within effective bombing distance of Japan herself. But it would be a year before the Americans could accumulate sufficient land, air, and naval strength to launch these offensives.

Meantime the Japanese, suffering from what one of their admirals called the "victory disease," planned to knock out the remnants of Allied power in the Pacific. In May, 1942, they struck at the American fleet in the Battle of the Coral Sea, in the waters just north of Australia. It was a conflict unique in character; "the first naval engagement in naval history," as Admiral King said, "in which surface ships did not engage a single shot," and it set the pattern for the future. All the fighting was done by carrier-based planes. The Japanese sank the carrier *Lexington*, a destroyer and a tanker, while American planes damaged two Japanese carriers, sank the carrier *Shoho* and a number of other ships. A few weeks later came the decisive battle of Midway (June 4–6). On June 4, American planes spotted an immense Japanese force of about fifty transports and thirty warships, including four carriers, moving on the American air and naval base on Midway, a small atoll about 1500 miles west of Hawaii. As Japanese planes roared on to Midway, American carrier-based planes struck at the invasion fleet and sank all four of its carriers, two heavy cruisers, and three destroyers, and crippled three battleships. The next day the Japanese fled, pursued by dive bombers which inflicted still further damage on the crippled fleet. It was the first major naval defeat Japan had ever suffered, and a foretaste of what was to come. It was, too, the turning point in the Pacific war. The United States was not yet ready to mount an offensive, but the momentum of the Japanese offensive was definitely checked.

Yet the Japanese were unwilling to acknowledge that they had been stopped. With a view to attacking the small Allied forces on the eastern tip of New Guinea they moved down the Solomons and began to build air bases at Tulagi and Guadalcanal. On August 7 a small force of American marines landed on Guadalcanal and seized the airfield there, renaming it Henderson Field. The Japanese reaction was sharp;

two days later a Japanese cruiser force surprised and all but wiped out the American and Australian fleet protecting the landing operation. With this Battle of Savo Island began a six months' fight for Guadalcanal—one of the toughest campaigns in American military history, and one of the most memorable. It was a campaign marked by a series of major naval engagements, by a dozen ferocious ground actions, and by almost daily air battles. The decisive action came in mid-November, 1942, with the naval Battle of Guadalcanal, which cost the enemy two battleships, a cruiser, two destroyers, and ten transports. Two more months of heavy fighting were ahead, but by February, 1943, the Japanese had evacuated the 'Canal, and thereafter the initiative in the southern Pacific passed to the Americans.

Thanks to the foresight in Washington which had laid down many new keels in 1938–1941, and to the spectacular success of the shipbuilding and ship-repair program thereafter, naval supremacy in the Pacific passed to the United States by the spring of 1943. One token of the new situation was the operations in the fog-bound Aleutians where the Japanese were driven from Attu in May and from Kiska the following August; with these victories all danger of attack by way of Alaska disappeared. Another was the Battle of the Bismarck Sea (March 2, 1943), which cost the Japanese an entire troop convoy and the life of Admiral Yamamoto, Japan's ablest military commander. A third was the launching of a full-scale offensive in the central Solomons and a series of devastating raids on the Japanese bastion at Rabaul, which were designed to protect MacArthur's forces from interference from that quarter. All this prepared the way for the full-scale offensive which was to reach its climax in the reconquest of the Philippines and the seizure of Iwo Jima and Okinawa.

The Battle of the Atlantic

THUS by almost superhuman efforts, the Americans, with such aid as the British Dominions and the Dutch could contribute, had staved off disaster in the Pacific and paved the way for victory. Meantime the war in the European theater, too, was going well. As we have seen, the basic decision of the war was to contain Japan until Germany could be knocked out. But before the United States or even Britain could come to grips with the Nazis, or their Italian allies, they had to solve the great problem of logistics. Obviously Germany could not be attacked from America. It could not even be attacked from Britain unless the United States could keep Britain going with food, ships, planes and other materials of war and then transform that island into an impregnable military base for their own operations. The first task, then, was to win control of the Atlantic.

The Battle of the Atlantic, upon the outcome of which depended victory or defeat, actually opened well before Pearl Harbor. Perhaps its opening gun, or gambit, was the farsighted decision—taken, to be sure, with dubious authority—to exchange overage destroyers for bases in the Atlantic and the Caribbean, and the subsequent acquisition of bases on Greenland and Iceland. Even the fighting phase of the battle began three months before formal entry into war, when President Roosevelt made the U-boat attack on the U.S.S. *Greer* the occasion for issuing a "shoot-on-sight" order to the United States Navy. The battle between German submarines, surface-raiders, and mine-layers, and the British and American navies and air forces thus begun, continued until the end of the war. Victory finally rested with the Allies, but by the narrowest of margins. The first phase of that contest, from 1941 to 1943, was one of the decisive battles of history.

It was a formidable task to beat the U-boats that swarmed like wolf-packs through the North Atlantic and eventually into the South Atlantic, along Atlantic coastal waters, and even into the Caribbean Sea. The British attempted to hem them in along the French, German, and Norwegian coasts, or to bomb their pens at St. Nazaire, Brest, Bremerhaven, and other ports, but without much success. All through 1941 and 1942 losses to submarines mounted alarmingly, and to these were added losses to enemy mines strewn by the thousand along the perilous approaches to Britain. By the end of 1940, shipping losses totaled about five million tons; in 1941, U-boats and mines took another four million tons. American entry into the war added to the U-boats' risks, but it also added to their potential victims. During the first four months of 1942 the U-boats sank 82 ships with a total of half a million tons, in the North Atlantic alone; then they shifted their main attack to the Gulf and the Caribbean and knocked off another 142 ships totaling almost three quarters of a million tons. And during this six months' period the Allies managed to sink only twenty submarines—less than a single month's production.

What fighting off U-boat attacks was like is told by S. E. Morison, historian of the American Navy in the Second World War:

Take a westbound convoy in February, escorted by United States coast-guard cutters *Spencer* and *Campbell*, five Canadian and British corvettes, and a Polish destroyer. Captain P. R. Heineman, USN, was the commander. Head winds slowed speed of advance to 4 knots; yet the escorts managed to fuel under way in tempestuous seas from tankers in the convoy. On 21 February the two cutters and a Liberator flying from the United Kingdom sank a U-boat. During the next three days when the convoy was outside the range of air protection, it suffered six attacks by a large wolf pack of submarines and lost five ships. Polish destroyer *Burza* depth-charged one U-boat which dove to 130 fathoms; its commander then blew all tanks, surfaced at a steep angle, and was promptly rammed and sunk by the *Campbell*. The rest of the wolf pack continued to snap at the convoy for two days more, but the energy and skill of the escort got the ships through with the loss of but one more. Heineman's escort unit, relieved by the Canadian navy south of Newfoundland, had barely tasted the uneasy shelter afforded by Argentia harbor when it had to go out and take charge of an eastbound convoy of 56 ships. Westerly gales with hail and snow battered this convoy for nine days running. Though the escorts were now experts and the merchant crews showed both courage and discipline, six ships were lost in so rough a sea that few survivors could be rescued.

From the moment of the German invasion, Russia had clamored loudly for aid from both Britain and the United States and, pressed as they were, the western Allies did their best to meet these demands. Until the Persian Gulf route was opened in 1943 all war material to Russia had to be shipped across the Arctic to the ports of Murmansk and Archangel. Exposed as it was to ceaseless attacks from German planes, submarines, and cruisers based in Norwegian waters, this was the most perilous of all convoy routes; in

1942 no less than one fourth of all the ships that ran this gauntlet were lost. Yet in that year nineteen convoys fought their way through ice, fog, and Nazi attacks to the northern Russian ports.

Gradually the Allies got the upper hand in this grim see-saw battle between surface and underwater ships. They established convoys to protect their merchant and troop ships across the perilous waters, and of the thousands of ships escorted by cruisers, destroyers, corvettes, and other warships, only a dozen or so were sunk. They established air patrols out from Newfoundland, Iceland, Brazil, Bermuda, Ascension Island, and, eventually, the Azores. They used sonar to spot the U-boats and "hedgehog" depth charges to sink them; they devoted over a thousand ships to sweep up mines, and equipped their ships with "degaussing" irons to give warning of mines or submarines. By these and other methods losses were cut sharply, and by the summer of 1943 the Allies were sinking an average of one submarine a day.

There was still trouble ahead, to be sure. Notwithstanding incessant bombings on German industrial cities, submarine production increased steadily, reaching its peak in 1944 with the launching of 387 U-boats. And Hitler's scientists were working feverishly to put into production the new 250-foot electric-driven "Schnorkel" U-boat which could make seventeen knots an hour and stay under water indefinitely. Fortunately these did not get into full production until the very end of the war—too late to affect its outcome. By midsummer of 1943 the Allies had definitely won the Battle of the Atlantic, and were in position to build up for a large-scale offensive on the continent.

North Africa and Italy

IN JUNE, 1942, even as the Pacific Fleet was repelling the Japanese at Midway and the Allied convoys were fighting their way across the precarious Atlantic, Roosevelt and Churchill met at Washington with the Combined Chiefs of Staff to plan Hitler's downfall. The Americans wanted to open a "second front" on the continent in 1942 or, at the latest, 1943; the British, who had made their own island impregnable to invasion and were very conscious of the risks of a premature attack on *Festung Europa,* wished to put off the second front until the Allies had built up adequate reserves and won complete mastery of the air. The decision to launch an offensive on the shores of North Africa was in the nature of a compromise between these two points of view.

It was, nevertheless, a bold decision. There were only four months in which to plan and execute the grand design —to train soldiers for amphibious warfare, stockpile supplies, find hundreds of merchant vessels, transports, and warships and protect them through the submarine-infested waters, conduct delicate negotiations with the Free French, with Vichy France, with Franco's Spain. The plan required, moreover, the most delicate co-ordination of invasion forces sailing from ports in the United States and the British Isles and arriving simultaneously at harbors thousands of miles distant, and of General Alexander's Eighth Army in Egypt.

Yet if the risks were great, the rewards were tempting. If the operation could be carried through to success it might ward off the danger of Spanish entry into the war on the side of the Axis, rally Free French forces in the homeland and in Africa and encourage resistance forces everywhere, assure control of the Mediterranean and thus shorten greatly the lifeline to the Near East, clear North Africa of Axis forces, and furnish a springboard for an invasion of Italy and the "soft underbelly" of Europe.

Command of Operation Torch, as it was known, was entrusted to General Dwight D. Eisenhower, then commanding American forces in the European theater. Once started, the whole complex plan went off like clockwork—all but that part of it which called for French co-operation. By midnight of November 7 three vast Allied fleets stood outside the harbors of Casablanca, Oran, and Algiers, and the next morning, as ships and planes pounded the defenses, the troops splashed ashore. They had expected to be met with open arms; instead they were met with shot and shell. The landings at Algiers were relatively easy, but those at Oran involved stiff fighting, while Casablanca was not reduced until Admiral Hewitt had sunk most of the French fleet defending its harbor. Fortunately for the military situation Admiral Darlan, a top Vichy official then in North Africa, issued a cease-fire order

on November 11, and brought his forces over to the Allies.
He was promptly disavowed by the doddering Pétain who was
still convinced that the Axis powers were bound to win the
war. For a time repercussions of this "deal" with the notorious Darlan threatened to be serious, but his assassination a
few weeks later cleared the air. After an abortive attempt
to place the legendary General Henri Giraud in command,
the Allies recognized the claims of the heroic Charles de
Gaulle, who had first raised the standard of resistance, to
head the provisional government of French North Africa and
to speak for the Free French forces everywhere.

The invasion caught the Germans by surprise, but they
reacted swiftly and effectively. They promptly took over the
whole of Vichy France, though failing to get the French
fleet at Toulon before it was scuttled. They flew twenty
thousand men across the Sicilian Straits into Tunisia, seized
the major ports of Tunis and Bizerte, set up airfields in the
interior, and prepared to make the Allies pay a high price
for the sands of Africa.

Then the race for Tunisia began. Already General Bernard
Montgomery had launched that famous offensive which was
to carry the Eighth Army from Egypt to Tunis—and beyond.
At El Alamein, one of the decisive battles of the war (Oct.
23–Nov. 3, 1942), he had overwhelmed Rommel's mixed
German and Italian army, and then taken up a relentless
pursuit of its remnants across Cyrenaica and Tripolitania.
Now General Eisenhower pushed across the five hundred
miles of rugged country from Algiers to Tunis. By the end
of November he had reached Mateur, only 55 miles from
his goal. But he had overextended himself. His communications were stretched thin; the weather turned foul; the Germans controlled all the good airfields. The Axis held. Then
in February, 1943, they counterattacked at Kasserine Pass,
threw the green American troops back in confusion, and
threatened to cut the Allied armies in two. Reinforcements
were rushed to the scene; the air force came out in strength;
and the Allies rallied and recovered the initiative.

Meantime Montgomery had brought Rommel to bay along
the strongly fortified Mareth Line just inside Tunisia. In
one of the most brilliant actions of the war he struck the
enemy front and rear, forced him out of his defenses, and
sent him reeling back towards Sfax along the Gulf of Gabès.

Now the American, British, and French armies closed in for the kill. On May 7 both Tunis and Bizerte fell; six days later a quarter of a million dazed German and Italian soldiers surrendered on Cape Bon. The conquest of North Africa was complete, and the way to Europe lay open.

The propitious outcome of this campaign did not catch the Allied leaders by surprise. They had already made their plans to exploit victory. In January, 1943, Roosevelt, Churchill, and their staffs met at Casablanca in one of the important conferences of the war. For the first time since 1939 the auspices were favorable. The Americans had won Guadalcanal and wrested the initiative from the Japanese in the Pacific. The embattled Russians had scored a decisive victory at Stalingrad, graveyard of a great German army and of German hopes, and were now poised for their massive counteroffensive. Montgomery had beaten Rommel and there was every prospect that the Axis would be thrown out of Africa and that the Mediterranean would be cleared. It was, as Churchill said, "the end of the beginning." It was, as we can see now, the turning point of the war. Against this background the Allied leaders made their fateful decisions: to invade Sicily and Italy at the first possible moment; to step up the antisubmarine warfare; to build up strength in the Pacific for a major offensive, and to end the war only on the basis of unconditional surrender.

This formula, which won general approval at the time, was later to come in for a great deal of criticism. It was argued that by leaving no room for negotiation and holding out no hope of easier terms it discouraged rebellious groups within the Axis nations, stiffened Axis resistance, and thus prolonged the war. Of course we never know "what might have happened" in history. But the formula did not delay Italian surrender; there is no evidence that anti-Hitler forces in Germany or anti-Emperor forces in Japan were ever strong enough to amount to anything; and neither Hitler nor the Japanese war lords were prepared to negotiate. In all likelihood unconditional surrender neither hastened nor prolonged the end of the war.

The plans formulated at Casablanca were swiftly put into execution. Early in June, General Eisenhower launched a large-scale attack on Sicily, the Americans landing on the southwest coast, the British at Syracuse on the east. Italian resistance was negligible, but the Germans put up a stiff fight. Within forty days the Allies overran the entire island, capturing one hundred thousand Italian prisoners and vast quantities of war material at a loss to themselves of about 25,000 men.

Even as the remnants of the German divisions were being ferried across the Straits of Messina, the Allies were planning to knock Italy out of the war. That weakest of Axis partners was already groggy from the blows that had been rained upon her, her people sick both of the war and of the tyrant Mussolini who had led them to a series of disasters unparalleled in their history. On July 25 Mussolini was deposed and the next month a provisional government opened peace negotiations with General Eisenhower. On September 3, 1943, just as the victorious Allies stormed across the Straits of Messina onto Calabria, Italy surrendered unconditionally. It was, as Roosevelt said, one down and two to go.

Yet this was, in a sense, premature. Italy was out of the war, to be sure, but the Germans were still in Italy and prepared to contest every yard of ground. The Italian campaign proved one of the toughest of the war. It opened, auspiciously enough, with the savagely contested amphibious landings on Salerno beach, thirty miles south of Naples. This beachhead once secured, the American Fifth Army and the British Eighth Army pushed swiftly on to take Naples itself and the invaluable Foggia airfields, from whose landing strips their bombers could hammer the Balkans, Austria, and southern Germany. But after the fall of Naples the campaign lost momentum. Taking advantage of the mountainous terrain of southern and central Italy, the Germans had erected a series of frowning defense lines—the Volturno, the Winter, the Gustav, and the Hitler; these, with geography and weather, combined to present almost insuperable obstacles to Allied tanks, planes, and armor. It required eight months of the hardest kind of fighting and a series of pitched battles, of which Monte Cassino and Anzio Beach were the toughest, to cover the eighty miles from Naples to Rome. Not until May, 1944, did the Allies finally crack the Cassino defenses and break through the German ring around Anzio Beach. On June 4, just as the vast invasion armada was getting ready to set out for the Normandy beaches, the victorious Allies entered Rome.

The Great Invasion

THE GRAND STRATEGY of the war, and of the invasion of the continent, had been worked out in a series of conferences between the Allied war leaders in 1943. The Casablanca Conference set up a combined planning staff in London, and the Trident Conference in Washington, in May, 1943, fixed the tentative date of the invasion one year ahead. In August a full-dress Anglo-American conference at Quebec canvassed "the whole field of world operations," and, as the official statement recited, "made the necessary decisions . . . to provide for the forward actions of fleets, armies and air forces." In September, Russia was for the first time successfully brought into the general plan by a gathering of foreign ministers in Moscow. This group set up a European advisory commission with headquarters in London to make plans and recommendations for joint action in the international sphere, and issued a declaration committing themselves to a postwar international organization for peace. The most important conferences came at the end of the year, in Teheran and Cairo. At Teheran (in Persia) Churchill and Stalin discussed the grand strategy of the war and laid definite plans for a series of mighty concerted movements of Russian and Anglo-American forces the following year; Cairo was largely concerned with plans for the war in the Pacific and the eventual settlement of Far Eastern affairs.

Thus Operation Overlord, as the invasion came to be called, had been planned both in broad strategic principle and in detail for fully a year before it was launched. Among other things it was decided that as the United States would contribute the largest proportion of men and material, the supreme commander should be an American. Eisenhower's success in Africa, Sicily, and Italy, and his popularity with the civil and military leaders of all the Allied nations, made him the logical choice for the job. In January, Eisenhower moved his headquarters to London, and with General Sir Frederick Morgan as chief of his planning staff began detailed preparation for the invasion.

No more formidable task ever confronted the military forces of any nation or combination of nations. Hitler himself had been unable to leap the English Channel even in 1940 and 1941, when he had overwhelming superiority in men and planes, and when the British defenses were still largely makeshift. And he had had four years in which to make the defenses along the French coast impregnable. For the Allies to breach those defenses, land and maintain an army in hostile territory, and build it up to strength where it could meet the Wehrmacht anywhere on the continent on even terms, required the accumulation of massive land and naval strength and of immense reserves of supplies and materials of war.

It required, too, one other essential: command of the air. Not only of the air over the Channel and the French coast, but over the whole of the continent as far east as Berlin and Vienna. Before the Allies could embark upon an invasion with any hope of success they would have to batter German industry, disrupt German communications, and ground the German air forces. This was their chief concern and their chief military accomplishment in the European theater in 1943, and the early months of 1944.

The real beginning of the air attack on Germany came on May 30, 1942, with a thousand-bomber raid on the great industrial city of Cologne. This was followed by a whole series of punishing raids on the cities of the Rhineland and the Ruhr and deep into the heart of Germany. Not until 1943 did the American air force really join in the battle, though it had participated in token raids in the previous year. Thus, during 1942 the Royal Air Force dropped a total of 75,000 tons of bombs on German-held Europe; the United States Air Forces based on Britain dropped 2000 tons of bombs. The American build-up, however, was rapid. In 1943, American bombers hurled 123,000 tons of bombs against the enemy, and the British an additional 213,000 tons. In 1944 the Allied bombing rose to a crescendo. By that time the British had developed a technique of saturation bombing, and the Americans of precision and through-the-clouds bombing. Day after day giant Flying Fortresses and night after night Halifaxes, Lancasters, and Stirlings sailed out over Germany, Austria, and Occupied France, smashing great cities into rubble, destroying factories, railroads, canals, U-boat

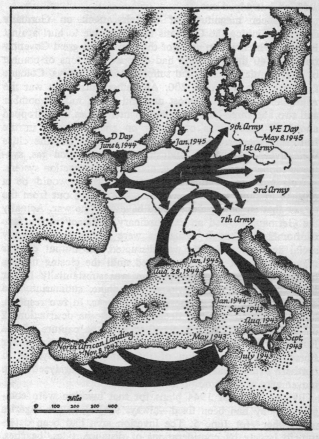

The Invasion of Nazi Europe
(This map does not include the armies of the United Kingdom,
the British Commonwealth, and other allies.)

pens, and a hundred other targets. Every major city in Germany was partially destroyed, and before the war was over Hamburg, Bremen, Cologne, Frankfurt, Essen, and others were all but wiped out.

The sheer magnitude of the air attack on Germany dwarfed anything the Germans had been able to hurl against Britain in the first two years of the war. In the great Coventry raid of 1940 the Luftwaffe had dropped 200 tons of bombs; by that standard Berlin had suffered 363 Coventrys, Cologne 269, and Hamburg over 200. Altogether during the war the Allied air forces flew almost one and a half million bomber and two and three-quarter million fighter sorties, and dropped about 2,700,000 tons of bombs on enemy targets in the European theater. The principal targets were not the cities themselves, but such key industries as oil, aviation gas, synthetic rubber, and ball-bearing, and the transportation system.

Yet immense as this achievement was, it would be a mistake to suppose that Germany was knocked out from the air, or that air power alone could have won the war. Actually the Germans showed an extraordinary resiliency in the face of bombing. Though casualties were heavy and ordinary social and economic life was disrupted, the output of war material was not seriously affected until the closing months of 1944. German war production was substantially higher in 1944 than in any previous year; plane, submarine, and ordnance production all increased that year. In two respects, however, the air war had decisive results: the destruction of oil and aviation gasoline, together with the capture of the Rumanian oil fields, grounded much of the German Air Force, and the disruption of the transportation system in northern France and western Germany all but paralyzed troop movements at the time of the invasion.

By the spring of 1944 plans for that invasion were complete. D-day had been fixed—always subject to the vagaries of weather—for June 5. The invasion area had been determined, largely by considerations of distance, tides, beaches, and shore defenses, as the Normandy coast at the hinge of the Cotentin Peninsula; the eastern sector of this was assigned to the British, the western to the Americans. The Allies had gathered a vast host of almost three million soldiers, sailors, and airmen. An armada of four thousand warships and boats of all kinds was ready to ferry the invasion army across the Channel and keep it supplied with the mountains of material necessary for a full-scale campaign; eleven thousand planes prepared to protect the invaders and pin the German Air Force to the ground. There were new weapons, specially contrived landing-boats, artificial harbors, and a hundred other things designed to make the landings a success. So heavy was the stockpile of supplies in Britain that the balloon barrage alone, it was said, kept the island from sinking into the sea. "All southern England," wrote General Eisenhower in *Crusade in Europe,*

was one vast military camp, crowded with soldiers awaiting final word to go, and piled high with supplies and equipment awaiting transport to the far shore of the Channel. The whole area was cut off from the rest of England. . . . Every separate encampment, barrack, vehicle park, and every unit was carefully charted on our master maps. The scheduled movement of each unit had been so worked out that it would reach the embarkation point at the exact time the vessels would be ready to receive it. . . . The mighty host was as tense as a coiled spring, and indeed that is exactly what it was—a great human spring, coiled for the moment when its energy should be released and it would vault the English Channel in the greatest amphibious assault ever attempted.

Foul weather threatened the whole plan, but Eisenhower gambled on clearing skies and gave the word to go on June 5. That night planes hammered the whole of northern France from Belgium to Brittany, a fake fleet sailed for the Pas de Calais area to deceive the Germans, and three airborne divisions parachuted behind German lines on the Normandy coast. Then early in the morning of June 6 the invasion armada approached the beaches and, breaking through formidable underwater obstacles, the Allied soldiers swarmed ashore.

The Germans, who had expected the main attack to come in the Pas de Calais area, were taken by surprise. Though they continued for some time to regard the Normandy invasion as a diversionary attack, they reacted to it vigorously enough. But Allied command of the air prevented any aerial interference with the invasion fleet, while the destruction of railroads and bridges all the way back to Paris made it

impossible for the German commander, Von Rundstedt, to
rush up reinforcements in time to deny the Allies a beachhead. By the close of D-day the Allies had breached the
Atlantic Wall, landed a total of 120,000 men, and begun to
work their way inland to link up with the gallant paratroopers. Within a week they had over 300,000 men and
100,000 tons of supplies on shore, and controlled an area
seventy miles in length and five to fifteen miles deep. Then
the Americans struck westward, cut across the Cotentin
Peninsula, and by June 26 captured the great port of Cherbourg.

During the next month the Allies won the Battle of Normandy. On the east the British took the key city of Caen;
on the west the Americans captured Saint-Lô, gateway to
the south. By the end of the month there were a million men
ashore, and the supply problem had been largely solved by
the construction of great artificial harbors and of pipe lines
to pump oil to the motorized divisions. Now, with clear
numerical superiority over the enemy and with unchallenged
command of the air, the Anglo-Americans were ready to
break through the German defenses and fan out over the
whole of northern France.

On July 25 the battle for Normandy was over, and the
battle for France began. With irresistible force General
Patton's Third Army smashed through the German defenses
west of Saint-Lô, raced to Coutances ten miles to the south,
seized Avranches, and ground up a German counterattack
in the so-called Falaise Gap. Then, with the battered remnants of the German army in headlong flight toward the
Siegfried Line, one wing of the American army swept up all
of Brittany but a few harbor towns, and another rolled eastward along the Loire toward Paris, while the British and
Canadians raced along the coast to Belgium and Holland.
Paris was liberated on August 23; a few days later the British
captured Brussels and the great port of Antwerp; and by
September 11 the American army had liberated Luxembourg
and penetrated into Germany at Aachen. Meantime another
invasion force had landed on the southern coast of France,
overcome feeble German resistance, and with the assistance
of the Free French captured the great ports of Toulon and
Marseilles and swept north along the Rhône Valley to the
borders of Switzerland. By mid-September all France was

cleared of the enemy. It was one of the most spectacular victories in the history of warfare.

Everywhere that summer and fall the Axis was in retreat. Stalin had promised to co-ordinate his offensive with that of the western Allies, and even as the Americans were battering their way to Cherbourg he launched a vast offensive along a thousand-mile front. On the far north Finland was invaded and forced out of the war; at the center the Russian armies smashed across the Ukraine and Poland to the gates of Warsaw; on the south they overran Rumania and fought their way into Yugoslavia and Hungary. In Italy, too, the Germans were in desperate trouble. After the fall of Rome, Allied armies had moved northward toward Lombardy, seizing one great city after another, and by September they reached the storied Po Valley. And in the Pacific MacArthur had landed on the Philippines, and the Navy had inflicted on the Japanese the worst defeat in their history. If the victories in North Africa had been the end of the beginning, this series of victories was the beginning of the end.

Victory in Europe

BY SEPTEMBER, 1944, the Allied armies had gone so far and so fast that they had outrun their supplies. They had to stop to consolidate their gains, reorganize their forces, clear ports, build up supplies, construct airfields, rebuild roads and bridges, and prepare for the campaign that should carry them across the Rhine into Germany. Their hardest fighting, as it proved, was still ahead, for the Germans defended their homeland with fanatical courage. The powerful Siegfried Line stretched from Holland to the Swiss border, and behind it lay the broad Rhine. A spectacular attempt to flank the Siegfried Line by a large-scale airdrop on Arnhem and Nijmegen in Holland failed by a hairbreadth, and the opposing armies settled down to a slugging match. That fall of 1944 saw fighting in the hills and woods of Belgium, Luxembourg, Alsace, and Lorraine much like that in the Wilderness of Virginia eighty years earlier. There was a whole series of bitterly-fought battles, each one as savage as any in which Americans had ever been engaged and each one as costly: the Battle of the Scheldt Estuary—fought largely by the British and Canadians—which opened Antwerp to Allied shipping; the battle for Aachen and the Roer River dams which involved fighting in the savage Hürtgen Forest and which was not finally won until the following February; the battle for the great fortress city of Metz and the Saar Basin; the battle for Strasbourg and Alsace. By mid-December Eisenhower's forces had largely won all of these battles and stood ready to plunge to the Rhine.

Then came a setback that for a short time threatened serious consequences. Against the advice of his top generals, Hitler decided to use all his remaining resources in the west on a last desperate gamble: a large-scale counterattack designed to split the Allied armies in two and carry the Wehrmacht back to the Channel coast or even to Paris. It came at the dawn of December 15 along a fifty-mile front on the snow-clad hills of the Ardennes, and won startling initial success. Within ten days the Germans had run over the thin American defense lines, surrounded the garrison at Bastogne, and plunged a spearhead fifty miles through the Ardennes to the river Meuse. For a moment there was grave danger of a complete break-through. But the American rally was swift. The defenders on the edges of the bulge held firm; the intrepid garrison at Bastogne, hurriedly reinforced by the 101st Airborne Division, was surrounded and cut off but put up a resistance that threw the whole German timetable out of gear and won for itself enduring fame. The German advance was stayed, then beaten back. By mid-January the Germans had forfeited all their gains, and had paid 120,000 men and hundreds of tanks and planes for their ill-advised gamble.

Then just as the Russians launched their great winter offensive destined to carry them to the gates of Vienna and Berlin, the Allies prepared to plunge across the Rhine and close in on Hitler from the west. The Germans retired across the river, destroying the bridges as they went, but the watch on the Rhine was faulty and on March 7 an American task force found the Ludendorff Bridge near Bonn still intact, and seized it. Within a few days the Americans had five divisions across the river and began to fan out north and south. Two weeks later, to the accompaniment of the greatest aerial bombardment of the war, the whole Allied army vaulted the Rhine from Cleve to Mannheim. Once across they stabbed through the German lines at breakneck speed, one armored division covering ninety miles in a single day. The American First and Ninth Armies drew a giant noose around the Ruhr, trapping over 300,000 Germans. Patton's Third Army sped toward Kassel and the Elbe River. To the south Patch's Seventh Army drove through Bavaria to the Czechoslovak border, and to the north Montgomery's British and Canadian troops raced along the coast through Bremen and Hamburg to the Baltic.

It was the end. With the Russians closing in from the east and the south, and the Americans and British from the west, and with the Germans in Italy throwing down their guns, the Wehrmacht began to crumble into fragments. On April 25, Russians and Americans met at the Elbe, and the two armies that had started on the beaches of Normandy and the banks of the Dnieper, 2000 miles apart, cut Germany in twain. Fanatical defenders put up a last-ditch fight for Berlin; when it was clear that the city was doomed Hitler committed suicide. Already Mussolini had been murdered by infuriated Italians. On May 7 what was left of the German army surrendered unconditionally. Thus the Reich that was to have lived a thousand years crashed to ruin.

One of the architects of the victory was no longer alive to see the vindication of his plans or the triumph of his cause. Franklin D. Roosevelt had died on April 12.

Even as the Allied armies were fighting their way into Normandy in the summer of 1944, the two major political parties had made nominations for the fall presidential elections. The Democrats turned, almost inevitably, to the man who had three times led them to victory and who was now leading the United Nations to victory, and renominated Roosevelt on the first ballot. The Republicans, repudiating Wendell Willkie as too close to the New Deal in his domestic views, too much of an internationalist in his foreign, and in any event too much of a political maverick, turned to Governor Thomas E. Dewey of New York, a party regular mildly liberal on domestic questions and apparently converted by the pressure of events to internationalism. Although the campaign was bitterly fought its outcome was never seriously in doubt. The President carried 36 states with 432 electoral votes; Dewey carried 12 states with 99 electoral votes; in the popular vote Roosevelt had a plurality of three and a half million.

In his fourth inaugural address Roosevelt pledged himself not alone to victory but to the construction of a firm international order after victory was achieved. "We have learned," he said,

that we cannot live alone, at peace; that our own well-being is dependent upon the well-being of other nations far away. We have learned that we must live as men and not as ostriches, nor as dogs in the manger. We have learned to be citizens of the world, members of the human community.

More and more, as victory approached, Roosevelt's thoughts had been turning to this great problem of peace and international law, and more and more his energies had been devoted to its solution. In February, 1945, he had taken the long trip to Yalta in the Crimea to confer with Stalin, Churchill, and their military and civilian advisers about the war and the postwar settlements. Already it was clear that the war in Europe was drawing to a close, and though it was expected that the defeat of Japan would require another year or two, it was clear that that defeat was ordained. So while much of the business of the Crimea, or Yalta, Conference was concerned with such purely military matters as Russia's entry into the Pacific war, much of it, too, was devoted to planning for the postwar world. And when Roosevelt and his military advisers returned from Yalta they believed, so Harry Hopkins tells us, that

this was the dawn of the new day we had all been praying for and talking about for so many years. We were absolutely certain that we had won the first great victory for peace—and by we I mean all of us, the whole civilized human race.

Even during the presidential campaign the opposition had criticized Roosevelt as a "tired old man." The characterization was correct, for the war had taxed his energies and strained even his buoyant spirit. He returned from Yalta obviously a sick man and, for the first time, gave his report to Congress from his wheel chair. Then he went to his winter home at Warm Springs, Georgia, to rest and to prepare for the opening of the first United Nations conference in San Francisco. On April 12 as he was drafting a Jefferson Day address he suffered a cerebral hemorrhage and died. The last words he wrote were a fitting epitaph to his own life: "The only limit to our realization of tomorrow will be our doubts of today. Let us move forward with strong and active faith."

Victory in the Pacific

THE RECONQUEST of Guadalcanal was, in a sense, a holding operation designed to block off the Japanese advance, get bases for an intensive bombing of Rabaul, and clear the way for the major offensive scheduled to begin in November, 1943. That offensive was to take two forms: an attack by MacArthur along the New Guinea coast to Halmahera and the central Philippines, and an advance by Admiral Nimitz up the island ladder to within bombing distance of the Japanese home islands. Both were amphibious operations, but the Army played the largest role in the first, the Navy and Marine Corps bore the burden of the second. A third possible approach to Japan was through Burma and over the Burma Road to China. But the problem of transportation and supply here proved insuperable, and little aid was forthcoming from the Chinese Nationalists; although Burma was eventually cleared of the enemy, that campaign had no effect on the outcome of the war.

The offensive jumped off, as planned, with an amphibious attack on the island of Bougainville in the northern Solomons on November 1, 1943. Alive to the danger of this thrust toward Rabaul, the Japanese struck back, but at the Battle of Empress Augusta Bay they were roundly defeated. From Bougainville the Americans moved on to islands east and west of Rabaul, and by incessant bombings largely neutralized that bastion. With their flank thus secured MacArthur was able to leapfrog along the New Guinea coast, and Admiral Nimitz to start on the long sea lanes that led to Okinawa.

The basis for the advance on Japan was the spectacular growth of the American navy and naval air arm to the point where it not only had supremacy over Japan but was stronger than the combined navies of all the warring powers.

Indeed, Admiral Halsey's famous Task Force 58 (alternately called 38) alone was more powerful than the entire Japanese navy. By midsummer of 1944 the American navy totaled over four thousand ships, including 613 warships. Seven great new battleships had joined the Pacific fleet since Pearl Harbor, and almost one hundred carriers with thousands of planes—the Grumman Wildcat and Hellcat, the Curtis Helldiver, the Douglas Dauntless, and many others.

Now this mighty force was ready to strike a series of prodigious blows. Admiral Nimitz had no intention of trying to reduce each of the scores of little enemy-held atolls scattered throughout the southern and central Pacific. His strategy was to capture key islands in each of the major island groups, build air bases on them, and then leapfrog on to another island hundreds of miles closer to Japan, leaving the Japanese garrisons on the outlying islands to "wither on the vine." Eventually it proved possible to bypass even such great islands as Mindanao in the southern Philippines and Formosa off the coast of China. The Japanese, who had made the original error of over-extending themselves, compounded that error by dissipating their strength.

The first blow was aimed at Tarawa in the Gilbert Islands. This tiny atoll was garrisoned by some 3000 Japanese marines, and protected by the most elaborate system of defenses that the Americans had yet encountered; its reduction was a bloody affair that cost the Americans almost a thousand dead and two thousand wounded. Two months later the Navy moved on to the Marshalls, hundreds of miles to the north. Kwajalein atoll, garrisoned by 8000 fanatical Japanese, was the first objective. The marines landed on January 31, 1944, and within three days had conquered the island and wiped out the enemy. Then they moved on and mopped up Eniwetok, 350 miles to the west.

Now with Rabaul and Truk neutralized and the Gilberts and Marshalls in American hands, the Fifth Amphibious Force headed for the Marianas 1200 miles west and only 1500 miles from Tokyo. The chief objectives here were Saipan, which the Japanese had converted into a powerful air and naval base, and Guam, wrested from the Americans in the offensive of December, 1941. With the approach of Admiral Spruance's task force into what were practically home waters, the Japanese navy came out to fight. The ensuing Battle of the Philippine Sea (June 19–20, 1944), fought entirely by carrier-based planes, destroyed the enemy carrier fleet and badly crippled its battleships and cruisers. Then the Marianas were systematically reduced, but only after some of the hardest fighting in the Pacific war. Saipan took three weeks and cost the Americans 15,000 casualties, and Guam was almost as hard a nut to crack. By August, however, the Marianas were in American hands, and soon giant B-29s were sailing out from their airstrips to bomb the Japanese home islands.

These victories in the southern and central Pacific opened the way to a direct assault on the Philippines. So successful had the American island-hopping technique proved itself that General MacArthur decided to bypass Mindanao and strike for the heart of the islands. On October 20, 1944, a vast fleet of 600 vessels, including transports with more than one hundred thousand soldiers, sailed into Leyte Gulf. MacArthur splashed ashore. "People of the Philippines," he said, "I have returned . . . Rally to me." He had, and they did. Within a short time he had a couple of hundred thousand men in the Philippines, and these were joined by loyal Filipinos who had long waged guerrilla warfare against the hated Japanese conquerors.

This was a challenge that the Japanese could not ignore, and in desperation they flung everything they had at the Americans. The Battle of Leyte Gulf (Oct. 23–25) was the last and greatest naval battle of the war. It was really three separate engagements, and in each of them the Americans were victorious. The Japanese fleet never recovered from the beating it took in this battle, and thereafter it opposed only negligible resistance to the American advance. MacArthur swiftly overran Leyte, then moved on to Luzon; Manila fell in February, 1945, and by April all the islands were liberated.

Even as MacArthur was reconquering the Philippines the Navy had taken the next long step toward Japan. The tiny island of Iwo Jima was only 800 miles from Tokyo. For a month planes subjected it to daily bombing; and for a week a task force of six battleships, cruisers, and destroyers pounded its defenses. Then on February 19 the Marines stormed the beaches. It took a month and five thousand casualties to wipe out the Japanese defenders, but by mid-

March American bombers were taking off from its airstrips for Tokyo, on a series of incendiary-bomb raids that did as much damage as the great British raids on Hamburg. Then the Army and Navy moved on to the first of the Japanese home islands, Okinawa in the Ryukyus. In desperation the Japanese resorted to kamikaze, or suicide, plane attacks, but though these did immense damage to the American fleet they could not halt the invasion. Fighting from cave to cave, the defenders resisted for almost three months; not until the end of June was Okinawa finally conquered.

By that time the European war was over, and the sands were running out for Japan. American submarines had all but wiped out the Japanese merchant fleet and the Japanese economy was shattered; navy planes sailed over harbors sinking remnants of enemy shipping; Admiral Halsey's task force ranged at will up and down the coast; Tokyo was a charred wasteland and most of the large industrial cities had been reduced to ruins by incendiary raids. The Japanese leaders knew that they were beaten, but they were afraid to tell their people the truth and hoped that by threatening to fight on to the bitter end they could get better peace terms from the Allies.

But the Allies were in no mood to negotiate. Now they could mass the whole of their armed might against Japan and they knew, too, that Russia was about to enter the Pacific war. And in July the first atom bomb had been detonated in the New Mexico desert, and this ultimate weapon was now ready for use against Japan. Whether it should have been used, or whether it should have been used first in a demonstration test, are questions that will long be debated. Seven of the scientists concerned with the making of the bomb advised against its use, but Secretary Stimson, upon whose advice the President relied heavily, and many of his military advisers, urged that only the prompt use of the bomb could bring the war to an end without staggering losses in American forces. All these considerations were the background of the ultimatum that the Allied leaders, meeting at Potsdam in Germany, issued to Japan: surrender or be destroyed. The Japanese government ignored the ultimatum. Then on August 6 a lone B-29 sailed over the industrial city of Hiroshima and dropped an atom bomb;

three days later a second bomb was dropped on Nagasaki. Both cities were wiped out, and casualties ran to well over one hundred thousand. Confronted by the threat of total destruction, Japan capitulated on August 14, and on September 2 signed an unconditional surrender on the decks of the U.S.S. *Missouri*. Thus came to an end the most terrible of all wars.

It ended, fittingly enough, in such a holocaust as made clear that humanity could not survive another war. Civilized men everywhere had hoped that the First World War would be the war to end wars. In that hope they were tragically disappointed. After twenty troubled years evil and ambitious men had ventured once again to gain their ends by violence and terror. They had almost succeeded. Yet in the end they had failed calamitously, proving once again that all they that take the sword shall perish with the sword. Whatever the military reasons for that failure, the deeper reason for it is clear enough. The Axis nations had been defeated because they repudiated human values and human faith and thus raised up against them all those forces in the world that still cherished humanity. In the end it was those who had faith in the virtue, intelligence, and dignity of man who triumphed.

The qualities which in the end brought victory to the free peoples of the world were not exhausted by the agony of war. "The true goal we seek," President Roosevelt had said in his war message, "is far above and beyond the ugly field of battle. When we resort to force . . . we are determined that this force shall be directed towards ultimate good as well as against immediate evil."

That the Second World War frustrated "immediate evil" is clear beyond dispute. That it brought "ultimate good" is still for the future to decide. Certainly it created conditions in which men might, if they would, seek good. To the American people it brought such responsibility as neither they nor any other people had known before. Upon them came to rest, in large measure, the task of rehabilitating the war-ravaged world, rebuilding the civilization of western Christendom, strengthening democracy and sustaining free peoples everywhere on earth, and constructing an international organization strong enough to guarantee peace. In the five years after the war they fulfilled many of these responsibilities. They contributed generously to the reconstruction of the western world, supported democracy and freedom in far quarters of the globe, and took the lead in establishing and sustaining a United Nations organization to keep the peace. Yet the world was still troubled by war and rumors of war, and the horizons were dark.

CHAPTER 25

The Cold War

Harry Truman

THE SUCCESSOR to Roosevelt in the White House was momentarily overwhelmed by the weight of his responsibilities; but only momentarily. Harry S. Truman had qualities of decision, self-confidence, and determination that belied his colorless personal appearance. Our second President from west of the Mississippi, he had been reared in western Missouri with a rural background and high-school education. His experience had been varied: bank clerk, farmer, artillery officer in France during the First World War, haberdasher, Kansas City politician, judge (actually a county administrative officer), and finally United States Senator. In the Senate he had supported the New Deal, taken special interest in farm and labor legislation, and during his second term achieved national prominence as the efficient chairman of a special committee investigating defense expenditures. His nomination for the vice-presidency had disappointed several

Democrats who thought they had better claims, including Henry Wallace and James F. Byrnes. Truman partly consoled the first by keeping him as Secretary of Commerce, and the second by presently appointing him Secretary of State.

Events soon proved that Truman had remarkable qualifications for not only national but international leadership. In small matters, to be sure, he blundered, making some poor appointments, standing by old friends after they betrayed his trust, and uttering various irresponsible offhand statements. His speeches lacked eloquence and his written papers elegance; it was in rough-and-ready talks of the political-rally, rear-platform variety that he excelled. He tended to oversimplify current situations, and often let partisanship get the better of his judgment. But he possessed a clear and decisive mind; he was better educated than many Presidents, for he had read widely, especially in American history; he had a passion for democracy, and as deep a conviction as Wilson or Franklin D. Roosevelt that the United States must be its energetic guardian in world affairs. Few Presidents have been so industrious; over long stretches he worked sixteen hours a day. He believed fervently in action and leadership. And when crises came, this peaceable-looking man rose with instant decision and fierce fighting power to meet them.

On his accession to power in April, 1945, fighting in Europe was almost ended, and peace in Asia was only four months distant. A vast complex of postwar problems, however, loomed ahead. They proved all the more difficult because they were temporarily underrated. As after the First World War, Americans talked too readily of a new age in world affairs, placed too much faith in the machinery of collective security, and showed a reckless alacrity in bringing the soldiers home and easing economic controls. Most people thought Uncle Sam could soon turn to home concerns alone. They were to be rudely disillusioned.

Truman himself shared briefly in the rash optimism. He yielded to the pressure for "normalcy" by rashly signing a paper which halted lend-lease shipments so abruptly as to injure and deeply offend some of our allies. He responded to the demands of business conservatives by terminating most price controls. Both steps he almost immediately regretted. His administration began demobilizing with precipitate zeal and divested some European areas of troops who should have stayed there. More happily, he also helped complete the work of building the United Nations as a permanent agency of international co-operation. If America expected rather too much from the UN, it at least assisted in giving that body a power for good which it had refused to give the League of Nations. The country had learned a lesson since Wilson's day.

The United Nations

THE UN had begun as an alliance against Germany, Italy, and Japan which eventually numbered sixty countries. In the midst of the conflict (October, 1943) the foreign ministers of the United States, Britain, and Russia (joined later by Nationalist China) had signed an agreement to convert this alliance into a permanent body. Congress had strongly supported this undertaking, a former Republican isolationist, Senator Arthur H. Vandenberg of Michigan, helping to lead the way. Then in the late summer of 1944, a gathering of experts met at Dumbarton Oaks in Washington, and hammered out the main framework of the proposed UN Charter. In most respects it was a simplified and strengthened version of the League. A Security Council was to shoulder the main burden of maintaining world concord; an Assembly was to offer a wide forum for complaint and discussion; a World Court was to adjudicate proper questions; and a Secretary-General and staff were to serve in a variety of ways. The Council was to have five permanent members—America, Britain, Russia, France, and China—and six others chosen for two-year terms by the Assembly. Any permanent member of the Council could veto its measures.

The first great occurrence of the Truman administration was the session of the UN Conference on International Organization in San Francisco, beginning April 25, 1945, to debate the Dumbarton Oaks plan. The forty-eight nations represented divided into three main groups: Russia, the great Western Powers, and certain small Western nations led by Australia. Russia played a generally obstructive role, trying to extend the veto and to keep the UN too weak to interfere seriously with an aggressor; her hope was to use it to confuse and divide the world. Molotov, the Russian foreign minister, also stubbornly but unsuccessfully opposed the entry of Argentina as a member. The main Western Powers, with Anthony Eden the principal British spokesman, and E. R. Stettinius, Harold Stassen, and Vandenberg the chief American representatives, labored earnestly to make the UN a strong and honest instrument for peace. The Australian foreign minister, Herbert Evatt, was a doughty champion of the minor nations, which wished it even stronger than it became. The conference finally decided that while the permanent Council members might veto action on substantive or concrete issues between nations, they could not veto "procedural" discussion on the means of taking them up. This decision helped to strengthen the UN as a forum where world opinion might be aired and exerted.

Senate action on the UN was prompt and decisive. The Charter was ratified by a vote of 89 to 2. This accurately reflected public feeling on the question, and when the UN chose its permanent home in New York City overlooking the East River, American interest and approval became greater than ever. Indeed, some observers later complained that many Americans thought the United Nations an American rather than a world agency! Isolationism was by no means dead, but it was everywhere on the defensive. The country understood at last that war anywhere menaces all nations everywhere and that peace is indivisible.

The Fair Deal

TRUMAN, trying in the summer of 1945 to turn his attention to the home front, was determined to keep the nation on the progressive path. The country was emerging from the war with a tremendous debt, but also with a tremendous increase in its productive capacity. The techniques of mass production, assisted by scientific discovery and engineering advance, were working greater wonders every year. At the peak of the war, in 1944–1945, all records in manufacturing, agriculture, and transport were broken by wide margins. Production was estimated at two and a half times what it had been in 1929. As a hungry, impoverished world demanded all that America could provide, fears that demobilization might result in acute unemployment proved quite unfounded. But as production continued to increase (in 1950 national income was $275 billion, as against $40 billion in the depth of the depression), would it be equitably shared? Would social justice prevail?

A disciple of Roosevelt, Truman naturally wished to keep the New Deal moving. In September, 1945, he gave a defiant answer to those who declared that the time had come for retrenchment and consolidation. Addressing Congress, he offered a program which he called the Fair Deal. It embraced government action, if needed, to provide full employment, a rise in minimum-wage rates, a broadening of the social-security system, Federal expenditures for slum clearance and better housing, higher crop price-supports, and duplicates of the TVA on the Missouri, Columbia, and other rivers. Clearly, he wished to maintain the old New Deal alliance of labor and farmers to give the country a dynamic social and economic democracy. But he encountered difficulties. Agricultural and laboring groups, never really congenial, fell apart as farm prices began to drop while wages continued to rise. Conservative business and professional elements wanted fewer government controls and lower taxes; many white Southerners were alarmed by Truman's requests for Federal legislation against the poll tax and lynching, and for a continuance of the wartime Fair Employment Practices Committee to give the Negro a full share of jobs. In Congress, Truman soon faced an iron wall of Republican conservatives and Southern Democratic Bourbons.

Probably the most important immediate result of the Fair Deal program was that it protected the New Deal gains already won. It gave progressives a rallying point, and served notice that the administration would fight every backward step. In the long run most of Truman's proposals went on the statute books. But a ten-year fight, many vicissitudes, and the leadership of many other men, Republicans as well as Democrats, had to be recorded before this happened. The vital fact is that the country did not experience such a postwar reaction as occurred after the Civil War and First World War.

Efforts at Peacemaking

HIGH GOVERNMENT OFFICIALS were quicker than the general public to comprehend that the establishment of a peaceful world would be a difficult and perhaps impossible task. Before his death President Roosevelt had begun to recognize the aggressive designs of Stalin's regime. Ambassador Averell Harriman and others stationed in Russia were quick to warn Truman. The President attended the tripartite conference at Potsdam July 17–August 2, 1945, in a watchful mood. East and West quickly deadlocked on important issues, and adjourned after handing over the continued work of peacemaking to a Council of Foreign Ministers, on which the United States, Britain, France, Russia, and China were represented. American forces occupied a zone of almost 40,000 square miles in southwestern Germany, the British 42,700 square miles, and the French 16,700, while the Russians held 46,600 square miles in East Germany. The city of Berlin inside the Russian zone was under occupation of the four Powers. Austria, too, was divided into four zones. Japan was kept under the strong hand of General Douglas MacArthur as Supreme Commander for the Allied Powers. Korea, which was promised her independence, was divided, Russia controlling the northern half, the United States the southern.

It quickly became evident that Russia was intent on establishing a broad zone of satellite states about her, on reaching the Dardanelles and Mediterranean, on getting a hand in the management of the Ruhr and its huge manufacturing facilities, and on using Communist parties in France, Italy, and other war-weakened nations to paralyze, if not control, their governments. Secretary Byrnes exerted himself, like Foreign Minister Ernest Bevin in Britain, to reach a modus vivendi with the Soviet government. He was in fact all too hopeful. Compromise was a word alien to the Russian vocabulary; Moscow took everything it could get, and yielded little in return. Particularly highhanded was the course of the Soviet Union in Poland, which the Western Powers hoped to make a truly democratic, self-governing nation. Not content with annexing some 78,000 square miles of the old Poland, Russia used its military occupation to strike down representatives of the London government-in-exile, establish a constitution on the Soviet model, and create a subservient Communist regime under Boleslav Bierut. While the Western Powers drastically reduced armaments, Russia increased its fighting power, consolidating her forces early in 1946 under General Nikolai Bulganin.

To meet the Russian menace, the United States steadily stiffened its attitude. At conferences held in London in the fall of 1945, Moscow that December, and Paris from May to October, 1946, American representatives showed increasing stubbornness. Treaties were concluded respecting Hungary, Bulgaria, and Rumania which Stalin at once misused (against American and British protests) to gain control of those countries. Finland was freed, but shortly compelled to sign a ten-year mutual assistance pact with Russia. Italy alone, which became a republic in 1946 and later accepted a peace treaty stripping her of all her colonies, was saved to the Western group. The free territory of Trieste was garrisoned by American and British troops under jurisdiction of the UN Security Council. Anglo-American action also excluded the Russians from any voice in the management of the Ruhr, in the British zone. Russia refused to agree to any treaty for the liberation of Austria, which Moscow wished to use to extract wealth from her occupation area, and as an excuse for maintaining troops along supply lines in Eastern Europe and the Balkans.

One matter on which the West and Russia did agree was punishment of the highest Nazi leaders. Indictments were framed and twenty-two war leaders were brought to trial in Nuremberg, in November, 1945. The case, fully argued on both sides, dragged on until September 30, 1946. Eleven men were sentenced to hang October 1. Hermann Goering committed suicide by poison in his cell; the other ten, including Foreign Minister Joachim von Ribbentrop, died on the gallows. Opinion in the United States was much divided on the justice and expediency of this unprecedented international action. The crimes of the Nazis were unspeakably foul, but they might have been punished by a German tribunal. Moreover, many of the German crimes were paralleled by Russian offenses of equal heinousness, and Germany and Russia, raising the signal for the Second World War in the Ribbentrop-Molotov pact of 1939, had invaded and devastated Poland in arrogant partnership. The cold-blooded murder of 7,000 captured Polish officers, attributed by the Russians to Hitler, almost certainly was ordered by Stalin.

America Takes a Firm Stand

AMERICAN SENTIMENT toward Russia, at first slowly, then rapidly, changed. The country lagged for a time behind Truman, who, outraged by Stalin's duplicity, exclaimed even in 1945: "It's time to stop babying the Soviets!" In March, 1946, Winston Churchill visited Fulton, Missouri, to deliver a speech denouncing Russian aggression and calling on the West to resist. Much American sentiment was shocked, but Truman on the platform and many leaders elsewhere applauded. Stalin replied to Churchill on April 30 by declaring that "international reaction" was planning a new war. But he revealed more of his hand when, on August 12, he sent Turkey a note demanding a share in the control of the Dardanelles. In Paris, Byrnes struggled all summer with the Russians in the Conference of Big Four foreign ministers, and on August 15 openly denounced their "repeated abuse and misrepresentation" of American policy.

A dramatic occurrence lighted up the changing situation. While Byrnes was contending with Molotov and our government was expostulating with Communist-led Yugoslavia for the shooting down of three unarmed American planes, Secretary Wallace prepared a speech which he delivered September 12 in Madison Square Garden vigorously attacking the "get-tough-with-Russia policy." Truman had indiscreetly approved the written text without reading it carefully. Secretary Byrnes, angered by what he regarded as a stab in the back, served notice that if Wallace did not resign he would; and Truman at once ousted Wallace on the ground of a "fundamental conflict" in foreign policy views. Public sentiment upheld Truman. Feeling between Byrnes and the President, however, remained strained. Their intercourse was less candid than it should have been, and early in 1947 Byrnes resigned on the ground of ill-health, giving way to one of the truly great figures of the period, General George Marshall.

Because the Paris Conference reached no agreement on Germany and Austria, Russia was left with powerful forces holding all Eastern Europe and menacing the West. That fall France adopted a new constitution; and when, in November, Communists seized the largest bloc of seats in the new National Assembly, a tremor ran through the free nations. But the focal point of uneasiness was now Germany. The Russian policy was to drain from Germany, as reparations, large quantities of manufactured goods, to prevent or delay German recovery, and by systematically producing poverty, disorganization, and despair, cause the people to turn to Communism. The Anglo-American policy, on the contrary, was to restore Germany to industrial health, re-establish prosperity, maintain order, and train the people in political democracy. Western Germany had a population of about 45,000,000 people; Eastern Germany, about 17,000,000. A large and constant influx of refugees swelled the West German numbers. Normally East Germany would have sent foodstuffs to the rest of the country, but the Russians cut off such shipments. The Western Powers therefore had to import great quantities of food for their various zones, America and Britain shouldering the heavy burden. The essential result was that as fast as the West pumped money and resources into their two thirds of the country, Russia pumped equivalent amounts out of her one third.

This was an intolerable situation. The Allied Control Council in Berlin became the scene of incessant bickering between the Anglo-American and the Russian representatives. For the United States, General Lucius D. Clay furnished a signally statesmanlike administration, winning the regard of the German people and the admiration of British colleagues. On December 2, 1946, the United States and Britain signed an agreement for an economic merger of their zones, and the nearly 80,000 square miles of "Bizonia" became much more viable than before. This was a development disconcerting to the Russians. So was the steady relaxation of Anglo-American controls over German industry, the embargo on shipments to Communist-controlled nations, and the general stimulation of German recovery. The first free municipal elections since the rise of Hitler were held under American and British auspices in 1946.

Early in 1947 the breach over Germany became complete and open. On March 10 the Council of Foreign Ministers began a conference in Moscow on Austro-German peace terms. After acrimonious debate, it adjourned six weeks later without agreement on a single issue of importance. Marshall, Bevin, and Bidault stood their ground without budging; Molotov stood his. When Marshall reported to the American people that Stalin had told him that all differences could be adjusted by conference, a guffaw rolled from coast to coast; the public had taken Stalin's measure. The German question was temporarily shoved aside. Deadlock was accepted there, and the immediate center of attention moved to Greece and Turkey.

Problems of Defense

THE COLD WAR showed that American armaments would have to be augmented. Even before this became clear, Americans were much concerned with improving the efficiency of defense planning and administration. The war had shown an urgent need for unification of forces and staff. The Truman administration supported the campaign for this objective, and Congress finally assented.

On July 26, 1947, Truman signed the act placing the army, navy, and air force in a new Department of Defense, of which he made James Forrestal the first head. Integration had been carefully and broadly planned. Each of the three forces had its subordinate Secretary, who did not, however, hold a place in the Cabinet. A National Security Council was established (consisting of the President, Secretaries of State, of Defense, and of the three armed forces, and the Chairman of the National Security Resources Board) to study the foreign situation and recommend policies. The National Security Resources Board, which had little to do in peacetime but would be vitally important in war, was to study and organize resources, production, and manpower. A Munitions Board was to take over functions previously exercised by the army and navy boards of the same name. A Research and Development

Board was to deal with scientific research. Finally, a Central Intelligence Agency was to give the nation for the first time a pool of information on the armaments and armed activities of other countries. This CIA became in time a powerful body, its activities secret and even independent.

Unfortunately, it proved easier to devise paper plans for unification than to make them work. Forrestal, who had directed much of the battle, envisaged a rather small Defense Department, which would command the friendly co-operation of all three branches. Instead, the new department became cumbrously large, and the three forces wrangled jealously over appropriations and power. Experts differed sharply over the roles of atomic weapons, of warships, and of planes if a new war occurred. When, in the fall of 1946, a B-29 flew from Honolulu to Cairo in a nonstop journey over the North Pole of 9425 miles, many accepted the feat as proof that huge naval units were outmoded. But the navy insisted that future conflicts would be fought largely by jet planes of great size, speed, and complexity, and that it must have huge and costly supercarriers to house and launch them. Congressmen, who were inclined to think that the atom bomb had inaugurated a new era in warfare, cherished a belief that Russia could not make a bomb until 1952, and were economy-minded with other weapons.

Trying to meet the difficulties of organizing the Defense Department, of composing the squabbles of the three forces, of wringing adequate appropriations from Congress, and of answering unjust political attacks, Forrestal broke down. His retirement was quickly followed by his tragic death. Few figures of the postwar period appear in retrospect more gallant than this devoted statesman, a man of uncommon cultivation and sensitiveness. Louis Johnson of West Virginia, who succeeded him, showed great force and energy but little tact or perception. With Truman's approval he continued an economy policy which, as the cold war grew sharper, proved dangerous. He quarreled with Congress, with the State Department, and with the services. He halted the construction of the supercarrier which had been authorized under Forrestal. Before long he had to be dropped as a political liability. The question of the proper military policy of the country remained unresolved, so that when peril became acute, the government dealt with it by vastly expensive increments in the strength of all three branches—a policy of dubious wisdom.

Atomic weapons and atomic energy were problems of the most exigent national and international concern. The United Nations and Congress tried to deal with them almost simultaneously. The UN Security Council created an Atomic Energy Commission of ten members, on which Warren Austin represented the United States; Sir Alexander Cadogan, Great Britain; and Andrei Gromyko, Russia. To this body Bernard Baruch presented in 1946 an elaborate plan for world control of atomic weapons. Since the United States alone then possessed them, his scheme reflected a highly generous attitude. It proposed the creation of an international atomic authority which should take entire control of the field; own or manage all atomic-energy installations which offered a potential threat of aggressive action; inspect, license, and regulate all other atomic activities; control atomic research; and stimulate useful and constructive use of atomic energy. The UN Commission, with Gromyko alone standing out, gave its approval to the plan.

A month later, in July, 1946, Congress passed the McMahon Atomic Energy Act establishing an Atomic Energy Commission of five men, an independent agency which within a year had five thousand employees. Its duties were to oversee the manufacture of atomic weapons, and the application of atomic power to a great variety of other uses: submarine engines, power plants, medicine, and agriculture. That summer the United States exploded its fourth atom bomb in Bikini Atoll in the Pacific and its fifth under water, both weapons of unprecedented destructiveness.

Yet Russia flatly refused to accept the Baruch Plan or any feasible modification thereof. One reason was that the Soviet masters felt perfectly safe. They knew that the United States would not use its bombs aggressively, and that they were near the completion of their own atomic weapons. Another was that Russia could not tolerate two of the Baruch proposals. Free inspection of plants all over the Soviet Union would break down what Churchill had termed the Iron Curtain and expose to global view mysteries and iniquities that Russia had to keep veiled; it was incompatible with Russian denials of freedom. The stipulation that no member of the UN Security Council could use the veto to obstruct action by the Atomic

Energy Authority was equally unacceptable: the Russians had
developed the veto habit. When Russia presently brought forth
her own plan of atomic control, it called for a general ban on
these terrible weapons without anything but intermittent and
partial inspection.

Counterbalancing Russian Might

STALIN'S DEMAND upon Turkey for a share in the control of
the Dardanelles coincided with a covert assault upon the freedom of Greece. When that country was cleared of Germans
in 1944, the king and cabinet had resumed power. But a
vicious civil war among partisan bands broke out, plunging
much of the country into disorder. Communists in Bulgaria,
Albania, and Yugoslavia took a hand, alternately fighting and
retreating over their borders, supplying rebels against the
Athens government, and kidnaping thousands of children. The
British, who had assumed the task of keeping order in Greece,
found the financial and military burden beyond their means.
Early in 1947 they notified the American government that
they must withdraw their forces and end their subsidies. There
was a great danger that the Communist guerrillas, using
terroristic methods, would take control of the country. As
Russia was maintaining her pressure on Turkey, and menacing Iran—whose northernmost province, Azerbaijan, abutted
on Soviet territory—the collapse of Greece might be followed
by a general Soviet advance in the Middle East.

Truman rose instantly to the crisis. To a joint session
of Congress he explained that the existence of Greece was
threatened by Communist-led bands; that the survival and
integrity of that country and Turkey were vital to the maintenance of order and freedom throughout the region; and
that the cost of American aid would be trifling compared
with that of war. He enunciated the Truman Doctrine, that
nations striving to maintain their independence, and com-
bating efforts at control by armed totalitarian minorities,
would receive American military and economic aid. "The
seeds of totalitarianism are nurtured by misery and want,"
he declared. "They reach their full growth when the hope of
a people for a better life has died. We must keep that hope

alive." A bill appropriating $300,000,000 for Greece and $100,000,000 for Turkey and authorizing the President to send military, naval, and economic advisers to both countries passed in May.

This intervention unquestionably saved Greece and helped Turkey. The Greek ruling groups, reactionary and selfish, were compelled by stern American pressure to grant some much-needed reforms; the Turkish government co-operated much more readily and loyally, and Turkey remained one of the bulwarks of freedom in the Near East. The United States meanwhile helped create another bastion in Palestine, where the Republic of Israel was proclaimed May 14–15, 1948, the date of British withdrawal. The Truman administration immediately recognized the new nation, and gave it moral support during the desperate struggle which followed between the Israelis and the Arab states. American Jews naturally furnished money, arms, and military assistance in that struggle. When a truce ended the fighting, Israel had staked out boundaries broad enough to guarantee national existence. Another factor in stabilizing the situation in the Balkans and the Near East was the revolt of Yugoslavia against Soviet control. When her dictator, Marshal Joseph Broz (Tito), quarreled with Stalin, the danger of Communist aggression in the great belt from Albania to Afghanistan diminished.

But the Truman Doctrine and the Greek-Turkish Aid bill were not enough: they were too limited. The enforced British withdrawal in that part of the world was proof that all Europe was in sad straits. Great Britain, the heart of a huge commonwealth and empire, was still a world power, still stable, still possessed of great industrial potentialities. But Italy and France had been ravaged by war, torn by civil strife, and deprived of much of their dignity and moral strength. Other nations, like Holland, Belgium, Denmark, and Norway, had lost men, capital, machinery, cultural institutions, and confidence. The task of rebuilding ruined cities and smashed industries was beyond their strength. They needed money—and America seemed to have it all; they needed hope and courage. Germany and Austria, too, must be lifted out of their rubble and despair. One nation alone could save Western civilization with speed and certainty— but it must show an unexampled vision and generosity.

The Marshall Plan

THESE QUALITIES, the essentials of a world renascence, were happily available. The United States had not forgotten the lessons of lend-lease, when the Allied nations pooled their resources in a tremendous common effort. Such a pool was to be reconstituted in a new war: a contest against poverty, inanition, and collapse. Ideally, the United Nations should have been the instrument of regeneration. But Russia had crippled that organization in every effort to advance the world toward peace and prosperity, using the veto to block action and incessant propagandist speeches to confuse thought.

This time Secretary Marshall announced the policy. Speaking at Harvard University on June 5, 1947, he pledged the United States to make substantial contributions toward a plan of co-operative European revival. The European Recovery Program, as it became known, included the offer not only of money but machinery, blueprints, raw materials, and experts versed in American technology. European nations were to assist each other by loans, exchange of special facilities, and a quickening of international trade. Tariffs were to be torn down or sharply reduced all over the free world. It was hoped that out of the program would come fresh progress toward that never-realized dream, a United States of Europe. And Marshall made it clear that Europe must furnish most of the initiative and energy.

Would Europe respond? And would Congress, jealous of American spending, fulfill Marshall's pledge?

The answer to the first question was quickly given. The British and French foreign secretaries invited all European nations, including Russia, to a Paris conference to discuss a unified program of reconstruction. Russia not only declined, but forbade her eight satellites to attend. Sixteen nations, however, from Iceland to Turkey, attended and, on September 22, 1947, adopted a co-operative plan of reconstruction which called for the use of nearly twenty-two billions of dollars in the next four years. Some of this money was to come from the International Bank for Reconstruction and Development, and some from various nations, but most of it from the United States. The plan pledged the sixteen participating nations to "a wide range of actual and potential mutual help." The task could not be completed in less than four years—but when it was finished, Europe would be far in advance of its prewar stage of economic development.

Congress was not quite as prompt. Meeting at the beginning of 1948, it marked time for two months. Then the Communist seizure of power in Czechoslovakia stimulated it to action. On April 3, 1948, Truman signed the Economic Co-operation Act, which authorized $6,098,000,000 for the first year, saying: "This is the answer to the challenge facing the free world." He immediately ordered a billion dollars made available to start the program, and appointed Paul G. Hoffman, an automobile manufacturer and a Republican, as head of the Economic Co-operation Administration.

Economic co-operation developed satisfactorily in Europe, and recovery was steady. When ECA ended its four years of activity, in 1951, the United States had loaned or given twelve billion dollars for its work, and the continent was back on its feet. A new stage of American-European relations had then been reached, and large new grants of money and material were being made. By the middle of 1950, the Marshall Plan countries had raised their industrial-production index to a level one fourth higher than that of 1936–1938; by the end of 1951, it was one half higher. In fact, the factories and farms of Western Europe reached the highest rate of production in all their history. This crowded area, thanks in part to more liberal tariff arrangements in the United States and other lands, seemed sure of selling enough goods to support a steadily improving standard of life. Most countries were lifting their industrial output by from seven to nine per cent annually. Unhappily, one great counterbalancing factor had come into existence. It had been necessary for the whole West to rearm, and the high taxes and inflation resulting from armaments expenditure were a heavy brake on continued progress.

Certain tensions are inseparable from any co-operative program in which one side does most of the giving and the other most of the receiving. Many Americans thought that Europeans showed insufficient gratitude; many Europeans felt that Americans expected too much. Some Europeans resented the pressure of advisers for reform, effort, and innovations— they preferred old ways even if inefficient; some Americans

were disappointed that Europe made so little progress toward
unity. French suspicion of Germany in particular was deep
and persistent. In a few European countries class interest
interfered with social justice and economic prosperity. In
short, frictions and resentments appeared. On the whole, however, the various governments showed patience. Hoffman and
his principal aides were models of tact, and apart from constant trouble-making by Communist groups, little real difficulty materialized. Western Europe was in process of getting
superficially Americanized, adopting American slang, jazz,
soft drinks, food, and dress along with machine tools and
mass-production techniques.

New Russian Aggressions

STALIN REALIZED that the Marshall Plan spelled the end
of Russian hopes of prostrating and disrupting Europe.
Moscow made its chagrin and resentment plain in a variety
of ways. In October, 1947, the Communist Information Bureau was organized to help guide the satellite nations, furnish
a strict control to Communist parties abroad, and stimulate
propaganda. The seizure of Czechoslovakia a few months
later was so arrogant that all the Western Powers immediately protested. Under Soviet instructions, Communist elements tried to paralyze France by strikes and Italy by rioting.
Then on April 1, 1948, the Soviet Union played what it
hoped would be a trump card: severe restrictions on rail
and road traffic between West Berlin and the American,
French, and British zones of West Germany. This blockade
was expected to bring about the surrender of Berlin to Russian control, when it might be made the capital of a strong
German Communist nation. The Soviet excuse was that the
West had violated certain agreements, but the real reason
was that the West was acting to restore Germany economically and politically as an important part of a rehabilitated
Europe.

Not for a moment did the Americans or British think of
submitting. General Lucius D. Clay and General Sir Brian
Robinson at once began checkmating the roadblock by an
air lift. Declaring their forces would never leave Berlin, they
built a series of new airfields and launched a vast fleet of

cargo planes to the rescue of Berlin. By fall nearly a thousand Anglo-American planes were arriving at Berlin airfields at three-minute intervals, carrying at least three thousand tons a day, and building up reserves not only of food but fuel. The effort was finally entrusted to a Combined Air Lift Task Force, with an American commander and British deputy commander. When the Russians adopted provocative tactics, fear arose that an untoward incident might trigger a war. The British thereupon announced that they would furnish fighter protection for their planes. Berliners showed their admiration for the gallant Allied effort when in December, 1,330,000 of them voted in an election held in defiance of Communist threats, and gave the anti-Communist Social Democrats sixty-five per cent of the vote.

Indeed, anti-Soviet feeling flamed throughout all Western Europe. The Russian government finally gave up the blockade, once more demanding a share in control of the Ruhr, and once more being refused. West German elections in August, 1949, resulted in the choice of a moderate government under Konrad Adenauer. During the same year the Western Allies replaced their military control by a civilian high commission; and the United States sent John J. McCloy to replace General Clay.

Collapse of Nationalist China

A MOMENTOUS ANNOUNCEMENT came from Truman in September, 1949: "We have evidence that . . . an atomic explosion has occurred in the U.S.S.R." Though it would be some time before the Russians accumulated a stock of bombs, they were on their way to equality with the United States. And this same year witnessed an equally momentous development in the Far East. The Communist forces there, sweeping across China with astonishing rapidity, brought an end to the civil war which had raged for twenty years.

When the year began, the Kuomintang Nationalists under Chiang Kai-shek held about half the area and population of mainland China. But their regime was riddled by corruption and their grip weak. The Communist armies, capturing Chiang's capital, Nanking, on April 24, moved forward to take the other principal cities, Canton, Chungking, and Shanghai. As they went they captured large quantities of American arms given to Chiang. The story of American relations with that leader is highly complex. During the war the American government had tried to unite the more moderate elements among both Communists and Nationalists into a dominant party of the center. After Japan's defeat Truman had continued to support that aim. George Marshall, going to China and arranging various short-lived truces between the two sides, had done his best to create a compromise government. Unfortunately, neither Chiang nor the opposition groups under Mao Tse-tung had wanted compromise, and the Truman administration became completely disillusioned with both leaders. The Communists believed that whether the civil war ended in complete victory or complete chaos, they were certain to triumph. Chiang, for his part, believed that no matter how wretched his government or weak his strategy, the United States in the end would have to make an all-out effort on his behalf. He did not realize that American public opinion, however hostile to Mao Tse-tung, would never countenance throwing millions of men into the Chinese morass.

The United States therefore looked helplessly on as Mao's well-disciplined forces completed their conquest of the country, and Chiang's remnant army fled to the island of Taiwan (Formosa). Washington had to write off as an almost total loss aids which the State Department estimated as aggregating two billion dollars for the postwar period, but which were probably not quite so large. The victorious Mao called a "consultative conference" or constitutional convention in Peiping, which, without any real debate, approved a framework of government already drafted by Communist chieftains. Thus came into being the Chinese People's Republic, with a heritage of contempt for democracy, militarism, and hatred of the West, particularly America. Before 1948 ended, Mao visited Moscow to conclude political and economic agreements amounting to a close alliance, and the world had to concede that over five hundred million people had been added to the Communist bloc. The Nationalists still had China's place in the UN; the Communists had China itself.

Staggered by this major setback, the United States ruefully surveyed the past without being able to affix the blame on any American group. A White Paper issued by the State Department offered more than a thousand pages of explanation and analysis, from which Chiang emerged as the major culprit. While great forces of reform and renovation had been asserting themselves among the Chinese, the dishonest and inept Nationalists had ignored them and the Communists had skillfully exploited them. The British government followed its historic policy of recognizing *de facto* governments by sending to Peiping an ambassador, who was treated with neglect. The British view was that by tactful treatment the new Chinese government could be led to assert a healthy independence of Moscow. But the United States continued to treat Chiang's regime as the true representative of the Chinese people and true holder of China's seat in the UN Security Council. The State Department warned Mao that we would resist any attack upon the freedom of the small countries of Southeast Asia. Mao for his part regarded America with defiance.

All this constituted one of the unhappiest chapters of the postwar period. For generations the United States had been the principal Western friend of China. John Hay had stood against its partition; American philanthropy had built colleges and hospitals, trained Chinese students, and carried out health programs. It was sad to see this record obliterated. Of more immediate importance was the potential accession to Soviet strength at the very moment that Russia gained the atomic bomb. Clearly, the situation called for new measures in both the Western and the Pacific area.

Birth of NATO

FORTUNATELY, the West had already taken preliminary steps toward a unification of power. Long before Mao's victorious march and the breakdown of the Big Four Conference of May, 1949, in Paris, Ernest Bevin and certain Benelux (Belgium, Netherlands, Luxembourg) leaders had discussed plans for a close defensive union. The United States, Canada, and other nations had been drawn into the negotiations. On April 4, 1949, the foreign ministers of the United States, Britain, France, and nine other countries signed the memorable compact creating the North Atlantic

Treaty Organization (NATO). "The parties agree," declared
the treaty, "that an armed attack against one . . . shall be
considered an armed attack against all." In the event of
such an attack, the twelve nations would rally together "to
restore and maintain the security of the North Atlantic
area."

NATO brought together about 350,000,000 people, occupying the most highly industrialized areas of Europe and
North America, in an alliance to raise new troops, choose
common weapons, select common commanders, and meet
force with force. Never before had the United States gone
so far in a practical, concrete surrender of part of its sovereign powers. Never before had it so clearly recognized that
its frontier henceforth lay far overseas, along the lines that
divided the free nations from Soviet dominion. The overwhelming public sentiment in favor of the pact was measured by the alacrity with which the Senate, rejecting all
reservations, ratified it by the vote of 82 to 13. And as it was
ratified, the Truman administration proposed a Military Assistance Program, giving it authority to spend $1,450,000,000
within the next year in furnishing arms and advice to the
other NATO signers, to Greece and Turkey (which would
soon join NATO), to Iran, still threatened by Russian encroachment, and to Korea and the Philippines. Some thought
the sum too large; some, including Senator Robert Taft, believed the grants should be withheld until the NATO Defense Council had matured its plans. But the administration
bill became law.

The NATO Command

THESE MEASURES were taken in the nick of time. Events
in Korea soon revealed that the danger of a third world war
was real and terrible. Weakness on the part of the Western
nations would have invited Stalinist attack in many parts
of the globe. Russia had more than five million men under
arms, with 15,000 aircraft and 30,000 tanks, and could
rapidly mobilize 175 divisions of her own with scores more
from her satellite nations. Her fleet of snorkel submarines had
great cruising power; her guided missiles, fired from advance

bases in East Germany and Czechoslovakia, might reach every Western city. Subsequent revelations by Russian leaders have established the utter irresponsibility, ruthlessness, and mendacity of Stalin. Had he not been deterred by fear of American atomic might, his cohorts might rapidly have overrun all Europe to the Channel and Gibraltar.

The year 1950 saw NATO rapidly gather coherence, and make a beginning in armed power. Its Council early in the year approved plans for an integrated defense. The first American shipments of arms reached Europe in April. Britain, improving her air and tank forces, promised that she would have nearly 700,000 men under arms the following spring. The French inaugurated a three-year rearmament program, which it was hoped would soon give the republic twenty divisions ready for instant action. The contingent of the United States in the NATO army was set at six divisions, of which two were already in Europe. A military mission from the United States gave Turkey expert advice in training and equipping forces numbering some 600,000 men. Finally, in December, General Eisenhower agreed to accept command of all NATO land operations and soon afterward landed at Cherbourg to a tumultuously enthusiastic reception. He established headquarters near Paris, and set to work with characteristic energy, grasp, and optimism.

The State Department by this time was in the hands of Dean G. Acheson, one of the ablest of all its recent heads. The son of an Episcopal bishop, an experienced attorney, and a man of wide cultivation, he had held important positions in the department during the war. His brilliance and somewhat chilly intellectualism made enemies, but amid a rising storm of unjustified partisan attack he held the helm firmly and wisely. It was Acheson who represented the United States in the NATO Council meeting in Ottawa in 1951 which admitted Turkey and Greece. Eisenhower sent that meeting a message emphasizing the urgency of preparations to meet the Russian menace, and calling on certain unnamed NATO members to recruit more troops, establish more arms factories, and raise the output of weapons during the next year by one third. Such demands, stated in the American Senate with still more vigor by Robert Taft, aroused protests in some European countries. Finance ministers and economic experts asserted that they could not make greater sacrifices without danger of an internal crash; they had to think of the peril of bankruptcy as well as the Soviet peril.

It was evident by this time that West Germany must play a key role both in the prosperity and defense of Western Europe. The German people, systematic, industrious, and skilled in the newest technologies, were experiencing a remarkable economic resurgence. The West needed their iron and steel, their skilled manpower, and the troops they could raise. It knew that a price would have to be paid: political freedom for West Germany; it shared with France a fear of a reawakened militaristic temper. The world situation in 1951, however, made it feasible to take risks. During the summer the three Occupation Powers reached a decision to restore a broad measure of German sovereignty. They would negotiate with the Bonn republic under Konrad Adenauer an agreement conferring general autonomy. They would, however, still control West Berlin and maintain troops in the Reich, have the sole conduct of negotiations with Russia over German unification, possess a veto power over basic policy changes harmful to the West, and be empowered to intervene to prevent any Communist or Fascist coup. These proposed conditions offended many Germans.

At the same time, the three Western governments brought forward a treaty of mutual security. Under its provisions, Germany would be allowed to raise a substantial army, which, however, would be made part of an international instead of a national force. That is, they would be incorporated into a multinational army of French, Italian, German, and Benelux soldiers. This European army was to serve alongside the separate national armies of the NATO countries under Eisenhower and his successors; the West would thus get the benefit of German manpower without too much danger of German aggression. This ingenious plan emanated primarily from the French. It was by no means certain, when 1951 closed, that either France or Germany would accept the whole scheme. But that West Germany would soon gain nearly independent status under her own government, and that plans for German divisions would be pressed, as Eisenhower desired, was entirely clear. Russia had forfeited all rights to object.

An Asiatic Front

DURING THE WAR some American groups had insisted that the Pacific front was really more important than the Atlantic; after it ended they returned to that view. When Chiang lost continental China, and India as well as Britain recognized Mao, a violent debate broke out in the United States. Many Americans agreed with the British and Indians that Communist China should be admitted to the UN. Some further held that the United States should send an ambassador to Peiping to try to regain some of China's former friendship and drive a wedge between the Chinese and Russians, old historic enemies. Secretary Acheson seemed to favor such a course. A majority of Congress, however, and a large part of the American people, were adamant in their hostility to the Mao government.

The Truman administration for a time held a middle course. It took no step toward recognition of Communist China. On the other hand, it refused (January, 1950) to pledge the use of American sea and air power to protect Chiang in Formosa from attack. The Joint Chiefs of Staff had reported that the island was not essential to American defense. Meanwhile, the administration tried to strengthen the American position elsewhere.

Freedom was given to the Philippines on the promised date, July 4, 1946, and the United States supplied money (over 600 million), materials, and experts generously for reconstruction. In return, the Philippines agreed to free trade with the United States for half a dozen years, and granted a ninety-nine-year lease on military bases.

Conquered Japan was treated with wise moderation. The United States had no intention of letting that country frustrate the firm but mild control exercised through the Supreme Commander for the Allied Powers, General Douglas MacArthur. Though MacArthur was required to keep close liaison with Washington and submit to its directives, his great prestige among the Japanese, his imperious temper and real sagacity gave him a large degree of freedom. His humorless self-esteem, aloofness, and single-minded concentration on his job irritated many American observers but impressed the island people over whom he presided. They respected authority, dignity, reserve, and dedication.

The Japanese, moreover, had little difficulty in reconciling themselves to the measures which MacArthur initiated and promoted. This was the easier because he kept himself and most subordinates so completely in the background. The Mikado remained Emperor, though he was stripped of whatever claims his adherents had ever made for a semidivine status. The Japanese government was maintained in its old form, though it was of course required to obey American decisions made by or transmitted through the Supreme Commander. Making no parade of his own supremacy, MacArthur refused to let Americans advertise their position as victors. However much some Japanese resented Hiroshima, they were grateful that the American forces had indulged in no conduct remotely akin to the excesses of the Nazis in Russia or the counterexcesses of the Russians in Germany, and they knew that compared with the way their own troops had behaved in Nanking, Malaya, and the Philippines, the Yankee doughboys were admirably restrained.

Nor did the Japanese object to American policies. It was the intention of Washington and MacArthur to recast the island institutions in a more democratic mold. Disarmament was carried out with great completeness. Fortresses were dismantled, ships sunk, equipment destroyed, the troops returned to civilian life. Trials of war criminals resulted in the execution of a small number of high dignitaries, including the former prime minister, Tojo, and some hundreds of lesser figures. The largest Japanese cartels or monopolies were (temporarily) struck down. Great land holdings were divided among peasants. The educational system was reformed, and the teaching of democratic principles made one of its principal functions. Labor unions were given an opportunity to put down vigorous roots. The status of women was brought abreast of that in Occidental countries. For much in the Oriental character MacArthur had deep respect, but he shared the view of most Americans that the Japanese had submitted too slavishly to regimentation and needed to cultivate the virtues of individualism. While MacArthur was innately conservative, his policy of excluding former warlords, imperialists, and monopolists from power gave unexpected opportunity to left-wing elements to move into positions of power.

Despite wartime losses, the population of Japan rose until in 1950 it reached the figure of 90,000,000; a formidable total in view of the nation's scanty resources since the loss of Korea, Manchuria, and other holdings. Expenditures for and by American troops aided the island's precarious economy. But if Japan was to be kept from falling into the Communist maw, the country must be brought back to prosperity; and the American authorities of necessity paid decreasing attention to reform, increasing attention to recovery. An Economic Stabilization Program, the rough counterpart of ECA in Europe, was instituted in 1949 and proved genuinely helpful. Large business units were permitted to rise again and to curb excesses of competition. The demands of labor leaders were kept within bounds, for Japan could not yet afford a Western standard of living. Since the Japanese found many of their markets for textiles, ceramics, and other consumer goods closed, American advisers assisted them to establish heavy industries, and they began shipping machinery to eager Asiatic markets. Within a few years their production had surpassed that of the early 1930's and was rapidly increasing.

The United States was hopeful that it could make and keep Japan one of the bastions of freedom in the Pacific. As with Germany, restoration and eventual rearmament involved risks. The small nations which had suffered from Japanese aggression in the past were even more acutely conscious of the fact than the Americans. What if Japan, once she gained independent sovereignty, decided it would be more profitable to join Communist China and Russia? While this fear did not materialize, the Japanese did become increasingly reluctant to embrace American foreign policies uncritically, and increasingly restive at being denied access to the markets of China.

Korea

VIEWING THE CATACLYSMIC CHANGES and general ferment in Asia, most Americans down to 1950 paid little attention to that minor area called Korea. They were engrossed in more spectacular parts of the panorama. India, given full freedom by Attlee's Labor government in London, had established herself as a nation with remarkable speed and success. Under Prime Minister Nehru, the new republic had conquered most of its political and many of its social and economic difficulties. Pakistan and Ceylon, also free, remained, like India, members still of the (British) Commonwealth of Nations. Burma had used its liberation less successfully. Dutch Indonesia had been given equal status with the Netherlands as a free nation under the Dutch crown, but was fighting for, and soon achieved, complete independence. French Indo-China was now autonomous in all domestic affairs, and facing an uncertain future as civil war, partly inspired by Communists, racked it. The whole great continent seemed in a state of sullen upheaval. A billion people, all the way from Syria to Celebes, were in various stages of revolt against colonialism, color lines, and their own poverty and misery.

Korea, a small, mountainous, half-barren peninsula of that continent, was in a specially unhappy plight. It had been divided between Russian and American control on the wholly artificial line of the thirty-eighth parallel. All efforts to unite the country had failed, for the Russians, as in Germany, would not consent to free elections. The American-controlled half had most of the population and agriculture, the Russian-controlled half a major share of the industry. The United Nations, on application of the United States, had finally tried to compose the difficulties. It had sent in a commission to organize a government. The Russians barred this body from their zone. The commissioners then did all that was possible: they held South Korean elections, oversaw the writing of a constitution, and helped install a government in Korea under Syngman Rhee, an able, elderly, stubborn-willed conservative. The Russians and Americans both withdrew their troops in 1948–1949, but both left behind military equipment and military advisers. From their vantage post just beyond the Yalu River, Soviet officials and army officers, acting in complete secrecy, could plan whatever measures they liked.

President Truman has recorded in his memoirs that early in 1950 watchers in Washington were deeply apprehensive of a sudden armed conflict. They knew that Russia had forces poised to strike at a dozen points: in Germany, Austria, the Balkans, Greece, Turkey, Iran, and so on across the map to Kamchatka. Nobody knew what the morrow would bring. It was obvious that the Communists did not wish to wait until NATO grew powerful. The spots of greatest uneasiness were in Europe and the Near East; the Joint Chiefs of Staff had explicitly said that no points beyond Japan and the Philippines were of vital or critical character in our defense. But prediction was impossible. On June 26, news broke upon the startled country that the North Korean army, with Russian airplanes, Russian tanks, and Russian-trained officers, had thrust across the thirty-eighth parallel and was at the gates of Seoul.

But before we deal with the Korean War, we must turn back to a consideration of domestic events under Truman.

CHAPTER 26

Postwar Problems, 1946—1952

Prosperity and Inflation

THE NATION passed from war into a great and prolonged boom. Production, employment, income, and profits during the first three years after victory reached extraordinary levels. The demand for goods by the government, domestic users, and foreign nations almost continuously outpaced supply. A slight recession which appeared early in 1949 never became a big one. Henry Wallace shortly before the conflict ended had brought out *Sixty Million Jobs,* a book which many thought rash in its demand for vigorous government measures to ensure full employment; but full employment came without special stimulants, and carried the total of wage earners well past the sixty million mark.

Almost inevitably, the boom was accompanied by rising prices and an inflation which brought hardship to large sections of the population. President Truman in his economic report to Congress at the beginning of 1947 pointed to many encouraging factors: an enlarged and improved industrial plant, a greater and more highly trained labor force, ample capital for industrial growth, and a huge backlog of unfilled orders. But on the other side of the ledger he noted the reduction in purchasing power caused by high price levels, the discontent of important labor elements and consequent danger of strikes, and the possibility that investment might fall off. In the autumn of 1947 wheat sold in Chicago well above three dollars a bushel, the highest point in a generation; that November the Bureau of Labor Statistics reported the consumers' price index 165 per cent above the 1935–1939 level. Population was expanding spectacularly—19 million during the decade of the forties—and this increased the pressure on supplies and prices.

Congress vs. President

TRUMAN had inherited from Roosevelt a Democratic Congress, but the fact did him little good. A coalition of Republicans and Southern Bourbons presented an impenetrable wall to his Fair Deal proposals. And in the fall of 1946 the scene changed. By a vigorous and well-financed campaign the Republicans, chanting "Had enough?," carried the Senate 51 to 45, and the House 246 to 188. In the new Eightieth Congress the conservatives were able to pass legislation over Truman's veto. They at once enacted a Labor-Management Relations Act (1947), popularly called the Taft-Hartley Act, which with some salutary features combined provisions that the labor unions pronounced intolerable: a ban on closed-shop agreements and restrictions on strikes and picketing. William Green, John L. Lewis, and the other labor leaders promptly launched a battle for repeal or drastic modification of the law, but in vain. Congress also submitted to the states an amendment to the Constitution forbidding any President to serve more than two terms. This vote of no-confidence in the judgment of the American people, partly a slur on Roosevelt and partly an effort to bring moral pressure on Truman not to aspire to a third term (though he as current incumbent was excepted), was ratified and in 1951 became the Twenty-second Amendment.

Disturbed by inflation, Truman requested legislation which would permit the government to ration scarce goods, impose price and wage ceilings where urgently needed, control exports, regulate commodity speculation, apportion transportation facilities, hold down rents, and take other steps. Republican leaders insisted that the President was trying to make political capital out of the situation, and did not really wish such far-reaching powers. As a matter of fact, plenty of politics was evident on both sides. The bill finally passed was too mild to be effective. Withholding from the President the power to control prices or wages and ration goods, it merely permitted voluntary agreements among business, labor, and agriculture for the restraint of inflation. Truman called it "pitifully inadequate," and though he signed it, events proved that he was right. Inflation continued.

The Eightieth Congress in fact refused to do most of the things for which Truman asked. It balked at a permanent Fair Employment Practices Act, at an increase in minimum wages from forty to sixty-five cents an hour, at a bold housing program, at the expansion of social security, and at the admission of displaced persons from Europe. It did pass a new presidential succession act which the administration desired. This provided that if both President and Vice-President died, the chief magistracy should go in turn to the Speaker of the House, the president pro tempore of the Senate, and Cabinet members in the order of the creation of their departments. Congress and Truman quarreled sharply on tax reduction. Both houses, to curry favor with the voters, passed bills lowering the tax burden by about four billion dollars, which the President twice vetoed as premature and badly framed.

National spending, in fact, continued at so high a level —the appropriations for the fiscal year 1948–1949, more than forty-three billion dollars, set a peacetime record— that tax reduction would have been grossly improper. One anomaly of the period was that despite prosperity, it proved impossible to reduce the national debt. That actually increased, reaching in December, 1949, the record mark of two hundred and fifty-seven billion dollars. Annual budgetary deficits were almost the rule. Truman declared late in 1949 that borrowing must end. But the international situation made high expenditures unescapable, and in time the economy of the country became increasingly dependent on government spending.

Truman and Loyalty

THE FIRST WORLD WAR had been followed by a great campaign for loyalty, conformity, and hundred per cent Americanism in which many patriotic and liberal people suffered. The same phenomenon now reappeared in even more virulent form. Though the Communist party in the United States had at most seventy-five thousand members, a number rapidly diminishing, a clamor arose for outlawing it, and for an indiscriminate investigation of alleged disloyalty, especially in the government, the press, education, and the amusement industry. The movement threatened basic civil rights, and the nation's wiser leaders tried to combat it.

Radically different positions were taken by the House Committee on Un-American Activities in the Eightieth Congress, under Representative J. Parnell Thomas of New Jersey, and President Truman's special Civil Rights Committee, both of which reported in 1947. The Thomas Committee asserted that it had uncovered a number of Communist "fronts," such as the American Youth for Democracy; had forced into the open ten Hollywood screen writers and directors, who were indicted for contempt of Congress; had brought about the conviction and sentencing of Eugene Dennis, secretary of the Communist party; and had exposed such notorious Communist agents as Gerhart and Hans Eisler. The methods of this committee were open to the gravest criticism. In an admirably written document, the President's committee, headed by Charles E. Wilson, president of General Electric, asserted that in the name of security, one fundamental civil right after another was being invaded. This happened, it said, all over the country. "At various times practically every region . . . has had its share of disgraceful interference with the rights of some persons." The committee listed the more flagrant abuses and recommended corrective measures.

In the fall of 1946, Truman issued an executive order creating the President's Temporary Commission on Employee Loyalty, which he asked to draft a program. The following year an elaborate machinery was created. The Civil Service Commission established regional loyalty boards throughout the country; persons accused of disloyal or subversive activities were given hearings before a loyalty board, with counsel; and if dissatisfied, they might appeal to a Loyalty Review Board of twenty-three men appointed by Truman, with Seth Richardson, a conservative Republican, as head.

This program for safeguarding governmental agencies had stopgap merits, but also serious defects. It was based on the postulate that the holding of any government appointment is not a right, but a privilege. It accepted the principle that a person might be refused or removed from employment if "reasonable grounds exist for believing that the person involved is disloyal." A handful of suspected men hastened to resign from the government; others were weeded out. But as Truman later wrote, even if a man was cleared of charges, all of the data about him remained in the files. Every time he moved from one post to another his file was reviewed, and he had to clear himself again. "This," wrote Truman, "is not in the tradition of American fair play and justice." The situation was to grow worse.

Truman's Re-election

THE PRESIDENT'S BATTLE with the Eightieth Congress aroused sympathy for him in progressive circles and the labor camp. In the spring of 1948 he met a considerable popular response when he toured the country denouncing the "do-nothing" Congress. Nevertheless, Democratic chances in the presidential campaign were almost universally regarded as poor. One reason was that Henry A. Wallace had announced his candidacy on a third-party ticket, and though he attacked both Republicans and Democrats, he was expected to draw votes mainly from the latter. Another reason was that Southern Democrats were in open revolt against Truman's program of civil rights for Negroes. A strong movement developed to place the party nomination in the hands of Dwight Eisenhower, for whom Truman would have stepped aside. Nobody knew in which fold the General stood. But when Eisenhower proved adamant against running on either ticket, the Democrats had no choice but to turn back to the President.

In July, the Democratic Convention in Philadelphia nominated Truman without important dissent and without the slightest enthusiasm. Truman alone showed undaunted fighting spirit. He had insisted on a platform which nailed the Fair Deal flag to the party mast. His acceptance speech offered no quarter to his enemies. He dismayed the Republicans by announcing that he would call a special session of the Eightieth Congress to give it a chance to redeem the liberal pledges the Republicans were now making. If necessary, Truman would carry on the battle alone.

For a time he seemed very much alone. Already the Republicans, who also met in Philadelphia, had renominated Thomas E. Dewey, and rallied all elements of the party behind him. For a time it had seemed that Senator Robert A. Taft, son of the former President, and a man said to have "the best mind in Washington until he makes it up," might defeat the New Yorker. But though Taft had some streaks of liberalism, the main cast of his mind and character was too doggedly conservative for the times; his prewar isolationism and postwar frigidity toward the United Nations were too clearly remembered; and his quirks and prejudices made him, for all his stubborn honesty, seem capricious and uncertain. Dewey was younger, more attractive, more liberal—and equipped with the better machine. Nominated on the third ballot, he had for his partner the able and popular Governor Earl Warren of California, who was expected to bring his state into line. The Republican platform stood for internationalism but was equivocal on important domestic issues.

To darken Truman's prospects, diehard Southern Democrats held a rump convention and nominated Governor J. Strom Thurmond of South Carolina and Governor Fielding L. Wright of Mississippi. Gulf-state oil interests were eager, like California, to bring tideland areas under state control; resenting Truman's veto of a bill for that purpose, they helped supply funds for the "Dixiecrat party." Most Southern conservatives clung to their ancient party allegiance, but if Thurmond carried even a few states, the election might go into the House. Wallace, meanwhile, was nominated by a hurriedly organized Progressive party and began a speaking tour in which he attacked Truman as about to plunge the country into war with Russia. As fast as Communists flocked to his side, most true liberals left it. All the polls indicated a smashing Republican victory. Most voters seemed apathetic.

Yet the President never lost heart, and in a series of extensive speaking trips used the vernacular of the masses in denouncing the Eightieth Congress, attacking Dewey, and defending his own record. His one-man campaign aroused admiration. Dewey, meanwhile, was so confident of victory that he skirted the real issues, talking of little but national unity. His colorless tactics inspired nobody and repelled many.

The day after election the nation awoke to one of the most startling upsets in its history. Truman had won with more than 24,000,000 popular and 303 electoral votes; Dewey had received not quite 22,000,000 popular and 189 electoral votes. Thurmond had carried Louisiana, Mississippi, Alabama, and South Carolina. Wallace carried not a single state. Some credited the result to the fact that only three fifths of the voters had turned out—too many Republicans had played golf; some to Dewey's flabby campaign—he had snatched defeat from the jaws of victory! Probably a larger reason was that Americans admire an indomitable fighter. And the theory that the country now basically leaned to the Democratic side gained strength from the Congressional results: the new Senate was Democratic 54 to 42, and the new House 263 to 161. For Truman this did not mean much; a Dixiecrat-Republican coalition would still be in control.

The Fair Deal Fades

A PRESIDENT more tactful and imaginative than Truman might have done more with the Eighty-first Congress, which met just after his election. Though in January, 1949, he again laid before Congress his Fair Deal program continuing and enlarging the New Deal, he made little progress with it. Most Presidents meet more difficulties in their second than in their first terms. Truman's influence in Congress in 1949–1952 sank about as low as Taft's in 1911–1912, though not as far as Cleveland's in 1895–1896 or Hoover's in 1931–1932.

In the field of race relations Southern members remained obdurate against his proposals. A weak Fair Employment Practice bill and a bill outlawing poll taxes passed the House but failed in the Senate. The deadlock over Federal aid to schools persisted. Truman was quite unable to modify, much less repeal, the Taft-Hartley Act. Congress did pass a Housing Act (April, 1950), which authorized the use of as much as one and a half billion dollars in slum clearance and the erection of low-cost housing. It took an important step in creating a National Science Foundation to devise a national program for basic research in engineering and all the exact sciences. It raised the minimum wage from the old forty-cent level to seventy-five cents an hour (1949). Most important of all, it broadened the Social Security Act, making it apply to almost forty-five million people instead of the thirty-five million previously covered (1950). But Congress refused to deal with such matters as Truman's request for TVA-style projects in other great valleys.

Meanwhile, inflation strode on with little check. Under the Defense Production Act of 1950, an Economic Stabilization Agency was established, headed first by Dr. Alan Valentine and later by Michael DiSalle. Valentine tried to establish selective controls, getting manufacturers and dealers to hold prices in a given commodity at fixed levels; DiSalle attempted sweeping price limitations. Neither achieved much success. After the opening of the Korean War, the familiar spiral of wages chasing prices and prices chasing wages reappeared. Salaried people, workers not protected by powerful unions, farmers, and others unable to hoist their incomes suffered badly.

Altogether, the problem of inflation was extremely complex. Yet something had to be done. "If runaway inflation were to take hold in America, the nation would go bankrupt and Stalin would realize his dreams of conquest without firing a shot," said Charles E. Wilson of the Defense Mobilization Office. In January, 1951, the administration issued orders for the control of prices and wages at set levels, but the orders contained many exceptions and proved temporary. The best defense against inflation was the rise in taxation, corporate and private, which began that year.

Communism and Security Again

JUST AFTER TRUMAN'S ELECTION a series of spectacular events riveted public attention on Communist activities at home and helped arouse a feverish public feeling which some feared might lead to an anti-Red hysteria.

Eleven Communist leaders, the "Politburo" of the party, were brought to trial in 1949 on the charge of violating the Smith Act of 1940, which made conspiracy to "advocate and teach" the violent overthrow of the government a crime. The trial posed a number of questions: Was the Communist party a conspiracy? Did it take its orders from Moscow? Did it preach the overthrow of the government by force? Judge Harold Medina, who presided with impartiality and decorum, summed up the evidence in a masterly charge of sixteen thousand words, and directed the jury to assume the constitutionality of the Smith Act, then in question but later upheld. The jury found all eleven defendants guilty, and ultimately they went to jail.

At almost the same time Alger Hiss, formerly a man of some importance in the State Department and more recently head of the Carnegie Endowment for International Peace, went on trial. He was charged with perjury in denying to a Federal grand jury that he had ever given secret State Department papers to Whittaker Chambers, himself a former Communist. The trial had sensational elements of mystery. After one jury disagreed, another found Hiss guilty, and he was sentenced to five years in a penitentiary. The next year, 1951, two New Yorkers, Julius and Ethel Rosenberg, were sentenced to death as traitors for giving Russian agents important data on the atom bomb in the critical years 1944–1945; the fullest evidence against them being furnished by Mrs. Rosenberg's brother, who was given a fifteen-year term in prison. The Rosenbergs were electro-cuted in 1953. Meanwhile, the government deported a number of aliens charged with Communist activities. Various states considered, and some passed, bills requiring em-ployees, including public-school and university teachers, to take loyalty oaths. In New York the sweeping Feinberg Act made possible the dismissal of teachers belonging to organizations labeled as subversive by the State Board of Regents, but it aroused a wave of protest and was annulled.

Many Americans feared that, under the impact of passions aroused by the Korean War, the movement to guard against internal dangers would get out of hand and do far more damage than Communist spies and plotters could possibly inflict. They believed that an atmosphere of panic, suspicion, and repression was enveloping the country; that in the name of security, our freedom of speech, of publication, of public assemblage, and of dissent was being grievously abridged. Reasonable public leaders pointed out that "guilt by association" was unjust and indefensible; that nobody could make a fair list of "subversive organizations"; and that any wholesale effort to expel disloyal people from schools, universities, mass media, and government offices would ruin many innocent people and do irreparable damage to the institutions affected. The Truman administration in general did its best to resist public hysteria, but Congress was less careful. Senator Pat McCarran's Internal Security Subcommittee in 1951–1952 showed more zeal than discretion, while the House Un-American Activities Committee continued its reckless course.

An opening was presented for a demagogue, and Senator Joseph R. McCarthy of Wisconsin came forward in 1950 to fill it. Blatant, unscrupulous, and adroit, he saw that he might achieve national prominence—even power—by wild charges, fake evidence, brazen attacks, blows below the belt, and appeals to prejudice. His pugnacious features, rasping voice, and use of the big-lie technique soon became familiar to television audiences. He had a gift for the headlines. He made his first big splash by charging that the State Department under Acheson harbored over two hundred "known Communists," and by the accusation that Owen Lattimore, professor at the Johns Hopkins University and former deputy director of Pacific operations in the Office of War Information, had been "Russia's top espionage agent in the United States." No Communist could be found in the State Department. A special Senate subcommittee, after prolonged inquiry, exonerated Lattimore. All charges against him, pressed with vindictiveness by the Eisenhower administration, were subsequently dismissed by the courts. But McCarthy's fulminations in the Senate, following the conviction of Hiss and the disclosure that a British physicist, Klaus Fuchs, had given atomic secrets to Russia, deceived many people. He was ready to play a larger role if the Republicans gained Congress.

So long as McCarthy used his smear procedure on the Senate floor, he was immune from prosecution for slander. Some utterances were so outrageous that they recoiled upon him. In 1951, for example, he attacked Defense Secretary George Marshall for tolerating a gigantic Communist conspiracy in the United States. He assailed ambassadors, editors, and even fellow-senators of high integrity. Whenever his falsehoods were exposed, as when a Senate subcommittee in 1950 declared his main charges "a fraud and a hoax," he asserted that his opponents were whitewashing Communism. His diatribes against the administration weakened the dignity and effectiveness of government in general. Worst of all, the uproar he aroused did the United States incalculable harm in the rest of the world, which believed that a Fascist movement might be under way.

Out of the sense of panic in wide circles came the McCarran-Nixon bill, passed in 1950 over the President's veto. It required the registration of all members of Communist "front" organizations, excluded Communists from employment in plants connected with national defense, and provided for the arrest of Communists and other "subversives" in time of war. It also debarred from the United States any person ever affiliated with a totalitarian organization. This excluded the British poet Stephen Spender, who in a youthful impulse had embraced Communism for one day and at once repented; it excluded great numbers of reputable Germans, Hungarians, Italians, and others once connected with Fascist groups; it excluded numbers of men who had fought in Resistance movements against Nazi occupation. The law was followed in 1952 by the McCarran Act, again passed over Truman's veto, revising the immigration statutes. Although this had some sound features, the President wrote, they were embedded in a mass of legislation which would perpetuate old injustices and hamper American efforts to rally the world to the cause of freedom. Eisenhower took the same view. America had always meant hope to oppressed aliens, he said, "yet to the Czech, the Pole, the Hungarian who takes his life in his hand and crosses the frontier tonight . . . the ideal that beckoned him can be a mirage because of the McCarran Act."

Altogether, as the Truman administration drew to a close, danger existed that wartime strains and a reaction from New Deal days might usher in a period of excessive conservatism and reaction. The pressures were almost irresistible: impatience with the burdens of world power, an almost psychotic fear of subversion, resentment of the rising demands of minority groups, and a desire for "business as usual," lower taxes, and higher profits. If liberal values could properly be protected in what Eisenhower called "an age of danger," all would be well, but that seemed increasingly unlikely.

From domestic affairs we must turn back to the darker foreign page.

CHAPTER 27

The Korean War: The Hydrogen Bomb

Truman Rallies the Free World

WHEN ON JUNE 26, 1950, they invaded South Korea, the Communists doubtless believed the moment ripe for a demonstration that they could dominate Asia. Mao ruled China; the Viet-Minh hoped with his aid to take over French Indo-China; Communist plotters were directing a bitter guerrilla warfare in British Malaysia; the Communist-inspired Huks were still formidable in the Philippines. All spring the Peiping government had been massing junks and other vessels at Foochow and other ports for an attack on Formosa. If they conquered Korea, cleared Southeast Asia of Western influence, and destroyed Chiang Kai-shek, the Communists could overawe all Asiatic peoples.

Stalin probably believed that the United States would not even try to intervene. The American mainland was seven thousand miles distant, only a few divisions were in fighting trim, and commitment of troops in Asia would weaken Western Europe. Secretary Acheson had omitted South Korea from his definition of the defensive perimeter of America, and MacArthur had said anybody who wished to involve our forces in Asia should have his head examined.

Fortunately, Truman, Acheson, and their advisers understood the moral value of immediate action. Had they delayed, panic might have overspread Europe. Within 24 hours the President announced he was sending American air and naval forces to aid the South Koreans, and had ordered the Seventh Fleet to protect Formosa. Later that day the UN Security Council called on member nations to repel the Communist aggression. Thereupon, Truman ordered American troops to the battle front. He had no time to lay the matter before Congress, nor was this necessary. The American public saw that the attack on the free world had to be resisted, and the UN sustained.

Other democracies took rapid action. In the first days of July Britain, Australia, New Zealand, and the Netherlands began to dispatch troops. Canada soon followed; so, before long, did France, Turkey, Thailand, the Philippines, and Brazil. When on July 7 the Security Council asked the United States to establish a unified command, Washington immediately appointed General MacArthur. A draft was instituted to fill American ranks. Before long the UN flag waved over a motley world army, the first in history, resisting the aggressor. The South Koreans at first constituted the largest single body of fighters; the Americans, next in number, were the best armed and most effective; the British, Canadians, Australians, and others soon made up a Commonwealth Division; and the remaining nations gave good service. Even India contributed a hospital unit. The absence of Russia from the Security Council had made possible this instant call to arms without fear of a veto. At once the UN gained a prestige which the League had never commanded.

Retreat and Advance

FOR NEARLY SIX WEEKS the South Korean, American, and other units were pushed down the peninsula so steadily that observers feared they would be flung into the sea before their lines held. The invaders evinced a fanatical bravery. Many of them had fought in Chinese, Japanese, or Russian ranks during the Second World War; they had excellent Soviet equipment, especially in tanks; they had learned from the Japanese an art of night attack and infiltration which was hard to resist. Above all, they had superior numbers. The hand-to-hand fighting often became desperately confused. "I'll be damned if I know who's got who surrounded!" an American officer exclaimed. The presence of American veterans in Japan and large naval contingents in Far Eastern waters had permitted the rapid landing of reinforcements, but they were too few. Over jagged mountains three to five thousand feet high, over malodorous rice paddies, over tangled ravines, the defenders retreated toward the tip of Korea nearest Japan.

But General Walton Walker's delaying battle accomplished his purpose. Early September found him pent within an irregular rectangle of sixty by one hundred miles, supplied by the port of Pusan. Here his Eighth Army fighters held firm, while more troops landed and new naval units came up. An incomplete tally of American casualties reached nearly 7000, while the North Koreans had lost far more. When sufficient forces and weapons had arrived, on September 15 the UN troops shifted suddenly to the offensive. "We are about to go," President Syngman Rhee had announced —and they went in a way that startled the world.

MacArthur had planned his blow far to the north, at Inchon Harbor on the west coast near Seoul. An armada of more than 260 vessels was gathered in Japanese ports. American, British, and Australian fliers began pounding the enemy with high-explosive bombs, incendiaries, and missiles filled with jellied petroleum (napalm). American and British warships poured shells into exposed coastal areas.

The first Marine Division took Wolmi Island at dawn, swept into devastated Inchon, and joined the Seventh Infantry Division in a rapid march on Seoul. Simultaneously, General Walker's troops in his Pusan rectangle moved forward against the North Koreans, while South Korean forces landed on the east coast to march inland. The battleship *Missouri*, which had steamed eleven thousand miles from Norfolk, brought its heavy guns into play. The enemy were in imminent danger of having their communications cut. It is not astonishing that all the North Korean fronts collapsed and their armies fled.

Seoul was in UN hands on the afternoon of September 26, and President Rhee was able to re-establish his government in his old capital while South Korean and UN troops pursued the invaders back across the boundary. MacArthur broadcast to the foe a summons to lay down their arms "under such military supervision as I may direct." They ignored him, but it was plain to the world that Communist aggression had been frustrated.

A crucial question now had to be answered. Should the UN forces halt on the thirty-eighth parallel, or push on until they had subjugated all North Korea and unified the country? Opinion in the Western nations was divided. MacArthur was convinced that if he did not pursue the enemy to the Yalu River, the boundary with Manchuria and Siberia, they would reassemble in the mountains, gather new recruits, obtain more tanks and planes from Russia, and renew the attack. The State Department agreed to a thrust beyond the parallel. UN forces moved rapidly forward, captured the North Korean capital Pyongyang, and by late October were deep in the northern boundary belt, the line actually touching the Yalu at one point. Just after the first American units moved, the General Assembly of the UN passed a resolution approving the step, and the British foreign minister, Ernest Bevin, asked that "all Korea" be given a free government.

It seems clear that in his rapid advance MacArthur went farther, however, than the Truman administration or other UN nations expected. One embarrassing factor was that Chiang Kai-shek had plucked up hope that the United States would assist him in invading the Chinese mainland. Whether MacArthur gave him any encouragement, and whether MacArthur expected and desired war with China, are questions which remain to be fully clarified. At any rate, from an early moment in MacArthur's new operations the Chinese Communists began to bristle. The foreign minister, Chou En-lai, told the Indian Ambassador that if any but South Korean forces crossed the old boundary, China would send troops to aid the North Koreans. Similar reports came from Moscow and Stockholm.

If China did intervene, MacArthur's headlong thrust had placed the UN forces in a vulnerable position, for his center was open to attack. President Truman was so worried by the situation that he ordered MacArthur to meet him on Wake Island October 15, where they discussed grand strategy. MacArthur assured the President that the victory was won in Korea, that the Chinese Communists would not attack, and that it would be possible to send one division from Korea to Europe the following January. In fact, he expected to withdraw the Eighth Army to Japan by Christmas. If the Chinese did intervene, said MacArthur, they could not get more than sixty thousand men into Korea, and without air power they would be slaughtered.

Communist China Attacks

INTERVENE THEY DID, and on a massive scale. Soon fanatical Chinese troops were pouring over the Yalu, and it was clear that the Chinese were ready, if necessary, for general war. Such a war neither the United States nor the UN wanted. As General Bradley said, it would be the wrong war at the wrong time in the wrong place. But could it be avoided?

The Communists maintained the fiction that the heavy Chinese forces were volunteers for the rescue of North Korea. "Like Lafayette, like Rochambeau!" a Russian spokesman derisively told the UN. That fiction both sides respected to the extent of not declaring war though war it really was. For it was clear that the Chinese attack was a ruse to stop American aid in reconstructing Europe. Truman regarded Europe as the key to world peace, and had no intention of letting American efforts be diverted from the Western theater. The UN carefully avoided military sanctions against Peiping.

MacArthur, anxious to ascertain the strength, direction, and objects of the Chinese effort, ordered the Eighth Army to begin what he called a "general offensive" on November 24. It quickly broke down, and Chinese forces, pouring down in overwhelming numbers, completely separated the two American wings, while a South Korean corps was ground up and almost disappeared. By December 3 MacArthur was reporting the situation of the Eighth Army as "increasingly critical." It was soon in full retreat toward the Seoul area, and parts of it were so badly mauled that American, British, and Turkish reserves were rushed up to assist it, only to find themselves in danger of being overwhelmed. Though the Defense Department declared that the situation was "not catastrophic," Washington buzzed with anxious conferences.

By the end of 1950 the UN forces held a precarious line between Seoul and the thirty-eighth parallel. No unit had been cut off, though many had been decimated and some almost destroyed. Lieutenant General Matthew B. Ridgway, who succeeded to the field command under MacArthur after General Walker was killed, headed tough infantry forces of about 325,000, of whom about 200,000 were Americans; air and naval personnel brought the total to 350,000. Enemy forces were estimated at nearly if not quite a half million, with huge reserves north of the Yalu. The superior fire power and air power of the UN army, however, enabled it to trade lives in battle at the rate of one to five, and to cripple enemy transport facilities.

The Chinese Drive Defeated

THE WINTER AND SPRING of 1951 brought a succession of Communist attacks, and a grimly successful effort by the UN to slow them down, bog them in blood, and finally halt them. Ridgway shortly opened a counterattack which carried the UN army north past Seoul again, until by mid-April the Americans and their allies had pushed a dozen miles above the thirty-eighth parallel, and had occupied part of the "Iron Triangle" which was the center of Communist power in Korea.

The winter fighting was perhaps the cruelest in all American history. The fierce cold and blinding storms; the rugged terrain of abrupt mountains, treacherous swamps, and unbridged streams; the ferocity of the enemy, giving no quarter, and fighting on until their troops stood behind high windrows of corpses; the power of the Russian tanks and strength of the Russian-built jet planes which brought down in flames many American B-29 bombers; the desperate nature of many of the battles, like that in which a British Gloucestershire regiment was practically exterminated; the well-grounded fear that UN prisoners would get even more inhuman treatment than that which the Russians had given German and Japanese prisoners—all this made the conflict a terrible ordeal. But American and British airplanes maintained a clear superiority; flying sometimes more than a thousand sorties a day, they blanketed the enemy with bombs, machine-gun bullets, and napalm.

April and May witnessed two ferocious Red counterattacks, which finally ground to a halt after a loss of some 200,000 men. Then, in June, came a massive UN counteroffensive. Moving steadily forward, the Eighth Army crossed the parallel, regained the greater part of the "Iron Triangle," and took up positions which almost defied assault. The fighting gradually died away.

On June 25, the first anniversary of the Korean War, the Communists held 2100 fewer square miles than when they began their attack. At some points the new UN boundary reached forty miles above the thirty-eighth parallel. North Korean towns were in ruins, and North Korean industries dead. The price of this was proportionately heavier than in the First or Second World War. While the UN forces were estimated to have lost well over 400,000 men killed, wounded, and missing (South Koreans 260,000, Americans 135,000, other nations 12,000), the Reds lost about four times as many—at least 1,500,000. In short, this was one of the bloodiest wars in history. Epidemics, too, had ravaged Red ranks. The free world had shown its unconquerable fighting power; the UN had vindicated its position as a shield of small nations against wanton aggressors.

MacArthur Deposed

WHILE THIS DRAMA of assault and counterassault was being enacted, a dramatic struggle between Truman and MacArthur reached its climax. Recalling Lincoln's difficulties with the temperamental McClellan, it was a struggle between a chief of state who had to think of many global considerations, and a general who thought only of military objectives; between a President determined to keep control of the situation, and a commander using political pressure to force the government's hand.

MacArthur, when his armies met defeat, took it badly. He reported to the Army Chief of Staff that three possible courses existed: continued action against the Chinese in Korea alone, acceptance of the thirty-eighth parallel as an armistice line (if the Chinese consented), and a vigorous offensive against China in every feasible sphere. He was for the third. He would blockade the Chinese coast, bomb the mainland, and use Chiang Kai-shek's army to invade South China and reinforce South Korea. It was obvious that if the United States landed Chiang's men on the mainland and bombed Chinese cities, a general war would ensue. Russia was bound by treaty to aid China. Truman was unwilling to risk a third world war. He broadcast a message (December 15, 1950) to the American people: "Our goal is not war but peace. Throughout the world our name stands for international justice and for a world based on the principles of law and order." The President had the full support of the Joint Chiefs of Staff in pronouncing for a *limited* war, and so far as China went, an undeclared war.

MacArthur, however, did not accept the administration policy. When March brought a turn in the tide of war, Truman prepared to meet the new state of affairs with an announcement that, South Korea having been substantially cleared of invaders, the time was at hand to stop the fighting and discuss a settlement. MacArthur was duly informed that this statement was almost ready. The State Department, Joint Chiefs, Secretary of Defense, and others helped Truman put the final touches on it. As the President was about to release it, all his work was set at naught: Mac-

Arthur on March 24 gave the world a statement of his own so completely at variance with Truman's that men would have been hopelessly confused had both appeared. The general asserted that Red China had been defeated; that she lacked the resources to carry on war much longer; and that if the UN decided on a mighty new effort, "through an expansion of our military operations to its coastal areas and interior bases," China would risk imminent collapse. In short, he coupled threats with a demand that China agree forthwith to a truce.

Truman had made up his mind to dismiss the general, when on April 5 a new incident occurred. Joseph W. Martin, Republican leader in the House, read the chamber a private letter in which MacArthur repeated his views on the necessity for summary treatment of Communist China. To talk about the paramount importance of Europe, he wrote, was folly. People should remember that "here we fight Europe's war with arms, while the diplomats there still fight it with words; that if we lose the war to Communism in Asia the fall of Europe is inevitable; win it, and Europe most probably would avoid war and yet preserve freedom." He added: "There is no substitute for victory."

Truman had but one course to follow. With the full agreement of his military and civilian advisers, he announced, on April 11, 1951, the removal of the recalcitrant general. The general's tremendous prestige, his connection with Republican elements hostile to Truman, and his supposed political ambitions made the event doubly dramatic. MacArthur came home for the first time in fourteen years to receive a tumultuous reception in San Francisco. On April 19 he addressed a joint session of Congress while the nation listened on the radio; next day he rode up Fifth Avenue to the cheers of millions. For a time his political star seemed to be rising.

Joint hearings by a Senate and a House committee early in May, however, placed his dismissal under the cold light of reason, and with the passing of time it became increasingly clear that Truman's decision had been dictated by wisdom as well as by necessity, and that it had vindicated, once again, the principle of the superiority of the civilian to the military authority.

Neo-Isolationism

THE GREAT DEBATE over MacArthur left the administration policy unshaken and probably strengthened it. For one reason, government spokesmen made it clear that while they wished to avoid perilous courses, they would stand no nonsense from the Communists. American patience was stretched about as far as it would go. Public sentiment approved this position. But the Congressional hearings did bring a new type of isolationism into the open.

MacArthur, protesting that he had "no political aspirations whatever," made it plain that he did have strong political opinions. He was for a policy which regarded America's interests alone. In his view, we did not particularly need allies in the West; we should boldly rely on our own strength, and strike hard with it. He made it clear that he leaned toward Senator Robert Taft rather than General Eisenhower as the next Republican candidate for the presidency, for Taft was head of the quasi-isolationists of the party. Some of his references to Eisenhower were stinging. MacArthur took comfort in the position of Herbert Hoover, who earlier that year had advocated withdrawal of our forces from the European continent, and the establishment of a "Western Hemisphere Gibraltar" in the two Americas, with Great Britain as an advance outpost. This was while Eisenhower was requesting four more divisions for Europe.

But the time when isolationism might be dangerous had passed. Eisenhower spoke before both houses of Congress just after Hoover's plea, describing his work for NATO and arguing that the North Atlantic sphere was our primary concern. We could not spare Western Europe's pool of skilled labor, the greatest in the world, he said; we must keep her huge industrial potential. He reported an encouraging rise in European morale. Early in April the Senate by a vote of 69 to 21 carried resolutions hailing the North Atlantic Treaty as a turning point in history, and declaring that the nation should station in Europe "such units of our armed forces as may be necessary and appropriate to contribute our fair share" to Western defense.

The administration promptly pressed forward its program for rearming America and helping rearm Europe. The plan at home was to increase national production by about one fifth within three (later four) years. Investment in new plants of clear value in war was encouraged by tax exemptions, and, where necessary, by the loan of government money. Normal civilian consumption was to be maintained intact, but vast additional quantities of guns, planes, tanks, and other weapons were to be produced. The cold war obviously might last for decades or even generations, and the United States would be better equipped for the long pull than Russia. But the burden was nevertheless heavy in two directions. For service and training about 3,500,000 men would have to be kept in uniform; for costs forty to sixty billion dollars would have to be raised annually. High expenditures and taxation meant a disquieting inflation.

Yet, the fact that rearmament, inflation, and prosperity seemed tied together undoubtedly helped account for the failure of the neo-isolationism of MacArthur, Hoover, and certain Midwestern and Western Senators. More important was the fact that circumstances sternly dictated adherence to the policies marked out under Roosevelt, Truman, Marshall, and Eisenhower. Any schism between the United States and the other NATO members would be fatal to both.

The Korean Truce

BY JUNE, 1951, the Korean conflict had reached a stalemate, and when the Soviet delegate to the UN remarked that the Kremlin was ready to discuss an armistice, the way was open for a cessation of the murderous war. Early in July military leaders of the UN and Communist armies began a series of discussions which then dragged on for month after weary month. The specific issue on which it proved impossible to reach agreement was the question of prisoners. Most of the UN prisoners in Communist hands had died or been killed; most of the Communist prisoners in UN hands did not want repatriation to North Korea or China. The real difficulty, however, was that it suited Russia's book to postpone peace. Intermittent fighting kept UN forces pinned down in Korea and delayed the NATO powers in their effort to rearm Europe. It increased Chinese dependence on Russia, and furnished a training ground for Chinese troops and Russian pilots.

The United States and UN for their part were unwilling that a partial or false peace should be made in the Far East. Korea could not be considered apart from Indo-China and Malaysia, where Russia and China were furnishing money, supplies, and advisers to Communist rebels. If Mao withdrew his army from North Korea only to put equivalent forces into action in Southeast Asia, the free world would gain nothing. Russia's object was apparently to use puppet states to carry on harassing conflicts in the Orient while Moscow waged the cold war in Europe. The UN negotiators wanted proof of a change of heart, not a change of front. War-weariness grew in the United States, Britain, and other Western nations. for the Korean fighting seemed largely futile. But evidence appeared that war-weariness was still greater in China.

As it grew, the death of Stalin and the ensuing struggle for power in Russia between Malenkov and Beria presented a new situation. By the early weeks of 1953 China and the Soviet Union were showing a more conciliatory temper. Negotiations at Panmunjom, which had been broken off, were resumed. That stubborn old patriot, President Syngman Rhee, created difficulties by insisting that all Korea must be united under his government, and by arranging the "escape" of about 20,000 North Korean prisoners who wished to stay in the South. But finally the Communists gave way sufficiently to accept a plan of voluntary, not compulsory, repatriation. On June 27, 1953, the truce was finally signed. The war was over.

At great cost, the West had won a substantial victory. Tens of thousands of American, British, South Korean, and other soldiers lay in their graves; hundreds of thousands were mutilated or weakened by disease and hardship: most of Korea was a litter of wreckage. But as Winston Churchill put it, the West had achieved a "checkmate"; it had defeated the Communist aggression by bringing it to a standstill. Had the Soviet Union succeeded in its experimental thrust in Korea, it would quickly have followed it by others. Stalin had made his time table for conquest in Malaysia, Indo-China, Formosa, and if all went well, Western Europe. It had been frustrated. Western rearmament had been accelerated. The world front against Communism was immeasurably stronger than it had been when the North Koreans attacked.

The Hydrogen Bomb

DURING THE LAST PHASES of the war the United States not only tested larger atom bombs, but at Eniwetok Atoll exploded the first hydrogen bomb in history. The blast that morning of November 1, 1952, was brighter than ten suns; the flame, two miles long and a thousand feet high, completely burned out the island on which the bomb was planted. "Such a weapon," wrote W. L. Laurence of *The New York Times*, "exploding with a force equal to that of twenty million tons of TNT, could devastate an area of more than 300 square miles by blast and 1200 square miles by fire. If encased in a shell of cobalt it could produce a radioactive cloud equal to five million pounds of radium, spreading death and devastation over thousands of square miles."

In short, a hydrogen bomb could almost completely obliterate London, Moscow, or New York. The significance of the new weapon was gradually comprehended by the world. Lethal as the atom bomb was, war with such missiles was still possible. But the hydrogen bomb, as air currents carried deadly atomic clouds hither and thither, was almost as dangerous to the power using it as to the power attacked; and a war of hydrogen bombs might depopulate the entire globe. Man had at last found a weapon so devastating that only madmen could contemplate an unrestricted conflict. A new age had opened.

Eisenhower vs. Stevenson

THE PRESIDENTIAL CAMPAIGN of 1952 offered an opportunity to debate war and defense. Both issues and personalities promised to be engrossing. Republicans blamed the Democratic administration for corruption and the debasement of governmental standards; for excessive taxes and reckless expenditures; for inflation and bureaucratic meddling with business; for tolerance of subversives; and, above all, for letting the Korean War run on needlessly. Their opponents attacked the Republican party for its reactionary and isolationist elements. They recalled the bad record of the Republican-controlled Eightieth Congress, and harked back to sour memories of the Harding, Coolidge, and Hoover administrations.

Both parties were troubled by serious internal divisions. On the Democratic side Southern conservatives had become more incensed than ever with Truman, while farm voters were losing the attachments formed under Franklin D. Roosevelt. Truman's announcement in March that he would not run again was hailed by many Democrats as ridding the party of an old-man-of-the-sea. On the Republican side the Old Guard, led by Robert Taft and cheered on by Hoover and MacArthur, was antagonistic to the progressive elements, who believed that they must accept the main features of the New Deal and support internationalism as represented by the United Nations, NATO, and foreign aid programs. A Young Guard appeared, of which far-from-young Eisenhower was the leader, and behind the general rallied such politicians as Thomas E. Dewey.

From the beginning Eisenhower dominated the Republican scene. His announcement in February that he would take the nomination if offered, and his resignation of the NATO command to take up political activities, were greeted with popular enthusiasm. Unquestionably he was the most popular man in the country. His machine was amateurishly managed, his knowledge of history and politics was slight, his understanding of our economics, government, and social problems left much to be desired. But people had tremendous faith in his ability, grasp, conscientiousness, and international experience. Rival aspirants like Harold Stassen, Robert Taft, and Governor Earl Warren of California made little impression on the public.

When the Republican Convention met in Chicago in early July, Governor Dewey marshaled the Eisenhower cohorts; wavering delegates fell in line under a conviction that only "Ike" could be certain of winning; and the general was uproariously named on the first ballot, with Senator Richard Nixon of California for Vice-President.

The leading figure among the Democrats, Governor Adlai E. Stevenson of Illinois, had the advantage of a name well known in the party (his grandfather had been Vice-President in Cleveland's second term), of experience in various

Washington posts, and of service as a UN delegate. He had given his state an efficient and progressive administration. Witty, highly cultivated, genial, and energetic, he possessed rare gifts of personality. President Truman pressed Stevenson to be a candidate, and when Harriman on the third ballot transferred the New York delegation to him, he was chosen. Hurrying to the scene, Stevenson made a televised acceptance speech which by its charm, eloquence, and sense made a deep impression.

The campaign which followed was neither closely fought nor highly dramatic. When great numbers of intellectuals joined most labor leaders in supporting Stevenson, the Republicans derisively attacked the "eggheads" as advocates of Socialism and working-class legislation. Taft, after sulking for a time, met Eisenhower in mid-September in the president's house at Columbia University, and emerged with a statement which seemed to imply that the general had met most of his demands. Both presidential candidates made a series of long tours, undertook arduous radio and television campaigns, and reduced themselves by autumn to exhaustion. While "Ike" suffered with liberals for his willingness to hobnob with such demagogues as McCarthy of Wisconsin and William E. Jenner of Indiana, Stevenson suffered with conservative voters from Truman's rough use of the shillelagh against Eisenhower in an October whistlestop circuit.

This was the first campaign in history in which television played an important part, and the first in which advertising and public-relations firms were hired on a large scale to organize publicity. The Republicans had a heavy advantage in campaign expenditures, estimated at thirty-five millions, and in use of the press, fully eighty per cent of the newspapers and magazines supporting Eisenhower. Though Stevenson's speeches had a rare intellectual content and literary polish, and Eisenhower maintained a position of great dignity and fairness, the contest as a whole was depressing. A huge and costly effort resulted in singularly little public enlightenment. The best features of the struggle were two: Stevenson's combination of candor with hard sense—he proved one of the most completely honest candidates in our annals—and Eisenhower's courageous acceptance of the main policies of the Roosevelt and Truman administrations: "We are not going to turn the clock back."

The result was a landslide in favor not of the Republicans, but of Eisenhower. He carried thirty-nine states with a popular vote of 34,000,000 and an electoral vote of 442. Stevenson carried only nine states, all Southern or border, with a popular vote of 27,300,000 and an electoral vote of 89. Eisenhower swept Texas, Florida, Virginia, Tennessee, and Oklahoma. Nearly everywhere he ran ahead of other Republicans, and usually far ahead. It was plain that, moved by his fame, his great services to the nation, and his engaging personal qualities, the people were in the mood expressed by the popular slogan "I like Ike."

The New Administration

THAT IT WAS A PERSONAL, not a party, victory was made plain by the narrowness of the Republican margin in Congress. The new House would stand 221 to 211; the new Senate 48 to 47. Had not Eisenhower's great vote assisted numerous Republican members who stood on the verge of defeat, the Democrats would have controlled both chambers. Eisenhower made it clear that his great hope would be to unite the party, unite the country, and unite the Western nations. Indeed, many men had supported him as a symbol of national and international unity at a time when the world needed above all else a harmonious America behind a harmonious and well-led NATO.

His appointments were of moderate and conservative men, all but one identified with business, finance, or corporation law. He made John Foster Dulles of New York, who had been a staunch advocate of bipartisan foreign policy and a representative of the United States in the UN Assembly, his Secretary of State. This act confirmed the internationalism of the new administration. The post of Secretary of Defense went to Charles E. Wilson, president of General Motors Corporation. Another business leader, George M. Humphrey of Cleveland, became Secretary of the Treasury. Douglas McKay of Oregon, no friend of conservation, became head of the Interior Department; and the cautious Ezra T. Benson of Utah was made Secretary of Agriculture. More important than most of these Cabinet appointments was Eisenhower's selection of Sherman P. Adams as his personal assistant. Adams, a dour Yankee from New Hampshire, became in time Eisenhower's *éminence grise*, more powerful, on most routine matters, than almost any member of the new administration.

It was evident that the new administration would be conservative, prudent, and divorced from strong political partisanship. It was also plain that the international outlook of the administration would be as enlightened as Truman's. The position of Mutual Security Director went to Harold Stassen, who shared the views of the President-elect and of Dulles on the importance of maintaining a strong Western alliance. The nation as Eisenhower took the helm was in the full tide of prosperity and industrial growth, and he intended to keep it there. The stability of the free world depended in large measure upon the stability of the United States, economic and political.

CHAPTER 28

The Eisenhower Administration

Lines of Policy

FOR THE FIRST TIME in twenty years, the Republicans were in power. A revolution had occurred in both domestic and world affairs since Hoover had gloomily left the White House, and the President at least was ready to accept it.

Few Americans had seen so much of the foreign scene as Eisenhower, or understood so clearly the necessity of welding the free nations against Communist attack. His inaugural address declared that America had a mission of "world leadership" which it would execute "not with confusion, but with confidence." Warning the people not to expect lower budgets or taxes, but to be ready for greater sacrifices, he pledged Western Europe a continuance of aid, and declared that the United States was ready to reduce tariffs to foster trade. He called on Europeans to bear their share of financial burdens, and to press forward in raising production and arming themselves.

In home affairs, Eisenhower outlined his fundamental ideas in his first long message to Congress. He wished to restrict bureaucratic interferences with the life of the people. Except in time of crisis he would leave business to the workings of natural economic law. The true role of the government was "to stabilize the economy and encourage the free play of our people's genius for individual initiative." Debt reduction was more important than tax reduction. Inflation should in general be met by limitations on credit, not by wage and price ceilings. In the labor field, he would keep the government out of rooms in which management and unions were bargaining, unless some shutdown threatened the national welfare. In the agricultural field, he thought it probable that when the law establishing rigid price supports expired in 1954, these should be replaced by flexible supports. He was for amendment of the unhappy McCarran Act just passed, and for further extensions of social security. As for the vexatious loyalty issue, he followed Truman in holding that primary responsibility for keeping subversives out of the government rested with the executive, not Congress.

All in all, Eisenhower's views and conduct were those of a moderate, or, as he shortly put it, of a believer in "dynamic liberalism" of a moderate type. He liked to speak of himself as moving down the middle of the road, although he was obviously to the right of the middle. He regarded himself as a grand national harmonizer, who would do all he could for both party unity and national unity. Like Washington, he would keep above the clash of policies and hold himself aloof from the strife of jealous contenders for power; he would be a moderator or umpire. This meant that he did little to lead Congress or direct public opinion, and resolutely refused to give battle to most opponents. He was a President of the type of McKinley or Taft. That he accurately gauged the temper of the country is clear; few occupants of the White House have been as popular as he remained throughout his eight years.

The first session of the Eighty-third Congress accomplished some of the moderate tasks which Eisenhower requested it to perform. It established a Department of Health, Education, and Welfare, to which he appointed Mrs. Hobby of Texas as head. It put an end to the Reconstruction Finance Corporation, substituting a Small Business Administration which could make loans of not more than one hundred fifty thousand dollars each. It simplified the customs system; extended the farm price-support program; and voted a one-year extension of the Reciprocal Trade Agreements Act which, since its institution by Cordell Hull, had done so much to stimulate international commerce. Not without a struggle, Eisenhower also persuaded Congress to appropriate four and one half billion dollars for foreign aid, which with large uncommitted balances from previous appropriations made a total of six billion six hundred million dollars available.

Other measures desired by the President, such as Hawaiian statehood and the amendment of the Taft-Hartley Act, did not get through. But Eisenhower was willing to proceed deliberately. He believed that in highly critical fields, like farm policy, a year of study should precede final recommendations. He was unwilling to prod Congress sharply, as T.R. and Wilson had done. While popular admiration and affection for Eisenhower steadily grew, he was sharply criticized as lacking industry and as hesitant in the formulation of new ideas and in leadership.

Ending the Korean War

EISENHOWER had promised during the campaign that he would halt the cruel, grinding Korean War. This task was made the easier by Stalin's death, and by Chinese war-weariness. But positive administration steps contributed to the declaration of a truce. The administration let the Communists know, through Prime Minister Nehru of India, that if the conflict did not soon end, UN forces would begin bombing Chinese supply lines. In other words, Eisenhower and Dulles were ready to make tactical use of atomic weapons in China proper, even at the risk of bringing Russia into the struggle and opening a third world war! At this point the Chinese government yielded: perhaps because it really wanted a truce, perhaps because the new government in Moscow after the end of Stalin's blindly bellicose regime brought pressure upon Peiping, perhaps because Nehru's influence counted. Under the truce declared on July 27, 1953, the Communists gave up their cruel contention that war prisoners in the hands of the UN should be forced, even when frantically unwilling, to return to Communist control. A new line between North and South Korean territory was fixed, giving South Korea a net gain of about 1500 square miles. Moreover, an inspection system was arranged under which the South Koreans would gain some advance warning of any new attack. The truce was supposed to be followed at once by a political conference, a treaty, and a permanent peace, but these proved a mirage. The world got an end of fighting, but it did not get a settlement, and Korea did not gain unity.

But the free world had made one momentous gain to balance all the lives it cost; it had demonstrated that it could and would stop Communist aggression.

When in 1954 a conference of nineteen nations met in Geneva to take up both the Korean and Indo-Chinese problems, it resulted rather in losses than gains for the free world. Korea was shoved aside; agreement there was impossible, for the West insisted on free elections, which were anathema to the Communists. Coastal Indo-China (Viet-Nam) was divided at the center. The northern half, where French forces had met defeat after defeat at the hands of Communist rebels, was placed in Viet-Minh or Red hands. The southern half was made for the time being an independent state. Nobody knew what the final fate of the region, or of all Southeast Asia, would be; the one certainty was that twelve million people in northern Viet-Nam had passed under the Communist yoke. Many Americans were deeply disturbed, and Secretary Dulles at once took steps to hold a conference of the free nations of the area in Manila, where they formed the Southeast Asia Treaty Organization (SEATO). It was meant to be a counterpart of NATO, but it had no comparable strength.

Under its new heads, the Soviet Union undertook a peace offensive, which obviously lacked sincerity but which impressed some wavering neutral areas. A revolt of the East

German workers on June 17, 1953, and dissension among the Communist leaders, probably played a part in this move. The West was ready to meet it. Late in 1953 the United States, Britain, and France proposed to Russia an early meeting of foreign leaders. When this suggestion was rebuffed, Eisenhower clung to the initiative. In a forcible speech to the UN Assembly in December, he offered the first important new approach to the atomic problem since the rejection of the Baruch Plan. All the governments chiefly concerned, he suggested, should pool uranium and fissionable metal in a great joint stockpile administered by the UN. The agency charged with its care should see that it was used for medicine, agriculture, and engineering, and to provide abundant power in parts of the globe lacking coal or hydroelectric energy. Russia at first showed chilliness, and though she later entered discussions of the subject, she was unwilling to take a real forward step.

Congressional Activity

BY PATIENT but certainly not strenuous effort, the administration slowly gained a part of the program on which Eisenhower had set his heart, and he could assert by the end of 1954 that he had really given the nation some "dynamic" measures. The most important enactment of the year was a complete overhaul of the whole Federal tax system, the first since Rutherford B. Hayes's day. Business found it stimulating, for it granted larger and more flexible allowances for plant depreciation. It also gave industry liberal treatment for research expenditures; and in various ways it made the tax burden more equitable, though without touching upon the built-in privileges. The President also gained a victory for flexible price supports for the basic agricultural products. The administration policy was to scale down supports slowly and moderately, so as to make the transition to the new system easy. It tried in vain to reduce the huge and wasteful crop surpluses held in government storehouses. But agrarian discontent grew, and fundamentally the farm problem remained unsolved.

Clearly in line with the President's preference for state rather than Federal control and for private rather than pub-

lic activity in the economic realm was the decision to waive
Federal title to the tideland oil resources off the shores of
Texas, Louisiana, and California—a position Eisenhower had
announced during the campaign. To many people it marked
an unhappy retreat from the conservation policies so energetically pressed by the two Roosevelts. The Supreme Court
had declared the offshore deposits the property of the nation, and President Truman had assigned them to the Navy
as a reserve. Now they were "restored" to the states. Elsewhere, too, by cutting down on appropriations to the TVA,
by supporting private rather than public hydroelectric development, by permitting grazing lands to revert to private
hands, and by pressing to exempt natural gas from Federal
regulation, the administration displayed its suspicion of
"creeping socialism" and its preference for the encouragement of individual or corporate initiative. And just before
he left office Eisenhower vetoed a bill to provide national
aid in checking the pollution of rivers by industrial waste
on the ground that this was primarily the responsibility of
the states and localities, not of the general government.

Both parties in Congress supported the President's program for wider coverage and larger benefits under the social-
security laws. Both also helped him carry (May, 1954) a
long-delayed measure for partnership with Canada in building the St. Lawrence-Great Lakes seaway. Canada was ready
to build the seaway alone, moreover, and the United States
wished it under international control. The seaway, with fifteen
new locks, was completed and open to navigation by 1959. A
bipartisan coalition, with the Democrats rather more prominent than the Republicans, defeated the Bricker amendment
to the Constitution. Bricker's proposal was that no treaty
or other international agreement should become effective as
internal law (unless the Senate specifically waived the two-
thirds rule) without legislation by Congress. The amendment
would have seriously crippled the treaty-making power of
the President and returned the United States to the situation
that prevailed during the period of the Confederation. After
an eleventh-hour intervention by the President the amendment was defeated by the narrowest of margins.

It was by a spasmodic and powerful movement that Mc-
Carthy was finally crushed in 1954. As head of the Permanent Senate Subcommittee on Investigations, he had gained

a position of considerable power. Growing more and more arrogant, he made the mistake of insulting both a general and the patriotic but clumsy Secretary of the Army over a trifling issue, the loyalty of an Army dentist. The Army struck back by a set of countercharges, and an inquiry by another Senate committee ensued. Through April and May and into June, the nation watched the proceedings of this inquiry over its television sets; and as it watched, its disgust with the exhibitionism and reckless violence of McCarthy grew. The principal counsel for the Army, Joseph Welch, brought out the weaknesses of the Senator's case in a most damaging way. At one point Eisenhower intervened. McCarthy demanded that the President supply him with certain documents which were rightly deemed confidential; and the President tartly asserted that he would maintain the rights of the executive, which "cannot be usurped by any individual who may seek to set himself above the laws of our land." When McCarthy made an indefensible personal assault on one of Welch's young assistants, public sentiment decisively turned from him.

The result was the appointment of a special new Senate committee under Arthur V. Watkins of Utah. It inquired into McCarthy's conduct under very narrow restrictions, dealing not with the flagrant mendacities which had made him a dangerous enemy of civil rights and of the international repute of the nation, but merely with his breaches of Senatorial decorum. But narrow as its action was, it cut to the heart of much of the evidence, and brought in a report flatly recommending that the Senate censure McCarthy. That censure was voted three to one, and in utter discomfiture, the offender all but disappeared from the public scene. His influence was almost completely dead. In any event he would have lost his committee chairmanship, for in the Congressional elections that fall the Democrats recaptured control of both houses.

Elsewhere, too, the tide of hysteria over the alleged Communist danger began to ebb. Organizations such as the American Civil Liberties Union and the Fund for the Republic dramatized the danger to traditional liberties inherent in much of the antiradical agitation. In a series of eloquent opinions the Supreme Court resolutely reaffirmed the validity of the Bill of Rights, curbing the excesses of Congressional committees, vindicating the right of citizens to passports, requiring due process even in security investigations, and striking down censorship by legislation or intimidation.

Eisenhower at Geneva

As WORLD TENSIONS SHOWED no relaxation, the United States had to meet crisis after crisis as best it could. The detonation of two hydrogen bombs in the Pacific in 1954 gave the country no sense of security, for the Russians proclaimed that they also had the hydrogen bomb. The Eisenhower administration did its utmost to strengthen the defenses of Western Europe. A treaty creating the European Defense Community, with a merger of military forces of six nations (France, West Germany, Italy, Holland, Luxembourg, and Belgium) into one army, was brought close to general acceptance in the summer of 1954. Then the French Assembly defeated the treaty in what Eisenhower called "a major setback" to our policy. The fact that the Soviet Union was desperately anxious to smash EDC added to American chagrin. But on the initiative of Anthony Eden, British foreign secretary, a substitute organization called European Union was brought into existence, Great Britain pledging herself to keep large forces on the continent unless an acute overseas emergency arose.

The rearmament of West Germany, under control of the Union, then went forward. To the alarm not only of her eastern neighbors but of France, that nation was given the right to raise half a million troops, to be commanded by the supreme NATO head. Even half that number, combined with the American and British divisions in Europe and the Italian, French, and Benelux troops, would make a strong army. In April, 1955, the new arrangement was completed.

The following July occurred a memorable meeting at Geneva of the principal Western and Soviet leaders: Eisenhower, Eden (now Prime Minister), Dulles, Faure, Premier Bulganin, Communist party head Nikita Khrushchev, and Defense Minister Georgi Zhukov. Their object was to explore the ground for bases of possible agreement. Disarmament and German unification were the key issues. "We shall be tolerant," said Eisenhower, "because this nation does not seek to impose our way of life on others." The President rapidly became the dominant figure of the conference, and made a particularly favorable impression on world opinion by his earnest presentation of an "open skies" inspection plan which Nelson Rockefeller and a group of experts had formulated; a plan under which authorized agents would be allowed to carry out continuous photographic reconnaissances of the major powers from the air, on agreed lines, to make sure that armaments were kept within pledged limits. America, declared Eisenhower, would freely open its whole area to aerial photography if Russia would do as much. For a brief period the frank exchange of views at the conference generated so happy an atmosphere that men hailed "the Geneva spirit." But the generalities of the sessions were never converted into practical steps, and the spirit soon evaporated.

The Election of 1956

MEN HAD BEGUN to discuss the coming presidential election when, on September 24, 1955, Eisenhower suffered a heart attack; his rapid recovery ended the talk that he might not run again. He resolved to accept renomination because he still had measures to carry, he hoped to confirm the ascendancy of his liberal "New Republicanism," his international prestige seemed useful, and he agreed with party leaders that he was the only Republican who could assuredly win. To his great satisfaction he balanced the budget for the fiscal year 1955–1956 and chalked up a small surplus. Some opposition arose to Nixon's renomination for Vice-President, but it melted before the sun of Eisenhower's approval. It was soon evident that the slogan "We Like Ike" proclaimed a widespread sentiment.

The Democrats turned once again to their most distinguished leader, Adlai Stevenson. In an eloquent acceptance speech Stevenson called for a New America dedicated to world peace, the abolition of poverty, and the realization of freedom for all, without respect to race or creed. The last days of the campaign found the gaze of Americans suddenly diverted to affairs in the Near East. To consolidate his shaky position, the new ruler of Egypt, Colonel Gamal Abdel Nasser, had seized the Suez Canal and threatened war against Israel. On October 29, before Nasser could mount an offensive, an Israeli army invaded Egyptian territory, and Britain and France immediately presented an ultimatum to the Egyptian government, which they followed by hasty military action. At the same time, the stored dynamite of discontent in Soviet-controlled Hungary blew up. These explosions overseas benefited the Republican ticket by giving it a "don't change horses in midstream" argument. Though Stevenson had conducted a campaign marked by masterly analyses of national problems, Eisenhower won a massive victory. He carried forty-one states against Stevenson's seven, and commanded more than fifty-seven per cent of the popular vote; his column even included the five Southern states of Virginia, Florida, Texas, Tennessee, and Louisiana. Yet the Democrats retained their control of Congress with a decisive majority in the House and a narrow margin in the Senate: clearly the election was a personal, not a party, triumph.

Foreign Affairs: The Suez Crisis and After

IMMEDIATELY after Eisenhower's re-election the government had to face the repercussions of the Israeli and Anglo-French attacks on Egypt. For the unhappy course of events the United States had some responsibility. The State Department disliked the semi-dictatorial regime of Gamal Abdel Nasser in Egypt, and hoped for his downfall. In mid-July, 1956, Washington canceled a $70,000,000 loan to help pay for a high dam at Aswan on the Nile, a step which gave Cairo intense chagrin. A week later Nasser startled Western nations by nationalizing the Suez Canal, long a lifeline between Europe and Middle Eastern oil supplies, and between Britain and France and their dependencies on the Pacific and Indian oceans. Australia, New Zealand, Thailand, and the Philippines all felt their interests threatened. A sharp rise of Soviet influence in the Arab world seemed imminent. Patience and calm were needed to avert a crisis.

It was at this moment that Israel invaded the Sinai Peninsula and Britain and France threw troops into the canal zone. Washington resented the fact that the Anglo-French movement was taken without the slightest advance warning, for precipitate action ignored the need for close unity among all NATO members. Moreover, it gave the Communists ready propaganda material against the "imperialists" and "aggressors" of the West; material all the more useful after the popular revolt in Hungary, which Soviet troops suppressed with grim brutality. Thousands of terrorized Hungarian refugees poured into Austria and Yugoslavia, while riotous anti-Soviet demonstrations simultaneously took place in Poland. The Russians naturally made all possible use of the Suez affair; and on October 31 the Security Council of the United Nations witnessed the strange sight of the United States and the Soviet Union voting together for a cease-fire resolution which France and Britain then vetoed.

Prime Minister Bulganin's proposal of joint Russian-American military intervention was rejected by Eisenhower as "unthinkable," and "an obvious attempt to divert world attention from the Hungarian tragedy." When early in November the United Nations General Assembly met the situation by voting 64 to 5 for a modified cease-fire resolution, Britain and France acquiesced, and in considerable humiliation, shortly removed their troops. To make this easier, Washington arranged an oil pool to augment the British supply of petroleum, for the canal was blocked by ships sunk by the Egyptians. Though it proved difficult to get Israeli troops out of the Sinai Peninsula—for Israel insisted on assurances of a right of transit through the Gulf of Aqaba—by the end of 1956 the Middle Eastern situation was fairly stable. Nasser, who had been taught a severe lesson, demonstrated his capacity to operate the Suez Canal efficiently, so that other nations accepted his control under explicit promises of good behavior. But he persisted in his refusal to open the canal to Israeli ships and Dulles failed to fulfill his guarantees to Israel.

Meanwhile the Russians in Hungary, after killing thousands of workers and intellectuals, murdering Imre Nagy, the head of a short-lived democratic government, and suppressing all freedom, installed a new puppet government in Budapest. In Poland too, after quelling desperate riots, the Soviet authorities regained their dominance, though here they had to make important concessions to the proud Polish people.

The defeat of the Anglo-French descent upon Egypt created a power vacuum in the Middle East, and Eisenhower and Dulles thought it essential for the United States to fill the gap. A special presidential message of January 5, 1957, embodied what became known as the Eisenhower Doctrine. "We seek not violence, but peace," the President said. He asked Congress, however, to authorize him to use force in the Middle East, if necessary "to secure and protect the territorial integrity of any nations requesting such aid against overt armed aggression from any nation controlled by International Communism." He also asked $200,000,000 for immediate aid to nations of the region in economic development and defense. The House at once complied, and though a handful of Senators offered rough opposition, that body also approved the Eisenhower Doctrine early in 1957 by a vote of 72 to 19. Applauded in the West, the new doctrine aroused hostility in the Middle East, sharp criticism from Nehru, and prompt counteraction by the Soviets.

The Negro and His Rights

ALL THROUGH THE DECADE Negro citizens were showing a new militancy in their battle for civil rights and social justice. In 1955 Negroes had begun boycotting public buses in Montgomery, Alabama, because the bus lines segregated the races in compliance with state law and city ordinances. Bus lines wilted under loss of revenue. The boycott continued stubbornly throughout 1956, though white authorities attempted to stop it by arrests and jail sentences, and though one judge enjoined the Negroes from using car pools for transit. Finally, in November, 1956, the Supreme Court held the segregation laws invalid as violations of the Fourteenth Amendment, thus once more rejecting the doctrine of "equal but separate facilities," first set forth by the Court in Plessy vs. Ferguson in 1896. Efforts by Southern states to destroy or interfere with the National Association for the Advancement of Colored People were frustrated by a series of court decisions vindicating a citizen's right to join that organization. The NAACP flourished under persecution, and in 1960 launched an effective boycott of retail stores which practiced segregation at their lunch counters.

The right to vote was guaranteed by the Fifteenth Amendment but was persistently and flagrantly denied to Negroes; and in 1956 Eisenhower proposed legislation to protect it, a step which helped bring many Negroes back into the Republican party in the fall elections. The next year the President renewed his recommendation in more emphatic terms; though Southern Senators offered angry opposition, he gained bipartisan support, and a compromise bill finally passed both chambers by overwhelming majorities. Eisenhower thus had the satisfaction of signing, on September 9, 1957, the first Civil Rights Act since the Grant administration. The new bill created a Commission on Civil Rights, which had power to subpoena witnesses in its investigations of all violations of the right of citizens to vote based on color, race, religion, or national origin, and which was to report to the President. The act also provided for an Assistant Attorney General in charge of a Civil Rights Division in the Department of Justice, who was responsible for prosecuting apparent breaches of the law. Enforcement moved slowly and unevenly, and within a short time it became apparent that new and stronger legislation was required if the Negro was to win the franchise.

Equally important was the right to equality in education. Here the battle was savage and prolonged. On May 17, 1954, the Supreme Court had handed down the most momentous decision in the history of race relations: Brown vs. Topeka. Speaking for a unanimous Court, Chief Justice Warren had declared that segregation in public schools must end. Rejecting the old doctrine of "separate but equal" facilities, it held that separation was in itself unequal, and it called upon the state and local school authorities to end segregation "with all deliberate speed." All along the border, from Baltimore to Kansas City, and down into Texas, authorities undertook—sometimes with more deliberation than speed—to conform to this decision. But a line of embittered resistance ran from Virginia to Louisiana. In 1956 the University of Alabama admitted a young woman, under court order, as its first Negro student, but yielded to mob violence and expelled her. Eight Southern states in 1956 passed laws of various kinds aimed at maintaining segregation, almost all of them plainly unconstitutional. Then in 1957 came an explosion of violence in Little Rock, Arkansas.

The school board in that city had made careful preparations for admitting nine Negro pupils to its Central High School, and most people expected integration to proceed quietly. It would have done so had not Governor Orval E. Faubus, the day before classes opened, thrown National Guardsmen around the school to exclude Negro children, alleging that this was necessary to prevent mob disorders. This provoked segregationists from outside Little Rock to gather and create the expected disturbance. On September 23 President Eisenhower ordered all those obstructing national authority in Little Rock to desist and disperse. Faubus defied the administration. In effect, he reasserted the doctrine of "state interposition" that Calhoun had enunciated and that the Civil War had knocked into supposed oblivion. President Eisenhower, who had no intention of tolerating such defiance, immediately ordered the Arkansas National Guard sworn into Federal service, to be used in sustaining court authority, and he followed this step by dispatching a thousand United States paratroopers to Little Rock. Thus checkmated, Faubus tried another course. In 1958 he convened a special session of the legislature, got it to confer on him autocratic powers over the school system, and in September closed all four Little Rock high schools. This hurt white pupils so much that enlightened public resentment ultimately forced him to give way. His display of demagoguery had injured the city and state, given America a bad name abroad, and intensified racial antipathies and frictions; but it had also led to a demonstration that Federal authority is paramount and that segregation was on the way out.

In other states, notably Virginia, some local authorities resorted to closing schools to prevent enrollment of Negro pupils, a policy which did comparable injury to white children—and to the whole of society. Virginia's effort at "massive resistance" to integration by cutting off state funds to desegregated districts failed, for the state supreme court declared such action a violation of the state constitution, but one county, Prince Edward, decided to close down its schools altogether. Everywhere in the deep South the progress of desegregation was painfully slow. By 1958, 790 biracial school districts out of 1890 in the border and Southern states had integrated their systems, but they enrolled only 400,000 Negroes. Yet that year a Negro woman was elected to the board of education in Houston, Texas, and began helping plan desegregation in that large city. And when in 1960 Negro students were admitted to the high schools of Atlanta, Georgia, only three states were without at least token integration—Mississippi, Alabama, and South Carolina. In 1962 Mississippi witnessed the admission of the first Negro student to its state university, though once more an obstreperous governor compelled the use of Federal force to protect the registrant; and early the next year the first Negro student registered in Clemson College, South Carolina—without untoward incident.

In 1960–1961 large numbers of Negroes voted in such Southern cities as Memphis and Atlanta, as well as throughout the North. The new Kennedy administration appointed a number of Negroes to high posts, including Robert C. Weaver as head of the Housing and Home Finance Agency, George L. P. Weaver as an Assistant Secretary of Labor, Thurgood Marshall as a judge of the Second District Court of Appeals, John B. Duncan as a commissioner of the District of Columbia, and Carl T. Rowan as Ambassador to Finland.

The struggle for Negro rights gathered force after 1960. Negroes sought to compel organized labor throughout the nation to give them fuller recognition; they fought against virtual school segregation in large Northern cities; they demanded better housing, for such slums as those of Harlem and South Chicago were among the worst in the world. During 1961 a spectacular drive was conducted by "Freedom Riders" to assure equal facilities for Negroes in interstate bus travel. Insisting upon use of restrooms, waiting rooms, and lunchrooms without segregation, the riders met arrest and harsh sentences in Alabama and Mississippi. They gained their main point when the Interstate Commerce Commission on September 22, 1961, required equal and unsegregated seating on all interstate buses and unsegregated facilities in all terminal stations, and eventually their position was vindicated in the courts.

Domestic Difficulties, 1957–1960

THE FOUR YEARS of Eisenhower's second administration were troubled and even unhappy. An economic recession which started late in 1957 reached full dimensions in 1958; and though it proved as short as it was sharp, the number of unemployed rose for a time above five million, or nearly eight per cent of the labor force. Partly as a result, the government deficit, which had been less than three billion in 1957–1958, rose slightly above twelve and a half billion in the fiscal year 1958–1959—the largest deficit in peacetime history. In 1957 the American people had also to face the fact that they must make immediate and far-reaching improvements in their scientific and educational systems. The success of the Soviet Union late that year in launching the first artificial satellite of the earth, well equipped with instruments, showed that the United States was lagging in a field of vital importance. During 1958 the country caught up in the space-age race by thrusting its Vanguard and Explorer satellites into the heavens; but it was clear that the nation needed both a far larger and a more expert corps of scientific workers.

In carrying its measures in Congress, the administration continued to depend on a coalition of liberal Democrats and Republicans, with the urbane Lyndon B. Johnson as Democratic leader in the Senate giving it more help than the grimly conservative minority leader, William F. Knowland, and with Democratic Speaker Samuel Rayburn in the House more co-operative than the minority chief, Joseph W. Martin. At times the Democrats complained of a want of executive leadership and took the initiative themselves. The second session of the Eighty-fifth Congress in 1958 was especially fruitful in moderate nonpartisan legislation. It again extended the Reciprocal Trade Agreements Act, this time for four years; authorized about three and a third billion dollars for mutual aid; created a Federal Aviation Agency to control the now crowded airways and a National Aeronautics and Space Administration to direct government activities in exploring outer space; and conferred statehood on Alaska. President Eisenhower had been much troubled by the rivalries of the military, naval, and air services, and asked for a defense reorganization bill which would end them by giving the Secretary of Defense and the Joint Chiefs of Staff greater authority. This passed in compromise form.

Though the success of Russia's Sputnik dramatized the importance of greater support for education, particularly for scientific education, little was accomplished. The President urged Federal aid to school construction, but when Congress did finally pass a bill providing for such aid he vetoed it on the ground that it interfered unduly with local autonomy! Congress did, however, enact a National Defense Education Act authorizing the government to use 887 million dollars for aiding gifted college students, chiefly by loans at low rates of interest. This was, to be sure, wholly inadequate, but the Congress still reflected Eisenhower's own conviction that outright Federal aid to education, at all levels, was both undesirable and unconstitutional.

Regulating the Economy

THE REPUBLICAN PARTY had come to power, after twenty years, pledged to put an end to "creeping socialism" and to restore "private enterprise." Republicans thought the "welfare state" was something on the road to Communism; that an unbalanced budget was an invitation to anarchy; and that organized labor and "do-gooders" together were leading the nation down the road to ruin. President Eisenhower was quite unprepared to espouse such reactionary views, but he gave aid and comfort to them by asserting that the "true role of government was to stabilize the economy," by his preference for going down what he called "the middle of the road," and by "dynamic conservatism" which proved more conservative than dynamic. The new conservatism took the form of hamstringing the independent regulatory commissions, or packing them with members who did not believe in government regulation; yielding offshore oil to the states; farming out the operation of atomic-energy plants to private enterprise; jettisoning the plan for a Federally constructed and controlled dam at Hell's Canyon on the Snake River in favor of small dams to be built and operated by private power companies; hamstringing the Tennessee Valley Authority; ending price and rent controls; and defeating the Federal Water Pollution Control Act.

For twenty years the Democrats had favored labor, and it was no wonder that the Republicans thought it high time to curb the privileges and the powers which labor now enjoyed—and misused. During 1958 Senator McClellan's Senate committee on the improper activities of labor conducted searching investigations into the strike of the United Auto Workers against the Kohler Company of Racine, Wisconsin, and the conduct of James Hoffa of the powerful but ruthless Teamsters' Union. The committee accused Hoffa of perjury and other crimes, and his union of a brutal repression of those members who sought to oust their corrupt leaders. To make labor unions more democratic in organization and punish misuse of union funds Congress passed, in 1959, the Landrum-Griffin Bill, which the President readily signed. This bill gave union members full protection in speaking and voting on labor-management issues, compelled unions to file complete financial statements, restricted picketing, and outlawed the secondary boycott. While this legislation was generally effective, it did little to cure the grave ills that afflicted the Teamsters' Union; not until the Kennedy administration was the arrogant leader of that union brought before the bar of justice and sentenced to prison for his crimes.

Eisenhower Loses His Chief Lieutenants

THROUGHOUT HIS ADMINISTRATION Eisenhower had leaned heavily on two men: John Foster Dulles, whose wisdom in foreign affairs he implicitly trusted, and Sherman Adams of New Hampshire, whom he called "my right hand" in conducting routine White House affairs and who gave him shrewd Yankee advice. Within eight months he lost both men. Dulles had faced many difficult crises, including those over the Korean truce terms in 1953, the French defeat by Communist forces in Indo-China in 1954, and the threatened Chinese attack on Formosa in 1954–1955. He had cherished the unity of the Western allies, helped build NATO to enhanced strength, collaborated with Anthony Eden in bringing West Germany into the free-world defense system, and been the principal creator, at the Manila conference of September, 1954, of the Southeast Asia Treaty Organization. He had been a firm advocate of American leadership in the democratic world, and of American generosity in assisting weaker lands. His belief in the nation's destiny, his consci-

entious sense of duty, and his devotion to his chief had won
the regard even of men who thought him stubborn and autocratic, or who distrusted what Adlai Stevenson had called
"brinkmanship"—his readiness to risk a world war—and
who resented that air of moral superiority which he habitually wore.

Sherman Adams had earned the dislike of most of Congress, and of official Washington, by his coldness and taci-
turnity, and by the rigor with which he guarded access to the
President. In 1958 he became a political liability. A House
subcommittee, investigating the independent regulatory commissions, published records showing that a Boston industrialist named Bernard Goldfine had paid substantial hotel
bills for Adams and his family at a time when Goldfine was
involved in proceedings before the Federal Trade Commission and the Securities and Exchange Commission. Adams
admitted accepting other gifts, but denied any wrongdoing.
Many Republicans facing re-election contests that fall asked
for his removal, and after Maine went heavily Democratic
in September, he resigned. The affair possibly figured in the
decisive Democratic victory that autumn, the party gaining
thirteen seats in the Senate and fifty in the House. Eisenhower, who had said of Adams, "I need him," felt the loss
severely. The death of Dulles from cancer on May 24, 1959,
was of course far more serious. His place as head of the
State Department was taken by Christian Herter of Massachusetts, but Eisenhower kept foreign affairs mainly in his
own hands. In his last year and a half the President showed
increased self-reliance and gave the country stronger leadership.

Loyalty in Government

WHEN EISENHOWER BEGAN his tenure of the White House,
Senator McCarthy was making the most of the almost wholly
spurious issue of Communists in government. He continued
his attacks on the State Department even after Dulles took
charge, and went so far as to assail Eisenhower for including Britain in the mutual security system after that country
had recognized Red China. The President detested him, but
refused to fight him openly. Meantime McCarthy continued

to harass public officials, hurl baseless charges at honest men, and terrorize American State Department officials overseas, in a series of irresponsible acts which Secretary Dulles bore with astonishing pusillanimity. McCarthy's downfall in 1954 was generally accepted as in the public interest. Even timorous people had been reassured by the practical collapse of the Communist party. Yet though its membership fell to some 10,000, J. Edgar Hoover of the F.B.I. continued to proclaim that it was a deadly enemy to American security!

The Internal Security Act passed in 1950 to deal with disloyal public officers was fortified in 1954 by a Communist Control Act, which outlawed the Communist party. Attorney General Herbert Brownell put decidedly excessive rigor into the activities of the Justice Department, as his abortive effort to indict the scholar Owen Lattimore showed—an effort rebuked by the Federal courts. To the end of the decade fear of betrayal by subversive officeholders, and of corruption by subversive books, ideas, films, magazines, and television programs, tormented many Americans, and gave rise to spasms of intolerance and persecution. In the Truman administration the government had dealt with "disloyalty risks"; in the Eisenhower administration it broadened its concern to include "security risks"; this shift deepened and exacerbated the semantic confusion. The Supreme Court remained a citadel of defense for the rights guaranteed by the First Amendment. In 1956, for example, it invalidated a state security program in Pennsylvania on the ground that the national government had pre-empted the field; and in 1958 it annulled a California law requiring clergymen to take loyalty oaths in order to gain tax exemption for their churches. But the Court itself was divided. While one group of liberals, led by the venerable Justice Black, was prepared to strike down any legislation which appeared to violate the First Amendment, another group, led by the distinguished Justice Frankfurter, felt that true liberalism required judicial continence even in the face of legislation palpably pernicious.

The Fiftieth State

THE YEAR 1960 dawned upon a nation of fifty states, for in March, 1959, the Hawaiian statehood bill passed by overwhelming majorities in both houses. As a result, the Senate shortly welcomed its first member of Oriental ancestry, a Hawaiian-Chinese, and the House saw the oath administered to its first member of Japanese ancestry.

CHAPTER 29

New Frontiers: The Challenge

Which Party in Power?

No GREAT NATIONAL ISSUE dominated the presidential campaign of 1960; no heated international issue gave it suspense. The days when the electorate had divided fiercely on the free-soil question, the tariff, the currency, or relations with Britain, Spain, or Germany, lay far in the past. Bipartisanship had lately stamped the action of Congress on most domestic questions, and bipartisanship had been carefully cherished in foreign affairs. Formidable problems confronted the nation, and men were not of one mind on how to solve them; most important differences, however, were not between Democrats and Republicans, but between the liberal and conservative wings in each party. Voters were troubled by the difficulties of racial integration in the schools and in public services; tempers flared high on the question. Yet both major parties necessarily stood for an end to segregation. Men were similarly divided by varying ideas on taxation, on defense spending, on the proper mode of dealing with subversion, and on labor legislation; but the two parties approached these matters in the same moderate way. At the water's edge, practically all Americans faced Russia with one determination:

to seek a peaceful adjustment of controversies, but to defend to the last the national heritage of freedom and to give aid and protection to our free allies.

After eight years of Eisenhower's passivity and of Congressional obstruction, the country was hungry for leadership, for more boldness, imagination, and thrust in Washington. It hoped that the presidential contest would bring forward men able to reduce the tensions between Washington and Moscow and lighten the appalling burden of armaments. It wanted a leader who would accelerate the nation's economic growth, which was plainly lagging, defend civil rights more energetically, bring more imagination to the solution of the baffling agricultural problem, champion larger expenditures on education, and meet the needs arising from rapid population growth. A new generation was taking control of the country. Many members of this generation wanted moral leaders who would awaken the people from self-indulgent lethargy and lead a crusade for social justice and equality of opportunity. The country was spending too much on private luxury, and far too little on farsighted public provision for the future, too much on the private and too little on the public economy.

Anyone who looked about could see imperative challenges. They appeared in the swift growth of great cities, giving America a thorny set of urban problems; in the space race with the Soviet Union; in the desperate effort of Negroes to get an equitable place in public facilities, public schools, the universities, employment, and the ballot box; in statistics showing that one per cent of the people held half the wealth; in the vulgarity that defaced television and the movies; in the inadequacy of most of the press; and in increasing juvenile delinquency. Any nation from time to time needs a regeneration. After the sacrifices of the Second World War the United States had spent a sufficient period resting and recuperating; the hour had struck to resume its forward march. But who should bear the banner?

The Candidates and the Campaign

NONE OF THE PRECONVENTION SUSPENSE was on the Republican side. The Republicans had already forfeited almost sure victory by pushing through what Eisenhower himself called an act of retroactive vindictiveness: the Twenty-second Amendment, which denied another term to Eisenhower. Now Vice-President Richard Nixon, a shrewd politician, used Eisenhower's blessing, the feeling that he would continue the Eisenhower policies, the support of state political machines, and the friendship of big business to make certain of the nomination. Few had confidence in his character or ability, but the President's recommendation on the ground of experience counted heavily—though, when questioned, he could not remember a single national decision of importance that Nixon had helped make. Governor Nelson A. Rockefeller of New York, an abler and more independent man, plainly aspired to the nomination. But when exploratory trips about the country revealed that business thought him too liberal, and that Nixon had enlisted all the political stalwarts, he quietly withdrew. The Republican Convention, held in Chicago, nominated Nixon by a vote of 1,321 to 10, and gave him as running mate Henry Cabot Lodge, grandson of President Wilson's old-time opponent.

Only one hour of excitement enlivened the Republican gathering. This came when Rockefeller insisted that Nixon support him in rewriting vital parts of the draft platform submitted by a routine committee. This revision translated a moderate statement on civil rights into a forthright, liberal plank, pleasing to Negroes but irritating to many Southern whites; and it gave the party a stronger statement on the strengthening of national defense. Nixon in his acceptance speech declared that the major problem before the next administration would be to alert the people to the "mortal danger" lurking in an insidious Communist propaganda which offered false promises of peace, plenty, and hope.

By contrast, the Democratic choice was so uncertain that the convention battle riveted the attention of the entire country. Principal aspirants were the adroit Lyndon Johnson of Texas, veteran of many political encounters; Stuart Symington of Missouri, a supposed expert on defense; and Senator Hubert Humphrey of Minnesota. Above these figures towered Adlai E. Stevenson, with his well-earned intellectual prestige and long experience, and the dashing, self-possessed young John Fitzgerald Kennedy, Senator from Massachusetts, who had vainly tried to seize the vice-presidential nomination four years earlier. Stevenson was handicapped by the fact that he had twice lost a national election, and by his refusal to declare himself an active candidate. Kennedy had apparent handicaps in the fact that the nation had never chosen a Roman Catholic as President, and only once a member of the Senate. But he had planned his campaign with consummate foresight and boldness. After a careful survey of the country, he had mobilized a hard-working organization and had enlisted a number of able Democratic leaders, from Chester Bowles of Connecticut to Governor Mike DiSalle of Ohio. What is more, he conducted a vigorous and imaginative campaign, making assets of his youthfulness, his intellectual elegance, and even— by his appeals for religious toleration—of his Catholicism. Boldly entering the primaries in seven states, he swept them all, and came to the convention the leading contender.

The galleries in the July convention in Los Angeles were with Stevenson; but the delegates on the floor were for Kennedy. Nominated on the first ballot, he at once proved his political acumen by decreeing that his rival Lyndon Johnson, influential throughout the South, should be named for Vice-President, and persuading Johnson to take the place. He roused his followers by saying in his acceptance speech, in Stevensonian phraseology: "We stand today on the edge of a New Frontier . . . the choice our nation must make [is] between the public interest and private comfort—between national greatness and national decline."

The Kennedy Victory

NOT SINCE THE 1880's had an election been so close. Kennedy's popular majority was only 118,000 out of 68 million votes, and though his majority in the electoral college was decisive—303 to 219—even here a few thousand votes in Illinois and Texas made the difference between defeat and victory. Yet it was not the narrowness of the victory that was astonishing, but the victory itself. Kennedy accomplished the almost unprecedented feat of turning the ruling party out of office at a time of both peace and prosperity; he overcame not only the heavy handicap of Catholicism, but the immense popularity of Eisenhower.

Almost everything about the new President caught the imagination of the people, and his Inauguration was no exception. The ceremonies were held out of doors; a blustery wind blew across the platform as the venerable Robert Frost —the first poet ever to be invited to participate in an Inauguration—read: "The land was ours, before we were the land's." Then, in an address suffused with idealism and eloquence, Kennedy dedicated the nation to its revolutionary heritage:

Let the word go forth from this time and place, to friend and foe alike, that the torch has been passed to a new generation of Americans, born in this century, tempered by war, disciplined by a hard and bitter peace, proud of our ancient heritage and unwilling to witness or permit the slow undoing of those human rights to which this nation has always been committed. . . . Let every nation know, whether it wishes us well or ill, that we shall pay any price, bear any burden, meet any hardship, support any friend, oppose any foe, to assure the survival and success of liberty.

But the address was not merely a call to battle but an invitation to peace as well. "Let us never negotiate out of fear," said the President, "but let us never fear to negotiate." Cooperation is better than conflict; let us then substitute cooperation for conflict:

Let both sides explore what problems unite us instead of belaboring those problems which divide us. . . . Let both sides seek to invoke the wonders of science instead of its terrors. Together let us explore the stars, conquer the deserts, eradicate disease, tap the ocean depths, and encourage the arts and commerce. Let both sides unite to heed . . . the command of Isaiah to "undo the heavy burdens and let the oppressed go free."

The first President to be born in the twentieth century, and the youngest ever to be elected to the presidency, Kennedy was not only spokesman for a new generation, but symbol as well. He brought to the presidency not only an alert intelligence, immense personal charm (what it became fashionable to call charisma), a warm and generous humanitarianism, and a sophisticated grasp of political realities, but also a lively awareness of the immense potentialities of presidential leadership. In the faltering hands of Eisenhower, presidential authority had all but disintegrated; Kennedy reimported vigor and power into the office, and brilliance as well: not since the days of Theodore Roosevelt had the White House been so much the center of national interest and excitement, or Washington the center of political gravity. He had something of Theodore Roosevelt's sense for power, something of Franklin Roosevelt's ability to reach out to the whole people; and to these he united an interest in the arts and the social graces as instinctive as that of Jefferson.

The Kennedy administration brought a new era of political thought as well as of political personalities, for Kennedy himself was young in mind as in years, and he instinctively rejected the weary clichés which for almost a decade had corrupted much of American political discussion: hackneyed denunciations of Communism, the arrogant emphasis on "loyalty" and the frantic search for "subversion"; irrelevant rhetoric about "private enterprise" and "creeping socialism," about "centralization" and "states' rights." He recognized that the nation faced a host of new problems, and that old problems had taken on a new character and required new ideas and techniques for their solution.

The task was prodigious, and the new President called upon men from both parties to help him. For the post of Secretary of State the President bypassed such obvious choices as Adlai Stevenson and Senator Fulbright, and appointed instead Dean Rusk, who had been president of the Rockefeller Foundation and who combined judiciousness with administrative talent. Robert S. McNamara, who had been president of the Ford Motor Company, became Secretary of Defense, and a Republican, Douglas Dillon, who had served under Eisenhower, took on the Treasury. One of the most interesting appointments was that of Arthur Goldberg, a noted expert on industrial relations, to the important post of Secretary of Labor (Goldberg later went on to a distinguished career on the Supreme Court and in 1965 became Ambassador to the United Nations). Adlai Stevenson, still in many respects the intellectual leader of the party, was

appointed to the increasingly important post of Ambassador
to the United Nations. In some ways the most important
appointment—as it was certainly the most unorthodox—
was that of Robert F. Kennedy, the President's brother, to
the Attorney-Generalship, an appointment dictated not only
by a recognition of the importance of the civil rights issue,
but by the President's desire to have a friend and counselor
constantly by his side. For already in the making was a
Kennedy dynasty which would match in power the Adams
and Roosevelt dynasties; another year and a third brother,
Edward Kennedy, would be elected Senator from Massachusetts. And it was an indication of the decline of anti-intel-
lectualism that a presidential "brain trust" recruited heavily
from Harvard and Oxford (the historian Arthur Schlesinger, Jr., as special assistant, Dean McGeorge Bundy as
adviser on foreign affairs, the economist John Kenneth Galbraith as Ambassador to India) and from the Massachusetts
Institute of Technology (Walt Rostow and Paul Samuelson)
commanded general acclaim.

The President and Congress

ALTHOUGH THEY HAD lost some twenty seats in the lower
house, the Democrats still had a firm grip on Congress. But
with a popular majority so slim that it raised questions about
the validity of the electoral mandate, could the new President carry through that program of liberal social and economic reform to which he and his party were committed?
Would he fare any better than had Presidents Truman and
Eisenhower in dealing with the familiar coalition of conservative Southern Democrats and reactionary Republicans
that had so long exercised a veto on progressive legislation?
That coalition was the product of an apportionment system
which discriminated against urban majorities, poll taxes
which denied Southern Negroes a fair voice in government,
and an anachronistic seniority system which threw control
of almost all important Congressional committees to aged
Southern Democrats. All of these things were being changed,
to be sure, but the changes would not be effective for another decade.

As it turned out, the President met with only limited

success in getting his program through Congress, though we can see now that it was in part his zeal and eloquence that prepared the way for its ultimate enactment. One by one his major proposals were blocked by the intransigent coalition, yet in each case something was achieved. Kennedy asked for a vastly expanded program of Federal aid to school construction and teachers' salaries. The Senate passed his bill, but in the House the measure ran into the roadblock of the religious issue. The Roman Catholic Church asked that the government provide some relief to its overcrowded parochial schools; after all, Catholics pointed out, they had been relieving taxpayers of a substantial part of the burden of public education for a long time; it was high time that the public recognize this and come to their relief. But the President subscribed to the traditional view that Federal aid to parochial schools would violate the constitutional requirement of separation of Church and State. A group of Catholic Representatives joined Republican conservatives in blocking the much-needed legislation.

In the welfare field, too, the President met with a setback when, responding to the massive propaganda campaign of the American Medical Association and to the lively fear of any form of "socialism," Congress failed to act on the bill providing medical care for the aged under the social security system. The administration did, however, succeed in pushing through a medical health program with substantial provision for research and for construction of community mental health centers, and an appropriation of over two hundred million dollars for medical education, which was lagging far behind public needs. There was some progress, too, in the realm of urban renewal. Many cities— Pittsburgh, Philadelphia, St. Louis, and Boston most strikingly—had attempted to arrest the urban blight which was rapidly reducing them to vast sprawling slums, but it was clear that the task was too great for local resources, and the ailments which afflicted most cities were rapidly becoming incurable. Congress defeated President Kennedy's proposal for the creation of a Department of Urban Affairs with cabinet rank, but the President persuaded it to pass a Housing Act, which made some five billion dollars available over a four-year period for urban renewal. These programs were, to be sure, expensive, and Congress was

economy-minded, yet the cost of Federal welfare programs
was almost negligible when compared with the cost of
national defense, which ran to some fifty billion dollars a
year.

Kennedy and the Arts

NOT SINCE JEFFERSON had any President been so interested in art, letters, and learning, or himself so involved in
them. Himself an historian—his *Profiles in Courage* won
nationwide acclaim—he was at home with scholars. He not
only surrounded himself with intellectuals but attracted
scholars, scientists, and artists to Washington, which now,
perhaps for the first time, became a cultural as well as a
political and social capital. It was characteristic that Kennedy should have asked the venerable Robert Frost to participate in the Inauguration ceremonies, and that he should
have seized the opportunity of a dedication of the Robert
Frost Library at Amherst College to call for an "America
which will not be afraid of grace and beauty . . . which
will reward achievement in the arts as we reward achievement in business or statecraft, which commands respect
throughout the world not only for its strength but for its
civilization as well." To dramatize his respect for the arts
Kennedy instituted the Presidential Medal of Freedom, a
kind of American Order of Merit; among the recipients
of this medal were artists like Marian Anderson, Pablo
Casals, Rudolf Serkin, and Andrew Wyeth, writers like
Thornton Wilder, T. S. Eliot, Carl Sandburg, and Lewis
Mumford, educators and scholars like James B. Conant,
Walter Lippmann, and Samuel Eliot Morison. While Mrs.
Kennedy restored the White House to something of its earlier
dignity and beauty and redesigned the White House gar-
dens, the President gave support to the plan to create a
great national arts center in Washington and to restore
the capital itself to what Major L'Enfant, Jefferson, and
Latrobe had hoped that it might be.

These were not mere gestures; they were part of a philosophy which accepted the arts as an essential part of civilization. Speaking at Amherst, just a few months before his
death, the President, who had a deep instinct for power, said:

Robert Frost saw poetry as the means of saving power from itself. When power leads man towards arrogance, poetry reminds him of his limitations. When power narrows the areas of man's concern, poetry reminds him of the richness and diversity of his existence. When power corrupts, poetry cleanses. For art establishes the basic human truths which must serve as the touchstone of our judgment.

The Struggle for Civil Rights

As THE CENTENARY of the Civil War and emancipation approached, Negroes in the South and in large parts of the North as well were still second-class citizens, deprived of fundamental rights and subject to ceaseless indignities. Negro children were fobbed off with schools that were not only segregated but inferior; Negro youths were denied entry to state universities; Negroes were required to sit in segregated cars, eat at segregated lunch counters, play in segregated playgrounds, and swim on segregated beaches, and even to worship God in segregated churches. They were assigned inferior jobs at inferior pay, and shunted off into slums and ghettoes that were breeding places for crime and delinquency. If lynching had died out, murder had not, and in the deep South white men could murder Negroes with impunity. Back in 1944 the Swedish economist Gunnar Myrdal had called the Negro problem *an* American Dilemma; twenty years later it was *the* American Dilemma—and still unsolved.

But the revolution which had been inaugurated by the Second World War and given constitutional respectability, as it were, by the historic Supreme Court decision of Brown vs. Topeka (1954) was now gathering a force which promised to be irresistible. Three things contributed to that promise. First, a long series of Supreme Court decisions disposing of the last remnants of the "separate but equal" fiction, striking down the more overt forms of discrimination, giving some reality to the long-ignored guarantees of equality, and implementing the right of suffrage at every level. Second, an aroused conscience in the North, and along with it an aroused awareness of the potential power of the Negro vote, particularly in the large cities, where Negroes now constituted a dominant political group. Third, and most important, the decision of Negro leaders like the Rev. Martin Luther King, A. Philip Randolph, Thurgood Marshall, James Baldwin, and others to take leadership of the crusade for equal rights into their own hands. By the sixties this crusade had achieved the proportions of a peaceable revolution. Chanting their battle hymn, "We Shall Overcome," Negroes conducted a crusade reminiscent of the Populist uprising of the nineties, a movement that was almost independent of the earlier equality crusades, which had been dominated by liberal whites. They took an active part in politics everywhere, embarked upon a vigorous campaign of publicity and education, conducted sit-in demonstrations and marches in Mississippi, Alabama, Georgia, and eventually in the national capital, used the tactics of the economic boycott, and fought every case of discrimination or denial of rights in the courts.

The Civil Rights Bill of 1957 had been, as predicted, inadequate and ineffective; clearly the party that had written emancipation and Negro rights into the Constitution a century earlier had muffed its chance. No issue meant more to President Kennedy than civil rights; as a descendant of the Irish he knew something of the history of persecution, as a Catholic he had met and fought a prejudice not greatly different from that which was the daily experience of every Negro. He had, too, a lively sense of history, and he knew that the United States was in danger of forfeiting her moral leadership in large parts of the globe by her injustices to her Negro citizens. "We face a moral crisis," the President warned, in his moving appeal of June, 1963, just a few months before his death. "It cannot be met by police action. It cannot be met by increased demonstrations in the streets. It cannot be quieted by token moves or talk. It is time to act in the Congress, in your state and local legislative bodies, and in all our daily lives." But, alas, the Congress did not choose to act. The police brutality, the injustice, the frustration, the discrimination, went on, and so, too, the demonstrations and marches and protests—protests which came to a climax in a massive "march on Washington" of some two hundred thousand Negroes in the mid-summer of 1963.

President Johnson, who inherited so much of Kennedy's legislative program, inherited, too, his passion for equality and for social justice. "Until justice is blind to color," he said in an address at Wayne University early in 1964, "until education is unaware of race, until opportunity ceases to squint its eyes at human pigmentation, emancipation will be a proclamation, but it will not be a fact." He was determined to make it a fact. The shock of Kennedy's assassination and the association—fortuitous to be sure, but none the less dramatic—of that desperate act with the South, did much to galvanize public opinion into action, while the new President's masterly ability to get his way with Congress was responsible for translating action into law. The Civil Rights Act of 1964 was the first really effective civil rights bill in almost a hundred years. It outlawed discrimination in public facilities of all kinds—hotels and motels, restaurants, playgrounds, theaters, public libraries—in employment, and, equally important, in labor unions. To take the "deliberate" out of the injunction to carry through school desegregation with "all deliberate speed," it authorized the withholding of Federal money from any school which persisted in segregation. And to overcome the notorious sabotage of the Fifteenth Amendment in most Southern states, it outlawed discrimination in the application of voting laws or practices in any election where a Federal official was on the ballot, and provided that six grades of school should be presumptive evidence of literacy. Together with the outlawing of the poll tax in Federal elections by the Twenty-fourth Amendment, these provisions went far toward guaranteeing that the Negro would vote in future elections. And the election of 1964, in which millions of Negroes voted, provided a dramatic illustration of the power of the Negro in American politics.

The Courts and Civil Rights

ONE OF THE MOST striking developments of the fifties and the sixties was the abandonment of the practice of judicial continence, and the re-emergence of the Court as a decisive force in American government and society. For some twenty years—ever since the Court fight of the Roosevelt administration—the Supreme Court had tended to lean over backward to avoid interfering in the political or the economic

arena; these were presumed to be exclusively the business
of the political branches of the government. With the accession of Earl Warren to the Chief-Justiceship in 1953, the
Court assumed a more activist role, particularly in the realm
of civil liberties. Justice Frankfurter had argued that the
Court should exercise the same rule of self-restraint in this
realm that it displayed in the economic, but increasingly
the Court adopted that position foreshadowed by Justice
Stone in his famous Carolene Products dictum of 1938:

It is unnecessary to consider now whether legislation which restricts those political processes which can ordinarily be expected
to bring about repeal of undesirable legislation, is to be subjected to a more exacting judicial scrutiny under the general
prohibitions of the Fourteenth Amendment than are most other
types of legislation. . . . Nor need we inquire whether similar
considerations enter into the review of statutes directed at . . .
racial minorities . . . whether prejudice against discrete and
insular minorities may be a special condition which tends seriously to curtail the operation of those political processes ordinarily to be relied upon to protect minorities, and which may
call for a correspondingly more searching judicial inquiry.

It was the threat of McCarthyism, with its far-reaching
implications for the integrity of "those political processes
ordinarily to be relied upon," that brought the Court to the
endorsement if not always the application of this dictum.
While it still refrained from intervening in economic arrangements made by the political branches of the government—more often than not even refusing jurisdiction—it
took an increasingly active part in the defense of civil rights
and liberties. By the sixties something like two thirds of the
business of the Court was taken up by this problem. With
growing confidence the Court acted to protect citizens
against their governments and against themselves, and with
the appointment of Justices Brennan and Goldberg, the
center of judicial gravity moved from the more conservative
to the more liberal, or from the more passive to the activist
wings of the Court. The Warren Court wrote substance into
the guarantees of equality in the Fourteenth Amendment
and of the "equal protection" clause as well; sustained the
rights of citizens to travel abroad; circumscribed importunate

interference with freedom by security-conscious bureaucrats and legislative "loyalty" committees; and made some progress toward clarifying newly emergent rights of privacy and of academic freedom. It upheld guarantees of free speech and press against all kinds of censorship, notably in striking down a libel charge against *The New York Times* by officials of the city of Birmingham, Alabama, who argued that reporting racial injustice in that city libeled the officials responsible. It protected the right of association against attacks by Southern states which sought to destroy such organizations as the NAACP and the Civil Liberties Union, and insisted on procedures in criminal trials which read more realistic meaning into the concept of due process.

Equally important were judicial contributions to democracy, indirect to be sure, but none the less effective for that. Almost everywhere in the United States rural areas were over-represented and urban areas under-represented in state legislatures until, in the end, most state legislatures were controlled by minorities—minorities whose position and power seemed impregnable. Indeed, in many states permanent under- and over-representation had been frozen into the constitutional arrangements. Back in 1946 the Supreme Court had dismissed a suit challenging malapportionment in the Illinois legislature for want of jurisdiction (Colegrove vs. Green). Sixteen years later the Court boldly risked intervention in the political processes by accepting jurisdiction in a case challenging malapportionment in Tennessee. The decision in Baker vs. Carr (1962) held that discriminatory apportionment for representation in the lower house of the legislature violated the equal protection clause of the Federal Constitution. Two years later the Court extended this ruling to the upper houses as well, thus establishing for state governments everywhere the principle of "one man, one vote," neither more nor less. These decisions promised to work a revolution in American politics comparable to that inaugurated by Brown vs. Topeka a decade earlier in the social realm. Together with civil rights legislation stiffening the guarantees of the Fourteenth and Fifteenth Amendments, they ushered in the day when all Americans would have the right to vote and when all votes would count equally. This meant a shift in the center of gravity from rural to urban America, and from agriculture to labor, and a more honest recognition of the Negro. Now, in the sixties, it seemed possible that the promises of equality and democracy might be realized only a century or so after they had been made.

Latin America and the Alliance for Progress

IF AMERICAN POLICY toward Europe in the postwar years had been a conspicuous success, and toward Asia a disappointing balance between success and failure, it could be said that the most conspicuous thing about relations with Latin America was the absence of any policy. Franklin Roosevelt, to be sure, had launched a "Good Neighbor" policy, but being a good neighbor was, it seemed, a negative rather than a positive affair, a matter of keeping hands off the internal concerns of the Latin American countries and of making the Monroe Doctrine, in form at least, multilateral. All through the postwar years the states of Latin America—Mexico and Chile were partial exceptions—were in the throes of major economic and social crises. Population was growing faster than in any other part of the globe, without a comparable increase in wealth or productivity; the gap between the poor and the rich was widening; and as the rich and powerful turned to the military for the preservation of order and privilege, the poor turned to revolution. Deeply involved in other quarters of the globe, the United States paid little attention to the fortunes or misfortunes of her neighbors to the south, and when she did intervene it appeared to be on the side of order and the *status quo* rather than on the side of reform. So frightened was the United States of "Communism" in Latin America that it preferred military dictatorship to reformers who might drift too far to the "left," and sustained a Batista in Cuba, a Trujillo in the Dominican Republic, a Perón in Argentina, and a Jiménez in Venezuela.

In his last two years President Eisenhower had tried to mend his Latin American fences. Though rejecting a Brazilian proposal of a Marshall Plan for Latin America, he did take the initiative in setting up an Inter-American Development Bank with a capital of one billion dollars, almost half of it supplied by the United States. Other government investments in Latin America ran to some four billion dollars, while private investments exceeded nine billion. Yet though to most Americans all this seemed a form of economic aid, many Latin Americans regarded it as economic imperialism. In September, 1960, came a co-operative plan that could not be regarded as other than enlightened: the Act of Bogotá, which authorized a grant of half a billion dollars to subsidize not only economic but social and educational progress in Latin America. "We are not saints," said President Eisenhower when he visited Santiago de Chile. "We know we make mistakes. But our heart is in the right place."

But was it? President Kennedy was confronted by the same dilemma that had perplexed his predecessors. Clearly it was essential to provide large-scale aid to the countries south of the Rio Grande, but should this aid go to bolster up established regimes and thus help maintain the *status quo,* or should it be used to speed up social reform, even at the risk of revolution? As early as 1958 the then Senator Kennedy had asserted that "the objective of our aid program in Latin America should not be to purchase allies, but to consolidate a free and democratic Western Hemisphere, alleviating those conditions which might foster opportunities for communistic infiltration and uniting our peoples on the basis of . . . constantly increasing living standards." This conviction that raising the standards of living was the best method of checking Communism now inspired President Kennedy's bold proposal for the creation of the Alliance for Progress—a ten-year plan designed to do for Latin America what the Marshall Plan had done for Western Europe. It was to be "a peaceful revolution on a hemispheric scale . . . a vast co-operative effort, unparalleled in magnitude and nobility of purpose, to satisfy the basic needs of the American people for homes, work, and land, health and schools." To achieve this the United States pledged an initial grant of one billion dollars, with the promise of additional billions for the future.

But even as the President promised further aid, he observed that "no amount of external resources, no new inter-American institutions, can bring progress to nations which do not have political stability and determined leadership." Did this mean that the United States would use the Alliance

for Progress to bolster existing regimes or to resist those
deep currents of social and economic revolution which
threatened everywhere to break forth into turbulence and
violence? So it had often been in the past. Now Cuba was
to provide a new challenge and a new test, but one which,
alas, threw light on the real problem.

For a century and a half Cuba had been a kind of King
Charles's head to those who conducted American foreign
policy. Jefferson had thought it properly within the American sphere of influence; John Quincy Adams had looked
forward with confidence to its eventual incorporation into
the United States; the notorious Ostend Manifesto of 1854
had tried to pressure Spain into selling the island to the
United States, and on the eve of the Civil War a Senate
committee had announced that "the ultimate acquisition of
Cuba may be regarded as a fixed purpose." Though the
United States did not choose to intervene in the Ten Years'
War, 1868–1878, it did intervene in the revolution which
broke out again in 1895, this time decisively. The Spanish-
American War brought independence to the troubled island,
but it remained, nevertheless, within the American sphere
of influence, and the United States reserved a naval base
at Guantánamo. In 1906 and again in 1917 the United
States intervened forcibly in Cuban affairs in order to protect American property. But thereafter, for almost forty
years, the United States followed a policy of hands off.

All through the fifties the island was a source of growing
anxiety to the United States as it became apparent that
the Cuban people would inevitably rise up against the cruel
tyrant, Fulgencio Batista, who had taken office in 1952.
In 1956 a student leader, Fidel Castro, sailed from Mexico
to rally his followers to rebellion; two years later he had
succeeded in ousting Batista and setting himself up in his
place. The Castro revolution was, at first, hailed with enthusiasm in most of the American republics; but it quickly
became apparent that he proposed to erect a tyranny of the
Left to match Batista's tyranny of the Right. He refused to
hold elections; suppressed civil liberties; executed hundreds
of war prisoners after trials that were a mockery of justice;
plunged the Cuban economy into confusion by hasty and
ill-considered reforms; and expropriated American and foreign land, businesses, utilities, and banks. These actions

might have been tolerated had he not made clear that he proposed to set up a quasi-Communist state in Cuba, attach himself closely to the Soviet Union, and embark upon a program of subverting other states of Latin America.

The American people had by now grown sensitive to Communist encroachments on Latin America. During the early fifties the government established by Jacobo Arbenz in Guatemala had taken on a Communistic coloration; it had confiscated lands, made fools of labor unions, put the press under close censorship, and, to intimidate popular discontent, imported arms from Poland. Guatemala's proximity to the Panama Canal made this situation a serious matter, and after trying in vain to check Communist infiltration through the Organization of American States, Secretary Dulles armed and encouraged an invasion of Guatemalan rebels from Honduras which overthrew the Arbenz regime and replaced it with a conservative government. This rough-hewn solution of the problem quieted apprehension in the United States but at the cost of widespread disapproval throughout Latin America.

After 1959 thousands of refugees from Cuba poured into the neighboring lands. Those who went to the Dominican Republic received a cordial welcome from General Trujillo, who sympathized with his fellow dictator, Batista, and some of them soon staged an invasion of Cuba which was stopped dead on the Dominican coast. Large numbers of refugees fled to Florida, where, with official American sanction and support, they plotted and prepared to return to their home island and overthrow the dictator. In the meantime Castro had moved closer to Communism and to the Soviet Union, and in February, 1961, Soviet Deputy Prime Minister Mikoyan visited Cuba and arranged for large-scale economic and military assistance to the island. Clearly it was the hope of the Soviet Union that Cuba might serve as a powerhouse for the exportation of Communist ideology and subversion throughout Latin America. The United States promptly broke off diplomatic relations with Castro, and twelve Latin American states followed her example.

Shortly after President Kennedy took office, a rash step imperiled the American moral position in the Cuban crisis. Contrary to both the United States and international law, the Central Intelligence Agency of the Eisenhower administration, under Allen Dulles, had covertly armed and drilled large numbers of Cuban refugees. On April 17, 1961, some fifteen hundred of these, sailing from Central America and from Florida, supported by American ships but not by American planes, attempted an invasion of Cuba at the Bay of Pigs. The invasion failed ignominiously, and Castro, who had first accused the Americans of "cowardly aggression," was able to proclaim his superiority over the Americans. He immediately accepted the Lenin Peace Prize awarded by the Soviet Union and offered to exchange some 1200 captured prisoners for cash and farm machinery; perforce the United States paid some 53 million dollars. It was an awkward way to give foreign aid.

This was the background of events in the autumn of 1962.

For some time the State Department kept up the fiction that the United States was not directly involved in the Bay of Pigs fiasco. Yet at the same time President Kennedy refused to concede that the United States would not, in any situation, take military action. Speaking early in September, 1962, he warned:

If, at any time, the Communist build-up in Cuba were to endanger or interfere with our security in any way . . . or if Cuba should ever attempt to export its aggressive purposes by force or the threat of force against any nation in this hemisphere, or become an offensive military base of any significant capacity for the Soviet Union, then this country will do whatever must be done to protect its own security and that of its allies.

That moment arrived sooner than had been anticipated. In the early weeks of October, American reconnaissance planes discovered that the Soviets had installed in Cuba rockets capable of carrying nuclear warheads to any spot in the hemisphere from Canada to Peru, and of destroying all major American cities. Not since the ill-fated Maximilian venture in Mexico just a century earlier had there been so overt a challenge to the Monroe Doctrine as this. "We owe it to candor," President Monroe had announced in 1823, "and to the amicable relations existing between the United States and those [European] powers, to declare that we should consider any attempt on their part to extend their system to any portion of this hemisphere as dangerous to our peace and safety." Here was just such an attempt. President Kennedy responded to this threat with firmness and courage. He readied air and ground forces for action, reinforced the Guantánamo naval base, and ordered the Navy to patrol Cuban waters and establish a "quarantine" against the importation of arms and other dangerous materials. More important, he demanded the immediate dismantling of all rocket sites and the removal of Russian weapons and airplanes from the island. In a dramatic broadcast on October 22, 1962, the President warned the American people—and the rest of the world—of the dangers ahead.

The path we have chosen for the present is full of hazards, as all paths are, but it is the one most consistent with our character and courage as a nation, and our commitments around the world. . . . Our goal is not the victory of might, but the vindication of right; not peace at the expense of freedom, but both peace and freedom, here in this Hemisphere, and we hope, around the world.

For a few days the world hovered on the brink of a nuclear war. But clearly Khrushchev was no more desirous of such a war than was Kennedy. The Soviets found it wise to accept Kennedy's demands, and in return obtained from the United States a pledge that she would end the "quarantine" and assurances that she would not invade Cuba. By November the President was able to assure the American people of progress toward a restoration of peace in the Caribbean, and in January, 1963, he could announce that the Cuban missile crisis was at an end. There were still some thousands of Soviet troops on the island, and their presence inspired partisans like Senators Dirksen and Goldwater to demand a more belligerent policy, but the President allowed the Soviets to save face by a gradual and orderly withdrawal.

The President's firm stand had taught the Soviet Union a new respect for the strength and determination of the United States, and at the same time it had cleared the air and improved chances for peace. As a result, there came a slight thaw in the cold war. Prime Minister Harold Macmillan of Great Britain had for some time urged an end to tests of nuclear weapons in the atmosphere, where they polluted the air with poisonous fallout—a fallout which did not discriminate between those involved in nuclear rivalries and innocent bystanders. Now President Kennedy joined him in calling for this enlightened step. After long negotiations the United States, Great Britain, and the Soviet Union signed, on August 5, 1963, a treaty ending all nuclear tests except those conducted underground. Eventually one hundred other nations signed the agreement. De Gaulle held aloof. So too, more ominously, did China, which was rapidly on the way to becoming a nuclear power. The nuclear test-ban treaty passed the Senate by a bipartisan vote of 80 to 10, and on October 10 President Kennedy was able to proclaim what was, in all probability, the most important achievement of his administration.

Crisis in the Far East

AFTER LOOKING INTO the pit of nuclear war, both antagonists, the United States and Russia, retreated somewhat sobered into a less belligerent mood. The nuclear test-ban treaty was merely the most dramatic manifestation of this. There were others: the sale of surplus wheat to Russia, the negotiation of cultural exchange between the two countries, co-operation in medicine and in scientific research and—though nothing came of it—President Kennedy's proposal for joint exploration of outer space.

Two major developments help account for this thaw in the cold war with the Soviets. First, with the passing of Stalin, Russia had begun to move out of the more turbulent and primitive stage of revolution and toward stability and sophistication. The Revolution was, by now, an accomplished fact, and Russia, after her triumph over Hitler, was an acknowledged power in the world. As she felt more secure, she lost something of her crusading fervor, and was more ready to involve herself with the community of Western Europe. Second, China was now looming up as potentially the strongest of Communist nations, ready to challenge Russian hegemony to her north and Russian influence everywhere in Asia. To Russia, the challenge from China came to seem more formidable than the challenge from the West.

The thaw in Russian-American relations did not, to be sure, abate either hostility to or obsession with Communism in the United States, but rather transferred the objects of that animosity to Castro's Cuba and to China.

Hostility to China was, by now, deep-seated and constantly aggravated; doubtless the Chinese felt the same way. The Korean War had almost escalated into a major war with China—had General MacArthur had his way, that is what would have happened. With the uneasy truce in Korea, hostilities had shifted to Formosa, where American power and resources maintained the aging Chiang Kai-shek in power. Mainland China was, naturally enough, determined to extend her authority over Formosa, while the Americans were no less determined to preserve its independence. It was this issue which, more than any other, aggravated hostilities between the two great powers.

Like Britain, France, and Germany in the nineteenth century, the Communist powers of the twentieth were expansionist, imperialistic, and militaristic. Russian expansion had carried her to the Elbe and the Danube in the West, and to the shores of the Pacific in the East, while her influence was strong throughout the Middle East. Now China, with a population of some seven hundred million, was pressing at her own borders—Siberia, Tibet, India, Korea, Burma, Laos, and Viet-Nam—and trying to extend her influence and her power to the Indonesians, the Indians, and the Japanese. Sometimes that pressure took the form of overt aggression —as against Tibet and India; more commonly it used the techniques of infiltration and subversion.

First Laos and then Viet-Nam was the battleground in which Americans unexpectedly found themselves contending. Here, in what had been French Indo-China, the French had sought, in vain, to defend local autonomy and their own interests. When, in 1954, the French departed, the Americans moved in, though neither their interest nor the nature of their commitment was entirely clear. And soon the Americans were confronted with all of those problems which had confronted, and confounded, the French.

During the fifties and the early sixties it was Laos that appeared to be the center of trouble and danger. A fourteen-power agreement had set up a shaky coalition regime, but this coalition was continually on the point of collapse and it appeared that Laos would surely come within the Chinese sphere of influence. To bolster up the shaky Laotian government the United States sent in a task force of the Seventh Fleet and a contingent of marines, and peace, of a sort, was restored.

Vietnam presented a more serious problem and one which did not yield to any solution which successive administrations were prepared to accept. The Geneva agreement of 1954 had drawn a line across the middle of that war-torn country, leaving the North to Communism and the South to whatever non-Communist government was able to survive. The North Vietnamese agreed to free elections in 1956. Their cadres to the South, the Vietcong, as they would be called, were instructed to undertake "political struggle" with the South Vietnam government of President Ngo Dinh Diem, which would culminate in the 1956 election which the North expected to win. The election itself never came. Buddhist-Catholic conflict, economic discontent, a corrupt and incompetent government, and the growing strength of local Communist political forces prompted both Saigon and Washington to conclude that the Communists would indeed be victorious at the polls and that the election should therefore be postponed. Although the United States could have accepted the mounting turbulence in South Vietnam as part of the growing pains of a new nation, the national security bureaucracy that controlled American foreign policy embraced the "domino" theory—that if one country in Southeast Asia fell to the Communists, all others would topple over like so many dominoes. So reasoned four successive Presidents—Eisenhower, Kennedy, Johnson, and Nixon. And each responded to his own fears with mounting intransigence.

And under the dubious authority of the SEATO agreement —which pledged its signatories to protect Southeast Asia against outside aggression and which were implicitly directed against China—the United States moved in to take over the responsibilities the French had been unable to fulfill. Thus, Americans found themselves more and more deeply involved in a kind of twilight war against the North Vietnamese and against guerrillas in the South—a war which was never formally declared and never endorsed by the American people.

President Eisenhower, who had resisted pressure to commit the United States to rescue the French forces in Vietnam, took Americans fully across the Asian Rubicon by pledging to support President Diem. President Kennedy inherited this policy and chose to pursue it. And Hanoi inevitably became increasingly dependent upon both China and the Soviet Union.

Persistently disavowing any desire to get more deeply involved in the Asian quagmire, Kennedy, nonetheless, stepped up military and economic aid to South Vietnam. His program of counter insurgency, designed to avoid the need for significant American ground forces, embraced teams of "unconventional warfare" experts skilled in sabotage and terrorism. The CIA "coordinated" security; United States operations missions furnished technical aid; United States military advisors trained South Vietnam's troops; the Agency for International Development supplied the money and became a financial bonanza for Saigon's officials. Kennedy secretly ordered 500 "Green Berets"—an elite counter-insurgency strike force that he had promoted—into Vietnam, and also more military "advisors," a euphemism for troops who, he admitted in February 1962, were now "firing back" in self-defense. By this time, too, Americans were committed to occasionally training South Vietnamese troops ". . . under combat conditions," as Secretary of Defense Robert McNamara revealed. By October 1963, some 16,000 American troops were in Vietnam; helicopters were now flying combat support missions; American pilots were strafing "enemy targets"; "advisors" were supervising raids upon the North, defoliation operations, and population removal—the "strategic hamlet" program, which forced the peasants to resettle and thus destroyed traditional village life. Under President Johnson, the "advisors" kept increasing, and so, too, did their clandestine military operations. In 1958, a CIA-inspired revolt in Laos had toppled the neutralist regime in that country: it was replaced with a right-wing general and additional "advisors," and military aid also began spilling into that beleaguered land.

Diem had begun to put out peace feelers toward Hanoi. Finding his behavior unacceptable, South Vietnamese generals, with the tacit encouragement of the American ambassador in Saigon and the open support of the CIA, successfully maneuvered his overthrow.

Lyndon Johnson, who had campaigned in 1964 as a "peace candidate," inherited and expanded the Vietnam policy of his predecessor. Like Kennedy, he feared being charged with another "loss" to Communism; soon he became almost inextricably entangled in what speedily took on the character of a major war. Notwithstanding a stream of optimistic reports, the military and political situation grew steadily worse. Johnson's response was to step up support for the new South Vietnam regime. This increased involvement led to such practices as intelligence gathering and commando raids along the coast to blow up bridges and coastal installations. One such raid produced the Tonkin Gulf incident of August 24, 1964, which in turn was used, fraudulently as we now know, to obtain the historic Tonkin Gulf Resolution providing the President with badly needed congressional authority for war-making. Passing the Senate with only two dissenting votes, and the House without opposition, it gave the President authority to use "armed force" in Vietnam, to protect any state in the region that sought assistance "in defense of its freedom." Lyndon Johnson speedily launched the continuous bombing north of the demilitarized zone, which indiscriminately destroyed military and civilian targets in that besieged and pre-industrial country.

In so doing, President Johnson brushed aside successive CIA reports that such bombings would have "no measurable direct effect" on Hanoi's ability to support military operations, nor prevent further Communist gains. He preferred to listen to his National Security Council, which proposed more of the same military actions. Johnson's response in the spring of 1965 was to order in marine combat units. This action, "for defensive purposes only," marked a turning point in American policy. The number of troops increased until it eventually reached 550,000. So did the combat operations as well as the bombings—everything now became fair game. "We seek no wider war," the President proclaimed, and then with complete illogic launched three years of steadily escalating air raids. Huge populated areas of South Vietnam were designated "free fire zones," in which American planes were authorized to shoot at anything that moved. Thus began the most savage air war in history. We were, an Assistant Secretary of Defense asserted, "proceeding on the assumption that the way to eradicate the Vietcong is to destroy all the village structures, defoliate all the jungle, and then cover the entire surface of South Vietnam with asphalt." As early as the close of 1966, bomb tonnage in Vietnam exceeded that dropped in the Pacific Theater of Operations in World War II. Before the war was over, the United States had dropped on Southeast Asia three times the total tonnage of the entire duration of the Second World War. By 1968 over half a million ground and air force units were in Vietnam. Together they destroyed villages, chemically defoliated an area equal to Massachusetts, and shattered in turn both South and North Vietnam.

Little wonder that by 1968 the peace movement in the United States had taken definite shape and the nation was racked by draft resistance. Johnson's hopes for another term in office were undone in part by this growing unrest, in part by the TET offensive of January 31, 1968. The spectacular and widespread TET attack by the North Vietnamese demonstrated the bankruptcy of official American military strategy and was a humiliating blow to Johnson's Vietnam program. Following TET in quick succession were the surprising primary victories of Democratic antiwar candidates and the startling request of General William Westmoreland, army commander in South Vietnam, for 260,000 more troops. Clearly the war was unwinnable without the escalation of troops and bombing which might precipitate conflict with China and the Soviet Union, a risk that even Johnson was not prepared to take. "Deeply shaken" by TET and by rising criticism from his closest advisors, the President announced a bombing cutback on March 31, and accompanied it with a statement of withdrawal from the forthcoming presidential race.

Nixon campaigned on the promise of ending the war, but his victory in November 1968 produced nothing new. To the contrary. He declared the American military involvement in Southeast Asia the nation's "finest hour" and sought a staunchly anti-Communist government for Saigon. Faith in victory through air power persisted. Indeed, shortly after assuming office, Nixon ordered B-52 bomber raids against officially neutral Cambodia, an action that went on for fourteen months. These raids were concealed from the public by falsification of air force records. Secret, too, were the training of Cambodian units by the CIA in Greece; the incursions by South Vietnamese rangers and American Special Forces into Cambodia; the commando raids by Green Berets into North Vietnam; the "Ferret Flights" of American aircraft into China and Laos. But the President did begin slowly to withdraw ground forces, though he compensated by strengthening South Vietnamese army units and increasing bombing raids—both part of Nixon's heralded "Vietnamization," which meant a continued military involvement, merely shifting casualties from American to Vietnamese troops.

On April 30, 1970, the President launched American forces in an invasion of neutral Cambodia on the ground that it was a staging area for enemy troops. Defending this decision, contrary to both United States and international law, Nixon declared: "We will not be humiliated. We will not be defeated." And, he continued: "If . . . the U.S. acts like a pitiful helpless giant, the forces of totalitarianism and anarchy will threaten free nations and free institutions throughout the world." This arbitrary expansion of the war generated acrimonious criticism in the Senate, which on January 5, 1971, passed the Cooper–Church amendment prohibiting American combat troops in Cambodia after June 30 as well as American air support for Cambodian military forces. The "incursion" (the official term for the Cambodian attack), revelations about My Lai—atrocities committed by American troops—and an exposé of conditions of North Vietnamese prisoners on the American-directed island prison of Con Son contributed to a bitter public mood. So did the South Vietnamese attack on Laos, a military strike against Hanoi's supply lines supported by American air power. Yet Nixon, in effect, succeeded in his immediate objective; he defused protest at home by withdrawing combat troops and filling the skies with American planes.

Meanwhile, a broad and powerful North Vietnamese offensive during Easter of 1972 sent South Vietnamese forces reeling and ended all remaining bombing restrictions. Hanoi was retargeted, Haiphong harbor was mined, and the air offensive set a record level of bombing runs. Nixon claimed these moves were ways "to win the war in Vietnam and end it." The new aggression came after a settlement with North Vietnam had been negotiated in Paris in October 1972. This settlement, which presidential foreign policy advisor Henry Kissinger had designed, included a provision allowing Hanoi to maintain troop forces in South Vietnam. President Nguyen Van Thieu, the last in a line of South Vietnam rulers, had not been consulted and, outraged by these terms, refused to sign the peace agreement. The twelve-day bombing raids of Christmas 1972, of an intensity unprecedented in the annals of warfare, were planned primarily to placate Thieu and persuade him to accept the Paris settlement. They succeeded in their purpose. Hanoi made some minor concessions and Thieu agreed to an accord in January 1973, in substance identical with that of three months earlier. He had, however, no serious intention of respecting it. Under the terms of this presidential agreement, the United States promised to withdraw all its armed forces from Vietnam but undertook to re-supply Saigon with much that it needed in the way of military armaments and equipment. As a result of what the United States left in the South and what it proceeded to "replace," South Vietnam could boast one of the largest navies in the world, the fourth largest army, and the sixth largest air force.

Thus, President Nixon could claim that he had somehow wrested "peace with honor" out of ten years of warfare in stricken Southeast Asia: events were to speedily demonstrate that there was neither peace nor honor in the arrangements. In three years of Nixon's presidency, more bombs had been dropped on Vietnam than on Europe and Asia combined in World War II. The administration sacrificed an additional 15,000 American lives, with 110,000 wounded, $50 billion more squandered, and 600,000 South Vietnamese civilians dead and wounded, in order to emerge with "honor." All together, the conflict had taken some 55,000 American lives and an additional 350,000 casualties. The financial cost was over 160 billion dollars; the cost in misspent resources and energies —material, intellectual, and moral—was incalculable. A Senate Committee reported that the toll of South Vietnamese troops was close to half a million, and that of "enemy" forces was a million, and civilian casualties ran to over one and a half million. Cambodia and Laos, too, had been wasted by more than a decade of warfare, with vast amounts of acreage rendered uninhabitable by defoliation, carpet bombing, and the destruction of village life.

The agreement, however, did not bring peace; both North and South Vietnam openly violated the agreement and so, too, did the United States. Without active American aid, the South could not maintain itself, for the Thieu government commanded neither the loyalty of the people or of the army, nor, for that matter, the administrative, intellectual, or moral resources to gain such loyalty. Increasingly through the year, North Vietnam pressed on the South until, by the beginning of 1975, it became clear that only a massive infusion of American aid could maintain Thieu's corrupt and incompetent government. The administration did its best to re-supply the South, but open assistance had been prohibited by a congressional act, and covert assistance was not enough. In the end Thieu's collapse came with astonishing suddenness. All through the winter and spring of 1975, the North Vietnamese forces, with the ever more open support of large elements in the South, pushed down toward Saigon, while the authority of South Vietnam's government visibly evaporated. There were desperate cries for last-minute military aid, and even for open intervention. President Ford asserted somewhat wildly that renewed United States assistance could still salvage and reverse the desperate situation. Neither the majority of Congress nor of the American people put any stock in these arguments: Americans and, it appeared, the Vietnamese, too, were sick of the war and wanted an end to it on almost any terms. Certainly the Communist forces in Vietnam (as in Cambodia at the same time) proceeded swiftly to demonstrate how preposterous were the hopes of salvaging the South by capturing most of the American-provided planes, tanks, and other military equipment, and by routing the South Vietnamese forces, sending them fleeing South toward Saigon, a disorderly mob rather than a disciplined fighting force. The United States recognized the inevitable too late and undertook to evacuate its own staffs and what it could of its Vietnamese friends and associates; all together, perhaps 130,000 South Vietnamese were successfully transferred to the United States. By now Cambodia had fallen to the Nationalist-Communist forces of the Khmer Rouge, and their equivalent had also taken over in Laos. On April 30, 1975, the North Vietnamese and their southern allies entered Saigon. Thus, the twenty-five-year struggle for an independent and unified Vietnam came to another climacteric. For the United States, the twenty-year intervention and the decade of war was not only a military defeat; it was a political, diplomatic, psychological, and moral disaster.

Vietnam derived from an unchanging self-image of America's moral duty as well as from a geo-political philosophy that had two decades of uninterrupted momentum. Consequently, the overseas policies of Johnson and Nixon were different from the cold-war policies of their predecessors only in degree and in cost. They had a common provenance, the same familiar and unwavering sources: commitments that had become global, rather than domestic, as with Jefferson, or limited to the Western Hemisphere, as with Polk and Cleveland; and their criteria were ideological, not practical. Increasingly, since the late 1940s, American Presidents had responded almost automatically to challenges—real and imagined—sometimes without consulting Congress and, whenever "freedom" was threatened by "Communism," with its uncritical approval.

Small wonder, then, that in such "threatened" nations as Bolivia, Peru, Cuba, and Santo Domingo the Green Berets and other American military forces carried out counter-insurgency operations. Fearing new Munichs and finding dominoes about to fall on every troubled landscape, administration decision-makers and the CIA pressed forward with the training of local counter-insurgency forces. Between 1950 and 1968, the United States trained over 40,000 Latin Americans to provide, as Secretary of Defense Robert McNamara stated, "the needed domestic security." Such policies often led to the support of repressive military regimes wherever they were in power or took power, just as it did in Spain and in Greece. Thus, when in 1964 Brazil's generals, proclaiming that they thereby saved the nation from Communism, rebelled against the democratically elected President, Joao Goulart, Johnson promptly recognized the new military regime.

Washington policy makers were more directly involved in the affairs of the Dominican Republic. In 1965, an army coup on that troubled island overthrew the legally elected President, Juan Bosch. When street crowds in turn threatened the short rule of the military junta, the American ambassador urged "armed intervention." Without bothering to consult Congress, Johnson responded by dispatching 23,000 marines who effectively suppressed Bosch's constitutionalist forces and saved the military regime. In justification, Johnson claimed that intervention was prompted by the need to protect American lives; an amended explanation argued that the popular democratic revolution had fallen into the hands of Communist conspirators. These conspirators could not be found,* but Johnson's unilateral actions, in defiance of obligations to the OAS, and his usurpation of executive power eroded America's moral authority in the Western Hemisphere.

Latin American policy, then, indicated that the nation that had once mounted a revolution and later defied the Holy Alliance had become a powerful bulwark against revolution. To maintain the status quo, it stationed over a million troops abroad by 1968; 33,000 planes in airports around the world; tens of thousands of military personnel aboard its naval vessels; an unknown number of covert CIA operators in some sixty countries, and a global network of almost 2,000 bases. In addition, the United States armed or subsidized about two million troops elsewhere, many of them commanded by military dictators, supplied well over 50 billion dollars in military assistance to scores of nations, and wove a network of five regional and forty-two bilateral defense alliances.

The Nixon years saw more of the same in every quarter of the globe. His administration supported military dictatorship in Greece and encouraged the overthrow of Archbishop Makarios on Cyprus; sold jet aircraft to South Africa and to Portugal, then engaged in a protracted struggle to eliminate counter-insurgency in its African colonies; violated United Nations sanctions against Rhodesia, and granted economic credits to South Africa, which was then being boycotted by many democracies for its apartheid policies. As to Chile, the top-secret 40 Committee, headed by the then presidential advisor Henry Kissinger, undermined the democratically elected socialist regime of Salvador Allende. The World Bank, over which the United States has virtual veto power, denied loan applications to Chile; the United States Export-Import Bank did the same; and the CIA was given eight million dollars to further a "destabilization" campaign authored by Kissinger, newly appointed as Secretary of State. All this contributed to a 1974 military coup that overthrew President Allende and

---

* The list of Communist participants included some people who were dead, abroad, already in prison, and a child of six.

installed a military dictatorship.* In Asia, American military assistance helped maintain repressive client governments in South Vietnam, Taiwan, the Philippines, and South Korea. Determining to "tilt toward Pakistan," the Nixon administration poured money and arms into that country during its savage decimation of the East Bengal population while at the same time cutting aid to India. Here, again, the United States aligned itself with a military dictatorship—this time against what was then the world's largest democracy.

Throughout the frenetic cold-war years, Nixon had denounced Communist wickedness and tirelessly insisted that United States policy toward China must be frozen in enmity, that Chiang Kai-shek's regime on Taiwan must be recognized and supported, and that mainland China must be barred from the United Nations. These policies seemed irreversible. But following a familiar pattern—de Valera making terms with Britain, Eisenhower ending the Korean war, de Gaulle pulling out of Algiers—Nixon did decide to give up on Taiwan and come to terms with China. How much his reversal of policy owed to his able, shrewd, and sedulous advisor, Henry Kissinger, we do not know. An uncompromising hard-liner, Kissinger had a clear vision of great-power relationships. Communism, he concluded, could not be dislodged in China or Russia and it was time for the United States to recognize realities and seek a classic three-cornered balance-of-power arrangement in which it might occupy a favored intermediate position. In his State of the World address of February 25, 1973, the President declared that "the United States is prepared to see the People's Republic of China play a constructive role in the family of nations." In quick succession, the United States suspended its destroyer patrol in the Formosa Strait, Kissinger flew secretly to a Peking rendezvous, and the President announced a visit to China before May 1972. When it became obvious, by November 1972, that a U.N. majority would vote to unseat Taiwan's delegation and replace it with one from Peking, the United States offered only token resistance and accepted what was in effect a stinging defeat.

Nixon's policy reversal had other attractions, as well. His

---

* When this gross violation of the constitution of the Organization of American States and of the charter of the United Nations finally came to light, President Ford shrugged it off as not being important.

Vietnam strategy of continuous support of the corrupt Thieu regime had seriously eroded Republican Party strength: a "voyage of peace" to Peking might be of great advantage at home. Such a voyage, moreover, was part of Kissinger's larger global blueprint—which included, likewise, a détente with Russia designed to stimulate trade with that rapidly developing country and to slow down the nuclear arms race. Always seeking the recognition of common world goals, especially that of international stability, Kissinger apparently persuaded the President that the Soviet Union as well as China could be softened up with favors, and that by using the carrot of trade as leverage, the United States could get away with the Haiphong blockade, the intensive bombings of Hanoi, and the crushing of other Asian opponents at no great risk.

Besides greater freedom of maneuver, this policy reversal brought additional gains. Mostly, it eased global tensions. Russia and the United States negotiated a vast wheat-trade deal and reassured each other about potential nuclear attack by agreements flowing from the renewed SALT talks. American businessmen streamed into Moscow in search of business deals, and China—no longer part of a diabolical Communist conspiracy—was hailed for its social and economic accomplishments.

"There Is No Armor Against Fate"

FACED WITH CONGRESSIONAL INTRANSIGENCE, and with widespread hostility to his civil rights and welfare programs in the South, the President planned, in November, 1963, to take his case to the people. He selected Florida and Texas as key states: Florida had voted Republican in the 1960 election, and only the presence of Lyndon Johnson on the ticket had held Texas in the Democratic column. The President's combination of high spirits and deep seriousness made a tremendous impression in Florida, and on November 21 he took off for Texas in a jubilant mood. In San Antonio, in Houston, and in Fort Worth he received tumultuous ovations. Then on Friday, November 22, 1963, he flew to Dallas. As his cavalcade was driving from the airport into the city, the President was shot through the head and killed by an unbalanced young man named Lee Harvey Oswald. Vice-

President Lyndon Johnson at once took the oath of office as President. For three days the nation—and the world—sat in stunned silence as it watched and heard the solemn funeral of the man who was loved as no other American of his time.

Thus died a victim of senseless hatred, a great gentleman, a devoted patriot, a wise statesman, one who combined gaiety with dignity, patience with ardor, compassion with courage, and poetry with power.

The assassination of the President by the wretched Oswald seemed too aimless, too capricious, to be credible; the American public simply could not believe that anyone would perpetrate a deed so foul with so little motive. It was not surprising, then, that almost at once the popular imagination conjured up plots and conspiracies to account for the assassination, and for the murder of Oswald himself, two days later, by a grubby night-club operator named Jack Ruby. Surely these deeds which seemed to shake the very firmament must have some meaning! Had the assassination been planned by Southern extremists? Was it all part of a Communist plot? Was it directed, perhaps, by Castro? To dispose of rumors and fears President Johnson appointed a commission under the chairmanship of Chief Justice Warren to investigate the assassination in all its ramifications. In due time the commission presented a monumental report which completely disposed of rumors of plot and conspiracy, and made clear that Oswald acted alone, and so too Jack Ruby, and that the whole thing was a nightmare of madness and fortuity, a tale told by an idiot. It could not be said, however, that it was a tale signifying nothing, for it did dramatize, in the most sobering and ominous fashion, the manner in which a climate of hatred could engender violence.

President Lyndon B. Johnson

AMERICAN POLITICS PRESENTS few more dramatic contrasts than that between Presidents Kennedy and Johnson, the one a New Englander, a Catholic, born to wealth and to privilege, educated at private schools and at Harvard, the other still, in some ways, a frontiersman, educated at country schools and at a state teachers' college, really self-educated and self-made. The style of the two men was as different as their backgrounds and their training: Kennedy brilliant, incisive, charismatic, affluent, cosmopolitan; Johnson homespun, easygoing, gregarious, and provincial; the one in the Jefferson tradition, the other in that of Lincoln.

But as it turned out, it was not the differences but the similarities that proved significant. The two men entertained much the same political philosophy, were committed to much the same program. The tragedy at Dallas, coming at a critical moment in the conduct of foreign policy, threatened a sharp break in American history, but it did not produce a break even politically; it was the continuity that was impressive, not the change.

In the domestic arena President Johnson speedily revealed an almost unparalleled ability to win a "consensus" and to persuade Congress to do what he wanted done. This was in part a matter of style—where Kennedy had been belligerent, Johnson was conciliatory—and in part a matter of technique: after all, Johnson had lived for thirty years in the Congress; he knew how to deal with the Congress, and the Congress knew how to deal with him. The result was that within a few months Johnson managed to push through almost the whole of the original Kennedy legislative program, and more, too. A sweeping civil rights bill passed the Congress by whopping majorities, and if it did not mark the end of Southern sabotage of the Fourteenth and Fifteenth Amendments, it marked the beginning of the end. A far-reaching educational bill, providing Federal underwriting of education at every level from pre-school to graduate school, went through after a decade of bickering. Medical care for the aged, bitterly fought by the American Medical Association, triumphed by a sizable vote in both houses. The President had declared a "war on poverty," and an anti-poverty bill, directed chiefly to the stricken area of Appalachia and to the slums of great cities, commanded support from both parties, and to help implement it Congress adapted the Peace Corps—one of President Kennedy's most imaginative inventions—to the domestic scene. Not since the "Hundred Days" of the Roosevelt administration had the country witnessed anything like the tidal wave of welfare state legislation.

It was against a background of unprecedented prosperity

and of unprecedented welfare legislation that the country prepared to elect a President in 1964.

Traditionally, American parties had been very much alike in character, policies, and membership. For a hundred years the Democratic and Republican parties had represented, or attempted to represent, a cross section of the American public; both of them had, customarily, been moderate, and had avoided issues that threatened to be divisive. When, on two occasions, 1860 and 1896, the parties had abandoned these characteristics and clashed sharply on issues, the country found itself torn by dissension and by class and sectional animosities. Most Americans concluded that though Europeans might indulge themselves in parties that represented conflicting groups, interests, faiths, and ideologies, they could not.

In 1964, however, as on these two previous occasions, Americans did so indulge themselves, and with consequences disastrous to one of the parties. President Johnson, to be sure, sought, as always, a "consensus." Nominated by acclamation, he deliberately turned to the darling of the Northern liberals, Hubert Humphrey of Minnesota, for his running mate, and he went into the campaign with a program that appealed to every section of the country, every interest, and almost every class.

The Republicans chose a different course. Driven frantic by Democratic success at the polls, the repudiation of the *laissez faire* philosophy, the growing power of the national government at the expense of the states, the mounting national debt, "me-too-ism" in politics, the abandonment of isolationism and the growth of internationalism, and by what they conjured up as "the Communist menace," at home as abroad, extremist elements in the party inaugurated a campaign which rapidly took on the dimensions of a crusade.

The idol of this rule-or-ruin element in the party was Senator Barry Goldwater of Arizona, who was quite sincerely persuaded that the nation was on the road to ruin. Softspoken, gentle, and honorable, he came to embody, to his infatuated following, the virtues of a bygone America, the America of the frontier, of the self-made man, of simple virtues and simple morals, and simple solutions to all problems. In almost everything but honesty and integrity he was a sharp contrast to his chief rival, Governor Nelson Rockefeller of New York. Picking up votes in Southern and Western states, Senator Goldwater won the all-important primary in California, and the momentum of that victory carried him to nomination on the first ballot at the party convention in San Francisco. Organized and directed by extremists in the party who howled down all opposition, insulted all competing candidates, and even voted against a civil rights plank in the platform, that convention provided the first shock to the rank and file of Republicans throughout the country, and started that defection which soon became something of a stampede.

The campaign speedily took on a nightmare quality. In the gentlest and most reasonable manner, Senator Goldwater advocated what seemed like hair-raising policies and programs—"seemed like" because there was so little rationale or consistency in his campaign. He had voted against the nuclear test-ban treaty and against the civil rights bill, and had no use for either, or for what they symbolized. As he swept from one part of the country to another he almost deliberately courted defeat, until some observers wondered openly whether he really had any intention of taking his own candidacy seriously. Though it was abundantly clear that without the support of the industrial states of the North, organized labor, and the Negroes, no candidate could possibly win, Goldwater either neglected these or went out of his way to antagonize them. To the voters of the Tennessee Valley he proposed selling the TVA to private power interests. To the unemployed of the industrial North he suggested that they go back to work and get off social security and unemployment compensation. To organized labor he advocated the hated "right to work" laws. While he ceaselessly argued for a reduction in public expenditures, he called at the same time for an increase in the military, an extension of the war in Vietnam, a tough policy toward Cuba, and a renewal of nuclear experiments in the outer air. The recklessness of his advocacy, his seeming inability to formulate any real program, his readiness to court the extremists and the racists and the militarists, dismayed moderate Republicans everywhere.

Early in the campaign it became clear that Johnson would

win: the only question was the size of the victory and the chances of survival of Republican moderates. As had been predicted, the victory was of landslide proportions. Johnson carried the country by a popular majority of over fifteen million votes, and carried every state but six in the electoral college, while traditionally closely balanced states like New York, California, Michigan, Ohio, and Pennsylvania went Democratic by majorities of over a million. A block of five states in the deep South, Louisiana, Mississippi, Alabama, Georgia, and South Carolina (along with his home state, Arizona), moved into the Goldwater column. It was a sobering fate for the party that had fought to hold the Union together to free the blacks! And the suicidal surrender of the Republican party to its Neanderthal elements brought something of a revolution in Congress as well. Out of 35 Senatorial contests, the Democrats carried all but 7, and they carried the lower house by the almost unprecedented majority of 295 to 140. Not since the Democrats had turned from Bryan to Alton B. Parker, in 1904, had a candidate led his party to a debacle so complete. But did they have a Bryan who could lead them out of the wilderness of reaction?

In his Inaugural Address as President in his own right, Lyndon Johnson called upon the Congress and the people to help him build the Great Society:

In a land of great wealth, families must not live in hopeless poverty. In a land rich in harvest, children must not go hungry. In a land of healing miracles, neighbors must not suffer and die unattended. In a land of great learning and scholars, young people must be taught to read and write.

The outlines of the Great Society were already familiar from presidential recommendations and Congressional enactments during the past year, and indeed over the past generation. For President Johnson's Great Society did not differ from the New Deal and the Fair Deal in spirit or in purpose. But it did differ in style and in method. First, the idea of the welfare state was by now generally accepted, and Johnson did not need to debate the ideological issue. That had somehow settled itself in that mysterious fashion in which controversies are settled in America—by being put aside. The President could therefore devote his ample energies to application instead of argument. Second, where many of the earlier programs were based on the assumption that redressing injustice called for a redistribution of wealth through taxation or other forms of regulation, Johnson now assumed that it was possible to expand wealth and resources almost limitlessly, and that society could therefore finance the most far-reaching welfare programs out of the wealth generated by the process itself. "No longer," said the President, "need capitalist and worker, farmer and clerk, city and countryside, struggle to divide our bounty. By working shoulder to shoulder, together we can increase the bounty of all." President Kennedy had sensed something of this and had coupled his own recommendations for welfare programs with proposals for tax reduction. But it remained for President Johnson to provide proof that the theory actually worked. Even while winning support for his programs of education and public health, he had persuaded the Congress to reduce income, corporate, and excise taxes. The result was an upsurge of prosperity which not only increased private and corporate income, but government income as well. In an economy which thus invoked both Adam Smith and John Maynard Keynes as presiding geniuses, and where the private and the public economy were integrated for their mutual advantage, the American people might hope, without undue optimism, to realize the Great Society.

The Great Society

SUCH LOFTY RHETORIC notwithstanding, the Great Society programs were hardly radical. Medicare depended upon a regressive payroll tax and assisted only the aged; it was weaker than Truman's health program. The war on poverty, directed by the Office of Economic Opportunity, ignored millions of aged, sick, and disabled Americans. In sum, the Administration programs simply did not go far enough; unlike the one in Vietnam, this war was not adequately funded, a consequence in part of the mounting military and financial commitment to Saigon. Presidential protestations to the contrary, the nation learned that it could not wage war on two fronts.

Nor were inadequate social welfare programs alone in demonstrating that all was not well with the republic. In response to proposals from student organizations, hundreds of white volunteers spent the summer of 1964 in Mississippi, registering black voters and organizing blacks into a Mississippi Free Democratic Party, efforts that the white community countered with intimidation and violence. The next year Congress enacted a Voting Rights Act, the passage of which owed much to widespread ghetto riots that summer, and to civil rights workers and black political leaders like Martin Luther King, Jr., who joined in dramatizing voter rights by undertaking freedom marches in Selma and Montgomery, Alabama. A 1966 Civil Rights Act failed to pass, and civil rights enthusiasm began to wane. Southern school officials defied the Supreme Court's integration orders; Northerners resisted open-housing ordinances, and Congress continued to grant federal funds to public-housing projects guilty of discrimination. Though blacks made impressive gains in the realms of politics and education, their economic progress was painfully slow. They were the last to be hired and the first to go; they remained at low-skill and low-paying jobs. Angry, resentful, and alienated from the expectations of American society, many of them turned to violence.

Another portent of trouble, antiwar protests, occurred in the fall of 1964—among white middle-class youths at the Berkeley campus of the University of California and among those who had earlier protested against discriminatory practices in the Bay area or in Mississippi. By September 1965, spontaneous resistance to the draft had spread to the most prestigious of the nation's colleges, and protests against ROTC, military recruiters, and defense-oriented university research became endemic. The Students for a Democratic Society (SDS), the premier radical youth organization and surrogate for the entire New Left, doubled its number of college chapters, and in April 1966 it was able to mount the largest antiwar demonstration in Washington's history. Deepening American involvement in Vietnam was paid for by loss of cohesion at home. Radical violence became widespread, and black militants transformed the nonviolent SNCC into a revolutionary, or at least black nationalist, organization. In April 1967, Martin Luther King, Jr., led a protest march in Washington that symbolically linked the antiwar and civil rights crusades. King, not content with symbols, pointedly declared:

This madness must cease. . . . I speak as a child of God and brother to the suffering poor of Vietnam. I speak for those whose land is being laid waste, whose homes are being destroyed, whose culture is being subverted. . . . I speak as a citizen of the world, for the world stands aghast at the path we have taken. I speak as an American to the leaders of my own nation. The great initiative in this war is ours. The initiative to stop it must be ours.

The summer of 1967 brought further racial disorders: the Newark and Detroit riots were the worst in a century, those in Detroit taking a toll of forty-three dead, two thousand injured, and fifty million dollars' worth of property damage. Though immensely destructive, the riots produced little corrective action beyond prompting local police departments to acquire weapons with deadlier fire power and making black nationalism a major target of the law-and-order campaign that candidate Richard Nixon had then adopted.

Worlds apart from black militants, though frequently living in seedy quarters near the violence-prone ghettoes, a new breed of American, called hippies or flower children, espoused life-styles radically different from those of their parents. In Haight-Ashbury in San Francisco and the East Village in New York they enjoyed rock music, drugs, sexual freedom, "guerrilla" theater, tarot cards, astrology, health foods, underground newspapers, and lived in "crash pads." Among the hundred thousand who participated in the antiwar march on the Pentagon in October 1967 were Zen Buddhists and flower children who put daisies in the barrels of the soldiers confronting them.

In March 1968, a beleaguered Lyndon Johnson astonished the nation by dramatically withdrawing from the upcoming election campaign; by then, Senator Eugene McCarthy had already begun his challenge on the war and brought thousands of student volunteers to his ranks. Meanwhile, the Poor People's Campaign of April 1968—the march of rural and urban poor that terminated in the nation's capital—caught the public imagination. Then, on April 4, civil rights leader Martin Luther King, Jr., was shot down in Memphis, Tennessee. His assassination sparked riots in urban centers across the country.

The week-long protests, with their looting and violence, were followed in quick succession by the June assassination of Robert Kennedy, then a candidate for the Democratic Party's nomination, and by the convergence of thousands of radicals upon Chicago for the Democratic national convention. This gathering touched off a series of savage encounters—later called a "police riot" by a presidential commission—between youthful radicals and Chicago's police. The televised sight of white middle-class Americans being battered down by society's defenders produced a deep impression on the public and on history.

The Nixon Presidency

THE NOMINATION of Hubert Humphrey resulted in widespread disaffection among liberal Democrats; those who had endorsed McCarthy were now unwilling to campaign for a candidate who, as vice president, had a record of support of United States policies in Vietnam. The Republican right, however, was neither demoralized nor in ideological disarray. Nixon, having "retired" after his 1960 and 1962 defeats, reentered the political arena and, brushing aside a challenge from Governor Nelson Rockefeller of New York, won the GOP nomination. His platform emphasized a "peace plan" for Vietnam and an anti-busing plank that enchanted Southern delegates. His running mate, part of the party's Southern, strategy, was Maryland governor Spiro Agnew. Nixon's campaign, given impetus by campus disorders and climbing crime statistics, was in behalf of, as the candidate stated, "the Forgotten Americans . . . those who do not break the law, people who pay taxes and go to work, who send their children to school, who go to their churches, people who love this country." He blamed the Supreme Court for permissiveness, pledged safe streets, stricter law enforcement, and, most important, a "plan to end the war"—which, he hastened to add, would "win the peace" as well. These pledges carried the Republicans to a surprisingly narrow victory: they received 43 percent of the vote; Humphrey had 42.7 percent, and George Wallace, who had campaigned as the third-party candidate of the reactionary American Independent Party, only 13.5%. Nixon captured the entire West, the Upper South, and the Border states, as well as some of the mid-West industrial states.

This triumph notwithstanding, there were those who held strong reservations about the new chief executive. The antiwar critics had no confidence in the sincerity of his "peace plan," and their doubts were speedily confirmed when bombing was escalated. On October 15, 1969, an estimated two million people participated in the Vietnam Moratorium—with a quarter million marchers in Washington, and record crowds in other urban centers. In Vietnam itself, military morale eroded, drug use climbed, desertions mounted, officers were killed in "fragging" incidents, and whole units refused to go into battle. The Cambodia "incursion" of April 30, 1970, relit the embers of revolt, touching off some of the most intense and widespread protests in American history. Demonstrations erupted within an hour of Nixon's announcement of troop entry into Cambodia. At Kent State University, the ROTC building was burned down, the National Guard was brought onto campus and, on May 4, advancing guardsmen fired into a student antiwar rally, killing four and wounding nine.

Despite public restlessness and the announced desire for peace, proclaimed by the administration, the war went on inexorably. Its economic consequences proved as serious as the political, social, and moral outcomes. The national debt skyrocketed to $395 billion, cities and states went ever deeper into debt, and public services, like transportation and health, deteriorated. In the meantime, major corporations tightened their grip on the nation's economy: by 1971, one percent of American business controlled 86 percent of the net assets of manufacturing corporations (and, in 1973, less than one percent of the total number of corporations, some 500, accounted for 75 percent of all profits). Many of these corporations were involved in defense work, and defense expenditures jumped quantitatively in these years. Indeed, defense remained the most profitable business in the United States. In the 1973 budget, the average American family's federal taxes totaled over $1,300 for military-related programs, but only $130 for education and $65 for housing and other community needs.

In other respects, too, the economy was inequitable. Taxation continued to be regressive. The wealthiest one percent of the population paid taxes at a lower rate than did most Americans, owing to a variety of tax breaks, incentives, and loopholes—and in 1969, 300 persons with incomes over $300,000 paid no federal income taxes at all. President Nixon himself set an example, underpaying his taxes by more than $400,000.* Tax loopholes and exemptions as well as subsidies —such as the oil depletion allowance—to airlines, shipping, railroads, and oil companies also helped the corporations to get richer and more powerful. More than ever before, vast corporate and financial networks interlocked—not only nationally but globally, with multinational giants like International Telephone and Telegraph preeminent among them. Huge agri-businesses, with the help of government subsidies, accelerated the end of the family farm and the decline in the number of farmers—who by 1970 had dipped to three million—while the average farm increased in size from 215 to 380 acres. Thus, in 1971, the wealthiest seven percent of the farms received about 63 percent of the total government subsidies and the poorer half got only 9.1 percent. The median family income climbed from $5,600 in 1960 to $9,590 in 1970, but inflation neutralized part of the gain, and the gap between rich and poor widened. Other statistics reflected the same inequities: a decade after poverty (defined as $3,700 or less for a family of four) had been discovered in America, the Census Bureau reported that more than 27 million lived in poverty, including a fourth of the nation's elderly, one seventh of its children, and a third of its blacks.

Such figures reinforced the general sense that, despite some minority advances, the quality of life in America was eroding. The Kerner Commission report on city life contained no surprises: welfare rolls were climbing; housing was bad; air was polluted; crime soared. Most cities suffered from poverty, slums, drug addiction, and lawlessness. Among nations of the world the United States now ranked twelfth in maternal mortality, fourteenth in infant mortality, and seventeenth in male life expectancy.

The break with the old order by so many of the nation's youth, and their changing life-style, encouraged new kinds of relationships between whites and blacks, old and young, policemen and citizens, bishops and clergy, men and women.

---

* Nixon was eventually required by the law to pay this amount in back taxes.

Women's liberation challenged the usual housewife-mother role of women and was a moving force behind the campaign to legalize abortion and the fight for passage of the Equal Rights Amendment which by 1975 lacked five states' approval for passage. The development of the Pill was inseparably related to the changing status of women. It enabled women to decide for themselves whether and when to bear children, allowed unmarried women greater sexual freedom without the risk of pregnancy, lessened the possibility of illegitimate pregnancy, and contributed to the decline in the birth rate, from 23.7 per 1,000 in 1960 to about 15 per 1,000 in 1974, the lowest in our nation's history.

The winds of change were blowing across other areas as well: the brutality of life behind bars touched a growing number of Americans. They were sensitized in part by the inmates themselves, since the prisoners, mostly black and poor, clamored for reform of prison conditions and clashed with unyielding administrators. Prison riots became familiar occurrences, the most conspicuous of them being the tragic clash at Attica, New York, in September 1971—which resulted in the death of thirty-three inmates and ten prison guards.

Jefferson had boasted, in his first inaugural address, of "land enough for our descendants to the thousandth and thousandth generation." By the last quarter of the twentieth century, it was clear that not only the land but almost the whole of the nation's resources were eroded or wasting away. The conservation movement launched by Theodore Roosevelt and Gifford Pinchot at the beginning of the century and renewed by Franklin D. Roosevelt in the 1940s ran out of steam. Many factors combined to threaten the very survival of the nation: the destructive work of logging companies and strip miners; recurrent oil spills along the coastal waters; the industrial pollution of lakes and streams—which threatened to make the Great Lakes "dead" seas, and which actually set Cleveland's Cuyahoga River afire; smog that threatened the health of city dwellers; the universal use of detergents and insecticides, which killed off fish, birds, and wildlife in general; the growing depletion of oil reserves. During the Johnson and Nixon administrations, environmentalists could boast a few victories: a 1970 Water Quality Improvement Act, which sought to tighten safeguards against sewage infection, water pollution, and thermal wastes; the National Air Quality Act, which required an eventual 90 percent reduction in automobile emission pollutants; some tentative and ineffective restrictions on strip mining; efforts by cities to create traffic-free malls and by states to outlaw billboards. But these measures did little to arrest environmental abuses. The energy crisis and the recession of 1974 and 1975 demonstrated how eagerly Americans, and their governments, would sacrifice environment for jobs and profits—that is, how readily they would sacrifice the interests of posterity to their own immediate needs. What, they seemed to ask, has posterity ever done for us?

Even religion responded to the social ferment of these years. There was a return to the "socialization of Christianity," so prominent at the turn of the century; and—under the leadership of Pope John XXIII—a remarkable modernization of the Catholic Church occurred. Modern language was substituted for Latin in the Mass. Some clergy rebelled against celibacy and left their vocations to marry; a number of nuns defied archdiocese authority and established secular orders. Larger numbers embarked on full-time careers of political and social activism. Nor were the Catholic and Protestant churches alone in religious ferment. Many, especially college-age youth, turned to contemplative Eastern theology or to emotional and non-intellectual religious expression.

Nixon's spectacular popular majority of 17 million (60.7 percent of the vote) in 1972 emboldened him to shed all political inhibitions in his second term. After November, he began to impound monies appropriated by Congress for social programs in such areas as education, social services, urban and ecological problems—but not for defense, with the Pentagon getting all it asked for. This impoundment practice challenged the Congress's constitutional power over the pursestrings.

Nixon's most interesting and innovative first-term reform measures—the family assistance plan, which was designed to provide a minimum income for all families with dependent children ($1,600 for a family of four); and the "new federalism," a revenue-sharing plan that would distribute a portion of federal funds to state and local governments—became mired in difficulties. The first proposal was rejected by Congress in 1972; the second, when coupled with drastic federal cutbacks and freezes, threatened to leave local governments worse off than before. Discouraged, or indifferent, the President turned away from these experiments. Sympathetic to corporate business and comfortable with Southern conservatives, he responded increasingly to their desires. As early as March 1970, he had opposed any compulsory busing of pupils for the purpose of achieving racial balance, and declared that school boards should be left alone to "formulate plans of desegregation that best suit the needs of their own localities." The following year the Supreme Court unanimously upheld the constitutional requirement of busing as a proper method to achieve racial balance in the schools of Charlotte, North Carolina. Nixon responded by asking Congress to impose a moratorium on court-ordered busing. The Justice Department opposed extension of the 1965 Voting Rights Act, ended guarantees of enforcement in the South, and intervened to delay school desegregation in Mississippi.

On another domestic front, Nixon liquidated the Office of Economic Opportunity, perhaps the centerpiece of the Great Society program; withdrew support from the fair housing enforcement program; proposed cutbacks in programs for students, farmers, veterans, unemployed, and the mentally ill; ended assistance to consumer protection and to environmentalist proposals; fought strip-mining regulations; vetoed an anti-water pollution measure to which the administration had been pledged. And when this bill was passed over his veto, he impounded the congressional appropriation for it.

In 1967, Defense Secretary Robert McNamara had ordered a task force to investigate what went wrong with the war in Asia; its findings were presented in some forty volumes known as the Pentagon Papers. One of those involved in the project, Daniel Ellsberg, had access to these papers as an employee of the Rand Corporation, which McNamara commissioned to make the study. Ellsberg concluded that neither the government nor the people had an accurate picture of events in South Vietnam. Persuaded that publication of the project's papers could no longer compromise, but might enhance, national security, and that in any event the American people had a right to know what was in them, he made Xerox copies of them and made them available to *The New York Times* and the *Washington Post*. These Pentagon Papers were a chilling account of decisions made in the Johnson years, to which they were limited, and confirmed the worst suspicions of the war critics. They told of secret military decisions that contrasted with the official administration positions, and exposed a record of calculated deception unprecedented in our history. The administration obtained a temporary injunction blocking publication of the papers, an action which, for the first time in our history, imposed prior restraint upon the press. The Supreme Court ruled six-to-three against the government, and publication was resumed. The administration then charged Ellsberg with theft, espionage, and conspiracy. After evidence of government prevarication, suppression of evidence, and concealment of witnesses—as well as burglary of the office of Ellsberg's psychiatrist—the judge threw out the case.

The Pentagon Papers decision was a striking victory for freedom of the press. But the Supreme Court was not always on the libertarian side. It did, to be sure, sustain the exemplary record of its predecessor on such politically volatile issues as school integration and school busing. It even broke new ground in some areas: the capital punishment and abortion cases, and the limits imposed on presidential power to wiretap and bug "subversives" without warrant. But the Nixon Court's opinions in other areas often reflected a turning away from the liberalism of the Warren Court. That was only natural, for Nixon had reshaped the Court in his own image. He replaced Earl Warren, who had resigned, with Warren Burger, a hard-line Appellate Court judge who had a record of dissents from the majority criminal justice opinions of his fellow judges on this bench. He appointed three additional conservative justices: Harry Blackmun, who had a mixed record on civil rights; Lewis Powell of Virginia, a highly respected conservative lawyer; William Rehnquist, deputy attorney general, who represented the Goldwater wing of the Republican Party. Their presence meant a sharp modification of the innovative and liberal decisions of the Warren Court. Now, according to Justice Douglas, "a 'law and order' judicial mood" prevailed and decisions made by this newly constituted court gradually undermined earlier liberal gains, especially in the field of criminal justice. To expedite criminal cases, it approved six-man juries, non-unanimous verdicts, and even the elimination of jury trials for prosecutions involving prison terms of six months or less. It also sanctioned courtroom use of illegally acquired evidence, and permitted warrantless searches and seizures unrelated to the cause of arrest.

Meanwhile, political and administrative invasions of privacy and due process of law mounted ominously. The Justice Department lobbied successfully for the 1968 Crime Control and Safe Streets Act, with a wiretap provision designed, according to the Attorney General, John Mitchell, to curb the "many revolutionary elements in society." The Department permitted Internal Security Division prosecutors to use the grand jury as a political weapon, and attempted to force journalists to reveal the sources of their information. This measure enabled the Department to compile dossiers on thousands of suspected radical and antiwar critics as well as on the Catholic left, and to jail suspects to compel testimony rather than to punish for a crime. Criminal conspiracy trials were launched against antiwar activists and critics, and these trials revealed the widespread use that had been made of *agents provocateurs* and entrapment practices. The government had an almost unbroken record of failure in such prosecutions, which raised the suspicion that they were undertaken not to obtain convictions, but to harass, intimidate, and bankrupt the defendants.

The Watergate Affair

THE PRESIDENT had proclaimed that no man can "set himself above the law in the name of justice," but he misused for political purposes national security and intelligence agencies, and set up a personal and extra-legal investigative force funded by taxpayers but accountable only to the President himself. "The plumbers," as a group of these White House operatives came to be called, burglarized private files, tapped the phones of reporters, and arranged for attacks on antiwar demonstrators, while the executive branch carried on a widespread campaign of political espionage, planting *agents provocateurs* to incite radicals to illegal activities, faking evidence against political opponents, and using the Internal Revenue Service for political harassment. Headed by the former Attorney General, John Mitchell, the Committee for the Reelection of the President collected a campaign chest of some $60 million, including large contributions illegally donated ("laundered" was the term) by oil, airline, and other corporations.

Such "laundered" funds as well as the bag of "dirty tricks" used in the 1972 presidential primaries were, as it turned out, quite unnecessary. Senator George McGovern, after being easily nominated on the first ballot, bungled the campaign that followed. The Democratic platform called for an end to the Vietnam war, diversion of substantial defense funds into social welfare programs, and the elimination of tax loopholes. After George Wallace, campaigning for the Democratic Party nomination in the Maryland primary, had been shot, Nixon wooed Wallace's nominally Democratic supporters—by assuring them that, if elected, he would end "the age of permissiveness" and would urge legislation that would prohibit arbitrary court-ordered busing of children. To appeal to voters of other persuasions, he shrewdly announced that the war was over and played up his diplomatic initiatives in China and Russia. The mood of the country had turned conservative and Nixon was elected with a popular majority of 17 million; he carried every state except Massachusetts, and the District of Columbia.

The Republicans, it is obvious, did not require political espionage or illegal contributions in order to win. Nor did they need those covert operations that ended with the destruction of the President. It all began on a minor key—when a gaggle of former CIA agents broke into Democratic headquarters at the Watergate Hotel in Washington, installed phone taps, and photographed documents. After another raid on the night of June 17, 1972, the team was apprehended inside the darkened offices. This seemingly unimportant event—presidential press secretary Ronald Ziegler dismissed it as only a "caper"—might have been just that, had it not involved the very highest echelons in the administration and had not the administration committed itself to covering up the nature of the crime. As it was, Watergate was to ignite a fuse that exploded two years later into the greatest political scandal in American history.

In the spring of 1973, a Senate Select Committee began a two-month probe of the Watergate affair as well as of the larger issue of presidential authority. Its hearings appeared on daytime television and it soon became apparent to millions of enthralled viewers that the drama—with its intricacy of plot, tangled motives, deceitful relations, unpredictable behavior, knaves and sycophants—was in fact part of the real world rather than the dramatic world of television. A parade of former cabinet officers, executive aides, FBI and CIA agents, Justice Department officials, GOP functionaries and fund raisers marched into the Senate chamber. Their testimony was confusing, and even contradictory, but their political philosophy was simple: loyalty to the President came before loyalty to the laws or to the Constitution. What emerged was a demonstration of how easily the democratic process could be subverted to private and partisan ends. Presidential counsel John Dean described in precise terms Nixon's involvement in the cover-up: his concealment of evidence; encouragement of hush-money payments to the imprisoned Watergate burglars; promise of executive pardons—and his testimony was devastating. When Alexander Butterfield, a presidential aide, informed the committee that Nixon had actually taped White House discussions of Watergate strategy, the fat was in the fire. When Archibald Cox, who headed the newly established office of the Special Prosecutor, requested these tapes, the President dismissed him. It was the beginning of the end. On July 24, the Supreme Court, in *United States vs. Nixon,* unanimously ordered Nixon to give up sixty-four tapes and documents. Now the Republicans began slipping from the bonds of loyalty to their chief. The last act of his drama was at hand.

Meanwhile, Vice President Agnew, a self-proclaimed paragon of law and order, and apparently "clean" in the Watergate affair, had come under investigation in Maryland for acccepting payoffs on state contracts while he had been Governor. When brought to trial, he pleaded *nolo contendere* to one count of tax evasion, received a lenient sentence, and resigned his office in disgrace.

All the while, the investigators of the Special Prosecutor as well as of the Senate Committee continued their tough probing into an ever-widening number of areas. By this time, there had been fifteen resignations from the administration, four indictments, three pleas of guilty, and countless retreats to the protection of the Fifth Amendment. Two separate grand juries were sitting, four Senate committees and a House Committee were conducting investigations, three civil suits were in the courts, and a Los Angeles federal grand jury had indicted a number of former White House aides for the attempted burglary of the office of Ellsberg's psychiatrist. By now, unexplained events had surfaced that made Watergate more than just another political scandal: the Ellsberg break-in; interference with the judicial process; the "laundering" of campaign funds; the use of the FBI, the CIA, and the Internal Revenue Service for political purposes; the tapping of the phones of presidential candidate Edmund Muskie on the pretext of "national security reasons"—these all added up to what many people thought were the undermining of the constitutional and political processes of democracy.

The discovery that the transcripts of the tapes submitted to the Special Prosecutor were both incomplete and inaccurate —and also included erasures—forfeited public and Party support, and Nixon's refusal to comply fully with further subpoenas from the Senate Committee or from the House Judiciary Committee all combined to make impeachment proceedings unavoidable. On July 31, 1973, Massachusetts Congressman Robert Drinan offered a formal motion to impeach the President "of high crimes and misdemeanors." The charges were not limited to complicity in Watergate, but also included the secret bombing of Cambodia, impounding of funds voted by Congress, and highly questionable expenditures on improvements of presidential homes in Florida and California. It was also reported that Nixon had paid only $800 in taxes on a $200,000 income, attempted to deduct $5,000 for his daughter Tricia's masked ball as "expenses incurred in the performance of official functions as President of the United States," and also deducted over $480,000 for a gift falsely described in a tax return and dependent upon a back-dated deed. It was alleged, too, that the presidential tapes had been tampered with, thus subverting the integrity of the legal process, and these very tapes indicated that Nixon had advised his chief aides to commit perjury and engage in conspiracy to violate federal laws. Obstruction of justice, misprision of a felony, and subornation of perjury were among the charges filed against the President and heard by a bewildered and troubled nation. Possibly the most serious charge of all, however, was the larger wrong from which these sprang—the abuse of power.

All through the spring and summer of 1974, the legal and judicial mills ground on relentlessly. District Court Judge John Sirica formally sentenced six of the original Watergate defendants. President Nixon was not himself indicted only because the Special Prosecutor counseled the grand jury that such an action was of doubtful constitutionality. But, in a sealed report sent to Judge Sirica, Nixon was named as an unindicted co-conspirator, suggesting the measure of his involvement and culpability in the jurors' eyes.

The proceedings continued to be hindered by presidential delaying tactics on the release of tapes and transcripts. Then, too, White House counsel rejected the contention that broad abuses of the public trust were grounds for impeachment. But by this time both the public and the Congress had had enough. When the publication of tapes that Nixon had unsuccessfully sought to conceal proved irrefutably that he had known all along of the Watergate cover-up and had perjured himself by proclaiming ignorance and innocence, the House Judiciary Committee voted two articles of impeachment on July 30, 1974. These articles had bipartisan support, with the vote being 27 to 11 (on the quasi-criminal obstruction-of-justice charge of Article I), as some of the President's staunchest supporters deserted him.

Aware that his strength in the House had eroded, the President did not wait for further developments. On December 6, 1973, he had replaced Agnew with Gerald Ford, the veteran Michigan lawmaker and House minority leader. Now, on August 8, 1974, he resigned from office and departed for his home in San Clemente, California. Just one month later, the new President, departing from his earlier assurances, granted an unconditional pardon to the man who had nominated him to the Presidency.

The Ford Administration

IF GERALD FORD had been running for election in 1974 the only plank necessary to his presidential platform would have been "to restore confidence in the Chief Executive!" That was the major task confronting him when he assumed office. It was a task unaccomplished when Jimmy Carter triumphed over him two years later. True, Gerald Ford's presidency did have a healing effect on the Watergate-inflicted wounds of domestic politics; his two years in office, however, failed to reverse what was perhaps the most sustained impact of Watergate, the decline of public confidence in government. Instead those years produced a deepening of the crisis in legitimacy. This was, in part, because of the deteriorating economy at home and the continuing decline of American prestige abroad; and, in part, because of popular disapproval of Ford's premature (September 8, 1974) pardon of Richard M. Nixon.

Notwithstanding the new President's contention that "there was no deal" and that only the "laws of God and the needs of the national interest" guided his decision to grant the pardon, many Americans concluded that it was but another instance of presidential cover-up. Ford did, to be sure, attempt to balance the pardon with a limited amnesty to young men who had fled the Vietnam draft, but the vague and quixotic terms of the amnesty program were in sharp contrast to the Nixon pardon. Such a divisive gesture, justified on the grounds that it was needed to get Nixon out of public consciousness so that Gerald Ford might get on with the job, did not augur well for the Administration. And the problems confronting it were many and importunate.

The War in Vietnam was dragging to its miserable conclusion, but it still needed to be liquidated; that was a long-term task. Nor was Vietnam the only problem which Ford inherited. Spiraling inflation—which was, to a great extent, the result of the refusal of both Lyndon Johnson and Richard Nixon to levy taxes to pay for the War—increasing unemployment, and soaring oil prices, all threatened traditional American prosperity. Furthermore, the effect of years of exploiting natural resources and polluting soil, air and water in the name of "Progress" forced Americans, for the first time, to face the fact that their resources were finite, not infinite. No wonder that by 1974 many Americans, disillusioned by Vietnam and Watergate, and discouraged about the prospects for the future, called for a return to traditional values and to the good old days of Eisenhower and less government, the era when Americans could take their superiority throughout the world for granted.

On balance, Gerald Ford was most successful in satisfying this nostalgia. If his presidency did little to solve the problems which he had inherited, and failed to restore dignity or authority to the office of chief executive, it did manage to achieve respectability. Nixon had betrayed those longing to step backward into history, Gerald Ford did not. Unimaginative and uninspiring, he believed, like former Presidents Coolidge and Eisenhower, that the chief executive should be a caretaker, not a leader. And he did, indeed, prove to be a caretaker-President; marking time, or so it seemed, until the election of 1976.

Though Nixon was out of office both his policies and his appointees continued to dominate government. Ford's solutions to the formidable problems of a deteriorating economy and declining prestige were simple: spend less at home, be strong abroad! If his simplicity earned him both affection and respect, it did not change governmental policy from what it had been during the previous six years. Nixon, too, had preached fiscal austerity except for increased monies to the military. "Law and Order" which had been axial to Nixon's Administration continued to be so during Ford's. While Nixon-appointed judges on the Supreme Court furthered its cause domestically, Nixon's Secretary of State, Henry Kissinger, sought to enforce "Law and Order" in the foreign arena.

Among those unresolved problems inherited from the preceding Administration, the most urgent was the wrap-up of Vietnam. Although Nixon had concluded a cease-fire with the Vietnamese and begun the withdrawal of American troops as early as March of 1973, it was left to Gerald Ford to negotiate a final settlement. The negotiations proved protracted, largely because U.S. policy was wholly lacking in that farsightedness and magnanimity shown toward Japan and Germany after World War II; but then Americans were not used to losing wars. Even if the Ford Administration had been predisposed to pay for the much vaunted "Peace with Honor," acknowledgment of defeat or culpability would have found little popular support.

Protracted treaty negotiations were not the only legacy of the Vietnam War; more important were the emotional, the physical and the psychological scars which the country suffered as a result of its posturing as an Asian power. Destruction of life and depletion of resources; disillusionment with government at home and distrust of the United States as a world power abroad; and a nagging sense of guilt for a war wholly without justification either in its cause or its conduct, made Vietnam the most cataclysmic event in American history since the Civil War. And unlike the Civil War where a defeated South managed to turn military defeat into a moral or psychological victory, Vietnam offered no such sop to the American people. Though in 1980, Republican presidential candidate Ronald Reagan was to earn applause from veterans' groups by proclaiming Vietnam a "noble cause," few outside the convention halls joined in that applause. Vietnam had proved the United States vulnerable—both militarily and morally. Soon it was to prove the nation vulnerable economically and socially as well.

The perceived loss of their status as Number One caused many Americans to clamor for a "militarization" of American society. The Cold War, diminished somewhat by Nixon's overtures toward China, seemed to take on added vindictiveness by concentration on the Soviet Union. Vietnam had demonstrated that the United States was unprepared; if America were to regain her "credibility" it was essential that she build up the military to protect her interests against the Soviet "threat" elsewhere in the world.

The Ford Program, if it can be called that, preached fiscal austerity and a limit on Big Government. The only exception to restricted funding and deregulation was—as it had been under Nixon—the military. Urging "fiscal discipline" in his veto of the 1976 Education Appropriation Act, Ford, in the same year, requested an eleven billion dollar increase in military spending. He had assured the people that his objective was to "get the Federal Government as far out of your business, out of your lives, out of your pocketbooks, and out of your hair as I possibly can," but he accepted without question that the American people and the American economy should serve the military. What Eisenhower had termed the "military-industrial" complex expanded under Nixon and Ford to a "military-industrial-financial-labor-academic" complex. If this contradictory policy failed to excite serious public protest it was because the majority of Americans, like their President, considered "national security" to be the top priority of government; and because national security, which had once meant *social* security, had by 1974 come to mean *military* security. By favoring the military at the same time he vetoed a host of social measures—a federal jobs bill, a comprehensive public works bill, a federal aid-to-education measure and a school lunch program among them—Ford confirmed this narrowing definition of "security."

Although few Americans challenged the Administration's generosity to the military, they were not happy with the consequences of austerity in other areas. By the end of 1976, over half of the eight million or more unemployed received no unemployment compensation; the elderly and others on fixed incomes were losing their fight against inflation. Major cities—New York, Cleveland, Detroit among them—denied federal funds, faced bankruptcy. Black and Hispanic minorities, long encouraged to enter through the door of the Great Society, now found that door closed to them; unemployment among black youths rose to forty percent. If political fences were mended during the Ford Administration, hard times furthered that fragmentation of society inaugurated by the Vietnam War, aggravated by the sharp economic recession and specifically favored by a neo-conservatism which was prepared to reject the whole concept of the Great Society.

The only clear-cut winners of Ford's fiscal conservatism, besides the military, were the large industrial conglomerates. Fearful of further cutbacks in employment, the President bowed to pressure from Detroit and postponed until 1976 implementation of the ninety percent reduction in the level of auto pollution stipulated by the 1970 Clean Air Act. Faced with a worsening "energy crisis" occasioned by the rise in oil prices and public hostility to either a rationing system or increased taxation, he vetoed price controls and urged deregulation. The "neo-conservatism" of the mid-1970s failed to embrace conservation of the nation's people or its environment.

Gerald Ford began his administration under a cloud of suspicion and secrecy engendered by his predecessor. His unassuming manner and his apparent honesty did much to dissipate that cloud at home. Neither he nor Henry Kissinger, however, were prepared to do so abroad. To be sure, nothing of the magnitude of the CIA's covert operations in Chile which brought about the downfall of President Salvador Allende in 1973 or their secret attempts to assassinate Fidel Castro occurred during Ford's tenure in office. When Senate investigators uncovered the excesses of CIA operations, however, Ford failed to instruct his Attorney General, Edward Levi, to take any action against the agencies of the CIA and FBI or its members. More overtly, he approved funneling CIA funds into Portugal and Angola and, most lavishly, into Italy in attempts to control their internal policies.

In the conduct of foreign affairs, Henry Kissinger's *Realpolitik* dominated the Ford Administration as it had Nixon's Administration. In his pursuit of "national security" for a "Free" America, Secretary Kissinger not only courted repressive allies like General Pinochet of Chile and General Park of South Korea, but, in 1975, urged passage of a 4.7 billion dollar military aid packet to support them as well. While Secretary of Defense James Schlesinger encouraged Pentagon demands for increased stores of military hardware in order to provide the U.S. with a "first strike capability," Kissinger encouraged the military of other nations to look upon America as munitions supplier of the world. Peace, of a sort, and the continued flow of oil in the Mideast was bought with large arms sales to Iran and Saudi Arabia. Thus the cost of peace in the Middle East was high: the proliferation of arms throughout the area. A measure of peace, however, was achieved. Kissinger's so-called "shuttle diplomacy" did restore U.S. prestige, at least temporarily, in the Arab world and set an Arab-Israeli dialogue in motion for the first time. Furthermore, it provided Americans with some renewed hope that they were, once again, leaders of the free world.

Re-establishment of American superiority was, from the beginning, of paramount importance to the Ford Administration and reflected the desires of the American public. This became all too evident in the handling of one of the dramatic—though in itself unimportant—episodes of Ford's two years: the capture, by a Cambodian torpedo boat, of the American freighter *Mayaguez*. Despite the some 250,000 tons of bombs dropped and the four billion dollars spent to create the Khmer Rouge guerillas by the United States, military involvement in Cambodia had been only a sideshow to the main event being staged in neighboring Vietnam. American activity there was skidding to a halt when, in May 1975, the *Mayaguez* was seized while sailing in Cambodia's territorial waters. The effrontery of Cambodia outraged Americans; even congressional "doves" like Senators Church and Case spread their wings like "hawks" and welcomed the chance to show the American giant not helpless after all. Cambodian allegations that the vessel carried top-secret intelligence equipment and data were disregarded. So, too, was the message that the crew had already been released. In direct violation of the 1973 War Powers Act, the Administration sanctioned a savage air-land rescue attack. When the gas and smoke had cleared and the body count——38 American dead——finished, American "credibility" had suffered rather than been strengthened by her "triumph" over the Cambodians. The giant might not be helpless, but it was hysterical.

The *Mayaguez* incident notwithstanding, the Ford years were colorless. As a caretaker-President, Ford provoked no amelioration of the national malaise centered on the defeat suffered in Vietnam, nor did he provide solutions for the domestic difficulties——inflation, unemployment, pollution and limited energy supplies——which by the election of 1976 were gravely troubling the American people.

The 1976 Election

AFTER THE DEBACLE of the Vietnam War and the infamy of Watergate and its attendant deceptions and crimes, the prospect for a Democratic victory in 1976 seemed promising. But the Democrats had no candidate who both inspired confidence and captured the imagination of the people, while "Jerry" Ford had proved to be a kind of Eisenhower Redivivus, an amiable and comfortable figure who would provide just that quiet and decency which the nation so sorely needed. His only serious Republican contender was former Governor Ronald Reagan of California, one-time moving picture idol and himself something of a father figure. But in the end, and after a heated and close contest, it was to Ford that the Republicans turned.

The Democratic contest was, by contrast, almost a free-for-all with a dozen candidates, some of them relatively unknown, aspiring to fill what was a most surprising political void. In the end the contest came down to four: Senator "Scoop" Jackson of Washington, Governor Jerry Brown of California, George Wallace of Alabama——a perennial candidate, now all but disqualified by the wounds of a would-be assassin——and the veteran Senator Hubert Humphrey, who had been so narrowly defeated by Nixon in 1968. Into this galaxy of familiar politicians came a brash newcomer, "Jimmy" Carter, one-time Governor of Georgia and peanut farmer. To the astonishment of all the professionals, it was the outsider who, in the end, captured the prize. What explains his victory? Perhaps, it was because he seemed a David fighting against so many Goliaths; perhaps, because the nation was weary of professional politicians and officeholders; perhaps, because his evangelical piety appealed to an instinct in the American people for simple morality and faith in public life. In any event, when the Democratic Convention met in New York, Governor Carter won handily on the first ballot—a triumph hitherto enjoyed only by incumbent Presidents. He chose for his running-mate a man whose integrity and ability had long been familiar to the American people, Senator Walter Mondale of Minnesota.

Polling only two percent more than his rival, Carter won narrowly in the Electoral College. (If Ohio and Hawaii—where the margins were most narrow—had gone the other way, Ford would have been the victor.) Carter's chief support came from the remnants of the old Franklin Roosevelt coalition: labor and blacks, both of whom had mounted intensive efforts, and Southerners, who rejoiced in the contemplation of the first President from the "Deep South" since Zachary Taylor.

Election day, then, was by no means a runaway victory for the Democrats. Furthermore, the election had both ominous as well as gratifying features. Ominous was the fact that only fifty-three percent of the electorate bothered to vote—one of the lowest percentages in twentieth-century history and one which contrasted shockingly with the customary turnout in western European elections of from seventy-five to ninety percent. Ominous, too, was the revelation of a potential division in the country along geographical lines: Ford carried every state west of the Mississippi except Minnesota and Texas. Those who remembered the geographical division of 1860 and the later emergence of the "Solid South" contemplated this with concern. That black voters went in unprecedented numbers to the polling booths and that the election returned so many blacks to city and state offices were two of the few gratifying features of the election.

In mind and character, James Earl Carter—who preferred to be called "Jimmy"—was closer, perhaps, to President Wilson than to any other twentieth-century chief executive. Carter shared Wilson's complexity of both character and experience. Born and raised in a little country town, almost symbolically named Plains, Georgia, he had graduated from the Annapolis

Naval Academy and worked closely on the nuclear submarine program with that exacting taskmaster Admiral Hyman Rickover. By profession an engineer, by practice a peanut farmer, by instinct a politician, he had served, like Woodrow Wilson, for one term as Governor of his state. He was an "outsider" both excluded from, and suspicious of, the Washington Establishment; and he promised to provide a more positive government than that of Gerald Ford, whose brief administration, relying as it did on the veto power (Ford had issued over fifty vetoes—most of them directed at liberal social and economic programs—while in office), had appeared negative.

During the campaign Carter pledged honesty in government and reductions of the swollen governmental bureaucracy, of military spending and of overseas armament sales. On the positive side, he promised bold programs of health care, environmental protection and rescue for the beleaguered cities. Yet, his Inaugural Address warned against expecting too much from government and consisted mostly of eloquent generalities: "to renew our search for humility, mercy and justice"; "to strengthen the American family"; "to provide equal treatment under the law for the weak and the powerful"; and "to enable our people to be proud of their government once again."

Displaying his own humility and simplicity, the new President concluded his Inauguration and walked, hand in hand, with his wife Rosalynn, from the Capitol to the White House, just as, two hundred years earlier, Thomas Jefferson had walked from the still unfinished Capitol to his boardinghouse after his own Inauguration.

The Carter Administration

A BORN-AGAIN BAPTIST, Carter also appeared to be a born-again Populist. Despite his long apprenticeship to Southern racial mores, Carter had won the black vote by being sensitive to the needs of blacks and showing respect for those on welfare rolls. He had deplored FBI and CIA excesses and had promised stricter enforcement of long neglected anti-trust laws, the creation of public service jobs for the unemployed, greater equity in the tax structure, respect—and legal protection—for the rights of women. In all this he was confident that he would be aided by a Congress dominated by the Democratic party which had chalked up a more clear-cut victory in the Congressional races than it had in the Presidential, winning twenty-one Senate seats to the Republicans' eleven, and 292 in the House to its rival's 143. Watching their new President walking back to the White House, Americans felt confident that he would keep his campaign promises. But the Georgia farmer turned President proved far more complicated than his campaign image had suggested.

A former member of David Rockefeller's Trilateral Commission which represented the most powerful corporate interests in the western world, Carter confounded some of his supporters by recruiting many of his chief advisors from that commission and its affiliates. His choice of cabinet members revealed that side of him very much at home with the business establishment and with Washington's elite.

To the post of Secretary of State, the President appointed Cyrus Vance, a product of Main Line Philadelphia and Yale University. A Wall Street lawyer, one-time President of the New York Bar Association and trustee of the Rockefeller Foundation, Vance had served as an advisor to President Johnson whose Vietnam policies he supported, although without enthusiasm. The new Secretary of Defense, Harold Brown, had much the same credentials: Air Force Secretary under President Johnson, and, later, President of the prestigious California Institute of Technology, Brown had been more imperative than Vance on bombing Vietnam "without the present scrupulous concern for collateral civilian damage or casualties." The new National Security Council head, Zbigniew Brzezinski, plucked from Columbia University, was likewise a member of the Trilateral Commission and the Foreign Policy Association Establishment; and to his ill-defined position he brought not so much the cool objectivity of the technocrat as a relentless hostility to the Soviet Union and a limitless faith in the power of armaments to intimidate that nation.

But it was not entirely "business as usual" in the White House. Carter's complexity of character was reflected in other top-level appointments which went to his Georgia associates. Bert Lance, an Atlanta banker, became head of the Bureau of the Budget; Griffin Bell was named to the post of Attorney General—a post as much political as legal; and two young political strategists, Hamilton Jordan and Jody Powell, were given the job of running the day-by-day affairs of both the White House and the Democratic party. It was hard to know what to make of these and others of the same ilk with whom the new President surrounded himself but it soon became clear that these presidential advisors did not constitute a born-again revolution of the excluded, the obscure and the perishing classes of American society.

If Carter's complexity of character was to confound his supporters, so, too, was history to confound Jimmy Carter. His Inaugural Address, like Wilson's sixty years earlier, looked almost wholly to domestic issues, and his solutions were encompassed within the framework of domestic politics. But world affairs were to intrude on Carter as they had on Woodrow Wilson. The center of gravity, as Carter quickly discovered, was not America but the globe: even those problems which appeared to be purely domestic, such as the depletion of oil resources, inflation and unemployment, were rooted in, precipitated by, and inextricably connected with circumstances and crises elsewhere on the globe. It quickly became apparent even to the most provincial eye that none of these could be solved within the insulated chambers of the American states or nation. Philosophers had long recognized that science and art were one; now statesmen had to accept and adapt to the reality that politics, economy, society and morality were one; and that, if civilization was to survive, nations everywhere would have to respect this elementary truth. Who would have imagined, a generation earlier, that by the mid-1970's the oil-rich nations of the Middle East could hold the United States in thrall; that uprisings in Cuba or in Angola could involve the greatest of global powers in ideological, and even in military conflicts; that the struggle between Israel and the Arab States could loom up as the major concern of American foreign policy; that nuclear experiments in China could threaten North America and Europe with poisonous fallout; that runaway population growth in Mexico and the Caribbean could profoundly affect the economy and politics of the whole of North America; that atomic secrets could not be kept secret, nor out of the hands of rival nations or of terrorists; that the value of the American dollar, long thought to be the standard throughout the world, would be determined in London, Zurich and Frankfurt; or that a revolution in distant

Iran could precipitate major economic, political and military crises within a nation which had long deluded itself that it was the most powerful nation on the globe.

All this called inexorably for a profound modification of traditional thinking and conduct. It was no use intoning the old political litanies—the necessity of being Number One, the reliance on military power to solve international problems, the illusion that our own resources were inexhaustible, or the Tocquevillian assumption that Democracy was an irresistible wave of the future. These and similar assumptions were palpably invalid. What was called for was resourcefulness, boldness, imagination and energy to adjust to new domestic and global problems. Not since Franklin Roosevelt had these qualities distinguished American statesmanship. The new President, for all his eloquence and his good intentions, gave little promise that they would distinguish his regime.

What was true in the realm of international relations was no less true in the domestic arena: here, too, the old litanies were irrelevant. By the election of 1976 the traditional concepts of "conservative" and "liberal" had been drained of meaning, and those who invoked them to solve political issues found that, instead, they obfuscated these issues. The generation which had created the Republic and written its Constitution had displayed a sophisticated grasp of the nature of the political problems they were called upon to solve. Thus they knew that the fundamental problem of the scope and the limits of government was one of principle, but that the question *which* government—state or national—should exercise political authority, and in which areas, was one of practical experience. Few of those who debated these issues since World War II had demonstrated either interest in or understanding of these distinctions. Thus the campaigns of 1976 and later that of 1980 were conducted with guerilla tactics rather than with disciplined strategy of reason or philosophy. Party differences on major issues such as the role of government in public health, employment, housing, education, the environment, the administration of the penal codes, or the rights of minorities and of women (who constituted a majority) were rhetorical, fortuitous, and evasive, rather than logical or consistent. Republicans, traditionally the party of nationalism and centralization, viewed government with suspicion and the national government with alarm, while privately exalting over public enterprise.

They were, at the same time, the special champions of corporate business, the military and the "intelligence community"—all of these the most centralizing of institutions. Democrats, traditionally the party of States Rights, localism and laissez-faire now took a far more favorable attitude toward Big Government, public enterprise and the welfare state than had Thomas Jefferson and his successors through most of the nineteenth century. President Carter found himself almost irresistibly drawn into both camps.

The "neo-conservatism" so carefully cultivated by Richard Nixon and so thoughtlessly embraced by Gerald Ford found Jimmy Carter's White House a hospitable place, his campaign pledges notwithstanding. The Nixon-Ford policy of reducing government regulation over private enterprise proved non-partisan; so, too, did the policy of increasing military allocations, often at the expense of social programs. By 1980, the ever-smiling "outsider" of 1976, who had waged war against the "same group of insiders, the same unkept promises," had lost both his smile and his belief that anyone outside of government could run government. If, during his White House years, Carter lost faith in outsiders, many of his former constituents had lost faith in Carter. While many came to doubt his ability to lead the country anywhere, others viewed him as leading it ever deeper into an economic decline from which there was no retreat. Disaffected intellectuals, minorities, women, the mayors of major American cities and those who opposed the insatiable demands of the Pentagon, all suffered more than a loss of faith. They felt betrayed by the born-again Populist who had promised so much and delivered so little.

It remains one of the curiosities of national politics that Americans often condemn or praise the President as if there were no other branches of government. There is, in effect, a sort of schizophrenia when it comes to the chief executive: should the White House formulate policy or should it merely *execute* those policies dictated by Congress? The answer seems to lie somewhere in the middle and depends on whether or not the individual citizen approves of what the President proposes. No President, unless he deliberately circumvents Congress and sidetracks the Constitution, can effect policies without legislative cooperation. If Jimmy Carter furthered the "crisis in leadership" it was because of his initial failure to gain that cooperation. Gerald Ford had spent much of his two years in office vetoing acts of Congress. Jimmy Carter spent much of his Presidency being vetoed by Congress.

He began his presidency by proclaiming that "as we prepare for the major problems of putting the American people back to work . . . control inflation, energy policy, defense matters, tax reform, welfare reform . . . we will work intimately with Congress on a bipartisan basis to achieve these goals." The Hill proved reluctant to work at all with Mr. Carter and his loyal, but politically ineffective, Georgians. New restraints on Presidential authority, such as the Budget Act of 1974 which tightened Congressional control of the purse strings, gave Congress the upper hand in its clashes with the President. The result of all this was that although his four years in the White House were years of great executive activity, they were also years of little achievement.

The Carter Administration got off to a good enough start; the promised pardon for draft evaders was signed on January 21. Proposals for stimulating the economy, overhauling the welfare system, abolishing the Electoral College and providing public funding for Congressional as well as Presidential elections followed in rapid succession. Most of these, while admirable, were greeted with passive resistance, if not open hostility, by the Congress.

It was in energy conservation that the President suffered his worst defeat, both in the Congress and in public response. Rightly considering that this was the most important of domestic issues, he had, in March 1977, created a new cabinet post, Secretary of Energy, to which he appointed Nixon's Secretary of Defense James Schlesinger. The reaction, both to the new cabinet post and to its far-from-new head, was lukewarm. In his public exhortations Carter emphasized the need both to increase production and to cut consumption of oil; but he was, as yet, unprepared to recommend effective governmental intervention to achieve these elusive ends. Instead of regulation he proposed deregulation—thus stealing a march on his Republican opponents—and instead of rationing, self-sacrifice. There was some excuse for this. Neither the Congress nor the people were prepared to accept effective taxes or rationing. Congress, indeed, displayed its contempt for reality by voting down the mild ten-cent-a-gallon tax on gasoline proposed by Carter.

Nothing contributed more to inflation than the high cost of importing oil, and public opinion had already relegated energy to second place and assigned to inflation the distinction of first priority. And no wonder: by 1979 inflation had risen from a modest seven percent, when Carter succeeded to office, to a troublesome twelve percent. Responding to the mood of the country, both outraged and sullen, Congress made gestures toward curbing inflation and chose to do this in the area of federal expenditures for social welfare. "Defense" expenditures escaped the Congressional axe.

Inflation was to persist, notwithstanding the efforts to control it. This was, no doubt, inevitable: the basic causes of inflation appeared to elude control both at home and abroad. These basic causes in the United States were an increasingly unfavorable balance of trade with the oil-producing countries; a budget deficit of fifty-nine billion dollars and a national debt of some eight hundred billion dollars by 1979; and a decline in productivity caused, in part, by failure to modernize factories and production technologies, in part by the distraction of a large percentage of research science, engineering and technological skills from the productive arena of the economy to nonproductive military research and manufacture.

Congress, in its resistance to Carter's proposals and in its handling of inflation, faithfully reflected the national mood of "conservatism" and a sullen hostility to almost all forms of government initiative. Thus economic difficulties nourished that special brand of neo-conservatism which looked with suspicion on Big Government, but welcomed with enthusiasm Big Corporations, national and multinational. Myriad single-interest groups, which had first emerged during Nixon's Administration, gained strength during Carter's first term and furthered the conservative cause; political action committees (PACs) crusaded against abortion, gun-control, the Equal Rights movement and demanded the return of capital punishment and prayer in the schools and legislation to enforce morality. For the first time since the Protestant campaign against Alfred E. Smith in 1928, evangelical groups boldly entered the political arena, prepared to break down the wall of separation between church and state. With this went a moral McCarthyism against individuals, groups or policies judged to be outside the mainstream of American life; and a revival of racial prejudices which embraced Blacks, Hispanics and what Theodore Parker had called the "Perishing and Dangerous Classes" in its animosity.

By 1980 most of this conservative resentment focused on the party in power, and especially upon President Carter who had promised to give the government back to the people and whose appeal had been so ostentatiously moral. Jimmy Carter's campaign commitments to social welfare, to a gradual abatement of the Cold War and a decrease in the military budget proved illusory and so he lost the "down-and-outs" and liberals who had helped elect him. That he had made those commitments at all angered conservatives who thought him "soft" on criminals and communists. Unable to balance the budget or halt inflation, Carter also failed to inspire public support for his energy programs—a support which was necessary if he was to circumvent Congressional delays. There was disillusionment, too, with the day-by-day conduct of the Presidential office. The enforced resignation of Budget Director Bert Lance, whose political and financial integrity was questioned by press and public alike; the illiberal policies of another of his Georgia associates, Attorney General Griffin Bell; Carter's abrupt dismissal of that outspoken champion of women's rights, Bella Abzug; and the 1979 reshuffling of his entire cabinet conjured up recollections of the Nixon Administration.

By the end of his first year in office, opinion polls indicated that less than one half of the American people thought Jimmy Carter an effective leader; by the middle of his third year, that sobering figure slipped to under one third. It would take an external force—the Iranian hostage crisis—to reverse somewhat ambiguously his fall from favor.

Carter's Foreign Policy

ONE HUNDRED AND FIFTY YEARS ago that greatest of all interpreters of democracy, Alexis de Tocqueville, wrote with reference to the United States, "Foreign politics demand scarcely any of those qualities which are peculiar to democracy. They require, on the contrary, the perfect use of almost all those in which it is deficient. Democracy is favorable to the increase of the internal resources of the state; it diffuses wealth and comfort, promotes public spirit, and fortifies the respect for law in all classes of society. All these advantages which have only an indirect influence over the relations one people bears to another. But a democracy can only with great difficulty regulate the details of an important undertaking, persevere in a fixed design and work out its execution in spite of serious obstacles."

These observations had not, on the whole, proved valid for the conduct of American policy during most of the nineteenth and the first half of the twentieth century. But in the second half of the twentieth century a long series of miscalculations, vacillations and blunders had brought the conduct of foreign policy into general disrepute at home and abroad: misguided intervention in Guatemala, the Dominican Republic and Cuba, the intervention of the CIA in the internal affairs of a score of nations throughout the globe, the readiness to use foreign "aid" for political purposes, hostility to the People's Republic of China and the stubborn insistence over a twenty-year period that the real China was the island of Taiwan, the exacerbation of the Cold War and Russia and, to climax it all, the agonizing castastrophe of the ten-year war in Vietnam and Cambodia. By the close of the seventies, judicious students of American foreign policy like George Kennan and Hans Morgenthau, who did not see eye to eye on most matters, could agree that American foreign policy was a shambles and that it had forfeited respect at home and abroad.

Did the decline of American prestige and authority reflect a failure in leadership or did it demonstrate that the rivalry between the Communist and non-Communist worlds had become so acrimonious, competition for alliance with the Third World so intense, the struggle for access to dwindling natural resources so violent, and a world of one hundred and fifty nation-states so disorderly, that the firm and consistent conduct of foreign policy was now unmanageable?

However damaging to American prestige or power the debacles of the sixties and the seventies, the United States could not evade or disown its responsibilities as a world power. Its interests were worldwide and so, too, its commitments. Even the Nixon Administration, which had so little to its credit in the domestic arena and so much to its discredit in the foreign, made striking contributions toward setting on the road to solution two problems which had loomed large on the world horizon: the Cold War with China and the nuclear arms race which threatened to get out of control.

Notwithstanding relentless opposition from what had been the "China Lobby" wing of his own party, Nixon abandoned his earlier position that recognition of the Communist regime in China was a form of "treason." Early in 1972 he took the dramatic step of visiting China for a summit meeting with Mao Tse-tung, where the leaders of both nations agreed to end hostilities and work toward reconciliation. Both Presidents Ford and Carter embraced this new "opening," and pursued it to its gratifying conclusion. On January 1, 1979, Carter was able to proclaim full diplomatic recognition of the People's Republic of China. This involved abrogation of our defense treaty with the island republic on Taiwan—an executive action which raised interesting constitutional questions of the authority of the executive to cancel a treaty originally made with the advice and consent of the Senate.

The new China policy brought immediate rewards in healing a festering sore, reducing the likelihood of Chinese intervention in the affairs of Korea, and encouraging large-scale exports of grain, machinery and technology to what might some day develop into the world's largest market. It brought, at the same time, an exacerbation of relations with the Soviet Union, and the danger that the American government might once again be tempted to "play the China card"—as if the United States was engaged in an international poker game and China was our "card" to play.

Notwithstanding his long history of paranoia toward Communism in its Russian, as in its Chinese form, it was Nixon who—with the guidance and support of Henry Kissinger—made the first effective move for slowing down the ruinous arms race with the Soviet Union. In 1972 came the First Strategic Arms Limitations Treaty (SALT I). If it did not actually reduce armaments, it did place ceilings on the manufacture of some categories of nuclear arms.

In his Inaugural Address Carter had gone even further by pledging his administration "to move toward our ultimate goal—the elimination of nuclear weapons from this earth." No other words of that address excited more enthusiastic approval. Yet it was not until June 1979 that, after protracted negotiations, the President was able to join President Leonid

Brezhnev in Paris to sign a second treaty—SALT II. The terms were, if anything, favorable to the United States, calling on the Soviet Union to reduce its existing stockpile of missiles and bombers, limiting the number of multiple warheads on these, and restricting, for a time, the development of anti-ballistic missile systems. It was a fair and sensible agreement and kept the door open for further compromises and adjustments; a move, said Carter, "that happens to serve the goals both of security and of survival, that strengthens both the military position of the United States and the cause of world peace."

On his return to Washington, the President made a stirring plea for early ratification of the treaty:

The truth of the nuclear age is that the United States and the Soviet Union must live in peace, or we may not live at all. From the beginning of history the fortunes of men and nations were made in unending cycles of war and peace. That pattern must now be broken forever. Between nations armed with thousands of thermonuclear weapons, each one capable of causing unimaginable destruction, there can be no more cycles of war and peace. There can be only peace.

His logic was irrefutable, but the forces supporting the Cold War were no longer susceptible to logic. SALT I had been ratified by an overwhelming majority. But now a coalition of unreconstructed Cold Warriors, spokesmen for the military-industrial complex, and intransigent Republicans eager to win the next presidential race and indifferent to the real needs of defense, launched a campaign to convince the American people that the Soviet Union now had clear military superiority over the United States and that they were prepared to use it. The inability of the United States to intervene to protect its embassy in Iran that same year, and the Russian invasion of Afghanistan the following year, seemed to confirm these fears. Despairing of ratification, the President acknowledged temporary defeat and withdrew the treaty from Senate consideration. He did not, however, abandon it, and in his presidential campaign of 1980 promised to reintroduce it if reelected. That was not to be.

Meantime a host of other problems competed for presidential concern. In the Caribbean and Latin America the new administration found itself in part the prisoner of past mistakes, some of which President Carter was prepared to correct, others which he seemed ready to make worse.

It was the Bay of Pigs which haunted American relations with Castro's Cuba. Neither the Johnson nor the Nixon Administrations were prepared to make amends for that folly or to initiate overtures for the restoration of normal relations; on the contrary the United States persisted in its embargo on trade with Cuba through four administrations. Confronted with what he thought unappeasable American hostility, Castro turned, naturally enough, to the Soviet Union which provided it with essential economic aid and in return exacted from it support for its own ventures in Africa.

Carter did make some tentative gestures toward relaxing hostilities but abandoned these when he "discovered" the presence of three thousand Russian "advisors" who had, as it turned out, been there since 1961. For domestic political purposes, the President made a great show of resentment by staging a display of military strength at the American-held Guantanamo Bay. A more serious contretemps came the next year when Castro, in a show of generosity, released thousands of Cubans from jail or safe-keeping and allowed other thousands to rejoin family and friends in the United States. The result was an influx of tens of thousands of Cubans onto the beaches and ports of Florida, which was unprepared to receive them. The resultant resentment and rioting did little to enhance the Carter Administration's prestige.

Nor were American responses to turbulence in Central America more reassuring. For years the United States had supported the dictatorial and corrupt regime of Anastasio Somoza in Nicaragua, providing it with modern arms and training its officers. When in July 1979 a long-drawn-out revolution finally triumphed and Somoza was forced to flee the country, taking with him a substantial part of its liquid wealth, the Carter Administration did have the wisdom to recognize the new regime. Congress, however, was reluctant to provide any aid for the new government. A similar revolt in San Salvador was also greeted with lukewarm enthusiasm by the State Department.

Panama, by contrast, provided one of the signal diplomatic triumphs of the Carter Administration. Ever since Theodore Roosevelt had boasted in 1902 that "I took Panama," control of that state—which had seceded from Colombia—and of the zone in which the United States built the canal had been a matter of dispute between the two countries. Not surprisingly Panama wanted freedom from American domination, and greater profits from the Canal itself. Changes both in the size and tonnage of ships, and modern strategies of warfare, made control of the Canal of declining importance. President Carter responded to Panamanian demands by negotiating a treaty which restored control over the Canal Zone and the Canal itself to Panama, with full control being established by the year 2000. Against determined opposition both in the Congress and elsewhere, the treaty was ratified in April 1979 by the margin of a single vote.

The large and amorphous issue of human rights was, from the beginning, one of President Carter's major concerns. "Because we are free," he said in his Inaugural Address, "we can never be indifferent to the fate of freedom elsewhere." And, therefore, "our commitment to human rights must be absolute." The vindication of human rights throughout the globe did indeed enlist Carter's energies, but that commitment was not, in fact, "absolute." It was directed toward the Soviet Union and its satellite states; to Cuba, Chile, Argentina and, within limits, to South Africa. Whether for reasons of prudence or of futility, "friendly" countries like South Korea, the Philippines, Indonesia, Brazil and Iran where systematic repression of human rights was notorious and where American influence might have had some impact escaped presidential displeasure. Perhaps the most sobering reflection on the President's advocacy of human rights was that though he had signed treaties committing the United States to the International Declaration of Human Rights, the United Nations Covenant on Civil and Political Rights and the Convenant on Social and Economic Rights, he was unable to persuade the Senate to ratify any of these.

For three administrations, the center of gravity of American policy had been in the Middle East. As that austere publication *The Annual Register* (launched by Edmund Burke in 1758) observed in its 1977 edition, "In terms of time and energy, the deep-rooted problems of the Middle East proved to be the greatest preoccupation for the United States, but a remarkable amount of advice, exhortation, influence and inspiration had not achieved discernible progress." That, as it turned out, was an understatement.

For years the Middle East—a term embracing Egypt as well as the largely Arab nations eastward to Pakistan—had been a powderkeg, exploding from time to time in religious, racial, ideological and economic warfare. Three times war had broken out between Israel and her Arab neighbors, while Palestinian Irredentists, determined to win back part of the homeland which they had lost, conducted relentless guerilla warfare. And because the Arab nations, including those along the southern Mediterranean, controlled what were, in all likelihood, the world's largest oil reserves, almost every industrial nation on the globe had a stake in its politics and its economy.

It was in this turbulent area that the Carter Administration scored its most striking success and suffered its most serious setback. The success, as yet not final, was in the settlement of hostilities between Israel and Egypt which threatened to erupt into another full-scale war. The setback was the revolution in Iran which, after overthrowing the hated Shah, turned the full force of its hostility against the United States which had been responsible for putting the Shah on his throne in the first place, and had been, for long, his staunchest friend and supporter.

After the short war of 1973, Israel had occupied Egyptian territory in the Sinai Peninsula and proposed to establish permanent settlements and military outposts there. It was a threat which Egypt could not accept and whose persistence, therefore, promised a revival of hostilities as soon as the Arab states felt strong enough to renew the attack on that nation which they had sworn to destroy. Clearly the United States, largely responsible for the creation of an independent Israel, and with the largest Jewish population of any nation on the globe, could not stand aside from this crisis. By a dazzling "shuttle diplomacy" between Cairo and Jerusalem, Secretary Kissinger had succeeded in persuading the opponents at least to mark time. When Carter came to office, the time was running out. Then in a dramatic gesture, President Sadat of Egypt made a surprise trip to Jerusalem in November 1977. Early in 1978 Carter flew to Egypt to discuss with President Sadat a solution to what appeared to be an intractable problem, and there, Anwar Sadat committed himself to the principle that in return for formal recognition, Israel should restore territory seized from Egypt and recognize the "legitimate rights" of the Palestinians to participate in the settlement of their future. This

was followed some months later by a dramatic invitation to
President Sadat and Prime Minister Begin of Israel to meet
with Carter at his presidential retreat, Camp David, for a final
effort at resolving a conflict which threatened not only the life
of the two contending nations but the peace of the world. After
two weeks of intensive negotiation the three leaders emerged
on September 17, 1978, with a series of agreements which
promised peace. It took another six months before the two
nations were prepared to sign the actual treaty—an event
which took place on March 26 at the White House. None of
the other Arab nations, however, were prepared to embrace
this solution, so the prospect of permanent peace remained
uncertain.

The revolution in Iran, in part caused by United States
policy, came, nevertheless, as a surprise. It was the United
States which had been instrumental, back in 1953, in restoring
the Shah of Iran to his throne; thereafter we had been the
Shah's most loyal supporter. After all, we depended on Iran
for oil and looked to Iran and Saudi Arabia to counterbalance
Soviet influence in the Middle East and therefore overlooked
the tyranny and torture which distinguished the Shah's regime.
The Shah, on the other hand, depended on the United States
for some one-and-a-half billion dollars' worth of armaments.
When a popular revolution, inspired by the revered religious
leader Ayatollah Khomeini, toppled the Shah from his throne,
he became an exile. It was while living in Mexico that the
Shah applied for admission to the United States for cancer
treatment. Though warned by the American Embassy in
Teheran that admission of the Shah to the United States might
bring retaliation, the Administration decided to go along
with the recommendation of Republican statesmen like Henry
Kissinger and David Rockefeller and admit him.

Retaliation was swift. Militant Iranian "students"—given a
free hand by the new Iranian government—seized the American Embassy and took some fifty of its members hostage.
President Carter responded by freezing all Iranian assets in the
United States and expelling Iranian diplomats, thus breaking
off diplomatic relations. The United Nations condemned the
Iranian kidnapping and the World Court pronounced it illegal.
All in vain! The Iranians became, every day, more intransigent
and their terms for the release of the hostages—an American
apology, return of all the Shah's wealth in America and re-

sumption of military supplies—more uncompromising. Desperate for action, President Carter authorized a rescue mission in early 1980. It failed both in its primary and its secondary purpose. It failed to rescue the hostages and it failed to revive President Carter's declining popularity.

The Iranian revolution, with its threat to the oil supply and to the stability of the Middle East, created apprehension in Russia as well as in the United States. This was not unexpected. Iran bordered on Afghanistan and Pakistan, both Islamic countries, the one co-terminous with China, the other barring the road to India. The Soviet Union had long held an interest in each. The possibility of a volatile Islamic anti-communism spreading across this vast territory, or penetrating into the Moslem areas of Russia, was alarming. Late in 1979 the Soviet Union reacted with an invasion of Afghanistan, designed to stabilize a situation rapidly getting out of control. Because the Afghans fought back, rather than acquiescing, the episode quickly took on the character of Communist imperialism and terrorism.

President Carter denounced the invasion as a blatant violation of international law and a grave threat to peace and cancelled American participation in the Olympics which were to be held in Moscow. It had, he said, "lifted the scales from his eyes" and confronted the United States with the most serious threat to world peace since the Second World War. There was widespread support for this view on Capitol Hill; even liberals like Senators Muskie and Church joined in the chorus of denunciation of such "international cannibalism." The consequences were fateful. The Carter Administration, which had made sincere attempts to mitigate the ravages of the Cold War, now repented of its moderation, resumed the Cold War and revived the arms race.

The 1980 Election

TOTALITARIAN GOVERNMENTS are not troubled by elections—only by revolutions; Parliamentary governments can generally manage to stave off elections until such time as seems propitious for them. These luxuries are not available to government or administration in the United States. The Presidential elections of 1980 could not have come at a more inauspicious time for the Carter Administration. Inflation was running at twelve percent; unemployment had climbed to over six million; the budget appeared to be permanently in deficit; oil prices had skyrocketed and promised to go higher; the conduct of foreign affairs was rarely effective, often futile—the most dramatic proof of this was the continued captivity of the hostages in Iran. Critics at home and abroad persuaded themselves that the United States could no longer be relied on to pursue clear or consistent policies; and Carter himself commanded neither the affection nor the respect which he had inspired four years earlier.

The 1980 campaign began fully one year early, and dragged its tortuous way through primaries, conventions, and polls against the background of a Niagaralike flow of speeches, almost all of which were addressed to prejudice and fear rather than to issues and solutions.

With the President's prestige (as revealed in polls not always accurate) lower even than that of Nixon after Watergate, Senator Edward Kennedy thought the prospects bright for taking over leadership of the party and the nation. The political signs were auspicious; not only did Senator Kennedy bear a name which had a certain magic, but he had himself, in three terms of the Senate, achieved an enviable reputation for his advocacy of the Roosevelt-Kennedy brand of liberalism. He was, in addition, an eloquent speaker and a skillful politician. He had not, however, taken sufficient account of two factors which were, in the end, to frustrate his candidacy: the memory of the tragedy of Chappaquiddick which now rose to haunt him, and public fear of his outspoken liberalism—a term which now, for the first time in our history, had become pejorative. State endorsements of anti-abortion legislation and of capital punishment, state and local hostility to busing blacks and whites to each other's schools, state reaction to more enlightened, but expensive, anti-pollution and environmental laws and a widespread revolt against taxes, all dramatized the growing impatience with "liberal" reform and the growth of governmental regulation. Thus Kennedy, even if he was forgiven for Chappaquiddick, would have to swim against the conservative tide. The Democratic primaries proved him unsuccessful. President Carter was to stand for the party.

The prospects for the Republicans looked bright, and a dozen candidates were ready to embrace them: ex-Governor Reagan of California, ex-Governor John Connally of Texas, former

Congressman and Director of the Central Intelligence Agency George Bush, and Robert Dole, 1976 Vice-Presidential candidate, among them; with ex-President Ford standing modestly in the wings awaiting a curtain call. In the end, the nomination went to Ronald Wilson Reagan, former sports announcer, actor, and two-term Governor of California.

CHAPTER 30

The Reagan Years

The Elections

RAISED IN SMALL TOWNS in Illinois, Ronald Reagan, in his early years, seemed a confirmed Democrat: he had voted four times for FDR and, in his own words, "bled for liberal causes." It was during the late 1940s that he began to move politically to the right and, by the mid-1950s, while president of the Screen Actors Guild, the major union representing Hollywood talent, he had moved all the way to the right, warning against big government, high taxes and an encroaching Communism. In the mid-sixties a group of farsighted Republican Californian businessmen picked—and packaged—Reagan to challenge the incumbent Democratic governor. Easily elected to two terms as governor, Reagan in office turned out to be more of a pragmatic compromiser than his rhetoric had foretold. Eventually, however, his philosophy was to catch up with his rhetoric.

Reagan was not the only candidate running against incumbent Jimmy Carter. The labels "Democrat" and "Republican" had meant little during the election of 1976. The prospect of yet another meaningless choice between the two major parties' candidates encouraged small-party and independent contenders to enter the field. Three of them—Barry Commoner, a champion of environmental protection; Edward Clark, a self-styled Libertarian in the tradition of philosopher-scientist Herbert Spencer; and Ellen McCormack, an activist in the anti-abortion movement—offered no threat to the major parties. The fourth, John Anderson of Illinois, a Republican congressman, ran as an Independent. Thoughtful and eloquent, Anderson won support from liberals, especially among academics and the young. Largely because Americans are reluctant to "throw away" their votes, Anderson ultimately garnered a surprisingly low seven percent of the vote, enough to qualify for post-election public financing but not seriously to influence the outcome.

With Carter and Reagan seemingly not far apart on most major issues, the campaign came to depend on popular impressions of leadership. Though most Americans saw Carter as a man of intelligence and integrity, they also viewed him as lacking the ability to communicate his ideas or to lead Congress or the nation. Capitalizing on these perceptions, Reagan decried Carter's "failures" to deal with the economy—although in retrospect, he dealt better with it than Reagan was to do; with the hostage crisis in Iran—although in the end, every one of the hostages came home unharmed; and with the preservation of the military strength of America—although she remained the strongest nation on the globe. Carter retaliated by charging Reagan with simplistic solutions to complex economic and domestic problems and warned that his three major objectives—a substantial military buildup, a massive tax cut and a balanced budget—were mutually incompatible. But Americans were tired of complexity and doubt and eager for simple solutions: in an election that turned on personalities more than on ideas, Ronald Reagan's mastery of television's techniques gave him an inestimable advantage.

So in 1980, as in 1976, voters again rejected the incumbent in favor of an "outsider" who promised more dynamic leadership. In contrast, however, to the 1976 contest in which Carter narrowly defeated Ford, the 1980 result was a landslide: only twice since the Civil War had Presidents been denied re-election by a larger popular vote—Taft in 1912 and Hoover in 1932. Though the turnout was the lowest since 1948, with only 53 percent of voters going to the polls, the Reagan victory was impressive. Even if Carter had won every vote that went to Anderson, Reagan would still have won with more than 300 electoral votes.

Now, too, for the first time in a quarter of a century, the Republicans, who picked up 12 seats, controlled the Senate. Four of the six liberals who had been prime targets of the conservatives (Senators Birch Bayh of Indiana, John Culver of Iowa, George McGovern of South Dakota, and Frank Church of Idaho) were defeated—a stunning victory for the "new conservatism." In the House, the rightward movement of the electorate and Reagan's long coattails, cost the Democrats a net loss of 33 seats. Although the Democrats still held a technical majority there, the combination of 192 Republicans and more than 30 mostly Southern and avowedly conservative Democrats—or "Boll Weevils"—augured well for the new President's legislative proposals.

While the 1980 elections did not define a fundamental political realignment, they did indicate a widespread conservative trend: a leader considered well to the right for his support of Barry Goldwater in 1964 was moving into the White House. If he had toned down, he had not abandoned the views which had first brought him to political prominence. Reagan's most avid supporters belonged to the so-called "New Right" or, as they themselves preferred, "neo-conservative" camp—a movement comprised largely of middle and upper–middle class voters who thought themselves over-taxed in order to pay for misguided "liberal" experiments. This New Right was distinguished from traditional conservatism—for which economic issues are paramount—by its passionate concern for such social and moral issues as school prayer and abortion. Ever since the Supreme Court ended racial segregation, imposed fair political representation in the states, approved such "socialist" legislation as the Tennessee Valley Authority and Social Security, this economic-moralistic "fundamentalism" had developed an aggressive vitality. Thus the Equal Rights Amendment—explicitly providing that "Equality of rights under the law shall not be denied or abridged by the United States or by any State on account of sex"—and the Supreme Court's decision in *Roe* v. *Wade* (1973)—striking down state anti-abortion laws as violations of the right to privacy—generated hostility that was activist, tenacious, and, in the case of the anti-abortion movement, found expression in numerous acts of terrorism against abortion clinics.

One of the most ominous features of "neo-conservatism" was the emergence of a "Christian" Right, ominous because it introduced religious controversies directly into politics, something Americans had avoided since the campaign against Al Smith in 1928. Popular evangelists formed a loose alliance of Christian Fundamentalists with political conservatives. The religious "Right" registered new voters, mobilized clergy, raised money, and appealed to the public through their own wide television networks. Relying on the Bible to guide their political activity, they agitated for voluntary prayer in public schools, federal aid to private (denominational) schools and the elimination of the theory of evolution from school textbooks. What they opposed was as significant as what they proposed: federal intervention to prevent racial or sexual discrimination in private schools, abortion, homosexual rights, and in some areas, the Equal Rights Amendment. By far the most visible of these groups was the Moral Majority, headed by the Reverend Jerry Falwell, which by the elections of 1984 claimed some five million members.

Although President Reagan had begun to experience some difficulties with Congress over the deficit, and aid to the *contras* in Nicaragua, as his first term drew to a close, the most memorable feature of the presidential campaign of 1984 was the predictability of its outcome. Responsibility for failure of policies or programs rarely stuck to Reagan—a condition that caused critics to dub him the "Teflon President." Moreover, after four years, many Americans felt themselves to be better off: inflation, which had lingered in the double digits, had fallen to eight percent; unemployment figures, although including only those still actively seeking work, declined, and employment itself increased. Americans welcomed what they saw as a return to "normalcy." The President had survived an assassination attempt with courage and magnanimity and he had faced the Russian Bear with defiance. Now, at last, after the disillusionment of the Vietnam War, Americans were achieving a new self-confidence.

Even if Reagan had not maintained much of his popular appeal, it is unlikely that the Democratic candidate, former Vice-President Walter Mondale, could have emerged victorious. Though thoughtful, experienced, resolute and honorable, he was an indifferent orator and did not come across well on the television screen. Moreover, his honesty in insisting that the growing national deficit would inevitably require an increase in taxes made him seem "a prophet of doom."

Although the race between Reagan and Mondale contained few surprises, the campaign itself is historically interesting for three features. First, it gave us, in Jesse Jackson, the first Black candidate for the presidency. Jackson, unfortunately, was no Martin Luther King. Although he sought to form a "Rainbow Coalition" of all races, he proved unable to do so: instead, he antagonized the traditional southern White voter and, by his rhetorical violence, many northerners as well. He failed equally to appeal to the Hispanics, who had heretofore been faithful to the Democratic party but were now moving over to the Republican side. A second innovation was the choice of Geraldine Ferraro, three-term Congresswoman from New York, as Mondale's running mate—the first time that any major party had selected a woman for that position. Although this bold act excited a lot of interest, it failed to garner substantial support for Mondale's faltering campaign; indeed, that gesture appeared to antagonize as many voters as it appeased. The third feature was quantitative, but with qualitative implications: the unprecedented sums of money expended in the election. The official estimate was something over two hundred million dollars spent by the two candidates—by far the larger part by the Republicans. When, in 1896, Mark Hanna had admitted to spending something over three million dollars to defeat William Jennings Bryan, champions of democracy had been alarmed at the implications of that precedent. Their premonitions were justified; now it was taken for granted that money was the prime essential.

As in 1980, the outcome of the election was never seriously in doubt. When the votes were counted it was clear that Reagan—rather than the Republican party—had won an overwhelming victory. The Electoral College vote was 525 to Mondale's 13. Though the discrepancy in the popular vote was by no means so great, it was decisive: some 52 million voted for Reagan, only 36 million for Mondale. Obviously much of the southern vote, traditionally Democratic, had swung again to Reagan, and a substantial part of the labor vote as well. That this represented a permanent shift in loyalties is improbable. Democrats actually picked up two seats in the Senate, continued to control the House, and held more than two-thirds of state governorships and over one-half of the legislatures. Nor is it clear that the vote represented a lasting ideological shift in American politics. Individual presidents may confess ideologies—as does President Reagan—but the American temperament is practical. It votes programs and policies or personalities, rather than ideas. In that lies one of the secrets of the strength of the Union. A nation as large and diversified as the United States cannot afford ideological conflicts; the struggle between Slavery and Emancipation made that clear.

The Reagan Administration

THE GREATEST ASSET Ronald Reagan brought to the elections and to the presidency was his personality. Not since Eisenhower had a President enjoyed such general popularity as did Reagan. But that popularity was, like that of Harry Truman and even Eisenhower himself, not so much a tribute to accomplishments as to character and personality. Reagan's simplicity, affability, humor, and mastery of the television medium won him almost limitless popular affection. Employment and the deficit might mount, but the general public did not seem to mind too much as long as they perceived the President as a man who spoke their language. What Ronald Reagan could do better than almost anyone else was to present himself as a good man who could make Americans "feel good about their country." Where William Jennings Bryan had gloried in the title "The Great Commoner," Reagan was to become the "Great Communicator": as with Bryan it was the rhetoric and the eloquence and not the substance of the communication that proved most significant.

The lavish Reagan inaugural in 1981 was reputed to be the most expensive in history, as the election itself had been. Clearly the advent of the Reagans brought a tone of opulence to the White House. This was to be an administration not only of the rich but of those rich unashamed to display their wealth. Formally, they might adopt Adam Smith as their patron saint, but their true philosopher was Thorstein Veblen, whom few had read, and fewer approved.

If coming to Washington began in a fairy tale setting for the new President and his wife, Nancy, the private demons of an unbalanced youngster, John W. Hinckley, tumbled them back to reality. On March 30, 1981, as the President and his entourage were leaving a Washington hotel, Hinckley fired several shots in their direction. Shot in the chest, Reagan underwent two hours of emergency surgery. That he was able to return to the White House in less than two weeks was testimony to his courage and his resiliency, and deservedly added to his popularity. It was at this time, too, that public opinion largely critical of Mrs. Reagan for her expensive tastes began to change: not only did she win admiration for her courage in the midst of the crisis and for her obvious devotion to her husband, but later for her dedication to fighting drug abuse. Curiously enough, the tragedy brought no abatement of either the Reagans' or the general public's long-time opposition to gun-control legislation.

Reagan's Domestic Policies

THE PRESIDENT'S OVERARCHING GOAL in the arena of domestic policy was to reduce the role of the federal government, a policy traditionally associated with the party of Jefferson, not that of Lincoln. Confident that individual initiative would produce an economic revival in the private sector, Reagan early avowed commitment to lower taxes, a cut in domestic (non-defense) spending, the liquidation of administrative regulations, and an increased role for the states. In his view, government was the problem, not the solution. The basic obligations of the federal government, as Reagan perceived them, were limited to providing a strong military defense and a "safety net" for the truly weak and needy. He quickly found it impossible simultaneously to reduce taxes, increase defense spending, and balance the budget. Inevitably his deficits proved the largest in American history.

President Reagan's first priority was to balance the budget and lower inflation, and he enjoyed early success in getting his legislative program for these enacted. There was broad bipartisan support for the idea of doing "something" about an economy seemingly mired in chronic high inflation, high interest rates and high unemployment—but little agreement on what thing. The Reagan Administration was able to build upon these sentiments by making innovative use of "reconciliation" procedures intended to strengthen the role of Congress in the budgetary process, a program quite unnecessary as the Constitution had already assigned Congress the primary role. David A. Stockman, Reagan's Budget Director, was the architect of a strategy which truncated and streamlined the legislative process, supposedly limiting the opportunities for interest groups to make their cases. Cuts were made in both authorization and appropriation bills, and these cuts, affecting nearly all federal domestic programs, were packaged by the House and Senate

Budget Committees into a single bill sent to the floor under strict debate limits. In effect this pretty well flouted the Constitutional mandate that all appropriations are to originate in the lower House. But, in any case, in a single vote—for or against the President's program—each house passed legislation mandating massive, across-the-board cuts in all areas of non-defense spending: a total of $130.6 billion in reductions in the fiscal years 1981–84.

Once the Reagan Administration achieved these spending reductions, it built on that momentum to make the case for massive (if selective) tax reductions. By the middle of the summer of 1981, Reagan was able to sign a bill cutting individual income taxes by twenty-five percent, improving business depreciation writeoffs and providing incentives to personal savings. It was projected that the new law would reduce tax revenues by $750 billion over the next five years. A substantial part of these were at the expense of the poor, of social services, of the environment, and of education.

All this was natural enough in a period of growing disillusionment with the Welfare State. The primary concern was no longer those whom Franklin Roosevelt had called "forgotten"—the "ill-housed, ill-clad, ill-nourished," and, he might have added, "the ill." It had shifted now to national security, which in some curious fashion came to mean not Social Security, as under FDR, but "military" security. The link between individual welfare and the government's responsibility for "general welfare" as set forth in the Constitution was conveniently ignored. Unemployment, to be sure, declined to some eight million, but this was in part because those who had given up any hope of finding employment were no longer counted. Infant mortality had declined, but while it was below ten per thousand for white babies, it was twenty per thousand for black babies. New housing "starts" were rising, but every major city acknowledged that its slums spread like a miasma. All this was thought necessary to ensure peace, but the cost of peace itself went up inexorably: it cost more to stay at peace in 1984 than it had cost to fight a global war in 1944!

As the national budget mounted to a thousand billion, the deficit to two hundred and fifty billion, the foreign trade deficit to some sixty billion dollars a year, and as the United States became the greatest debtor nation on the globe, Congress took alarm. Some began to contemplate with sympathy Thomas Jefferson's proposition that as no one generation had a right to bind its successors, or to impose heavy burdens upon them, all public debts should be paid off or wiped out every twenty years. Each new generation, then, could start with a clean slate! A somewhat more practical, if unnecessary, proposal was a Constitutional amendment which would, quite simply, forbid a deficit—or deficit spending; an amendment which, if passed, would probably have had the force of a New Year's Resolution. Another, and on the surface more tempting, solution was the Gramm-Rudman bill which required statutory limits to the federal deficit for five years, and mandated automatic cuts if that limit was breached. Under that proposal—eventually enacted (but then held in part unconstitutional)—half the cuts would come from domestic programs—with Social Security exempted—and half from the military. The Gramm-Rudman bill boasted many loopholes, and it seemed improbable that, even if revised, the budget would in fact be balanced within the foreseeable future.

Reagan's Foreign Policy

IN THE REALM of foreign policy, President Reagan's leadership represented both a resurgence of chauvinistic nationalism and a return to the intellectual simplifications of the Cold War. His presidency demonstrated how enduring were the historic forces of American exceptionalism. Reagan exalted the idea of America as a special land with a special history and a special destiny—a "city on a hill." Americans were seen to be "God's chosen people;" their country, "the promised land;" their government, "the last best hope of earth"—all concepts, to be sure, nourished by earlier generations. Reagan came to office vowing that the United States would once again command the respect of both adversaries and allies, which, he asserted, previous administrations had frittered away. His method was to be tough, and to build up the military.

Reagan's foreign policy views were dominated by ideological anti-Communism and a "hard-line" approach to the Soviet Union. As he saw it, the world was divided between two great ideological and power groups, one dedicated to freedom, the other to slavery. The United States represented the first, while the Soviet Union represented the second. According to Reagan, Communism, especially the Soviet variety (for he seemed to have no trouble with Communism in Hungary, Rumania, or

China) was not only dedicated to the enslavement of men but was godless and immoral. The Soviet Union, he believed, was engaged in ceaseless aggrandizement; it could never be relied upon to keep its word; it made a mockery of international law and human dignity; and it trusted only force. Reagan's focus upon Communism as the inveterate enemy, and the USSR as the implacable foe was scarcely disturbed by developments which to many produced a world less easy to paint in black and white. Among these were the long-standing Sino-Soviet conflict, the US rapprochement with China, Third World neutralism, the emergence of new power centers in the Middle East, the reluctance of some members of the "Free World" to respect the freedom of their own people—for example South Africa and Chile. Looming behind all this, was the threat of a world population doubling every fifty years, and the steady erosion of its natural resources. But from Reagan's perspective America's main problem in the international arena was to combat the expansion of Soviet power around the world; to substitute diplomacy or reliance on international arbitration at the expense of the exercising of power might lead Americans into a trap from which they could not extricate themselves.

This simplistic world view was blind to the forces of nationalism, particularly in the Middle East and Central America; ignored the unique characteristics of situations in almost every country; and promoted polarizing approaches to local and regional disputes. This perspective, furthermore, encouraged a tendency to tolerate human rights abuses committed by dictatorial but anti-Communist regimes like those in Chile, Haiti, Pakistan, the Philippines, and South Korea, while registering outrage against those committed by leftist regimes, like the Soviet Union and Castro's Club. The "Kirkpatrick doctrine"—after Jeane Kirkpatrick, Reagan's Ambassador to the United Nations—postulated a distinction between "totalitarian" (Communist) and "authoritarian" governments. Authoritarian regimes, it asserted, held out more hope of reform and were better for American interests than totalitarian, or Communist, regimes, which inevitably became a menace to their neighbors. Even in 1986, after he had looked sympathetically on the removal of right-wing pro-American dictators—Duvalier in Haiti and Marcos in the Philippines—President Reagan refused to abandon the Kirkpatrick doctrine.

From the outset of the Reagan Administration "détente," like "liberalism," became a pejorative term, and the President's rhetoric, increasingly combative, reflected a breakdown in civility. Nonetheless, Reagan's hawkishness was tempered by the need to respond to domestic economic concerns and to pressures from more sophisticated European allies. Thus, in April 1981, Reagan yielded to pressure from the farm belt to lift a grain embargo against the USSR—the embargo which Carter had imposed after the invasion of Afghanistan. A similar practicality influenced American policy towards Poland. In December 1981, when the Soviet-selected government of Poland decreed martial law and suspended operation of "Solidarity," that nation's independent trade union, Reagan imposed a series of economic sanctions on both Poland and the USSR. The most damaging of these appeared to be the prohibition of exports for construction of a natural gas pipeline from Siberia to western Europe, but it proved damaging to the United States, not to its intended victims; for it not only penalized American industry but antagonized America's European allies, who instructed their firms to continue to provide the Soviets with essential materials. This setback to relations with non-Communist Europe and pressure from American farmers losing millions of dollars forced the President to beat a retreat from his position. All in all neither American rhetoric nor policies had serious impact on the Polish economy and none on the Soviet.

The central issue of both domestic and foreign policy remained, as it had for many years, the problem of nuclear arms. Though the two superpowers had been military allies in two World Wars, both believed that the other represented a mortal threat. In the flurry of military buildups, both countries refused to recognize that the issue was not one that concerned just them, but one that inevitably concerned the whole of mankind. Negotiations, which might have been carried on through agencies like the United Nations, were left to diplomats of the two superpowers. The two nations were determined to bargain from a position of "strength," which to both meant military rather than economic, social, scientific or even moral strength. President Reagan proved even less willing than his predecessors to negotiate with the Soviets, for he was convinced that only by achieving military superiority would the United States be in a position to influence the outcome of future talks on arms control.

At a time when the two superpowers already controlled some fifty thousand nuclear weapons—sufficient to kill every person on the globe twelve times over—continuous enlargement of nuclear capability might well be seen as a manifestation of contagious insanity. Scientists around the globe offered chilling visions of a world condemned to "nuclear winter," the end of all life as a result of fallout. It was a grudging recognition of this protest, coupled with Congressional reluctance to continue to vote billions on the controversial but unproven MX missile and similar programs, which persuaded President Reagan to embrace as a substitute for the arms race the so-called "Star Wars" defense program: an anti-nuclear system based on exotic technologies and designed to search out and destroy all incoming offensive weapons. In a televised address to the nation in 1983 Reagan proposed this "Strategic Defense Initiative," which, he implied, would make all existing nuclear missiles "impotent and obsolete." Though critics charged that the system would never be feasible, Congress endorsed a five-year research program which was expected to cost some $30 billion. The long-range program called for trillions.

Concentrating as he did on the "East-West" conflict, Reagan was slow to immerse himself in the problems of the Middle East; however, they soon commanded his attention. The new President did not challenge the accepted Middle-East policies of earlier administrations: an unswerving commitment to the security and survival of Israel and with it support to "moderate" Arab leaders, and protection of the Persian Gulf oil fields from the Soviet Union. Any differences came in the means he chose to further those goals.

At Camp David, President Carter had played a decisive role in promoting a peace between Israel and her neighbors that had achieved a temporary stay against disaster. The Reagan Administration, initially de-emphasizing the problem and later relying on force, proved equally incapable of providing a lasting solution to the intransigent Palestinian problem. Neither was Reagan able to control the increasingly bellicose Middle-East states.

In 1982, determined to create a twenty-five-mile buffer zone between Israel and the Palestinians, Israel's President Menachem Begin launched an invasion of southern Lebanon which in the end continued all the way to the outskirts of Beirut. A special American emissary negotiated an agreement for the gradual withdrawal of both Palestinians and Israelis, but the agreement was doomed from the start. Syrian forces moved in from the north to occupy Beirut; the Palestinians fought every effort to crowd them out of what they considered their ancestral lands; and Lebanon remained in turmoil, teetering on the brink of anarchy.

When, the next year, the situation threatened to get out of hand, Congress supported sending 1,200 Marines to join an international peacekeeping force in Beirut. In October of that year a bomb-laden truck, driven by a Moslem "suicide martyr," crashed through the frail barriers of the American headquarters and exploded, killing 241 Marines as they slept. Two months later, after the first direct clash between American and Syrian forces, the tide turned against further United States military involvement. After Vietnam, Congress was unprepared to let American blood be shed in a protracted and futile conflict whose relation to American interests was murky. The President moved swiftly to "redeploy" US forces to offshore ships. The futility of force seemed about to command general recognition.

It was in the tiny Caribbean island of Grenada, with a population of 113,000, that President Reagan decided to demonstrate that America could still "stand tall." On October 25, 1983 (only two days after the tragic bombing in Beirut), some 4,600 US troops landed in Grenada. The intervention followed a coup in which hard-line Marxists overthrew and subsequently murdered the soft-line Marxist Prime Minister, Maurice Bishop, and was prompted by a request from the Organization of Eastern Caribbean States to reestablish law and order in Grenada, and the perceived need to "rescue" the nearly 1,000 Americans studying at an American-run medical school. Within three days the US had arrested the leaders of the coup and overcome the resistance of a handful of soldiers and some 700 armed Cuban construction workers. By mid-December all American troops except a small peacekeeping force had been evacuated, and the criticism and questions concerning the legality of the venture died down. An American public, still remembering the frustrations of the war in Vietnam and the Iranian hostage crisis, rejoiced in a return to the style of the "Rough Riders."

Heroic as the Reagan intervention seemed to certain of the Caribbean nations, many of their neighbors in Central America viewed such conduct differently. And if the President's popular appeal and rhetoric continued to please large segments of the American public, his policies towards Central America became a source of serious dissension in and out of Congress and in Europe.

United States interest in Central America had abated since

the heyday of the "Big Stick" and "Dollar Diplomacy" in the early years of the century, but it increased markedly after 1979 when the Sandinistas (named after Augusto Sandino, a national hero of the 1920s and an early foe of US intervention) ended the forty-six-year tyranny of the Somoza family in Nicaragua. That same year, in El Salvador, young military officers toppled a conservative dictatorship. Abandoning the more tempered approach of the Carter Administration, Reagan was soon deeply entangled in the internal struggles of both countries in an attempt to turn what he saw as a Communist tide.

In El Salvador, the moderate government imposed by the military coup gave way rapidly to a right-wing dictatorship. Poor and desperate, many Salvadorans joined the ranks of leftist guerrillas. As the fighting spread, the government relied increasingly on "death squads" responsible for killing thousands of opponents, civilian and military alike. Adhering to the Kirkpatrick doctrine, the President refused to withdraw support from a government so staunchly "anti-Communist." Congress, concerned both with humanitarian issues and increasing American military involvement, finally insisted on progress in human rights as a condition for continued aid. Although fighting persisted, the specter of American soldiers being sent to defend El Salvador against Communist guerrillas faded with the election in 1984 of José Napoleón Duarte, a former President and political moderate.

Nicaragua proved a far more intractable problem. Here the United States chose not to defend a government in power but attempted to topple one that enjoyed wide popular support within its own boundaries. Charging that the Sandinistas, mere pawns of the USSR and Cuba, were attempting to export revolution (a charge made against the United States in the early years of the Republic) and set up a "privileged sanctuary for terrorists and subversives just two days' driving time from Harlingen, Texas," the President suspended the Carter Administration's program of economic aid, and authorized US support—through the CIA—to Nicaraguan exiles fighting against the Sandinistas. Based on Honduras and Costa Rica, these "contras," as they came to be called, numbered some 10,000 men by the summer of 1983, and came to depend heavily on the United States for arms, supplies, money, and military guidance. Many Americans refused to share the President's unqualified support for these Nicaraguan "freedom fighters." While censorship, mismanagement and alleged mistreatment of the Miskito Indians eroded sympathy for the Sandinista regime itself, the *"contras,"* many of them former followers of the Somozas, waged war against civilians and wasted or embezzled the funds sent to them—some illegally—from the United States.

Meantime, the leaders of Mexico, Colombia, and Venezuela sought to negotiate a settlement of the seemingly endless conflict. Reagan dismissed this effort at arbitration out of hand and instead intensified his quasi-war against the Sandinista regime by mining Nicaraguan waters. When Nicaragua brought its case before the World Court, the United States first denied the Court's jurisdiction, then withdrew from the Court itself; two years later the Court handed down a unanimous decision against the United States. Instead, Reagan made money available to the *"contras"*—only presumably limited to non-military activities. When that money ran out—the steam seemed to be running out of the *"contra"* offensive—the President once again displayed his almost matchless effectiveness with Congress by persuading them to vote another hundred million dollars to the *"contras."* The theory behind this continued support was clear: the Sandinistas were supported by the Soviet Union; with that support they might infect the whole of Central America, endanger the Panama Canal, subvert Mexico, and confront the United States at the Rio Grande. It was, needless to say, a fantasy, but with Vietnam now safely in the past the nation seemed ready once again to embrace fantasy.

While the situation in Central America dragged on in its incoherent course, events in the Middle East and the Mediterranean provoked another international crisis, and another flexing of American military muscle.

Throughout the eighties the Middle East provided the locale, its extremist political factions, religious sects, and ethnic groups the source, of an epidemic of terrorist attacks. Because the United States had a special relationship with Israel, she was, almost inevitably, the prime target for such attacks, not only from Palestinians but from fundamentalist Moslems opposed to the growth of Western economic and political imperialism. Terrorism, to be sure, was nothing new. It had, in a sense, been introduced and all but universally accepted with the first mass raids on large civilian populations in the Second World War, beginning with that on Hamburg in 1943 which cost over thirty thousand civilian lives; it was enhanced by the firebombing of great cities like Tokyo, by the dropping of an atomic bomb on Nagasaki, and by the saturation-bombing of Vietnam with seven million tons of bombs in the sixties and seventies. With governments almost everywhere setting the example, it was no wonder that desperate religious or nationalist fanatics should follow suit. By the mid-eighties terrorism had become an almost universal technique of fanatical groups who had no alternative resources with which to vent their anger against nations and peoples they both hated and feared.

Terrorism presented many problems, none more difficult than that of responsibility. Who, after all, was accountable? How were the criminals to be found, how brought to punishment? How guard against attacks which were random and whose sponsorship was for the most part almost undetectable?

In June 1985 a group of hijackers—probably Palestinian or Syrian—boarded a TWA flight from Athens to Rome with 104 Americans aboard; the hijacking was frustrated by American intervention carried through with admirable dispatch and effectiveness. That October a cruise ship, the *Achille Lauro,* was boarded, Americans held hostage, and one murdered. Here too the criminals were apprehended. Increasingly President Reagan focused on Libya and its flamboyant head of state, Colonel Qadaffi as responsible for stimulating international terrorism. After simultaneous terrorist attacks on the airports at Rome and Vienna in December 1985 killed and wounded 110 victims, the US launched an economic boycott against Libya. Dismissing Colonel Qadaffi's claim that the Gulf of Sidra was Libyan waters, in March 1986 the President ordered military maneuvers in the Gulf, thus provoking a Libyan response; this, in turn, led to a US attack on Libyan missile sites and the sinking of two Libyan patrol ships. A month later, after the explosion of a bomb in a West German nightclub frequented by American military personnel was linked to Qadaffi's regime, the United States launched a lethal nighttime air strike against targets in and around the Libyan capital. The aim of such attacks, the Administration asserted, was to make the sponsoring of terrorists too costly. With the exception of Great Britain, few of America's allies supported this latest display of military might, and many Americans likewise expressed concern that America, in the words of Senator Lowell Weicker of Connecticut, had climbed into the "same gutter" as Colonel Qadaffi. Yet, while thousands of citizens, fearful of terrorist reprisals, canceled their European and Mediterranean vacations, the Administration's actions clearly gratified the general public, who took vicarious pride in Reagan's toughness and effectiveness.

After six years in office President Reagan's popularity was still unabated, and his influence on his own party and on recalcitrant members of the Democratic party all but irresistible. In most matters of both foreign and domestic affairs he had his own way: even his most controversial policies—those associated with "Star Wars" for example, or with intervention in Central America—commanded popular approval and Congressional acquiescence, and his most dubious appointees were routinely confirmed. He had, it seemed, imposed his pejorative meaning of the term "liberalism" on a substantial body of the people and persuaded them to accept—in theory at least—his concept of "conservatism"—one closer to that of Herbert Spencer than to that of Edmund Burke. He had vindicated—again, in principle—his repudiation of the "Welfare State," his concept of national security based primarily on military superiority, his philosophy of States' Rights—a philosophy inspired by nostalgia rather than by constitutional law—and he had some success in limiting the effectiveness of the national government while strengthening that of state government. And, even though the actual budget was more grossly unbalanced than at any previous time in our history, Reagan had achieved an emotional, rhetorical, and almost constitutional endorsement of that darling objective which gave all those who contemplated it a sense of achievement. Yet while all these objectives had been accepted, none had been realized. The "Welfare State" was still pretty much as FDR had left it, "security"—as a military objective—was still far in the future, and Americans had never before felt so insecure. Thanks to the impact of militarization on the economy—and to the American passion for Bigness—government, economy, finance, and science itself were more highly centralized than ever before. Contemplating all of this President Reagan might have concluded, with Emerson, that "things are in the saddle and ride mankind."

Suggested Readings

I • GENERAL

1. Large Co-operative Works

Adams, James Truslow, ed. / THE DICTIONARY OF AMER-
ICAN HISTORY, 5 vols.

Boorstin, Daniel J., ed. / THE CHICAGO HISTORY OF CIV-
ILIZATION. In progress.

Commager, H. S., and Morris, Richard B., eds. / THE NEW
AMERICAN NATION, c. 50 vols.

Gabriel, Ralph, ed. / THE PAGEANT OF AMERICA, 15 vols.

Gannett, Lewis, ed. / THE MAINSTREAM OF AMERICA
SERIES, 12 vols.

Hart, A. B., ed. / THE AMERICAN NATION: A HISTORY,
28 vols.

Johnson, Allen, and Malone, Dumas, eds. / THE DICTIO-
NARY OF AMERICAN BIOGRAPHY, 22 vols.

—— *and Nevins, Allan, eds.* / THE CHRONICLES OF
AMERICA, 56 vols.

Skinner, Constance L., and others, eds. / THE RIVERS OF
AMERICA, c. 50 vols.

2. Major Individual Works

Beard, Charles and Mary / THE RISE OF AMERICAN CIV-
ILIZATION, 3 vols.

Morison, Samuel E., and Commager, H. S. / THE GROWTH
OF THE AMERICAN REPUBLIC, 2 vols.

3. Documentary and Handbooks

Commager, H. S., ed. / DOCUMENTS OF AMERICAN HIS-
TORY

——, *ed.* / LIVING IDEAS IN AMERICA

Hart, A. B. / AMERICAN HISTORY TOLD BY CONTEMPO-
RARIES, 5 vols.

Morris, Richard B., ed. / THE ENCYCLOPEDIA OF AMERICAN
HISTORY

U.S. Department of Commerce / HISTORICAL STATISTICS OF
THE UNITED STATES, COLONIAL TIMES TO 1957

Important Works on Special Aspects of American History

Allen, Harry C. / GREAT BRITAIN AND THE UNITED STATES:
A HISTORY OF ANGLO-AMERICAN RELATIONS, 1783–
1952

Bailey, T. A. / DIPLOMATIC HISTORY OF THE AMERICAN
PEOPLE

Bemis, Samuel F. / DIPLOMATIC HISTORY OF THE UNITED
STATES

Brooks, Van Wyck / MAKERS AND FINDERS: A HISTORY OF
THE WRITER IN AMERICA, 5 vols.

Commons, John R., and others / HISTORY OF LABOR IN
THE UNITED STATES, 4 vols.

Curti, Merle / GROWTH OF AMERICAN THOUGHT

Davidson, Marshall / LIFE IN AMERICA, 2 vols.

Gabriel, Ralph / THE COURSE OF AMERICAN DEMOCRATIC
THOUGHT

Handlin, Oscar / UPROOTED: GREAT MIGRATIONS THAT
MADE THE AMERICAN PEOPLE

Hansen, Marcus / THE IMMIGRANT IN AMERICAN HISTORY

Kirkland, Edward C. / HISTORY OF AMERICAN ECONOMIC
LIFE

Kohn, Hans / AMERICAN NATIONALISM

Larkin, Oliver / ART AND LIFE IN AMERICA

Link, Arthur S. / AMERICAN EPOCH: A HISTORY OF THE
UNITED STATES SINCE THE 1890's

McLaughlin, A. C. / CONSTITUTIONAL HISTORY OF THE
UNITED STATES

Nevins, Allan / AMERICAN SOCIAL HISTORY AS SEEN BY
BRITISH TRAVELERS

Parrington, V. L. / MAIN CURRENTS OF AMERICAN
THOUGHT, 3 vols.

Pochmann, Henry / GERMAN CULTURE IN AMERICA

Spiller, Robert E., and others / LITERARY HISTORY OF THE
UNITED STATES, 3 vols.

Stokes, Anson Phelps / CHURCH AND STATE IN AMERICA, 3
vols.

Sweet, W. W. / STORY OF RELIGIONS IN AMERICA

Swisher, Carl / AMERICAN CONSTITUTIONAL HISTORY
Wittke, Carl / WE WHO MADE AMERICA
Wright, C. W. / ECONOMIC HISTORY OF THE UNITED STATES

5. Magazines
AMERICAN HERITAGE, ed. by Bruce Catton

II • THE COLONIAL PERIOD

1. General
Becker, Carl / BEGINNINGS OF THE AMERICAN PEOPLE
Boorstin, Daniel J. / THE AMERICANS: THE COLONIAL EX-
PERIENCE
Brebner, John B. / NORTH ATLANTIC TRIANGLE
Bridenbaugh, Carl / CITIES IN THE WILDERNESS; (with Jes-
sica Bridenbaugh) REBELS AND GENTLEMEN: PHILA-
DELPHIA IN THE AGE OF FRANKLIN
Fiske, John / NEW FRANCE AND NEW ENGLAND; DUTCH
AND QUAKER COLONIES IN AMERICA; OLD VIRGINIA AND
HER NEIGHBORS; THE BEGINNINGS OF NEW ENGLAND
Nettles, C. P. / ROOTS OF AMERICAN CIVILIZATION
Parkman, Francis / FRANCE AND ENGLAND IN NORTH
AMERICA, especially:
PIONEERS OF NEW FRANCE; JESUITS IN CANADA; LA
SALLE AND THE DISCOVERY OF THE GREAT WEST; A
HALF CENTURY OF CONFLICT; MONTCALM AND WOLFE
Rossiter, Clinton / SEEDTIME OF THE REPUBLIC
Savelle, Max / SEEDS OF LIBERTY

2. Discovery and Exploration
Bakeless, John / THE EYES OF DISCOVERY
Brebner, John B. / EXPLORERS OF NORTH AMERICA
De Voto, Bernard / THE COURSE OF EMPIRE
Fiske, John / THE DISCOVERY OF AMERICA
Lorant, Stefan / THE NEW WORLD
Mirsky, Jeannette / THE WESTWARD CROSSINGS
Radin, Paul / STORY OF THE AMERICAN INDIAN
Rowse, A. L. / THE EXPANSION OF ELIZABETHAN ENGLAND

3. Special Works
Adams, James Truslow / FOUNDING OF NEW ENGLAND
Andrews, Charles M. / COLONIAL FOLKWAYS

Bolton, Herbert E. / THE RIM OF CHRISTENDOM; THE
   SPANISH BORDERLANDS

Jones, Howard Mumford / O STRANGE NEW WORLD:
   AMERICAN CULTURE, THE FORMATIVE YEARS

Miller, Perry / THE NEW ENGLAND MIND, 2 vols.; ERRAND
   INTO THE WILDERNESS

Morison, Samuel E. / BUILDERS OF THE BAY COLONY; THE
   PURITAN PRONAOS

Tyler, Moses Coit / HISTORY OF AMERICAN LITERATURE,
   1607–1765, 2 vols.

Wertenbaker, T. J. / THE FIRST AMERICANS; THE FOUND-
   ING OF AMERICAN CIVILIZATION, 4 vols.

Wright, Louis / THE ATLANTIC CIVILIZATION

4. Biographies

Brockunier, S. H. / THE IRREPRESSIBLE DEMOCRAT: ROGER
   WILLIAMS

Fisher, S. G. / THE TRUE WILLIAM PENN

Morison, Samuel E. / ADMIRAL OF THE OCEAN SEA, 2 vols.

Murdock, Kenneth / INCREASE MATHER

Van Doren, Carl / BENJAMIN FRANKLIN

Winslow, Ola / JONATHAN EDWARDS

III • THE REVOLUTION AND THE MAKING
OF THE CONSTITUTION

1. General: Revolution

Alden, John / THE AMERICAN REVOLUTION

Channing, Edward / HISTORY OF THE UNITED STATES, Vol.
   III

Fisher, S. G. / STRUGGLE FOR AMERICAN INDEPENDENCE, 2
   vols.

Lecky, W. E. H. / THE AMERICAN REVOLUTION

Miller, John C. / ORIGINS OF THE AMERICAN REVOLUTION;
   TRIUMPH OF FREEDOM, 1775–1783

Morris, Richard B. / THE PEACEMAKERS

Namier, Lewis / STRUCTURE OF POLITICS AT THE ACCES-
   SION OF GEORGE III

Nevins, Allan / AMERICAN STATES DURING AND AFTER THE
   REVOLUTION

Trevelyan, George O. / THE AMERICAN REVOLUTION, 6
   vols.

2. Special Aspects of the Revolution

Allen, Gardner / NAVAL HISTORY OF THE AMERICAN REVOLUTION

Becker, Carl / THE DECLARATION OF INDEPENDENCE

Jameson, John F. / AMERICAN REVOLUTION CONSIDERED AS A SOCIAL MOVEMENT

Kraus, Michael / THE ATLANTIC CIVILIZATION

Swiggett, Howard / WAR OUT OF NIAGARA

Tyler, Moses Coit / LITERARY HISTORY OF THE AMERICAN REVOLUTION, 2 vols.

Van Tyne, Claude H. / CAUSES OF THE WAR OF INDEPENDENCE; THE WAR OF INDEPENDENCE

3. The Confederation and the Constitution

Adams, James Truslow / NEW ENGLAND IN THE REPUBLIC

Beard, Charles A. / ECONOMIC INTERPRETATION OF THE CONSTITUTION

Farrand, Max / FATHERS OF THE CONSTITUTION

Fiske, John / THE CRITICAL PERIOD IN AMERICAN HISTORY

Jensen, Merrill / THE NEW NATION

McLaughlin, A. C. / CONFEDERATION AND CONSTITUTION; FOUNDATIONS OF AMERICAN CONSTITUTIONALISM

McMaster, John B. / HISTORY OF THE PEOPLE OF THE UNITED STATES, Vol. I

Roosevelt, Theodore / THE WINNING OF THE WEST, 4 vols.

Schuyler, Robert L. / THE CONSTITUTION OF THE UNITED STATES

Van Doren, Carl / THE GREAT REHEARSAL

Warren, Charles / THE MAKING OF THE CONSTITUTION

4. Biographies

Allen, Herbert S. / JOHN HANCOCK: PATRIOT IN PURPLE

Beveridge, Albert J. / JOHN MARSHALL, 4 vols.

Bowen, Catherine D. / JOHN ADAMS

Boyd, James / MAD ANTHONY WAYNE

Brant, Irving / JAMES MADISON, 6 vols.

Chinard, Gilbert / HONEST JOHN ADAMS

Flexner, James / BENEDICT ARNOLD

Forbes, Esther / PAUL REVERE AND THE WORLD HE LIVED IN

Freeman, Douglas S. / GEORGE WASHINGTON, 6 vols.

Goodman, Nathan / BENJAMIN RUSH

Haraszti, Zoltán / JOHN ADAMS AND THE PROPHETS OF
        PROGRESS
Kimball, Marie / JEFFERSON: THE SCENE OF EUROPE
Malone, Dumas / THOMAS JEFFERSON AND HIS TIMES, 2
        vols.
Miller, John C. / ALEXANDER HAMILTON
Morison, Samuel E. / JOHN PAUL JONES
Pell, John / ETHAN ALLEN
Smith, Page / JOHN ADAMS, 2 vols.
Van Doren, Carl / BENJAMIN FRANKLIN
Warfel, Harry / NOAH WEBSTER

IV • THE EARLY REPUBLIC:
JEFFERSON TO JACKSON

1. General

Adams, Henry / HISTORY OF THE . . . ADMINISTRATIONS
        OF JEFFERSON AND MADISON, 9 vols.; 2 vols. ed. by
        Herbert Agar
Bond, Beverly / CIVILIZATION OF THE OLD NORTHWEST
Boorstin, Daniel J. / THE AMERICANS: THE COLONIAL EX-
        PERIENCE
Bowers, Claude G. / JEFFERSON AND HAMILTON; JEFFER-
        SON IN POWER; PARTY BATTLES OF THE JACKSON PERIOD
Brooks, Van Wyck / THE WORLD OF WASHINGTON IRVING
Dangerfield, George / THE ERA OF GOOD FEELINGS; AWAK-
        ENING OF AMERICAN NATIONALISM
Flexner, James / DOCTORS ON HORSEBACK; STEAMBOATS
        COME TRUE
Fox, Dixon Ryan / YANKEES AND YORKERS
Hammond, Bray / BANKING AND POLITICS IN AMERICA
Harlow, Alvin / OLD TOWPATHS
Hulbert, A. B. / PATHS OF INLAND COMMERCE
Livermore, Shaw / THE TWILIGHT OF FEDERALISM
McMaster, John B. / HISTORY OF THE PEOPLE OF THE
        UNITED STATES, 8 vols.
Morison, Samuel E. / MARITIME HISTORY OF MASSACHU-
        SETTS
Nye, Russel B. / CULTURAL LIFE OF THE NEW NATION
Roosevelt, Theodore / NAVAL WAR OF 1812
Schlesinger, Arthur M., Jr. / THE AGE OF JACKSON
Tucker, Glenn / POLTROONS AND PATRIOTS, 2 vols.

2. Biographies

Adams, Henry / ALBERT GALLATIN

Bemis, Samuel F. / JOHN QUINCY ADAMS, 2 vols.

Beveridge, Albert J. / JOHN MARSHALL, 4 vols.

Brant, Irving / JAMES MADISON, 6 vols.

Cresson, W. P. / JAMES MONROE

Hamlin, Talbot / BENJAMIN LATROBE

James, Marquis / ANDREW JACKSON, 2 vols.

Mirsky, Jeannette, and Nevins, Allan / THE WORLD OF ELI WHITNEY

Schurz, Carl / HENRY CLAY, 2 vols.

V • THE MIDDLE PERIOD: JACKSON TO LINCOLN

1. General

Johnson, Gerald / AMERICA'S SILVER AGE

McMaster, John B. / HISTORY OF THE PEOPLE OF THE UNITED STATES, Vols. IV–VII

Nevins, Allan / ORDEAL OF THE UNION, 2 vols.; EMERGENCE OF LINCOLN, 2 vols.

Tocqueville, Alexis de / DEMOCRACY IN AMERICA, ed. Phillips Bradley

Turner, Frederick J. / THE UNITED STATES, 1830–1850

2. Special Aspects

Adams, James Truslow / NEW ENGLAND IN THE REPUBLIC

Branch, E. D. / THE SENTIMENTAL YEARS, 1836–1860

Brooks, Van Wyck / FLOWERING OF NEW ENGLAND; WORLD OF WHITMAN AND MELVILLE

Clark, Arthur Hamilton / THE CLIPPER SHIP ERA

Eaton, Clement / GROWTH OF SOUTHERN CIVILIZATION, 1790–1860

Foreman, Grant / INDIANS AND PIONEERS

Gates, Paul W. / THE FARMER'S AGE: 1815–1860

Hamlin, Talbot / GREEK REVIVAL ARCHITECTURE IN THE UNITED STATES

Hansen, Marcus / THE ATLANTIC MIGRATION

Matthiessen, Francis O. / AMERICAN RENAISSANCE

Mumford, Lewis / GOLDEN DAY; STICKS AND STONES

Parrington, V. L. / THE ROMANTIC REVOLUTION
Phillips, Ulrich B. / LIFE AND LABOR IN THE OLD SOUTH
Riegel, R. E. / YOUNG AMERICA
Robbins, R. M. / OUR LANDED HERITAGE
Stampp, Kenneth / THE PECULIAR INSTITUTION
Taylor, George R. / THE TRANSPORTATION REVOLUTION: 1815–1860
Tyler, Alice Felt / FREEDOM'S FERMENT

3. Biographies

Bemis, Samuel F. / JOHN QUINCY ADAMS, 2 vols.
Commager, H. S. / THEODORE PARKER
Fuess, Claude M. / DANIEL WEBSTER, 2 vols.
Nevins, Allan / FRÉMONT, THE WEST'S GREATEST ADVENTURER
Nye, Russel B. / GEORGE BANCROFT
Rusk, R. L. / RALPH WALDO EMERSON
Shepard, Odell / BRONSON ALCOTT
Tharp, Louise / THE PEABODY SISTERS OF SALEM; UNTIL VICTORY: HORACE MANN AND MARY PEABODY
Van Deusen, Glyndon G. / HENRY CLAY; HORACE GREELEY
Weaver, R. M. / HERMAN MELVILLE
Wiltse, C. M. / JOHN C. CALHOUN, 3 vols.

VI • THE WESTWARD MOVEMENT

1. General Accounts

Billington, R. A. / THE FAR WESTERN FRONTIER
————— *and Hedges, J. B.* / WESTWARD EXPANSION
Briggs, N. E. / FRONTIERS OF THE NORTHWEST
Clark, Dan / THE WEST IN AMERICAN HISTORY
De Voto, Bernard / THE COURSE OF EMPIRE; THE YEAR OF DECISION
Dick, Everett / VANGUARDS OF THE FRONTIER; THE SOD-HOUSE FRONTIER
Hulbert, A. B. / SOIL: ITS INFLUENCE IN AMERICAN HISTORY
Quiett, G. C. / THEY BUILT THE WEST
Riegel, R. E. / AMERICA MOVES WEST; STORY OF THE WESTERN RAILROADS

Turner, Frederick J. / THE FRONTIER IN AMERICAN HISTORY

Webb, Walter Prescott / THE GREAT PLAINS

Winther, Oscar / THE GREAT NORTHWEST

2. Personal Accounts

Dana, Richard Henry / TWO YEARS BEFORE THE MAST

Garland, Hamlin / A SON OF THE MIDDLE BORDER

Gregg, Josiah / COMMERCE OF THE PRAIRIES, 2 vols.

Irving, Washington / ASTORIA; CAPTAIN BONNEVILLE

Langford, Nathaniel P. / VIGILANTE DAYS AND WAYS

Parkman, Francis / THE OREGON TRAIL

Sandoz, Marie / OLD JULES

Taylor, Bayard / EL DORADO

Twain, Mark / ROUGHING IT; LIFE ON THE MISSISSIPPI

3. Special Aspects of the West

Anderson, Nels / DESERT SAINTS

Branch, E. D. / THE COWBOY AND HIS INTERPRETERS; HUNTING THE BUFFALO

Caughey, John / GOLD IS THE CORNERSTONE

Cleland, R. G. / THE CATTLE ON A THOUSAND HILLS; THIS RECKLESS BREED OF MEN

Dobie, J. Frank / CORONADO'S CHILDREN; THE LONGHORNS

Duffus, R. L. / THE SANTA FE TRAIL

Ghent, W. J. / THE ROAD TO OREGON

Horgan, Paul / THE RIO GRANDE, 2 vols.

Hough, Emerson / THE STORY OF THE COWBOY

Hulbert, A. B. / FORTY-NINERS

Lavender, David S. / BENT'S FORT

Monaghan, Jay / THE OVERLAND TRAIL

Osgood, Ernest S. / DAY OF THE CATTLEMEN

Quiett, G. C. / PAY DIRT: PANORAMA OF THE GOLD RUSHES

Webb, Walter P. / THE TEXAS RANGERS

4. Biographies

Bakeless, John / DANIEL BOONE

Barker, Eugene C. / THE LIFE OF STEPHEN F. AUSTIN

Brodie, Fawn M. / NO MAN KNOWS MY HISTORY: LIFE OF JOSEPH SMITH

Elliott, C. W. / WINFIELD SCOTT

James, Marquis / THE RAVEN: LIFE OF SAM HOUSTON

McCormac, E. I. / JAMES K. POLK

Morgan, Dale / JEDEDIAH SMITH
Nevins, Allan / FRÉMONT
Porter, Kenneth / JOHN JACOB ASTOR, 2 vols.
Rourke, Constance / AUDUBON; DAVY CROCKETT

VII • THE CIVIL WAR AND RECONSTRUCTION

1. General: Civil War

Adams, James Truslow / AMERICA'S TRAGEDY
Benét, Stephen Vincent / JOHN BROWN'S BODY
Catton, Bruce / GLORY ROAD; MR. LINCOLN'S ARMY;
    STILLNESS AT APPOMATTOX; THIS HALLOWED GROUND
Channing, Edward / HISTORY OF THE UNITED STATES, Vol.
    VI
Coulter, E. Morton / THE CONFEDERATE STATES OF AMER-
    ICA
Eaton, Clement / THE CONFEDERACY: A HISTORY
Fish, Carl R. / THE CIVIL WAR
Fiske, John / MISSISSIPPI VALLEY IN THE CIVIL WAR
Horn, Stanley / THE ARMY OF THE TENNESSEE
Leech, Margaret / REVEILLE IN WASHINGTON
Monaghan, Jay / CIVIL WAR ON THE WESTERN BORDER
Nevins, Allan / THE WAR FOR THE UNION, 4 vols.
Randall, James G. / CIVIL WAR AND RECONSTRUCTION
Wiley, Bell / JOHNNY REB; BILLY YANK
Williams, Kenneth / LINCOLN FINDS A GENERAL, 4 vols.

2. General: Reconstruction

Bowers, Claude G. / THE TRAGIC ERA
Buck, Paul / ROAD TO REUNION
Coulter, E. Merton / SOUTH DURING RECONSTRUCTION
Du Bois, W. E. B. / BLACK RECONSTRUCTION
Dunning, William A. / RECONSTRUCTION
Fleming, W. L. / SEQUEL OF APPOMATTOX
Franklin, John Hope / RECONSTRUCTION AFTER THE CIVIL
    WAR
Henry, Ralph S. / STORY OF RECONSTRUCTION
Josephson, Matthew / THE ROBBER BARONS
Milton, George F. / THE AGE OF HATE
Nevins, Allan / EMERGENCE OF MODERN AMERICA
Randall, James G. / CIVIL WAR AND RECONSTRUCTION
Stampp, Kenneth / THE ERA OF RECONSTRUCTION

VIII • FROM RECONSTRUCTION TO THE FIRST WORLD WAR

Bryce, Lord James / THE AMERICAN COMMONWEALTH, 2 vols.

Buck, Paul / THE ROAD TO REUNION

Commager, H. S. / THE AMERICAN MIND

David, Henry / THE HAYMARKET AFFAIR

Filler, Louis / CRUSADERS FOR LIBERALISM

Fine, Sidney / LAISSEZ FAIRE AND THE GENERAL-WELFARE STATE

Goldman, Eric / RENDEZVOUS WITH DESTINY: A HISTORY OF MODERN AMERICAN REFORM

Hechler, Kenneth W. / INSURGENCY: PERSONALITIES AND POLITICS OF THE TAFT ERA

Hicks, John D. / THE POPULIST REVOLT

Hofstadter, Richard / THE AGE OF REFORM

Josephson, Matthew / THE POLITICOS, 1865-1896; THE PRESIDENT MAKERS: THE CULTURE OF POLITICS AND LEADERSHIP IN AN AGE OF ENLIGHTENMENT, 1896-1919

Leech, Margaret / IN THE DAYS OF MCKINLEY

Millis, Walter / THE MARTIAL SPIRIT

Mowry, George / THE ERA OF THEODORE ROOSEVELT

Mumford, Lewis / THE CULTURE OF CITIES

Schlesinger, Arthur M., Sr. / THE RISE OF THE CITY

Shannon, F. A. / THE FARMERS' LAST FRONTIER

Tarbell, Ida / THE NATURALIZATION OF BUSINESS

Webb, Walter P. / THE GREAT PLAINS

Woodward, C. Vann / THE RISE OF THE NEW SOUTH

2. Autobiographies, Memoirs, and Letters

Addams, Jane / FORTY YEARS AT HULL-HOUSE

Bryan, William Jennings / MEMOIRS

Carnegie, Andrew / AUTOBIOGRAPHY

Riis, Jacob / THE MAKING OF AN AMERICAN

Roosevelt, Theodore / AUTOBIOGRAPHY; LETTERS, selected and ed. by Elting E. Morison and John M. Blum, 8 vols.

Steffens, Lincoln / AUTOBIOGRAPHY, 2 vols.

Washington, Booker T. / UP FROM SLAVERY

White, William Allen / AUTOBIOGRAPHY

Whitlock, Brand / FORTY YEARS OF IT

3. Biographies

Barker, Charles Albro / HENRY GEORGE

Barnard, Harry / EAGLE FORGOTTEN: JOHN PETER ALTGELD

Beer, Thomas / HANNA

Bowen, Catherine D. / YANKEE FROM OLYMPUS: OLIVER WENDELL HOLMES

Bowers, Claude G. / BEVERIDGE AND THE PROGRESSIVE ERA

Croly, Herbert / MARK HANNA

Dennett, Tyler / JOHN HAY

Dorfman, Joseph / THORSTEIN VEBLEN AND HIS AMERICA

Edel, Leon / HENRY JAMES, 3 vols.

Garraty, John / GENTLEMAN FROM MASSACHUSETTS: HENRY CABOT LODGE

Harbaugh, William H. / POWER AND RESPONSIBILITY: THE LIFE AND TIMES OF THEODORE ROOSEVELT

Howe, Mark D. / JUSTICE OLIVER WENDELL HOLMES, 2 vols.

Jessup, Philip / ELIHU ROOT, 2 vols.

Johnson, Walter / WILLIAM ALLEN WHITE'S AMERICA

La Follette, B. and F. / ROBERT M. LA FOLLETTE, 2 vols.

Link, Arthur S. / WOODROW WILSON, 5 vols.

Mason, Alpheus T. / BRANDEIS

Nevins, Allan / GROVER CLEVELAND; JOHN D. ROCKEFELLER, 2 vols.; HENRY WHITE; HENRY FORD, 3 vols.

Perry, Ralph B. / THOUGHT AND CHARACTER OF WILLIAM JAMES, 2 vols.

Pringle, Henry / THEODORE ROOSEVELT; LIFE AND TIMES OF WILLIAM HOWARD TAFT, 2 vols.

Putnam, Carleton / THEODORE ROOSEVELT: THE FORMATIVE YEARS, 1858–1896

Samuels, Ernest / HENRY ADAMS, 3 vols.

Woodward, C. Vann / TOM WATSON: AGRARIAN REBEL

IX • WORLD POWER: WILSON TO LYNDON JOHNSON

1. Normalcy, Depression, and the New Deal

Allen, Frederick Lewis / LORDS OF CREATION; ONLY YESTERDAY: AN INFORMAL HISTORY OF THE 1920's

Faulkner, Harold U. / VERSAILLES TO THE NEW DEAL

Fuess, Claude M. / CALVIN COOLIDGE, THE MAN FROM VERMONT

Galbraith, John / THE GREAT CRASH, 1929

Gunther, John / INSIDE U.S.A.

Hofstadter, Richard / THE AGE OF REFORM: FROM BRYAN TO F.D.R.

Jackson, Robert / STRUGGLE FOR JUDICIAL SUPREMACY

Leuchtenberg, William E. / FRANKLIN D. ROOSEVELT AND THE NEW DEAL, 1932–1940

Link, Arthur S. / WOODROW WILSON, 5 vols.

Lynd, Robert and Helen / MIDDLETOWN; MIDDLETOWN IN TRANSITION

Mason, Alpheus / HARLAN FISKE STONE

May, Henry F. / THE END OF AMERICAN INNOCENCE

Mitchell, Broadus / DEPRESSION DECADE

Perkins, Dexter / THE NEW AGE OF FRANKLIN D. ROOSEVELT, 1932–1945

Pusey, Merlo J. / CHARLES EVANS HUGHES, 2 vols.

Rauch, Basil / HISTORY OF THE NEW DEAL; ROOSEVELT: MUNICH TO PEARL HARBOR

Roosevelt, Franklin D. / PUBLIC PAPERS AND ADDRESSES, 1928–1940, compiled and collected by Samuel L. Rosenman, 9 vols.

Schlesinger, Arthur M., Jr. / THE CRISIS OF THE OLD ORDER; THE COMING OF THE NEW DEAL; THE POLITICS OF UPHEAVAL

Sherwood, Robert E. / ROOSEVELT AND HOPKINS, AN INTIMATE HISTORY

Soule, George Henry / PROSPERITY DECADE

Sullivan, Mark / OUR TIMES, 6 vols.

Wecter, Dixon / AGE OF THE GREAT DEPRESSION

2. World Power and Foreign Policy

Acheson, Dean G. / THE PATTERN OF RESPONSIBILITY, ed. by McGeorge Bundy from the records of Secretary of State Dean G. Acheson

Adler, Selig / THE ISOLATIONIST IMPULSE: ITS TWENTIETH-CENTURY REACTION

Dulles, Foster R. / AMERICA'S RISE TO WORLD POWER

Feis, Herbert / THE ROAD TO PEARL HARBOR: THE COMING OF THE WAR BETWEEN THE UNITED STATES AND JAPAN

Haas, W. H. / THE AMERICAN EMPIRE

Langer, William, and Gleason, E. / THE CHALLENGE TO ISOLATION; THE UNDECLARED WAR

Lippmann, Walter / U.S. FOREIGN POLICY

Nevins, Allan / THE UNITED STATES IN A CHAOTIC WORLD; NEW DEAL AND WORLD AFFAIRS

Perkins, Dexter / AMERICA AND TWO WARS
Pratt, Julius W. / AMERICA'S COLONIAL EXPERIMENT
Stimson, Henry L., and Bundy, McGeorge / ON ACTIVE
    SERVICE IN PEACE AND WAR
Weinberg, Albert K. / MANIFEST DESTINY
Willkie, Wendell / ONE WORLD

3. The World War

Baxter, James P. / SCIENTISTS AGAINST TIME
Buchanan, Russell / THE UNITED STATES AND WORLD WAR
    II, 2 vols.
Cant, Gilbert / THE NAVY IN WORLD WAR II
Churchill, Sir Winston / THE SECOND WORLD WAR, 6 vols.
Clark, Mark / CALCULATED RISK
Eisenhower, Dwight D. / CRUSADE IN EUROPE
Hall, Walter P. / IRON OUT OF CALVARY
Hersey, John / HIROSHIMA
Hunt, Frazier / MACARTHUR AND THE WAR AGAINST JAPAN
Merriam, Robert E. / DARK DECEMBER
Morison, Samuel E. / HISTORY OF UNITED STATES NAVAL
    OPERATIONS IN WORLD WAR II, 15 vols.
Pyle, Ernie / BRAVE MEN
Wilmot, Chester / STRUGGLE FOR EUROPE

4. The Postwar World

Albertson, Dean, ed. / EISENHOWER AS PRESIDENT
Bailey, Thomas A. / AMERICA FACES RUSSIA
Bowles, Chester / AMERICAN POLITICS IN A REVOLUTION-
    ARY WORLD
Carleton, William G. / THE REVOLUTION IN AMERICAN
    FOREIGN POLICY
Clay, Lucius D. / DECISION IN GERMANY
Dean, Vera M. / EUROPE AND THE UNITED STATES
Donovan, Robert J. / EISENHOWER: THE INSIDE STORY
Goldman, Eric F. / THE CRUCIAL DECADE: AMERICA
    1945–1955
Kennan, George / AMERICAN DIPLOMACY 1900–1950; RE-
    ALITIES OF AMERICAN FOREIGN POLICY
Rossiter, Clinton / THE AMERICAN PRESIDENCY
Stevenson, Adlai / A TIME FOR GREATNESS; WHAT I THINK
Welles, Sumner / SEVEN DECISIONS THAT SHAPED HISTORY
White, Theodore / FIRE IN THE ASHES; MAKING OF THE
    PRESIDENT 1960; MAKING OF THE PRESIDENT 1964

5. Autobiographies and Memoirs

Byrnes, James Francis / SPEAKING FRANKLY; ALL IN A LIFETIME

Eisenhower, Dwight D. / MANDATE FOR CHANGE; WAGING PEACE

Farley, James / JIM FARLEY'S STORY

Forrestal, James / THE FORRESTAL DIARIES

Grew, Joseph / MY TEN YEARS IN JAPAN; THE TURBULENT YEARS, 2 vols.

Hoover, Herbert / MEMOIRS, 3 vols.; ADDRESSES ON THE AMERICAN ROAD

Hull, Cordell / MEMOIRS, 2 vols.

Ickes, Harold L. / THE SECRET DIARY, 3 vols.

Leahy, W. M. / I WAS THERE

Roosevelt, Eleanor / MY STORY

Rosenman, Samuel / WORKING WITH ROOSEVELT

Schlesinger, Arthur M., Jr. / A THOUSAND DAYS

Sorensen, Theodore / KENNEDY

Truman, Harry S. / MEMOIRS, 2 vols.

Index

Q

R